UTAH MOLLUSK IDENTIFICATION GUIDE

Utah Mollusk Identification Guide

Eric J. Wagner

THE UNIVERSITY OF UTAH PRESS | *Salt Lake City*

The publisher gratefully acknowledges the following organizations for their generous support of *Utah Mollusk Identification Guide*:

The Western Division of the American Fisheries Society

and

David C. Richards, Ph.D., with Wasatch Front Water Quality Council and with OreoHelix Ecological, "Dedicated to Evaluating the World's Ecological Health, Integrity, and Well Being…One Snail at a Time"

Copyright © 2023 by The University of Utah Press. All rights reserved.

The Defiance House Man colophon is a registered trademark of the University of Utah Press. It is based on a four-foot-tall Ancient Puebloan pictograph (late PIII) near Glen Canyon, Utah.

Names: Wagner, Eric J., author
Title: Utah Mollusk Identification Guide / Eric J. Wagner.
Description: Salt Lake City : University of Utah Press, [2023] | Includes bibliographical references.
Identifiers: LCCN 2023935304 | ISBN 9781647690878 (hardcover : alk. paper) | ISBN 9781647690892 (ebk) | ISBN 9781647690885 (paperback : alk. paper)
LC record available at https://lccn.loc.gov/2023935304

Errata and further information on this and other titles available online at UofUpress.com

Printed and bound in the United States of America.

*To the malacologists
upon whose work I humbly stand
and who have generously shared their time,
data, and photographs*

Contents

Preface xiii
Acknowledgments xv
What's in the Guide xvii

Introduction 1
Utah Gastropoda Key 5
Family Keys for Aquatic Snails 14
Terrestrial Snail Keys 29

The Freshwater Snails 44
    Amnicolidae 44
        Amnicola limosa 46
        Colligyrus greggi 48
    Cochliopidae 49
        Tryonia porrecta 50
    Hydrobiidae 51
        Pyrgulopsis anguina 52
        Pyrgulopsis chamberlini 53
        Pyrgulopsis deserta 55
        Pyrgulopsis fusca 56
        Pyrgulopsis hamlinensis 58
        Pyrgulopsis inopinata 59
        Pyrgulopsis kolobensis 61
        Pyrgulopsis lindahlae 63
        Pyrgulopsis nuwuvi 64
        Pyrgulopsis peculiaris 65
        Pyrgulopsis pilsbryana 67
        Pyrgulopsis pinetorum 69
        Pyrgulopsis plicata 71
        Pyrgulopsis santaclarensis 73
        Pyrgulopsis saxatilis 74
        Pyrgulopsis variegata 75
    Lithoglyphidae 77
        Fluminicola coloradoense 77
    Tateidae 80
        Potamopyrgus antipodarum 80
    Lymnaeidae 83

Galba	84
Hinkleyia and *Polyrhytis*	84
Lymnaea	87
Radix	88
Galba bulimoides	88
Galba dalli	91
Galba humilis group	92
Galba humilis	94
Galba techella	101
Hinkleyia caperata	102
Hinkleyia montanensis	105
Hinkleyia pilsbryi	107
Polyrhytis bonnevillensis	109
Polyrhytis utahensis	110
Polyrhytis elodes	114
Lymnaea stagnalis	118
Radix auricularia	121
Physidae	123
Aplexa elongata	123
Physella microstriata	125
Physella acuta	126
Physella gyrina	130
Physella utahensis	133
Physella zionis	134
Physa megalochlamys	135
Physa skinneri	136
Planorbidae	138
Gyraulus circumstriatus	139
Gyraulus parvus	141
Helisoma anceps	142
Helisoma newberryi	144
Menetus opercularis	145
Promenetus exacuous	146
Planorbula campestris	147
Planorbella binneyi	148
Planorbella oregonensis	149
Planorbella subcrenata	150
Planorbella trivolvis	151
Ferrissia rivularis	153
Valvatidae	154
Valvata humeralis	155
Valvata utahensis	158
Viviparidae	159
Cipangopaludina chinensis	159

Thiaridae	161
Melanoides tuberculata	161

The Terrestrial Snails 163
Achatinidae 163
Rumina decollata 163
Helicidae 164
Cornu aspersum 165
Polygyridae 166
Polygyra cereolus 166
Thysanophoridae 167
Microphysula ingersolli 167
Gastrodontidae 169
Glyphyalinia indentata 170
Glyphyalinia umbilicata 172
Perpolita electrina 173
Zonitoides arboreus 175
Zonitoides nitidus 176
Oxychilidae 177
Oxychilus cellarius 178
Pristilomatidae 179
Hawaiia minuscula neomexicana 180
Hawaiia minuscula 182
Pristiloma subrupicola 182
Agriolimacidae 184
Deroceras laeve 184
Deroceras reticulatum 186
Limacidae 187
Limacus flavus 187
Limax maximus 188
Vitrinidae 189
Vitrina pellucida 189
Discidae 191
Discus shimekii 191
Discus whitneyi 193
Helicodiscidae 194
Helicodiscus eigenmanni 195
Oreohelicidae 196
Oreohelix strigosa group 198
Oreohelix haydeni 198
Oreohelix parawanensis 201
Oreohelix peripherica 202
Oreohelix strigosa 204
Oreohelix subrudis group 207

Contents

    Oreohelix subrudis 207
    Oreohelix yavapai group 209
    Oreohelix eurekensis 209
    Oreohelix hemphilli 211
    Oreohelix yavapai 212
Punctidae 214
    Punctum minutissimum 215
Cochlicopidae 216
    Cochlicopa lubrica 217
Pupillidae 218
    Pupilla blandi 219
    Pupilla hebes 221
    Pupilla syngenes 223
    Pupoides albilabris 224
    Pupoides hordaceus 225
Valloniidae 226
    Vallonia cyclophorella 227
    Vallonia gracilicosta 229
    Vallonia perspectiva 230
    Vallonia pulchella 231
    Zoogenetes harpa 232
Vertiginidae 234
    Columella columella 234
    Gastrocopta ashmuni 235
    Gastrocopta cristata 236
    Gastrocopta pellucida 237
    Gastrocopta pilsbryana 239
    Gastrocopta quadridens 240
    Vertigo arizonensis 241
    Vertigo arthuri 242
    Vertigo berryi 243
    Vertigo coloradensis 243
    Vertigo modesta castanea 244
    V. modesta concinnula 244
    Vertigo ovata 246
    Vertigo cf. utahensis 247
    Vertigo ventricosa 248
Succineidae 249
    Catinella avara 251
    Catinella stretchiana 252
    Oxyloma haydeni 253
    Oxyloma nuttalliana 256
    Oxyloma retusa 258
    Succinea grosvenorii 260
    Succinea missoula 262

    Succinea oregonensis 263
    Succinea rusticana 264
  Euconulidae 265
    Euconulus alderi 265
    Euconulus fresti 266
    Euconulus fulvus 268

Utah Bivalvia Key 271
Mussels and Clams 276
  Margaritiferidae 276
    Margaritifera falcata 277
  Unionidae 278
    Anodonta nuttalliana 279
    Pyganodon grandis 281
    Utterbackia imbecilis 283
  Cyrenidae 285
    Corbicula fluminea 286
    Corbicula fluminalis 289
  Dreissenidae 291
    Dreissena rostriformis 291
  Sphaeriidae 294
    Genus *Musculium* 295
    Musculium lacustre 296
    Musculium partumeium 297
    Genus *Pisidium* 299
    Pisidium casertanum 299
    Pisidium compressum 303
    Pisidium insigne 305
    Pisidium lilljeborgii 306
    Pisidium milium 308
    Pisidium rotundatum 309
    Pisidium subtruncatum 311
    Pisidium variable 312
    Pisidium ventricosum 314
    Genus *Sphaerium* 316
    Sphaerium nitidum 316
    Sphaerium occidentale 318
    Sphaerium striatinum 319

Bibliography 323
Glossary 371

Preface

The present work was created to provide better guidance for identification of animals in the phylum Mollusca within the state of Utah, where possible. Some species can be identified at a glance, but others may require genetic analysis or microscopic examination of the animal's anatomy. Dedicated malacologists (those who study mollusks) have been describing species since before Linnaeus (1707–1778) initiated the binomial scientific name convention. A previous guide, entitled *Mollusca of Colorado, Utah, Montana, Idaho, and Wyoming*, was published in 1924 by Junius Henderson. In 1929 Ralph Chamberlin and David Jones published the first Utah guide, *A Descriptive Catalog of the Mollusca of Utah*, using data from their own collections and museum specimens, and summarizing the works of others that preceded them. In addition, some identification guides of broader scope have been published, for example, Josiah Keep's *West American Shells* (1904), Pilsbry's monumental works on terrestrial mollusks (1939, 1940, 1946, 1948), Burch's *North American Freshwater Snails* (1989), Clarke's (1981) *The Freshwater Molluscs of Canada,* Mackie's (2007) *Biology of Freshwater Corbiculid and Sphaeriid Clams of North America,* and Burke's (2013) *Land Snails and Slugs of the Pacific Northwest.* The latest effort was initiated by biologists in the native aquatic species program of the Utah Division of Wildlife Resources; the second edition of *Mollusks of Utah*: *A Simple Guide* was published in 2017. That work updated the taxonomy of most of the species, noted key shell characteristics, added modern photos, and summarized what species to expect in the state, including relatively new invasive mollusks. It is possible that new species may appear via recent introduction or may be discovered for the first time due to greater survey effort; *Zoogenetes harpa* was discovered in Utah for the first time in 2021. I also found *Cryptomastix magnidentata* and *Arion* slugs living in the foothills near Richmond, Utah, on 2 May 2022—too late to add to this guide (see Burke 2013 for more). *Cepaea nemoralis*, recently found in Holliday, Utah, is also a new addition to the Utah checklist.

Acknowledgments

This work would not have been possible without the initial efforts of all those who created and supported the *Mollusks of Utah: A Simple Guide* (Wilson, Wheeler, and Bertram 2017), including Kevin Wheeler, Krissy Wilson, Erin Bertram, Robert Hershler, Sarah Seegert, George Oliver, Mark Ports, David Richards, and Donald Sada. Like many scientific works, this guide benefits from the efforts of those who have previously contributed to biology and science through their studies and published works. The bibliography of this effort is large and is the product of a wide variety of individuals who I collectively thank for their individual contributions to this summary volume. Many images of type specimens from the Academy of Natural Sciences in Philadelphia (ANSP) are used in this book, thanks to the Academy's Malacology Department. Paul Callomon is especially thanked for his assistance with visits to the Academy, for access to the collections, and for use of the shell images. The superb images of *Pyrgulopsis* species were generously provided by Yolanda Villacampa, U.S. National Museum of Natural History. Additional images were obtained from the University of Michigan Museum of Zoology, via an intermuseum database available at www.invertebase.org. I also thank the other providers of excellent photographs and figures, including iNaturalist.org, Robin Delapena at the Chicago Field Museum, Anna Chinn at the Chicago Academy of Science (Peggy Notebaert Nature Museum), Christina Piotrowski at the California Academy of Sciences, Ellen Strong of the Smithsonian Institute, Leanne Elder at the University of Colorado Museum, Jeff Nekola, G.T. and P. Poppe, Veronika Horsáková, Michal Horsák, Krissy Wilson, Chance Broderius, Mark & Lois Ports, Rick Fridell, Jordon Detlor, Maxim Vinarski, Kevin Wheeler, and Henry A. Pilsbry via his works. Thanks also to Christine Bills at the Natural History Museum of Utah and Shawn Clark, Monte L. Bean Life Science Museum, Brigham Young University, for help and access to mollusk collections. Images used in this volume are credited below each image or in footnotes. I am indebted to the Biodiversity Heritage Library website and program for digital access to many historical documents that are increasingly rare and fragile. I thank my wife, Professor Patricia Lambert, for her help in obtaining literature, gifts of equipment and books that aided my studies, and general support for the guide and mollusk research. I am grateful to Peter Hovingh, Kate Holcomb, Karen Mock, George Oliver, Kevin Wheeler, and Jeff Nekola for their input regarding taxonomy and constructive critique of the manuscript. Thanks also to Robert Dillon for advice on physid anatomy. I want to also thank Glenda Cotter and her team of editors at the University of Utah Press for improving the quality of this work. The Western Division of the American Fisheries Society and David Richards, Oreohelix Ecological and Wasatch Front Water Quality Council, generously donated funds to help defray publishing costs.

What's in the Guide

The focus of this work is on extant species, so fossil species are generally not presented, though a few are listed or discussed. The guide provides taxonomic keys to help identify mollusk species. The initial keys will lead to families or genera that are listed separately later in the key section. In some cases, there is only one species represented by the family in Utah, or shell characters are such that family or generic-level grouping was not possible (e.g., for most of the glossy, disc shells), so keys went to the species level. The bivalve key is at the beginning of the bivalve section. The guide uses shell characteristics as much as possible for identification, but be aware that animal dissection may be needed to identify a snail to species. For animal dissection, see Taylor (2003) and Hershler and Liu (2017) for details on methods. Some keys offer three options. The parentheses in the keys provide the number of the couplet preceding that one, so the key may be followed backward if desired.

This guide contains original descriptions of each species, where possible. Latin descriptions were not given in the interest of reducing pagination, but the translation is given. Supplementary descriptions provide more details to aid identification. Data are also given under separate headings for size, type location, and junior synonyms (including taxonomy notes). General data for families are provided, such as genera, generic and family-level characters, distribution, and life history. The Notes include comments to help the reader differentiate similar species and miscellaneous data on ecology, life history, and genetics.

With regard to the distribution data, I have simply listed sites in Utah where species have been reported, inasmuch as distribution data are woefully inadequate and outdated for accurate mapping of most species. Other states, Canadian provinces, and countries/regions are also listed where appropriate. In the future, when more accurate and complete distribution data are available, more definitive distribution maps may be presented. The distribution data reported in this work are based on historical articles, museum records, personal observations, and collections.

The museum and database abbreviations in this book include the following:

ANSP (Academy of Natural Sciences of Philadelphia)

CAS-IZ (California Academy of Sciences, Invertebrate Zoology Department)

CM (Chicago Academy of Sciences)

DMNH (Delaware Museum of Natural History)

FMNH (Field Museum of Natural History)

What's in the Guide

Ibase (invertebase.org)

INHS (Illinois Natural History Survey, biocoll.inhs.illinois.edu/portal/collections/list.php)

Mbase (molluscabase.org)

MCZ (Museum of Comparative Zoology, Harvard)

UCM (University of Colorado Museum of Natural History)

UMMZ (University of Michigan Museum of Zoology)

UMNH (Natural History Museum of Utah)

USNM (National Museum of Natural History at the Smithsonian)

Measurement abbreviations include the following:

ApL = aperture length

ApL/SL = ratio of aperture length to total shell length expressed as a percentage

ApW = aperture width

dia. = diameter

SL = total shell length or height

SW = shell width

umb. = umbilicus diameter

W/L = ratio of SW over SL

Other abbreviations include standard U.S. state abbreviations and other miscellaneous abbreviations such as SPF = superfamily; *s.l.* = *sensu lato*, that is, in a broad sense; and s.s. = *sensu stricto*, that is, in the strict sense or narrower interpretation of the taxa. For errors that may have been overlooked, please feel free to send any suggestions to Eric Wagner at fishcreekut@gmail.com; future editions will update the errors and add taxonomic and distributional updates.

The guide includes a glossary in the back, with figures, in order to help readers learn the lexicon of the malacologist. With regard to the references that have been provided, much effort has gone into trying to obtain and correctly reference historical documents. Budding and professional malacologists alike will appreciate having these references in one place.

TAXONOMIC NOTES

The taxonomy of snails and bivalves has changed many times over the last few centuries as new species have been discovered and new data have arisen. In the past, many species were described from a single shell, with little understanding of the natural variation of shell form in a population or of the animal's anatomy. These data gaps still exist for many species. Genetic data is known for only a handful of species and for a limited number of genes, though more data are being generated. Hermaphrodism in mollusks complicates interpretation of genetic data. Some shell traits have evolved multiple times in different species in similar habitats. This convergent evolution has led to species that appear similar but are not genetically related. Hence, it is fully expected that there will be more taxonomic turmoil ahead.

This guide follows Bouchet and Rocroi (2005) for mollusk classification (family level and above), Bouchet et al. (2017) and Bank (2017) for gastropods, and Bouchet et al. (2010) for bivalves. At the species level, Johnson et al. (2013) was generally followed for standard common and scientific names for freshwater snails in the United States and Canada. However, where new data suggested changes, these have been adopted (e.g., synonymy in Physidae demonstrated by hybridization studies; genetic studies in Lymnaeidae and Oreohelicidae). For Lymnaeidae, see the discussion under that family for the guide's rationale for taxonomic revisions, including elevation of *Hinkleyia* to genus level and use of *Polyrhytis* for North American stagnicoline species and synonymy. Other taxonomic decisions are discussed in the relevant species or family section. An effort was made to convene some Utah malacologists to reach some consensus on the taxonomy of some taxa, such as *Polyrhytis bonnevillensis* and *P. utahensis*.

Introduction

Utah's mollusks are a diverse group, occupying both aquatic and terrestrial habitats. Some species are found worldwide, while many others are only known in Utah. Some introduced mollusks, like the quagga mussel, are invasive and have the ability to significantly alter ecosystems, negatively affect native mollusk populations, and seriously interfere with water delivery systems and lake recreation. Although often overlooked, snails provide useful ecosystem services. They are primary consumers (e.g., grazing algae and bacteria) and detritivore consumers (e.g., helping to break down leaf litter), providing protein and energy for animals up the food chain. Some are predatory, eating other snails or invertebrates. Bivalves can contribute greatly to water quality by collective filtration of large quantities of water.

Mollusks in Utah can be divided into two easily recognized groups: bivalves (class Bivalvia), which have two shells, and gastropods (class Gastropoda; i.e., snails, limpets, and slugs), which have a single shell (internal and reduced in slugs). Gastropods are divided into freshwater and terrestrial groups, though there are multiple evolutionary lines within both groups, so genetic relatedness crosses this artificial division. Aquatic gastropods may have gills and are often operculate, whereas terrestrial snails lack gills and operculae. All mollusks require moisture to survive, so the term *terrestrial* is a relative one. Most mollusks are found in or near water or in moist habitats, though some have evolved mechanisms for aestivating during summer droughts and winter cold.

For identification of mollusks, this guide relies as much as possible on shells and their characteristics. However, some species like the *Pyrgulopsis* and some succineids may require genetic analysis or microscopic examination of the animal's anatomy. Much of the formal taxonomic classification of snails has relied on characters of the animals themselves, especially differences in the jaw, lingual membrane, and genitalia (e.g., Pilsbry 1939, 1948; Tillier 1989; Thiele 1998). The jaw is a hard structure in the upper mouth that may be a single piece, one piece with an accessory quadrate piece attached to its upper margin, or separate detached pieces, free on their lower edges but united above (Binney 1876).

The lingual membrane, in the lower mouth, serves as a rasp to scrape food into its mouth. The teeth are referred to as radula. They are arranged like chairs in an auditorium, with each row replicated front to back, replacing worn teeth at the front with newer ones behind. Each row has a variable number of teeth, arranged palindromically. A central tooth is flanked by lateral teeth, which are flanked by intermediate or transitional teeth and marginal teeth, moving away from the center. While the number of teeth in a row, number of rows, and tooth length vary somewhat with size (Weaver et al. 2008; Yakhchali and Deilamy

2012), the characteristics of the individual teeth—for example, number of cusps and their shape—are consistent enough, even in younger snails, to be used as a diagnostic character. "Formulas" for radular teeth will show the number of marginals, transitionals, and laterals about the single central tooth. For instance, 18–4–3–1–3–4–18 indicates that the row has 18 marginal, 4 transitional, and 3 lateral teeth on either side of the central tooth and that there are 51 total teeth in the row. In some literature, the number of cusps (or range) is indicated as a denominator below the number.

Regarding genitalia, it is primarily the male organ that is used for diagnosis, though the length of the seminal vesicle duct is a helpful character differentiating among *Radix* species (Glöer 2019). Variations in spermatheca characteristics can also be diagnostic (Meier-Brook 1983). The penis varies in the presence or absence of a penial appendix, sheath, or glands. Differences in size, proportion of various subparts, and number and position of glands also can be diagnostic. Variation in the muscles used for retraction and extension and in the way the vas deferens connects (terminally central or laterally) are additional characters. Some terminology bears reviewing, including verge = penis; penis sac = preputium; and penis sheath = epiphallus. Subparts of the male reproductive system include the prostate, sperm duct, penis sheath, preputium (when present), and penis. The sperm storage organ is variously known as the spermatheca, bursa copulatrix, or seminal receptacle.

I encourage you to explore the wide world of mollusks, and hopefully this guide will be helpful in that endeavor. As you go afield, please bear in mind a few suggestions that may minimize your impact and protect your shells.

1. Don't take a live animal unless you are doing research on the animal. Photograph the animal in situ and let it live. Note that aestivating animals may appear dead, though they are still alive. If the shells are stuck to anything, or if they have a clear or whitish membrane or operculum over the opening, they are likely aestivating and alive.
2. Take only a few empty shells for your collection. Put shells in rigid containers to prevent breakage. Separate large and small shells into separate vials. Putting shells in water with some alcohol (e.g., 70%) will help reduce breakage, bacterial degradation of the spire, and odors in your shells. Clean, rinse, and dry the shells a day or two after collection. Keep records about their location with the samples, including collection date, specific location, microhabitat, abundance, and name of collector(s). If possible, determine the latitude/longitude with a Global Positioning System (GPS) device.
3. Leave the site as undisturbed as possible, returning overturned logs, rocks, and the like, to their former position. Return live bivalves in the same orientation as you found them.

Please contribute to the overall knowledge of mollusks. Add your photos to the iNaturalist.org database, where naturalists record their observations. It is easy to sign up on the website, where you can document species distributions, the habitats they are found in, and their abundance, and also note other observations. There is still a lot to learn about our native mollusk fauna, and you can help add to the body of knowledge. This guide is a summary of some of what is known to date.

Utah Gastropoda Key

1	No shell or shell internal (slugs)...2	
1'	Short limpet-like shell lacking spirals (limpets, Fig. K1*a*)...*Ferrissia rivularis* (Planorbidae)	
1"	Complete or partial helical shell...3	
2(1)	>25 mm (to 100–200 mm) with black stripes and spots (*Limax maximus*) or yellowish-green-gray body (*Limacus flavus*)...Limacidae (p. 187)	
2'	15–50 mm, mottled gray body lacking stripes and spots, mantle with concentric ridges; pneumostome (breathing hole) in the posterior half of the mantle...Agriolimacidae (*Deroceras*) (p. 184)	
3(1")	Shell taller than wide...4 (3 choices)	
3'	Shell wider than tall...18	

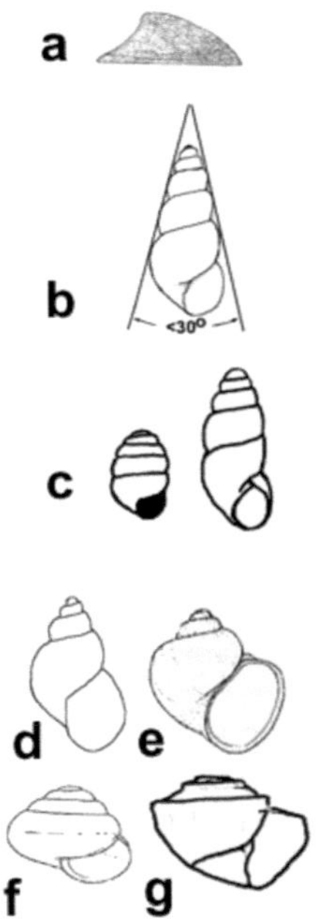

FIG. K1. Shell shape comparison. Credit: E. Wagner.

SHELLS TALLER THAN WIDE

4(3)	Narrow conical shells with an acute spire (<30°, Fig. K1*b*)...5
4'	Columnar or pupae-shaped shells with a rounded apex (Fig. K1*c*)...9
4"	Shell with spire angle >30° (e.g., globose Fig. K1*d*), subglobose (e), beehive-shaped (f), or depressed conic (g), (not narrowly conical or columnar)...10
5(4)	Shell 30–40 mm long, or could be if spire was not broken off...6
5'	Shell <30 mm, usually <20 mm...7

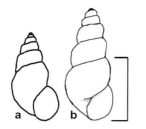

FIG. K2. Comparison of *Potamopyrgus* and *Tryonia* shells. Credit: E. Wagner.

FIG. K3. *Cochlicopa lubrica* shell. Credit: E. Wagner.

FIG. K4. Rimate umbilicus (bottom view). Credit: Pilsbry 1948.

6(5)		Shell nearly always with a broken spire, mottled brown and horn color . . . Subulinidae 1 spp. (*Rumina decollata*)
6′		Shell entire, with rust-colored streaks (found in isolated warm springs) . . . Thiaridae 1 spp. (*Melanoides tuberculata*)
7(5′)		Sinestral shell (aperture opens to the viewer's left) . . . Physidae (p. 23)
7′		Dextral shell (aperture opens to the right) . . . 8
8(7)		Shell 8–10 mm, apex rounded, 7–8 whorls, aperture not offset; body whorl ~57% of total length (Fig. K2*b*) . . . Cochliopidae 1 spp. (*Tryonia porrecta*)
8′		Shell typically 3–6, rarely 8 mm, spire apex acute, 5–7 whorls, rarely 8, aperture often offset a little to the right of imaginary tangential line connecting spire whorls, body whorl ~68% of total length (Fig. K2*a*) . . . Tateidae 1 spp. (*Potamopyrgus antipodarum*)
9(4′)		Shell imperforate (lacking an umbilicus); oblong, tapering to a rounded spire; aperture lip not expanded; columella slightly sinuate or truncate at base; no teeth present (Fig. K3) . . . Cionellidae 1 spp. (*Cochlicopa lubrica*)
9′		Shell rimate (umbilical indentation more fissure-like than circular; see Fig. K4) or umbilicate; pupae- or column-shaped shells (Fig. K1*c*); teeth may or may not be present; aperture lip may or may not be expanded/flared . . . Pupiloid shells (p. 34).
10(4″)		Shell sinestral (aperture opens to the observer's left) . . . Physidae (p. 23)

10'	Shells dextral (aperture opens to the right)...11
11(10')	Shells large, >25 mm dia., typically globose to sub-globose shaped (Fig. K5)...12
11'	Shells smaller, <25 mm, shell shape varied...13
12(11')	Shells 25–40 mm dia., bands of amber and brown, no operculum...*Cornu aspersum* (Helicidae)
12'	Shells up to 65 mm, uniform smooth shell without colored bands, with operculum...*Cipangopaludina chinensis* (Viviparidae)
13(11')	Shells with a carinate (ridged) terraced spire and an angular aperture that is broad above, narrow below (Fig. K6)...*Helisoma newberryi* (Planorbidae)
13'	Shell spire not terraced, if carinate, the aperture is round, oval or elliptic...14 (3 choices)
14(13')	Tiny shells <1–4.5 mm tall with 3–5 smooth whorls (no radial costae), globose or subglobose in shape, usually found in springs...Amnicolidae/Hydrobiidae (p. 14)
14'	Tiny globose shells <4 mm tall, with ~4 whorls and radial costae (ribbing); terrestrial (leaf litter, moss, in wooded sites or wetland margins)...*Zoogenetes harpa* (Valloniidae) (Fig. K7)
14"	Adult shells >4 mm tall, various shapes...15
15(14')	Shells with a depressed conic shape, spire whorls with a carinate ridge

FIG. K5. Globose shell shape. Credit: E. Wagner.

FIG. K6. Outline of *Helisoma newberryi*. Credit: E. Wagner.

FIG. K7. *Zoogenetes harpa*. Credit: Jordon Detlor.

Utah Gastropoda Key

FIG. K8. *Valvata* showing carinate ridge. Credit: E. Wagner.

FIG. K9. Subglobose shape of *Fluminicola*. Credit: E. Wagner.

FIG. K10. Typical shape of Succinea shells. Credit: E. Wagner.

FIG. K11. Representative lymnaeid shape. Credit: E. Wagner.

	that does not quite reach the aperture (Fig. K8)...*Valvata* (Valvatidae, in part p. 154)
15'	Shells globose, subglobose, or elongate oval in shape, rounded whorls lacking carinate ridges...16
16(15')	Shell subglobose, opaque, 7–9 mm (Fig. K9)...*Fluminicola* (Lithoglyphidae, p. 77)
16'	Shell globose or elongate oval, opaque or translucent...17
17(16')	Translucent delicate shell of 2.5–4 whorls, apertures >½ of shell height, often oblique (offset to right of shell spire axis); shell shape is elongate oval (succineid shape, Fig. K10); animal has four tentacles...Succineidae (p. 38; 249)
17'	Opaque or translucent, up to 7 whorls; shells with apertures <½ shell height or if >½; shells are globose with a rotund body whorl; columella (inner lip) often with a fold, but outer lip simple; two triangular tentacles; shell shape globose, depressed globose, or subglobose (Fig. K11)...Lymnaeidae (p. 17 (animal key); 18 (shells); 83)

SHELLS WIDER THAN TALL

18(3')	Shells only ~1–1.5 mm in diameter with 4 whorls...Punctidae (Fig. K12; p. 214)
18'	Shells >1.5 mm in diameter...19
19(18')	Shells beehive-shaped, 2–4 mm dia. (Fig. K13)...Euconulidae (p. 29; 265)
19'	Shells discoidal or depressed-conic

shaped, size variable ... 20

20(19')   Shells with 1–3 pairs of "teeth" present on distal inner surface of body whorl or aperture (Fig. K14a, b) ... 21

20'   Shells lacking teeth in the aperture ... 22

21(20)   Shells with 6–8 whorls, delicately ribbed; adults often with a columellar "tooth" in the aperture (see arrow, Fig. K14a) ... Polygyridae 1 sp. *Polygyra cereolus*

21'   Shells ± flat, striations parallel with spiral, not ribbed; with ~5 whorls and a broad open umbilicus ... *Helicodiscus eigenmanni* (Fig. K14b; Helicodiscidae p. 194)

22(20')   Depressed conical-shaped shell, solid, opaque, dextral (Fig. K15) ... 23 (3 choices)

22'   Discoidal shell with a spire that is sunken, level, or slightly convex ... 24

23(22)   Shells >8 mm in diameter, aperture broadly rounded ... Oreohelicidae (Fig. K15; p. 30; 196)

23'   Shells <8 mm in dia., aperture roughly rhomboidal, animal without an operculum ... *Menetus opercularis* (Planorbidae)

23"   Shells <8 mm in dia., aperture rounded; animal with an operculum ... *Valvata humeralis* (Fig. K16)

24(22')   Small discoidal shell (≤6 mm dia.) with a sharp keel (Fig. K17) ... *Promenetus exacuous* (Planorbidae)

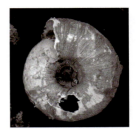

FIG. K12. Representative Punctidae shell. Credit: ANSP.

FIG. K13. Beehive shape of *Euconulus*. Credit: E. Wagner.

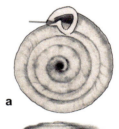

FIG. K14. Examples of Polygyridae (a), Helicodiscidae (b). Credit: Pilsbry 1939–1948.

FIG. K15. Example of depressed conical-shaped shell (*Oreohelix*). Credit: E. Wagner.

FIG. K16. *Valvata humeralis.* Credit: E. Wagner.

FIG. K17. *Promenetus exacuous.* UMNH 1.003757. Credit: E. Wagner, courtesy UMNH.

FIG. K18. Examples of Planorbidae. Credit: E. Wagner.

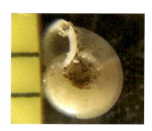

FIG. K19. Example of a *Vallonia* shell. Credit: E. Wagner.

24'		Discoidal shells of various sizes; whorls are convex, and if keeled, the ridge is not as acutely angled and is on larger shells...25
25(24')		Spires sunken (Fig. K18), shell usually sinestral (if dextral, see *Helisoma*)...Planorbidae (in part; see p. 26; 90).
25'		Spire flat, or very slightly convex; aperture is dextral...26
26(25')		Shells ≤3.5 mm, often in rotten wood, but may be found in stream drift; aperture reflected (flared, Fig. K19) or simple...27 (3 choices).

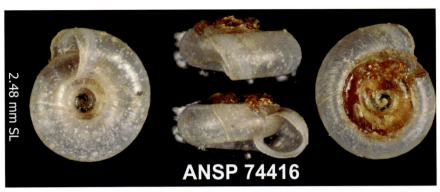

FIG. K20. *Hawaiia minuscula*, ANSP lectotype 74416. Credit: ANSP.

26′	Shells >3.5 mm, usually 4–9 mm dia., aperture lip unreflected (not flared)...28
27(26)	Aperture abruptly everted (Fig. K19) or if not everted, aperture ±round, the peristome entire or nearly so (ends nearly touching); 3.3–4 whorls...Valloniidae (p. 40; 226)
27′	Aperture simple, not everted or thickened, aperture lunate, ends not approximating (lower end at about the middle of the base of penultimate whorl); 3.5–4.5 whorls... Pristilomatidae (Figs. K20, K21; p. 34; 179)
27″	Aperture narrowly lunate, taller than wide, whorls 5.5–5.75...*Microphysula ingersolli* (Thysanophoridae, p. 167)
28(26′)	Shell diameter 9–12 mm, whorls 5–6, umbilicus narrow (~6X in diameter)...*Oxychilus cellarius* (Oxychilidae, p. 177)
28′	Shell diameter <9 mm, usually 4–7 mm; whorls 3.5–4.5, umbilicus variable...29
29(28′)	Umbilicus indented, fissure-like (Fig. K21)...30

FIG. K21. *Pristiloma subrupicola*, ANSP 178008 Topotype. Credit: ANSP.

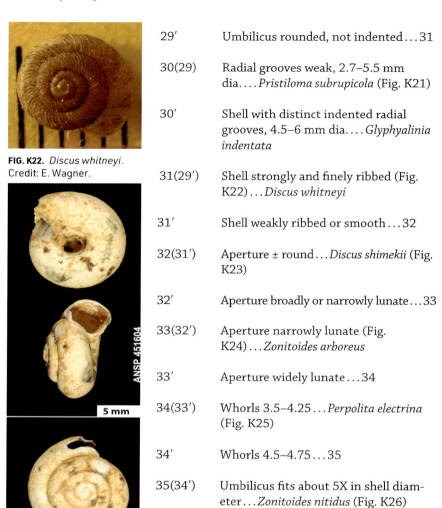

FIG. K22. *Discus whitneyi.* Credit: E. Wagner.

FIG. K23. *Discus shimekii.* ANSP 451604. Credit: ANSP.

29'	Umbilicus rounded, not indented...31
30(29)	Radial grooves weak, 2.7–5.5 mm dia....*Pristiloma subrupicola* (Fig. K21)
30'	Shell with distinct indented radial grooves, 4.5–6 mm dia....*Glyphyalinia indentata*
31(29')	Shell strongly and finely ribbed (Fig. K22)...*Discus whitneyi*
31'	Shell weakly ribbed or smooth...32
32(31')	Aperture ± round...*Discus shimekii* (Fig. K23)
32'	Aperture broadly or narrowly lunate...33
33(32')	Aperture narrowly lunate (Fig. K24)...*Zonitoides arboreus*
33'	Aperture widely lunate...34
34(33')	Whorls 3.5–4.25...*Perpolita electrina* (Fig. K25)
34'	Whorls 4.5–4.75...35
35(34')	Umbilicus fits about 5X in shell diameter...*Zonitoides nitidus* (Fig. K26)
35'	Umbilicus smaller (>5X; Fig. K27)...*Glyphyalinia umbilicata*

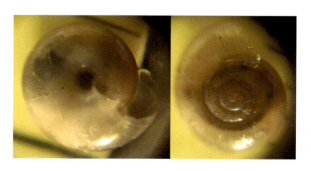

FIG. K24. *Zonitoides arboreus.* Whiskey Spring, Daniel's Canyon, Utah. Credit: E. Wagner.

FIG. K25. *Perpolita electrina.* Cache Valley, Utah. Credit: E. Wagner.

FIG. K26. *Zonitoides nitidus.* Cache Valley, Utah. Credit: E. Wagner.

FIG. K27. *Glyphyalinia umbilicata.* Credit: iNaturalist.org (left image by Ben Schwartz, San Marcos, TX; right by Sam Kieschnick).

Family Keys for Aquatic Snails

AMNICOLIDAE/HYDROBIIDAE/LITHOGLYPHIDAE
(Keys Adapted From Burch and Tottenham 1980; Hershler and Liu 2017)

1	Globose, convex shell to 7–9 mm tall, with a teardrop-shaped aperture; penis simple without any accessory lobes...subfam. Lithoglyphinae (1 species in Utah, *Fluminicola coloradoense*, Fig. K28).
1′	Shells ≤4.5 mm tall, globose, subglobose, ovate, or narrowly conic, with convex or carinate whorls; apertures round, oval, or teardrop-shaped; penis with accessory lobes...2

FIG. K28. *Fluminicola coloradoense*, Rich Co., UT. Credit: E. Wagner.

2	Penis with a single duct and one or more accesory lobes (Hydrobiinae; one genus in Utah, *Pyrgulopsis*)...4
2′	Penis with two ducts, Fig. K29 (Amnicolinae)...3
3	Shell 3.0–4.5 mm tall; aperture oval to slightly teardrop-shaped; penial lobe medially positioned; bursa copulatrix large relative to albumen gland (Fig. K30);...*Amnicola* (one species in Utah, *Amnicola limosa*, Fig. K31)
3′	Shell 1.3–3.3 mm tall; ovate or circular aperture; spire whorls often shouldered; penial lobe basally positioned; bursa copulatrix small relative to albumen gland (Fig. K30)...*Colligyrus* (1 Utah species, *Colligyrus greggi,* Fig. K32)
4(2)	Shell subglobose...5
4′	Shell globose to ovate, to 4.5 mm...6
5	Shell to 1.4 mm tall, endemic to Gandy Warm Spring (Fig. K33)...*Pyrgulopsis saxatilis*

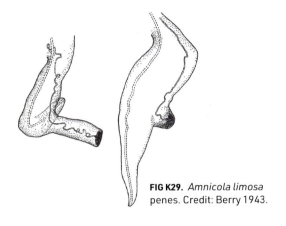

FIG K29. *Amnicola limosa* penes. Credit: Berry 1943.

FIG. K31. *Amnicola limosa*, Utah Lake. Credit: E. Wagner.

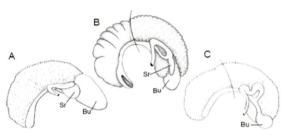

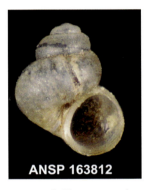

FIG. K30. Female glandular oviducts of amnicolid snails. A. *Amnicola limosa*. B. *Colligyrus convexus*; anterior to left. C. *Lyogyrus* sp. Bu=bursa copulatrix, Sr = seminal receptacle. Credit: Hershler and Liu 2017.

FIG. K32. *Colligyrus greggi*. Credit: ANSP.

5′	Shell to 3.5 mm tall, endemic to springs of Lake Creek, Iron County, Utah (Fig. K34)... *Pyrgulopsis anguina*
6	Whorls carinate, endemic to upper Sevier River drainage (Fig. K35)... *Pyrgulopsis inopinata*
6′	Whorls roundly convex, not carinate...7
7	Other *Pyrgulopsis* not already identified in the lines above are similar enough in shell morphology that identification based on shell characters is not possible without further study of variation among shells within and between populations. DNA analysis is recommended for proper identification of *Pyrgulopsis* species. Hershler and Liu (2017) have summarized the GenBank accession numbers and, through their research, have laid the groundwork for further study of the spring snails. Characteristics of the animal may also be studied for differentiating species. Glands found on the penis of some of the southeastern Utah species are contrasted in Fig. K36.

Family Keys for Aquatic Snails

FIG. K33. *Pyrgulopsis saxatilis.* Gandy Warm Springs, UT. Credit: E. Wagner.

FIG. K34. *Pyrgulopsis anguina.* Credit: Yolanda Villacampa, Dept. Invertebrate Zoology, USNM (Hersler 1998, left), Krissy Wilson (right).

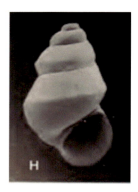

FIG. K35. *Pyrgulopsis inopinata.* Credit: Yolanda Villacampa, Dept. Invertebrate Zoology, USNM, Hersler 1998.

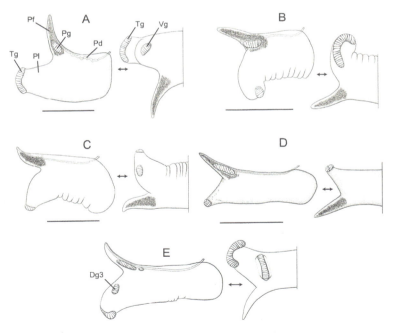

FIG K36. Penes (dorsal aspect shown at left, ventral view, right) of some southeastern Utah *Pyrgulopsis* species: A. *Pyrgulopsis kolobensis.* B. *Pyrgulopsis pinetorum.* C. *Pyrgulopsis lindahlae.* D. *Pyrgulopsis nuwuvi.* E. *Pyrgulopsis santaclarensis.* Note diagnostic glandular patches (Tg = terminal gland, Vg = ventral gland, Dg3 = dorsal gland 3) that vary in size, position, and orientation. Note also the length of the penial filament (Pf) relative to penial lobe (Pl), as well as the sinuosity of the penial duct (Pd; i.e., sinous in *P. kolobensis*, straight in the other species). Credit: Hershler et al. 2017.

KEY TO UTAH LYMNAEIDAE
Animal Key to Lymnaeidae Genera

1   Penis sheath narrow (about 14 times longer than its breadth at the base; not much greater in diameter than the vas deferens; Fig. K37A, B); 16 or 17 haploid chromosomes... *Radix* (1 spp., *Radix auricularia*)

1'   Penis sheath wider (2–3 times width of vas deferens; Fig. K37C); 18 haploid chromosomes... 2

2   Penis sheath less than half the length of the preputium, penis with a ring-like swelling; prostate with ≥2 internal folds... *Lymnaea*

2'   Penis sheath about 2/3 of, and up to 1.5 times, the length of the preputium; ≤1 prostate fold... 3 (3 choices)

3   Vas deferens notably stout; penis with a muscular swelling/knot distal to midlength, terminal part conical; lower prostate weakly folded, roughly D-shaped; lateral teeth bicuspid... *Hinkleyia*

3'   Vas deferens not as stout; penis sheath about 2/3 of, up to slightly longer than, preputium length; tricuspid and bicuspid lateral radular teeth; folds of prostate none, 1 feeble, or 1.... *Galba*

3"   Vas deferens not as stout; lateral teeth bicuspid; penis sheath from 2/3 of, and up to about as long as, the length of the preputium; one internal fold in prostate... *Polyrhytis*

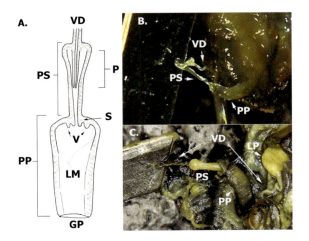

FIG. K37. Comparison of Lymnaeid penial complex morphology. **A.** Diagramatic longitudinal cross section of penial complex (retractor muscles not shown). GP = genital pore, LM=longitudinal muscle, P = penis, PP = preputium, PS = penis sheath, S = sarcobellum, V = velar flaps, VD = vas deferens. **B.** Penial complex of *Radix auricularia*. Black bar on left is 3 mm wide. **C.** Penial complex of *Polyrhytis;* LP = lower prostate. Credit: E. Wagner.

Shell Key to Utah Lymnaeidae

1   Shell with a large ear-shaped *ultra-dextral* (jutting out to the right of the shell) aperture (Fig. K38); up to 23–30 mm total height; total shell height/shell width ratio about 1.1–1.4 (greater in small shells)...*Radix auricularia*

FIG. K38. *Radix auricularia*. Credit: E. Wagner.

1'   Aperture elongate-oval (aperture width is about 47–60% of the aperture height), not ultra-dextral, height/width ratio typically >1.4; height variable...2

2(1')   Aperture about 26% of total shell length, shell narrowly conical-columnar (Fig. K39)...*Hinkleyia pilsbryi*

2'   Aperture >30% of shell length; shell globose to elongate-oval, often with a rotund body whorl...3

3(2')   Shells small (≤9 mm) with 4.5–5 whorls...4

3'   Shell length >9 mm with ≥4 whorls (if <9 mm, with <4.5 whorls)...5

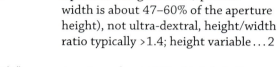

FIG. K39. *Hinkleyia pilsbryi*. Credit: F. C. Baker 1911.

4(3)   Inner lip more erect, with a "denting in" or constriction at point of juncture of inner lip and parietal wall; shells typically 3.25–4.25 mm (max. 6 mm) (Fig. K40, left)...*Galba dalli*

4'   Inner lip not "dented in," creating an aperture with a smoother oval outline; shells typically 5.5–6 mm tall. Young *G. humilis* have fewer whorls for shells of the same size as *dalli*...*Galba humilis* (*parva* form) (Fig. K40, right)

5(4)   Adult shells greater than 20 mm tall...6

5'   Adult shells <20 mm tall...7

6(5)   Shell large (20–57 mm) with an inflated body whorl and a long acute spire much narrower than the body whorl; L/W ratio 1.68–2.22 (Fig. K41)...*Lymnaea stagnalis*

FIG. K40. *Galba dalli*, CM-INV 23125 (left, Credit: CM / Peggy Notebaert Nature Museum's collections) & *G. humilis* (*parva* form; ANSP 113038. Credit: ANSP).

6'	Shell body whorl not inflated, shells 20–37 mm long, L/W ratio 2.47–3.11 (Fig. K42)...*Polyrhytis elodes*
7(5')	Shells often featuring longitudinal ridges (Fig. K43), 4–4.5 whorls (length-to-width [L/W] ratios averaging about 1.7 (1.54–2.0)); effuse lower lip; Bonneville Basin distribution...*Polyrhytis bonnevillensis* (fossil) and *P. utahensis*
7'	Shells lacking the longitudinal (axial) ribbing, 4.5–6 whorls; L/W ratios 1.3–3.2; statewide...8
8(7')	Spire whorls turreted, bulimoid to oblong shell (*G. humilis; H. caperata, H. montanensis*)...11
8'	Spire whorls not turreted, subglobose to globose shell (*G. bulimoides, G. techella*)...9
9(8')	L/W ratio <1.54...*Galba bulimoides* form *cockerelli* (Fig. K44)
9'	L/W ratio >1.54...10
10	Small, slightly perforate umbilicus, short spire, 5 whorls, surface

FIG. K41. *Lymnaea stagnalis*. Credit: E. Wagner.

FIG. K42. *Polyrhytis elodes*, Cache Valley, Utah. Credit: E. Wagner.

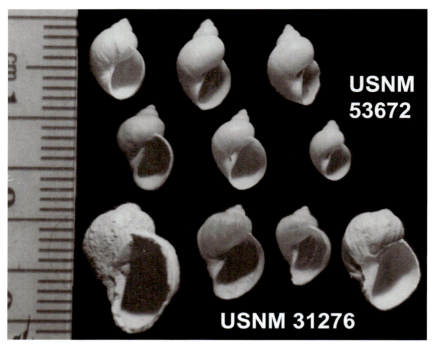

FIG. K43. *Polyrhytis utahensis* paratypes. USNM 53672 & 31276. Credit: Peter Hovingh, courtesy USNM.

	not as smooth as in *techella*; marginal teeth undetermined . . . *Galba bulimoides s.s.*
10′	Large umbilicus, acute pyramidal spire, 5–6 whorls, smooth shell; dagger-like-tricuspid marginal teeth . . . *Galba techella* (Fig. K45)
11(8)	Shell sculpture has spiral grooves creating blade-like ridges in the periostracum; spherical egg capsule . . . *Hinkleyia caperata* (Figs. K46, K47)

FIG. K44. *Galba bulimoides cockerelli.* Credit: ANSP 84287.

11′	Periostracal sculpture not as above, elongate egg mass . . . 12
12(11′)	Shell reaching to 19.5 mm long, strongly shouldered, oblong (L/W 1.91–3.20), body whorl not very rounded . . . *Galba humilis* (*obrussa* form) (Fig. K49)
12′	Shells smaller, 6–12 mm long, L/W 1.6–2.4; spire shouldering not

FIG. K45. *Galba techella*. 30: Bixby, CA; 31, 33-35: Bardsdale, CA; 32: Rockwell Co., TX. Credit: F.C. Baker 1911, Plate 27.

FIG. K46. *Hinkleyia caperata*, lectotype ANSP 58824. Credit: E. Wagner, courtesy ANSP.

FIG. K47. *Hinkleyia caperata*. 176578. Credit: UMMZ.

FIG. K48. *Hinkleyia montanensis*. UMMZ shell collected by D. Taylor. 1 Credit: UMMZ.

FIG. K49. *Galba humilis obrussa*. Left: lectotype ANSP 58700; right: ANSP 104176. Credit: ANSP.

FIG. K50. *Galba humilis rustica*, holotype USNM. Credit: USNM, Dept. of Invertebrate Zoology.

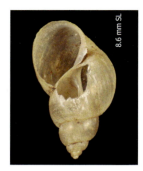

FIG. K51. *Galba humilis*. ANSP lectotype 58754. Credit: ANSP.

FIG. K52. *Galba humilis modicella*. ANSP 191340, Saratoga, UT. Credit: ANSP.

	as pronounced; bulimoid with a rounder body whorl (reduced or inflated)...13
13(12')	Shell shape subfusiform/elongate; umbilicus imperforate (closed)...*Galba humilis* (*rustica* form) (Fig. K50)
13'	Shell umbilicate, bulimoid...14
14(13')	Shell dull, typically 7–10 mm tall, rarely 12 mm; columellar fold slight; tricuspid lateral teeth; penis sheath about as long as penis sac (preputium); snails of marshes and muddy stillwater at lower elevations...*Galba humilis* (s.s. [Fig. K51] and *modicella* form [K52])
14'	Shell shiny, columellar fold often absent or low; penis sheath length 75–100% of preputium length; bicuspid lateral teeth; snails usually found in montane areas in clear flowing creeks/springs...*Hinkleyia montanensis* (Fig. K48)

Family Keys for Aquatic Snails

KEY TO UTAH *PHYSIDAE*

1   Aperture about half the length of the shell; shell elongate, spindle-shaped (Fig. K53)... *Aplexa elongata*

1'   Aperture length greater than half the total shell length; often with rotund body whorl... 2

2(1')   Shell wider than tall, small (≤5 mm), with ultra-sinestral aperture... *Physella (Utahphysa) zionis* (Fig. K54)

2'   Shell taller than wide, usually >5 mm shell height, aperture sinistral... 3

3(2')   Shell narrow, spindle-shaped, with the body whorl not inflated (L/W ratio ~2.2), whorls slightly more than 4 (known only from Fish Lake, Sevier Co.)... *Physella microstriata* (Fig. K55)

3'   Shell globose (Fig. K56, L/W ratio <2.2), whorls 4–6, with an enlarged body whorl and short spire... 4

4   Spire apex bluntly rounded (e.g., Fig. K57), whorls 4–4.5, shells ≤12 mm... 5

4'   Spire apex acute, whorls 4–6, shell size variable... 6

5   Whorls 4, maximum size ~9 mm, aperture 60–69% of shell length, shell glassy, mantle with narrow elongate projections (length of several about 2X width)... *Physa skinneri*

5'   Whorls 4.5, maximum size ~12 mm, aperture ~75% of shell length, shell silky, rounded mantle projections not elongated (typically L/W <2)... *Physa megalochlamys* (Fig. K57).

FIG. K53. *Aplexa elongata.* Credit: E. Wagner.

FIG. K54. *Physella (Utahphysa) zionis.* Credit: ANSP.

FIG. K55. *Physella microstriata.* Credit: E. Wagner, courtesy Monte Bean Museum, Provo, Utah.

FIG. K56. Typical form for *P. acuta* & *P. gyrina*. Credit: E. Wagner.

FIG. K57. *Physa megalochlamys.* Paratype, CAS 146099. Credit: Taylor 2003, Revista de Biologia Tropical.

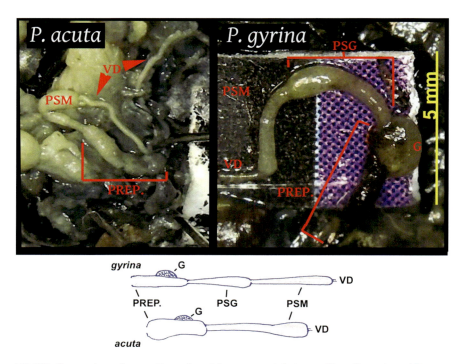

FIG. K58. Comparison of proportions of penial components between *Physella acuta* and *P. gyrina*. G = preputial gland; PREP=preputium, PSG = glandular penis sheath; PSM = muscular penis sheath, VD = vas deferens. Credit: left, E. Wagner; right, redrawn from Wethington 2004.

6	One-part penial sheath; spire whorls moderately convex, shell less stout, with a moderately wide to narrow aperture; statewide ... *Physella acuta* (Figs. K58, K59)
6'	Two-part penial sheath; spire whorls only slightly convex; shell less stout with a moderately wide to narrow aperture; statewide ... *Physella gyrina* (Figs. K58, K60)
6"	Stout, opaque shell with a nearly straight columellar axis and wide aperture, spire whorls only slightly convex; Utah Lake drainage (Fig. K61) ... *Physella utahensis*

FIG. K59. *Physella acuta*. Credit: E. Wagner

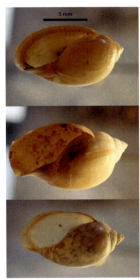

FIG. K60. *Physella gyrina*. Cache Valley, Utah. Credit: E. Wagner.

FIG. K61. *Physella utahensis*. Credit: E. Wagner.

KEY TO UTAH *PLANORBIDAE*

1	Shell not spiraled, convex conical cap-like shape (limpet)...*Ferrissia rivularis*
1'	Shell spiraled, stout, about as tall as it is wide, sharply angled shoulders and angular aperture (Fig. K62)...*Helisoma newberryi*
1"	Shell spiraled, fragile, wider than tall, aperture ovate, crescent shaped, or rounded...2
2(1")	Shell small (≤8 mm dia.)...3
2'	Shell larger (>8 mm dia.)...6
3(2)	Shell carinate (keeled)...4
3'	Shell with rounded whorls, not carinate...5
4(3)	All whorls in the same plane, very flattened (Fig. K63)...*Promenetus exacuous*
4'	Last whorl descending/ascending, keeled but still convex (Fig. K64)...*Menetus opercularis*
5(3')	Body whorl not rapidly enlarging; shell usually flattened, planispiral (whorls all in the same plane), umbilical and apical views similar (Fig. K65)...*Gyraulus circumstriatus*
5'	Shell not planispiral, umbilical and apical views different, last whorl enlarging rapidly (Fig. K66)...*Gyraulus parvus*
6(2')	Shell thin, shell diameter about 3X the shell height, aperture about as tall as wide (Fig. K67)...*Planorbula campestris*
6'	Shell thicker, body whorl not depressed; shell diameter: shell height

FIG. K62. *Helisoma newberryi.* Bear Lake, UT. Credit: E. Wagner

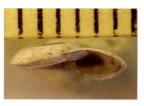

FIG. K63. *Promenetus exacuous.* Newton Reservoir, UT. Credit: E. Wagner.

FIG. K64. *Menetus opercularis.* Credit: ANSP.

FIG. K65. *Gyraulus circumstriatus*. Credit: ANSP.

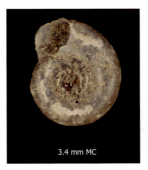

FIG. K66. *Gyraulus parvus*. Credit: ANSP.

FIG. K68. *Helisoma anceps*. Credit: ANSP.

FIG. K67. *Planorbula campestris*. Credit: E. Wagner, courtesy ANSP.

ratio <3. Aperture lunate or auriculate and taller than wide ... 7

7(6') Shell dextral, carinae (ridges) on upper and lower surface of the body whorl, 4–19 mm dia. ... *Helisoma anceps* (Fig. K68)

7' Shell sinestral, spire (left side, when aperture is ventral) not strongly inverted (depression shallow, no depression, or raised above body whorl); spire side of body whorl with or without carinae (ridges). Up to 32 mm dia. (*Planorbella*) ... 8

8(7') Whorls 6, sharp radiating ridges ... *Planorbella subcrenata* (Fig. K69)

8' Whorls 3–5 ... 9

Family Keys for Aquatic Snails

FIG. K69. *Planorbella subcrenata.* Fish Springs National Wildlife Refuge, Utah. Credit: E. Wagner.

FIG. K70. *Planorbella binneyi ursalacustre.* Credit: ANSP.

FIG. K71. *Planorbella oregonensis.* Credit: ANSP.

FIG. K72. *Planorbella trivolvis.* Credit: E. Wagner.

9(8')   Whorls 4–5, "strap-like" (compressed so height > width), with elevated lines of growth, giving a rough appearance; widely umbilicate...*Planorbella binneyi* (Fig. K70)

9'   Whorls 3–4, subcylindrical, not "strap-like," umbilicus deep and funnel shaped...10

10(9')   Whorls increasing rapidly in size, sunken spire with each whorl rising above the other, shell smaller (~9 mm dia.) (Fig. K71)...*Planorbella oregonensis*

10'   Whorls increasing moderately in size, shell to 15–30 mm dia.; sunken spire nearly level (Fig. K72)...*Planorbella trivolvis*

Terrestrial Snail Keys

KEY TO UTAH *AGRIOLIMACIDAE*

1   Sheath of eye stalks indicated by black lines extending backward from their base under the edge of the mantle, white ring around breathing pore, tubercles on dorsal side outlined with black, mucus milky; up to 50 mm...*Deroceras reticulatum*

1'   Sheath of eye stalks not visible except when stalks are withdrawn, breathing pore not circumscribed with a white band, though it may be whitish within, whole dorsal area usually blackish, mucus watery; 15–25 mm long...*Deroceras laeve*

KEY TO UTAH *EUCONULIDAE*

1   Shell dark cinnamon-brown (Fig. K73-1, 2), very glossy; animal black . . . 2

1'   Shell a lighter yellow-brown (Fig. K73-3, 4), glossy; animal gray...*Euconulus fulvus*

2   Protoconch with rounded, widely spaced radial ribs (Fig. K73-2)...*Euconulus alderi*

2'   Protoconch smoother, with weak ribbing to none (Fig. K73-1)...*Euconulus fresti*

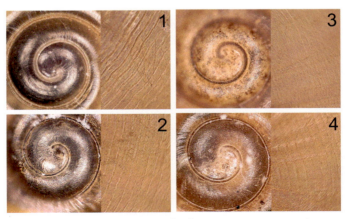

FIG. K73. Comparison of protoconch (left) and shell base microsculpture (right) among 1) *Euconulus fresti*, 2) *E. alderi*, 3) *E. fulvus fulvus*, & 4) *E. fulvus egenus*. Credit: © Michal Horsák (Horsáková et al. 2020).

KEY TO UTAH *OREOHELICIDAE*
(*Oreohelix*; adapted from Pilsbry 1939)

1	Shell has a coarse spiral structure, color light ashy gray, aperture crenulated by the spirals ... *Oreohelix haydeni* (Fig. K74)
1'	Shell with coarse radial striae, wrinkles or ribs along lines of growth, small umbilicus (~6.5 times in the shell diameter) ... *Oreohelix peripherica* (Fig. K75)
1"	Shell ± smooth or striate along growth lines, often with fine spiral lines; umbilicus larger (3–5 times in diameter) ... 2
2(1")	Shell with a peripheral keel (Fig. K76) (note that immature specimens (<4 whorls) of other *Oreohelix* will appear keeled, so use larger shells in population for key); anterior half of the penis decidedly swollen ... 4 (3 choices)
2'	Periphery rounded or weakly keeled; anterior part of penis not, or just slightly, swollen ... 3
3(2')	Internally plicate (pleated folds) part of the long penis decidedly less than half of the entire length; internally costate part of the penis shorter than the papillose part ... *Oreohelix strigosa* (Fig. K77)
3'	Internally plicate parts of the penis ≥ ½

FIG. K74. *Oreohelix haydeni*. UMNH 1.012125, Morgan Co. UT. Credit: E. Wagner, courtesy UMNH.

FIG. K75. *Oreohelix peripherica*. Left: UMNH 1.003839, Echo Reservoir, UT. Credit: E. Wagner, courtesy UMNH. Right: ANSP 11357. Credit: ANSP.

FIG. K76. Keeled shells. Left, *Oreohelix hemphilli* lectotype, ANSP 23060; center, *Oreohelix eurekensis*, UMNH 1.012095; right: *O. yavapai*, UMNH 1.00111. Credit: left, ANSP; center and right, E. Wagner, courtesy UMNH.

FIG. K77. *Oreohelix strigosa*. Cache Valley, Utah. Credit: E. Wagner

FIG. K78. *Oreohelix subrudis*, UMNH 1.012140, Salt Lake County, UT. Credit: E. Wagner, courtesy UMNH.

	total penis length. Anterior half of the penis not or slightly swollen; internally costate part of the penis longer than the papillose part ... *Oreohelix subrudis* group (Fig. K78)
3″	Penial morphology unknown. Diagnosis based on location. Shells in the Brian Head Peak area east of Parawan, Utah ... *Oreohelix parawanensis*
4(2)	Body whorl above or below the keel flat to concave; umbilicus diameter ~5 times in diameter of shell; in Bonneville Basin ... *Oreohelix hemphilli* (Fig. K76, left)
4′	Body whorl with a flat face or slightly convex, above and below keel; umbilicus ~3.75–4.0 times in diameter of shell (south and southwest Utah, Arizona, New Mexico; Fig. K76, right) ... *Oreohelix yavapai*
4″	Body whorl with a flat face or slightly convex; umbilicus diameter is 4.4–5 times in shell diameter; shell small for an *Oreohelix* (~9–11 mm dia.)(Fig. K76, center) ... *Oreohelix eurekensis*

Table K.1 Comparison of characters of *Galba* species within Lymnaeidae. ND = no data, L = length, W = width, SL = shell length (data from Baker 1911, 1928; McCraw 1957, 1961; Hubendick 1951; Hibbard and Taylor 1960; Taylor et al. 1963; Clarke 1973).

	G. dalli	G. humilis (parva form)	G. bulimoides	G. b. cockerelli	G. techella	G. humilis	G. humilis (rustica form)	G. humilis (modicella form)	G. humilis (obrussa form)
SHELL									
Adult SL (mm)	3.25–6.0	5.5–6.0	10–14	8–13.5	8–14	6–12.5	7.5–10.5	7–12	8–19.5
Whorls	4.5–5.0	4.5–5.0	5	4.5	5–6	5–nearly 6	5.0–5.5	4.5–5.0	5–5.5
L:W	1.36–2.12	1.8–2.02	1.54–2.00	1.29–1.54	1.56–1.79	1.60–1.89	1.87–2.25	1.7–2.4	1.91–3.20
Shape	turreted ovate-conic	sub-turreted, pyramidal	bulimoid	subglobose	narrow bulimoid	ovate conic, turreted	sub-fusiform	turreted, elongate oval	turreted ovate-sub conic
Aperture (% of SL)	45–55, slight angle at columella	33–47, round oval	50–70	54–75	52–62	46–56	44–53	36–64	33–58
Umbilicus	chink	deep, open	small	large	large	open	imperforate	narrow	large
ANIMAL									
Radula formula	21-1-21 to 22-1-21	24-1-24	ND	21-1-21 to 24-1-23	ND	ND	20-1-20	25-1-25	25-1-25 to 26-1-26
Lateral teeth	3 bicuspid	4 tricuspid	bicuspid	bicuspid	bicuspid, irregularly serrate	Tricuspid or bicuspid	6 tricuspid	6 tricuspid	8 tricuspid, long
Intermediate teeth	tricuspid (5)	2 with 4 cusps	ND	tricuspid	tricuspid, daggerlike	ND	2 with 3–4 cusps	1/4 cusps	2 with 3–4 cusps
Marginal teeth	6 cusps	18 ≥4 cusps	ND	4–7 cusps	ND	ND	12 with 4–6 cusps	18/5–6 cusps	16 with 4–7 cusps
Penis	ND	2/3 length of penis sac	ND	2/3 length of penis sac	about as long as penis sac	about as long as penis sac	as long as or slightly longer than penis sac	as long as or slightly longer than penis sac	as long as or slightly longer than penis sac
Prostate folds	ND	1 feeble	No fold	ND	No fold	1	ND	ND	ND

Table K.2 Comparison of large lymnaeid species' shell and animal characters (data from Baker 1911, 1928; Chamberlin 1933; Hubendick 1951; Taylor et al. 1963; Russell 1971; Clarke 1973; author's unpublished data; ND = no data; SL = shell length; L = length; W = width).

	Lymnaea stagnalis	Polyrhytis elodes	Polyrhytis utahensis	Hinkleyia caperata	Hinkleyia montanensis	Hinkleyia pilsbryi
SHELL						
Adult SL (mm)	38–52	21–37	13–17	9–17	7–15	7–16
Whorls	6–7	6–7, wider than high	4.0–4.5	4.75–5.75	5.0–6.0	6.25–9.0
L/W	1.68–2.22	2.47–3.11	1.45–2.07	1.71–2.40	1.78–2.15	2.03–2.91
Shape	narrow spire, fat body whorl	narrowly conic, elongate	globose, effuse lower lip	suboval to elongate, turreted	globose, turreted	narrow conical
Aperture (% of SL)	53–62	38–52	54–83	41–50	49–61; angular at columella	26
Umbilicus	imperforate to small chink	usually imperforate	"somewhat umbilicated"	wide, triangular	narrowly open	small chink
ANIMAL						
Radula formula	40–1–40 to 54–1–54	34–1–34	As for elodes	32–1–32	23–1–23	ND
Lateral teeth	bicuspid	bicuspid		bicuspid	bicuspid	
intermediates	tricuspid	tricuspid		tricuspid	tricuspid	
Marginal teeth	serrate	3–5 cusps, long, narrow			"many and smaller cusps"	
Penis sheath to preputium ratio	0.33	0.52–1.0	0.75–1.0	0.66–1.0	0.75–1.0	ND
Penis	ring-like muscular swelling on penis	muscular ridge ~2/3 the circumference	penis sac length 59–76% of the preputium	knot distal to mid-L; stout vas deferens; short blade-like papilla	knot distal to mid-L; stout vas deferens; short blade-like papilla	ND
Other	columella twisted usually forming a fold; prostate with bulbous end and many folds	prostate with one fold; seldom found out of water; with vegetation	Bonneville Basin distribution; Prostate with 1 fold	vaginal sphincter; spherical eggs; tentacle and foot slender; D-shaped prostate; subequidistant, unique shell sculpture	vaginal sphincter; tentacles and foot slender; D-shaped prostate; habitat: clear mountain streams, springs, pools, not mudflats	presumed extinct

KEY TO UTAH *PRISTILOMATIDAE*

1   Shells small (<3.2 mm dia.), with umbilicus about $1/3$ the shell diameter (Fig. K79)... *Hawaiia minuscula*

1'   Shells larger (2.7–5.5 mm dia.), umbilicus is rimate (Fig. K80)... *Pristiloma subrupicola*

FIG. K79. *Hawaiia minuscula. Cowley Canyon, UT.* Credit: E. Wagner.

FIG. K80. *Pristiloma subrupicola*, topotype, ANSP 178008. Credit: ANSP.

KEY TO COLUMNAR PUPILLOID SPECIES IN UTAH

1   Angle and parietal lamellae fused (parietal tooth may appear to be a single lamella but is usually thicker and with a wider base than seen for a single parietal tooth; see Figs. K84–K88)... *Gastrocopta*

1'   No teeth or angle (if present) and parietal lamellae distinct and separate... 2

2   Shells with 4 or more teeth... *Vertigo* (p. 42)

2'   0 to 3 teeth in the aperture... 3

3   Tapered spires, aperture with no teeth, whorls increasing regularly in size, shell length up to ~5 mm (Fig. K82, left)... *Pupoides* (p. 38)

FIG. K82. Comparison of shapes of *Pupilla* (upper right) and *Pupoides* (upper left and lower). Credit: Pilsbry 1948.

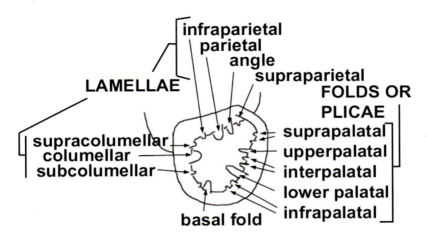

FIG. K81. Notation for aperture features in pupilloid shells. Credit: E. Wagner, after Pilsbry & Vanatta (1900).

3'	Shells more keg or columnar shaped, whorls increasing more slowly (Fig. K82, upper left and lower shells), 0–3 teeth, ≤3.5 mm SL...4
4	Last three whorls of shell about the same diameter (Fig. K83), columnar, with a domed apex, up to 7.5 whorls and ~3.5 mm long, no teeth...*Columella columella* (Vertiginidae)
4'	Shells with body whorl slightly smaller or larger than penultimate whorl, shell length typically <3.5 mm; whorls fewer; with or without teeth...5
5	With or without a weak angle lamella, 0–2 weak palatals, and/or basal tooth, 4.5–5.5 whorls...*Vertigo modesta castanea*
5'	Lacking teeth, or if present, no angular or basal teeth, palatal and columellar teeth tubercular or weak; 6–8 whorls...*Pupilla* (p. 37)

FIG. K83. *Columella columella*, dorsal view, ANSP 43910. Credit: ANSP.

KEY TO UTAH *GASTROCOPTA*

1	Angle and parietal lamellae fused, forming a wide single anguloparietal tooth...*Gastrocopta ashmuni* (Fig. K84)
1'	Anguloparietal tooth much narrower (e.g., as in Fig. K85)...2
2	Aperture with 4 teeth, each ±equal in size...*Gastrocopta quadridens* (Fig. K85)
2'	Aperture with 4–6 teeth, if 4, then not ± equal in size...3
3	Anguloparietal tooth sometimes bi-lobed at tip, aperture with 3–4 small palatal teeth recessed from lip (Fig. K86)...*Gastrocopta pellucida*
3'	Parietal tooth simple, not bilobed; 2–3 palatal teeth closer to lip...4
4	Aperture with a strong crest, often a subcolumellar tooth (Fig. K87)...*Gastrocopta cristata*
4'	Crest lacking or weak, no subcolumellar tooth (Fig. K88)...*Gastrocopta pilsbryana*

FIG. K84. *Gastrocopta ashmuni*. ANSP 78690. Credit: ANSP.

FIG. K85. *Gastrocopta quadridens*. Syntype, ANSP 74567. Credit: ANSP.

FIG. K86. *Gastrocopta pellucida*. ANSP 114028. Credit: ANSP.

FIG. K87. *Gastrocopta cristata*. ANSP 78694. Credit: ANSP.

FIG. K88. *Gastrocopta pilsbryana*. Lambs Canyon, Utah. Credit: E. Wagner.

KEY TO UTAH *PUPILLA*

1	Aperture is sinestral (although there are dextral forms), spire cylindrical, often club-shaped (wider near the top of spire); 8 whorls (Fig. K89P–Q)...*Pupilla syngenes*
1'	Aperture is dextral, spire cylindrical to broadly tapering; ≤7 whorls...2
2	Shell shiny, apex domed, delicately striate, sutures shallow (row 1, Fig. K89)...*Pupilla blandi*
2'	Shell silky, apex domed, but tapering to a greater degree; with sharp minute striae, sutures moderate to deep (rows 2 and 3, Fig. K89)...*Pupilla hebes*

FIG. K89. *Pupilla blandi* (A-D), *Pupilla hebes pithodes* (E-H), *P. hebes* (I-M), *P. sonora* (N), *P. syngenes* (P-Q). (See Fig. T47, p. 220 for more details). Credit: © Jeff Nekola.

KEY TO UTAH *PUPOIDES*

1	Shell conical, smooth, lacking ribbing...*P. albilabris*
1′	Shell cylindrical-ovoid, with widely spaced ribs...*P. hordaceus*

KEY TO UTAH *SUCCINEIDAE*

1	Whorls 4, columella bent in and twisted, shell somewhat opaque...*Succinea grosvenorii* (Fig. K90)
1′	Whorls 2.5–3.75, shell translucent, columella curved, not twisted...2
2(1′)	Shell L/W ratio ≥2, shells usually ≥12 mm (*haydeni; nuttalliana, retusa, missoula, rusticana*)...5
2′	Shell L/W ratio 1.2–1.8, whorls convex, shell length usually <12 mm (*oregonensis, stretchiana, avara*)...3
3(2′)	Whorls not as strongly convex, shell length typically 6 mm (8.5 mm max); aperture 50–80% of shell length...*Catinella stretchiana* (Fig. K91)
3′	Whorls strongly convex, with very impressed sutures; aperture length <75% of total shell length; to 7–11 mm long...4
4(3)	Spire elevated...*Catinella avara* (Fig. K92, left)
4′	Spire not as elevated...*Succinea oregonensis* (Fig. K92, right)
5(2)	Columella with a distinct fold...*Succinea rusticana* (Fig. K93)
5′	Columella lacking fold...6 (*retusa, nuttalliana, haydeni, missoula*)
6(5′)	Penis lacking an appendix, seminal vesicle entire (not bilobed)...*Succinea missoula*
6′	Penis with an appendix, seminal vesicle bilobed or with a black lateral projection...7
7(6′)	Shell L/W ratio about 2.0, lengths to 13 mm, aperture >80% of shell height; seminal vesicle with a black lateral projection...*Oxyloma nuttalliana* (Fig. K94)

FIG. K90. *Succinea grosvenorii.* ANSP 183154, 65369, jr. synonym types of *S. greerii* and *S. mooresiana.* Credit: ANSP.

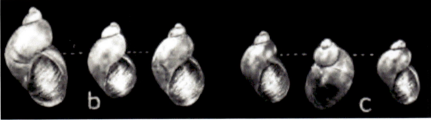

FIG. K91. *Catinella stretchiana.* Credit: Pilsbry 1948.

FIG. K92. Left: *Catinella avara*, ANSP 144611. Credit: ANSP. Right: *Succinea oregonensis.* Credit: Pilsbry 1948.

FIG. K93. *Succinea rusticana.* ANSP 12485. Credit: ANSP.

FIG. K94. *Oxyloma nuttalliana.* ANSP 5609. Credit: ANSP.

FIG. K95. *Oxyloma retusa.* ANSP 8289. Credit: ANSP.

FIG. K96. *Oxyloma haydeni.* Credit: UMNH 1.003742, E. Wagner, courtesy UMNH.

7'	Shell L/W ratio about 2.10–2.25, lengths to 18 mm; aperture about 75% of shell height, seminal vesicle bilobed, but lacking black lateral projection ... 8
8(7')	Penial appendix short (<0.6 mm) ... *Oxyloma retusa* (Fig. K95)
8'	Penial appendix long (0.6–1.0 mm) ... *Oxyloma haydeni* (Fig. K96)

KEY TO UTAH *VALLONIA*

1	Shell surface smooth. Aperture crescent shaped, forming 4/5–5/6 of a circle (not transversely elongated), with ends of margins distant, little or moderately inclined and oblique; suture not markedly descending to the aperture ... *V. pulchella* (Fig. K97)
1'	Surface with distinct axial ribs or rib-like striae. Aperture with margins near each other, either ± circular, transversely elongate, elliptic, or pear shaped; suture more descending ... 2
2(1')	Aperture circular, nearly round ... *V. cyclophorella* (Fig. K98)
2'	Aperture transversely elongate or oblique ... 3
3(2')	Umbilicus wide (>$1/3$ of shell diameter) showing all whorls, lip continuous, shell small (≤2.1 mm dia.) ... *V. perspectiva* (Fig. K99)
3'	Umbilicus <$1/3$ of diameter, shell larger (2.5–2.6 mm dia.), lip strongly everted and whitish ... *V. gracilicosta* (Fig. K100)

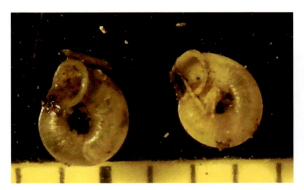

FIG. K97. *Vallonia pulchella.* Currant Creek Reservoir, Utah Credit: E. Wagner.

FIG. K99. *Vallonia perspectiva.* Lectotype, ANSP 109594. Credit: ANSP.

FIG. K98. *Vallonia cyclophorella.* Credit: iNaturalist.org (Kevin Wheeler).

FIG. K100. *Vallonia gracilicosta.* Parley's Creek, Utah. Credit: E. Wagner.

KEY TO UTAH *VERTIGO*

1	Shiny ovate (egg-shaped) shells with weak, blunt, minute striae; columellar tooth is long; moderate to strong sinulus (indented lip) usually present...2 (3 choices)
1'	Shells cylindrically ovate, dull to silky or shiny, striae blunt to sharp, columellar tooth peg-like; sinulus none to weak...3
2(1)	Angular and long infrapalatal teeth lacking; basal fold none to strong; SW 1.0–1.2 mm...*Vertigo ventricosa*
2'	Angular tooth none to strong, often with long infrapalatal tooth and 2 basal folds; SW 1.0–1.4 mm...*Vertigo ovata*
2"	Angular tooth present; 1–2 basal folds; infrapalatal tooth short; SW 1.2–1.5 mm...*Vertigo berryi*
3(1')	Shell length >2 mm, striae irregular...4
3'	Shell length <2 mm, striae regular...5

FIG. K101. Utah *Vertigo* species/subspecies. Credit: © Jeff Nekola.

4(3)	Strong angular tooth; sometimes with a moderate basal tooth; keg-shaped shell, dull to silky...*Vertigo modesta concinnula*
4'	Angular tooth weak or absent; teeth not well developed in general; ovate-cylindrical shell; shiny...*Vertigo modesta castanea*
5(3')	Lower palatal tooth inserted further into aperture than palatal tooth; basal fold none to strong...*Vertigo arthuri*
5'	Lower palatal tooth situated ±same distance as palatal from aperture lip; no basal fold...6
6(5')	Strong angular tooth...*Vertigo arizonensis*
6'	Angular tooth weak or absent...7
7(6')	Lacking a weak angular lamella...*Vertigo coloradensis*
7'	With a weak angular lamella...*Vertigo* cf. *utahensis*

The Freshwater Snails

CLASS: Gastropoda
SUPERORDER: Hygrophila
CLADE: Littorinimorpha
SUPERFAMILY: TRUNCATELLOIDEA Gray, 1840

Amnicolidae Tryon, 1863

DESCRIPTION (Binney 1865b; Tryon 1870; Berry 1943): Shell small, higher than wide, dextral, unicolor, of few whorls, globular or elongated; generally umbilicated. Aperture broadly oval to rounded, lip continuous. Operculum subspiral or concentric. Animal with elongated tentacles, with eyes at their outer bases; foot oblong, truncate before, rounded or pointed behind. Sexes separate; penis exserted, situated on the back behind the right tentacle; gills both pallial, the right one short, broad, and composed of few laminae which are broader than high. See Berry (1943) for data on the radula characteristics. Insights from genetic analysis (e.g., Wilke et al. 2000, 2001, 2013) led to separation of Amnicolidae, Cochliopidae, and other former subgenera from Hydrobiidae, which had become a "catch-all" taxon for small spring snails. Amnicolidae now contains 21 genera (including a few marine), 3 of which are found in the western United States: *Amnicola*, *Lyogyrus*, and *Colligyrus* (Hershler and Liu 2017).

COLLIGYRUS (Hershler 1999, p. 206): "A northwestern American amnicoline group having a small, globose to conical shell and paucispiral operculum. Female coiled oviduct simple; glandular oviduct large, ventrally closed; bursa copulatrix large, posteriorly positioned; seminal receptacles, 2. *Colligyrus* differs from other amnicolines in that females have three sperm pouches: a posterior bursa copulatrix and two small seminal receptacles.

Shell small (up to 3.3 mm in length), thin, globose to conical, umbilicate. Whorls, 3.5–4.5, convex, narrowly shouldered, sutures impressed. Shell clear to white, periostracum thin. Shell apex nearly flat; protoconch of about 1.5 whorls, sculptured with weak spiral lineations. Teleoconch smooth except for faint growth lines. Aperture medium-sized, ovate or circular; outer lip thin; parietal lip complete across body whorl, thin; columellar lip sometimes slightly thickened. Umbilicus narrow to perforate. Operculum flat, thin, ovate, paucispiral. Outer margin of operculum without a rim; attachment scar and callus weakly developed. Body pigmentation well developed. Salivary glands long, simple tubes. Radula ribbon elongate (ca. 15 times longer than wide), coiled behind buccal mass. Cutting edge of central teeth straight or weakly concave, bearing 9–15 short cusps. Central cusp pointed, slightly larger than lateral cusps. Basal cusps, 1–2 (sometimes absent on one side), innermost cusp largest. Lateral margins of central teeth angled about 40° to vertical axis of tooth, slightly thickened, distally expanded, projecting slightly beyond V-shaped base of tooth. Lateral teeth with 2–4 inner cusps and 3–5 outer cusps; basal process well developed. Lateral wing of lateral teeth rather broad, somewhat longer than cutting edge. Marginal teeth with relatively numerous cusps; cusps on inner marginals larger than those on outer marginals. Dorsal folds of esophagus short, straight. Cephalic tentacles medium length in preserved material. Ctenidium absent, reduced to a vestige, or well developed, with small, triangular filaments. Osphradium medium-sized, narrow. Hypobranchial gland well developed along rectum.

Renal organ with prominent pallial bulge. Stomach longer than style sac, posterior caecal appendix absent; anterior stomach chamber larger than posterior chamber. Rectum straight in pallial roof. Cephalo-pedal ganglia weakly pigmented; cerebral and pedal commissures short. Testis large. Prostate gland small, walls of medium thickness. Penis small to medium-sized relative to head, bifurcate. Lobe slightly shorter than filament, arising from inner edge at or near base, usually posteriorly oriented, weakly folded along most of length. Lobe containing weakly coiled duct which enters small muscular sac distally and exits as eversible papilla through cup-shaped opening. Duct exits base of lobe into nuchal cavity, broadening to form a large mass of blindly ending glandular loops above the salivary glands; gland lined with thin muscular coat. Penial filament straight or coiled to left, tapering to pointed tip. Penial duct medium width, with thick muscular coat, straight or weakly undulating basally, positioned along outer edge of filament. Females oviparous. Ovary small. Glandular oviduct consisting of subequal albumen and capsule glands. Albumen gland with short pallial component. Coiled oviduct a single, posteriorly arched loop opening to anterior portion of albumen gland. Bursa copulatrix medium-sized, positioned posteriorly, partly overlapped by albumen gland. Bursal duct ciliated, short to medium length, originating from anterior edge, opening to oviduct slightly behind pallial wall. Posterior seminal receptacle pouch-like, opening to distal arm of coiled oviduct; anterior seminal receptacle ovate to circular, pressed against ventral edge of albumen gland, opening to oviduct just distal to connection with bursal duct. Capsule gland with narrow, vertical lumen. Sperm tube narrow, separated from capsule gland along most of length, but distally fused to form a common genital aperture."

AMNICOLA Gould and Haldeman, in Haldeman 1840: type species is *Paludina porata* Say, 1821 (=*Amnicola limosa* Say, 1817). Shell usually less than 5 mm tall, conical or ovate-conic, 4–5 whorls, aperture subcircular or ovate, umbilicus perforate (Berry 1943). Radular central tooth wider than high, with 1–3 basal denticles. Penis simple or bifid, secondary lobe and accessory duct present or absent. Animal oviparous. Found in fresh or brackish water (Berry 1943). Six species are known, one of which is found in Utah, *Amnicola limosa*.

The Freshwater Snails

FIG. 1. *Amnicola limosa*, top left: lectotype, ANSP 57057 (*Amnicola pallida*); bottom left: lectotype, ANSP 283866 (*Paludina porata* Say). Credit: ANSP.

Amnicola limosa Say, 1817 Mud Amnicola

DESCRIPTION (Say 1817; Berry 1943): *Shell*: broadly conic, subumbilicate, dark horn colored, generally encrusted with a blackish irregular covering on the spire and sometimes on the body, which completely obscures the obsoletely wrinkled epidermis. *Whorls*: 4.5, apex blunt, nuclear whorl in same plane, later whorls round and somewhat shouldered, sutures impressed, whorls increasing gradually in size, body whorl round. *Aperture*: ovate-orbicular to subrotund, 1.52 wide × 1.88 mm high, peristome continuous, joined to the body by a thin callus.

SIZE: about 4.5 mm high × 3 mm wide.

ANIMAL: whitish; head brown; tentacula orbits, and a streak on each side of the neck, white; tentacles filiform, more than half as long as the base of the animal; rostrum about half as long as the tentacle, annulate, with darker lines above; foot white, brownish above, short, suboval, truncated before, and rounded behind. Penis is as shown in Fig. 2 (Berry 1943).

RADULA: 64 rows, long in proportion to the animal (1.2 × 0.18 mm); central tooth almost twice as broad as high, with four short, sharply pointed side cusps; lateral

Amnicolidae

FIG. 2. Penis of *Amnicola limosa*. Left: distended penis and secondary lobe (flagellum sheath) relaxed. The secondary duct exits at the upper margin; the lower duct is the vas deferens. Right: penis coiled around erected secondary lobe. Credit: Berry 1943.

FIG. 3. Radula of *Amnicola limosa*. Credit: Berry 1943.

tooth with a wide peduncle, basal ridge strong, one prominent basal cusp at the arch and one tubercle (sometimes developing into denticle) on the ridge.

TYPE LOCATION: Delaware and Schuylkill rivers, between low- and high-water marks.

JUNIOR SYNONYMS (Stewart 2006; Hershler and Liu 2017): *Paludina limosa* Say, 1817, *Paludina porata* Say, 1821; *Amnicola porata*; *Amnicola ferruginea* Calkins, 1880; *Amnicola orbiculata* Lea, 1844; *Amnicola limosus*; *Amnicola pallida* von Martens, 1874 (in part, i.e., U.S. shells assigned to it).

NOTES: Mature shells tend to be larger than those of *Pyrgulopsis* and *Colligyrus* but comparison of penial morphology (e.g., Fig. 2) is recommended for differentiation from *Pyrgulopsis* species. For identification of western springsnails, I recommend obtaining the keys produced by Hershler and Liu (2017), which are accompanied by excellent anatomical figures and images of shells. GenBank accession numbers: AF213348, AF212903, and AF212916.

DISTRIBUTION: Atlantic Coast to the Rocky Mountains, Labrador to Florida (Burch and Tottenham 1980). Utah records from Box Elder County, lower Provo River, Utah Lake, Spring Lake, Tooele County, and Fairfield, Utah (ANSP; Ibase; Jones 1940a; Hovingh 2018). The author has also found shells in Cache County. No living Amnicola have been noted in Utah (Call 1884).

Colligyrus greggi Pilsbry, 1935 Rocky Mountain Duskysnail

DESCRIPTION (Pilsbry 1935; Hershler 1999): *Shell*: small, conic, umbilicate (narrow to perforate), with rather obtuse summit (nearly flat apex), dull green, clear to white, with a thin periostracum. *Whorls*: 4 (3.5–4.5), nearly smooth, convex, narrowly shouldered, joined by a very deeply impressed suture; protoconch ~1.5 whorls with weak spiral lineations. *Aperture*: broadly oval to circular, narrower in the posterior part, but not angular there; peristome continuous (thin parietal lip is complete across the body whorl), but adnate above for a short distance, the outer margin thin; columella distinctly calloused; operculum paucispiral, the outer margin lacking a rim, attachment scar and callus weakly developed. Parietal margin thickened in old shells.

SIZE (Pilsbry 1935; Hershler 1999): SL 2.3 mm (1.7–3.3 mm), dia. 1.8 mm, ApL 1.1 mm.

ANIMAL (Hershler 1999): Body pigmentation well developed; Tentacles light gray to black, snout light gray. Foot pale; neck pale or pigmented with scattered gray granules; pallial roof and visceral coil black.

GENITALIA: Female coiled oviduct is simple; glandular oviduct is large, ventrally closed; bursa copulatrix large, posteriorly positioned; 2 seminal receptacles. Penial lobe rises near the base of the penis. Prostate gland bean-shaped. Basally, the penial duct narrows somewhat and undulates but is otherwise straight.

RADULA: about 15× longer than wide (1.5 mm × 94 μm), coiled behind buccal mass, with ~155 rows of teeth. Central teeth with 9–15 short cusps. The central cusp is pointed and slightly larger than lateral cusps. Lateral cusps 4–7, basal cusps 1–2, the innermost the largest. Lateral margins of central teeth angled about 40° to vertical axis of tooth, slightly thickened, distally expanded,

FIG. 4. *Colligyrus greggi*. ANSP 163812, holotype. Credit: ANSP.

projecting slightly beyond V-shaped base of the tooth. Marginal teeth with numerous cusps (27–27 inner, 25–33 outer).

TYPE LOCATION: Cliff Creek Canyon, a fork of Hoback Canyon, about 29 miles south of Jackson Hole, Wyoming in the Snake River drainage. Holotype in ANSP (163812); paralectotypes ANSP 375735.

JUNIOR SYNONYMS: *Hydrobia greggi* Pilsbry, 1935; *Amnicola greggi* (Pilsbry) Taylor 1966; *Lyogyrus greggi* (Pilsbry) Burch and Tottenham, 1980; The species was transferred to the new genus *Colligyrus* by Hershler (1999).

FIG. 5. *Colligyrus greggi*, China Row Spring, Logan Canyon, UT. Credit: E. Wagner.

NOTES: Small, globose to conical shell with a paucispiral operculum. Smaller shell than *Amnicola limosa,* and the penial lobe arises closer to the base of the penis. Similar to other hydrobiids, but with a thicker columella, more developed spire and deeper sutures (Pilsbry 1935). Differs from *Lyogyrus* in that females have two sperm pouches rather than one. The penis lacks surficial glands that are found in *Pyrgulopsis*. Lives in springs and small streams.

DISTRIBUTION: Upper Snake River Basin and northeastern Bonneville Basin. The genus occurs in the Willamette River, Harney-Malheur, Klamath and Pit River drainages, indicating that the distribution in Utah is likely associated with the Pleistocene connection of the Bear River with the Snake River (Hovingh 2018). In Wyoming in the Hoback River drainage (Sublette County) and Lincoln County (Sublette Creek). In Idaho in Bannock, Bear Lake, Caribou, and Franklin counties (Hershler 1999).

Records in Utah from Cache County springs, Logan and Bear rivers, and Tooele County (UMNH; Hershler 1999; Hovingh 2018). The shell in Fig. 5 is a shell from China Row Spring in Logan Canyon, 2019.

Cochliopidae Tryon, 1866a

The family consists of 5 genera, *Eremopyrgus, Ipnobius, Littoridinops, Spurwinkia*, and *Tryonia*. The first four contain but a single species found in the western United States (Hershler and Liu 2017). *Tryonia* contains 14 species, only one of which is found in Utah.

Tryonia Stimpson, 1865 (from Hershler and Thompson 1987): "Shell colorless, transparent, elongate-conic to turreted, 1.7–7 mm tall with 4.0–8.0 whorls; typically high spired with rounded whorls and indented sutures. Aperture simple, unthickened, and complete. Umbilicus narrow or absent. Sexual dimorphism pronounced, with males often half of female shell height. Protoconch flat or slightly protruding, smooth or slightly wrinkled. Teleoconch sculpture consisting of fine growth lines, sometimes coupled with weak spiral lines or collabral striations or varices. Central tooth of radula broader than tall, with 1–3 pairs of basal cusps. Digestive gland without anterior lobe. Cephalic tentacles with several elongate ciliary tracts. Flattened penis is elongate and slender with a single enlarged glandular (mammiform) lobe at its base and 1–4 smaller glandular lobes on the inner curvature. Distal portion of penis ciliated to varying degrees, base sometimes also ciliated. Tip of penis with blunt swelling on inner curvature. Female ovoviviparous, with 3–15 embryos brooded in enlarged capsule gland. Capsule gland with muscle sphincter at anterior end. Pallial oviduct reflected posteriorly; albumen gland reduced in size. Small-sized bursa copulatrix and seminal receptacle ventral to albumen gland; coiled seminal receptacle duct opens into short spermathecal duct."

Tryonia porrecta Mighels, 1845 Desert Tryonia

DESCRIPTION (Mighels, 1845{published 1848}): *Shell*: elongated, turreted, thin, smooth, greenish, imperforate. *Whorls*: 6, very convex, suture deep. *Aperture*: ovate, lip continuous. In Gould's (1855) description, there are 7–8 rounded whorls.

SIZE: SL 5.7 mm, dia. 1.7 mm.

ANIMAL: The penis has multiple papillae, including one located on inner edge (Hershler and Liu 2017).

TYPE LOCATION: Oahu, Hawaii.

JUNIOR SYNONYMS (Hershler and Liu 2017): *Paludina porrecta* Mighels, 1845 (1848); *Amnicola protea* Gould, 1855; *Tryonia protea* (Gould) Binney, 1865b; *Melania exigua* Conrad, 1855; *Paludestrina protea* (Gould) Chamberlin & Jones 1929; *Pyrgulopsis imminens* Taylor, 1950; *Pyrgulopsis blakeana* Taylor, 1950; *Pyrgulopsis cahuillarum* Taylor, 1950; Russell, 1971.

NOTES: More narrowly conic than other shells in Hydrobiidae and Amnicolidae in Utah. Shells of the more common New Zealand mud snail also are similar in shape, but these tend to be darker brown in color, with a rounder aperture often (not always) jutting out beyond an imaginary tangential line connecting all the upper whorls. It may be confused with juvenile shells of *Melanoides tuberculata*, but these juveniles have more ornamentation and ribbing that are readily observed on close inspection. Recent surveys after 2011 have failed to find *T. porrecta* where they were previously reported at Horseshoe, Muskrat, or Warm Springs; the invasion of New Zealand mud snails (Horseshoe Spring

FIG. 6. *Tryonia porrecta*, lectotype, ANSP 27965 (orginal combination Melania exigua). Credit: ANSP.

FIG. 7. *Tryonia porrecta*. Fish Springs National Wildlife Refuge, UT. Credit: E. Wagner.

survey by E. Wagner, 2019), the introduction of bass into Horseshoe Springs, and desiccation from groundwater pumping are correlated with their disappearance (Hovingh 2018).

DISTRIBUTION (Hershler and Liu 2017): Lower Colorado River Basin (AZ, CA, Mexico), Great Basin (NV, UT), San Francisco Bay, California, Hawaii. In Utah, reported from Blue Lake complex, and Skull Valley (Horseshoe and Muskrat Springs, Tooele County; Russell 1971; Hovingh 2018). *T. porrecta* were found live in Delle Spring, Tooele County and Fish Springs National Wildlife Refuge in 2021 (J. Holcomb, Utah Division Wildlife Resources, personal communication 2021).

Hydrobiidae Stimpson, 1865

The family contains many genera, including *Pyrgulopsis*, that contains 126 species found in the western United States. The type species is *P. nevadensis* Stearns, 1883. Characteristics of *Pyrgulopsis* Call and Pilsbry, 1886, include (Hershler and Thompson 1987): Shell subglobose, globose, to elongate-conic, 1.2–8.0 mm in height, with 3.0–6.0 whorls. Aperture simple, sometimes loosened from body whorl. Umbilicus absent to open. Protoconch partly or totally covered with wrinkled pits (for figures, see Thompson 1977; Hershler 1985). Teleoconch smooth or uni-carinate on periphery, usually with fine growth lines. Radula with basal cusps on the central teeth. Mantle and/or penial filament often with distinctive pigment markings. Penis with small, distal lobe and narrow, elongate filament. Penial surface with 1–15 glandular ridges, sometimes on stalked crests. Females oviparous; capsule gland with two tissue sections and a near-terminal opening (Thompson 1977; Hershler 1985).

Oviduct with a single anterior coil on the left side of the albumen gland into which opens the seminal receptacle. Bursa copulatrix typically enlarged and partly posterior to albumen gland; bursa duct and oviduct jointly open into anterior portion of albumen gland. *Marstonia* Baker, 1926, was previously synonymized under *Pyrgulopsis*, but the genus was resurrected by Thompson and Hershler (2002) to include some eastern spring snails that differed morphologically from *Pyrgulopsis*. Previously described genera now considered junior synonyms of *Pyrgulopsis* include *Fontelicella, Natricola, and Microamnicola* Greg and Taylor, 1965; *Savaginius* Taylor, 1966; *Nymphophilus* Taylor, 1966, *Mexistiobia* Hershler, 1985; *Apachecoccus* and *Yaquicoccus* Taylor, 1987 (Hershler and Thompson 1987; Hershler and Liu 2017). For genetic analyses of *Pyrgulopsis* species and their GenBank codes, see Hershler and Liu (2017).

Pyrgulopsis anguina Hershler, 1998 Longitudinal Gland Pyrg

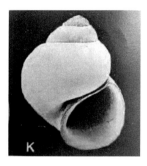

FIG. 8. *Pyrgulopsis anguina.* Credit: Y. Villacampa, Dept. Invertebrate Zoology, USNM (Hershler 1998).

DESCRIPTION (Hershler 1998): *Shell*: medium sized, with subglobose to ovate-conic shell, the apex often eroded. *Whorls*: 3.0–5.0; protoconch 1.25 whorls, dia. 0.30 mm, weakly wrinkled at the apex, otherwise smooth; teleoconch whorls medium to highly convex, shoulders narrow or absent, sculpture including faint spiral striae; body whorl often slightly disjunct behind the aperture. *Aperture*: pyriform, adnate or disjunct; inner lip slightly thickened in larger specimens, often forming narrow columellar shelf; outer lip thin, slightly prosocline, without sinuation. Umbilicus shallowly perforate. Periostracum tan-green. Operculum ovate, amber, nuclear region slightly reddish; nucleus eccentric; dorsal surface frilled; attachment scar often thick all around.

SIZE: SL 2.0–3.5 mm, SW 1.7–2.4 mm, and W/L 70–95%.

ANIMAL: Tentacles unpigmented to medium brown. Snout and foot are light to medium brown; pallial roof and visceral coil uniformly dark brown or black.

GENITALIA: Penial filament darkly pigmented along almost the entire length; black granules sometimes scattered on remainder of penis. Penial filament and lobe short. Penial ornaments: a medium-sized terminal gland, large penial gland, medium-large dorsal gland (Dg) 1, large Dg2, medium-large Dg3, additional dorsal gland, and large ventral gland. Bursa copulatrix as long and wide as albumen gland, ovate-pyriform, longitudinal, with most or all of the length posterior to the gland.

RADULA: 820 × 120 µm, with 62 rows of teeth; central tooth 26 µm wide, with medium-highly indented dorsal edge; lateral cusps 5–7; Lateral tooth formula 2(3)–1–4(5).

TYPE LOCATION: Big Springs, Snake Valley, White Pine County, Nevada. Holotype USNM 883848, paratypes USNM 860710.

JUNIOR SYNONYMS: none

NOTES: Similar to *Pyrgulopsis chamberlini*, but *P. anguina* has a broader shell, larger penial lobe, a longitudinal orientation of terminal gland, and a stronger Dg3 and ventral gland. GenBank accession number EU700466. Closest genetic relative is *P. kolobensis* (Hershler and Liu 2017).

DISTRIBUTION: Snake Valley (Bonneville Basin, Millard County, Utah and Nevada).

Pyrgulopsis chamberlini Hershler 1998, Smooth Glenwood Pyrg

DESCRIPTION (Hershler 1998): *Shell*: ovate-conic; umbilicus absent or narrowly rimate; periostracum light green. *Whorls*: 4.5–6.0; protoconch 1.25 whorls, diameter 0.33 mm; very weakly wrinkled at apex, otherwise smooth. Teleoconch whorls medium convexity, shoulders well developed, often having a broad shelf; body whorl often slightly disjunct behind the aperture. *Aperture*: ovate, slightly disjunct in largest specimens. Inner lip slightly thickened, columellar shelf medium width; outer lip usually thin, but slightly thickened in largest specimens, prosocline, without sinuation. Operculum ovate, amber, with a reddish, eccentric, nuclear region; dorsal surface weakly frilled. Attachment scar thick all around, broadly so between nucleus and inner edge.

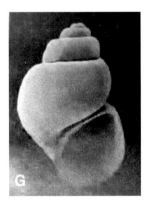

FIG. 9. *Pyrgulopsis chamberlini*. Credit: Y. Villacampa, Dept. Invertebrate Zoology, USNM (Hershler 1998).

SIZE: SL 2.3–4.3 mm, SW 1.8–3.1 mm, W/L 64–78%

ANIMAL: Tentacles unpigmented or light brown; proximal section unpigmented. Snout light to dark gray-brown. Foot light brown. Opercular lobe light gray along inner edge, sometimes all around. Neck very light gray. Pallial roof, visceral coil dark brown or black, sometimes uniformly pigmented. Penial filament darkly pigmented along almost entire length; distal base often similarly pigmented. Stomach as long as style sac; anterior stomach chamber larger than posterior chamber. Stomach caecum small.

GENITALIA: Ovary 0.75–1.0 whorl, filling 50% of digestive gland behind stomach, abutting or slightly overlapping posterior stomach chamber. Albumen gland has a medium large (33% or more) pallial component. Capsule gland shorter, narrower than albumen gland, having distinct pigment patch alongside genital aperture, subglobose in section; rectal furrow weak. Ventral channel broadly overlapping capsule gland; longitudinal fold well developed. Genital aperture a terminal pore mounted on small papilla, having short anterior extension. Coiled oviduct of two overlapping, posterior-oblique loops, distal loop having dark pigmented streak. Oviduct and bursal duct joining a little behind pallial wall. Bursa copulatrix long, medium width, lying along ventral margin of gland, ovate, longitudinal, 50–75% of length posterior to gland. Bursal duct originating from anterior edge at midline, 50% of length of bursa, medium width. Seminal receptacle small, with an elongate pouch, rarely folded, overlapping anteriormost portion of bursa.

Testis, 1.25 whorls, filling more than 50% of digestive gland behind stomach, overlapping posterior stomach chamber. Prostate gland large, elongate bean-shaped, pallial portion short, ovate in section. Proximal pallial vas deferens having well-developed, reflexed loop. Penis large; base rectangular, often elongate, smooth or weakly folded along inner edge, usually constricted proximally; filament medium length, narrow, gently tapering, oblique; lobe short, broadly rounded, longitudinal, or slightly oblique. Terminal gland medium sized, ovate, rarely bifurcate, usually transverse, ventral. Penial gland filling most of the length of the filament and small portion of the base, almost as wide as filament. Dg1 (dorsal gland) large, narrow, raised on a low pedicel, longitudinal (although proximal part sometimes oblique), borne along outer edge proximally, rarely abutting the penial gland, sometimes accompanied along inner side by small, circular raised gland. Dg2 small, ovate, distal. Dg3 small, ovate-elongate (sometimes dot-like or absent), slightly raised. Dorsal surface having 1–6 additional longitudinal glands proximal to Dg2, units usually dot-like or ovate, but also often including 1–2 elongate glands near inner edge. Ventral gland small, ovate, transverse, borne on low swelling, positioned near base of lobe; sometimes accompanied by dot-like or small, circular gland proximally. Penial duct straight, near outer edge.

RADULA: 710 × 100 μm, with 62 rows of teeth. Central tooth 28 μm wide, with highly indented dorsal edge; later cusps, 4–6; central cusp narrow (sometimes long), dagger-like; basal cusps medium sized. Lateral tooth formula 2(3)–1–3(4); neck weakly flexed; outer wing 175% of cutting-edge length. Inner marginal teeth with 26–30 cusps; cutting edge occupying 40% of length of tooth. Outer marginal teeth with 32–34 cusps; cutting edge occupying 25% of length of tooth.

TYPE LOCATION: Spring, Glenwood, Sevier River drainage, Sevier County, Utah. Holotype USNM 883576, paratypes USNM 860729.

JUNIOR SYNONYMS: none

NOTES: Penial ornaments include a medium-sized terminal gland, large penial gland, large Dg1, small Dg2, small Dg3 (sometimes absent), 1–6 additional dorsal glands, and a small ventral gland. GenBank accession number EU700468. Closest genetic relative is *P. variegata*, differing by 1.9% (Hershler and Liu 2017).

DISTRIBUTION: Known only from the type locations, 2 springs in the Sevier River drainage near Glenwood, Utah.

Pyrgulopsis deserta Pilsbry, 1916 Desert Springsnail

DESCRIPTION (Pilsbry 1916a; Hershler and Landye 1988): *Shell*: small (1.2–2.2 mm tall), globose to ovate conic, perforate, corneous, translucent, thin, with a glossy surface very minutely marked with delicate growth lines. Spire outline is convex, the apex somewhat pointed. *Whorls*: 3.5, strongly convex, the last more rapidly descending close to the aperture. *Aperture*: ovate, somewhat oblique, angular above. Peristome continuous and free from preceding whorl.

SIZE: SL 2.4 mm, SW 1.7 mm; ApL 1.25 mm. Another shell measured 2.2 × 1.6 mm (4 whorls).

ANIMAL: Penis with an enlarged filament bearing dorsally an elongate glandular ridge; ventral penial surface with 2–3 more ridges.

TYPE LOCATION: Washington County, Utah. Holotype ANSP 121112.

JUNIOR SYNONYMS: *Amnicola deserta* Pilsbry, 1916a; *Fontelicella deserta* (Pilsbry 1916a) Gregg and Taylor, 1965.

NOTES: Taylor (1987) suggested that the lack of a specific type location should invalidate this species. The description closely agrees with Taylor's (1987) description of *P. kolobensis* and *P. pinetorum*, which are from the same area.

FIG. 10. *Pyrgulopsis deserta*. ANSP 121112. Credit: ANSP.

However, later genetic analyses indicated that *P. deserta* is a distinct species (Hurt 2004). GenBank accession numbers for *P. deserta:* DQ251077, AY485534-AY485539 (Hershler and Liu 2017). Hershler et al. (2017) noted that "*P. lyndahlae* differs from *P. deserta* by 7.8–8.4% COI sequence divergence (*P. deserta* sequences from Hurt 2004, Liu and Hershler 2007) and is also readily distinguished from this species by its larger size and the absence of a penial gland."

DISTRIBUTION: In Utah, it is found in springs in the lower Virgin River in the St. George area (Hershler et al. 2017). There is also an ANSP record from Grapevine Springs, Zion National Park, though this record is likely *P. lindahlae*, since those springs are the type locality for that species. Also reported from near Littlefield, Arizona, in Virgin River and lower Colorado River (Hershler and Liu 2017).

Pyrgulopsis fusca Hershler, 1998, Otter Creek Pyrg

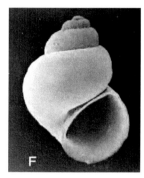

FIG. 11. *Pyrgulopsis fusca*. Credit: Y. Villacampa, Dept. Invertebrate Zoology, USNM (Hershler 1998).

DESCRIPTION (Hershler 1998): *Shell*: ovate- to elongate-conic, with a rimate or shallowly perforate umbilicus; periostracum dark tan. *Whorls*: 4.25–5.25; protoconch 1.5 whorls, diameter 0.40 mm, initial 0.75 whorl very weakly wrinkled, mostly near inner edge, otherwise smooth; remaining teleoconch whorls of medium to high convexity, shoulders narrow to broad, sculpture including faint spiral striae; body whorl often slightly disjunct from previous whorl behind the aperture. *Aperture*: ovate, adnate or slightly disjunct; inner lip thin, sometimes having a very narrow columellar shelf. Outer lip is thin, slightly prosocline, without sinuation. Operculum ovate, amber, with a reddish, eccentric nucleus; dorsal surface weakly frilled. Attachment scar is slightly thickened along inner edge and between nucleus and inner edge.

SIZE: height 2.5–4.4 mm, width 1.6–2.9 mm, width/height 61–73%.

ANIMAL: Tentacles dark brown or black, with narrow unpigmented streak centrally. Snout, foot, are medium brown or black. Opercular lobe sometimes dark along inner edge and/or along outer edge. Neck light to medium gray-brown. Pallial roof, visceral coil dark brown or black.

Ctenidial filaments, 19, pleated; ctenidium overlapping pericardium posteriorly. Osphradium small, narrow, centered well posterior to middle of ctenidium. Renal gland longitudinal; kidney opening slightly thickened. Rectum broadly overlapping pallial oviduct, slightly overlapping prostate gland. Stomach slightly longer than style sac; anterior stomach chamber larger than posterior chamber; stomach caecum small.

GENITALIA: Penial filament darkly pigmented internally. Ovary 1.0–1.25 whorls, filling more than 50% of the digestive gland behind the stomach, overlapping posterior stomach chamber. Albumen gland has a short pallial part. Capsule gland shorter, narrower than albumen gland, subcircular in section; rectal furrow medium depth. Ventral channel slightly overlapping capsule gland; longitudinal fold well developed. Genital aperture a terminal slit having a short anterior extension. Coiled oviduct usually of two overlapping posterior-oblique loops; proximal loop lightly pigmented internally. Oviduct and bursal duct joining a little behind pallial wall. Bursa copulatrix medium length and width, ovate, longitudinal, with most of length posterior to gland. Bursal duct originating from anterior edge at midline, 50% to almost as long as bursa, medium width. Seminal receptacle medium sized, pouch-like, curved or folded, overlapping anteriormost portion of bursa.

Testis with 2.0 whorls, filling almost all of digestive gland behind stomach, overlapping both stomach chambers. Prostate gland broad bean-shaped, pallial portion short, narrowly ovate in section. Proximal pallial vas deferens has a well-developed, reflexed loop. Penis medium sized; base elongate-rectangular, inner edge weakly folded or smooth; filament medium length, broad, tapering to point, longitudinal or slightly oblique; lobe short, truncate, longitudinal. Terminal gland small, subcircular, distal, ventral. Penial gland small (sometimes reduced or absent), narrower than filament, positioned on filament near base. Ventral gland small, subcircular or ovate (transverse), borne on low swelling, positioned near base of filament. Penial duct straight, near outer edge.

RADULA: 650 × 100 μm, with 50 rows of teeth. Central tooth 24 μm wide, with highly indented dorsal edge; lateral cusps 3–8, central cusp medium width, spoon-like; basal cusps small, sometimes accompanied by slight thickenings to outside. Lateral tooth formula 2(3,4)–1–3(4,5); neck weakly flexed; outer wing 220% of cutting-edge length. Inner marginal teeth with 21–28 cusps; cutting edge occupying 34% of length of tooth. Outer marginal teeth with 27–33 cusps; cutting edge occupying 28% of length of tooth.

TYPE LOCATION: Spring brook about 1.6 km above The Narrows, Otter Creek, Piute County, Utah. Holotype USNM 883439, paratypes USNM 860728.

JUNIOR SYNONYMS: none

NOTES: Medium-sized with ovate- to elongate-conic shell. Penis medium-sized; filament medium length; lobe short. Penial ornaments of small terminal, penial, and ventral glands. Specific name is derived from the Latin word *fuscus*, meaning dark or swarthy and referring to the black body pigmentation characterizing this snail.

DISTRIBUTION: Only known from Otter Creek in the Sevier River drainage.

Pyrgulopsis hamlinensis Hershler, 1998 Hamlin Valley Pyrg

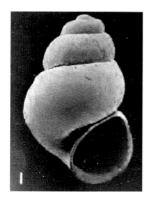

FIG. 12. *Pyrgulopsis hamlinensis*. Credit: Y. Villacampa, Dept. Invertebrate Zoology, USNM (Hershler 1998)

DESCRIPTION (Hershler 1998): *Shell* narrow-conic, periostracum light tan. *Whorls*: 4.25–5.0. Protoconch 1.25 whorls, diameter 0.34 mm, smooth except for a small area of very weak wrinkling at apex. Teleoconch whorls low-medium convexity, narrowly shouldered, often having pronounced angulation at base; body whorl often broadly disjunct behind the aperture. *Aperture:* ovate, usually disjunct. Inner lip thin, without columellar shelf. Outer lip thin, orthocline or weakly prosocline, without sinuation. Umbilicus rimate to shallowly perforate. Operculum ovate, amber; nucleus eccentric; dorsal surface weakly frilled. Attachment scar thick all around.

SIZE: SL 1.6–2.0 mm, SW 1.0–1.3 mm; W/L 59–69%

ANIMAL: Cephalic tentacles unpigmented or having very light gray pigment proximally. Snout medium gray. Foot light to medium gray. Opercular lobe dark along inner edge, sometimes along outer edge as well. Neck unpigmented except for scattered gray granules. Pallial roof, visceral coil near uniform black (pigment slightly lighter on genital ducts). Stomach as long as style sac; anterior stomach chamber larger than posterior chamber; stomach caecum small.

Ctenidial filaments, 15, weakly pleated; ctenidium connected to pericardium by short efferent vein. Osphradium small, narrow, positioned slightly posterior to middle of ctenidium. Renal gland longitudinal; kidney opening gray-white. Rectum broadly overlapping genital ducts. Ovary 0.75 whorl, filling less than 50% of digestive gland behind stomach, overlapping posterior stomach chamber. Albumen gland having medium (up to 33% pallial component). Capsule gland shorter, narrower than albumen gland, ovate in section; rectal furrow medium depth. Ventral channel slightly overlapping capsule gland; longitudinal fold well developed.

GENITALIA: Genital aperture a terminal slit, mounted on weak papilla, having short anterior extension. Coiled oviduct a posterior-oblique loop sometimes preceded by weak to well-developed posterior twist. Bursa copulatrix medium length and width, ovate, longitudinal, slightly less than 33% of length of posterior to gland. Bursal duct originating from anterior edge at midline, often poorly distinguished from bursa; short (up to 50% of bursa length), medium width. Seminal receptacle small, sometimes minute, pouch-like or subglobular, overlapping anteriormost section of bursa.

Testis with 1.5 whorls, filling more than 50% of digestive gland behind stomach, overlapping posterior and part of anterior stomach chambers. Prostate gland small, subglobular, pallial portion short, narrowly ovate in section. Proximal pallial vas deferens straight or having weak undulation. Penis small to medium-sized; base rectangular, weakly folded; filament 66% length of base, medium width, tapering to point, longitudinal or slightly oblique; lobe slightly shorter to as long as filament, club-like, longitudinal or slightly oblique. Terminal gland medium-sized, ovate or circular, rarely bifurcate, variably oriented, ventral. Penial duct straight, near outer edge. Penial filament darkly pigmented internally for most of its length.

RADULA: 560 × 95 μm, with 62 rows of teeth. Central tooth 23 μm wide, with highly indented dorsal edge; lateral cusps, 5–7; central cusp narrow, dagger-like; basal cusps medium-sized. Lateral tooth formula 3(4) –I–4(5); neck weakly flexed; outer wing 225% of cutting-edge length. Inner marginal teeth with 2–28 cusps; cutting edge occupying 33% of length of tooth. Outer marginal teeth with 25–30 cusps; cutting edge occupying 25% of length of tooth.

TYPE LOCATION: Springs 0.5 km east of White Rock Cabin Springs, Hamlin Valley, Beaver County, Utah. Holotype USNM 883215, paratypes USNM 860695.

JUNIOR SYNONYMS: none

NOTES: Small, with narrow-conic shell. Penis small to medium-sized, filament medium length, lobe short to medium length. Penial ornament a medium-sized terminal gland.

DISTRIBUTION: Limited to one spring complex in Hamlin Valley, Utah, and adjacent Lincoln County, Nevada.

Pyrgulopsis inopinata Hershler, 1998 Carinate Glenwood Pyrg

DESCRIPTION: *Shell*: ovate- to narrow-conic; umbilicus absent or rimate. Periostracum is tan. *Whorls*: 5.0–5.75; protoconch 1.25 whorls, diameter 0.34 whorls, smooth or very weakly wrinkled at apex. Teleoconch whorls flat to medium convexity, without shoulders, sutures shallow; final 2.0 whorls usually having weak to well-developed peripheral angulation or narrow keel, sculpture sometimes weaker on body whorl; body whorl often slightly disjunct behind the aperture. *Aperture*: ovate, usually slightly disjunct. Inner lip thickened in larger specimens, without columellar shelf. Outer lip thin, orthocline or slightly prosocline, weakly sinuate. Operculum ovate, amber, slightly darker in the eccentric nuclear region;

dorsal surface strongly frilled; outer margin having a weak rim; attachment scar strongly thickened all around.

SIZE: SL 2.9–3.5 mm, SW 1.4–2.1 mm; W/L 55–63%.

FIG. 13. *Pyrgulopsis inopinata*. Credit: Y. Villacampa, Dept. Invertebrate Zoology, USNM (Hershler 1998).

ANIMAL: Tentacles medium gray to black, unpigmented around eyes. Snout medium gray to black. Foot light gray to black. Opercular lobe diffuse black along inner edge. Neck light gray. Pallial roof, visceral coil medium gray to black, pigment lighter along genital ducts. Ctenidial filaments, 24, pleated; ctenidium overlapping pericardium posteriorly. Osphradium small, narrow, positioned slightly posterior to middle of ctenidium. Renal gland longitudinal, kidney opening gray-white. Rectum broadly overlapping genital ducts. Stomach longer than style sac; anterior stomach chamber larger than posterior chamber; stomach caecum small.

GENITALIA: Ovary 0.75–1 whorls, filling less than 50% of digestive gland behind the stomach, slightly overlapping posterior stomach chamber. Albumen gland has a short pallial component. Capsule gland shorter, slightly narrower than albumen gland, broadly ovate in section; rectal furrow deep. Ventral channel slightly overlapping capsule gland; longitudinal fold small. Genital aperture a terminal pore mounted on a slightly muscular papilla, having short anterior extension. Coiled oviduct of two small, posterior-oblique loops; proximal portion sometimes only weakly kinked. Oviduct and bursal duct joining a little behind pallial wall. Bursa copulatrix medium length and width, ovate, longitudinal, with 50% of length posterior to gland. Bursal duct originating from anterior edge at midline, 50% of bursa length, medium width, often shallowly embedded in albumen gland. Seminal receptacle small, pouch-like, overlapping or lateral (ventral) to anterior portion of bursa.

Testis 1.5–2.0 whorls, filling more than 50% of the digestive gland behind the stomach, overlapping posterior, and part of anterior, stomach. Prostate gland bean-shaped, pallial portion short, ovate in section. Proximal pallial vas deferens having well-developed, weakly reflexed loop. Penis medium-sized, base elongate-rectangular, folded; filament short, narrow, tapering to a point, longitudinal; lobe longer than filament (sometimes considerably so), rectangular, longitudinal. Terminal gland medium sized, ovate, transverse, largely ventral. Dorsal gland (Dg1) elongate, extending from middle of penis base near outer edge onto proximal half of filament, almost as wide as filament, slightly raised; longitudinal, but with proximal part slightly oblique. Dg2 small, circular, absent in about 50% of specimens, positioned near inner edge of lobe. Ventral gland medium-sized, ovate, borne on low swelling, transverse-oblique, positioned near base of lobe. Penial duct straight, near outer edge. Penial filament black along almost entire length; pigment often extending onto distal penis.

RADULA: 610 × 105 µm, with 55 rows of teeth. Central tooth 29 µm wide, with medium indented dorsal edge; lateral cusps 5–7; central cusp medium width, rounded or dagger-like; basal cusps small. Lateral tooth formula 3(4,5) –1–4(5); neck weakly to medium flexed; outer wing 160% cutting edge length. Inner marginal teeth with 23–27 cusps; cutting edge occupying 34% of length of tooth. Outer marginal teeth with 28–33 cusps; cutting edge occupying 27% of length of tooth.

TYPE LOCATION: Spring, Glenwood, Utah, Sevier County, Utah. Holotype USNM 883493, paratypes USNM 860730.

JUNIOR SYNONYMS: none

NOTES: Hershler and Liu (2017, Appendix) noted that the closest genetic relatives were *P. kolobensis* (differed by 2.6–3.6%), *P. marcida* (differed by 2.6%), and *P. plicata* (2.6%). Penial ornaments include a medium-sized terminal gland, large dorsal gland (Dg1), small dorsal gland (Dg2, often absent), small Dg3, and medium-sized ventral gland. Specific name derived from the Latin word *inopinatus*, meaning unexpected. Other carinate species of *Pyrgulopsis* include *P. nevadensis*, *P. archimedis*, and *P. carinata*, but *P. inopinata* differs in the pattern of dorsal glands on the penis. GenBank accession number AY426360.

DISTRIBUTION: Known only from three springs in the Sevier River drainage, Utah.

Pyrgulopsis kolobensis Taylor, 1987 Toquerville Springsnail

DESCRIPTION (Taylor 1987): *Shell*: elongately ovate-conic to broadly conic; periostracum tan. *Whorls*: 4 (3–4.5), regularly convex, forming a spire with a slightly convex outline. *Aperture*: peristome simply adnate or free; when adnate, largely or completely covering a narrow umbilicus. Operculum plane, amber, with a darker internal callus. Attachment scar has a discrete border all around that leaves no conspicuous spiral trace.

SIZE: (mean and range, n = 30) SL 3.14 mm (2.85–3.70), length of body whorl 2.55 (2.30–2.85 mm), ApL 1.57 mm (1.39–1.76), ApL/SL 50.3 (45–56)%, ratio aperture length to body whorl length 0.618 (0.57–0.66), W/L 70.1 (62–76)%, ratio of width to length of body whorl 0.862 (0.7–0.91).

ANIMAL (Taylor 1987; Hershler 1998): GENITALIA: Penis distinguished by the pattern of glands (see notes and figure). Penis large, filament short, lobe

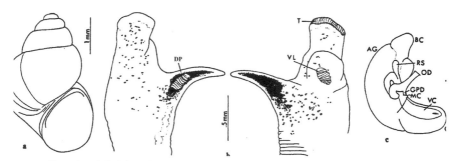

FIG. 14. *Pyrgulopsis kolobensis*. a: shell, b: penis; c: distal portion of female reproductive system. Abbreviations: AG = albumen gland, BC = bursa copulatrix, CG = capsule gland, DP = penial gland, GPD = gonopericardial duct, MC = posterior end of mantle cavity; OD = oviduct; RS = seminal recepticle; T = terminal gland; VC = ventral channel, VL = gland on ventral lobule. Credit: Taylor 1987, New Mexico Bureau of Geology and Mineral Resources.

medium-long. Penial ornament variable, but typically a large terminal gland, small penial gland, and large ventral gland. The terminal gland of the penis is usually fairly large and curved but may be short and either ovate or, rarely, circular. The penial gland is small or absent (Virgin River population) and confined to the base of the filament, but it may also be long, filling most of the filament and often extending a short or long distance onto the base. Ventral gland of penis varies from either a long or short strip to oval or dot-like. The free portion of the penis has a core of melanin granules but does not form the conspicuous black mass found in several other species. Bursa/albumin gland ratio in seven specimens ranged from 0.28 to 0.38. Loop of oviduct thickened and glandular; seminal receptacle club shaped. Bursa copulatrix is larger than that for *P. pinetorum*.

RADULA: no data

TYPE LOCATION: Toquerville Springs, Washington County, Utah. Holotype in Los Angeles County Museum of Natural History (LACM), 2216.

JUNIOR SYNONYMS (Hershler 1998): *Fontelicella kolobensis* Taylor, 1987; *Paludestrina longinqua* Gould, 1855; *Amnicola (Cincinnatia) cincinnatiensis* Anthony, 1840 (in Henderson 1924). Distribution of *P. longinqua* is limited to its type locality in the Salton Trough of southern California and does not appear to be closely related to the Bonneville Basin form (Hershler 1998).

NOTES (Taylor 1987; Hershler 1998): Differentiated from other pyrgs by the glandular patches on the penis: short penial patch on the proximal half of the free portion; accessory process with a long transverse terminal strip; a ventral lobule (VL) with a gland of variable size, and sometimes a papule on the ventral surface in front of the gland. Many shells were identified as *P. longinqua* or *P. kolobensis* (e.g., Liu et al. 2015) since there were few other species described at the time.

Bonneville Basin records for *kolobensis* have mostly been transferred to *P. pilsbryana* (Liu et al. 2018). GenBank accession numbers AY485532, AY485533, AY627939 (Hershler et al. 2017).

DISTRIBUTION (Jones 1940a, b; Hershler 1998; Hershler and Liu 2017): Currently, based on genetic analyses (COI; Hershler et al. 2017), which show genetic differences among populations even within the Virgin River headwater system, the species distribution is restricted to the type locality. *P. kolobensis* was formerly thought to have a much broader distribution, with earlier observations of *Pyrgulopsis* species being assigned to the species, for example, reports from the Bonneville Basin and lower Colorado River drainage of Utah, Colorado, and Nevada, and the Strawberry River drainage in Utah (e.g., Pilsbry 1899d; Jones 1940a; Russell 1971) and museum records (Hershler 1998; ANSP): counties of Box Elder, Cache, Davis, Iron, Juab, Millard, Morgan, Rich, Salt Lake, Sevier, Summit, Tooele, Utah, Wasatch, Washington, and Weber.

Pyrgulopsis lindahlae Hershler, Liu, Forsythe, Hovingh et Wheeler, 2017; Lindahl's Pyrg

DESCRIPTION: *Shell*: ovate- to narrow-conic; umbilicus absent or very small; periostracum tan. *Whorls*: convex, weakly shouldered. *Aperture*: parietal lip usually free, rarely adnate, last half whorl sometimes broadly disjunct. Operculum as for genus; muscle attachment margin variably thickened on inner side.

SIZE: SL (mean, range) 3.35 (3.03–3.74) mm; SW 2.24 (2.03–2.65) mm; height of body whorl 2.56 (2.37–2.76) mm, width of body whorl 1.89 (1.71–2.09) mm, ApL 1.47 (1.29–1.73) mm; ApW 1.33 (1.23–1.51) mm.

FIG. 15. *Pyrgulopsis lindahlae*. Credit: Y. Villacampa, Dept. Invertebrate Zoology, USNM (Hershler et al. 2017).

ANIMAL: GENITALIA: Penis large, distally bifurcate; filament rather short, lobe slightly longer than filament. Terminal gland overlapping both dorsal and ventral sides of lobe, present in 29 of 30 specimens; ventral gland small, positioned nearly centrally on lobe, present in 28 of 30 specimens. In females, the coiled oviduct is a small, circular loop preceded by a well-developed kink. Bursa copulatrix medium-sized, largely posterior to albumen gland; seminal receptacle overlapping proximal section of bursal duct.

RADULA: as for genus; lateral cusps 3–5, basal cusp 1. Lateral teeth having 1–3 cusps on inner, and 2–4 cusps on outer, side. Inner marginal teeth with 16–23 cusps, outer marginal teeth with 23–38 cusps.

TYPE LOCATION: Grapevine Spring, along west side of Left Fork of North Creek, Zion National Park, Washington County, Utah (37.28038°N, 113.09455 °W). Holotype USNM 905098; paratypes USNM 1409023.

JUNIOR SYNONYMS: None, though some previous collections were identified as "probably *Amnicola* sp." (Hamilton 1994) or *Pyrgulopsis kolobensis* (Hershler 1998).

NOTES: Distinguished from *P. deserta* by its larger size and the absence of a penial gland (Hershler et al. 2017). Named in honor of Alice Lindahl who first described the species during her ecological survey of Grapevine Spring (Lindahl 1976). Nearest relative appears to be *P. pinetorum* (Liu et al. 2018).

DISTRIBUTION: Known only from two springs about 100 m apart in an incised canyon at the base of a basalt escarpment along the west side of the Left Fork of North Creek, Washington County, Utah, a short distance upstream from the Right Fork confluence.

Pyrgulopsis nuwuvi Hershler, Liu, Forsythe, Hovingh et Wheeler, 2017 Nuwuvi Pyrg

DESCRIPTION (Hershler et al. 2017): *Shell*: narrow-conic; periostracum is tan. *Whorls*: 4.5–5 (mean, 4.7), convex, weakly shouldered. *Aperture*: parietal lip usually free, rarely adnate, last 0.5 whorl, sometimes broadly disjunct, narrow columellar shelf sometimes pesent; umbilicus, when present, is small. Operculum is as for genus, with an eccentric spiral nucleus; muscle attachment margin variably thickened.

SIZE: SL (mean, range) 3.63 (3.23–4.02) mm; SW 2.35 (2.22–2.47) mm; height of body whorl 2.68 (2.42–2.86) mm; width of body whorl 2.01 (1.81–2.16) mm; ApL 1.56 (1.40–1.69); ApW 1.40 (1.28–1.46).

FIG. 16. *Pyrgulopsis nuwuvi*. Credit: Y. Villacampa, Dept. Invertebrate Zoology, USNM (Hershler et al. 2017).

ANIMAL (Hershler et al. 2017): GENITALIA: Penis large, distally bifurcate; filament rather short, lobe about as long as filament. Terminal gland overlapping both dorsal and ventral sides of lobe, present in 50 of 50 specimens, varying from a narrow strip to a small oval. Penial gland overlapping proximal half of filament, present in 50 of 50 specimens. For females, the coiled oviduct is a posterior oblique loop preceded by a weak kink. Bursa copulatrix is medium-sized, about 50% of length posterior to albumen gland; seminal receptacle overlaps proximal section of bursal duct.

RADULA: As for genus; lateral cusps 2–5, basal cup 1. Lateral teeth having 2–3 cusps on inner, and 3–4 cusps on outer, side. Inner marginal teeth with 15–20 cusps, outer marginal teeth with 15–24 cusps.

TYPE LOCATION: Danish Ranch, Washington County, Utah (37.26527 N, 113.42797W; eastern foothills of the Pine Valley Mountains). Holotype at Bell Museum of Natural History.

JUNIOR SYNONYMS: *Fonticella pinetorum* Taylor 1987 (in part).

NOTES: Distinguished by the bifurcate penis with glands on the filament and along distal edge of penial lobe.

DISTRIBUTION: Known only from Danish Ranch, a private inholding within the Dixie National Forest, Washington County, Utah.

Pyrgulopsis peculiaris Hershler, 1998 Bifid Duct Pyrg

DESCRIPTION: *Shell*: ovate to narrow conic; periostracum light tan. *Whorls*: 3.5–5.0; protoconch 1.25–1.5 whorls, diameter 0.34 mm, initial 0.5–1.0 whorl finely wrinkled, latter portion smooth. Teleoconch whorls highly convex, shoulders weak to well developed; body whorl often slightly disjunct behind the aperture and having subsutural ramp bordered below by pronounced angulation. *Aperture*: ovate, usually disjunct, columellar shelf very narrow to broad. Outer lip thin or slightly thickened, slightly prosocline, without sinuation; inner lip slightly thickened. Umbilicus narrowly perforate. Operculum ovate, reddish; nucleus eccentric; dorsal surface weakly frilled; outer margin sometimes having weak rim. Attachment scar thick, sometimes broadly so, all around.

FIG. 17. *Pyrgulopsis peculiaris*. Credit: Y. Villacampa, Dept. Invertebrate Zoology, USNM (Hershler 1998).

SIZE: SL 1.7–3.0 mm, SW 1.3–2.1 mm, W/L 62–89%

ANIMAL: Tentacles, snout, and foot are light to medium brown. Opercular lobe dark along inner edge, often all around. Neck unpigmented except for scattered granules to light brown. Pallial roof, visceral coil uniform dark brown to black. Stomach larger than style sac; anterior stomach chamber larger than posterior chamber; stomach caecum small. Ctenidial filaments, 16, without pleats. Osphradium small, narrow, positioned slightly posterior to middle of ctenidium. Renal gland slightly oblique; kidney opening gray-white, slightly raised. Rectum broadly overlapping genital ducts. Ovary 0.5–0.75 whorl, filling less than 50% of digestive gland behind stomach, overlapping posterior stomach chamber. Albumen gland having very short pallial component. Capsule gland longer, but narrower than albumen gland, broadly ovate in section; rectal furrow medium depth. Ventral channel slightly overlapping capsule gland; longitudinal fold well developed.

GENITALIA: Genital aperture a terminal slit with a short anterior extension. Coiled oviduct a posterior-oblique to almost circular loop; proximal arm sometimes kinked, usually darkly pigmented. Oviduct and bursal ducts joining a little behind pallial wall. Bursa copulatrix as wide as albumen gland, pyriform, longitudinal, with almost entire length posterior to gland. Bursa duct bifid, consisting of duct originating from anterior edge at or near midline medium length, narrow; and much narrower duct (of same length) originating from anterior edge near ventral margin; ducts share common opening to oviduct. Seminal receptacle a small, narrow pouch folded into an inverted U-shape, overlapping middle of bursa copulatrix.

Testis 1.0–1.25 whorls, filling less than 50% of digestive gland behind stomach, overlapping posterior stomach chamber. Prostate gland large, elongate bean-shaped, pallial portion short, ovate in section. Proximal pallial vas deferens having well-developed, reflexed loop; duct broad. Penis base rectangular, expanded distally, with pronounced swelling along inner edge, inner edge folded; filament medium length, narrow, tapering to a point, usually oblique; lobe as long as filament, triangular, longitudinal. Terminal gland consisting of three short, ovate-circular units along edge of lobe (mostly ventral) unit along outer edge, often fused with distal unit, occasionally all three units fused. Penial gland small, narrow, positioned near base of filament. Dg1 large (rarely reduced), positioned medially, usually transverse, sometimes fused with either Dg3 or outermost of additional longitudinal glands. Dg2 large, distal, borne on expanded edge of lobe. Dg3 large, extending to near base of filament (abutting or fusing with Dg1), sometimes curving across lobe, portion on lobe raised. Dorsal penis also bearing 4–7 additional units (typically elongate, longitudinal, sometimes small, circular or dot-like) positioned between penial gland. Dg1 and Dg2; innermost units often fused distally. Ventral glands, two, large distal gland narrow (sometimes accompanied distally by raised dot-like unit), borne on large swelling, traversing most of width of penis near base of filament; proximal gland shorter, broader, borne on prominent swelling, transverse, positioned near base of penis. Penial duct straight, near outer edge. Penial filament darkly pigmented along most of length; adjacent portion of base similarly pigmented.

RADULA: 720 × 100 μm, with 57 rows of teeth. Central tooth 32 μm wide, with slightly indented dorsal edge; lateral cusps 4, central cusp medium width, dagger-like; basal cusps medium-sized. Lateral tooth formula 2–1–3; neck weakly flexed; outer wing 130% of cutting-edge length. Inner marginal teeth with 18–20 cusps; cutting edge occupying 36% of length of tooth. Outer marginal teeth with 27–31 cusps; cutting edge occupying 27% of length of tooth.

TYPE LOCATION: Maple Grove Spring, Round Valley, Millard County, Utah. Holotype USNM 883933, paratypes USNM 860703.

JUNIOR SYNONYMS: None

NOTES: Named for unique bifid configuration of the female bursa duct. Penial ornament a medium-large, fragmented terminal gland; small penial gland, large Dg1, Dg2, large Dg3, additional 4–7 dorsal glands, and two large ventral glands.

DISTRIBUTION: This springsnail has been found in six spring complexes in Millard County, Utah. Also known from two spring complexes in White Pine County, Nevada (Kevin Wheeler, Utah Division of Wildlife Resources, pers. comm.).

Pyrgulopsis pilsbryana Baily and Baily, 1951 Bear Lake Springsnail

DESCRIPTION (Baily and Baily 1951; Hershler 1998): *Shell*: ovate- to narrow-conic, narrowly umbilicate, smooth, periostracum tan. *Whorls*: about 4.5 (4.25–5.25), protoconch 1.4–1.5 whorls (1.25–1.3 whorls for *nonaria* variant), 0.35 mm dia.; teleoconch whorls very strongly convex; suture is deeply impressed; body whorl often slightly disjunct behind the aperture. Whorls of variant forms not as strongly convex. *Aperture*: broadly oval, often disjunct, outer lip thin, occupies about 40% of the length and is noticeably oblique (at an angle from shell axis). Umbilicus rimate to shallowly perforate. Operculum ovate with an eccentric nucleus. The columellar margin is slightly expanded.

FIG. 18. Pygulopsis pilsbryana. holotype on left, two paratype variants to its right. Credit: Baily and Baily 1951; P. pilsbryana var. nonaria (I), P. pilsbryana var. transversa (J), Credit: Y. Villacampa, Dept. Invertebrate Zoology, USNM (Hershler 1998).

Genetic analysis by Liu et al. (2018) showed that springsnails from many Bonneville Basin and Wasatch Front locations formerly ascribed to *Pyrgulopsis kolobensis* were all in one clade and were considered a single species. Among these Bonneville Basin samples were two snails formerly considered separate species, *Pyrgulopsis nonaria* and *P. transversa*. These had differences in penial gland characteristics that separated them. These characters (Fig. 19) are used herein to define the variants *P. pilsbryana* var. *nonaria* and *P. pilsbryana* var. *transversa*. The *transversa* form also was noted as having whorls that were not as convex as those of *P. pilsbryana*.

SIZE: *P. pilsbryana* holotype: SL 3.0 mm, SW 1.8 mm. *P. pilsbryana* var. *nonaria*: SL 2.5–2.9 mm, SW 1.6–1.9 mm; W/L 60–71%. *P. pilsbryana* var. *transversa*: SL 2.0–3.1 mm, SW 1.3–2.2 mm, W/L 58–78%.

ANIMAL: For variants *transversa* and *nonaria*, the tentacles are unpigmented to light gray-brown or dark brown; snout unpigmented to light or medium gray-brown, and foot light to medium gray-brown. Neck has scattered black or gray-brown granules. Pallial roof and visceral coil dark brown to black, often uniformly pigmented. For the *transversa* form, opercular lobe black along inner edge, sometimes all around. This lobe in the *nonaria* form usually dark brown-black all around.

GENITALIA: Penis large, filament and lobe medium length. Penial ornament a medium-sized terminal gland, very small to large penial gland, and tiny dorsal gland 3. For variant *transversa* the terminal gland on the penis is small-medium, circular-narrow, longitudinal-transverse, ventral; glandular smear seen on base of filament in one specimen; similar smear conforming to dorsal-gland 2 observed in one specimen. Ventral gland small, circular-ovate, often absent, borne near base of lobe on low swelling. Penial duct straight near outer edge. Penial filament usually lightly pigmented on proximal half; penis occasionally unpigmented. For variant *nonaria*, terminal gland large, narrow, slightly curved, transverse, largely ventral. Distal penis bearing two glandular dots (Dg2) in one specimen. Ventral gland large, narrow, transverse, borne on prominent swelling, positioned near base of lobe, sometimes accompanied distally by small, circular unit, also borne on swelling.

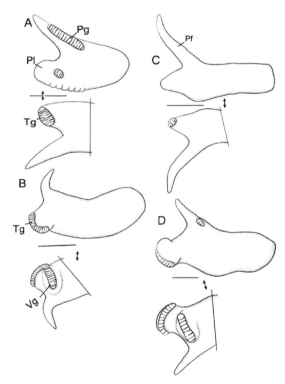

FIG. 19. Comparison of penial morphology among *Pyrgulopsis pilsbryana* variants. Dorsal and ventral views shown for: A. *P. pilsbryana* s.s., USNM 905389, spring, St. Charles Campground, Bear Lake Co. ID; B. *P. pilsbryana* var. *nonaria*, spring east of Ninemile Reservoir, San Pete Co., UT; C. *P. pilsbyana* var. *transversa*, USNM 860732, Sixmile Springs, Tooele Co., UT. D. *P. pilsbryana* s.l., spring, Parley's Summit, Salt Lake Co. Pf = penial filament, Pg = penial gland, Pl = penial lobe, Tg=terminal gland, Vg = ventral gland. Scale bar = 0.25 mm. Credit: Liu et al. 2018, Oxford Univ. Press.

RADULA: For the *transversa* variant, 650 × 110 μm, with 53 rows of teeth. Central tooth 26 μm wide, with highly indented dorsal edge; lateral cusps 4–5, central cusps medium width, dagger-like; basal cusps small. For *nonaria* variant: 750 × 120 μm, with 57 rows of teeth. Central tooth 32 μm wide, with medium indented dorsal edge; lateral cusps, 6–7; central cusp broad, dagger-like; basal cusps medium-sized. Lateral tooth formula 3(4) –1–3(4, 5); neck weakly flexed; outer wing 170% of cutting-edge length. Inner marginal teeth with 23–33 cusps; cutting edge occupying 39% of length of tooth. Outer marginal teeth with 29–39 cusps; cutting edge occupying 29% of length of tooth.

TYPE LOCATION: Lifton, Ideal Beach, Bear Lake UT-ID. Holotype ANSP 187691, paratypes ANSP 368401. For the *transversa* variant: Sixmile Springs, Simpson Mountains, Old River Bed, Tooele County, Utah. Holotype, USNM 883221; paratypes USNM 860732. For the *nonaria* variant: Spring along east side of Ninemile Reservoir, San Pete County, Utah. Holotype USNM 883566; paratypes USNM 860731.

JUNIOR SYNONYMS: *Amnicola pilsbryi* Baily and Baily, 1951; *Amnicola pilsbryana* Baily and Baily, 1951 (*pilsbryi* previously occupied by Walker 1906, so the specific name was changed to *pilsbryana*); *Fonticella pilsbryana*, *Fonticella pilsbryi* (Baily and Baily, 1951) Taylor, 1975; *Pyrgulopsis nonaria* Hershler, 1998; *P. transversa* Hershler, 1998. Transfer to *Pyrgulopsis pilsbryana* (Baily and Baily 1951) by Hershler and Thompson, 1987.

NOTES: Specimens from the Bonneville Basin previously referred to as *P. kolobensis* were shown to be synonymous with *P. pilsbryana* by Liu et al. (2018). However, *P. kolobensis* was described from the Virgin River drainage (Toquerville), so that population is still considered a distinct species, albeit with a distribution now restricted to the type location. GenBank accession number for the *nonaria* variant: EU700467.

DISTRIBUTION: Bear River Basin of Idaho and Utah; Lake Bonneville Basin of Utah. The *nonaria* variant was described from the San Pitch River drainage.

Pyrgulopsis pinetorum Taylor, 1987 Pine Grove Pyrg

DESCRIPTION (Taylor 1987): *Shell*: elongate-oval, narrow umbilicus consistently present; periostracum tan. *Whorls*: 4–4.5 (mean, 4.2), regularly convex, separated by an incised suture, forming a spire with a slightly convex outline. *Aperture*: rounded, peristome usually disjunct from previous whorl but sometimes adnate. Operculum plane, amber, with a dark internal callus; attachment scar has a discrete border that leaves no conspicuous spiral trace.

SIZE: SL (mean, range) 3.15 (2.79–3.64) mm; length of body whorl 2.48 (2.27–2.76) mm; ApL 1.43 (1.27–1.73) mm; ratio of ApL/length of body whorl 0.577 (0.52–0.68); W/L 68 (61–78)%; ratio of width/length of body whorl 0.864 (0.80–0.96).

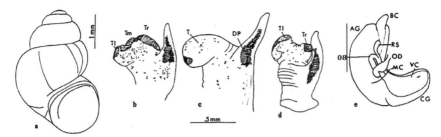

FIG. 20. *Pyrgulopsis pinetorum.* a. Shell, b-d, dorsal view of three penises showing variation in glands and terminal lobe; e, distal portion of female reproductive system. AG = albumen gland, BC = bursa copulatrix, CG = capsule gland, DP = penial gland, MC = mantle cavity (posterior end), OB = distal end of oviduct bend, OD = oviduct, RS = receptaculum seminis, T = terminal gland (left, middle, right segments noted with lower case letter), VC = ventral channel. Credit: Taylor 1987, New Mexico Bureau of Geology and Mineral Resources.

ANIMAL: GENITALIA: Penis (see Fig. 20) commonly with a bifurcate terminal lobe. Specimens with the standard terminal gland as a long strip have a terminal lobe set off by a subterminal restriction. The free portion of the penis has a core of melanin granules, partly masked by a glandular dorsal patch. The glands on the penis varied among the 50 specimens examined by Taylor (1987) and between the type locality and Danish Ranch, a private inholding within the Dixie National Forest. At the type locality, 40% had one long terminal strip, 18% had two separate segments on one lobe, 38% had two separate terminal segments on two lobes, and 4% had three segments. Dorsal penial glands also varied, with 22% having one long strip, 68% having one short strip, 2% having two short strips, and 8% having none. The Danish Ranch population (Washington County, Utah) was later described as a new species *P. nuwuvi* (Hershler et al. 2017).

In females, the bursa copulatrix is a slender sac indistinctly separated from its duct, projecting behind the albumen gland to a rounded tip. The full length of the bursal duct, and sometimes even the anterior part of the bursa, immersed in the albumen gland. Bursa/albumen gland ratio in six specimens ranged from 0.20 to 0.34, mean 0.27. Loop of oviduct thickened and glandular, with an anterior double kink and simple posterior distal bend. Seminal receptacle club-shaped, slightly curved to the right, projects well behind the distal bend and is appressed to the albumen gland over the bursal duct or anterior end of the bursa. Duct of the receptacle enters the oviduct distad of the distal bend. Albumen gland extends beyond the end of the mantle cavity by 1/3–1/4 its length. Bursal duct, of width equal to the oviduct, joins with it to enter a broad ventral channel.

TYPE LOCATION: Spring on Leeds Creek (37.3087°N, 113.42935°W), Washington County, Utah. Holotype is in Los Angeles County Museum of Natural History, No. 2217.

JUNIOR SYNONYMS: *Fonticella pinetorum* Taylor 1987, *Pyrgulopsis kolobensis* (in part) Hershler, 1994

NOTES: Hershler (1994) considered *Fonticella pinetorum* Taylor, 1987 to be a junior synonym of *P. kolobensis* but later resurrected *Pyrgulopsis pinetorum* as a distinct species based on new genetic data (Hershler et al. 2017). Separated from other similar pyrgs by the bifurcate terminal lobe and glandular patches on the penis: short dorsal patch on the proximal half of the free portion; terminal gland on accessory process that varies from an oval to a long strip or is divided into segments or two glands on two separate lobes; no ventral glands. Differs from nearby *P. kolobensis* by lacking the penial ventral glands and lobule consistently present in *P. kolobensis;* in females the bursa copulatrix is smaller than for *P. kolobensis*, and the anterior extent of the albumen gland is generally less (Taylor 1987). Differs from *P. kolobensis* and *P. nuwuvi* by its broader shell, frequently adnate inner lip, and generally larger gland on penial lobe (Hershler et al. 2017).

DISTRIBUTION: Known only from springs in the Pine Valley Mountains, Washington County, Utah.

Pyrgulopsis plicata Hershler, 1998 Black Canyon Pyrg

DESCRIPTION (Hershler 1998): *Shell*: broadly to ovate-conic; umbilicus rimate or shallowly perforate; periostracum light tan. *Whorls*: 4.0–4.5, protoconch 1.5 whorls, diameter 0.38 mm; initial 0.5–0.75 whorl very weakly wrinkled, otherwise smooth; the remaining teleoconch whorls have medium to high convexity, shoulders absent to medium developed; body whorl often slightly disjunct and strongly translated behind the aperture. *Aperture*: large, ovate, usually disjunct; inner lip thick, without a columellar shelf. Outer lip slightly thickened, orthocline or weakly prosocline, without sinuation. Operculum ovate, amber, with a reddish, eccentric nucleus; dorsal surface very weakly frilled; attachment scar thick all around.

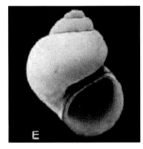

FIG. 21. *Pyrgulopsis plicata*. Credit: Y. Villacampa, Dept. Invertebrate Zoology, USNM (Hershler 1998).

SIZE: SL 2.3–2.9 mm, SW 1.8–2.2 mm; W/L 72–85%

ANIMAL: Tentacles medium to dark gray-brown or black. Snout light to dark gray-brown; foot light to medium gray-brown. Opercular lobe black along outer edge; inner edge medium to dark gray-brown. Pallial roof, visceral coil dark brown or black. Ctenidial filaments 17, without pleats. Osphradium small, narrow, positioned posterior to middle of ctenidium. Renal gland oblique; kidney opening gray-white. Rectum broadly overlapping genital ducts. Stomach longer than style sac; stomach chambers equal-sized; stomach caecum very small.

GENITALIA: testis 1.5 whorls, filling more than 50% of digestive gland behind stomach, overlapping posterior, and part of anterior, stomach. Prostate gland small, bean-shaped, pallial portion short, narrowly ovate in section. Proximal pallial vas deferens having large, well-developed loop, sometimes weakly reflexed. Penis base elongate-rectangular, proximal portion folded under remaining penis; inner edge folded; filament tapering to a point, slightly oblique; lobe short, hemispherical, longitudinal. Dg 1 large, narrow, raised; longitudinal (proximal part curves slightly across width of penis), borne along outer edge. Almost entire length of penial filament and distal penis, particularly the portion near outer edge—medium to darkly pigmented. See Hershler (1998) for figures of genitalia.

Ovary 0.5 whorl, filling less than 50% of the digestive gland behind stomach. Albumen gland with a short or no pallial component. Capsule gland shorter, narrower than albumen gland, broadly ovate in section; rectal furrow weakly developed. Ventral channel slightly overlapping capsule gland; longitudinal fold weakly developed. Genital aperture a terminal pore, slightly raised, having a short anterior extension. Coiled oviduct a tight, posterior-oblique loop. Oviduct and bursal duct joining a little behind pallial wall. Bursa copulatrix medium length and width, ovate, longitudinal, with 50% or less of length posterior to gland. Bursal duct originating from anterior edge at or near midline, 50% of length of bursa, narrow to almost as wide as bursa, duct sometimes shallowly embedded in albumen gland. Seminal receptacle small, overlapping or adjacent to anterior part of the bursa.

RADULA: 740 × 100 μm with 60 rows of teeth. Central tooth 26 μm wide, with medium to highly indented dorsal edge; lateral cusps 4–7; central cusp broad and dagger-like; basal cusps medium-sized, sometimes accompanied by weak swelling to outside. Lateral tooth formula 3–1–3(4); neck weakly flexed; outer wing 150% of cutting-edge length. Inner marginal teeth with 19–25 cusps; cutting edge occupying 38% of length of tooth. Outer marginal teeth with 24–30 cusps, the cutting edge occupying 30% of length of tooth.

TYPE LOCATION: Spring, Black Canyon, East Fork Sevier River, Garfield County, Utah. Holotype USNM 883494, Paratype USNM 860727.

JUNIOR SYNONYMS: None

NOTES: Differs from other pyrgs in the Sevier River drainage in the penial ornament, an elongate gland (Dg1). *Pyrgulopsis cruciglans*, from eastern Nevada, has a similar gland, but it is larger and transversely oriented.

DISTRIBUTION: Known only from a spring complex adjacent to the Sevier River, Garfield County, Utah.

Pyrgulopsis santaclarensis Hershler, Liu, Forsythe, Hovingh, and Wheeler, 2017 Santa Clara Pyrg

DESCRIPTION (Hershler et al. 2017): *Shell*: ovate- to narrow-conic, umbilicus absent or very small, periostracum tan. *Whorls*: 4.0–4.5 (mean 4.29), medium convex, weakly shouldered. *Aperture*: lip usually free from body whorl, rarely adnate; operculum as for genus; muscle attachment margin variably thickened on inner side.

SIZE: SL (mean, range) 3.48 (3.01–3.74) mm, SW 2.40 (2.15–2.56) mm, height of body whorl 2.68 (2.30–2.88) mm, width of body whorl 2.06 (1.84–2.21) mm, ApL 1.53 (1.29–1.73) mm, ApW 1.38 (1.19–1.52) mm.

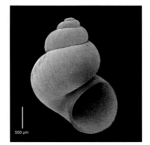

FIG. 22. *Pyrgulopsis santaclarensis*. Credit: Y. Villacampa, Dept. Invertebrate Zoology, USNM (Hershler et al. 2017).

ANIMAL: GENITALIA: Penis distally bifurcate; filament rather short; lobe slightly longer than filament. Terminal gland largely on ventral surface, sometimes consisting of two units (4 of 18 specimens); small gland (Dg3) frequently present on dorsal surface of lobe near outer edge (13 of 18 specimens); ventral glands large, positioned near base of lobe, slightly raised, 2–3 additional glandular units sometimes present (4 of 18 specimens). In females, coiled oviduct is a small circular loop preceded by a small kink. Bursa copulatrix medium-sized to large, about 33% of length overlapping albumen gland; seminal receptacle overlapping proximal section of bursa duct.

RADULA: as for genus; lateral cusps 3–5, basal cup 1. Lateral teeth having 2–4 cusps on inner and 3–6 cusps on outer side. Inner marginal teeth with 14–26 cusps, outer marginal teeth with 18–30 cusps.

TYPE LOCATION: Spring-fed ditch along Left Fork Santa Clara River, Pine Valley, Dixie National Forest, Washington County, Utah. Holotype, USNM 847209, paratypes USNM 1411243.

JUNIOR SYNONYMS: None

NOTES: Differentiated from other pyrgs in southeastern Utah by the longitudinal glandular patch located ventrally and transversely on the penis.

DISTRIBUTION: Known only from type locality.

Pyrgulopsis saxatilis Hershler, 1998 Subglobose Snake Pyrg

DESCRIPTION (Hershler 1998): *Shell*: subglobose, apex usually eroded in adult shells; periostracum eroded or absent. *Whorls*: 3.5–4.0, protoconch 1.25 whorls (diameter 0.29 mm, initial 0.75 whorl finely wrinkled); teleoconch whorls of medium convexity; shoulders well developed, final 0.25 whorl sometimes having pronounced subsutural angulation. *Aperture*: ovate-pyriform, adnate. Inner lip slightly thickened, columellar shelf medium width. Outer lip thin, prosocline, weakly sinuate. Umbilicus narrowly rimate to shallowly perforate. Operculum ovate, amber, slightly darker in nuclear region; dorsal surface smooth or weakly frilled; outer margin sometimes having a very faint rim. Attachment scar thick along inner edge and between inner edge and nucleus.

FIG. 23. *Pyrgulopsis saxatilis*. Credit: Y. Villacampa, Dept. Invertebrate Zoology, USNM (Hershler 1998).

SIZE: SL 1.0–1.4 mm, SW 1.0–1.4 mm; W/L 90–106%

ANIMAL (Hershler 1998): Tentacles and foot are light to medium brown; snout medium to dark brown; opercular lobe unpigmented or diffuse light brown. Neck is light to medium gray-brown. Pallial roof and visceral coil are uniformly dark brown or black. Stomach longer than style sac; stomach chambers poorly distinguished externally, but anterior chamber slightly larger; stomach caecum very small. Ctenidial filaments 12, without pleats.

GENITALIA: penis large, the base elongate-rectangular, smooth or weakly folded along inner edge; filament short, narrow, tapering to a point, longitudinal or slightly oblique; lobe as long as filament, club-like, but narrowing distally, longitudinal. Terminal gland small, circular to ovate (usually transverse), ventral. Dg1 small, ovate, longitudinal or slightly oblique, positioned just proximal to base of filament. Ventral gland large, narrow, slightly raised, angling across to base of lobe at inner edge. Dorsal and ventral penis also frequently having 6 tiny, variably positioned, glandular dots. Penial duct slightly undulating near outer edge distally. Penial filament darkly pigmented along most of length; base also containing scattered black granules. Bursa copulatrix is short, narrow, globular-pyriform, longitudinal, with most of the length posterior to gland. Bursal duct originating from anterior edge at midline, long, narrow to medium width. Seminal receptacle small to medium-sized, pouch-like, overlapping proximal to medial portion of bursal duct, often overlapped by albumen gland. Proximal pallial vas deferens with a well-developed loop.

RADULA: 480 × 65 μm, with 60 rows of teeth. Central tooth 15 μm wide, with highly indented dorsal edge; lateral cusps 5–7; central cusp long, dagger-like; basal cusps medium sized. Lateral tooth formula 3–1–4(5); neck weakly flexed; outer wing 200% of cutting-edge length. Inner marginal teeth with 22–25 cusps; cutting edge occupying 36% of length of tooth. Outer marginal teeth with 24–27 cusps; cutting edge occupying 29% of length of tooth.

TYPE LOCATION: Warm Springs, Snake Valley, Millard County, Utah. Holotype USNM 883237; paratypes USNM 860726.

JUNIOR SYNONYMS: None

NOTES: Differentiating characters include the relatively small subglobose shell, large penis with a short filament, short lobe, small terminal gland, small Dg1, and large ventral gland. *P. saxatilis* resembles *P. kolobensis*, but shell shape differs and *saxatilis* has narrower radular central cusps, more elongate outer wing on the lateral radular teeth, smaller penial lobe and filament, and weakly developed terminal gland. Specific Latin name refers to being "found among rocks." GenBank accession number AY627934.

DISTRIBUTION: Known only from the type locality.

Pyrgulopsis variegata Hershler, 1998 Northwest Bonneville Pyrg

DESCRIPTION: *Shell*: ovate- to narrow-conic; periostracum light or reddish-brown. *Whorls*: 4.25–5.0, protoconch 1.4–1.5 whorls (dia. 0.33 mm, smooth except for weak spiral striae along outer edge of whorl); teleoconch whorls medium to highly convex, shoulders weak or absent; body whorl often slightly disjunct behind the aperture. *Aperture*: ovate, usually disjunct; inner lip slightly thickened in largest specimens, without columellar shelf; outer lip thin, prosocline, without sinuation. Umbilicus rimate or shallowly perforate. Operculum ovate, amber, nuclear region reddish; nucleus eccentric; outer margins have a weak rim. Attachment scar thick all around.

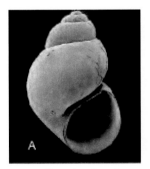

FIG. 24. *Pyrgulopsis variegata*. Credit: Y. Villacampa, Dept. Invertebrate Zoology, USNM (Hershler 1998).

SIZE: SL 2.2–3.0 mm, SW 1.5–2.4 mm; W/L 63–75%

ANIMAL: Tentacles unpigmented or having proximal light gray patch. Snout and foot are light to medium gray; opercular lobe black along inner edge. Neck is unpigmented except for scattered granules of black to medium gray. Pallial roof and visceral coil are medium gray to black, pigment nonuniform. Stomach longer than style sac; anterior stomach chamber larger than posterior chamber; stomach caecum small or very small. Ctenidium filaments 17, without pleats.

GENITALIA: Penis small to large, base rectangular, sometimes elongate; filament 50% to almost as long as base, tapering to point, longitudinal or slightly oblique; lobe shorter than filament, slightly narrower than base, knob-like, longitudinal. Terminal gland small, rarely dot-like, narrow, circular-ovate, usually transverse (rarely longitudinal), entirely ventral or partly overlapping dorsal surface. Penial gland very small or absent, narrow, positioned near the base of the filament. Ventral gland small or absent, ovate-narrow, often slightly raised, longitudinal, distal. Penial duct straight near outer edge. Proximal pallial vas deferens looped. Penial filament darkly pigmented; pigment granules scattered on the base.

Bursa copulatrix short, pyriform, often having a silvery sheen, longitudinal, with 50% or more of length usually posterior to gland, the dorsal edge sometimes overlapped by gland. Bursal duct originating from anterior edge at midline, slightly shorter to slightly longer than bursa. Seminal receptacle small, pouch-like, overlapping or slightly ventral to proximal portion of bursal duct.

RADULA: 665 × 105 μm with 62 rows of teeth. Central tooth 26 μm wide, with indented dorsal edge; lateral cusps 5–7. Lateral tooth formula 3(4) –1–3(4,5); neck weakly flexed; outer wing 185% of cutting-edge length. Inner marginal teeth with 25–31 cusps (basal cusp enlarged); cutting edge occupying 35% of the length of the tooth. Outer marginal teeth with 31–36 cusps, cutting edge occupying 25% of the tooth length.

TYPE LOCATION: 2.5 km south of South Patterson Spring, Pilot Valley, Box Elder County, Utah. Holotype: USNM 883627, paratypes, USNM 860723.

JUNIOR SYNONYMS: None

NOTES: Distinguishing characters include a small terminal gland on the penis, very small penial gland (often absent), and a small ventral gland (often absent). Differs from *P. kolobensis* in having a smaller penial lobe and penial glands that are reduced or absent. Populations of this species from the southern and western basin have relatively well-developed penial and terminal glands but weakly developed or absent ventral glands; conversely, those in the northern or eastern basin (e.g., Grouse Creek, Park Valleys) have a weak terminal gland, often lack a penial gland, and have stronger ventral glands. However, there is intergradation in these characters in some populations. GenBank accession number AY627937.

DISTRIBUTION: Found in the North-Central Great Basin and one site in the Snake River drainage (Elko County, Nevada; Box Elder and Tooele County, Utah).

Lithoglyphidae Tryon, 1866d

The family Lithoglyphidae contains 11 genera and 73 North American species (Johnson et al. 2013). Shells are usually globose to trochoid, rarely ovate- or narrow-conic, ranging in height from 2.5–12 mm, 3.5–5.0 whorls. Males feature a distinctive penis (Hershler and Ponder 1998). Females lay eggs singly in the spring, though for one species, *Lepyrium showalteri*, eggs are laid by multiple females in a "superclutch" (Johnson et al. 2013). A few Pliocene fossil species in the family have been named from Utah including (1) *Pilsbryus antiquus utahensis*, Yen, 1947 (transferred to *Lithoglyphus* by Taylor, 1966), and (2) *Fluminicola yatesiana utahensis*, Yen, 1947 (transferred to *Savaginius* by Taylor 1966, as a synonym of *Paludistrina nanna*; Chamberlin and Berry 1933); Both species were found in the Salt Lake Formation and Cache Valley Formation of Cache and Box Elder counties (Hershler and Frest 1996).

The genus *Fluminicola* Carpenter, 1864 (=*Heathilla* Hannibal, 1912) contains nine species (Hershler and Frest 1996), one of which, *F. coloradoense*, is found in Utah. The type species for the genus is *Paludina nuttalliana* Lea, 1839 (now *Fluminicola nuttalliana*). Hershler and Frest (1996) note that *Fluminicola* is probably paraphyletic, indicating that future taxonomic changes are to be expected. Species in the genus are found in northwestern North America from California north to British Columbia, east to South Dakota and the upper Colorado River drainage. *Fluminicola* prefer clear cold flowing water with high dissolved oxygen content. Many taxa graze periphyton on rocks but are intolerant of soft substrates and impounded waters. For more detailed characteristics of the genus, see Hershler and Frest (1996).

Fluminicola coloradoense Morrison, 1940, Green River Pebblesnail

DESCRIPTION (Morrison 1940; Hershler and Frest 1996): *Shell*: large (for the genus), subglobose-conic, smooth; spire short, periostracum tan. *Whorls*: 3.5–4.5, well rounded, separated by a deep suture; protoconch of 1.5 whorls; microsculpture of many strong spiral striae, some joining. Body whorl shouldered, often with a broad sutural shelf, rapidly enlarged. *Aperture*: teardrop-shaped, narrowly rounded above; widely, evenly rounded below, ~2/3 of shell height; parietal lip complete, usually thick, adnate or rarely slightly detached. Columellar lip thick, columellar swelling broad, often covering umbilical region. Operculum with an obvious rim; callus weak or absent. The umbilical chink is distinct; wider, and more prominent than that in *F. fusca*. Lighter colored than *F. fusca*; apex pinkish, the remainder of the shell a dirty white, not reddish or purplish throughout.

SIZE (holotype): SL 9.0 (6.5–10.8) mm, SW 8.3 mm, ApL 6.0 mm, ApW 5.0 mm; whorls 4.5.

ANIMAL (Hershler and Frest 1996): Brown-black pigment well developed on snout and tentacles (except for light patch around, and slightly posterior to, the eyes). Head light gray, foot gray-black and often dark along anterior and posterior edges. Pallial roof and visceral coil black. Ctenidium filaments about 38, tall, pleated. Osphradium about 40% of ctenidium length. Hypobranchial gland swollen on proximal genital duct. Stomach about as long as style sac. Ganglia pigmented.

GENITALIA: Testis 1.5 whorls, filling more than 50–67% of visceral coil behind stomach. Prostate gland with 33% of length in pallial roof. Vas deferens nearly straight in pallial roof and neck. Penis sickle-shaped, usually very tightly coiled, with strong folds along proximal 67% of length; base slightly narrowed; medial section gently tapering, bulbous distal section narrowing considerably to a short, pointed tip. Penial duct near center, of medium width, strongly undulating in basal and medial portion. Penis with dark epithelial pigment on proximal half of dorsal surface, rarely pale; black subepithelial pigment scattered along length of penial duct.

FIG. 25. *Fluminicola coloradoense*. Credit: E. Wagner.

Ovary 1.0 whorl, filling ~50% of visceral coil behind stomach. Coiled oviduct narrow, sometimes weakly pigmented, joining bursal duct just behind pallial wall. Bursa copulatrix about 50% of albumen gland length, pyriform, about as long as wide, with central section decidedly narrowed, positioned largely posterior to gland. Bursal duct about 67% of bursa length, originating slightly lateral to tip of organ. Seminal receptacle about 33% of bursa copulatrix length, lightly pigmented, positioned anterior to bursa copulatrix near posterior edge of albumen gland, partly or entirely overlapped by gland. Genital opening a subterminal slit fringed by small papilla.

RADULA: about 65 rows of teeth; ribbon length 0.3 mm; central tooth width 95 µm, with slight dorsal indentation; lateral cusps 2–3; median cusp broadly U-shaped, slightly broader and longer than laterals; basal cusps 2–3, narrow, originating near dorsal edge of lateral angles; basal tongue medium wide, basal sockets moderate depth. Lateral tooth with convex dorsal edge, very slightly indented centrally, dorsal edge about 50% of tooth width; lateral shaft shorter than height of tooth face; tooth face taller than wide; central cusp broadly U-shaped, lateral cusps 3 (sometimes 4 on outer side). Inner marginals with 9–11 cusps; outer marginal teeth with 10–11 cusps.

TYPE LOCATION: Green River, Wyoming. Holotype USNM 526631, paratypes USNM 526576.

JUNIOR SYNONYMS: *Lithoglyphus coloradoensis* (Morrison) Taylor 1975; *Lithoglyphus hindsii* Taylor 1966; Beetle 1989 (in part); *Fluminicola coloradoensis* (Morrison) Hershler and Frest 1996; *Fluminicola hindsi* Burch and Tottenham, 1980 (in part, Liu et al. 2013). Prior to the description by Morrison (1940), these shells were likely called *F. fusca*, which is native to the Snake River drainage. So, some previous records (in part) should be transferred to *F. coloradoense* (e.g., Binney 1865a; Ingersoll 1877; Pilsbry 1899d; Henderson 1924; Chamberlin and Jones 1929; Jones 1935; Henderson 1936; Beetle 1961).

Chamberlin and Jones (1929) listed *Fluminicola seminalis* Hinds 1842, as a Utah species. This species, from the Sacramento River, California, was described as having 4 whorls, a dark blue aperture, and eroded apex (Hinds 1842, 1844). Hershler (1999) synonymized Utah records of *F. seminalis* (Chamberlin and Jones 1929) with *F. coloradoense*. However, Hershler and Frest (1996) note *F. seminalis* as a valid species, though its known range is restricted to the Sacramento River Basin.

NOTES (Hershler and Frest 1996): Differentiated from similarly shaped shells in Utah with a teardrop-shaped aperture by the larger adult size and slightly stouter shells. All *Fluminicola* species have an umbilical region that often has a well-developed axial ridge, except *F. coloradoense* and *F. fusca*, which have a simple umbilical region. *F. dalli* and *F. turbiniformis* have protoconchs with weakly developed spiral striae, whereas other *Fluminicola* have strong spiral lines. These two species and *F. modici* have >20 cusps on inner marginal radular teeth compared to ≤17 for other *Fluminicola*. *F. coloradoense* is separated from *F. fusca* by the gray-white shell color, absence of either pronounced subsutural angulation or keel on the body whorl, weaker operculum callus, frequent presence of third pair of basal cusps on central radular teeth, bulbous distal penis, longer bursal duct, and greater overlap of seminal receptacle by albumen gland. Furthermore, a pigmented seminal receptacle, and occasionally a pigmented coiled oviduct, are unique to *F. coloradoense*, compared to other species in the genus. Unique characters of *F. fusca* include pigmented salivary glands, and position of the seminal receptacle entirely lateral to the albumen gland. Hershler and Frest (1996) suggested that *F. coloradoense* is limited to the Colorado River Basin, that *F. fusca* is found in the lower Snake and Columbia River drainage, and that Great Basin *Fluminicola* may be one or more separate species. Shells collected by the author in the lower Provo River drainage and Box Elder County lack the "strong subsutural angulation" described for *F.*

fusca. So, for now, Great Basin forms are considered *F. coloradoense* until future genetic testing and animal anatomical studies provide further data.

DISTRIBUTION (Morrison 1940; Liu et al. 2013) Snake and Owyhee River basins; USNM records: Bear River at Soda Springs, Idaho, Oneida County, Idaho, Harris Fork of Green River, Wyoming, and Bell's Fish Cliff, Horn's Peak, Wyoming. Utah records (Jones 1935; USNM, UMNH; iNaturalist.org): Malad River, Weber Canyon, Utah Lake, Kelton, and Salt Lake City. The author has collected shells from Springville, Box Elder County, Cache Valley, Utah Lake, and Bear Lake, Utah. K. Holcomb found live individuals in the lower Provo River (iNaturalist.org).

Tateidae Thiele, 1925

The family Tateidae was established by Thiele in 1925 in the superfamily Truncatelloidea. It contains 48 genera, mostly marine (www.marinespecies.org). One genus, *Potamopyrgus*, is represented by a single introduced species in Utah.

The genus *Potomopyrgus* was established by Stimpson (1865): "Shell ovate-conic, imperforate; apex acute; whorls coronated with spines; outer whorl nearly two-thirds the length of the shell; aperture ovate, outer lip acute. Operculum corneous, subspiral. Foot rather short for the length of the shell, broadest in front and strongly auriculated. Tentacles very long, slender, and tapering. Eyes on very prominent tubercles. Rostrum of moderate size." Winterbourn (1970) noted that the eyes were in bulges at the base of the tentacles and featured prominent pigment cups. Stimpson (1865) designated *Potamopyrgus corolla* as the type species, which accounts for the spines on the whorls in the genus description; however, these spines are lacking in *P. antipodarum* found in Utah. Based on Suter's (1904) and Winterbourn's (1970) observations of New Zealand *Potamopyrgus*, as well as observations of the progeny of ornamented forms (Warwick 1944), it appears that the presence of spines is an inconsistent shell characteristic, with both smooth and spinous forms found in a population. Chromosome number in diploids is 24 (Winterbourn 1970). *Potamopyrgus* was originally placed within the family Littorinidae (Gray 1843), and later placed within the family Hydrobiidae, but recent genetic analysis supported a transfer to Tateidae (Criscione and Ponder 2013).

Potamopyrgus antipodarum, Gray, 1843, New Zealand Mud Snail

DESCRIPTION (Gray 1843): "Shell ovate, acute, subperforated (generally covered with a brown earthy coat); whorls rather rounded, mouth ovate, axis 3 lines; operculum horny and subspiral: variety, spire rather longer, whorls more rounded." Suter (1904) noted that although shells varied, the elongately conical form, flatly convex whorls, and little-impressed sutures were fairly

Tateidae

FIG. 26. *Potamopyrgus antipodarum*. Credit: left: E. Wagner, right: ANSP.

constant characters. The aperture has a simple, continuous margin (Hutton 1880). The aperture is often offset a little to the right, such that the outer margin is outside of a tangential line along the right side of the acute spire. The shells of embryos are translucent and have 1.5 whorls when released from the brood pouch (Winterbourn 1970). The diameter of the first whorl at this age varied from 200 to 310 μm (Winterbourn 1970). The ovoid operculum is semitransparent, yellow to brown, with a subcentral nucleus. Subspiral lines of growth are clearly visible, and there is no distinct marginal area. In its native New Zealand, the snail has three general variants in form: one is carinate without any bristles, one is carinate with bristles, and one is like the form found in the United States, acarinate and lacking any other ornamentation.

SIZE: In New Zealand, the shell height has been reported to vary between 4 and 11.5 mm across many populations. Among the Utah shells found to date, shell height does not exceed about 6 mm (Wagner, unpublished data). The European form rarely exceeds 5 mm total height (Winterbourn 1970).

ANIMAL (Winterborn 1970): The broad gray foot has a stippled appearance, is rounded posteriorly, and truncated anteriorly. The anterior mucus slit is prominent and extends the width of the foot. The mantle skirt is black, with a well-defined, pale, anterior margin.

RADULA (Hutton 1882): The median radular tooth is trapezoidal, the inferior margin ± trilobate; the first lateral tooth is broad and escavated in the middle, contracted into a long peduncle, the denticles being nearly equal; Second lateral is pointed at the inner extremity, the shank broad and thickened on its outer margin. The third lateral has an inner extremity broad and rounded, constricted at its junction with the very broad shank, which is thickened on its outer margin; the number of transverse rows of teeth is 55–69.

TYPE LOCATION: New Zealand in freshwater.

JUNIOR SYNONYMS: *Amnicola antipodanum*, Gray, 1843; *Amnicola zelandiae* Gray, 1843 (see Suter 1904); *Hydrobia jenkinsi* Smith, 1889 (synonymy suggested by

Winterbourn 1970); *Hydrobia antipodum* von Martens, 1873; *Bythinella antipoda* Hutton, 1880; *Potamopyrgus antipodum* Suter, 1904. Winterbourn (1970) considered *Potamopyrgus corolla* Gould, 1846, to be a synonym of *P. antipodarum*, and this synonymy is reflected in the shell collection at the Academy of Natural Sciences in Philadelphia as well (Wagner, personal observation). However, others, for example, those who maintain the Wikipedia page for *Potamopyrgus*, still consider *P. corolla* a distinct species. Holotype is in the British Museum of Natural History.

NOTES (Winterbourn 1970; Cox and Rutherford 2000; Duncan and Klekowski 1967; Gerard et al. 2003; USFWS 2015): Small size (4–6 mm) and narrow conic acute spire will distinguish *P. antipodarum* from most Utah shells. Spire more acute than for *Pyrgulopsis* species and with more whorls. Similar to *Tryonia porrecta*, but *P. antipodarum* has a rounder, slightly ultra-dextral aperture and fewer, less shouldered whorls. *Cochlicopa lubrica* has a similar shape, but is not aquatic and has a more lustrous shell and narrower aperture.

P. antipodarum is ovoviviparous, parthenogenetic, and highly variable in shell size, shape, and ornamentation in its native home in New Zealand. Upper thermal tolerance of *P. antipodarum* is 31.0 ± 0.6°C (LT_{50}) under constant temperatures and 28.6 ± 0.4°C for diurnally fluctuating (10°C amplitude) temperatures. It tolerates salinities up to 26 ppt in the wild, and reproduction has been observed at 12–18 ppt. In laboratory tests evaluating tolerance to desiccation, *P. antipodarum* survived up to 51 days. The species is known to reproduce throughout the year; a single snail may have over 100 offspring in its brood pouch. In New Zealand, *P. antipodarum* occurs in a wide variety of habitats, including lakes, ponds, estuaries, springs, wells, seeps, creeks, ditches, and lowland rivers.

P. antipodarum is considered an invasive species outside of its native range. Densities can be high, exceeding 500,000/m^2 in some locations (Richards et al. 2001; Hall et al. 2003; Kerans et al. 2005). Due to their high densities, the snails can compete with native snails and insects for the same food items (Richards 2004; Hall et al. 2006; Vinson et al. 2007; Krist and Charles 2012).

DISTRIBUTION: *P. antipodarum* has spread from New Zealand to freshwater environments throughout the world (Smith 1906; Ponder 1988; Bowler 1991; Alonso and Castro-Diez 2012; Collado 2014). It was first discovered in the United States in 1987 in the Snake River near Hagerman, Idaho, in Lake Ontario and the St. Lawrence River in 1991, in the Columbia River estuary in 1996, and in Washington's Capitol Lake in 2009 (Bowler 1991; Bowler and Frest 1992; Levri et al. 2007; Bersine et al. 2008; Cheng and LeClair 2011). New Zealand mudsnails are now found in many major western rivers, including the Snake, Green, Colorado, Columbia, Owens, and Madison rivers (Bowler 1991; Dybdahl and Kane 2005; Vinson et al. 2007; Alonso and Castro-Diez 2012; USFWS 2015). In Utah, *P. antipodarum* are found in most of the major river drainages of the northern part of the state and in the Green River from just downstream of Flaming Gorge Dam to Dinosaur National Monument (Harju 2007; Vinson et al. 2007; Oplinger and Wagner 2016). Wagner et al. (2018) found additional populations in the Logan River, Weber River, Spring Creek (Springville and Loa, Utah), Jones Hole Creek, and Bicknell Bottoms. It is also found in central Utah in the Sevier River drainage and in southwestern Utah in the Virgin River Basin. Previous reports of *P. antipodarum* in the Strawberry River above the reservoir could not be confirmed in 2018 surveys (Wagner et al. 2018).

SUPERORDER: Hygrophila
SPF: LYMNAEOIDEA Rafinesque, 1815

Lymnaeidae Rafinesque, 1815

Rafinesque (1815) classified the lymnaeid snails in the subfamily Lymnidia, which was later elevated to the family level (Broderip 1839; Dybowksi 1903a). His original description was brief: "Spire roulée extérieurement, coquille oblongue ou ovale" (spire coiled externally, shell oblong or oval). Species within Planorbidae and Physidae were once included in Lymnaeidae but are now separate families. Baker (1911) separated out planorbid snails (genitalia on the left side, discoidal shells, with cylindrical appendage at the apex of the penis) from Lymnaeidae.

Shells of Lymnaeidae vary from patelliform in the *Lanx* genus to narrowly conic, elongate, bulimoid, and globose in other genera. The aperture has a simple outer lip, and the body whorl is typically inflated. Radulae feature a diminutive central tooth, bicuspid or tricuspid lateral teeth, and intermediate and marginal teeth of gradually diminishing size and variable dentition. The head has a broad, short muzzle, the mouth has one or more jaws, and tentacles are contractile, flattened, and triangular, with the eyes sessile at their inner bases. Excretory orifices are on the left side of the neck; respiratory orifice and genitalia are on the right side. Sexes are united internally, but male and female organs have separate external orifices (Binney 1865a).

Currently recognized subfamilies within Lymnaeidae include Amphipepleinae, Lymnaeinae, Lancinae, and the fossil group Valencienniinae (Bouchet et al. 2017). Genera within Lymnaeidae represented in Utah include *Galba*, *Hinkleyia*, *Lymnaea*, *Radix*, and *Polyrhytis* (formerly *Stagnicola*, which now applies to a more restricted group of lymnaeids in Eurasia). Assignment of species to genera is based on internal anatomy or DNA analysis (Baker 1911; Meier-Brook and Bargues 2002). Additional major reviews of the family by Hubendick (1951), Jackiewicz (1993), and Kruglov (2005), have a greater focus on European and Asian species.

Galba

Galba, originally erected as a genus by Schrank (1803), was a junior synonym to *Lymnaea*. Baker (1911), however, resurrected the genus in order to define a subset of lymnaeid snails that had small, smooth, turreted shells with a flat and expanded inner lip without a columellar fold. Baker (1928) noted that *Fossaria* (=*Galba*) has tricuspid lateral teeth (bicuspid in *Lymnaea* and *Stagnicola*), though some species have bicuspid laterals (e.g., *G. bulimoides*). Whorls gradually increase in size, with the last whorl not inflated; the aperture is moderate, the outer lip is not expanded or thickened, and the inner lip is not appressed; columella is not twisted or plicate, the axis minutely umbilicate (Dall 1905). The animal has a long-ovate prostate and a smooth penis slightly shorter than the penis sac. The genus *Galba* was previously named *Limnophysa* by Binney (1865a), *Limnaea* by Tryon (1870), *Simpsonia* by Baker (1911), and *Fossaria* by Westerlund (1885). A decision by the Zoological Nomenclature Commission (ZNC 1998) declared *Fossaria* a junior synonym of *Galba*. Chromosome number: 18 pairs.

Galba bulimoides has several form variations (e.g., *techella*, Haldeman 1867; *cockerelli*, Pilsbry and Ferriss 1906) that have been considered different species by some authors (Bequaert and Miller 1973; Hibbard and Taylor 1960). Baker (1911) listed these forms as races or synonyms of *Galba bulimoides*, which Pilsbry (Pilsbry and Ferriss 1906), as well as Clarke (1973), also supported. Baker (1911, p. 217) observed that "*techella* and *cockerelli* were once thought to be specifically separable from *bulimoides*, but the examination of a large series of both forms has proven conclusively that *techella* is but a race of *bulimoides*." To date, no *cockerelli* forms have been reported from Utah, though reports from neighboring states suggest it may be present. This guide follows the opinions of expert malacologists F. C. Baker, A. H. Clarke, and H. A. Pilsbry, and considers the *cockerelli* form a variant of *bulimoides*. The *techella* form is considered a species herein, based on differences in marginal radular teeth characteristics. Other taxonomic issues are discussed in the text for the species (Junior Synonyms section) or species group. See also the following section.

Hinkleyia and *Polyrhytis*

Recent changes in the taxonomy (Meier-Brook and Bargues 2002; Kruglov 2005; Vinarski 2012; Welter-Shultes 2012; Campbell et al. 2017; Glöer 2019), and phylogenetics (Bargues and Mas-Coma 1997; Remigio and Blair 1997a, b; Bargues et al. 2001; Remigio 2002; Correa et al. 2010; Bargues et al. 2012; Pieńkowska and Lesicki 2018) of Lymnaeidae have been considered and applied to this guide after consulting the rules of the International Code of Zoological Nomenclature, 4th edition (hereafter the Code). The rationale and background of the taxonomic changes related to the genera *Hinkleyia* and *Polyrhytis* are discussed below.

Phylogenetic studies demonstrated that North American *Stagnicola* were genetically distinct from the European species (Bargues et al. 2001; Correa et al. 2010), leading to creation of a new genus *Catascopia* Meier-Brook et Bargues, 2002, with *Lymnaea catascopium*, Say 1817, as type. *Catascopia* was subsequently changed to *Ladislavella*, Dybowski, 1913, with *Leptolimnaea terebra* var. *sorensis*, Dybowski, 1913, as type (Vinarski 2012). Code rules (Art. 23.3.5) require the name for the genus must be the oldest available name applied to that type, so *Catascopia* was incorrect since older names were available. However, the Code rules (Article 68.2) indicate that the type species for the new genus is *Lymnaea catascopium* Say, 1817, by original designation. Errors in name selection do not change the type (Article 67.8). So, the "First Reviser" action is nullified (Article 24.2.5). Following Article 42.3 of the Code, *L. catascopium* is the type that must be reviewed for historic generic names. *Limnophysa*, Fitzinger 1833, is the oldest available name, applied to the type *catascopium* by Beck (1837) and Tryon (1865b). *Limnophysa* was synonymized with *Stagnicola* Jeffreys, 1830 (Dall 1905; Baker 1911). The type for *Limnophysa* was not given by Fitzinger (1833), but later was designated as "*Limnaea palustris* Müll." (i.e., *Buccinum palustre* Müller, 1774) by Herrmannsen (1846). However, *Buccinum palustre* is also the type species for *Stagnicola*, in which the *Limnophysa* clade and *Lymnaea catascopium* were allocated before genetic analyses indicated a split was needed. *Stagnicola* is still a valid taxon, though with a more restricted distribution in Eurasia (see Kruglov 2005; Welter-Shultes 2012; Glöer 2019). Therefore, due to *Limnophysa* having the same type species as *Stagnicola*, it is ineligible.

The next name chronologically in the *Stagnicola* group for consideration is *Polyrhytis* Meek, 1876. Dall (1905) classified *Polyrhytis* as a subgroup of the subgenus *Lymnaea s.s.* within the genus *Lymnaea*. Baker (1911) provisionally classified *Polyrhytis* as a subgenus within *Stagnicola,* pending anatomical data. Anatomical study of *Stagnicola kingii* from Utah Lake (Utah Co.), and Conner Springs (Box Elder Co.), Utah, USA, by Chamberlin (1933) confirmed its proper placement in *Stagnicola*. Wagner (unpublished data) also dissected five specimens (12.8–20.6 mm long) from Conner Springs and noted the anatomy is consistent with Kruglov's (2005) description of *Polyrhytis* (prostate consistently has a single fold and the penis sac length varied from 59–76% of the preputium length). Kruglov and Starobogatov (1993) and Kruglov (2005) classified *Polyrhytis* as a subgenus of *Lymnaea*, using *Lymnaea kingii* Meek, 1876 as the type species. Campbell et al. (2017) used *Polyrhytis* instead of *Ladislavella* as a replacement for North American *Stagnicola*, based on the priority of *Polyrhytis*.

Kruglov and Starobogatov (1993) and Kruglov (2005) put six species within *Lymnaea* (*Polyrhytis*): *petersi* Dall, 1905 (type location: Koyukuk River, Alaska); *atkaensis* Dall, 1884 (type location: Atka Island, Alaska); *nuttalliana* Lea, 1841 (type location: Oregon); *kurenkovi* Kruglov et Starobogatov, 1989a; *azabatschensis* Kruglov et Starobogatov, 1989a; and *falsipalustris* Kruglov et Starobogatov, 1989a. *L. nuttalliana* was synonymized with *Stagnicola palustris* (Binney 1865–1867; Baker

1902; Baker 1911; Chamberlin and Jones 1929). *S. palustris* in North America has since been considered *Catascopium elodes* based on genetic testing (Bargues et al. 2001). *L. kurenkovi* has been reclassified as a subspecies of *Catascopia catascopium* based on genetic testing (Vinarski et al. 2016). So, there are at least two of the species in Kruglov's *Polyrhytis* group that are either identical to *C. catascopium* or very closely related (i.e., *elodes*, Correa et al. 2010).

So, given the priority of *Polyrhytis* over *Ladislavella*, as well as the occurrence and current use of *C. catascopium* and *C. elodes* already in the group, *Polyrhytis* is the proper genus name for North American *Stagnicola/Catascopia* species. *Polyrhytis* is defined as described by Meier-Brook and Bargues (2002) and differentiated from *Stagnicola* in Lymnaeidae by the length of the rDNA ITS-2 (internal transcribed spacer-2) sequences, which are shorter in *Polyrhytis* (444–449 base pairs) than in European *Stagnicola* species (468–484 base pairs). The descriptions of animal anatomy in Kruglov (2005) for the subgenus subgroup *Ladislavella* and *Polyrhytis* applies, but the characteristics are not necessarily limited to *Polyrhytis* per se. The type species is *Lymnaea catascopium* Say, 1817, as designated by Meier–Brook and Bargues (2002).

The characteristics of *Polyrhytis,* as newly defined, combine elements of Kruglov's (2005) subgroups *Ladislavella* and *Polyrhytis*. Species in the *Ladislavella* group were described as having shells with weakly convex, almost flat whorls in the spire; penis with the cylindrical sac a little shorter than the preputium, and one-half to three-quarters the thickness; distal part of prostate saccular, proximate part clearly separated and ribbon-like; Uterus round, after a small interception, it passes into a wide, trumpet-shaped section. Kruglov (2005) characterized species within *Polyrhytis* as having shells that were ovoid to elongate-oval, brown or yellow-brown, moderately stout, and often with malleated shell sculpture on the last whorl or axial ribbing. The spire is conical or highly conical, 25–50% of the shell height or more. The columellar fold closes the umbilicus, leaving a narrow or rather wide gap (in the personal experience of the author, the umbilicus is an inconsistent character, varying in a population of *Polyrhytis utahensis*). Aperture is higher than wide and less than 75% of total shell length. Distal part of the prostate is cylindrical or pear-shaped, with one fold. Penis sac is short, thick, and noticeably swollen at the proximal end. The penis narrows distally. The velum is more developed than the sarcobellum. Preputium is cylindrical, 1 to 3.5 times as long as the penis sac. Seminal receptacle lies at the pericardium and grows together with it. Sperm duct is long, often expanding to provagina. Seminal vesicle is of the alveolar type. Central radular tooth with one cusp, followed by 8–9 bicuspid teeth, 3–4 tricuspid teeth, and 15–17 marginal teeth gradually featuring 5–6 cusps.

Species assigned to *Polyrhytis* include those tested by Meir-Brook and Bargues (2002) and Remigio (2002), that is, *Stagnicola catascopium*, *S. emarginata, S. elrodi, S. elodes, S. hinkleyi,* and *S. utahensis* (*S. utahensis* was wrongly identified as *S. bonnevillensis* in the genetic analyses of Remigio [2002] and Correa et al. [2010]).

The fossil species *S. bonnevillensis* (Call, 1884) and *Lymnaea (Polyrhytis) kingi* (Meek, 1876) are probable ancestors of *S. utahensis* (Call, 1884), based on the unique shell morphology and geography common to all three species, and are included as well. The species of the *Ladislavella* group of Kruglov (2005; *Lymnaea* [*Stagnicola*] *vulnerata* Küster, 1862; *L.* [*Stagnicola*] *liogyra* Westerlund, 1897) are provisionally added, given that the type species of *Ladislavella*, *Leptolimnaea terebra* var. *sorensis* (Dybowski, 1913; junior synonym of *Polyrhytis terebra*), was previously synonymized with *S. occulta* (Vinarski and Glöer, 2008) and genetic work (Pieńkowska and Lesicki, 2018) has indicated a very close relationship between the two species. *Polyrhytis catascopium tumrokensis* (Vinarski et al., 2016), is also included as a member, given it is a subspecies of the type species. Other North American species not mentioned will need to be tested to determine their proper generic placement.

Bargues et al. (2001) suggested that *Stagnicola (Hinkleyia) caperata* was different enough from other North American *Stagnicola* to warrant elevation to its own genus, *Hinkleyia* Baker, 1928. This was also suggested by Remigio and Blair (1997b), Correa et al. (2010), Bargues et al. (2012), and Pieńkowska and Lesicki (2018). So, in this guide, the three North American species in the former subgenus *Hinkleyia* are now elevated to the genus level as recommended by the authors of the five articles noted above. The three species are *Hinkleyia caperata*, Say, 1829, *H. montanensis*, Baker, 1912, and *H. pilsbryi,* Hemphill, 1890a.

Hinkleyia (Baker 1928; Taylor et al. 1963) features shells that appear like those of *Polyrhytis* in general form, that is, elongate, with weakly convex spire whorls, a large convex body whorl, large nuclear whorl, and an elongate-oval aperture that is shorter than the spire. The shell typically has a deep umbilicus, a columellar axis that is not twisted and without a fold or weak, and a microsculpture of spiral lines and periostracum with a "hairy" appearance. Lateral radular teeth are bicuspid. Penis sheath (epiphallus) is about two-thirds the length of preputium, and thicker in diameter than that for *Polyrhytis*. Vas deferens is also notably stout. The penis is short and thick, with a muscular knot or constriction near its midlength. Oviduct more globose and prostate more ovate and shorter than for *Polyrhytis*; lower prostate flattened, weakly folded. Vaginal sphincter well-developed, somewhat eccentric, but not ball-like. Upper prostate has a large diverticulum appended to proximal end. Foot and tentacles slenderer than for *Polyrhytis*. Egg masses have a thin inconspicuous outer tunic, and individual egg envelopes are relatively thin. Distributed in upper North America. Type species is *Stagnicola caperata* Say, 1829. The genus is named in honor of malacologist Anson Hinkley of Illinois.

Lymnaea

Lymnaea, Lamarck, 1799 (Dall 1905; Baker 1911; Chamberlin and Jones 1929; Jackiewicz 1993), features shells that are ovately oblong or elongated, generally thin and brittle, the last whorl typically expanded, peristome thin and somewhat flaring; aperture ovate to oblong-ovate, sometimes ovately rounded; no true umbilicus, but occasionally there is a small chink; strongly gyrate columella, columellar callus closely appressed to the last whorl, forming a wide deposit. Penis is less than half the length of the penis sac, with a ring-like swelling; lateral teeth bicuspid. The type species for *Lymnaea* is *L. stagnalis* Linnaeus, 1758. Chromosome number: 18 pairs. Synonyms include *Lymneus* Cuvier, 1816; *Limnaea* Blainville, 1824; *Limnea* Link, 1807; *Limneus* Draparnaud, 1801; *Lymnula* or *Lymnulus* Rafinesque, 1819; *Lymnus* Montfort, 1810 (Burch 1982).

Radix

Radix Montfort, 1810 features shells that are globose, broadly ovate or rounded, with a short spire, large body whorl, very large aperture, simple outer lip, and strongly twisted columella (which may be concealed by a reflexed inner lip that forms an umbilical chink) (Baker 1911; Jackiewicz 1993). First laterals are tricuspid, and the balance bicuspid; penis longer by a fourth than the penis sac; penis sac retractor muscle bifid and narrow (Baker 1911). Synonyms of the genus include *Gulnaria* "Leach" Turton, 1831; *Xymorus* Gebler, 1829; *Neritostoma* H. and A. Adams, 1858; *Cerasina* Kobelt, 1881; *Auriculariana* Servain, 1881; *Acuminatiana* Bourguignat, 1889; *Cyclolimnaea* Dall, 1905; *Costolimnaea* Dybowski, 1913; and seven genera of Kruglov and Starobogatov 1989b: *Desertiradix, Iraniradix, Nopponiradix, Okhotiradix, Pamiriradix, Thermoradix,* and *Ussuriradix* (Vinarski et al. 2020). Chromosome number: 16–17 pairs (Vinarski 2013). See Askenova et al. (2018) for a recent genetically based revision of the genus.

Galba bulimoides Lea, 1841 Prairie Galba

DESCRIPTION (Lea 1846a, p. 9): "Shell ovately conical, rather thin, smooth, shining, diaphanous, brownish yellow, slightly perforate; spire rather short; sutures small; whorls five, slightly convex; aperture ovate. The aperture is more than half the length of the shell, and the fold obsolete. The deposit of the columella is wide, and nearly covers the perforation, which consequently is very small."

FIG. 27. *Galba bulimoides*, UMMZ collection. 73594: Idaho, 73606: Farmington, NM; 73611: Farson, WY. Credit: UMMZ.

Baker (1911) and Pilsbry and Ferriss (1906) note a few races of *G. bulimoides,* including *cockerelli* Pilsbry & Ferriss, 1906; *techella* Haldeman, 1867; *sonomaensis*, and *cassi* Baker, 1911. Based on radula characters, *Galba techella* is considered a valid species in this

Lymnaeidae

FIG. 28. *Galba bulimoides*, Holotype. Credit: Dept. Invertebrate Zoology, USNM.

FIG. 29. *Galba bulimoides cockerelli*, lectotype, ANSP 84287. Credit: ANSP.

FIG. 30. *G. bulimoides sonomaensis*, paralectotype, ANSP 330130. Credit: ANSP.

guide until more is known about the anatomy of *G. bulimoides* s.s.

The shell of *G. bulimoides cockerelli* Pilsbry and Ferriss, 1906 (Fig. 29) is subglobose, with a short spire, pale yellowish-corneous, composed of 4½ convex whorls, which are finely striate, but without spiral lines or malleation; last whorl large. Aperture short-ovate, its length $^3/_5$ to $^2/_3$ that of the shell. Columella broadly expanded, not folded. Umbilicus large.

SIZE (Lea 1846a; Pilsbry and Ferriss 1906; Baker 1911): *G. bulimoides* s.s. (mean, range): SL 10.3 (6.5–13.5) mm; SW 6.0 (4–8) mm; SL/SW ratio 1.72 (1.54–2.00); ApL 6.1 (3.5–9) mm; ApW 3.3 (2–4.5) mm; ApL/SL 59.6 (50.0–70.0)%. Lea's type had a total shell length of 9.7 mm, dia. 5.6 mm, aperture 6.5 × 3.5 mm. For *G. bulimoides cockerelli* (n = 8): SL 10.3 (8–13.5) mm; SW 7.3 (6–9.5) mm; SL/SW ratio 1.41 (1.29–1.54); ApL 6.5 (5.3–8.2) mm; ApW 4.0 (3.0–5.0) mm; ApL/SL 63.7 (54.5–75.0)%.

ANIMAL (Pilsbry 1896; Baker 1911; Hubendick 1951; Clarke 1973): The animal has a translucent, almost water-colored body, peppered with opaque white; eyes black, tentacles opaque white; a dark stripe on back starting between tentacles. For *G. bulimoides cockerelli*, the radula formula is 21–1–21 to 24–1–23 (7 bicuspid laterals, 4 tricuspid intermediate teeth, 10 marginals with 6–7 cusps); Penis is $^2/_3$ the length of the preputium. Even though *bulimoides* has bicuspid lateral teeth, genetic analysis by Burch and Lindsay (1972) indicated that it is properly allocated to *Galba*, not *Polyrhytis*.

TYPE LOCATION: Oregon for *G. bulimoides* Lea, 1841; Holotype (118647) is at the USNM. The holotype for *G. bulimoides cockerelli* (ANSP 84287) was from Las Vegas, NM.

JUNIOR SYNONYMS (Baker 1911; Clarke 1973): *Lymnaea bulimoides* Lea, 1846; *Limnaea adelinae* Tryon, 1863; *Lymnaea techella* Haldeman, 1867; *Lymnaeus bulimoides* Küster, 1862; *Limnophysa bulimoides* (Lea) Tryon 1865b; *Lymnaea cubensis* var. *bulimoides* Pilsbry, 1891; *Lymnaea bryanti* Baker, 1905b; *Lymnaea bulimoides cockerelli* Pilsbry and Ferris, 1906; *Lymnaea hendersoni* Baker, 1909; *Lymnaea cockerelli* Pilsbry and Ferriss, 1910; *Galba bulimoides cassi* Baker, 1911; *Galba alberta* Baker, 1919; *Fossaria perplexa* Baker and Henderson, 1929; *Stagnicola cockerelli* Bequaert and Miller, 1973.

NOTES (Baker 1911): Highly variable in form. The triangular and rolled over form of the inner lip and more rotund shape of the body whorl separates *bulimoides* s.s. from *Galba techella*. The *cockerelli* race is easily distinguished by differences in its L/W ratio (i.e., shorter, more globose shell), shorter spire, and the wide expansion of the inner lip. The shell of *Galba techella* is relatively shinier than *G. bulimoides*, and with a narrower spire. The shell is not as turreted as *G. humilis modicella* and *obrussa*, and it differs from these two taxa in anatomy (lateral teeth bicuspid in *bulimoides*, not tricuspid, and penis is shorter).

Hibbard and Taylor (1960, p. 91) considered *cockerelli* a distinct species based on "(1) morphological distinction, (2) occurrence of *S. cockerelli* in the same area with *S. bulimoides* and *S. bulimoides techella* without evident intergradation, and (3) distinct geographic distribution." However, given (2), then (3) is contradictory. Leonard (1943) also found *cockerelli* and *techella* in Kansas but in different sites; the *cockerelli* form was from an ephemeral pool. Baker (1911, p. 217) writes that "*techella* and *cockerelli* were once thought to be specifically separable from *bulimoides*, but the examination of a large series of both forms has proven conclusively that *techella* is but a race of *bulimoides*." Walter's anatomical observations in Taylor et al. (1963) indicated that *techella* has tricuspid marginal teeth, whereas *G. bulimoides cockerelli* has 4–7 cusps on the marginals (for *bulimoides* s.s., no data). For that reason, *techella* is considered a distinct species herein, distinguished primarily by the marginal teeth character. Pilsbry and Ferriss (1906) described a shell of Hemphill's from Sonoma County, California, as *L. bulimoides sonomaensis* Hemphill; Baker (1911) considered this form to be a distinct species, which he referred to as *Galba sonomaensis* (Fig. 30). The spire is not as acute, and the aperture is more patulous than *bulimoides* s.s. Baker (1911) also considered *Limnea ampla* Keep, 1887, *Radix ampla* var. *utahensis* Keep, 1904, and *Lymnaea perpolita* Dall, 1905, to be synonymous with *G. sonomaensis*.

G. bulimoides is an intermediate host to the sheep liver fluke *Fasciola hepatica* (Shaw and Simms 1929). It is found in dense aquatic vegetation in ponds, slow creeks, and ditches, surviving periods of drought in seasonally dried ponds

(Leonard 1943; Clarke 1973). Genetic analyses by Correa et al. (2011) show that *bulimoides* is distinct from *G. parva*, *G. humilis*, *G. cubensis*, *G. truncatula*, and some South American *Galba*.

DISTRIBUTION (Johnson et al. 2013; CM, ANSP): BC; AR, AZ, CA, CO, ID, KS, MN, MO, MT, NE, NM, OH, SD, TX, UT, WY, OR, WA. The *cockerelli* form has been reported from AZ, CA, CO, ID, KS, SD, OR, TX, and Alberta, but not in Utah. Utah records for *G. bulimoides*: Farmington, Tooele County (Snake-Hamblin and Skull Valleys), Box Elder County (Blue Spring Hills; Promontory; Park Valley; Pilot Creek), Bear, Sevier, Weber, Jordan, and Green rivers (Hovingh 2018). The *G. b. cassi* and *techella* forms were reported from Cedar Breaks National Monument and Zion National Park (Gregg 1940, 1941; Taylor et al. 1963).

Galba dalli Baker, 1907 Dusky Galba

DESCRIPTION (Baker 1907, p. 125): "Shell very small, thin, ovate-conic, turreted; color greenish or whitish-horn; surface dull to shining, marked by heavy crowded growth-lines, which are elevated into distinct ribs in some specimens; protoconch very small, flatly rounded, light-horn colored; whorls 4½ to 5, rounded and distinctly shouldered; spire generally obtusely conic, turreted, a trifle longer than the aperture; sutures very deeply impressed; aperture elongate, ovate or elliptical, the peristome continuous in many specimens; outer lip acute; inner lip forming a rather flat extension over the umbilical region, leaving a rather pronounced chink; the lower part of the aperture is somewhat effuse; the columellar extension of the inner lip is appressed so as to form a pseudo-plait; the inner edge of the outer lip frequently forms a rib-like ridge in very old specimens."

SIZE (Baker 1907; Clarke 1981): SL typically 3.25–4.25 mm (up to 6 mm), SW 2–2.1 mm (to 3.3 mm); L/W ratio 1.76 (1.36–2.12); ApL 1.25–2.0 mm (45–55% of SL), ApW 0.9–1.25 mm.

ANIMAL (Clarke 1973): Radula formulae of 22–1–21 and 21–1–21 (laterals bicuspid, intermediate teeth tricuspid, and marginals with 6 cusps).

TYPE LOCATION: James Lake, Steuben Co., Indiana; Holotype at Chicago Academy of Sciences; cotypes at ANSP and Smithsonian.

JUNIOR SYNONYMS (Baker 1911; Hibbard and Taylor 1960): *Lymnaea dalli* Baker, 1907; *Fossaria dalli* (Baker) Baker 1928); *Bakerilymnaea dalli* (Baker) Weyrauch, 1964, Clarke 1981 *Lymnaea turritella* Leonard, 1943. In Baker's (1905a) initial description, he thought the shell was *Lymnaea parva*, previously described by Lea. Baker later published a more detailed description of the shell (Baker 1907), which indicated it was a unique species, *Lymnaea dalli*. *Fossaria* Westerlund, 1885 was a genus to which species in *Galba* were formerly assigned; *Fossaria* is now considered a junior synonym (ICZN 1998).

FIG. 31. *Galba dalli.* Left: holotype CM:inv:23125.1 from the Chicago Academy of Sciences/Peggy Notebaert Nature Museum's collections. Credit: Robin Delapena, Insect Div., Field Museum, 27 Feb 2017. Above: topotype ANSP 90176; (L to R) apertural view, closer view of the umbilicus, and dorsal view. Credit: E. Wagner, courtesy ANSP.

NOTES (Baker 1907; Clarke 1973, 1981): *Galba parva* was recently synonymized with *Galba humilis,* based on new genetic information (Alda et al. 2021). Juvenile shells of *G. humilis* or shells in colder climes may appear similar to *G. dalli*. However, *G. humilis* shells are slenderer in outline, with a longer and narrower aperture, a smaller and less conspicuous umbilicus, and the whorls are not as turreted. Also, the variants of *G. humilis* have tricuspid lateral teeth, whereas *dalli* laterals are bicuspid. *G. dalli* does not normally occur out of water, differing from *G. humilis*, which is more amphibious. Identified by the large number of whorls for its small size, incised sutures, and roundly shouldered whorls. The specific name honors William Dall, former curator of USNM.

DISTRIBUTION (Johnson et al. 2013; ANSP records): Canada; AZ, IL, IN, KS, MI, MN, MO, MT, NY, NE, NV, OH, PA, ND, SD, VA, WI, WV, WY, NM, TX. In Utah, reported from Temple of Sinewava (Zion National Park) in 1977 (possibly misidentified?; Wilson et al. 2017).

Galba humilis group

Galba humilis Say, 1822, *G. humilis modicella* Say, 1825, *G. humilis rustica* Lea, 1841, and *G. obrussa* Say, 1825, share a common anatomy and a tumultuous taxonomic history. Each of these taxa has tricuspid lateral teeth, intermediate teeth of 3–4 cusps, marginal teeth with 4–7 cusps, and a penis that is about as long as the penis sac (shorter in other Utah *Galba*) (Baker 1911; McCraw 1957; Clarke 1973). Hubendick (1951) noted that the *L. humilis* he dissected frequently had bicuspid lateral teeth, so this may be a variable character or it may be due to differences in identification. Their distribution, based on museum records and literature, also overlaps. *Galba humilis* s.s. anatomy was published by McCraw (1957), showing similar penial anatomy to others in the group.

Recent genetic work (Alda et al. 2021) also suggests that the former species *G. obrussa, modicella,* and *obrussa* should be synonymized under *G. humilis,* which has priority. In addition, *G. parva* was also synonymized under *G. humilis.* Further sampling in North America is needed, especially in the West; For example, Alda et al. (2021) noted a potential new species of *Galba* in New Mexico. Based on the similar animal characteristics, as well as the recent genetic evidence, this guide considers *modicella, parva, obrussa,* and *rustica* as shell morphs and form variants of *humilis.* Whether these forms merit subspecific status will need to be determined by future research. The rationale is further reviewed below.

Haldeman (1840, p. 43) compared the *humilis* of South Carolina and the *modicella* form from Maine, Massachusetts, and Ohio. He concluded that "the shells are delicate and fragile, and differ considerably among themselves, but I cannot regard them in any other light than as well marked varieties." Baker (1911) considered *G. humilis* a southeastern U.S. lymnaeid that transitioned in the northern and western United States into the *G. humilis modicella* form; *Galba rustica* was also relegated to a subspecies of *G. humilis* based on anatomy. Baker (1911) listed *G. obrussa* as a separate species, with similar anatomy but distinctive shell characters. Baker (1911, p. 258) remarks: "A careful study of all available material, including Say's type, following Mr. Walker's suggestion, revealed the fact that typical *humilis* was not authentically known outside of the region east of the Appalachian Mountains. The fact also became apparent that *modicella* was simply a northern form of *humilis,* . . . . The spire in *modicella* varies greatly in length, the short-spired individuals being the form commonly known as *humilis.*" Henderson (1924) similarly considered *L. humilis* specimens from Colorado as *L. humilis modicella.* Baker (1928) later elevated *modicella* to species level based on shell characters, which was adopted by Chamberlin and Jones (1929). Burch (1989), like Baker (1911), considered *humilis s.s.* to be restricted to the Atlantic drainage from New Jersey to South Carolina, and *rustica, modicella,* and *obrussa,* as part of the *G. obrussa* group distributed over the rest of North America.

Hubendick (1951), who focused on anatomy, synonymized all the North American *Galba* species under *Lymnaea humilis.* Clarke (1973) listed *modicella* as *Lymnaea modicella* and considered *rustica* a junior synonym of *modicella.* Tryon (1865b) considered *rustica* and *modicella* to be junior synonyms of *Lymnaea humilis* Say, 1822. Baker (1905b) initially considered *G. rustica* to be a junior synonym of *Lymnaea desidiosa* var. *modicella* (= *Galba modicella* Say, 1825), but later (Baker 1911) considered it a subspecies of *Galba humilis.* Burch (1960a) and Inaba (1969) noted that *rustica* has 19 haploid chromosomes, the latter suggesting that it should be a separate species, differing from other Lymnaeinae, which have 18 chromosomes. Hibbard and Taylor (1960, p. 234) listed *Lymnaea humilis rustica* as a synonym of *Lymnaea (Galba) obrussa.* Notably, Burch still listed *rustica* as a subspecies in later work (Taylor et al. 1963; Burch 1989). Johnson et al. (2013) listed it as *Galba rustica.* McCraw (1957) noted that the penial morphology of *humilis* was like that of *modicella, rustica,* and *obrussa,* but failed to provide radular teeth data, which are still not available.

Data from Baker (1911, 1928), and Clarke (1973) show that *rustica*, *modicella*, and *obrussa* have radular characters in common, that is, tricuspid lateral teeth, intermediate teeth with 4–7 cusps, and marginal teeth with 4–7 cusps. Each of these forms is also turreted to varying degrees. Maximum size is similar among *humilis*, *rustica*, and *modicella* (1–12.5 mm), but *obrussa* reaches larger maximum size (19.5 mm SL; Baker 1911). *G. obrussa* also appears to have greater variation in the number, size, and position of marginal teeth cusps than the other forms (Baker 1911). The type is more strongly shouldered than the other forms, but Baker (1911, p. 281) notes variation in form for *obrussa*: "spire may be long or short, pointed or wide, and strongly shouldered. The whorls may be slender, scalar, or wide and corpulent, while the aperture varies from almost round to long and narrow." However, in the genetic study by Correa et al. (2010), *obrussa* appears to be synonymous with *humilis*; the latter is shown to be distinct from *G. bulimoides*. Alda et al. (2021) also demonstrated that topotypic *obrussa* from Cincinnati, Ohio, was synonymous with *G. humilis*. Remigio (2002) demonstrated some small differences between *obrussa* (i.e., *humilis*) and *bulimoides* in his phylogenetic trees based on 16S genes. Modern genetic data support the separation of the *Galba* group from other lymnaeid genera (Remigio 2002; Correa et al. 2011), but more work is needed within the genus.

So, given the similarity in radular teeth, penial anatomy, and preferred habitat, as well as overlapping distributions, the genetic data in support of synonymy, and variation in shell characteristics among lymnaeidae, herein, *obrussa*, as well as *parva*, *rustica* and *modicella,* are considered form variants of *humilis*. Given their previous status as species, data on the variants is presented separately below within *G. humilis*. Museum specimens listed as *Lymnaea humilis* or *Galba humilis* are found from Florida to western Canada.

Galba humilis Say, 1822 Marsh Galba

DESCRIPTION (Say 1822, quoted, p. 378; Baker 1911): "Shell ovate-conic, thin, translucent, with slight wrinkles; volutions nearly six, convex, terminal one very minute; suture well indented; aperture about equal in length to the spire; labium with an obvious plate of calcarious deposit; a distinct and rather open umbilical aperture; colour pale reddish-white or yellowish white." *Shell*: periostracum light yellowish horn; surface shining, sometimes polished; lines of growth crowded, prominent, spiral sculpture absent or but slightly indicated;

FIG. 32. *Galba humilis*. ANSP lectotype 58754. Credit: ANSP.

FIG. 33. *Galba humilis* form *modicella*. Left: ANSP holotype 58790, center and right: ANSP 191340, Saratoga, UT. Credit: ANSP.

FIG. 34. *Galba humilis* form *obrussa*, ANSP 104176, 58700. Credit: ANSP.

spire conic, turreted, apex as in *G. modicella*. *Whorls*: 5–5.5, convex, rather rapidly increasing in diameter, fat body whorl. *Aperture*: ovate or roundly ovate; peristome lip thin, inner lip reflected, creating a narrow triangular expansion, which may roll in toward the umbilical chink or stand somewhat erect; parietal callus well marked; axis smooth, forming a column.

FORM VARIANTS: For the *modicella* form (Say 1825; Baker 1911, Fig. 33) the shell is narrower than typical *G. humilis*, blackish, periostracum light yellowish horn, with 4.5–5 whorls, nuclear whorls 1.25.

In the *obrussa* form (Fig. 34), the shell is narrower than typical *G. humilis*, oblong, somewhat shouldered to strongly turreted, with 5–5.5 rounded whorls with deep sutures, nuclear whorls 1.25; light-yellowish periostracum.

For the *rustica* form variant (Fig. 35) (Lea 1846a; Baker 1911), the shell is subfusiform, thin, imperforate; spire rather elevated, very acute, and regularly tapering; sutures impressed. *Whorls*: 5–5.5, rather convex, nuclear whorls similar to *modicella*. *Aperture*: narrow elliptical and about half of total shell length. Lea (1846a) described *rustica* from a single shell (Fig. 35).

Lea's shell was covered with a red coating of iron oxide, giving it a rough feel that begat the specific epithet.

FIG. 35. *Galba humilis* form *rustica*, holotype USNM. Credit: USNM, Dept. of Invertebrate Zoology.

FIG. 36. *Galba humilis* form *parva*. Right: ANSP 113038; above: ANSP 90176 from Wheelon, UT. Credit: ANSP.

The *parva* form of *G. humilis* features a diminutive solid shell that is subturreted, thin, smooth; horn colored to translucent light brown or yellowish-white, subperforate; spire elevated, considerably longer than the aperture, turreted, forming an acute pyramid in some specimens and a broad pyramid in others; sutures impressed. *Whorls:* 4.5–5, more convex and with deeper sutures than for typical *Galba humilis*. *Aperture:* roundly elliptical and almost continuous. The inner lip is more erect in the *parva* form, causing the umbilicus to be round, deep, and open; the umbilical area is gracefully rounded. (Lea 1846a; Baker 1905b).

SIZE (Say 1822; Baker 1911; McCraw 1961): Type: 8.6 mm long. SL 6–10 (max. 12.5) mm, SW 3.5–5.0 mm, SL/SW ratio: 1.73 (1.60–1.89); ApL 2.75–4.5 mm, ApW 2.0–2.5 mm, ApL/SL 51.0 (46–56)%.

FORM VARIANTS: For the *modicella* form, total length 8.9 mm, breadth 5.1 mm, aperture length 5.1 mm. Data for 11 shells in Baker (1911; mean, range): shell length 8.9(7–12) mm, breadth 4.6(3.25–6) mm, L/W ratio 1.94(1.7–2.4),

FIG. 37. *Galba humilis* in UMMZ collection. Line spacing 1 mm. Credit: UMMZ: 1) 195550, Cache Co., UT; 2) 150721, Weber R. at Hennifer, UT; 3) 75942, Harney Cr., WY; 4) 75881, Umpqua R., OR; 5) 75841 Reno, NV; 6) 5482 Woodruff Cr., NV.

aperture height 4.66(4–5.75) mm, and aperture/total length percentage 53.5(35.8–64.3)%.

The *obrussa* form is noted to reach a longer shell length. Say's (1825) type: SL 11.4 mm, SW 5.1 mm (SL/SW 2.23); ApL 6.3 mm. Baker (1911): SL 8.0–19.5 mm, SW 4.5–12.5 mm, SL/SW ratio 2.24 (1.91–3.20); ApL 4–12.5 mm, ApW 2.0–5.0 mm; ApL/SL 49.4 (33–58)%.

The *rustica* variant reaches up to 7.5 to 10.5 mm tall × 3.8–4.8 mm wide, SL/SW ratio 2.09(1.87–2.25), aperture length 44–52% of shell length. Type specimen: shell 8.9 mm tall × 3.8 mm wide. Leonard (1943) noted that *rustica* in Kansas were all about 6 mm long (5.5 whorls).

For the *parva* form, typical specimens measure 5.5–6.0 mm × 3.0 mm wide, L/W ratio 1.93 (1.80–2.02); ApL 2.5 to 3.0 mm (43.2 {33–47}% of SL), ApW 1.25–1.75 mm. Holotype was 5.6 mm long by 3.0 mm wide.

ANIMAL (Baker 1911; Hubendick 1951; McCraw 1957): Body dark gray to blackish, lighter below, sometimes yellowish, the whole surface dotted with white or yellowish, especially around the eyes. Tentacles triangular, flat, short, semitransparent, the black eyes at inner base of tentacles; respiratory orifice on right side near angle of the peristome and body whorl. Foot 5 mm long × 3 mm wide. Portions of body appear pinkish through shell. Jaw about 3X as wide as high, arched, with rounded ends and a median convex swelling.

RADULA: central tooth small, spade-shaped, very asymmetric, with a hint of a side cusp; first two laterals bicuspid (stout mesocone and smaller ectocone); 10th tooth with 4–5 cusps. For the *modicella* form, the central tooth has 1 cusp, 6 tricuspid laterals, 1 intermediate with 4 cusps, and 18 marginal teeth with 5–6

FIG. 38. *Galba obrussa* lectotype, ANSP 58700. Credit: ANSP.

cusps. The *obrussa* form had 70 rows of teeth; 26–1–26, sometimes 25 per side. Central tooth with 1 cusp (or with another very short side cusp), 8 lateral teeth with 3 cusps, 2 intermediate teeth with 3–4 cusps, 16 marginal teeth with 4–7 cusps. For the *rustica* form, radulae (20–1–20) feature a unicuspid central tooth, 6 tricuspid laterals, 2 intermediate teeth with 3–4 cusps, and 12 marginals with 4–6 cusps. For the *parva* form, radulae (24–1–24) feature a central tooth with one long cusp, 4 tricuspid laterals, 2 intermediate teeth with 4 cusps, and 18 marginals with ≥4 cusps. Clarke (1973) noted radula ranging from 16–1–16 (4.2 mm long shell) to 23–1–22 (6.3 mm shell) among 7 different sites.

GENITALIA: Hermaphroditic duct becomes fine and hair-like distally, terminating in a bulbous expansion that joins the short, stout, pigmented albumen gland duct. For the female of the *parva* form, the seminal receptacle is roundly pyriform, its duct 1.75 mm long; albuminiparous gland long-ovate, placed near the vaginal opening. For *G. humilis s.s.*, the seminal receptacle is pear-shaped and bright orange in the living animal. Vas deferens narrows as it approaches the body wall, anterior to the vagina on the right wall.

Penis sheath about equal in length or slightly longer than the muscular preputium. The penis sheath/preputium length ratio for the *obrussa* form ranged from 1.0 to 1.5 (Baker 1911, n = 11). In the *parva* form, the penis was described (Baker 1911; Hubendick 1951) as two-thirds as long as preputium; narrow, with a rounded head; the sarcobellum and velum of ordinary size; 4 protractor muscles; Vas deferens 4 mm long. The preputium is broad and square-shouldered where it receives the penis sheath. Two penial retractor muscles, one attached to penis head, one attached to penis sac; 5 tiny protractor muscles on the penis sac.

The vas deferens enters the prostate without marked enlargement. Prostate small, short, flattened, long-ovate in front view, with one large fold. In the *parva* form, the prostate was described as elongate, ovate, flattened, rounded at both ends; one feebly developed fold; anterior end gradually narrows to meet the prostate duct, which is about 1 mm long.

TYPE LOCATION: South Carolina. For the *modicella* form, Susquehanna River near Owego, Tioga County, New York (ANSP #58790); for synonym *jamesii*, ponds near Cincinnati, Ohio (USNM 29106).

For the *obrussa* form, Harrowgate, Philadelphia County, Pennsylvania. *Lymnea philadelphica* Lea 1841, Schuylkill River near Philadelphia. *Lymnaea acuta* Lea 1837, pond four miles north of Philadelphia. The *rustica* type specimen was from Poland, Ohio; Holotype (#118652) is at USNM. The *parva* form holotype was from Cincinnati, Ohio.

JUNIOR SYNONYMS (Haldeman 1840; Baker 1911; Alda et al. 2021): *Lymnaeus humilis* Say, 1822; *L. modicellus* Say, 1825; *Lymnaea exigua* Lea, 1841; *Lymnaeus obrussus* Say, 1825; *Lymnaea rustica* Lea, 1841 (1846a).

SYNONYMS OF THE *MODICELLA* FORM: *Lymneus modicellus* Say, 1825; Tryon (1865b) considered *modicella* to be junior synonym of *Lymnaea humilis* Say; *Lymnaea desidiosa* var. *modicella* Baker, 1905; *Lymnaea obrussa modicella* Baker, 1906; *Lymnaea jamesii* Tryon, 1867. Baker (1911) also considered *obrussa* to be a subspecies of *G. humilis*, but later (Baker 1928) considered it a distinct species, *Fossaria modicella*, based on shell character differences. Burch (1989) considered it a form of *G. obrussa*, with which it shares a common anatomy.

SYNONYMS OF THE *OBRUSSA* FORM: *Lymneus obrussus* Say, 1825; *Lymnaea obrussus* (Say) Gould 1833; *Lymnaeus obrussa* (Say) Küster 1862; *Lymnaeus desidiosus* Sager, 1839; *Lymnea desidiosa* (Sager) Haldeman 1842; *Limnophysa desidiosa* (Sager) Beck 1837; *Lymnaea desidiosa* var. *acuta* Jay, 1852; *Limnaea adelinae* Tryon, 1870; *Lymnea philadephica, L. exigua, L. plica,* and *L. planulata* Lea, 1841; *Lymnaea galbana* var. *philadephica* Dall, 1905; *Lymnaea acuta* Lea, 1837; *Lymnaea pallida* Lea, 1856; *Limnophysa pallida* (Lea) DeCamp 1881; *Lymnaea plicata* D'Urban, 1859; *Limnophysa humilis* var. *exigua* Cooper, 1870; *Lymnaea truncatula* (Müller) Woodward 1856; *Fossaria obrussa* Baker, 1928; Genetic analyses (Correa et al. 2010; Alda et al. 2021) demonstrated that *G. obrussa* was synonymous with *G. humilis* Say, 1822; the latter has taxonomic priority. For more on *L. desidiosa*, see Binney (1865a) and Baker (1908).

SYNONYMS OF THE *RUSTICA* FORM: *Lymnaea rustica* Lea, 1841 (1846a); *Fossaria rustica* Westerlund, 1885.

SYNONYMS OF THE *PARVA* FORM: *Lymnaea parva* Lea, 1841 (Lea, 1846a); *Lymnaea curta* Lea, 1841 (Baker 1905b); *Lymnaea sterkii* Baker, 1905a; *Lymnaea parva sterkii* Baker, 1905a (Clarke 1973).

NOTES: Differentiated from *G. dalli* by its larger size. It is slenderer, more turreted, with a slightly shorter aperture than *G. bulimoides*, though these metrics overlap, so examination of the radula is recommended for proper identification (lateral teeth bicuspid in *G. bulimoides*, typically tricuspid in *G. humilis*). Differentiated from juvenile *Polyrhytis* species by its narrow triangular inner lip, forming an evenly rounded expansion (Baker 1911).

McCraw (1961) noted that *humilis* was more common on damp ground or muddy flats rather than in water. Egg masses in the field were first observed in April when water temperatures were 13°C (air, 20°C), continuing through the end of May or early June. Eggs were deposited in the water or less than half a meter from the water's edge. Hatched snails (from laboratory-held egg mass) averaged 0.68 mm × 0.54 mm. Snails did not oviposit if they were <4 mm long. Genbank accession numbers for *G. humilis*: FN182190-NF182199 (Correa et al. 2011; Bargues et al. 2012), AF485658 (Ontario), and DQ256737 (Alabama; Holzmagel et al. 2010).

FORM VARIANTS: The whorls of the *modicella* form are less shouldered, the sutures are less deeply impressed, and the shell length is shorter than the *obrussa* form. Compared to *G. humilis s.s.*, *modicella* has a longer and narrower aperture, narrower spire, straighter columella, and less obese body whorl (Baker 1911). Not as turreted as *S. caperata*. Habitat of *modicella*: wet, muddy, shoreline strips or small pools with vegetation or vegetated borders; not usually found in larger bodies of water (Chamberlin and Jones 1929). In Canadian surveys, the *parva* form was associated with thick to moderately thick vegetation around large mesotrophic lakes, in pools in permanent woods, shallow pools near large lakes, small permanent ponds, muskeg, logs near a river, muddy or grassy river banks, or river backwaters (Clarke 1973).

The *obrussa* form is identified by its narrow, pointed spire, compressed body whorl, and elongated and shouldered aperture, which is also strongly effuse at the anterior end; the inner lip is appressed to the body whorl about the middle of the aperture. The shell is larger and more elongated than the *modicella* form, the aperture is longer and narrower, and the last whorl is not as rounded. In shells of the same size, *modicella* has five whorls, while *G. obrussa* has four (Baker 1928).

Fig. 38 is Say's (1825) type specimen, though broken, in the ANSP collection. *Obrussa* variants summarized by Baker (1911) include *peninsulae* (Walker 1908) from Michigan with 6 whorls, SL 12.5–15.0 mm; *exigua* (Lea 1841) from Tennessee with 5 whorls, SL 5.5–11.5 mm; and *decampi* (Streng 1896) from Michigan with 5 whorls, SL 5–11 mm. Clarke (1973) considered the *decampi* form a distinct species that is more shouldered, with a narrower aperture and with a body whorl that is more flattened laterally near the outer lip; *decampi* also doesn't get as big (maximum length about 12 mm) and lives in coldwater lakes and rivers, whereas the *obrussa* form is found in ponds, creeks, and marshes. Egg masses observed in an aquarium were 7.5 to 8.0 × 2.0 to 2.5 mm, with 30–45 eggs in each.

The *rustica* form features a long, very acute spire and ovate aperture. Half-grown specimens of *obrussa* are similar in general form, but the upper outer lip of the aperture of *obrussa* is shouldered, whereas in *rustica*, this part of the lip forms a graceful curve. Leonard (1943) noted that *rustica* was found sparingly in grassy pools and in moist meadows around marshes, with occasional specimens found in brooks.

DISTRIBUTION (Ibase; ANSP): Kamchatka Peninsula; Canada from Newfoundland and Nova Scotia to British Columbia; widespread in the United States (AL, AZ, AR, CA, DE, FL, GA, ID, IL, IN, IA, KS, LA, ME, MD, MA, MI, MN, MO, MT, ND, NE, NV, NJ, NY, NC, NM, OH, OK, OR, PA, SC, SD, TN, TX, VA, VT, WA, WV, WI, WY). Utah records at UMMZ: Weber drainage (Hennifer, Chalk Creek, and Morgan), Lehi, Cache County, Garden City, and Provo; DMNH: Box Elder County and Fish Springs National Wildlife Refuge; ANSP: the mouth of Ogden Canyon; Fossil record from Kelton, Utah (Henderson 1924).

For the *modicella* form, there are fossil records from Kelton, Utah (Stearns 1893). Contemporary (Recent) Utah records (Chamberlin and Jones 1929; Chamberlin and Berry 1929; Hovingh 1993): Fillmore (Woolstenhulme 1942a), Lamb's Canyon (UMNH), Salt Lake City, Garden City, Morgan, Utah Lake, Logan, Logan Canyon, Dry Canyon, Big Cottonwood Canyon, Brighton, Fish Lake, Seven Mile Canyon (Fremont River drainage), Richfield, Wellsville, between Marysvale and Richfield, Rich county, Glenwood, Crystal Hot Lakes, Salt Lake County, Moroni, Panguitch Creek, Beaver, Torrey, Tremonton, Garland, Snake Valley, and Fish Springs Flat.

For the *obrussa* form, there are fossil records from marl deposits from Lake Bonneville in Utah (Baker 1911) and near Salt Lake City (Hayden 1872). Jones (1940a) found living specimens of this species at Fairfield, Utah. Other Utah records (Chamberlin and Jones 1929; Chamberlin and Berry 1930; Jones 1935; Brooks 1936; Woolstenhulme 1942a, b; Hovingh 2018): Sevier Lake and River, Utah Lake (southeastern shore), Jordan River, southern shore of the Great Salt Lake, south of Garden City and marsh west of Laketown (Rich County), Upper Bear River and also west of Tremonton, Salt Creek, Weber River, Fish Lake (Sevier County), Seven Mile Canyon (Fremont River drainage), Logan Canyon and Blacksmith Fork Canyon below Ballard Springs (Cache County); Ogden; Echo, Weber, Parley's, Lamb's, Big Cottonwood, and Provo Canyons; Kamas; Grantsville; Panguitch; Beaver; Marysvale; between Circleville and Junction; Juab; Glenwood; Navajo Lake; Moab; Duchesne County; and Fruita, Utah.

Utah records for the *rustica* form (Chamberlin and Jones 1929; Jones 1935, 1940b; Woolstenhulme 1942a): Weber River drainage, western Summit County, northern Utah County, 1 mile north of Vernal; Deception Lake, Kane County; live snails at Lake Point (near Tooele) and 2 miles west of there.

Utah distribution records for the *parva* form (Henderson and Daniels 1916; Baily & Baily 1951–1952; Hovingh 1993; UMNH; ANSP): Box Elder, Grand, and Tooele counties, Bear Lake, Logan River, Salt Creek, Utah Lake, Saratoga, Wheelon, Jordan River, Sevier River, Snake Valley, and Pine Valley (Beaver County).

Galba techella Haldeman, 1867 Smooth Prairie Galba

DESCRIPTION (Haldeman 1867, p. 94): "Surface smoother than in *L. bulimoides* Lea, of Oregon, with the lines of accretion less apparent, and the labium more angular. In

FIG. 39. *Galba techella*, lectotype, ANSP 59604. Credit: ANSP.

some individuals the shell is thick enough to be corroded." Pilsbry and Ferris (1906): *Shell* obese, with acutely conic spire, of five or six convex whorls; pale yellowish or light brown, finely striate and usually malleated, the flattened facets obliquely descending. Last whorl very ventricose (rotund), umbilicus large. *Aperture* short-ovate, about 3/5 the total length; basal lip expanded, columellar lip broadly dilated, without a fold. Umbilicus large.

SIZE: SL 8–14 mm, SW 5.1–9 mm, SL/SW ratio 1.56–1.79, ApL 4.9–8.8 mm (52–62% of total length).

ANIMAL (Taylor et al. 1963; Hubendick 1951): Bicuspid lateral teeth; tricuspid marginal teeth. Anatomically not stagnicoline but allied with *Galba*. Penis sheath about the same length as preputium. Velum and sarcobellum well developed. Prostate not folded.

TYPE LOCATION: Texas

JUNIOR SYNONYMS (Baker 1911; Hibbard and Taylor 1960): *Lymnaea techella* Haldeman, 1867; *Galba bulimoides cassi* Baker, 1911; *Lymnaea diminuta* Leonard, 1943; *Galba bulimoides techella* (Pilsbry & Ferriss 1906; Baker 1911).

NOTES (Taylor et al. 1963): *Galba techella* is larger than *G. dalli*. The triangular and rolled-over form of the inner lip (forming a larger umbilicus) and less rotund shape of the body whorl separates *G. techella* from *G. bulimoides* s.s. The *cockerelli* race is easily distinguished by differences in its L/W ratio (i.e., shorter, more globose shell), shorter spire, and the wide expansion of the inner lip. The shell of *Galba techella* is relatively shinier than *G. bulimoides,* and has a narrower spire. The shell is less turreted than that of *G. humilis,* and the *modicella* or *obrussa* forms and lateral teeth are bicuspid, not tricuspid. *G. techella* is the only *Galba* observed to have tricuspid marginal teeth (fewer cusps than the other species). Despite having bicuspid laterals, the anatomy is not that of *Stagnicola* or *Polyrhytis,* but rather like *Galba* species.

DISTRIBUTION (Johnson et al. 2013): Mexico; Canada: Alberta, British Columbia; United States: AL, AR, AK, CA, KS, LA, MO, NE, NM, NV, OK, SD, TX, WY; Utah records: Emery County (Hibbard and Taylor 1960); Cedar Breaks National Monument; head of Mammoth Creek in Garfield County (Gregg 1941, 1942). Brooks (1936) reported both *G. techella* and *G. obrussa* from a pond near 10,000 ft, 7 miles north of Farm Creek, Uinta County.

Hinkleyia caperata Say 1829 Wrinkled Marshsnail

DESCRIPTION (Say 1829; Baker 1911; Taylor et al. 1963): *Shell*: suboval to elongate-oval, a little oblong, turreted, rather solid, color obscurely yellowish horn to brown, sometimes black, surface dull to shining; spire half the length of the

FIG. 40. *Hinkleyia caperata.* UMMZ collection: 1) 176578 St. Louis, MO; 2) 197483 Stillwater R., OH; 3) 49783 Tooele, UT; 4) 189141 Salt Lake Co., UT (Hemphill); 5) 134541 Oconto Co., OH; 6) 150717 N. Platte R., WY. Line spacing = 1 mm. Credit: UMMZ.

FIG. 41. *Hinkleyia caperata.* Lectotype, ANSP 58824, Illinois, umbilical view. Credit: E. Wagner, courtesy ANSP.

mouth; apex acute. *Whorls*: 4.75–5.75 (Baker noted 6–6.5 very convex whorls); slightly wrinkled across, and with very numerous, equal, subequidistant, elevated, minute, revolving lines (seen under 10X magnification); nucleus of 1 1/3 whorls. *Aperture*: ovate, rather dilated, frequently reddish or purplish within; fold of the labium not profound, inner lip reflected over the umbilicus, forming a wide, smooth, triangular expansion without a columellar plait; parietal callus very thin, axis not twisted; umbilical chink open, generally wide and deep (Fig. 41). As in *Stagnicola, Polyrhytis, Lymnaea,* and *Galba*, there are 18 haploid chromosomes.

SIZE (Baker 1911, n = 17, mean, range): Type specimen: 12 mm long × 5 mm wide; ApL 5.0 mm, ApW 3.0 mm. SL 13.2 (9.0–17.0) mm; SW 6.6 (5.0–8.2) mm; ApL 5.9 (4.2–7.5) mm; ApW 3.2 (2.5–4.0) mm; ApL/SL 44.8 (41–50)%; SL/SW ratio 2.02 (1.71–2.40).

ANIMAL (Baker 1911; Chamberlin and Jones 1929): Black or bluish-black, lighter below, and minutely flecked with whitish dots that are scarcely visible except on the top of the head; head distinct, tentacles short, flat, triangular; foot short and wide (8 × 3 mm). Jaw wide and rather high, the median swelling occupying about a third of the width; ends bluntly rounded.

GENITALIA: Penis sheath about 2/3 as long as the cylindrical preputium; prostate ovately cylindrical, rounded at both ends. Spermatheca small, rounded, with a long duct; oviduct very large, somewhat bulbous, the lower portion very short.

RADULA: Central tooth with a broad spade-shaped cusp; lateral teeth bicuspid, intermediate teeth tricuspid. Formula 20 (5–7 cusps)–4(3–4 cusps)–8(2 cusps)–1–32. Over 85 rows of teeth (Baker 1928).

TYPE LOCATION: Near New Harmony, Indiana. Say's type specimen is not in existence, but Baker (1911) notes that shell specimen No. 58824 from Illinois in Philadelphia's Academy of Science is recognized as the lectotype for *Lymnaea caperata*. The synonym *S. smithsoniana* type location was Loup Fork of the Platte River; *S. ferrissi*, Joliet, IL.

JUNIOR SYNONYMS (Tryon 1870; Baker 1911): *Lymneus caperatus* Say, 1829; *Galba caperata* (Say) Baker 1911; *Limnophysa caperata* (Say) Morse 1864; *Limnophysa* (*Lymnaea*) *cubensis* Baker, 1897; *Limnaea ferrissi* Baker, 1897; *Lymnaea* (*Limnophysa*) *smithsoniana* Lea, 1864c; *Limnaea caperata umbilicata* Baker, 1906; *Stagnicola caperata* (Say) Baker 1928.

There was one historical record of a collection of *Stagnicola sumassi* from Echo Canyon (Weber River drainage) and one from the Jordan River (collection date unknown; Fig. K11). Herein, Utah records for *Stagnicola sumassi* Baird, 1863, described from the Sumass Prairie of British Columbia, are also considered junior synonyms of *S. caperata*. Dissection of specimens from Echo Canyon by the author revealed penial anatomy consistent with *S. caperata*, which has taxonomic priority. Shell morphology of type specimens of *S. sumassi* (see images in Baker 1911) is similar to *H. caperata* as well. Tryon (1870) considered *sumassi* to be a synonym of *Lymnaea palustris;* The *palustris* shells of the United States. were later determined to be *Polyrhytis elodes*, genetically distinct from their European counterpart *S. palustris*. Notably, *sumassi* is not listed in Clarke's (1973, 1981) guides to Canadian freshwater mollusks. The species is also not listed by either Burch (1982) or Johnson et al. (2013) in their lists of North American taxa.

NOTES: Similar to *H. montanensis*, which has the same anatomy but differs in surface sculpture (Fig. 43); Shells of *montanensis* are shiny without the raised spiral ridges of periostracum diagnostic of *caperata*. The ridges are easily rubbed off and may not cover the entire shell, so diagnosis may rely on a tiny portion of residual periostracum. *H. montanensis* is also found in different habitats (clear mountain streams, springs in water, not mudflats; Taylor et al. 1963). More turreted and with fewer whorls and a larger umbilicus than *S. elodes*. Penis of *H. caperata*, like *montanensis* and unlike *Polyrhytis*, has the penial knot distal to penis midlength (Baker 1928) and a stout vas deferens. *H. caperata* held in

FIG 42. Radula of *Hinkleyia caperata*. c = central tooth; 1 = 1st lateral, 9-12 = tricuspid intermediate teeth, 14-28 = representative marginal teeth. Credit: Baker 1928.

FIG. 43. Microsculpture of *Hinkleyia caperata*, Univ. Colorado Museum 22484 (*Lymnaea caperata warthini*). Credit: L. Elder, UCM.

captivity were observed to produce egg masses (11 × 2 mm) of 28 to 45 spherical eggs in each (Baker 1911). Taylor et al. (1963, p. 254) noted that the egg mass of this species is unique among lymnaids; that is, the "egg capsules are nearly spherical and rather small, while their individual sets of envelopes are more than twice as thick, relatively, as those of *Polyrhytis*. The egg mass, instead of having the common type of thick, firm and obviously differentiated outer tunic, has a thin one that is hardly visible." Genetic analyses by Remigio (2002) noted that *caperata* was more closely allied to *Galba* species than to North American *Polyrhytis*.

DISTRIBUTION: Found from Quebec to Massachusetts west to California, south to the Rocky Mountains and Maryland. In Utah, Gregg (1941) found this species at Cedar Breaks National Monument. There are also records from Box Elder, Cache, Juab, Garfield, Millard, Rich, Weber, Salt Lake, Summit, Tooele, Utah, and Beaver counties (Taylor et al. 1963; Woostenhulme 1942a; Hovingh 1993, 2018); Fish Lake, Seven Mile Canyon (Chamberlin and Berry 1930), Uinta Co. (Brooks 1936); Saratoga (Baily and Baily 1952), St. George, Heber City (UMNH records), Juab, Salt Lake City, St. George, Moab, and Torrey (Chamberlin and Jones 1929).

Hinkleyia montanensis Baker, 1912 Mountain Marshsnail

DESCRIPTION (Baker 1912; Taylor et al. 1963): *Shell*: thin, translucent, ovate-turreted; periostracum light horn color; surface shining, lines of growth distinct, crossed by very fine wavy spiral lines. *Whorls* 5.25–6.5, convex, the body whorl

FIG. 44. *Hinkleyia montanensis*. UMMZ shells collected by D.W. Taylor. 1) 207604, Franklin, ID; 2) 219300, Bear Lake, ID; 3) 219358, Nez Perce Co. ID; 4) 219284, Hayes Cr. MT; 5) 207602 Driggs, ID. Line spacing = 1 mm. Credit: UMMZ.

somewhat obese; sutures deeply impressed; spire acute, longer than the aperture. *Aperture:* ovate, outer lip thin; inner lip wide, somewhat triangular, reflexed over the umbilical region; there is no distinct axial plait, but the inner lip is slightly indented where it touches the parietal wall; the umbilical chink is narrowly open.

Taylor et al. (1963) also note that the spire outline varies from regularly conical to convex and bullet-shaped. The surface of the shell is conspicuously shiny except when covered by dirt or algae. Overall color is brownish horn. The nuclear whorl is larger than that in *Galba*, so the apex is more blunt. Body whorl is about two-thirds the total length of the shell. Columellar fold is often absent, or, when present, it is low and poorly defined; Columellar lip is broadly reflected, resulting in a narrow umbilical perforation. Parietal lip thin, appressed to the preceding whorl, and transitions smoothly into the columellar lip.

SIZE (Baker 1912; n = 4): SL 9–14 mm, SW 5–8 mm, SL/SW ratio 1.78–2.15, ApL 5–6.8 mm (49–61% of SL), ApW 3–4 mm (54–60% of ApL). Young specimens tend to be more obese. Measurements from four Idaho locations (Taylor et al. 1963): SL up to 14.3 mm, but averaged from 5.4–11.2 mm among sites; SL/SW ratio was 1.85–2.42 among all sites, and the ApL/ApW ratio was 1.4–1.8 among all sites. Whorl number varied somewhat with size: 5.25–5.5 for 8 mm shells to 6.0–6.5 whorls for shells 9.7–13.2 mm.

ANIMAL (Taylor et al. 1963): Foot about twice as long as wide; head–foot dark gray to medium gray; tentacles relatively slender. Prominent pigmentation (dusky flakes) in the pallial areas; larger specimens were darker. Groove along edge of mantle collar that divides the periphery into two shelf-like structures, one above the other, the lower sometimes projecting out more than the upper. These "shelves" are not as well developed in other lymnaeids. Kidney slender.

GENITALIA: *H. montanensis* has a comparatively short, bilaterally symmetrical penis, with a knot distal to its midlength; a comparatively robust, comparatively short penis sheath; a prostate pouch; and a well developed vaginal sphincter. Differs from *Polyrhytis* in having a very stout vas deferens, very short and stout penis, a gradual transition between the vaginal sphincter and musculature preceding it, and the penial knot placed more distally from the midlength.

TYPE LOCATION: Hayes Creek, near Ward, Montana, in the Bitterroot Mountains, altitude 3,825 ft. Holotype in UMMZ, 76196.

JUNIOR SYNONYMS: *Galba montanensis* Baker, 1912; *Lymnaea montanensis* (Baker) Walker, 1918; *Stagnicola montanensis* (Baker) Taylor et al., 1963.

NOTES: Inner lip is roundly and evenly reflexed over the umbilicus, lacking the twist characteristic of many lymnaeids. Resembles *Galba bulimoides cockerelli* and *H. caperata*, especially half-grown specimens, but the spiral lines and narrow umbilical chink of *H. montanensis* separates it from those species (Baker 1912). Taylor et al. (1963) note that surface sculpture and texture differentiate *montanensis* and *caperata*: "Relatively conspicuous raised spiral ridges of periostracum are diagnostic of *S. caperata* and a shiny surface without such sculpture, but with spirally arranged series of tiny crescents, of *S. montanensis*." Evenly rounded whorls, regularly tapering spire, and glossy shell surface help differentiate this from other lymnaids (Taylor et al. 1963).

This species occurs in small coldwater rivers or spring-fed tributaries to larger river systems and is not usually found in areas with mud, sand, or bedrock (Taylor et al. 1963; Stagliano et al. 2007). Taylor et al. (1963) noted that the animals had fully developed genitalia by the time the shells were ≥7 mm.

DISTRIBUTION: Found in the eastern Columbia River and northern Great Basin drainages (MT, ID, WY, NV; Taylor et al. 1963). In Utah, there are records from Cache, Summit (East Canyon), and Beaver counties (Taylor et al. 1963). Hovingh (2018) also notes records in UMMZ from the Bear and Weber rivers as well as formalin-preserved UMNH specimens from Mona Lake and the lower Sevier River (Juab County), Salt Creek (Box Elder County), Pilot Valley (Tooele County), and the San Pitch, Provo, and Jordan rivers.

Hinkleyia pilsbryi Hemphill, 1890 Fish Springs Marshsnail

DESCRIPTION (Hemphill 1890a, quoted, p. 25–26; Baker 1911): "Shell elongated, narrow, somewhat solid, smooth, of a light horn color; consisting of about six roundly-shouldered whorls, the last flattened on its sides and occupying a little

FIG. 45. *Hinkleyia pilsbryi*, syntype, ANSP 62293. Credit: ANSP.

FIG. 46. *Hinkleyia pilsbryi*, Fish Springs National Wildlife Refuge, 2019. Credit: E. Wagner.

more than half the length of the shell; lines of growth very delicate, suture deep; aperture oval, longer than wide, outer lip acute; inner lip subreflexed." Spire narrow, attenuated, greater than twice the aperture length, whorls inclined to be shouldered, with deep sutures; parietal callus thin; umbilical chink small, slightly emarginated by the inner lip; columella smooth, without a plait.

SIZE (Hemphill 1890a): SL 9.5 mm, SW 3.2 mm. Baker (1911): SL 8.0 mm, SW 3.0 mm, ApL, 2.1 mm, ApW 1.1 mm; ApL/SL 26%. Russell (1971, mean, range): SL 11.1 (7.1–16.3) mm, SW 4.3 (2.2–5.9) mm, SL:SW ratio 2.57 (2.03–3.36), ApL 3.9 (2.8–4.9) mm, ApW 2.4 (1.6–3.0) mm, aperture L:W ratio 1.38–1.74 (1.57), whorls 6.25–9, the number correlated with total shell length; immature specimen of 2.8 mm had 4.5 whorls.

TYPE LOCATION: Fish Spring, Nevada. Baker (1911) identified the site as being in Nye County, Nevada, but as Taylor et al. (1963) note, Hemphill's label describes the location as "Fish Spring Nevada between Austin and Salt Lake," indicating that Fish Springs, Utah (currently a national wildlife refuge) is the original type location.

JUNIOR SYNONYMS: *Lymnaea (Leptolimnea) pilsbryi* Hemphill, 1890a; Baker (1911) put this species within *Galba*. Taylor et al. (1963) transferred the species to *Stagnicola* (*Hinkleyia*) based on shell morphology (large nuclear whorl; shell sculpture as for *H. caperata* and *H. montanensis*). Clarke (1991) suggested this species is better classified within the subgenus *Bakerilymnaea* (genus *Galba*). The size, columella with only a slight trace of a fold, and turreted whorls also suggest this classification. Examination of the anatomy is needed to properly place the species.

NOTES: The narrowly conic shell, shouldered whorls, and the small oblique aperture distinguish this species from other lymnaeids (Baker 1911). The form is similar to *Tryonia porrecta*, but the aperture is more elongate. Known only from Fish Springs and three shells in the ANSP collection (the mature shell is shown above). Russell (1971) found 134 empty shells of *S. pilsbryi* at Fish Springs National Wildlife Refuge in 1970. Based on Russell's findings, a more in-depth survey was commissioned by the refuge and was conducted by the well-known malacologist and paleontologist Dr. Dwight Taylor. Dr. Taylor found old worn shells at three sites and eight other gastropod species but no live snails (Darling 1987). The author (Wagner) collected two shells from the refuge near South Spring in 2019 that appeared relatively fresh that could be *S. pilsbryi* . To date, records indicate that live specimens have never been seen. Currently, the species is presumed to be extinct.

DISTRIBUTION: Fish Springs National Wildlife Refuge, Utah; Fish Springs, Nevada.

Polyrhytis bonnevillensis Call, 1884 Bonneville Lake Snail

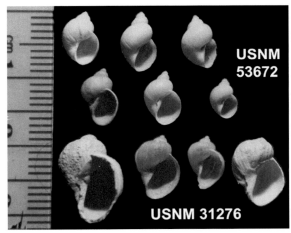

FIG. 47. *Polyrhytis bonnevillensis*. Above: ANSP syntype 73738, Credit: ANSP. Below: Rows 1 and 2, USNM 53672: paratypes; Row 3 USNM 31276, paratypes. Credit: Peter Hovingh, courtesy USNM.

DESCRIPTION (Call 1884, p. 48): "Shell umbilicated, elongate, ventricose (inflated) or bullate (bubbled), somewhat solid, faintly striate and very minutely reticulated below the suture, the last whorl bearing faint longitudinal ridges or costae; spire elevated, acute; suture deeply impressed; whorls 4 to 4½, very much rounded, sometimes tending to geniculation above, the last whorl equal to ¾ the whole length of the shell, rapidly increasing in size, much swollen, somewhat expanded at the base; columella somewhat plicate, slightly callous, regularly arcuate; columella and peristome continuous; peristome simple, margins joined by a heavy callus, which is continuous and so reflexed as to partially close the umbilicus; aperture broadly ovate, often patulous, equal to one-half the entire length of the shell, oblique, angled slightly behind." The form of the shell varies; some specimens are longer spired and others are shorter, with a more globose form. Smooth forms without the axial ribbing are also found.

SIZE (Call 1886, $n = 4$): SL to 9.4 to 18.5 mm, SW 5.2–7.8 mm. The SL/SW ratio ranged from 1.81 (smallest specimen) to 3.08 (largest specimen). Data from Homestead Cave (range, $n = 102$, Hovingh 2018): SL 5.08–15.5 mm, SW 3.0–10.5 mm, spire L 2.0–8.5 mm, SW/SL 0.531–0.913 (mean 62%), Spire L/SL 0.381–0.680 (mean 49%), Spire L/SW 0.517–1.058 (mean 81%).

TYPE LOCATION: Kelton, Utah; Bonneville Lake Quaternary bed. Holotype (53672) is in the Smithsonian Institute; cotypes are at ANSP (73738).

JUNIOR SYNONYMS: *Limnaea bonnevillensis* (Call) Stearns, 1902; *Galba bonnevillensis* (Call) Baker, 1911; *Stagnicola bonnevillensis* (Call) Burch, 1989.

NOTES: *Polyrhytis bonnevillensis* Call, 1884, is a fossil species and is the probable ancestral form for what, in the Recent period, is considered *Polyrhytis utahensis* (Chamberlin and Jones 1929; Burch and Tottenham 1980; Clarke 1991; Hovingh 2018). Hovingh (2018) separated the two species by the characteristics of the aperture, which in *P. bonnevillensis* is more patulous (ultra-dextral), relative to the more ovoid aperture of *P. utahensis*. See notes under *P. utahensis*.

P. bonnevillensis is known only as a Quaternary fossil in the Lake Bonneville shoreline beds and as extinct (Taylor and Bright 1987). Taylor and Bright (1987) suggested that the Snake River *Stagnicola hinkleyi* Baker, 1906, may have been an ancestor of *P. bonnevillensis*. The latter lived only during the Lake Bonneville pluvial cycle, its evolution and extinction shaped by the diversion of the Bear River from the Snake River to the Great Basin some 30,000 years ago and the later drainage of Lake Bonneville. A GenBank record (AF485655) of "*Stagnicola bonnevillensis*," collected by Peter Hovingh from the Blue Spring Hills complex north of the Great Salt Lake, was used by Remigio (2002) and Correa et al. (2010). This genetic sample should be considered *Polyrhytis utahensis* (Hovingh 2018). Similarly, in this guide, living forms that resemble ancestral *P. bonnevillensis* and *P. kingii* are considered to be *P. utahensis*. The close genetic relationship with *Polyrhytis elodes* and *P. catascopium* (Remigio 2002; Correa et al. 2010) and similarities in morphology (Chamberlin 1933; Clarke 1991) suggest that *P. bonnevillensis* was a recent derivative of a common ancestor.

DISTRIBUTION: Historically distributed in the Bonneville Basin (Call 1884; Baker 1911; Henderson 1924). Baker (1911) also noted samples from ancient Lake Lahontan (Rye Patch, Humboldt County, Nevada. Burch (1989) reported *bonnevillensis* in Wyoming, which Clarke (1991) considered an error. However, the connectivity of the Bonneville Basin with the Bear River system since the Pleistocene suggests it is possible. The distribution map for *bonnevillensis* in Taylor and Bright (1987) suggested the distribution did not extend into the Bear Lake Valley. Specimens from Blue Springs Hills, Box Elder County, collected live (UMZ 159949 and UMNH specimens), are considered to be *S. utahensis*.

Polyrhytis utahensis Call, 1884 Thickshell Pondsnail

DESCRIPTION: Call (1886, p. 5): "Shell globose, somewhat umbilicated, irregularly costate, light horn color, nearly pellucid; spire rather small, conical; whorls four to four and one-half, convex, somewhat flattened above, giving rather a shouldered appearance to the whorls, rapidly increasing in size, the last whorl being inflated, with numerous rather marked transverse costae, minutely wrinkled; suture somewhat deep, regularly impressed; aperture elongately ovate, effuse, approaching patulous, pearly white within; outer lip simple, the margin

FIG. 48. *Polyrhytis utahensis*, Bear Lake, UT. Credit: E. Wagner.

connected by a slight calcareous deposit; columella somewhat twisted, but straight in front. Dentition unpublished."

Clarke (1991), for shells from the Blue Spring Hills: shell whitish to pale brown (but appearing darker with soft parts within), with 6 whorls in mature specimens; aperture subaurate but variable in shape, its length varying from about 52–70% of the length of the shell, with a sigmoid, reflected inner lip that partly or completely obscures the umbilicus and with a thin, curved outer lip which in some specimens exhibits a reddish collabral band within. Nuclear whorls dark brown, mostly smooth, and of 1.5 whorls. Sculpture on the following whorls consists of fine to coarse collabral lines or ridges and, in many specimens, of broad, flat spiral bands that may be subparallel with the suture or may descend more or less obliquely across the whorls in a manner not seen in any other species.

SIZE: Length of largest specimen, 16.82 mm, SW, 8.88 mm; SL/SW ratio: 1.45 to 2.07. Means (n = 9): SL 13.4 mm, SW 7.1 mm, with about the same ratio for corresponding measurements of aperture. ApL 9.00 mm, ApW 5.90 mm; ApL/SL 54M–83%. Clarke (1991) observed shells up to about 30 mm in length, width varying between 50 and 60% of length; his shells, however, had up to 6 whorls, suggesting that perhaps it was a different lymnaeid species. Data from Blue Spring Hills and Big Spring, Bear Lake (range; Hovingh 2018): SW/SL 0.485–0.848, spire L/SL 0.278–0.728, spire L/SW 0.442–1.198. See Hovingh (2018, p.179) for site-specific data.

ANIMAL (Chamberlin 1933, p. 98): "The anatomy shows agreement with *Stagnicola*, as represented by *S. palustris nuttalliana* (Lea), in the essential generic features of radula, genitalia, and other internal parts." (Clarke 1991): Soft parts are whitish to pale yellowish to mottled; one highly pigmented specimen had a black mantle with yellowish blotches, yellowish tentacles, and a purplish, gray-black foot. The tentacles are flat and triangular. The radula from a 24 mm-long specimen had

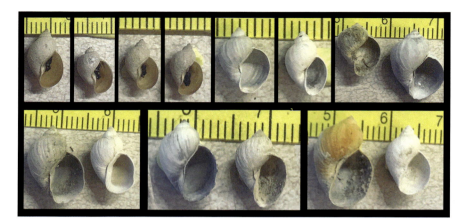

FIG. 49. *Polyrhytis utahensis*, UMNH P. Hovingh collection; First four shells on top row are fresh from Blue Hills Springs, UT; the rest are older shells from Utah Co., UT. Credit: E. Wagner, courtesy UMNH.

bicuspid first lateral teeth. The author (Wagner) has dissected 5 specimens (12.8 to 20.6 mm long) from Conner Springs, of which, all had a single fold in the prostate; the length of the epiphallus (penis sac) ranged from 59 to 76% of the preputium length.

TYPE LOCATION: Utah Lake, Lehi, Utah.

JUNIOR SYNONYMS: Call (1884) originally named this snail *Radix ampla* var. *utahensis* but later changed it to *Radix utahensis* (Call 1886). *Galba utahensis* (Call) Baker, 1911; *Polyrhytis utahensis* (Call) Chamberlin and Jones 1929 (elevating Meek's (1876) subgenus *Polyrhytis*); *Stagnicola kingii* (Meek) Chamberlin 1933. Chamberlin compared Meek's holotype in the National Museum with topotypes "without finding tangible grounds for separation." Baily and Baily (1952) referred to it as *Lymnaea (Polyrhytis) kingii utahensis* (Call). Burch (1989) listed it as *Stagnicola utahensis*. Records for *Lymnaea lepida* from Bear Lake should be transferred to *Polyrhytis utahensis*. Transferred to *Polyrhytis* in this guide (see discussion under Lymnaeidae).

NOTES: Fewer whorls (4–4.5) and the axial ribbing (costae) separate this from most other lymnaeids, though some *utahensis* specimens are smooth. Separated from *P. bonnevillensis* by the shape of the aperture, which is more ultra-dextral than in *utahensis*. Hovingh (pers. comm.), measuring shells from Homestead Cave (near the western side of Great Salt Lake; Hovingh 2018), also observed differences in the angle between the last and penultimate whorls; the angle was acute in *bonnevillensis* and wider (obtuse) in *P. utahensis*. The measurements given by Call do not match the figure he gave, which appears to be *Radix auricularia* but do conform with *P. utahensis* shells. Baker (1911) also noted his figure did not agree with USNM type specimens.

Chamberlin and Jones (1929) assorted a complete series of intergrades between "*Stagnicola palustris nuttalliana* (= *elodes* in the United States) and *P. utahensis*", suggesting natural variation in the species, which could include forms attributable to *bonnevillensis*. Clarke (1991) suggested that *utahensis* and *bonnevillensis* are possible synonyms.

F. Meek (1876; 1877, p.192) described a fossil, *Lymnaea (Polyrhytis) kingii*, from "Cache Valley, Utah; Tertiary, probably of the Miocene age" with the same longitudinal costae as *P. bonnevillensis*. Taylor (1966) later considered the mollusk bearing strata of the Cache Valley formation to be of the Blancan Age (late Pliocene and early Pleistocene, 2 to 5 million years ago) and pinpointed the type location to Mendon, Utah. Regarding possible synonymy of *utahensis* with *Limnaea (Polyrhytis) kingii*, we will likely never know if the two were different species, but for taxonomic purposes, some assumptions must be made. For this guide, given the age of Meek's fossil and differences in the environment over time, it is assumed that it was likely different from both present-day *Polyrhytis utahensis* and *P. bonnevillensis*. Clarke (1991, p. 63) writes, "Some authors (e.g., Chamberlin 1933; Henderson 1919; Taylor 1966; Burch 1989) consider *utahensis* to be a synonym of the Miocene species *Stagnicola kingii* (Meek 1877). Baker (1911) believed them to be separate species, however, with *kingii* as the probable ancestor of *utahensis*. After comparison of our Utah Lake specimens of *utahensis* with Call's holotype of *utahensis* (MCZ 4036) and Meek's holotype of *utahensis* (USNM 8097), I have concluded that Baker was correct (the axial costae are much more pronounced and more regular in *kingii* than in *utahensis*)." This guide follows the assessment of Baker (1911) and Clarke (1991) that *Polyrhytis kingii* is the probable ancestor of more modern *bonnevillensis/utahensis,* but a distinct fossil species, separated by about 2–5 million years in time. Furthermore, *P. bonnevillensis* is also considered an ancestral fossil form, distinct and separated in time from *kingii* by 1–4 million years and from modern *L. utahensis*. See also the notes for *P. bonnevillensis*. Clarke (1991) recommended that this snail be listed as endangered.

Habitat is small spring-fed ponds, though it previously survived in Utah Lake, its associated springs, and Bear Lake (Call 1884; Chamberlin 1933; Clarke 1991). Note that the *bonnevillensis* in genetic analyses by Remigio (2002), which were collected by P. Hovingh from Blue Hill Springs, are currently considered *utahensis*. In the cladograms of Remigio (2002), *utahensis* groups with other midsize North American lymnaeid species: *Polyrhytis elrodi, P. emarginata*, and *P. catascopium*. The cladogram of Correa et al. (2010) is similar but shows a closer relationship with *Polyrhytis elodes*. Given the consistent differences with *elodes* in whorl number (fewer), the shorter spire, axial ribbing, and wider aperture, *S. utahensis* is considered a distinct species herein until cross-breeding studies indicate otherwise.

DISTRIBUTION (Baily and Baily 1951–1952; Taylor and Bright 1987): Historical Bonneville Basin and Bear River distribution. In Utah, living specimens were reported in Conner Spring, Box Elder County, and Utah Lake, Utah, by Chamberlin (1933). Later collections by Hovingh (2018) recently confirmed that it is still living in Box Elder County springs, as well as in Big Springs south of Bear Lake. It is feared to be extirpated from Utah Lake.

Polyrhytis elodes Say, 1821 Marsh Pondsnail

FIG. 50. *Polyrhytis elodes*, lectotype, ANSP 58638. Credit: ANSP.

DESCRIPTION (Say 1821; Baker 1911, 1928): *Shell*: oblong, elongated, narrow, conic, gradually acuminated, rather thin. Periostracum light yellowish horn, frequently jet black; occasionally longitudinally striped; surface dull to shining; reticulate with transverse lines and longitudinal wrinkles. *Whorls*: 6–7 (5 whorls at 10 mm), whorls rather evenly increasing in size, typically flatly rounded, especially the body whorl. Body whorl on the back longer than the spire, which is long and acutely terminated; sutures moderately impressed. *Aperture*: elongate-ovate, shorter than the spire; inner lip submargin reddish-brown, calcareous deposit rather copious, not apressed at base, but leaving a linear umbilical aperture; inner lip narrow, reflected and appressed to the columellar region, forming a distinct plait and usually completely closing the umbilicus; parietal callus rather wide, heavy.

SIZE (Baker 1911; $n = 11$, mean, range): SL 29.1 (21–37) mm; SW 10.6 (8.5–14) mm; SL/SW ratio 2.74 (2.47–3.11); ApL 12.4 (11–16) mm; ApW 5.8 (4.5–8) mm, ApL/SL 42.9 (38–52)%.

Baker (1911) noted two subspecies that differed in shell morphology: *S. elodes shurtleffi* Tryon, 1866b (Fig. 51) and *S. elodes jolietensis* Baker, 1901 (Fig. 51). Tryon's shell (from Weatogue, Connecticut; originally published as *Limnaea shurtleffi*, 1866b) differs from typical *elodes* in that the upper spire whorls are shortened and the body and aperture are compressed; whorls 5–6. For *jolietensis*, originally published as *Limnaea reflexa jolietensis*, the subspecies had a sharp, attenuated spire, very convex whorls (6–7), 22–24 mm long, and the aperture is about 39% of the shell length.

FIG. 51. *L. elodes* synonyms. **LEFT:** *Stagnicola elodes jolietensis* Baker, 1901 syntype; center: *S. elodes shurtleffi* Tryon, 1866, lectotype. Credit: ANSP. Right: *Stagnicola impedita* Baker, 1934, paratype. Credit: L. Elder, UCM.

ANIMAL (Baker 1928): Black, lighter below, the body spotted with white which shows through the shell; foot wide and short, rounded before and behind; tentacles short and wide.

GENITALIA: Preputium muscular, cylindrical, 4.5 mm long × 1.5 mm greatest diameter; penis sheath 3 mm long, of equal diameter throughout, round, with thin walls; between the preputium and penis sheath is a thickened ridge, the sarcobelum. The vas deferens is 15 mm long; penis sheath retractor is long and narrow; preputium retractors are long, wide, ribbon-like, usually 6 in number. Prostate duct 5 mm long, slightly enlarged as it enters prostate; prostate flattened, much elongated, rounded at either end, the larger end receiving the prostate duct; the prostate gradually tapers to the point where the spermoviduct joins. The penis is wide where it receives the vas deferens, and below this portion there is a ridge that passes about two-thirds the circumference of the penis; below this ridge, the penis gradually narrows to a point, with the opening in the center.

In the female, the seminal receptacle is pear shaped, connecting with the oviduct with a duct 7 mm long, which enters the oviduct 1.25 mm from the vaginal opening; oviduct is long and narrow. The uterus is elongate-ovate, narrowing suddenly at both ends; it is creased in the center, longitudinally, where the prostate is attached. The nidamental gland is very small, rounded.

RADULA/JAW: Superior jaw wide and high, with a rounded median swelling on the ventral margin. Formula 34–1–34 (21 marginals with 3–5 cusps, 4 tricuspid

FIG. 52. Radula of *Polyrhytis elodes*. c=central tooth, 1-2 laterals, 10-14 intermediate teeth, 16-18 typical marginal teeth. Jaw is shown at the right. Credit: Baker 1928.

intermediate teeth, 9 bicuspid laterals with a long narrow mesocone and short wide ectocone, and a central tooth with a long sharp cusp; Fig. 52).

TYPE LOCATION: Canandaigua Lake, New York; Holotype (58638) in ANSP. *Lymnaea umbrosa* type from Missouri River near Council Bluffs, Iowa; Holotype 58504, ANSP. *L. palustris michiganensis* type from Wayne County, Michigan; cotypes 58690, ANSP. *L. shurtleffi* holotype (ANSP 58160) is from Weatogue, Connecticut. The *jolietensis* subspecies type was from Joliet, Illinois; holotype (23606) is in the Chicago Academy of Sciences.

JUNIOR SYNONYMS (Baker 1911): *Lymneus elodes* Say, 1821; *Stagnicola sumassi* Baird, 1863; *Lymnaea palustris* Binney, 1865a; *Limnaea palustris michiganensis* Walker, 1892; *Limnophysa elodes* (Say) Tryon, 1865b; *Lymnaeus elongatus* Say, 1821; *Lymnaea elongata* Gould, 1833; *Limnophysa elongata* (Gould) Beck, 1837; *Lymnaea palustris nuttalliana* (Lea) Chamberlin and Jones, 1929; *Lymnaea palustris elodes* (Say) Baker, 1928; *Lymnaea traskii* Tryon, 1863; *Limnaeus traskii* (Tryon) Clessin, 1886; *Lymnaea traski* (Tryon) Dall, 1905; *Galba traski* (Tryon) Baker, 1911; *Stagnicola hemphilli* Baker, 1934 (described from "near Salt Lake City"; holotype: CAS-IZ 60803; *S. impedita* Baker, 1934 (Fig. 51). Most shells in the United States that were historically identified as *S. palustris* are likely *S. elodes*. *S. palustris* is still a valid species, but it refers to a Eurasian counterpart to *S. elodes* with 4.5–6 whorls (10–18 mm, rarely >20 mm; Welter-Shultes 2012). In a genetic analysis, *elodes* separated from *palustris*, which was in a clade with other European lymnaeids (e.g., *Stagnicola turricola, fuscus,* and *corvus*), of which *S. turricola* is now considered a junior synonym of *palustris* (Bargues et al. 2005; Correa et al. 2010; Welter-Shultes 2012). *S. palustris* also differs from North American *Polyrhytis* in penis sheath/preputium length ratio (about as long as preputium in Europe, shorter in North America; Glöer 2019) and lateral teeth (bicuspid in North America, tricuspid in Europe; Baker 1911; Hubendick 1951). Some *palustris* synonyms in the United States include *Stagnicola palustris buttoni* Baker, 1934; *S. palustris magister* Baker, 1934.

Lewis (1860, pp. 18-19) remarked that *elodes* was found in canals, ditches, pools, and the like and that "varieties *emarginata* and *catascopium*, I have ascertained, may be produced from the eggs of *elodes*, by change of station. A small pool of stagnant water, formerly the bed of the canal previous to its enlargement, is populated by thousands of *Lymnaea* that formed part of the canal family. These vary in form in different seasons; some retain the form of *catascopium*, others diverge to *emarginata*, but a larger number are *elodes*." Terry and Duda (2021) reared *S. elodes* and *S. emarginata* in captivity in similar conditions; the two species remained morphologically distinct but differed significantly from wild-caught shells (captive shells were shorter and narrower for *S. elodes*, whereas captive *S. emarginata* were larger than wild counterparts).

FIG. 53. *Stagnicola traskii* (=*Polyrhytis elodes*). ANSP holotype 58519. Credit: ANSP.

Genetic analyses by Rudolph and Burch (1989; gene frequency analysis); Remigio and Blair (1997a; mitochondrial rDNA); Correa et al. (2010; concatenation of 16S ITS-1, ITS-2 gene data); and Bargues et al. (2003) suggested that *Polyrhytis catascopium* and *P. emarginata* are very closely related to *P. elodes*. Genetic data by Vinarski et al. (2017) suggested that *Polyrhytis elodes* and *P. emarginata* are synonymous with *P. catascopium*, which has taxonomic priority. Vinarski et al. (2016) synonymized two lymnaeid species from Kamchatka (*Lymnaea (Orientogalba) tumrokensis* Kruglov and Starobogatov, 1985 and *Lymnaea (Polyrhytis) kurenkovi* Kruglov and Starobogatov, 1989a) with the North American *L. elodes* group, which Vinarksi and his co-authors considered to be one species, *L. catascopium*. Data presented by Baker (1911) on the lengths of the penis sheath and penis sac (preputium) also show overlap among the three species in the penis sheath/preputium ratio, a character that has been used in lymnaeid taxonomy as a diagnostic character. The radula of *elodes*, *emarginata*, and *catascopium* also have the same number of cusps on central, lateral, and marginal teeth. In contrast, there are the breeding experiments by Burch and Ayers (1973), in which *L. elodes* was crossed with *L. emarginata*, producing offspring that had the same shape as the egg-laying parent. Also, second-generation snails in the same study maintained the same shapes as the original parent snail. The data suggest that the two forms are reproductively isolated and unique species.

Stagnicola traskii Tryon, 1863, is also considered a junior synonym. It was described from a single shell (Fig. 53). Later, California malacologist J. Cooper (1870) considered *traskii* a variety of *S. elodes*. Tryon himself later (1870) considered *traskii* to be a form of *Lymnaea proxima* Lea, 1856 (also Burch 1989; Hovingh 2018), which Clarke (1981) concedes might just be a subspecies of *P. elodes*. Notably, Tryon also recorded *H. caperata*, *L. fragilis* (synonym of *L. stagnalis*, Welter-Schultes 2012), *L. umbrosa*, and *L. reflexa* (form variant of *S. elodes*; Burch 1989) at the same location in California where the *traskii* form was found, suggesting that *traskii* may be a variant of another lymnaeid. Chamberlin and Jones (1929), in consultation with F. Baker, considered *L. reflexa*, *traskii*, and *proxima* to be synonyms of *Stagnicola palustris nuttalliana* (= *P. elodes*). Beetle (1989) and Tronstad and Andersen (2018) also considered *traskii* to be a synonym of *L. elodes*. Baker (1928) noted that the animal of *L. reflexa* Say, 1821, *L. umbrosa* Say, and *L. exilis* Lea, 1837, were the same as for *Stagnicola palustris* (= *L. elodes* in N. America), indicating these three are also synonyms. Trends in recent genetic studies and observations on lymnaeid shell variation also suggest that there are fewer species than have been named. Genetic and anatomical studies of specimens from the type localities for *sumassi* (Sumass Prairie, British Columbia) and *traski* (Mountain Lake, California) relative to other stagnicolines are needed to clarify whether these species are valid. A visit to Mountain Lake by the author (Wagner) in December 2021 revealed that the urban pond (in the Presidio, San Francisco) was subject to a major renovation project in 2013–2014, in which the soil substrate was removed to control invasive species. A search effort (about 2 h) for snails in the pond and upstream was unsuccessful.

NOTES: The relatively large shell size, narrow conical shape, large number of whorls, and lower aperture height/total length ratios separate this shell from other lymnaeids. Juvenile shells are harder to differentiate. The species inhabits ponds and other wet, marshy areas of still water. *Polyrhytis emarginata* is typically found in lakes on rocks, vegetation, and gravel, whereas *catascopium* and *elodes* are found on submerged vegetation, floating sticks, on stones, and muddy bottoms, but they are seldom found out of water (Baker 1928). Opportunistic feeder, grazing on vegetation and scavenging dead biota; is carnivorous as well (Baker 1928).

DISTRIBUTION (Baker 1911; Chamberlin and Jones 1929; Chamberlin and Berry 1930; Brooks 1936; Woolstenhulme 1942a; Roscoe 1964; ANSP): Ontario, Alberta, British Columbia, Northwest Territories, Quebec; Upper Mississippi River and Great Lakes states, St. Lawrence River drainage; ME, NY, PA, NJ, OH, MI, WI, SD, ID, MT, WY, CO, NV, CA, OR, WA. Widely distributed in Utah. Utah records (including *S. palustris nuttalliana*) from Salt Lake City, Kamas, Mt. Olivet Cemetery Reservoir (Salt Lake City), Mud Lake (Aquarius Plateau, Garfield County), 1 mile west of Lehi, Lynndyl (west of Sevier River bridge), Grantsville, Bonneville Basin, Sevier River, Fish Lake, Seven Mile Canyon, Fruita, Bicknell, Koosharem Reservoir, Richfield, Panguitch Lake, Uinta Mountains to 10,000 ft elevation, Navajo Lake, Glenwood; Cache, Daggett, Piute, Rich, and Uinta counties.

Lymnaea stagnalis Linneaus, 1758 Swamp Lymnaea Duskysnail

DESCRIPTION (Baker 1911): *Shell*: elongated or oval, enlarged at the anterior end, thin, yellowish-horn to brownish black; spire long, pointed, acute, occupying about half the total shell length; sutures distinct, sometimes impressed; surface shining, growth lines numerous, crowded, more or less elevated, crossed by many fine, impressed spiral lines; apex smooth, brownish horn color. *Whorls*: 6 to 7, rapidly increasing, all but the last two rather flat sided; last whorl very large, considerably inflated, inclining to form a shoulder. *Aperture*: large, broadly ovate, dilated, particularly at the upper part; aperture margin thin, acute, the anterior part rounded; parietal wall with a rather wide, spreading callus that is closely appressed to the body and either completely closes the umbilicus or leaves a very small chink; pillar of the columella gyrate, usually forming a more or less heavy, oblique, ascending plait.

Galba

FIG. 54. *Lymnaea stagnalis*. Upper row: ANSP 450703, syntype, Hungary. Lower row: a. UMMZ 80115, Logan, UT; b. Uinta Co., WY, UMMZ 229594; c. UMNH 1002588, Germany. Credit: upper row, ANSP. Lower row: a, b: UMMZ; c: E. Wagner, courtesy UMNH.

SIZE: SL up to 38–52 mm, SW 19–31 mm, ApL/SL 53–62%, ApW 42–62% of ApL. For *wasatchensis* form, SL 32.5–45 mm, SW 14–20 mm, ApL 15–22 mm (45.2–51.3% of SL), ApW 9.5–13 mm (59–63% of ApL).

ANIMAL (Say 1821; Crabb 1927b; Jackiewicz 1993): Foot pale, neck (above and sides) blackish.

GENITALIA: The preputium is an elongated narrow sac, its walls forming two invaginated longitudinal folds. The papillar fold, situated at the bottom of the bulbous termination of the preputium, is big and broad but relatively flat. The penis sheath is short, tube-shaped, with a bulbous swelling at the junction with the vas deferens. The length ratio of preputium to penis sheath is 3:1. The penis is 4 times longer than its breadth at the base and relatively thick. Its terminus, situated distally from the ring-like swelling, is stylet-shaped or wedge-shaped. The penis has characteristic tiny folds on its surface, especially at the proximal end. The prostate is large and strongly swollen at its distal end, where there are numerous tiny folds. The vas deferens exits the prostate gland apically.

RADULA: Central tooth is a single spade-like cusp; lateral teeth (1–19th) bicuspid, with a large, narrow, acute mesocone and a short spade-like ectocone; 16–19th teeth have a small cusp just above the ectocone; three intermediate teeth with an entocone formed by split of the mesocone. First 4–5 marginal teeth are serrate, with a small ectocone. Typical marginals are narrow and elongate, with very small cusps. Number of teeth varies with individuals (typically 46–1–46, varying from

40–1–40 to 54–1–54 (Baker 1911). *L. stagnalis* from Iran that were 35 mm long (± 4.3 mm, SD) had 27–1–27 radular teeth in 95.1 ± 2.1(SD) rows; the number of lateral teeth averaged 13 ± 2 (Yakhchali & Deilamy 2012).

FIG. 55. *Lymnaea stagnalis*. Little Creek Reservoir, UT. Credit: E. Wagner.

Baker (1911) considered the *L. stagnalis* described by Linnaeus to be circumboreal but limited in distribution in North America to north of the 40th parallel. Say's (1821) *Helix appressa* (now considered *Lymnaea stagnalis appressa*) is the typical form in the lower 48 states (Baker 1911). In Washington State, *L.s. occidentalis* Hemphill, 1890a occurs; this variant has a quadrangularly inflated body whorl, a long-ovate aperture that is more than twice the spire length, and 5 whorls. The *appressa* form is more fusiform and coniform in general shape, with the body whorl less shouldered and less inflated or rotund relative to previous whorls; *appressa* has a more oval, less angular aperture, and the columellar callus is more closely appressed to the parietal wall, giving the axis a conspicuous twist, which is absent in most typical *stagnalis* specimens (Baker 1911).

The *wasatchensis* form of *L. stagnalis* (collected by H. Hemphill) was described by Baker (1911): Shell much elongated, narrow, thin, spire very long, acutely pointed, occupying more than half the length of the shell; color light yellowish horn; surface with the characteristic sculpture of *stagnalis*. Whorls 6.5, flatly rounded, increasing slowly in size; last whorl small, generally not inflated, but well rounded; sutures well marked. Aperture small, roundly ovate; inner lip appressed tightly to the parietal wall and to the columellar region; no umbilical chink; axis with a strong plait as in *L. stagnalis appressa*.

TYPE LOCATION: Germany; *L. stagnalis wasatchensis* Hemphill, near Salt Lake City, Utah; *L. s. appressa* Say, 1821, Lake Superior.

JUNIOR SYNONYMS (Baker 1911; Kennard and Woodward 1926; Soler et al. 2006): *Helix stagnalis* Linnaeus, 1758; *Buccinum stagnale* (Linnaeus) Müller, 1774; *Turbo stagnalis* (Linnaeus) Mendes Da Costa, 1778; *Limneus major* Jeffreys, 1833; *Limnaeus turgidus* Menke, 1830; *Bulimus fragilis* (Lamarck) Gray, 1840; *Stagnicola vulgaris* Hartmann, 1840, *Stagnicola elegans* Leach, 1852; *Limnaea borealis, Limnaea elophila, Limnaea colpodia, Limnaea doriana,* and *Limnaea raphidia* Bourguignat, 1862; *Limnaea stagnalis* var. *arenaria* Colbeau, 1865; *Limnaea stagnalis* var. *variegata* Hazay, 1881; *Limnaea westerlundi, Limnaea locardi* (Coutagne), *Limnaea variegata, Limnaea turgida,* and *Limnaea coutagnei* Locard, 1893; *Limnaea lagorii* Dybowski, 1903b. *L. stagnalis jugularis* Say, 1821, was considered synonymous with *L. stagnalis appressa* by Baker (1911).

NOTES: The large size of this shell, the narrow spire, rotund body whorl, and (sometimes) with a somewhat angular upper lip distinguish this shell from other lymnaeids in Utah. The snail may serve as a host for trematode parasites (Karvonen et al. 2003; Correa et al. 2010). The species is also known to prey on live animals, such as a newt, leech, beetle (*Dysticus*) larvae, other snails, and minnows (probably sac fry); they will scavenge carcasses too (Baker 1911). Preferred habitat is standing to slowly flowing waters which are rich in vegetation, of basic pH (7–8, but tolerant of 6–9.5), and of high total hardness (Glöer 2019). Genetic data summarized by Correa et al. (2010) suggest a European origin for *L. stagnalis*. Remigio and Blair (1997b) and Remigio (2002) noted genetic divergence among *stagnalis* populations that warranted possible subspecies designations.

DISTRIBUTION (ANSP; Baker 1911; Ibase): Russia, Europe, United Kingdom, Canada; AZ, AK, CA, FL, ID, IL, IN, IA, KS, ME, MA, MI, MN, MO, MT, NM, NJ, NY, NV, ND, OH, OK, OR, PA, SD, TN, VT, WA, WI, WY. In Utah, the subspecies *L. stagnalis wasatchensis* has been collected near Salt Lake, Logan (Ballard Spring), Panguitch Lake, and Tooele County. Call (1884) collected semi-fossils from the Sevier Desert and noted living snails in Salt Lake City and Utah Lake at American Fork. Ingersoll (1877) also reported *stagnalis* from the south end of Utah Lake; specimens at the Monte Bean Museum, Provo, Utah, were collected from near the same location (South Meadows) in 1956 and in Sterling Reservoir (San Pete County) in 1927. Chamberlin and Jones (1929) reported it from Logan, Salt Lake City, Tooele County, and Laketown. The author has found it living in Rich County (Little Creek and Birch Creek reservoirs). Hovingh (2018) notes UMNH specimens from Chalk Creek in the upper Weber River.

Radix auricularia Linnaeus, 1758 Big-eared Radix

FIG. 56. *Radix auricularia*. Provo River, UT. Credit: E. Wagner.

DESCRIPTION: Baker (1911, p. 179): "Roundly ovate shell, inflated, thin; periostracum horn-color to pale gold; surface shining, lines of growth fine, wavy, crowded, with occasionally a heavy ridge representing a rest period; spiral, impressed lines present but very fine; whorls four, convex, inflated, the last large and spreading; spire short, conic, very small compared with the body whorl; sutures deeply impressed, channeled in some specimens; aperture very large, ovate, occupying 4/5 of the length of the entire shell, rounded above and flaring in old specimens; peristome thin, sharp; columella sigmoid, the axis strongly twisted forming an erect, sharp ascending plait; callus very thin, closely appressed to the body whorl; inner lip reflected and widely spreading in old specimens; umbilical chink very small in young or half grown individuals, but wide and deep in fully adult specimens. The epidermis is somewhat marked by light and dark lines of color, alternating. Nucleus of about 1¼ hyaline whorls." This species has 17 haploid chromosomes, compared to the usual 18 in lymnaids (Taylor et al. 1963). There are 4–4.5 whorls.

SIZE: Shells may reach 30 mm in shell height and breadth (Jackiewicz 1993).

ANIMAL (Jackiewicz 1993): Preputium is club-shaped, with two longitudinal folds within, with the proximal part markedly broadened. The papillar fold is shaped like a large, flat shield; there is granular dark pigment close to its border. The second fold is cupola-shaped, with a small aperture. The penis sheath is very narrow and long, and is about as long as the preputium. The penis is about 14 times longer than its breadth at the base. The distal part of the prostate has one large fold, the lumen of which is situated nearly regularly around the fold.

TYPE LOCATION: unknown, presumed to be Europe.

JUNIOR SYNONYMS (Kennard and Woodward 1926; Soler et al. 2006; Vinarski et al. 2020): *Helix auricularia* Linnaeus, 1758 (type species of the genus *Radix*); *Buccinum auricula* Müller, 1774; *Turbo patulus* da Costa, 1778; *Bulimus auricularius* Bruguiere, 1792; *Gulnaria monnardii* Hartmann, 1840; *Limnaea canalis* Dupuy, 1851; *Limnaea auricularia* (Linnaeus) Baker, 1905; *Lymnaea auricularia* (L.) Hubendick, 1951; Jackiewicz, 1993; and four species of Kruglov and Starobogatov (1989b): *Lymnaea* (*Radix*) *hadutkae*, *L.* (*Radix*) *hakusyensis*, *L.* (*Radix*) *thermobaicalica,* and *L.* (*Radix*) *thermokamtschatica*.

NOTES (Welter-Schultes 2012): Ultra-dextral aperture and narrow, sharp apex separate this shell from other Utah species. Considered to be an invasive species in Utah. Consumes mainly green algae and protozoans. About 30–80 oval eggs (1.5–1.8 mm) are laid in clutches of 15–30 mm between July and September. These egg cases are attached to aquatic plants or stones. Juveniles hatch in about 2–3 weeks. Lifespan about 1 year.

DISTRIBUTION: Native to Eurasia. Widespread in the United States from Arkansas to Maine, south to Arizona and Florida. In Utah, records from Fish Lake (DMNH 158855) and Utah Lake (UMMZ 219480). Recent surveys (iNaturalist.org) have found *R. auricularia* in the Price River drainage, Strawberry River, lower Provo River, Utah County, Mantua Reservoir, Mammoth Creek (Iron County), Koosharem Reservoir (Sevier County), Ouray, and Brigham City. Specimens in the Monte Bean Museum, Brigham Young University, collected from the Provo River drainage, indicate it has been in the state since at least 1950.

Physidae Fitzinger, 1833

Sinestral coiling, a pointed foot posteriorly, and slender tentacles separate Physidae from other family groups (Taylor 2003). Tentacles are rod-like, with eyes at their inner bases. Shells are smooth, polished, with a pointed exserted spire and longitudinal aperture with a sharp unreflected lip (Haldeman 1842). There are currently 23 genera within Physidae (Taylor 2003). The Physidae subfamily Aplexinae Starobogatov, 1967, is characterized by the absence of a preputial gland, whereas in Physinae Starobogatov, 1967, this gland is present. Further subgroupings were made by Te (1978) and Taylor (2003) based on penial morphology. Additional revisions to the family resulted from the genetic analyses of Wethington and Lydeard (2007). They noted that *Physa fontinalis* and *P. jennessi* (*P. skinneri* and *megalochlamys* are close relatives in Tribe *Physini* Taylor, 2003) were genetically distinct from the clade with species like *acuta*, *gyrina*, and *utahensis*. The former clade is *Physa* (based on *Bulla fontinalis* L. as type), and species in the latter clade are now considered *Physella*.

The type species for the genus *Physella* Haldeman, 1842, is *P. globosa* Haldeman, 1840, from Tennesee (Taylor 2003). The characteristics of the genus are (Taylor 2003): shell ovoid to subfusiform reaching 25 mm total length, dull to silky but not glossy or polished, with crescentic microsculpture. Aperture usually >50% of shell length. Parietal callus narrow. Suture distinct, either well impressed or scarcely so. Apex acute. Mantle not reflected over outer lip of shell, with triangular projections in two groups. Penial complex: preputium shorter than penial sheath. Penial sheath bipartite, with glandular distal portion and muscular proximal portion.

The genus *Physa* Draparnaud, 1801, is characterized by shells that are ovoid to elongate-ovoid, silky to polished and shining, with inconspicuous spiral sculpture, shallow to inconspicuous sutures, and with a broadly rounded apex. The aperture is >50% of shell length. Parietal callus broad or narrow. The penis sheath is unitary (not bipartite as in *Physella*), entirely glandular; penis thin and flagellar with a terminal lanceolate stylet; vas deferens between paragonoporal angle and penial sheath is shorter than the preputium. The type species is *Bulla fontinalis* L., 1758 (currently *Physa fontinalis* L.; Taylor 2003). Junior synonyms of the genus include *Bulla* L., *Phyza* Risso, 1826; *Physodon* Haldeman, 1840; *Bulinus* Adanson, 1757; *Rivicola* Fitzinger, 1833; and *Laurentiphysa* Taylor, 2003 (Paetel 1875; molluscabase.org). Like Lymnaeidae, this family is also in need of further work to sort out taxonomic relationships among putative species.

Aplexa elongata Say, 1821 Lance Aplexa

DESCRIPTION (Say 1821, p. 171): "Shell heterostrophe (sinestral), pale yellowish, very fragile, diaphanous (translucent), oblong; whirls [sic] six or seven; spire tapering, acute at the tip; suture slightly impressed; aperture not dilated, attenuated above, about half as long as the shell; columella much narrowed near the base, so that the view, may be partially extended from the base towards the apex."

SIZE: SL 17.8 mm, SW 7.6 mm.

ANIMAL: deep black, without spots, and with setaceous tentacles with a white ring at the base. Penial complex characterized by lack of a (or externally discernible) preputial gland. Penial sheath length is 2–3 times the length of the preputium (Te 1978).

FIG. 57. *Aplexa elongata*. Left: paralectotype, ANSP 329116, Credit: ANSP. Right: Downey, ID. Credit: E. Wagner.

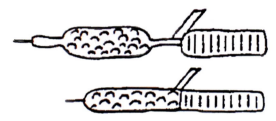

FIG. 58. Comparison of penial morphology between *Aplexa elongata* (upper) and *A. hypnorum*. Credit: Te 1978.

TYPE LOCATION: Illinois shores and stagnant ponds on the banks of the Mississippi River.

JUNIOR SYNONYMS (Burch 1982): *Physa elongata* Say, 1821; The genus *Nauta* Leach, 1852= *Aplexa* Fleming, 1820. Old U.S. records for *Aplexa hypnorum* may be referred to *A. elongata*.

NOTES: Shorter aperture than for *P. microstriata*; narrower and more elongate shape separates *elongata* from the other Utah physid species. As in other species within the subfamily Aplexinae, the preputium lacks a gland, whereas the preputium of species within the subfamily Physinae has a posterior gland (Taylor 2003). Found in stagnant ponds and marshes (Say 1821). Te (1978) studied Physidae in detail using 37 shell and 34 anatomical characters. Although radula characteristics and oral lappet shape were the same between the two species, Te (1978, p. 46) found that *Aplexa hypnorum* L. and *A. elongata* are similar, but distinct, taxa: "*Aplexa hypnorum*, previously considered to be a holarctic species, showed two major penial complex variations. In this study, the two variations are recognized as separate basic taxa." *A. hypnorum* is the palearctic (Eurasian) species, whereas *A. elongata* is the nearctic species native to North America. So, older North American specimens referred to as *hypnorum* are likely *A. elongata*. The two species can be differentiated by the penial morphology (Fig. 58, Te 1978). Te (1978) also noted differences in protoconch color and shape but did not give the details of how they differed. Data on *A. hypnorum* suggests that the snails spawn only once a year (Hartog and De Wolf 1962).

DISTRIBUTION (ANSP; Ibase; UMNH; Chamberlin & Jones 1929; as *A. hypnorum*): Canada; AK, CO, FL, ID, IL, IN, IA, ME, MI, MN, MT, NJ, NY, ND, OH, OK, OR, PA, SD, WA, WI, WY. Utah records from Box Elder County, Malad River, Weber and Ogden canyons, Fish Lake, Glenwood, marsh west of Laketown, Garden City, and Salt Lake City (slough near airport). Brooks (1936) found it in Uintah County (as *Aplexa hypnorum pilsbryi*, from a pond near the Whiterocks River at Paradise Creek). The author has encountered it in Cache Valley, Utah, Utah Lake, and Echo Canyon (Weber County Utah) wetlands. Idaho records from Bear Lake County.

Physella microstriata Chamberlin and Berry, 1930

Fish Lake Physa

FIG. 59. *Physella microstriata*. Left: ANSP Syntype #152657 (*Aplexa microstriata*) from Fish Lake, Sevier Co., UT. Credit: left: ANSP 152657. Credit: right: E. Wagner, courtesy ANSP.

DESCRIPTION (Chamberlin and Berry 1930): *Shell*: oval, elongated, very thin, fragile, pellucid, golden-yellow in color. *Whorls*: slightly more than 4, somewhat compressed, and are partially embraced by each succeeding whorl; the last whorl is characteristically compressed, is narrow, elongate, and about 4/5 of the shell length; nuclear whorls 1 1/3. The non-nuclear whorls have crowded, evenly spaced, minute revolving lines between the transverse lines, which deadens the lustre and portrays a satin periostracum. The transverse lines become deeper near the suture and form narrow grooves on the penultimate whorl. The sutures are exceedingly shallow and are narrowly banded by brown on each succeeding whorl. The spire is very short and acute. It is closely appressed to the body wall and often bordered by a narrow brown stripe. The columella is narrow but is longer in proportion to the size of the aperture, more twisted, and more oblique, than in *Aplexa hypnorum*. *Aperture*: narrow and elongated. The peristome is thin, sharp, and gently oval, following the general outline of the shell.

SIZE: SL 10.7 mm, SW 4.7 mm; ApL 7.6 mm long, ApW 2.9 mm; spire 2.3 mm long.

ANIMAL (Taylor 2003): The mantle, which is simple, is reflected over $1/3$ of the last whorl.

Preputium length about equal to bipartite penial sheath length.

TYPE LOCATION: "Abundant in shallow water along shore of portions of Fish Lake, Utah" (Sevier County).

JUNIOR SYNONYMS: *Aplexa microstriata* Chamberlin and Berry, 1930; *Stenophysa microstriata* Taylor, 1966; Genus *Utahphysa* erected by Taylor (2003), is now used as a subgenus.

NOTES: Narrow shell shape differentiates this from other Utah physids except *Aplexa elongata*, which has a shorter aperture. Mantle lacks projections and is broadly reflected on both sides (Taylor 2003). Species is allocated within the subfamily Physinae. Little is known about this species. It is presumed extinct (Clark 1991).

DISTRIBUTION: Known only from the type locality and seen alive only by the authors Chamberlin and Berry.

Physella acuta Draparnaud, 1805 Wandering Physa

DESCRIPTION (Taylor 2003): *Shell*: dull to silky, spire usually longer than wide. Reaches a typical length of about 13 mm. The *mexicana* form has a thin shell, is dull to polished, usually with little or no sculpture of the spirally aligned arcs characteristic in many species; the acute spire is 3/4 of the aperture length or longer. Shell features vary with habitat. In small streams, the shell spire is high, often with a concave outline, and the shell is thin, polished; the spirally aligned crescents are less evident than those for *Physella gyrina*. In a limestone habitat, the shells are thick, often with apertural thickenings (white bands). In areas with high gypsum content, shells are thick, narrow, and elongate, with shouldered spire whorls. The *integra* form has a convex spire, and shells are nearly white, but is similar in size.

SIZE: Measurements of shells from Texas and California populations range as follows: SL 13.4–18.8 mm, SW 7.4–11.1 mm, W/L ratio 0.50–0.65; whorls 4.75 to 6.

FIG. 60. *Physella acuta*. E. holotype of Draparnaud, Nat. Hist. Mus. Wein, Austria. ANSP 45871 (*Physella virgata* holotype), 329455 (*Physa mexicana* paralectotype), 99498 (*Physa baleata* [=*P. mexicana*] syntype). Credit: ANSP; NHMW holotype image courtesy of M. Vinarski (Vinarski and Eschner 2016).

Gould's (1855) description (translated from Latin) of synonym *P. virgata*: Shell small, firm, smooth, elongated-oval, gray-olive, lengthwise streak; pointed, elevated spire; 4–5 well-defined whorls; lunate-shaped aperture, ²/₃ the length of entire shell, columella is moderately folded, very calloused; reddish-yellow throat. Long. 2/5 (10.2 mm); lat. ¼ (6.3 mm) poll.

ANIMAL (Taylor 2003): Penial complex pigmentation is a light dusting of melanin on preputium and preputial gland, with practically none on either the penial sheath or vas deferens. The preputium is cylindrical, with the preputial gland entirely within the proximal half. The penial sheath is unitary, with a thin muscular sheath about three-fourths or more as long as the preputium, tapering gradually from a broader proximal end to a kink or abrupt curve at about ⁴/₅ the total length, then widening. The penis also tapers to a slender simple tip with no stylet or internal thickening. Within the preputium there is a large elongate sarcobelum with a minute papilla at the apex. Among shell variants, the nipple-like sarcobelum is a consistent character. Penial retractor muscles are inserted on ends of the penial sheath and are not connected by cross connections. The vas deferens between the paragonoporal angle and the penial sheath is ~³/₄ the length of penial complex.

TYPE LOCATION: Garonne River and its tributaries, France. Holotype at Naturhistoriches Museum Vienna (Austria), Draparnaud Collection 1820/XXVI/45 (Taylor

2003). The *Haitia mexicana* holotype was destroyed during World War II but was presumably collected near Mexico City.

JUNIOR SYNONYMS: *Physa virgata* from the type location in the Gila River of Arizona was shown to be able to hybridize with *Physella acuta* by Dillon et al. (2005) and so is considered a junior synonym of *P. acuta*. Cooper (1870) also considered the striping character of *virgata* an environmental effect of an alkaline habitat, not a species-worthy character. *Haitia mexicana* is also a junior synonym, which Taylor (2003) considered synonymous with *P. virgata*. Synonyms of *H. mexicana* (Taylor 2003): *Physa solida* Philippi, 1841; *P. squalida* Morelet, 1851; *P. humerosa* Gould, 1855; *P. anatina*, *P. forsheyi*, *P. grosvenori*, *P. halei*, *P. parva*, *P. striata*, *P. tenuissima*, and *P. traski* Lea, 1864d; *P. mexicana* var. *minima*, *P. mexicana* var. *minor*, *P. mexicana ovalis* (Wiegmann) and *P. mexicana* var. *parva* Martens, 1865; *P. distinguenda*, *P. polittissima*, and *P. sparsestriata* Tryon, 1865a; *P. dorbigniana* Lea, 1867; *Limnaea ambigua* and *L. compacta* Pease, 1870; *P. berendti* (Dunker) & *P. mexicana minor* Strebel, 1873; *P. boucardi* and *P. tehuantepecensis* Crosse and Fischer, 1881; *H. polakowskyi* Clessin, 1886; *P. mexicana* var. *acuttissima* Fischer and Crosse, 1900; *P. berendti* var *intermedia* Fischer and Crosse, 1900; *P. mexicana* var *plicata* and *P. mexicana* var. *tolucensis* Fischer and Crosse, 1900; *P. cupreonitens* Cockerell, 1889; *H. heterostropha* var. *penicillata* Hemphill, 1890a; *P. osculans rhyssa* Pilsbry, 1899a; *P. rhomboidea* Crandall, 1901; *P. virgata* mut. *alba* Cockerell, 1902; *H. gabbi* var. *orbignyana* (Lea) Keep, 1904; *P. crandalli* Baker, 1906; *P. balteata* Preston, 1907; *P. bottimeri* Clench, 1924; *P. marci* Baker, 1924; *P. humerosa interioris* Ferriss, 1920 (Pilsbry 1932a); and *P. californica* (Monterosato) Coen, 1945.

Hybridization studies have shown that *Physa heterostropha* and *P. integra* are also junior synonyms (Dillon et al. 2002). Other synonyms (Taylor 2003; Vinarski and Eschner 2016) are *Physa fluviatilis* Férussac, 1807; *Physa rivalis* Maton and Rackett, 1807; *P. subopaca* Lamarck, 1822, *P. borbonica* Férussac, 1827; *P. striata* Menke, 1828; *Bulla crassula* Dillwyn, 1817; *Bulinus acutus minuta*, *B. acutus normalis*, *Bulinus crassulus* (Dillwyn) and *Physa arctistropha* (Cristofori and Jan) Beck, 1838; *P. nana* Potiez and Michaud, 1838; *P. fontana* Haldeman, 1840; *P. inflata* Lea, 1841; *P. plicata* De Kay, 1843; *P. perrisiana* Dupuy, 1849; *P. rivularia* Dupuy, 1849; *P. elliptica* (Parryss) and *P. mediana* (Parryss) Dupuy, 1850; *P. buschi* Küster, 1850 (Küster et al. 1886); *P. charpentieri* Küster, 1850 (Küster et al. 1886); *P. venetzi* (Charpentier) H. and A. Adams, 1855; *P. acuta gibbosa*, *P. acuta* var. *minor*, *P. acuta* var. *subacuta*, and *P. acuta* var. *ventricosa* Moquin-Tandon, 1855; *P. acuta* var. *minor* Bourguignat, 1864; *P. lata* Tryon, 1865a; *P. primeana* Tryon, 1865a; *P. pisana* Issel, 1866; *P. fusca* (Rossmassler) Rigacci, 1866; *P. heterostropha* var. *gibbosa* and *P. heterostropha* var. *minor* Rigacci, 1866; *P. acuta* var. *acutior* and *P. acuta* var. *minor* Gassies, 1867; *P. melitensis* Mamo (Caruana 1867); *P. seychellana* Martens, 1869; *P. tenerifae*, *P. tenerifae* var. *fuerteventurae*, *P. tenerifae* var. *gomerana*, *P. tenerifae* var. *grancanariae*, and *P. tenerifae* var. *palmaensis* Mousson, 1872; *P. mamoi* and *P. elliptica* var. *minor* Benoit, 1875; *P. acuta* form *burriana*, *P. acuta* var. *fusca* (Rossmassler) and *P. acuta* var. *septentrionalis* Kobelt, 1879;

Physidae

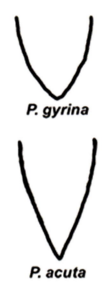

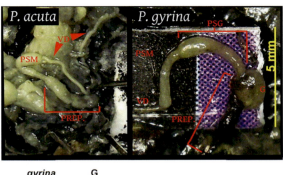

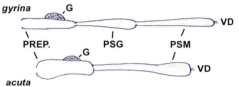

FIG. 61. Comparison of foot outline between *P. gyrina* (D) and *P. acuta* (E). Credit: redrawn by author from Te 1978.

FIG. 62. Comparison of penial morphology between *Physella acuta* and *P. gyrina*. PREP = preputium, PSG = glandular portion of penis sheath, G = preputial gland, PSM = muscular portion of penis sheath, VD = vas deferens; the penis is within the muscular portion of the penial sheath. Credit: photos by E. Wagner, drawing by E. Wagner, redrawn from Wethington and Lydeard 2007.

P. acuta major Locard, 1880; *P. dilucida* (Letourneaux) and *P. martorelli* Servain, 1880; *P. achaiae* Westerlund, 1881; *P. solidior* A. Costa, 1882; *P. acuta* var. *brevispira* Paulucci, 1882; *P. acroxa* and *P. saint-simonis* Fagot, 1883; *P. acuta* var. *minima* Cockerell, 1889; *P. acuta* var *minuta* (Parryss) and *P. aurata* (Draparnaud) Paetel 1889; *P. gallica* (Bourguignat), *P. massoti* (Penchinat), and *P. salteli* (Saint-Simon) Locard, 1893; *P. heterostropha* var. *alba* Crandall, 1901; *P. subopaca* var. *nilotica* Pallary, 1909; *P. castanea globosa, P. castanea major,* and *P. gibbosa rubella* Germain, 1903; *P. acuta* var. *bulla* and *P. acuta* var. *castanea* Schlesch, 1906; *P. syriaca* Germain, 1911; *P. caliban* Vanatta, 1910; *P. acuta* var. *thermalis* Boettger, 1913; *P. subopaca* var. *minor* Pallary, 1920; *Bullinus borbonicensis* (Férrusac) Germain, 1921; *P. acuta botanica* (Monterosato), *P. acuta brevispira thermalis* (Monterosato), *P. brevispira vinacea* (Monterosato), *P. acuta nostra* (Monterosato), *P. acuta panormitana* (Monterosato), and *P. opaca* (Lamarck) Coen 1945; *P. tonollii* Mirolli, 1958; *Physella acuta* (Draparnaud) Starobogatov, 1970; *Haitia acuta* (Draparnaud) Taylor, 2003; *Costatella acuta* Starobogatov, Bogatov, Prozorova, and Saenko, 2004.

NOTES (McMahon 1975; Taylor 2003; Dillon et al. 2004): Te (1978) observed that *acuta* has a more pointed foot tip outline (Fig. 61) and lacks white pigment granules observed in *P. gyrina*. *P. acuta* differs from *P. gyrina* in having more convex apical whorls and a two-part penial complex (versus 3 in *P. gyrina;* Fig. 62; Wethington and Lydeard 2007). Mean fecundity (eggs/week/pair) was 62, with

63% viable, hatching after about 2 weeks. The *mexicana* form may produce up to three generations per year. For additional descriptions of the animal, see Taylor (2003).

DISTRIBUTION (Taylor 2003; ANSP; Ibase): Native to North America and widely spread worldwide: Europe, Japan, Denmark, Dominican Republic, Cuba, Malaysia, Singapore, New Zealand, Mexico, Costa Rica, Peru, and North Africa. Widespread in United States and Canada. The snails formerly known as *P. virgata* or *P. mexicana* were found in Mexico, Central America, U.S. Virgin Islands, HA, AL, AZ, CA, CO, IA, ID, KS, LA, MI, NE, NV, NM, OK, OR, TN, TX, WA, WY. *P. integra* has been reported from the Great Lakes area, upper Great Plains states, and Colorado. In Utah, records (as *P. mexicana*) exist for Enterprise, Bear Lake (Ideal Beach), Newton, Great Salt Lake near Saltair, Fish Spring National Wildlife Refuge (Russell 1971, as *virgata*), Saratoga Lake, and Walker Lake (9 miles below Shurtz, Utah). UMNH records show *P. virgata* collected from Tooele and Iron (near Parowan) counties. Distribution data based on dissections to verify penial morphology, differentiating it from *P. gyrina,* are limited to Hovingh (2018), who found *P. acuta* (as *H. mexicana*) at Fish Springs National Wildlife Refuge, Snake-Hamblin Valley, and the Virgin and San Juan rivers.

Physella gyrina Say, 1821 Tadpole Physa

DESCRIPTION (Say 1821): *Shell:* heterostrophe (sinestral), oblong. *Whorls:* 5 or 6, gradually acuminating to an acute apex; suture slightly impressed. *Aperture:* more than one half but less than two-thirds of the total shell length; lip a little thickened on the inner margin. Synonyms *P. elliptica* and *Physa fragilis* had 4 whorls, a margined outer lip, and narrow aperture. Tryon (1870, p. 132, for synonym *P. propinqua*): "Shell large, fragile, inflated; spire short, apex acute; body whorl almost shouldered, very large, covered with distinctly elevated lines of growth on the adult specimens; the surface frequently exhibits several planes, instead of being uniformly rounded; columella a little twisted."

SIZE: SL 17–26 mm, SW 9.0–12.0 mm, ApL 11–14 mm, ApW 4.5–5.5 mm (Baker 1902, n = 5). For *P. elliptica* type, 12.7 mm × 5.1 mm wide (Lea 1834); For *P. hildrethiana* type (5 whorls): 19.0 mm × 10.2 mm wide; *P. propinqua*: 19 × 13 mm (Tryon 1870); *P. occidentalis* 18 × 11 mm (Tryon 1870). Utah specimens from Cache Valley (mean, range, n = 9, coll. 15 March 2019) had SL 16.8 mm (10.7–20.7 mm); SW 9.2 mm (6.4–11.9 mm), SL/SW ratio 1.848 (1.684–2.463), ApL 12.4 mm (7.6–16.1 mm); ApW 6.9 mm (4.8–9.2 mm), Apl/SL 73.8 (69.5–80.0%); body whorl height as % of shell length 88.1 (85.1–90.5%), whorls 4.25–5.25. A higher elevation site (9,300 ft), Duck Fork Reservoir in San Pete County, Utah, sampled in early July 2019, had smaller shells and shorter spires: SL 10.1 (6.8–14.5) mm, SW 6.2(4.2–8.8) mm; SL/SW ratio 1.649 (1.536–1.724); ApL 8.0 (6.0–11.5) mm, ApW 4.2(3.2–6.4) mm, ApL/SL 79.2 (71.9–87.5)%, body whorl height as % of SL 93.5 (89.0–99.8)%, 3.5–4.5 whorls.

Physidae

FIG. 63. *Physella gyrina*. Type specimens from the Academy of Natural Sciences of Philadephia of some species synonymized with *P. gyrina*: No. 17255 = *P. occidentalis*, 17276 = *P. coniformis*, 17278 = *P. propinqua*, 17298 = *P. cooperi*, 17300 = *P. malleata*, 58304 = *P. warreniana*, 17316 = *P. diaphana*, 58296 = *P. whitei*. Credit: ANSP.

TYPE LOCATION: Waters of the Missouri (Bowyer Creek, near Council Bluffs, Iowa).

JUNIOR SYNONYMS (Taylor 2003; Moore et al. 2014): *Physella elliptica* Lea, 1834; *Bulinus crassulus typica* Beck, 1838; *Physella aurea* Lea, 1839; *Physella sayii* Tappan, 1839; *P. margarita*, Lesson, 1840; *P. concolor* Haldeman, 1841; *P. hildrethiana* and *P. troostiana* (*troostenis* in February 1841 Proceedings of the American Philosophical Society) Lea, 1841 (Lea 1846a); *Physa cylindrica* (Newcomb) De Kay, 1843; *P. fragilis* Mighels and Adams, 1842; *P. obesa* De Kay, 1843; *P. virginea* Gould, 1846; *P. bullata* Gould, 1855; *P. triticea* Lea, 1856; *P. gabbi* Tryon, 1863; *P. altonensis, P. blandi, P. crocata, P. febigerii, P. hawnii, P. nicklinii, P. nuttali, P. parva,*

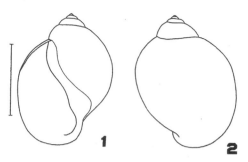

FIG. 64. *Physella gyrina*, aperture view (1), dorsal aspect (2). Credit: Clench (1926; published as *P. gyrina goodrichi*). Line=10 mm.

P. saffordii, P. smithsoniana, P. venusta, P. warreniana, and *P. whitei* Lea, 1864a; *P. ampullacea* Gould, 1855 (originally *bullata*, but preoccupied, changed by Binney 1865a); *P. cooperi, P. diaphana, P. malleata, P. occidentalis,* and *P. propinqua* Tryon, 1865a; *P. coniformis* & *P. oleacea* Tryon, 1866c; *P. deformis* Currier, 1867; *P. carltoni* Lea, 1869; *P. wolfiana* Lea, 1869; *P. amygdalus* Sowerby, 1874; *P. binneyana* Ancey, 1886 (new name for *diaphana* Tryon 1865a, preoccupied); *P. elliptica* var. *decollata* Cockerell, 1888a; *P. heterostropha* var. *heterostrophella* forma *elongata* and *P.h.h.* forma *brevis* Cockerell, 1889; *P. staffordi* (Lea) Paetel, 1889 (error for *saffordi* Lea, 1864a); *Physa gyrina albofilata* (Ancey) Crandall, 1901; *Physa elliptica minor* Crandall, 1901; *P. smithi* Baker, 1919; *P. smithiana* Baker, 1920 (new name for *smithi*, preoccupied); *P. goodrichi* and *P. johnsoni* Clench, 1926; *P. gyrina byersi* Crabb, 1927a; *P. bayfieldensis, P. chetekensis,* and *P. obrussoides* Baker, 1928; *P. plena, P. remingtoni,* and *P. salina* Clench, 1930; *P. gouldi* Clench, 1935; *P. jennessi athearni* Clarke, 1973.

NOTES: Probably the most common snail in Utah. Penial morphology or DNA testing should be used to differentiate between *acuta* and *gyrina*. See notes for *P. acuta*. Body whorl not as inflated as for *P. utahensis*. There are a number of genetic sample records (cytochrome oxidase I gene) for *P. gyrina* in GenBank, including one from Fish Lake, Sevier County, Utah (#EU038398; Moore et al. 2014) and one from California (18S: HQ659967; Dayrat et al. 2011). This species is highly variable in shell morphology. Dillon et al. (2004, 2011) noted that *P. acuta* and *P. gyrina* held together did not hybridize, indicating that each is reproductively isolated and is a unique species. Studies with *P. acuta* indicated that shell morphology is influenced by the environment; for example, under stream flow conditions, shells are more elongate with narrow apertures, whereas those in ponds have wider apertures and short spires (Taylor 2003; Gustafson et al. 2014).

P. gyrina can withstand high temperatures (35–40°C). Eggs do not survive prolonged exposure to 5°C; egg laying usually occurs when water temperatures reach 10–12°C. Adults produce one to two generations per year (Taylor 2003). Dillon et al. (2004) noted that fecundity averaged 21 embryos per pair; these eggs hatched in about 2 weeks. The life span is about 13–16 months.

DISTRIBUTION: *Physella gyrina* is widely distributed in Utah, and the United States. Distribution in Utah based on dissections to differentiate *gyrina* from *acuta* is limited to Hovingh (2018), which showed *gyrina* is the predominant *Physella* in Utah and is widespread.

Physella utahensis Clench, 1925 Utah Physa

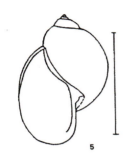

FIG. 65. *Physella utahensis*. Credit: above, original figure from Clench (1925); below, topotype, 2018, by E. Wagner.

DESCRIPTION (Clench 1925): "Shell sinestral, large, rhomboidal, slightly imperforate, slightly malleated, solid. Color light straw, varicose bands only slightly develop on a few individuals of type lot—not at all on the type. Whorls five, rounded. Spire slightly obtuse, nuclear whorl reddish. Aperture slightly elongate, columella margin straight. Lip not noticeably thickening in the type; six of the paratypes have a slight reddish-brown callosity a little behind the lip margin. Columella straight, not twisted, rather wide. Suture rather deep, slightly indented. Sculpture coarse, vertical growth lines on all last three whorls, a few not regularly spaced, more prominent, especially so toward superior border of the body whorl. Cross striae absent, a few coarse spiral lines on center of body whorl of type, but not on any of the paratypes."

SIZE (Clench 1925): type specimen (UMMZ 4257) SL 31 mm, SW 21.5 mm, ApL 22.5 mm × 11.5 mm wide. The paratypes (n = 11) range in size from 20 to 31 mm SL × 13.4 to 21.5 mm SW, SL/SW ratio 1.27 to 1.40, ApL/SL 53.8 to 83.6%, ApL/ApW ratio 1.25 to 2.10 (Clench 1925).

ANIMAL: No data

TYPE LOCATION: Utah Lake, Utah

JUNIOR SYNONYMS: Clench (1925) described shells found at Utah Lake as a subspecies (*Physa lordi utahensis*) of *P. lordi* Baird, 1863. Ingersoll (1877) classified the Utah Lake shells as *Physa sayii*, noting that the shells were "exact miniatures of *P. lordi* and *P. ancillaria*." Henderson and Daniels (1917) reported Utah Lake physid shells as *Physa lordi*. Chamberlin and Jones (1929) considered the Utah Lake physid as a distinct species, *Physella utahensis*. Johnson (2003) noted that the paratypes are UMMZ 229549 and MCZ 36541, 30982, but searches for these numbers on invertebase.org do not show these records. There is a 1916 INHS record for *P. lordi* from Utah Lake (74605). Te (1980) listed this species as *Physella utahensis*, distinct from

P. lordi and *P. gyrina*. Genetic studies by Wethington and Lydeard (2007) also supported putting this species in the genus *Physella*.

NOTES: Columellar margin of the aperture nearly straight, projecting further down (anteriorly) from the penultimate whorl than for *P. gyrina* or *P. acuta,* creating a long, extended aperture. Larger, stouter, and more opaque than other Utah physids. As far as is known, *P. utahensis* is restricted to Utah Lake and its lower drainage. Taylor (2003) considered *utahensis* a synonym of *P. gyrina*. *P. utahensis* is considered herein to be distinct from *gyrina* based on comparisons of the shell with typical *P. gyrina,* the observations of Te (1978), the evolution of *utahensis* in a large Pleistocene lake, as well as the descriptions and comments of Chamberlin and Jones (1929). However, although shells may still be found, *P. utahensis* is currently considered extinct.

DISTRIBUTION: Utah Lake and its lower drainage. *P. lordi* fossils from the Sevier Desert (Roscoe 1964) are also probably attributable to *P. utahensis*.

Physella zionis Pilsbry, 1926 Wet-rock Physa

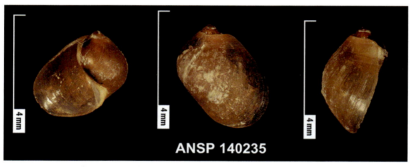

FIG. 66. *Physella* (*Petrophysa*) *zionis*. ANSP 140235. Credit: ANSP.

DESCRIPTION (Taylor 2003): Globose shell with obtuse spire less than $1/5$ the length of the large ear-shaped aperture. Surface dull, with sculpture of axial fine growth lines only. Mantle not reflected over the shell; projections reduced to a few inconspicuous, bluntly rounded projections on columellar surface.

SIZE: < 5mm long

ANIMAL: broad foot; relatively short, blunt tentacles with large post-tentacular flaps, reduced eyes, and reduced mantle projections. Insertion of distal penial retractor higher on the penial sheath than usual.

TYPE LOCATION: Zion Canyon, Utah

JUNIOR SYNONYMS: *Physa zionis* Pilsbry, 1926a; *Petrophysa zionis* (Pilsbry) Baker, 1928, Taylor 2003. Genetic analyses and similarities in penial morphology suggest that *zionis* belongs in the genus *Physella* (Te 1980; Wethington 2004).

NOTES: Shell shape is unique among snails in Utah and so is easily identified. Genetic tests have differentiated *P. zionis* from the Owyhee wet-rock physa from warm springs near Three Forks, Owyhee River, Oregon (Moore et al. 2014) and other physids available in the GenBank database. GenBank accession numbers for *P. zionis*: KF305417 to KF305427. Te (1978) has also segregated this species from other physids using multiple characters. Egg clutches vary from 1 to about 4 embryos (Wethington 2004). Found on rocks and vertical, wet, canyon walls in riparian areas.

DISTRIBUTION: Known only from North Fork Virgin River Narrows, Zion National Park, Washington County, Utah.

Physa megalochlamys Taylor, 1988 Cloaked Physa

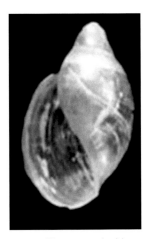

FIG. 67. *Physa megalochlamys.* Paratype, CAS 146099. Credit: Taylor (2003), Revista Internacional de Biologia Tropical.

DESCRIPTION (Taylor 1988a; 2003): *Shell*: thin and fragile, ovoid-fusiform; surface texture silky, sometimes shining; axial sculpture of spirally arranged fine growth lines and weakly raised threads; apex obtusely rounded, spire bluntly rounded. *Whorls*: 4.5, weakly convex, separated by a shallow, broadly attached suture. *Aperture*: about ¾ of total shell length, elongate-oval, rounded anteriorly, narrowed abruptly to an acute angle posteriorly, widest about $1/3$ of the length from the anterior end; outer lip thin, sharp, arched in the direction of growth, strongly retractive to the suture. Parietal wall and ventral-anterior aspect of body whorl with a broad, thin, translucent, closely appressed callus; edge of the callus crosses the axis of the shell opposite a point ~$3/4$ or more of the aperture length from anterior end. Columellar lip is a rounded ridge that enters the whorl cavity, forming a low fold.

SIZE (Taylor 1988a): Length of body whorl 10.5 (9.5–11.2) mm. Largest shells may have the apex eroded. Largest shell from type locale was 11.5 mm long (SL), SW 6.7 mm; ApL 8.6 mm.

ANIMAL: Mantle may cover the whole shell. Mantle projections rounded, numbering 2–17 (mean, 8.1) for columellar-parietal area, 0–9 (mean, 5.4) in the left posterior area.

GENITALIA: Preputium is translucent, melanin-flecked, shorter than the penial sheath; on its posterior side it has a preputial gland less than $1/3$ the length of preputium; within preputium is a large sarcobellum, $\sim 3/4$ as wide as long, with a small terminal papilla. Penial sheath is long and glandular, widest at the proximal third, narrowing distally, then enlarging at distal tenth; sheath is opaque creamy-white, and flecked with wisps of melanin. Penis is narrow, flagellar, $\sim 2/3$ the length of the sheath, bearing an elongate stylet that is not sharply set off from the shaft. Retractor muscles lack cross connections between them. Vas deferens length between paragonoporal angle and penial sheath is $< 1/4$ the sheath length.

TYPE LOCATION: Lily pond in Teton County, Wyoming.

JUNIOR SYNONYMS: None known.

NOTES (Taylor 1988a): This species is characterized by the elongate and thin shell with a narrow spire with a blunt apex and wide parietal callus. In living specimens, the mantle is broadly reflected over both sides of the shell, even covering the entire shell. Mantle projections are broadly rounded. Narrower, higher spire, broader parietal callus, with more convex growth lines and aperture profile than for *P. skinneri*, but with a less convex body whorl. *P. megaochlamys* also attains nearly twice the size of *skinneri*.

DISTRIBUTION (Taylor 1988a; Ibase): British Columbia, Saskatchewan; east of the Cascade Mountains of Oregon; Idaho, Montana, Wyoming, Minnesota, and Colorado. For Utah, Taylor (1988a) reported it from Snake Valley, Millard County. A subsequent visit by P. Hovingh and S. K. Wu (Hovingh 2018) was unable to confirm its presence. There is a specimen at FMNH (383103) from Meeks Cabin Reservoir in the Uinta Mountains. (Black's Fork of the Green River).

Physa skinneri Taylor, 1954 Glass Physa

DESCRIPTION (Taylor 2003): *Shell*: thin, narrowly ovoid to ovoid-fusiform, apex obtusely rounded; spire blunt with weakly convex whorls separated by a shallow, broadly attached suture. *Whorls* 4. *Aperture*: elongate-oval, about 60% of shell length, rounded anteriorly, acute posteriorly, widest about $1/3$ length from anterior end. Outer lip thin, sharp, sometimes with a white band of callus thickening within, convex in the direction of growth.

SIZE: Largest specimen (Ruby Lake, Nevada) was 8.8 mm long × 5.2 mm wide; ApL 6.1 mm.

ANIMAL (Taylor 2003): Mantle reflects narrowly off left side; mantle projections are narrow and elongate, numbering 6–8 (mode = 8) in the columellar-parietal area and 1–8 (mode = 5 or 6) in left posterior area.

Physidae

FIG. 69. *Physa skinneri.* ANSP 110787 from Deuel Co., SD. Credit: E. Wagner, courtesy ANSP.

FIG. 70. Acuminate shape of foot end of *Physa skinneri*. Credit: redrawn from Te 1978.

FIG. 68. *Physa skinneri* reared in culture from eggs from Mantua Reservoir, Utah: empty shell; egg cases; live individuals. Credit: E. Wagner.

GENITALIA: Preputium is translucent, flecked with melanin, and shorter than the penial sheath; the preputium has a gland $1/4$–$1/2$ the length of the preputium. The long penial sheath is entirely glandular, opaque creamy-white, and flecked with melanin. The penial sheath is widest at the proximal third, then narrows gradually to its minimum diameter at $9/10$ of the length and enlarges toward the preputium. Penis is narrow, flagellar, $1/2$–$2/3$ the length of the sheath and bears an elongate stylet sharply set off at its base from the shaft. Sarcobelum large, more than twice as long as the width, forming a prolate hemisphere; a terminal papilla is present but may be inconspicuous.

Retractor muscles on the ends of the penial sheath lack cross connections or multiple insertions.

TYPE LOCATION: Beaver County, Oklahoma, in Pleistocene deposits

JUNIOR SYNONYMS: None known.

NOTES: Smaller and narrower than *P. acuta* or *gyrina,* with a blunter apex. In a laboratory population derived from Comins Lake, Nevada, the number of eggs/capsules averaged 3.12 (range 2–5; Taylor 2003). Smaller than *P. megalochlamys*, with mantle reflected only on the left side (both sides for *P. megalochlamys*). Te (1978) noted that the foot terminus of this species is acuminate (Fig. 70). Te (1978), comparing multiple shell and animal characters, found that the closest relatives of *P. skinneri* were *P. jennessi* Dall, 1919 and *P. fontinalis* L.

DISTRIBUTION (ANSP; Ibase): From Alaska to Ontario, Canada. United States: CO, ME, MA, MI, NE, PA, SD, NV, WA, WY. In Utah, Taylor (1988) found specimens in Sevier County. FMNH 178572 from Salt Lake County airport; 360844 from 2 miles south of Garden City. The author (Wagner) found specimens in wetlands around Mantua Reservoir, Mantua, Utah.

SPF: **LYMNAEOIDEA Rafinesque, 1815**
Planorbidae Rafinesque, 1815

DESCRIPTION (Baker 1911, 1945; Burch 1989): Shell: mostly discoidal, mostly sinestral (though not readily evident due to sunken or flat spires; dextral in *Helisoma*). The limpet *Ferrissia rivularis*, featuring an uncoiled patelliform shell, also belongs in this family. The limpets were formerly separated into their own family Ancylidae, but genetic analysis has found that family to be polyphyletic and that placement of limpet tribes Ancylini and Laevapecini within Planorbidae is warranted (Albrecht et al. 2007).

The animal has a secondary gill present (pseudobranch) on left side; and long, filiform tentacles, with eyes at their inner base. The penis has a cylindrical appendage attached to the apex; the vas deferens enters the distal end of the appendage, reappearing at the junction of the appendage with the penis and enters the penis in a depression on the side. Penis with wide retractor and protractor muscles. Kidney very long and narrow. Mantle ridged. Genitalia on the left side.

Radula central tooth bicuspid, lateral teeth tricuspid.

Baker (1928, 1945) divided the family into subfamilies based on genital and prostate gland morphology as follows:

PLANORBINAE: The prostate diverticula are simple sacs placed in a single row along a prostate duct. The kidney is rounded and lacks a ridge. The ovotestis has the diverticula arranged in a double row, except in the genus *Australorbis* (Caribbean and South America) where the single row of glands is placed directly on the sperm duct and the prostate gland ends are branched.

SEGMENTININAE: The prostate diverticula are simple sacs placed in a single row along a prostate duct as in Planorbinae. The penial complex has one or two flagella placed at the end of the penis sac, and in addition several genera have a penial gland in the preputium. The kidney lacks a ridge.

HELISOMATINAE: Prostate diverticula compound or multiple, with a basal stem with branches grouping around a short prostate duct which is in intimate contact with the sperm duct. In cross section, the prostate is fan-like. Penial gland is always present with an external duct of greater or lesser length. Kidney is usually heavily ridged.

PLANORBULINAE: Prostate forms a finger-shaped pattern with few diverticula. The penial gland duct is inside the preputium, and the ovotestes have paired diverticula.

Tryon (1870) defined the subgroups (subgenera at the time, now known as genera) of *Planorbis* as (1) *Planorbella* Haldeman, 1840, shell with few whorls, aperture expanded, bell-shaped; (2) *Helisoma* Swainson, shell ventricose (swollen or distended), the spire sunk below the body whorl; whorls few, often angulated; (3) *Menetus* Adams and Adams, 1855 (1858), shell depressed, whorls rapidly increasing, periphery angulated; (4) *Adula* Adams and Adams, 1857 (1858), shell with the whorls rounded and very numerous, deeply umbilicated on the upper, and convex on the underside, aperture campanulate; and (5) *Nautilina* Stein, 1850, shell small, orbicular above, flat beneath; whorls few, rapidly increasing. Taylor (1966) raised *Planorbella* to generic rank that included the subgenera *Pierosoma* Dall, 1905 and *Seminolina* Pilsbry, 1934; these groups have sinestral shells. The left side is plane in early stages of growth, with a carina around the edge, and it becomes slightly concave only as successive whorls enlarge; The right side is not funicular but has a narrow umbilicus. In contrast, *Helisoma* s.s. have dextral shells; Taylor (1966) demoted *Carinifex* to subspecific rank under *Helisoma*, which still featured *H. anceps*. Taylor (1966) also considered the Utah fossil species *Vorticifex laxus* Chamberlin and Berry, 1933, an unrecognizable species, probably of Hydrobiidae. In Utah, there are 12 known species of planorbids.

Gyraulus circumstriatus Tryon, 1866 Disk Gyro

DESCRIPTION (Tryon 1866b; Baker 1928): *Shell*: small, rugose, light horn color; *Whorls*: 4–4.5, convex with a rounded periphery, but body whorl slightly flattened above, obtusely subangulate below; spire whorls rounded; whorls generally distorted in adult specimens (the whorls not proceeding in the same plane but elevated or depressed below it at times) increasing very slowly in diameter, with

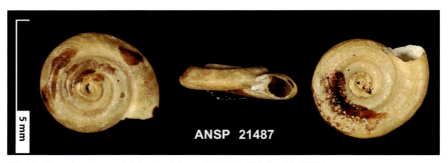

FIG. 71. *Gyraulus circumstriatus*, lectotype, ANSP 21487. Credit: ANSP.

deeply impressed suture, deflected toward the aperture; Umbilicus: concave but exhibiting all the volutions, with two or three raised revolving lines. *Aperture:* small, very oblique.

SIZE: Holotype dia. 6 mm, SL 1.5 mm. Baker (1928) noted similar dimensions for three shells: 5.0 mm dia., 1.3–1.5 mm SL, ApL 1.3 mm, ApW 1.4–1.5 mm.

ANIMAL (Baker 1945): Small narrow jaw has about 37 plates; radula formula is 14–1–14 with 105 rows of teeth. Center tooth bicuspid, 1–6 tricuspid laterals, intermediate teeth with ectocone split into two teeth, 9th tooth ectocone split into three cusps; marginal teeth with entocone split into two small cusps, the mesocone large and spade-shaped, and ectocone with three cusps. Prostate and spermatheca each with 12 diverticula.

TYPE LOCATION: Artificial pond at Weatogue, Connecticut

JUNIOR SYNONYMS: *Planorbis circumstriatus* Tryon, 1866b; *Torquis circumstriatus*; *Planorbis parvus walkeri* Vanatta, 1902. Last revision to *Gyraulus circumstriatus* by Baker (1928).

NOTES: *G. circumstriatus* has whorls that are more closely coiled than *G. parvus*, the last of which is not rapidly enlarged; there are also about 4.5 whorls in *G. circumstriatus* but less than 4 in *G. parvus* (Baker 1928). Epiphytic feeder, mostly in colder lakes, ponds, fens, and marshes (Frest and Johannes 2000). Normal somatic cell chromosome number is 72 (Burch 1960b; Thiroit-Quiévreux 2003), which Burch and Jung (1993) considered as tetraploid, when compared to other snails in Planorbidae, which typically have 18 chromosomes. Recent genetic analyses by Lorencova et al. (2021) included two *G. circumstriatus* specimens from Montana and Canada in a study comparing European *G. laevis* Alder, 1838, and *G. parvus* Say, 1817, from many locations including the U.S. Their data suggests synonymy of all three species. More sampling, especially from the type location of *circumstriatus* and other U.S. populations is needed to confirm the synonymy.

DISTRIBUTION (ANSP; Ibase): BC, Manitoba, Nova Scotia, Ontario, Quebec; AK, AR, CA, CO, CT, FL, IA, ID, IL, IN, LA, MA, ME, MI, MN, MT, ND, NE, NM, NV, NY, OH, OR, PA, SD, VT, WA, WI, WV, WY. Utah records from Emery Co., Rich Co. (Bear L.), Weber Co. (Morgan, Chalk Creek, Ogden Canyon), Utah County (Utah Lake), and Cache County.

Gyraulus parvus Say, 1817 Ash Gyro

DESCRIPTION (Haldeman 1844; Chamberlin and Jones 1929): *Shell*: small, discoidal, compressed, minutely striate, smooth, flat above, with the spire impressed; color light wood-brown, sometimes with a greenish tinge; left side with a broad shallow concavity. *Whorls:* 4, most visible to the center on both sides, with sutures equally impressed.

FIG. 72. *Gyraulus parvus*, ANSP 63303, Bear Lake, UT-ID (Hayden Survey, 1892); right: live animal, Mantua Reservoir, UT. Credit: left: ANSP. Right: E. Wagner.

SIZE (Chamberlin and Jones 1929 for *G. similaris*): Holotype: SL 2.5 mm, dia. 6.2 mm, aperture 2 × 2 mm; paratype: SL 1.7 mm, greatest dia. 4.7 mm, ApL 1.4 mm, ApW 1.5 mm.

ANIMAL (Baker 1928): Dark brown, lighter below; foot short, rounded, extending from the labrum to the center of the shell, rounded posteriorly, sides parallel. Tentacles whitish, with a dark line on the center of the dorsal surface; secondary branchia long, narrow, whitish. Spermatheca long, narrow, the duct 1.5X the gland. Male preputium long, narrow, similar diameter throughout; penis sheath 1.5X the length of the preputium, not enlarged at the distal end as in *exacuous* and *deflectus*.

TYPE LOCATION: Delaware River near Philadelphia, PA. *P. similaris* type location was Smartweed Lake, Colorado, altitude 8,575 ft; East Lake, near Tolland, altitude 8,850 ft (Baker 1919).

JUNIOR SYNONYMS: *Planorbis parvus* Say, 1817; *Planorbis elevatus* Adams, 1840; *Gyraulus vermicularis* Gould, 1846; *Planorbis parvus* var. *walkeri* Vanatta, 1902; *Gyraulus labiatus* Leonard, 1948; *Planorbis billingsi* Lea, 1864a, 1866; *Planorbis similaris* Baker, 1919 (Bequaert and Miller 1973).

NOTES: *G. parvus* can be differentiated from *G. circumstriatus* by the more rapidly enlarging body whorl, flattened and almost excavated lower surface of last whorl, and rounded body whorl, which is only slightly flattened above. This species is considered tetraploid (normal chromosome number is 72; Burch and Jung 1993). Found in quiet spots in lakes and rivers, and small pools (Baker 1928). Often associated with submerged aquatic vegetation.

DISTRIBUTION (Ingersoll 1877; Chamberlin and Jones 1929; Chamberlin and Berry 1929, 1930; Brooks 1936; Jones 1940a, b; Baily and Baily 1952; Roscoe 1964; ANSP; UMNH): Widely distributed in North America from Canada south to Florida and Mexico. Common in Utah. Records from Fairfield, Rush Lake, Bear Lake, between Springville and Provo, near Morgan, shore of Great Salt Lake, Spring Lake, Utah Lake (records for both *G. parvus* and *G. parvus similaris*), Zion National Park, Kamas, Koosharem Reservoir, Salt Lake City, Sevier Desert, Geneva, Saratoga, Provo, Toy, Topaz Lake, and Diaz Lake; Sevier, Summit, Box Elder, Millard, Rich, Cache, Uintah, and Weber counties.

Helisoma anceps Menke, 1830 Two-ridge Ramshorn

DESCRIPTION (Clarke 1973): *Shell*: medium-sized to large (up to ~17 mm diameter), compressed, ultradextral, relatively high, blackish brown to pale brown. Spire immersed to a variable extent but usually deeply recessed; umbilicus deep and narrow. *Whorls*: about 4, and in most populations with two prominent carinae, one on the upper surface of the body whorl and the other bounding the umbilicus. Upper and lower carinae (when present) rounded, sharp, or corded; the upper carina of variable position and located at the center of the whorl or close to, but not on, the shoulder. Periphery rounded. Spiral striae absent or present and of prominence varying from barely apparent to strong and obvious. Collabral sculpture present and fine to moderately fine. *Aperture:* ear-shaped, expanded in some populations, commonly thickened internally. Callus moderately thick on parietal wall.

FIG. 73. *Helisoma anceps*, lectotype, ANSP 45058. Credit: ANSP.

SIZE: Alberta shells were 7.0–10.8 mm dia., 4.1–6.0 mm height, umbilicus dia. 3.1–5.0 mm, ratio of umb. dia./shell dia: 0.43–0.54, whorls 3.4–3.8. A Saskatchewan population had diameters of 6.6–15.0 mm, height 4.3–8.7 mm, umbilicus

FIG. 74. Original figure for *Helisoma anceps*. Credit: Lister 1823.

dia. 3.3–7.1 mm, umb. dia./shell dia. ratio 0.40–0.54, whorls 3.3–4.5. A Minnesota population had similar data fitting within these ranges, but with whorls of 3.1 to 4.1. Width/height ratios among the varieties in Baker (1928, as *Helisoma antrosa*) ranged from 1.32 to 2.19 (mean 1.68, $n = 30$).

ANIMAL (Baker 1945): Yellowish or brownish, flecked with white; there are spots of color near the eyes and between the tentacles, and the mantle is spotted with dark mottling, especially over the kidney. The tentacles are long and filiform, and the velar area is notably developed. The shell is carried almost perpendicularly. Kidney has a ridge.

GENITALIA: Seminal vesicle short (~1 mm) and widely rounded; sperm duct about 6 mm long, sausage shaped, ~0.3 mm dia. Prostate is ovate, ~2.5 × 1 × 1 mm, fan-shaped in cross section, with 6–8 diverticula, each of which is branched 2–4x. Prostate duct is short, uniting sperm duct and prostate gland. Vas deferens is thinner than sperm duct, ~14 mm, but enlarges to form the epiphallus near the tip of the bullet-shaped penis sac (1.5 × 1 mm). The preputium is wide (1.7 mm) and about 2.5 mm long. The penis is typically short and wide, tapering abruptly to a narrow point, and with a small sharp papilla slightly below the tip.

RADULA: Tricuspid laterals, marginals multicuspid. Upper jaw arched, with rounded ends. See Baker (1945) for anatomy figures and additional details.

TYPE LOCATION: Not given.

JUNIOR SYNONYMS: *Planorbis bicarinatus* Say, 1817 (although Say predates Menke, the name was preoccupied for a Paris Basin fossil per Baker 1945); *Planorbis anceps* Menke, 1830; *Planorbis antrosus* Conrad, 1834a (Fig. 73 is *P. antrosus latchfordi*, ANSP lectotype #45058). Menke (1830) noted that this species was illustrated in "Lister Conch. table 139. Fig. 44." Martini Lister's *Synopsis Methodica Conchyliorum* was an early guide to European shells, published in several editions. In the third edition (Lister 1823), an index in English by Dillwyn lists the species published. For the figure referenced by Menke (see Fig. 74), Dillwyn suggests that the species "constitutes the *Helix* No. 269 of Schroeter's Einleitung, and appears to me to be an undescribed species." Mehnke (1830) does not provide a description but just lists the snail as a *Planorbis anceps*. Baker (1945) recognized 12 races of *H. anceps*.

NOTES: Differentiated from the other large ram's horn snails in Utah by the dextral coiling of the shell. Differs from *H. newberryi* by its rounder aperture lip and sunken spire. Usually found in permanent aquatic habitats, both lotic and lentic, associated with vegetation.

DISTRIBUTION (ANSP; Ibase): Found throughout North America from southern James Bay and Hudson Bay south to Georgia, Texas, and northwestern Mexico and west to Oregon and Alberta. There are no museum records for Utah for this species.

Helisoma newberryi Lea, 1858 Great Basin Ramshorn

DESCRIPTION (Lea 1858; Binney 1865a): *Shell* light horn colored, depressed, turreted, very minutely striated, above and below acutely carinated, broadly and deeply umbilicated. *Whorls:* 5, flat or slightly geniculate (stairstep-like). *Aperture:* large, light horn colored, subtriangular.

SIZE (Wagner, unpublished data, Bear Lake, UT-ID; mean, range, *n* = 20): SL 7.57 mm (6.1–10.3 mm); SW 9.62 mm (7.3–13.6 mm); SL/SW ratio 0.792 (0.665–0.982); ApL 5.89 mm (4.8–8.6 mm); ApW 4.28 mm (3.0–5.9 mm); ApL/SL 77.9 (65.5–83.8%); whorls 3.8 (3–4.25); umbilicus dia. 3.25 mm (2.3–4.4 mm), 33.9% of shell dia. (28.2–41.5%).

TYPE LOCATION: Klamath Lake and Canoe Creek, California

JUNIOR SYNONYMS (Henderson 1932a; Baker 1945; Taylor 1981): *Planorbis newberryi* Lea, 1858; *Carinifex newberryi* Binney, 1865a; *Carinifex ponsonbyi* Smith, 1876; *Megasystropha newberryi* (Lea) Walker 1918 (see Baily 1957 for ICZN Opinion 432 ruling in favor of *Carinifex* as genus. Lea [1864b] had proposed *Megasystropha* as an alternate name in case *Planorbis* was not the right genus for the species but provided no description). *Carinifex occidentalis* Hanna, 1924;

FIG. 75. *Helisoma newberryi.* Bear Lake, UT. Credit: E. Wagner.

Carinifex atopus Chamberlin and Jones, 1929; *Helisoma jacksonensis* Henderson, 1932a; *Carinifex newberryi subrotunda* Pilsbry, 1932b; *Carinifex newberryi malleata* Pilsbry, 1934; *Helisoma newberryi occidentale* Hanna and Henderson, 1934. Taylor (1966) moved *Carinifex* to subgenus rank under *Helisoma* based on the carinate and dextral shell characteristics of both.

NOTES (Frest and Johannes 1998; Hietala-Henschell et al. 2019): The angular aperture, carinate shouldered whorls, and stout shell with a deep umbilicus easily distinguish this shell from others. As the distribution data indicates, this species prefers lakes with high water quality; eutrophic sites that experience hypoxia will not support this species. In Oregon, *H. newberryi* was associated with cold spring complexes, creeks, and pools, often associated with submerged aquatic plants in muddy substrates with scattered gravel, and larger rocks.

DISTRIBUTION (ANSP; Ibase; Ingersoll 1877): France; CA, ID, ND, NV, OR, WY. Utah records from Bear Lake, Utah Lake, Fish Lake, Sevier Lake, and Spring Lake. Call (1884, p 20) reported that it was "discovered living in Utah Lake." It has not been reported live since then. An old shell was found by the author at China Row Spring in Logan Canyon in 2019.

Menetus opercularis Gould, 1847 Button Sprite

DESCRIPTION (Gould 1848b; Binney 1865a): *Shell*: small, very depressed, chestnut, flat above; depressed at the apex, subconvex, widely umbilicate, peripheral margin is bluntly carinate; *Whorls*: 4, with well-impressed sutures. *Aperture*: transversely subrhomboid. Lip above slightly declining, at periphery acute angled, beneath arched, lips embracing ¾ of whorl beneath the carina.

FIG. 76. *Menetus opercularis*, Oregon. ASNP 145110. Credit: ANSP.

SIZE: 6.3 × 1.6 mm

ANIMAL: Penial gland elongated, somewhat sausage-shaped when fully formed, and almost completely filling the preputial sac, which is regularly elongated. There is a cup-shaped termination opening at the proximal end from which a long narrow duct extends through the body of the gland to the distal end. The duct enters the muscular collar between the preputial and penial sacs. The vas deferens enlarges as it enters the penial sac, forming an epiphallus (this feature is absent in *Promenetus*).

TYPE LOCATION: Sacramento River, California.

JUNIOR SYNONYMS: *Planorbis opercularis* Gould, 1847.

NOTES: Differs from *G. parva* and *circumstriatus* by the presence of a blunt keel. Resembles *P. exacuous* but is larger, less compressed, and less delicate. The periphery has a blunt keel but is not acutely edged like *P. exacuous* (Gould 1848b). *M. opercularis* is the type species of the genus *Menetus* (Baker 1928).

DISTRIBUTION (Ibase; ANSP): BC; AK, CA, OH, OR, TX, WA. For Utah, there are no museum specimens or naturalist records for Utah.

Promenetus exacuous Say, 1821 Sharp Sprite

DESCRIPTION (Say 1821): *Shell*: discoidal, with an *acute edge*, dextral, depressed, but spire not impressed; wider than long, not elevated above the suture but a little flattened, sides obliquely descending to an acute lateral edge, below the middle. *Whorls*: 4, striated across, sutures not profoundly indented, body whorl flattened, though inner edge is rounded; umbilicus regular, showing all whorls to the apex. *Aperture:* transversely subtriangular; the lip angulated in the middle, arched near its inferior tip, the superior termination just including the acute edge of the penultimate whorl.

SIZE: Greatest breadth <6.3 mm.

ANIMAL: Blackish, with a rounded short foot. Penial gland short and rounded, the cup or opening extending the length of the gland, and there is no duct, as there is in *Menetus*. Male preputium large, pyriform, $2/3$ as wide as high; penis sheath longer than preputium, wide, and somewhat enlarged at the vas deferens end; penis very long, the spade-shaped head lodged in the upper part of the preputium and in the middle of the penis sheath. For figures of internal anatomy see Baker (1945).

TYPE LOCATION: Lake Champlain, New York.

FIG. 77. *Promenetus exacuous,* Newton Reservoir, UT Credit: E. Wagner.

JUNIOR SYNONYMS: *Planorbis exacuous* Say, 1821; *Planorbis exacutus* Haldeman, 1844; Binney, 1865a; *Paludina hyalina* Lea, 1839; *Menetus exacuous* (Say) Baker, 1928; Chamberlin and Jones, 1929. *Promenetus* genus established by Baker (1935).

NOTES: Distinguished from *P. parvus* and other small discoid planorbids by the acute periphery of the last whorl of the shell. Epiphytic feeder.

DISTRIBUTION (ANSP; Ibase; Chamberlin and Berry 1930): Alberta, British Columbia, Saskatchewan, Northwest Territories, Manitoba, Ontario, Quebec; CA, CO, CT, ID, IL, IN, IA, MA, MD, ME, MI, MN, MO, NC, ND, NV, NJ, NM, NY, OH, PA, RI, SD, TX, VT, WA, WI, WY. Utah records from Newton Reservoir and Meier's Pond, Cache County; Provo; Fish Lake, Sevier County; and Utah Lake (UMNH; UF; Chamberlin and Jones 1929; Baily and Baily 1951–1952). The author found it in Tony Grove Lake, Cache County.

Planorbula campestris Dawson, 1875 Meadow Ramshorn

FIG. 78. *Planorbula campestris.* Left: synonym *P. christyi* Dall, ANSP 217084, Teton Co., WY. Right: ANSP 152525, Manitoba, Canada. Credit: E. Wagner, courtesy ANSP.

DESCRIPTION: Dawson (1875, p. 349) originally categorized this species as a subspecies *Segmentina armigera* var. *campestris*: "This is a large fine variety characteristic of the prairie region, which I have distinguished by the above varietal name. The normal form, with the usual number of whorls (4) is abundant in the Lake of the Woods, and surrounding wooded region. Specimens seldom exceed 6.5 mm. The variety *campestris* occurs abundantly in some pools and coulees of the Red River Valley and prairie region westward. They are much larger, with more whorls, and only in young specimens show the teeth. Colour generally wax yellow or pale brown. Diameter of largest specimens from 10.5 mm to 12.5 mm, whorls often six, specimens to 7.5 mm often, but not invariably, show teeth; above this size no teeth were recognized." *Shell*: flattened, discoidal, sinestral. *Whorls*: rounded and without carinae; body whorl expanded near the aperture in the same plane or slightly lower than the penultimate whorl (but not sharply bent down as in *P. armigera*); spire flat or slightly concave centrally. Umbilicus: wide, deep, and funnel-shaped, showing all whorls. *Aperture*: ovate to subquadrate, at an angle of about 25° to the umbilical axis; lip thin (Clarke 1973). Adult shells lack denticles, but in juvenile shells there are up to 4 sets of denticles, each set with 5 tooth-like processes similar to those in

P. armigera, except that the small uppermost process seen in *P. armigera* is lacking in *P. campestris* (Clarke 1973).

SIZE: Typically about 7.5 mm, but up to 10.5–12.5 mm dia.; (Dawson 1875). Baker (1945; USNM #63393): SW/SL ratio = 3.09. Alberta shells were 5.7–11.7 mm dia., 0.34–0.44 mm SL, and 4.3–6.1 whorls (5.3 on average). Saskatchewan shells from two different populations ranged from 6.2–11.1 mm dia., 0.32–0.38 mm SL, and 5.5–6.2 whorls; the largest at a third site measured 12.3 mm dia., 4.6 mm high, with 6.3 whorls (Clarke 1973).

ANIMAL (Clarke 1973): Blackish, though paler on the long narrow tentacles and bottom of the foot. Radula formula (7.6 mm dia. specimen from Saskatchewan) was 23–1–23 (12 marginals with 4–7 cusps, 11 tricuspid laterals, and a bicuspid central tooth).

TYPE LOCATION: Pointe du Chéne, Dufferin, Trader's Road, and 500 Mile Lake, Manitoba.

JUNIOR SYNONYMS (Clarke 1973): *Segmentina armigera* var. *campestris* Dawson, 1875; *Segmentina (Planorbula) christyi* Dall, 1905.

NOTES: Smaller size and proportionally not as tall as other *Planorbella* or *Planorbula* species, and with more whorls.

DISTRIBUTION (Clarke 1973; ANSP; Ibase): In Canada from British Columbia east to Manitoba. *P. campestris* records in the United States: CA, ND, NE, MI, MN, MT, SD, and WY. Burch (1989) notes that the distribution is from Canada and North Dakota, south to New Mexico in the Rocky Mountains. No museum records for Utah.

Planorbella binneyi Tryon, 1867 Coarse Ramshorn

DESCRIPTION (Haldeman 1844, for *P. corpulentus*): *Shell:* large, composed of 4–5 strap-shaped, compact whorls, having a considerable transverse diameter (carina to carina), which much exceeds the diameter of the aperture, taken at right angles to the axis; the lines of growth are distant, elevated, and conspicuous, giving the surface a rough appearance. The right side is widely and deeply umbilicate and has a tendency to obtuse carination; the left side is carinated and presents a wide and rather deep cup. *Aperture:* angled very little from the shell axis; margins extend considerably to the right and left beyond the penultimate whorl; lip expanded.

P. binneyi ursolacustre Baily and Baily, 1952, from Bear Lake, UT-ID (Fig. 79) is not as tall as typical *binneyi*, but taller than *P. subcrenatum*. The umbilicus is deep and vortex-like, showing 2–3 whorls that are more rounded than for typical *binneyi*. The spire is shallow, with a prominent angulation on the periphery of the whorls,

FIG. 79. *Planorbella binneyi ursolacustre*, holotype, ANSP 187690, Bear Lake, UT-ID. Credit: ANSP.

though the body whorl tends to be rounded near the aperture, which is wider in proportion to its length than that of *P. binneyi* s.s. The surface is sculptured with coarse striae, generally well spaced, but sometimes locally crowded, especially near the aperture.

SIZE: To 20–30 mm dia. Holotype: 21.4 mm dia. × 10.5 mm tall.

TYPE LOCATION: Washington and Oregon.

JUNIOR SYNONYMS: *Planorbis binneyi* Tryon, 1867, 1870; *Planorbis corpulentus* Haldeman, 1844; *Helisoma trivolvis binneyi* "Tryon" Chamberlin and Jones 1929; *Planorbella binneyi randolphi* Baker, 1945; *Helisoma binneyi ursolacustre* Baily and Baily, 1952

NOTES: The distinguishing characteristics of this species, according to Haldeman (1844; describing *P. corpulentus*), are the width and flatness of the whorls.

DISTRIBUTION (Chamberlin and Jones 1929; Baily and Baily 1951–1952; ANSP): Ontario; CA, ID, IA, MN, MT, NY, OR, WA. Utah records from Bear Lake, mouth of the Bear River, Cache County, Salt Lake County, Utah Lake, Junction, and North Fork Provo Canyon (Salamander Lake).

Planorbella oregonensis Tryon, 1870 Lamb Ramshorn

DESCRIPTION (Tryon 1870): *Shell*: similar to *P. trivolvis*, but the whorls increase more rapidly in volume; thin, dark horn color. Striae not very close, coarse, and irregular. *Aperture*: oblique, ear-shaped, large, extending above and below the plane of the whorls.

SIZE: Holotype was 9 mm dia., height 4 mm.

ANIMAL (Baker 1945): GENITALIA: seminal vesicle ~1 mm long, ovisperm duct ~3 mm long, with short lateral vesicles for much of its length. Prostate ~2 mm long, with 16 rows of long, narrow diverticula. Spermatheca bulbous, 0.7 mm long, connecting to the long, narrow vagina with a duct just over 1 mm long. Penial complex with a pyriform preputium, penis sac ~1/2 of preputium length and swollen at the end. One retractor muscle (sometimes split in two) attached to lower preputium and one band of supporting muscle. Penial gland duct ~5 mm. Penial gland round, short, attached to preputium wall by a short, wide neck.

FIG. 80. *Planorbella oregonensis*. Left: lectotype ANSP 21339, Pueblo Valley, OR. Right: ANSP 7835, paralectotype, Oregon. Credit: left: ANSP. Right: E. Wagner, courtesy ANSP.

TYPE LOCATION: Pueblo Valley, near the boundary between Oregon and Nevada, 60 miles west of the east boundary of Oregon.

JUNIOR SYNONYMS: *Planorbis oregonensis* Tryon, 1870; *Helisoma oregonense* Baker 1945.

NOTES: *P. oregonensis* is a smaller ramshorn than *binneyi, subcrenata,* or *trivolvis*. Similar to *P. campestris* in general size and number of whorls but relatively taller. The holotype was found associated with a hot spring.

DISTRIBUTION (ANSP): ID, NV, OR. The only Utah record is from Tooele County (Salt Springs).

Planorbella subcrenata Carpenter, 1857 Rough Ramshorn

DESCRIPTION (Binney 1865a): *Shell:* tumid, very thin, horn colored. *Whorls*: 6, rounded, sutures impressed; with sharp radiating, somewhat crowded, and occasionally minutely crenulated, ridges. *Aperture:* rounded, parietal wall small, scarcely touching the penultimate whorl; lip scarcely deflected, brownish within, umbilicus deep.

SIZE (Carpenter 1857; Clarke 1973): Type was 24 mm dia., 9.1 mm tall. Can grow to 32 mm dia., 10 mm high. Canadian population data: Banff, Alberta, 16.8–24.8 mm dia. × 6.8–10.3 mm high, H/D 0.376–0.498, 11–20 riblets/5 mm; Saskatchewan, 13.5–21.1 dia, 6.1–9.1 mm high, H/D 0.369–0.498, riblets/5 mm 14–23; Manitoba, 17.1–23.4 mm dia, 6.7–9.7 mm high, H/D 0.375–0.480, riblets/5 mm 13–20.

ANIMAL (Baker 1945; Clarke 1973): GENITALIA: Seminal vesicle 2 mm long and wider than ovisperm duct, notable for its long vesicles bordering the gland; sperm duct short (2 mm), vas deferens narrow, about 7 mm long. Prostate 2 mm long with 24 rows of diverticula, arranged fan-wise when seen in cross section. Uterus about 1 mm wide, narrowed anteriorly. Penial complex 3.5 mm in adults, cylindrical penis sac slightly shorter than preputium; penial gland duct is 3–4 mm, normally coiled on the preputium.

RADULA: 29–1–29 (20.1 mm dia. shell) to 30–1–30 (21.6 mm dia.); central tooth bicuspid, 12–13 laterals with 3–4 cusps, and 16–17 marginals with 4–5 cusps.

TYPE LOCATION: Oregon

JUNIOR SYNONYMS: *Planorbis subcrenatus* Carpenter, 1857; *Helisoma subcrenatum* (Carpenter) Baker, 1945. Bequaert and Miller (1973) considered *P. binneyi* to be a junior synonym, but Baker (1945) recognized *binneyi* as a valid species.

FIG. 81. *Planorbella subcrenata*, ANSP 189016. Credit: E. Wagner, courtesy of ANSP.

NOTES: Differs from *P. trivolvis* in the acuteness of the ribs and their being more distant (Carpenter 1857; Binney 1865a). Clarke (1973) considered *subcrenata* to be a subspecies of *trivolvis*, differentiated by its shorter height (<10 mm, typically; >10–12 mm for *trivolvis*), more loosely coiled whorls, and deeper sutures. Also, there are more whorls in *P. subcrenata*. Rarely, some *subcrenata* also exhibit spiral pale colored streaks or irregular coiling (Clarke 1973). The genitalia of *subcrenata* differs from *trivolvis* in the greater number of prostate diverticula, shorter penial gland duct (adult), and the digitate vesicles in the seminal vesicle.

Clarke (1973) noted that *P. subcrenata* was found in a variety of habitats from lakes large and small to ponds, creek backwaters, and swamps, invariably where aquatic vegetation was present.

DISTRIBUTION (ANSP; Brooks 1936; Baker 1945; Baily and Baily 1951–1952; Russell 1971): Western Canada; United States: AK, CA, ID, CO, WA, WY. In Utah: Jordan River, Newton Reservoir, Bear Lake, Utah Lake, Fish Springs National Wildlife Refuge, Locomotive Springs, and "small pond in the Uinta Mts. along the Vernal-Manila road" (Brooks 1936, p. 14).

Planorbella trivolvis Say, 1818 Marsh Ramshorn

DESCRIPTION (Nicholson 1818; Say 1819; Haldeman 1844; Baker 1928): *Shell*: discoidal, sinestral, flattened laterally, spire concave and nearly level with last whorl, nucleus of about ½ turn, subcarinate above and beneath, particularly in young shells; Rufous to yellowish brown or chestnut. *Whorls*: 3–4, subcylindrical, with finely striated growth lines with grooves between them; lines of growth begin abruptly; sutures deep and V-shaped. Umbilicus: narrow, deep, funnel-shaped, large, with 2–3 rounded whorls visible with deep sutures between them. *Aperture*: broadly lunate, somewhat expanded below and with a V-shaped angle above; large, embracing a large portion of the body whorl, within bluish-white, vaulted anteriorly and slightly thickened within the margin, lip thin and rounded outward, often a little thickened on the inside and bordered within by a wide chocolate or yellowish band; both sides of aperture projecting beyond the planes of the shell.

SIZE: SL 6.3 mm, dia. 12.7 mm. In Baker (1928, n = 9), shell diameter ranged from 10.4 to 32 mm, SL 6.2–19.5 mm, dia./height ratio 1.64–2.27, ApL 6.0–14.5 mm, ApW 3.0–10.5 mm, ApW/ApL 0.33–0.75

ANIMAL (Baker 1945): Aquatic, dark ferruginous, with very numerous, confluent, pale yellowish points; tentacles long, setaceous, with confluent points; foramen on the left side.

GENITALIA: Long seminal vesicle (3.5 mm × 0.5 mm wide). Narrow sperm duct ~4 mm long. Prostate ~4.5 mm × 1 mm, fan-shaped in cross section, with 14 rows of diverticula emptying into a short prostate duct which connects to the sperm duct, which in turn connects to a long vas deferens (15 mm). There is a slight enlargement of the vas deferens (epiphallus) as it enters the penis sac. Penial complex ~5 mm long; preputium wide (1.5 mm) and cylindrical, narrowing where it connects with the penis sac. Penis sac is very narrow, about the same length as preputium. Penis sac doubles its diameter near the end where the vas deferens enters. Single wide retractor muscle, which may be split into branches; additional band of supporting muscle. Penial gland duct narrow, 8–9 mm long, normally coiled over preputium.

TYPE LOCATION: French Creek, near Lake Erie (*trivolvis*); for synonyms, Delaware River (*fluviatilis* Say); Cohoes Falls, New York (*planorbula* DeKay); near Lake

FIG. 82. *Planorbella trivolvis*. Above and below: Haldeman's types, ANSP. Credit: E. Wagner, courtesy ANSP. Center: Box Elder Co., UT. Credit: E. Wagner.

Ontario (*megastoma*); ponds near Mile-end-Gate, Montreal, Canada (*macrostomus*); United States (*regularis*) (Baker 1928).

JUNIOR SYNONYMS (Baker 1928): *Planorbis trivolvis* Say, 1818; *Bulla fluviatilis* Say, 1821; *Planorbis corpulentus* Say, 1824; *Physa planorbula* DeKay, 1843; *Planorbis regularis* Lea, 1841; *Planorbis megastoma* DeKay, 1843; *Planorbis macrostomus* Whiteaves, 1863; *Helisoma trivolvis* Baker, 1928; *Helisoma plexata* Ingersoll, 1876; *Helisoma trivolvis plexatus* (Ingersoll) Chamberlin and Jones, 1929; *Planorbis horni* Tryon, 1865a; *Helisoma trivolvis horni* (Tryon) Chamberlin and Jones, 1929.

NOTES: Recognized by its large size, flat spire, and expanded aperture. Older individuals that have made it a year longer than usual will often form a hump in the body whorl where new growth begins as temperatures warm up. Baker (1928) noted variation in form based on habitat; lake forms were smaller and more compact. In general, *P. trivolvis* prefers still waters and aquatic vegetation. Reproduction is achieved by either self- or cross-fertilization. Egg masses contain about 1–54 eggs; the number of egg masses was not related to body size, but the number of eggs/mass was positively correlated with size (Norton and Bronson 2006).

DISTRIBUTION (ANSP; Chamberlin and Jones 1929; Chamberlin and Berry 1930; Roscoe 1964): Widely distributed within the United States and Canada. Also reported from Mexico. Utah records: Fish Lake, Richfield, Glenwood, Junction (old pond south of town); Kolob Mountains, LaVerkin Breaks (Washington County); Kaibab Forest near Arizona state line; Sevier River, Fillmore Lake, Panguitch Lake, Seven Mile Canyon (Fremont River drainage), Provo Canyon, Salamander Lake, Pleasant Grove, near Salt Lake, Utah Lake, Cache County, Bear River, Bear Lake, and Deweyville; Smithsonian Institute records from the Sevier Desert and near Salt Spring Creek. Recent surveys by the author have found *trivolvis* living in several counties: Box Elder, Cache, Rich, Grand, and Uinta.

Ferrissia rivularis Say, 1817 Creeping Limpet

FIG. 83. *Ferrissia rivularis*. ANSP 21982. Credit: ANSP.

DESCRIPTION (Say 1819; Baker 1928): *Shell:* conic, not spiral, corneous, opaque, conic-depressed, apex obtuse and simple, nearer to, and leaning toward one side and one end; aperture oval, rather narrow at one end, entire; within milk-white, concave. Anterior slope convex, posterior slope concave below the apex, straightening toward the shell edge, which is usually quite flat. Apex is located about a third of the distance from the posterior end and radially striate; growth lines irregular, well marked.

SIZE: to 6.3 mm long.

TYPE LOCATION: Delaware and Susquehanna rivers, Pennsylvania.

JUNIOR SYNONYMS (Walther et al. 2010): *Ancylus rivularis* Say, 1819; *Ancylus parallela* Haldemann, 1841

FIG. 84. *Ferrissia rivularis*. Gandy Warm Springs, UT. Credit: E. Wagner.

NOTES: *F. rivularis* is the only limpet known to be in Utah, and so it is easily identified by its unique shape. Uncommon in Utah. Typically found adhering to stones in rivulets (Say 1817). Originally allocated to its own family (Ancylidae); anatomical and genetic studies led to its proper placement in Planorbidae (Hubendick 1978; Albrecht et al. 2007). Walther et al. (2010) noted separate western and eastern U.S. genetic clades of *F. rivularis*. A similar looking species, *Acroloxus coloradensis* Walker, 1925, may possibly be in the mountains of Utah based on its presence in Colorado; it is distinguished by having a more acute rosethorn-like apex than for *F. rivularis* (Clarke 1973; Paul and Clifford 1991; Ecosearch 1993).

DISTRIBUTION (ANSP; UMNH; Call 1884; Henderson and Daniels 1917; Jones 1935; Hovingh 2010): Mexico; Nova Scotia, Ontario; United States: AL, AZ, AR, CA, CO, DE, IL, IA, ME, MD, MI, MN, MO, MT, NV, NJ, NM, NY, NC, OH, OR, PA, SC, TN, TX, VT, VA, WA, WI, WY. Utah records: Salem Pond (Utah County; Monte Bean Museum, 1939 specimen), Utah Lake, San Juan and Weber River drainages. Russell (1971) reported finding *Ferrissia californica* Rowell, 1863, at Fish Springs National Wildlife Refuge but considered it might be synonymous with *F. rivularis*. Recently found living in Gandy Warm Springs Creek, Millard County (fig. 84).

SUBCLASS: **Heterobranchia**
SPF: **VALVATOIDEA Gray, 1840**

Valvatidae Gray, 1840

Valvatidae features operculate aquatic snails typically associated with aquatic vegetation. The dextral shells are small (4–8 mm dia.), turbinate or depressed, the aperture rounded, lip entire (Tryon 1870). The animal has an externally protruding bipectinate gill. There is also a tentacular appendage protruding from the mantle in addition to the two tentacles, which are elongated, with eyes at their

FIG. 85. *Valvata virens* Tryon, 1863 lectotype 12024, ANSP. Credit: ANSP.

outer bases. Foot is bilobed in front. Operculum multispiral, corneous. Hermaphroditic, with separate orifices for each gender; the male opening is the tip of the penis located on the head or neck, and the female opening is near the entrance into the mantle cavity (Burch 1989). Eggs are laid in strings (Rath 1988).

Worldwide, there are 8 genera in the family, including *Valvata* Müller 1773, which is the type genus of the family. *Valvata cristata* Müller, 1774, is the type species for that genus. There are 159 fossil and 37 Recent species of *Valvata* described worldwide (www.molluscabase.org), 10 of which are in North America (Johnson et al. 2013). Junior synonyms of *Valvata* include *Cincinna* (now a subgenus), *Aphanotylus* Brusina, 1894; *Costovalvata* Polinski, 1929 (also a subgenus); *Gyrorbis* Fitzinger, 1833; *Jelskia* Westerlund, 1886; *Ielskia* Bourguignat, 1877; *Heterovalvata* Munier-Chalmas, 1879; *Michaudia* Locard, 1883; and *Tropidina* Adams and Adams, 1854 (Dall 1905; www.molluscabase.org). The most recent summary of the family was by Hazprunar (2014) who catalogued the known fossil and Recent species without discussing any synonymy.

In Utah, there are two Recent species, *Valvata humeralis* Say, 1829 and *Valvata utahensis* Call, 1884. *Valvata virens* was reported (Roscoe 1964) from the Sevier Desert as a fossil that is in the USNM collection (111672); it was considered to be *V. humeralis*. Another shell (111678), originally labeled *Valvata sincera* Say, was later considered *V. virens*. Hannibal (1910) considered Call's Great Basin shells of *virens* to be *Valvata calli* Hannibal, 1910. *Valvata virens* (Fig. 85) was described from Clear Lake, California, by Tryon (1863) as turbiniform (5 × 5 mm), apex acute, of 4 rounded whorls with a periphery almost angulated; with a very wide umbilicus, oval to round aperture, and a closely striate surface; color bright to dark green. Yen (1947) described *V. incerta,* a low-spired Pliocene fossil from northwest Cache Valley, Utah.

Valvata humeralis Say, 1840 Glossy Valvata

DESCRIPTION (Say 1840, p. 22, for *V. humeralis*): "Shell subglobose, depressed; spire convex, not prominent; whorls 3.5, with the shoulder depressed, plane; wrinkled across, or rather with slightly raised lines; aperture appressed to the penultimate whorl, but not interrupted by it; umbilicus rather large. Differs from *V. sincera* Nob., of the Northwest Territories, in being more depressed and in having a shoulder or plane surface near the suture. The umbilicus is larger than that of *V. piscinalis* Mull., and the spire more depressed; that species is also destitute of the depressed shoulder." For the form described by Pilsbry (1908b), *V. humeralis*

FIG. 86. *Valvata humeralis.* ANSP 58064: Holotype, Mexico. ANSP 12023: Lectotype, *Valvata humeralis californica*, Big Bear L., CA. Credit: ANSP.

californica Pilsbry, 1908b, the spire is shorter than *V. humeralis s.s.* and the last whorl descends less. Also, whorls are rounded, not flattened or carinate.

SIZE: Greatest dia. less than 5 mm.

TYPE LOCATION: *V. humeralis s.s.*: Mexico; *V. humeralis californica*: Bear Lake, San Bernardino Mountains., California.

JUNIOR SYNONYMS: *Valvata californica* (Pilsbry) Hovingh, 2004

NOTES: *V. humeralis* differs from *V. utahensis* by its shorter spire, lacking the sharp ridge, and having a plane or shouldered surface near the suture. Regarding the latter character, as Hovingh (2004) noted, western U.S. shells are morphologically like *Valvata humeralis californica* Pilsbry, 1908b, that is, lacking the flattened shoulder of *humeralis s.s.*, but with round whorls and a shorter spire (Fig. 86, bottom row). Hovingh (2004) suggested that shells attributed to *V. humeralis* in Colorado and the western United States should be considered *Valvata californica*

FIG. 87. Valvata humeralis (left ANSP 61444) and V. humeralis var. patzcuarensis (ANSP 77192) from Lake Patzcuaro, Mexico, showing variation in spire height, size, and roundness of whorls. Credit: ANSP.

(Pilsbry, 1908b) *nov. comb*. This classification was based on differences in the shell morphology of western shells compared to the holotype (Fig. 86, upper row). However, images of shells from Lake Patzcuaro, Mexico (*Valvata humeralis* var. *patzcuarensis* Pilsbry, 1899c; Fig. 87), demonstrate considerable variation there too.

Hannibal (1910) suggested that *V. humeralis* probably replaced *V. sincera* and *V. lewisi* west of the Rocky Mountains. Referring to western *V. humeralis*, Taylor (1981, p. 147) notes "Northern and eastern limits of range uncertain; possibly synonymous with some species named from eastern North America." Museum specimens of *V. sincera* exist from British Columbia to Newfoundland, from Alaska to Maine south to Utah, Wyoming, and the Rio Grande drainage of Colorado (invertebase.org). *V. lewisi*, which differs from *sincera* in radula structure (Baker 1930), is also found in Canada from Quebec to British Columbia, from Alaska to Maine south to California, New Jersey, and South Dakota. Comparison of *V. sincera* shells from eastern locations (Fig. 88), shows that some are higher spired, but others are very similar in shell morphology to *V. humeralis*, suggesting they may be synonymous.

Herein, the Utah shells are considered to be *V. humeralis*. Further work is needed, comparing animal and shell morphology among putative U.S. *Valvata* species.

FIG. 88. *Valvata sincera*, showing variation among and within locations. UMMZ collection, Great Slave Lake, Canada (249322, 17336), Rio Grande R., CO (98034), Ithaca, NY (97970), Mill Cr., MO (197779) Lake Simco, Ontario, Canada (98040), Tinkeris Cr. OH (98035), Lake Maxinkuckee IN (97974). Credit: UMMZ.

DISTRIBUTION (ANSP; UMNH; UMMZ; Call 1884; Hannibal 1910; Chamberlin and Jones 1929; Chamberlin and Berry 1930; Woolstenhulme 1942a, b; Baily & Bailey 1951–1952; author's collection): Mexico; AZ, NM, NV, CA, ID, WA. Utah records: Bear Lake, Tony Grove Lake, Utah Lake, Salt Lake City, Spring Lake, Salem, Strawberry River, Emory, Fish Lake, Navajo Lake (Kane County); Sanpete, Rich, and Millard counties. Richards (2016) found both *V. humeralis* and *V. utahensis* shells in the Jordan River.

Valvata utahensis Call, 1884 Desert Valvata

DESCRIPTION (Call 1884): *Shell*: operculate, narrowly umbilicate, conical, with minute transverse striae, shining, somewhat pellucid, yellowish horn color at apex, white below; spire obtusely elevated, flattened at tip; suture well impressed. *Whorls*: four, convex, regularly increasing, the uppermost ones with a single well-marked carina, which becomes obsolete on the last whorl; the last whorl equals one-half the whole length of the shell. *Aperture*: circular, slightly angled posteriorly; peristome simple, continuous, joined to the next whorl above by a very slight calcareous deposit; within white. Operculum light horn color, corneus, spirally multivolute, slightly produced posteriorly to conform to the shape of the aperture.

SIZE: SL 4.8 mm, dia. 3.2 mm.

TYPE LOCATION: Utah Lake, Utah.

JUNIOR SYNONYMS: *Valvata sincera* var. *utahensis* Call 1884. Elevated to species status by Call (1886).

NOTES: *V. utahensis* is higher spired than *V. humeralis* and carinate. Baily and Baily (1952) described the subspecies *V. utahensis horatii* from Lifton, ID and Ideal Beach at Bear Lake (ANSP type 187689). The principal difference in this subspecies is that it is carinate both basally and above, rather than just above as in *V. utahensis* s.s. The intergradation in the bicarinate and unicarinate forms reported by Baily and Baily (1952) suggest that these two forms are simply within-population variation. Similarly, *Valvata sincera* (a smooth uncarinate species) has also been found in the same location as tricarinate forms (Lewis 1860; Goodrich

FIG. 89. *Valvata utahensis*. Holotype, ANSP 187689. Credit: ANSP.

1943); Lewis (1860) found that the *sincera* form was less common (0.1% of tricarinate form). The co-ocurrence of *V. utahensis* and *V. humeralis* in populations suggest that the two may be the same species (Hovingh 2004; E. Wagner, personal observation). However, genetic analyses by Miller et al. (2006a) indicated that there are distinct genetic differences between the two taxa. *Valvata utahensis* was listed in 1992 as a federally endangered species (USFWS 1992a).

DISTRIBUTION (ANSP; Ibase; Baily & Baily 1951–1952; Russell 1971): ID (Bear Lake and Snake River), CA (Kings County), Wyoming (Uinta County). Utah records: Fish Springs National Wildlife Refuge, Bear Lake, and Utah Lake. The author found old shells in Cache County and Fish Springs. Living *V. utahensis* are only known from the Snake River drainage (Hovingh 2004).

CLADE: **Caenogastropoda**
SPF: **VIVIPAROIDEA Gray, 1847**

Viviparidae Gray, 1847

This freshwater family contains about 150 species and 31 genera (Franke et al. 2007; Lu et al. 2014). Species in this family are ovoviviparous, producing live young. The shells are globose to globose-turbinate, imperforate to subimperforate, banded or unicolored, and with a corneous operculum. Respiration is with gills. There are four genera: *Lioplax* Troschel, *Campeloma* Rafinesque, *Tulotoma* Conrad, and *Cipangopaludina* Hannibal 1912 (=*Viviparus* Clench and Fuller, 1965, =*Bellamya* Smith, 2000a), varying in characteristics of the operculum and radula (Clench 1962). Within *Cipangopaludina* there are 11 species and 2 subspecies (Lu et al. 2014). In North America, there are three species: *C. georgianus* (native to eastern United States and Mississippi River drainage), *C. japonicus*, and *C. chinensis* (Clench 1962). See Lu et al. (2014) for a key to the species within the genus.

Cipangopaludina chinensis Gray in Griffith and Pidgeon, 1833
Chinese Mystery Snail

DESCRIPTION (Clarke 1981; Jokinen 1982; Burch 1989; Waltz 2008): *Shell*: large, smooth, globose, with a small round umbilicus; color is olive-green, greenish brown, brown or reddish brown, and lighter in juveniles. The periostracum of juveniles features rows of hooked "hairs" (2 apical and 3 body whorl rows), distinct ridges, and many other hairs with short hooks. *Whorls*: 6–7, convex. In juveniles the body whorl has a distinct carina, and shell grooves have about 20 striae/mm) between each groove. Umbilicus is small, round, covered in part by the reflected parietal lip. *Aperture*: ovoid, with a simple outer and inner lip; black pigmentation around the entire lip and somewhat within the aperture. Operculum with concentric markings.

SIZE: Typically about 40 mm tall × 30 mm wide but can reach 60–65 mm tall × 40 mm wide (W:H ratio of 0.74–0.82).

TYPE LOCATION: Not given, but presumably China based on specific name.

JUNIOR SYNONYMS (Lu et al. 2014): *Paludina chinensis* Gray in Griffith and Pidgeon 1834; *Viviparus malleatus*, *Idiopoma* (*Cipangopaludina*) *chinensis* Hannibal, 1912; *Lecythoconcha chinensis* Annandale, 1920; *Viviparus chinensis malleatus* Clench and Fuller, 1965; *Bellamya chinensis* (Gray in Griffith and Pidgeon 1833-1834) Smith 2000a; *Cipangopaludina wingatei*. *C. fluminalis* is now a subspecies of *C. chinensis*.

FIG. 90. *Cipangopaludina* (*Bellamya*) *chinensis*. Credits: left: original figure from Griffith and Pidgeon (1834). Right: E. Wagner, Goshen Warm Springs, UT, 2019.

The taxonomy of the genus has been revised many times (see Pace 1973 and Smith 2000a for a synopsis). Some authors recognize *Cipangopaludina* as the genus (originally presented as a subgenus of *Viviparus* by Hannibal 1912), whereas others have adopted the proposal by Smith (2000a) for placing both *japonicus* and *chinensis* within the genus *Bellamya*, which had been previously proposed by Rohrbach (1937). The most recent work by Lu et al. (2014) has recognized the validity of the genus *Cipangopaludina* based on shell characteristics. Genetic analysis is needed to sort out the taxonomy. For the present, the most recent update in this work is followed (Lu et al. 2014).

NOTES: This species is easily identified in Utah by its large size and lack of banding observed in *Cornu aspersum,* the brown garden snail. *Cipangopaludina chinensis* is an introduced species native to Eastern Asia that is considered invasive. In the United States, *C. japonicus* may also be found, though it is less common. It has a narrower, taller spire and carinae, but *chinensis* may have carinae in shells shorter than 35 mm; *C. japonicus* also has a branched vas deferens proximal to the testes, whereas in *chinensis* it is unbranched (Smith 2000a).

Its presence has been associated with decreases in macroinvertebrate densities (Behrens and Strayer 2007). It also is a host for intestinal flukes that affect humans and is a host for parasites that affect unionid mussels (Huchner and Etges 1977; Gangloff et al. 2008). The closely related snail *C. georgianus* was observed preying on largemouth bass eggs (Eckblad and Shealy 1972). *C. chinensis* can both filter feed and graze with its radula, feeding on algae, flagellates, and decaying organic matter. The preferred habitat is lentic freshwater, with sand or silt. The snails live up to 3–5 years and can produce at least 169 offspring per female during its lifetime; 102 embryos have been counted in a single female (Jokinen 1982). The operculum protects the snail from physical and chemical attack (Haak et al. 2014).

DISTRIBUTION (United States Geological Survey nonindigenous aquatic species database; accessed April 2019). AZ, CA, CO, CT, DE, FL, GA, HA, ID, IL, IN, IA, KS, KY, ME, MD, MA, MI, MN, MI, NE, NH, NJ, NY, NC, OH, OR, PA, RI, SC, TX, VT, VA, WA, WV, WI. In Utah, one record from Goshen Warm Springs in 1965 was confirmed in a 2019 survey, where the species was found live in abundance. Russell (1971) noted that it was in Fish Springs National Wildlife Refuge.

CLADE: **Sorbeoconcha**
SPF: **CERITHIOIDEA Fleming, 1822**

Thiaridae Gill, 1871

The freshwater snails of Thiaridae are operculate, with some species viviparous, others ovoviviparous (Animal Base 2019). Shells are conical with elongate apertures and often with ornamentation. The superfamily is characterized by the structure of the euspermatozoa, radula, a complex stomach with a style sac and gastric shield, open pallial gonoducts, aphallate males, and characters of the nervous system (Ihering 1909; Houbrick 1988). The family is composed of the following genera: *Melanoides* Olivier, 1804; (type species *M. fasciolata* Olivier, now *M. tuberculata*), *Aylacostoma* Spix, 1827 (Spix and Wagner 1827); *Esperiana* Bourguignat, 1877; *Holandriana* Bourguignat, 1884; *Melanopsis* Ferussac, 1807; *Microcolpia* Bourguignat, 1884; *Pachymelania* Smith, 1893; and *Thiara* Röding, 1798 (AnimalBase 2019). Haploid chromosome numbers in the family range from 16 to 60 (Houbrick 1988). In Utah, only one species is known to be present, the invasive snail *Melanoides tuberculata*.

Melanoides tuberculata Müller, 1774 Red-rimmed Melania

DESCRIPTION (Morrison 1954; Welter-Schultes 2012): *Shell*: large, narrow, conic, reddish-brown, with rusty streaks and spots; typically with distinctive radial ribbing. Spire is usually twice the length of the aperture or more. *Whorls*: 10–14, slightly convex. *Aperture*: oval, elongate. Operculum is paucispiral with the nucleus near the base.

SIZE: up to 30–40 mm long.

ANIMAL: Testes of males are reddish, noticeable through shells as a dark area in upper whorls. Female gonads are cream, orange, or yellow. There are no size differences between sexes, but male shells are narrower.

TYPE LOCATION: India

JUNIOR SYNONYMS (Bouchet and Rocroi 2005; AnimalBase 2019): *Nerita tuberculata* Muller, 1774; *Melanoides fasciolata* Olivier, 1804. Junior synonyms of the family include Melanidae Children, 1823; Semisinusinae Fischer and Crosse, 1891; Melanoididae Ihering, 1909; Pyrguliferidae Delpey, 1941; Aylacostomatinae Parodiz, 1969; and Pachymelaniidae Bandel and Kowalke, 1999. *Melania*, originally a genus established by Lamarck in 1799, was later elevated to the family level (Melanidae). However, *Melania* was later determined to be a junior synonym of *Thiara* Röding, 1798 (type genus of the family), so the family is now Thiaridae.

FIG. 91. *Melanoides tuberculata*. Credit: E. Wagner.

NOTES: Introduced species that is invasive in warmer climes. Limited to warm springs in Utah. Temperature tolerances (Mitchell and Brandt 2003): killed by exposure to 5°C for 1 day, 9°C for 2 days, 11°C for 8 days, and 13°C for 12 days; at 17°C and 32.5°C, about 10% of the snails died within 27 days. The snail is the intermediate host for the trematode parasite *Centrocestus formosanus* (liver fluke), which is a significant and potentially lethal parasite of fish, amphibians, and mammals (Chen 1942; Mitchell and Brandt 2003). The snail may also have significant impacts on native snail populations, as noted by H. Murray in Taylor (1970) for the Texas snail *Goniobasis comalensis*, which became extinct after *M. tuberculata* infestation. Ladd and Rogowski (2012) noted that *M. tuberculata* ate eggs of *Physella* spp. Reproduction is parthenogenetic or sexual. It is an ovoviviparous brooder, holding eggs until they hatch (Welter-Schultes 2012). At release, newborns are about 2 mm long. The snails tend to graze by night and stay burrowed by day (Morgan and Last 1982). They mature in about 100 days to 6 months. They can tolerate salinities as high as 17.9 ppt (Roessler et al. 1977).

DISTRIBUTION: Native to northern Africa and southeastern Asia. Known in the United States in Arizona prior to the mid-1950s (Dundee 1974); now in other states at sites where temperatures are suitable for their survival. Distribution in Utah is limited by its thermal requirements, so it is restricted to warm springs (Rader et al. 2003). Found in Utah's Fish Springs National Wildlife Refuge, Gandy Warm Springs, Blue Lake (Tooele County), Goshen Warm Springs, and the Boiler (Washington County), Utah.

The Terrestrial Snails

CLASS: **Gastropoda**
CLADE: **Geophila**
ORDER: **Stylommatophora**
SPF: **ACHATINOIDEA Swainson, 1840**

Achatinidae Swainson, 1840

Achatinidae are native to Africa. The family has about 12 subfamilies, 99 genera, and nearly 200 species (Raut and Barker 2002; marinespecies.org). Frequently, they are agricultural pests in tropical agriculture and are considered invasive species in Utah. Achatinidae synonyms include Ampullidae and Urceidae (Bouchet and Rocroi 2005). Swainson (1840) characterized the Achatinids as "shell spiral, aperture oblong or oval, always equal, and generally shorter than the spire." They are hermaphroditic and oviparous or ovoviviparous. One species in the genus *Rumina* has been introduced into Utah.

Rumina decollata Linnaeus, 1758 Decollate Snail

DESCRIPTION (Welter-Schultes 2012): *Shell*: Narrowly conic, decollate (spire broken off); in living specimens, brownish, shiny, with white lip; empty shells white. *Whorls:* hatched juveniles have 3 whorls initially, adding 6 more after 2 weeks, 9–10 whorls after 6 weeks. Decollation of the first whorls begins in the second month. These whorls are broken off by deliberate truncation, with the apical opening covered by a calcareous septum. Additional whorls are lost over time in 5 decollations (total loss of 8 whorls). *Aperture:* ovate, narrowed above.

SIZE (Welter-Schultes 2012): SL 25–40 mm, SW 10–14 mm.

ANIMAL (Dundee 1986; Welter-Schultes 2012): relatively short, whitish with dark pigments on the body except in the grooves, upper tentacles long, gray, and slightly transparent, lower tentacles very short. Jaw is arc shaped with coarse transverse ribbing. The radular teeth have little variation among central, lateral, and marginal teeth. For images of these and additional data on the internal anatomy, see Dundee (1986).

FIG. T1. *Rumina decollata*. ANSP 347037. Credit: ANSP.

TYPE LOCATION: Italy and India (Müller 1774).

JUNIOR SYNONYMS: *Helix decollata* L. 1758.

NOTES (Dundee 1986; Welter-Shultes 2012): Distinctive large narrowly conic shell with a broken spire separates this shell from others in Utah. It lacks the ribbed ornamentation of *Melanoides tuberculata* and is terrestrial, not aquatic. Between May and October, an average of 32 (7–64) eggs/snail/deposition period are laid in the soil over a period of several days; adult animals estivate in the soil or under rocks for 1–3 months, covering their eggs. Egg deposition may occur multiple times over a spawning season; in the U.S. Southeast, this occurs from February to June, followed by a nonreproductive period; Spawning resumes from September to November. Eggs hatch in about 10 days at 21–27°C. Adults begin mating in the first active days in spring, though previous-year offspring mate after their last decollation in June. Decollation is performed by creating tiny holes from the inside at a particular ring line, and then the animal withdraws from the section to be jettisoned and builds a new tap; the upper whorls are lost eventually in natural movements or by the snail banging against a hard object (Cooke 1895).

The Decollate Snail is found in dry and open habitats, between plants and under stones, or in the soil. In North Africa it is found in cultivated areas, grasslands, and semideserts up to 5–10 km from the coast. Foraging is mostly nocturnal, feeding on other snails, but also feeding on vegetation.

DISTRIBUTION (Welter-Shultes 2012; ANSP records; Ibase): North Africa, Southern Europe, Bermuda, Cape Verde Islands, Brazil, Uruguay, and Cuba. It was introduced into the United States: CA, AL, AZ, FL, GA, PA, NC, SC, MI, LA, NM, NV, TX, VA. In Utah, it has been found in Washington County (Wheeler 2018).

SPF: HELICOIDEA Rafinesque, 1815

Helicidae Rafinesque, 1815

Nicholson (1818) describes the genus *Helix* as "shell subglobose, suborbicular, broader than long, spire convex; aperture wider than long, diminishing above by the convexity of the penultimate whorl." From Pilsbry (1939), "large and medium sized shells, umbilicate or closed, varying in shape from globose to lens-shaped or rarely cylindric; one-colored or with 1–5 bands; peristome from simple to reflected. Genitalia: The penis contains a papilla or a short verge, is provided with a retractor muscle, continued in the epiphallus and usually with a flagellum. On the vagina there is one dart sac containing a 2- or 4-bladed dart; in the crotch between vagina and dart sac are inserted 2 mucous glands, which are tubular, varying from simple to many-branched. Spermathecal duct long, usually with a branch (the diverticulum), the spermatheca round or oval, lodged near base of the kidney, being caught over an artery. Jaw ribbed or rarely smooth." In Helicidae worldwide, there are currently 315 Recent and 46 fossil species among 57 Recent and 9 fossil genera recognized within subfamilies Arantinae, Helicinae, and Murellinae (Mbase). One introduced species is found in Utah.

Cornu aspersum Müller, 1774 Brown Garden Snail

DESCRIPTION: *Shell*: globose, thin, large, *Whorls:* ~4.5, with brown bands, increasing rapidly in size, descending in each and last whorl. *Aperture:* roundly ovate; imperforate (no umbilicus). The brown bands are broken by regular narrow yellowish streaks.

SIZE: to about 38 mm wide × 33 mm tall.

TYPE LOCATION: Italy

JUNIOR SYNONYMS: *Helix mazzulopsis*; *Helix aspera* Müller, 1774. The genus *Cornu* was named by Ignatii Born in 1778 for the snail he named *Cornu copiae*. Some European and Russian malacologists consider *Cantareus aspersus* or *Cryptomphalus aspersus* Charpentier, 1837, to be the appropriate name. Guisti et al. (1996) argued that the anatomical similarities between the brown garden snail and the singing snail *Cantareus apertus* (Born 1778) warranted that both belonged to the same genus, *Cantareus* Risso, 1826. Also, since the *Cornu copiae* shell was a deformed variant of *H. aspersa*, *Cantareus* should be the genus. See Welter-Schultes et al. (2013) and Cowie (2011) for more detail on the issue.

NOTES: Large globose shell with banding distinguishes this shell from other Utah species. It was introduced from Europe and is considered an invasive species and agricultural pest.

DISTRIBUTION: Widespread in the United States. Its date of introduction into Utah is unknown, but Hanna's record (1966) indicates that the species has been in Utah since at least 1966. Known to be in the Wasatch Front and St. George area of Utah.

FIG. T2. *Cornu aspersum*. Left: old shell. Right: with animal. Credit: E. Wagner.

Polygyridae Pilsbry, 1895

Polygyridae features shells that vary from discoidal or lens-shaped to globose-conic; color typically is yellow to brown, without color markings. A few species have a dark band above the periphery. The aperture has a continuous peristome; lip reflected (flared), the ends connected by either a raised parietal fold or by the diverging branches of a V-shaped parietal tooth. The penis lacks papillae. Spermathecal duct is short and slender. Genitalia lack the dart apparatus, the penis is simple or continued into an epiphallus, with a very short flagellum or none. The talon (seminal vesicle) is tuberculose. Spermathecal duct is unbranched, its length short to medium. The jaw is ribbed. Central and lateral radular teeth with ectocones (except in some species of *Mesodon*). Kidney narrow, ~2–3X the length of pericardium (Pilsbry 1940).

Widespread in North America from Canada to Mexico. There are currently 24 genera in the family, including *Ashmunella* (found in the southwestern United States), *Polygyra* (widely distributed), and *Allogona*, *Cryptomastix*, and *Vespericola*, endemic to the Pacific Northwest. Polygyridae has 281 Recent and 8 fossil species recognized worldwide (Mbase). Genus *Polygyra* has 3 fossil and 8 Recent species, one of which is found in Utah.

Polygyra cereolus
Muhlfeld, 1818, Southern Flatcoil Snail

DESCRIPTION (Pilsbry 1940): *Shell*: discoidal, apex varies from flat to slightly convex, umbilicate (vortex shape), white with radial streaks of gray or wood- to fawn-brown, delicately obliquely ribbed. *Whorls*: 7.5–9, first whorl prominent, body whorl slightly swollen at the aperture, keeled at its upper edge, the periphery strongly angular to subcarinate, weakening at the aperture; in the first half of the last

FIG. T3. *Polygyra cereolus*. Left: shell with animal, LA. Credit: iNaturalist.org. Right: St. George, UT. Credit: K. Wheeler.

whorl there is a narrow white lamina on the parietal wall. *Aperture:* bordered, one tooth present where inner lip is reflected and attached to ventral surface. Tooth absent in immature shells; peristome reflected and thickened within.

SIZE: 7.4–18.2 mm dia. × 3.6–4.6 mm height; H/D ratio 24.7–31.7%.

ANIMAL: As for family.

TYPE LOCATION: Key West, Florida.

JUNIOR SYNONYMS (Mbase): *Helix cereolus* Muhlfeld, 1818; *Helix carpenteriana* Bland, 1862; *Polygyra carpenteriana* Binney, 1878; *Helix cereolus* var. *laminifera* Binney, 1858b (*nomen nudum*); *Helix microdonta* (Deshayes) Binney, 1859; *Helix febigeri* Bland, 1866; *Helix volvoxis* Pfeiffer, 1846; *Polygyra septemvolva* var. *floridana* (Hemphill) Binney, 1892.

NOTES: The large number of whorls and the large parietal tooth distinguish this shell from other Utah snails.

DISTRIBUTION: Caribbean, Egypt, Iraq, Saudi Arabia, Mexico; SE USA west to CA, HI. In Utah, reported in St. George.

Thysanophoridae Pilsbry, 1926c

Snails in Thysanophoridae are found in North American woodlands bearing shells that are small, discoidal, fragile, glossy, and openly umbilicate. The family is defined by the anatomy of the animal: wider kidney than in related genera, penis lacking an appendix; spermathecal duct shorter than oviduct; and the absence of both a diverticulum and a stimulatory organ (Pilsbry 1926c). Pilsbry (1926c) created the subfamily Thysanophorinae within Sagdidae Pilsbry, 1895. More recent genetic analyses have led to taxonomic changes noted by Bouchet et al. (2017). They list Thysanophoridae as a family within superfamily Helicoidea and Sagdidae within SPF Sagdoidea. There are currently 34 species recognized in 10 genera, including the type genus *Thysanophora* Strebel, 1873 (Mbase). *M. ingersolli* is the type species for the genus *Microphysula*. The genus is characterized by discoidal, clear, glossy, smooth, flat (or very low spired) shells with a narrow crescentic aperture (Pilsbry 1940). Only one species of the family is found in Utah.

Microphysula ingersolli Bland, 1875a Spruce Snail

DESCRIPTION (Bland 1875a): *Shell:* umbilicated, discoidal, thin, translucent, nearly smooth, white; spire flat to slightly convex, summit subimmersed; suture impressed. *Whorls:* 5.5–5.75, rather convex, slowly increasing, the last not

FIG. T4. *Microphysula ingersolli*, ANSP 97366. Credit: ANSP.

descending, more convex below the periphery; breadth of umbilicus nearly 1 mm. *Aperture:* subvertical, higher than broad, lunate; peristome simple, acute, margins remote, columellar margin slightly reflexed, basal margin subsinuate.

SIZE: Greater diameter 4–5 mm, height 2.5 mm.

ANIMAL (Pilsbry 1940; Burke 2013): Whitish; jaw low, wide, slightly arcuate, ends slightly attenuated; whole anterior surface with about 22, broad, flat, separated ribs, whose ends denticulate either margin. Teeth about 16–1–16.

TYPE LOCATION: Southwestern Colorado; Logan Canyon, Utah, for var. *convexior* Ancey, 1887b.

JUNIOR SYNONYMS: *Helix ingersolli* Bland, 1875a; *Thysanophora ingersolli* (Bland) Dall, 1898; *Microphysa ingersolli* var. *convexior* Ancey, 1887b; last change to *Microphysula ingersolli* (Bland) by Ingersol (1877).

NOTES (Pilsbry 1940): Similar to the glass snails of Oxychilidae and Gastrodontidae, but more widely umbilicate than *G. indentata*, *G. umbilicata*, *N. electrina*, and *Pristiloma subrupicola*. The lunate aperture, tilted right of the shell axis, is slightly narrower than for the other discoid shells. The variety *convexior* was described by Ancey (1887b) from Logan Canyon, Utah (shell slightly smaller, spire neither flat nor subimmersed, distinctly convex. Whorls usually 5, not 5.5, regularly increasing in size more slowly; smaller umbilicus). Another subspecies, *M. ingersolli merionlais* Pilsbry and Ferris, 1910, has a wider aperture, about 5 whorls that are more loosely coiled, and an umbilicus that is about a fourth of the shell diameter. It has been reported from the Blue Mountains near Monticello, Arizona, and New Mexico. Preferred habitat is subalpine meadows, spruce forests, and aspen groves (Forsyth 2004), but it is also found in mountain brush and pinyon-juniper habitats (Ports 1996).

DISTRIBUTION (ANSP; Ibase; Chamberlin and Berry 1930; Gregg 1940; Jones 1935, 1940a; Woolstenhulme 1942a, b; Pilsbry 1946; Wheeler 2018): AZ, NM,

CA, CO, ID, OH, OR, TX, WA, WY, MT, NV, OR. Utah records from Box Elder, Cache, Daggett, San Juan, and Uinta counties; Logan, Ogden, and Weber canyons; Mount Nebo; City Creek, Red Butte, Big Cottonwood, Emigration, and Mill Creek canyons; Oquirrh Mts; Kamas; Provo; Fish Lake; Seven Mile Canyon; Fillmore; Monroe Canyon; Beaver; Brian Head Peak area; Cedar Breaks Nat. Monument; Zion National Park; LaSal, Blue, and Henry Mountains, and North Creek Gulch west of Monticello.

SPF: **GASTRODONTOIDEA Tryon, 1866a**

Gastrodontidae Tryon, 1866a

Gastrodontids are small snails with translucent, discoidal shells. They are called glosses or dagger snails. The latter refers to a dart sac in males used for stimulating females. They have four tentacles; the lower ones are very short, and the longer, upper ones have eyes at the tip. Tryon (1866a, p. 242) described the gastrodontids as: "shell thin, translucent, *striate* or ribbed, generally *depressed conical*, frequently lamellately toothed."

The taxonomy of Stylommatophora and Gastrodontoidea has been revised many times (Tillier 1989; Beiler 1992; Hausdorf 1998; Bank et al. 2001, Saadi and Wade 2019). H. B. Baker (1928) and Pilsbry (1946) differentiated the subfamily Zonitinae from Gastrodontinae based on the lack of the dart apparatus in zonitids, and the spermathecal duct, which is not forked anteriorly. Currently, 38 fossil and 136 Recent species are recognized worldwide within 20 genera in Gastrodontidae (Mbase). In Utah there are representatives from three genera, *Glyphyalinia*, *Perpolita*, and *Zonitoides*. Glyphyalinia E. von Martens, 1892 currently has 24 recognized species.

Junior synonyms of the genus include *Glyphognomon* H.B. Baker, 1930a (Mbase). Discoid shells in the genus are about 3.5–13 mm in diameter, depressed, thin, subtransparent, clear to amber-colored, umbilicate or imperforate; spire very low with a smooth apical whorl; aperture lunate, the lip thin. The long, narrow foot has a tripartite sole. Penis has an epiphallus; radula central tooth tricuspid, laterals 3–5, bicuspid, marginals unicuspid (Pilsbry 1946). A capsular gland (function is to produce a capsule around the egg), externally visible around the oviduct or vagina, is present (absent in other members of the subfamily Godwiniinae; Hausdorf 1998).

Perpolita H. B. Baker, 1930b taxonomy has been intertwined with that of *Nesovitrea* Cooke, 1921, and *Retinella* Fischer, 1877, so the reader may encounter species like *P. electrina* shown as *Retinella electrina* or more recently as *Nesovitrea electrina* (Burke 2013, for example). The rationale for the use of *Perpolita* in this guide follows herein. Cooke (1921) created *Nesovitrea* as a new genus for some Hawaiian glass snails, with *Helix pusillus* Gould, 1846 as type (preoccupied, so later renamed *Helix pauxillus* by Gould in 1852; now accepted as *Nesovitrea pauxilla*). *Nesovitrea* features "vitrea-like snails, whorls about four, the first whorl smooth, the rest minutely but distinctly striate. Aperture simple, outer margin thin, sharp. Umbilicus rather shallow, perspective showing all the whorls" (Cooke 1921, p. 271). H. B. Baker (1928) established the subgenus *Perpolita* within *Retinella* P. Fischer, 1877, designating *Helix hammonis* Strom, 1765, as the type species. However, this was not the "real" *Helix hammonis*, but a misidentified *Helix electrina* Gould, 1841 (Baker 1930; deWinter et al. 2015). Hence the type of *Perpolita* is *Perpolita electrina*. In the classification by Bank et al. (2001), *Nesovitrea* is a genus within Oxychilidae; *Perpolita* is a sub-genus within *Nesovitrea*. Schileyko (2003) however, restricted *Nesovitrea*, as a genus, to H. B. Baker's (1930b) Hawaiian species. H. B. Baker (1941, p. 328) himself similarly noted that Hawaiian *Nesovitrea* are morphologically distinct from *Retinella* s.s. and *Glyphyalina* Martens, 1892. *Nesovitrea* currently includes just four species: *N. hawaiiensis, N. molokaiensis, N. pauxilla,* and *N. subhyalina* (Mbase). Shileyko (2003) used *Perpolita* as a genus, composed of holoarctic species. In the classification of Bank (2017) *Nesovitrea, Retinella, Glyphyalinia,* and *Perpolita* are transferred to Gastrodontidae as separate genera. As this is the most current classification, it is used herein.

Glyphyalinia species feature an ovoid spermatheca and a well-developed epiphallus, whereas *Perpolita* species are characterized as having a poorly developed epiphallus (not distinctly differentiated from vas deferens), a sausage-shaped spermatheca, and shell sculpture of nearly uniform growth wrinkles lacking more widely spaced deeper grooves (H. B. Baker 1930b; Pilsbry 1946). The outer marginal teeth in *Glyphyalinia* are serrate, whereas in *Perpolita* they are thorn-like (Pilsbry 1946). The type species of *Glyphyalinia* is *Helix indentata* Say, 1822.

Zonitoides Lehmann, 1862 features shells that are small (4–8 mm dia.), thin, depressed, umbilicate, lightly or distinctly striate above (rarely ribbed), with 3.5–4.5 whorls that are convex, regularly increasing, the last rounded (whorls are more tubular than in *Oxychilus* or *Retinella*). The aperture lip is thin, lacking an internal callus or teeth. (Pilsbry 1946). The foot is long, narrow, with distinct pedal grooves and a slit-like caudal pore. The sole is not tripartite, lacks muscular waves, and moves arrhythmically. The central radula is tricuspid and of similar size to the lateral teeth, which are bicuspid; marginals are thorn-shaped. Spermatheca is oval, on a long duct. *Zonitoides* species are found in temperate areas around the world (Pilsbry 1946). The type species of the genus is *Helix nitida* Müller, 1774.

Glyphyalinia indentata Say, 1822 Indented Leaf Snail

DESCRIPTION (Say 1822; Morse 1864; Burch and Jung 1988): *Shell:* depressed, pellucid, highly polished. *Whorls:* 4–4.75, well-rounded, with regular distant,

FIG. T5. *Glyphyalinia indentata*. Credit: iNaturalist.org (left, Ben Hutchins, right: no name given).

FIG. T6. *Glyphyalinia indentata*, live. Credit: iNaturalist.org.

FIG. T7. Jaw of *Glyphyalinia indentata*. Credit: Morse (1864).

subequidistant, impressed lines across, of which there are about 28 to the body whorl, all extending to the base; embryonic whorls smooth except for periodic indented radial lines; suture not deeply indented. *Aperture:* rather large, lunate, with a simple unexpanded lip, terminating at its inferior extremity at the center of the base of the shell; umbilicus deeply "indented" or perforate.

SIZE: Greatest dia. 5(4.5–6) mm; height 3 mm.

ANIMAL: Blue-black to white and pearl-gray, immaculate, tentacles dark blue and superior tentacles unusually long and thick compared to the size of the body. Mantle collar has large right and left neck lappets and small, but distinct, umbilical shell lobe. Buccal plate slightly arcuate (Fig. T7), partially raised in the middle of the cutting edge; longitudinally striate in the center of the plate. Tricuspid medial tooth with a long and broad central cusp and smaller pointed cusp on either side; 3 tricuspid laterals, long and narrow, slightly curved, having one long broad denticle and one smaller outer denticle; marginals 36, with one long recurved hook, gradually diminishing to minute plates (see Fig. T8). Spermathecal duct short.

TYPE LOCATION: Harrigate (country residence of J. Gilliams, near Philadelphia)

JUNIOR SYNONYMS: *Helix indentata* Say, 1822; *Polita indentata* (Say) Vanatta, 1921; *Hyalina indentata* (Say) Binney and Bland, 1869; *Zonites indentatus* (Say) Binney, 1885; *Vitrea indentata* (Say) Chamberlin and Jones, 1929; *Retinella indentata* Pilsbry, 1946. H. B. Baker (1928) moved the species to *Glyphyalinia,* which Burch and Jung (1988) also recognized.

FIG. T8. Radula of *Glyphyalinia indentata*. Credit: Morse 1864.

NOTES: Rimate (fissure-like crack) umbilicus differentiates *indentata* from similar glossy discoid shells except *Pristiloma subrupicola*, which has weaker radial lines and the animal is whiter. Smaller foot relative to shell size when compared to *G. electrina*. Found under loose bark, rotting logs, stones, and leaf debris (Burch and Jung 1988).

DISTRIBUTION: Eastern Canada south to Florida and Mexico, west to KS, MO, TX, AZ, and NM. Utah records from 5 miles east of Kamas (Jones 1935), near the head of Provo Canyon, and North Fork Spring Creek near Vernal (Jones 1935); additional Utah records (ANSP; Ibase) from Emigration Canyon, southeast of Tooele, and War God Spring (Navajo Mountains, Kane County), and Zion National Park.

Glyphyalinia umbilicata Morelet, 1849 Texas Glyph

DESCRIPTION (Morelet 1849–1851; Martens 1901; Pilsbry 1946): *Shell* umbilicate, convex-depressed, corneous, translucent, smooth, incised radial lines (as if cut into the surface of the shell) on both sides. *Whorls:* 4.5, flattened, the penultimate subdilated, unreflexed. *Aperture:* oblique, lunate-oval, simple margin, acute.

FIG. T9. *Glyphalinia umbilicata.* Credit: iNaturalist.org, Ben Schwartz (right), Sam Kieschnick (left).

SIZE (Pilsbry 1946): 5–6 mm dia., rarely 7.1 mm; height 2–2.3 mm, rarely 3.2 mm.

ANIMAL: Spermathecal stalk more swollen basally than typical *indentata*. Epiphallus lumen weakly T-shaped; base more attenuate. Penis apical, papillate chamber teat-shaped, almost half as long as the entire organ; basal chamber relatively stouter than *indentata*.

RADULA formula 18–18–4–1–4–36; marginal teeth with very small serrations on inner border. Jaw crescentic with 3–5 vague plaits in the center.

TYPE LOCATION: near Salama, Guatemala.

JUNIOR SYNONYMS: *Zonites indentatus* var. *umbilicatus* (Singley) Cockerell 1899. Baker (1930a) considered *Z. indentatus* var. *umbilicatus* to be a junior synonym of the snail *Helix paucilirata* Morelet 1849 (later *Hyalina paucilirata M.,* Martens 1892) and put the species in the genus *Retinella* Fischer, 1877, as a subspecies, *Retinella indentata paucilirata*. H. B. Baker (1930a) noted that rimate individuals (i.e., typical *indentata*) occur in populations of *paucilirata* (i.e., umbilicate), suggesting that the two species are but variations of the same species. But he suggested that "*paucilirata* seems to be a fairly well-marked geographic race. In Tennessee and northern Alabama, I found it the prevalent form in the broader and drier valleys." Pilsbry (1946) also recognized this subspecific designation.

NOTES: Differentiated from *G. indentata* by the larger umbilicus. Not as large as *Z. nitidus* or *O. cellarius*, but larger than *Hawaiia* species. For *P. electrina*, the radial lines do not reach the base of the shell as in *G. umbilicata*; *M. ingersolli* lacks the radial lines.

DISTRIBUTION (Henderson and Daniels 1917; Jones 1940b; Pilsbry 1946; Ibase): Mexico; United States: AL, AR, AZ, CA, FL, IN, KY, GA, LA, MO, MS, NC, OK, NM, SC, TN, TX, VA. Utah records from Zion National Park, Tooele and Salt Lake counties.

Perpolita electrina (Gould) Binney, 1841 Amber Glass

FIG. T10. *Perpolita electrina*, ANSP 182162, St. Paul, MN. MC = maximum diameter. Credit: ANSP.

DESCRIPTION (Binney 1841; Morse 1864; Pilsbry 1946; Burke 2013): *Shell*: discoidal with a weakly convex spire, deeply umbilicate (ca. 1/6th of total dia.), transparent, with a faint yellow or green tint (in live animals the whole shell is yellowish, with a dark line below the suture); faint radially revolving lines on the shell surface (lacking in first whorl) not reaching the base, which is smooth except for faint growth-wrinkles; microscopic spiral striation is lacking or weak; slight folds in the periostraca, running obliquely across the incremental lines. *Whorls:* 3.75–4.25, increasing rapidly, the last convex below. Umbilicus funnelform, ~1/5–1/6 shell diameter. *Aperture:* rotund-lunate, a little wider than high.

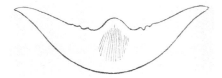

FIG. T11. Jaw of *Perpolita electrina*. Credit: Morse 1864.

FIG. T12. Radula of *Perpolita electrina*. Credit: Morse (1864).

SIZE: Type dimensions: 2.82 mm high × 5.15 (greatest) and 4.54 mm (smallest) diameter; umbilicus 4.4X in diameter. 4.5–5.2 mm dia. (Burke 2013).

ANIMAL (Morse 1864; Pilsbry 1946): The collar, back, and tentacles are almost black, the shade becoming lighter toward the foot edges and sole, which are dark gray. The sole is tripartite, the parts separated by impressed lines. The kidney is triangular, a little longer than the pericardium.

Buccal plate crescent shaped (Fig. T11), wide through the center with a central rounded beak having 1–2 smaller projections to either side of it. Lingual membrane 54–27–1–27. A Philadelphia specimen had 27–3–1–3–27. Central plate broad and long, tricuspid (one slender mesocone and smaller teeth on either side at its base), as large as laterals. The 3 laterals are bicuspid, the first 2 long and narrow, the third smaller; the lateral central cusp projects beyond the basal plate; three laterals have well-developed endoconal cusps borne high on the mesocones and ectocones. Marginals with one claw-shaped tooth (Morse 1864; Pilsbry 1946; Fig. T12).

Ovotestis: Four groups of ovoid alveoli with especially large connecting tubes; duct long, gradually swollen and convoluted near base; talon tapering toward the apex and recurved. Free oviduct very short, with a small elliptical mass of yellow, glandular tissue on columellar wall. Spermatheca sac long with a short duct. Vagina large and stout, with heavy whitish walls. Epiphallus: a slight, but distinctive, swelling with thinner walls and larger lumen just above apex of penis; penial pore on one side of apex of penis. Penis is relatively small with thick walls and many longitudinal folds and a bell-shaped apical region interrupted about $1/3$ the length from apex by a series of elliptic, sucker-shaped thickenings. Penial retractor has its insertion at apex of penis.

TYPE LOCATION: Shores of Fresh Pond, Cambridge, Massachusetts.

JUNIOR SYNONYMS (Pilsbry 1946): *Helix electrina* Gould, 1841; *Helix janus* Adams, 1841; *Zonites radiatulus* var. *alba* Jeffreys, 1872; *Zonites viridulus* 'Mehnke' Binney, 1878; *Hyalina pellucida* Lehnert, 1884; *Vitrea radiatula* (Alder) Dall, 1905; *Vitrea hammonis* (Ström) Walker and Pilsbry, 1902, *Retinella hammonis* (Ström) Baker, 1928 (in part); *Retinella electrina* (Gould) Pilsbry, 1946; *Nesovitrea electrina* (Gould) Bank et al. 2001.

NOTES: Not as tightly coiled as similar *Zonitoides* and *Oxychilus* species (Burke 2013). Wider aperture than for *M. ingersolli*. See data under the family heading for anatomical differences from other gastrodontids. Habitat is aspen forests, wet meadows, floodplains, and margins of ponds and marshes (Karlin 1961; Hubricht 1985).

DISTRIBUTION (Ibase): Southern Canada and widespread in the United States from Maine to California and Arkansas, south to Mexico. There is a Wyoming specimen from Fort Bridger (ANSP 11962). For Utah, Carnegie Museum specimens exist from Uinta and Daggett counties. Other Utah records exist from Weber County (Pilsbry 1946), Cedar Breaks National Monument (Gregg 1941), 2.8 miles west of Vernal (Brooks 1936; Oliver and Bosworth 2000), and Kane County (Meretsky et al. 2002).

Zonitoides arboreus Say, 1816 Quick Gloss Snail

DESCRIPTION (Say 1818; Pilsbry 1946): *Shell*: very thin, glossy, translucent, discoidal, spire slightly elevated, umbilicus large and deep, 4.5–5X in diameter; *Whorls*: 4.0–4.5, moderately convex, regularly increasing in size; embryonic 1.5 whorls are smooth, subsequent whorls have growth wrinkles that are weakly and irregularly sculptured; very faint, minute spiral striae; the base smoother. *Aperture*: deeply lunate, wider than high. Peristome thin, junction with the body whorl acute.

SIZE: Dia. 5–6 mm × 2.4–3.0 mm high.

ANIMAL (Pilsbry 1946): Eye tentacles are carried widely diverged, with tips bearing distinct black eyes that are slightly bulbous. The anterior of the animal is bluish-gray above and on the tentacles, paler toward the foot edges, the sides and tail not pigmented. The mantle collar is slate, flecked with white, and with two dorsal grooves on the back. The sole is white or gray, with paler flecks in a narrow border around the edge, but without division otherwise. Movement is without waves. This species lacks the connection between the spermathecal stalk and the free

FIG. T13. *Zonitoides arboreus. Lectotype.* ANSP 248104 (orginal comb. Hyalinia roseni, Russia). Credit: ANSP.

oviduct, which is present in *Z. nitidus*, and apparently does not develop a distinct oviducal sac. Radula formula is 19–6–1–25; 77 transverse rows counted. Central tooth tricuspid, noticeably larger than first laterals; laterals are bicuspid.

TYPE LOCATION: Not given in original publication.

JUNIOR SYNONYMS: *Helix arboreus* Say, 1816 (Nicholson's Encyclopedia); *Helix ottonis* Pfeiffer, 1840; *Helix breweri* and *Helix whitneyi* Newcomb, 1864; *Hyalina breweri* (Newcomb) Tryon, 1866a; *Hyalina whitneyi* (Newcomb) Binney and Bland, 1869; *Hyalina roseni* Lindholm, 1911; *Zonites arboreus* Binney, 1878; *Hyalina arborea* var. *viridula* Cockerell, 1888b; *Hyalina arborea* (Binney) Tryon, 1866a; *Zonitoides arboreus* (Binney) Henderson, 1924.

NOTES: Shell is smaller and more depressed than *Z. nitidus,* has a wider aperture, and the living animal is lighter colored. H. B. Baker (1928) notes that *Z. arboreus* lacks a connection between the spermathecal stalk and the free oviduct, which is present in *Z. nitidus*. Slightly larger than *M. ingersoli*. Sole is tripartite in *Perpolita electrina* but undivided for *Z. arboreus*. Found at 10,000 ft elevation in Colorado.

DISTRIBUTION: North America from Canada to Mexico, Central America, and in the West Indies. Utah records from the Oquirrh Mountains (Jones 1940a), at 11,000 ft on the slopes of Brian Head Peak and at Cedar Breaks National Monument (Gregg 1940, 1941); Zion Canyon, Fish Lake, Beaver, Weber Canyon, American Fork Canyon, City Creek Canyon, west of Wood's Cross, Chalk Creek, Red Butte Canyon, Clear Creek Canyon, Hidden Lake (Glendale); near Utah Lake; San Juan, Grand, and Wayne counties; (Ingersoll 1877; Henderson 1924; Chamberlin and Berry 1929; Jones 1935; Woolstenhulme 1942a, b; Wheeler 2018; ANSP records). UMNH records exist for Red Canyon, Orderville, Salt Lake City, Emigration Canyon, Brighton Trail to Lake Solitude, LaSal Mountains, Verdure, and Provo Canyon (Soapstone Basin).

Zonitoides nitidus Müller, 1774 Black Gloss

DESCRIPTION (Pilsbry 1946): *Shell*: discoidal, with slightly elevated spire, umbilicus contained 5X in diameter, olivaceous yellow, very glossy, somewhat transparent; *Whorls:* 4.5–4.75, convex, gradually widening, joined by a well-impressed suture; embryonic 1.5 whorls smooth, the rest finely, weakly marked by growth lines, the base smoother and more transparent. *Aperture:* lunate, the peristome thin; columellar margin narrowly dilated.

SIZE: Diameter 6.1–7.0 mm (rarely 8 mm) × 3.6–4 mm high.

ANIMAL (Pilsbry 1946): Black throughout except for some pale flecks along foot edge; mantle black. Foot acuminate but not protuberant, mucus pore in a groove just behind. Sole is long, narrow, and uniform. Mantle collar deep and thick in front

Oxychilidae

FIG. T14. *Zonitoides nitidus.* Left: ANSP 236818. Credit: ANSP. Center: live animal, Ogden River, UT. Credit: E. Wagner. Right: apical view of shell from Ulysses, NY. Credit: M. Coppolino, iNaturalist.org.

of lung; right neck lappet large and complex, left one small. Two types of copulatory organs have been described; one type (euphallic or "male") has a long and slender dart within a long, recurved dart sac; the dart bears a rounded coronal gland in mature specimens. The penis and epiphallus are well developed, and the prostate gland is conspicuous. In the second type, the dart sac and penis are markedly smaller and less developed, the sac is not reflexed posteriorly; the dart is lacking, no coronal gland is present, and the prostate gland is not distinguishable. For additional descriptions of the animal, see H. B. Baker (1928) and Watson (1934).

TYPE LOCATION: Fridrichsberg ("In muscosis humidis, praefertim in *Sphagno*, ac in scala lapídea horti Fridrichsbergensis").

JUNIOR SYNONYMS (Tryon 1866a; Pilsbry 1946): *Helix nitida* Müller, 1774; *Helix lucida* Draparnaud, 1805; *Helix hydrophyla* (Ingalls) Miles 1861; *Helix hydrophila* (Ingalls) Binney and Bland, 1869 (as synonym of *Hyalina nitida*); *Zonites nitidus* (Müller) Binney, 1878; *Zonitoides nitidus* (Müller) Dall, 1905.

NOTES: *Z. nitidus* is larger, less depressed, and a little more narrowly umbilicate that *Z. arboreus*; it also lacks the faint spiral lines on the shell and the base is more convex and the aperture rounder (Pilsbry 1946). Usually found around logs and leaf litter near water or in marshy areas, whereas *Z. arboreus* is found in upland woods.

DISTRIBUTION (ANSP; Ibase): Argentina; Widely distributed in Europe, Algeria, nearer Asia and Siberia; North America south to Georgia, Arkansas, Utah, and coastal California. Utah records from Daggett, Weber, Salt Lake, Utah, and Uintah counties; Ogden and Blacksmith Fork (Cache County).

Oxychilidae Hesse, 1927 (1879)

Oxychilinae Hesse, 1927 (1879), was elevated to family rank by Bank et al. (2001). Oyxchilidae has 25 genera within 5 subfamilies (Mbase). Utah has representatives from one genus, *Oxychilus* Fitzinger, 1833, that currently contains 87 species worldwide. Shells of *Oxychilus* are small to medium (5–16 mm diameter), depressed, biconvex, umbilicate, thin, translucent, glossy, of 4–6 whorls, increasing moderately to the last, which is much wider (Pilsbry 1946). The lateral and central radular teeth are tricuspid, marginals unicuspid; sole tripartite. *Oxychilus* was formerly in Zonitidae, which was split into other families, including Euconulidae, Oxychilidae, Pristilomatidae, and Gastrodontidae (Burke 2013). *Oxychilus cellarius* Müller, 1774 (formerly *Helix cellaria*), is the type species of the genus.

Oxychilus cellarius Müller, 1774 Cellar Glass Snail

DESCRIPTION (Binney 1840; Morse 1864; Burke 2013): *Shell*: discoid with a slightly convex spire, clear, corneous, glossy smooth with some weak striation; *Whorls*: 5–6, slightly rounded; Umbilicus: narrow, fitting about 6X in the diameter, whitish around umbilicus; *Aperture*: not dilated, transverse diameter the greatest, with a simple, acute lip.

FIG. T15. *Oxychilus cellarius*, apical and umbilical views. Credit: E. Wagner.

SIZE: dia. 9–12 mm (max. ~14 mm), SL 4.2 mm

ANIMAL: Light gray with pale sole; mantle is spotted with brown; buccal plate (Fig. T16) crescentic, with a point projecting in the center, with

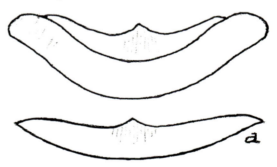

FIG. T16. Jaw of *Oxychilus cellarius*. Credit: Morse 1864.

longitudinal striae. In younger animals, the plate is not as crescentic (lower drawing). Lingual membrane 38–17–1–17–38; central plate very long and narrow, with 3 tiny teeth occupying nearly the center of the plate. First four laterals are irregular in shape, apparently bidentate; marginal teeth with long, single, aculeate denticles (Morse 1864). Penis sheath is not abruptly narrowed at its junction with the atrium as in *O. lucidus,* and the epiphallus is short and not twisted (Pilsbry 1946).

TYPE LOCATION: "In cellis vinarüs Havniae copiose" abundant in wine cellars of Copenhagen, Denmark.

JUNIOR SYNONYMS (Binney 1840): *Helix cellaria* Müller, 1774; *Helix nitida* Drapernaud, 1805; *Hyalina cellaria* Morse 1864.

NOTES: Larger size and whitish basal area distinguishes this species from other Utah members of the family. There is a similar species, *O. draparnaudi*, in the Northwest and in Colorado, that might be expected in Utah; it is larger (11–16.5 mm diameter), has a wider last whorl, and has a gray mantle (Welter-Schultes 2012; Burke 2013). Found in rotten wood and leaf litter. Between 25 and 45 eggs are laid between February and October, with juveniles hatching after 12–16 days. These juveniles mature early in the following year, but full shell size can occur in 4 months (Welter-Schultes 2012).

DISTRIBUTION: ANSP records from Great Britain, Europe, Asia Minor, Japan, New Zealand, Australia, northern Africa, Bermuda, and Chile. In North America from eastern Canada, New England south to the Carolinas, west to California (Pilsbry 1946). In Utah, recent surveys have found it in several Wasatch Front locations and Logan, possibly introduced with greenhouse plants.

Pristilomatidae Cockerell, 1891a

Shells of Pristilomatidae are small, glossy, depressed conical to nearly flat, translucent, closely coiled, and with or without an umbilicus; the aperture is lunate and may have conspicuous lamellae (section Pristinoides); lip simple and sharp (Ancey 1886; Pilsbry 1946). The type species is *Pristiloma stearnsi* (Bland) Ancey, 1886. Ancey (1886) first used *Pristina* as a subgenus within *Hyalina*, but it was already in use, so the name was changed to *Pristiloma* (Ancey 1887a). Cockerell (1891a) later elevated the status to a subfamily within Zonitidae; he noted that this group shared a similar radular teeth structure; that is, central and lateral teeth are ± quadrate, and marginal teeth are aculeate (simple pointed).

Worldwide 177 species are recognized within 15 Recent genera and 1 fossil genus in Pristilomatidae (Mbase). Species in this family were originally allocated to Zonitidae, which was later divided into other families, including Pristilomatidae, Euconulidae, Oxychilidae, and Gastrodontidae (Bank et al. 2001; Bouchet and Rocroi 2005). Vitreidae Baker, 1930, is a junior synonym. *Pristiloma* currently has 15 species recognized in the genus. Only one is known to exist in Utah. Animals in *Pristiloma* usually have a scalloped border of black along the sutural angle of liver mass. The foot has distinct, often coarse, tessellation (mosaic pattern); pedal grooves, and a very small caudal mucus pore. The sole is elongate, sides ± parallel. The left neck lappet is wider than high. Ureter is complete. Radula central and lateral teeth are tricuspid; transitional teeth bicuspid (H. B. Baker 1931; Pilsbry 1946). The genus *Hawaiia* was created by Gude (1911, p. 272) and described as "shell zonitoid, vitreous, finely and regularly costulate (ribbed), openly umbilicated." The type species of the genus is *Helix kawaiensis* Pfeiffer, 1855 (now *Hawaiia minuscula*). Within *Hawaiia* there are currently 5 accepted species, including one reported to be in Utah.

Hawaiia minuscula Binney, 1841 Minute Gem

DESCRIPTION (Binney 1841; Morse 1864; Pilsbry 1946): *Shell*: minute, depressed-convex discoidal, with a whitish epidermis; thin, pale gray or often flesh-colored above from the contained soft parts. *Whorls*: 4, convex, the last tubular; very distinctly impressed sutures and a large umbilicus {~$1/3$ the diameter of the shell}, not spread and showing not more than 2 volutions. The whorls widen gradually. Embryonic whorl is smooth, the rest distinctly, unevenly striate above, nearly smooth beneath; spiral lines wanting or quite indistinct. *Aperture:* nearly circular, lip simple and acute.

SIZE: greatest diameter <3.2 mm, height about 1.2 mm.

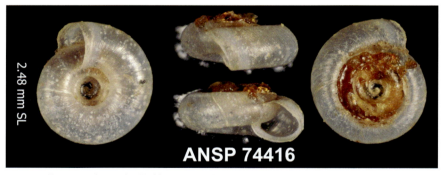

FIG. T17. *Hawaiia minuscula*, ANSP lectotype 74416. Credit: ANSP.

ANIMAL (Pilsbry 1946): Buccal plate nearly straight, rounded at ends, faintly striate longitudinally, slightly raised at the center of cutting edge. Radula: 57 transverse rows of 13–4–1–17. Central tooth tricuspid with squarish base, laterals bicuspid, with broad entoconal shelf; marginals unicuspid (Fig. T18).

TYPE LOCATION: Ohio, on the margins of streams, under chips or sticks in damp, shaded areas or under bark of decaying stumps near the surface of the waters.

Pristilomatidae

FIG. T18. *Hawaiia minuscula* radula. Credit: Morse 1864.

JUNIOR SYNONYMS (Dall 1885; Pilsbry 1946): *Helix minuscula* Binney, 1840; *Helix apex* Adams, 1849; *Zonitoides minusculus* (Binney) Binney 1878; *Pseudohyalina minuscula* (Binney) Morse 1864; *Chanomphalus minusculus* (Binney) Strebel 1873; *Psuedovitrea minuscula* (Binney) Baker 1928; *Hawaiia minuscula* (Binney) Baker 1941; *Zonites minusculus* var. *alachuana* Dall, 1885; *Pseudovitrea minuscula alachuana* (Dall) Baker 1930a; *Helix (Patula) unwini* (Brazier) Etheridge, 1889; *Helix kawaiensis* L. Pfeiffer, 1855. *Hawaiia minuscula* is the type species for the genus *Hawaiia* (originally *Helix kawaiensis* Reeve, 1854) (Welter-Schultes 2012). Other synonyms of the genus include *Johannesoconcha* and *Macgillivrayella* Preston, 1913 (Mbase).

NOTES: Smaller size separates this species from the disk-shaped shells of Oxychilidae and Discidae species; it tends to be larger than *Punctum minutissimum,* with a jaw that is nearly straight, not arcuate as in *Punctum*. The umbilicus is slightly larger in *H. minuscula neomexicana* (fits 2.5X in the shell diameter) than *H. minuscula s.s.* (3X in dia.). Occurrence in North American Pleistocene and absence in European deposits of the same age indicate that it is a North American native (Bequaert and Miller 1973). Karlin (1961) found *H. minuscula* in Engelmann spruce and lodgepole pine forests.

DISTRIBUTION: Widespread in North America from Maine and eastern Canada to Alaska south to Costa Rica. Utah records from ponds and aspen grove at Jensen (Uinta County), Utah (Carnegie Museum, 88590) and Zion National Park (ANSP 342117, 342118). The author (Wagner) found empty shells in Cowley Canyon, Cache County.

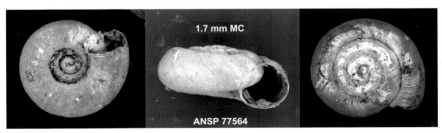

FIG. T19. *Hawaiia minuscula neomexicana*. Lectotype from Dripping Spring, NM, ANSP 77564. Credit: ANSP.

Hawaiia minuscula neomexicana (Cockerell and Pilsbry) Pilsbry, 1900a Minute Gem

DESCRIPTION (Pilsbry 1946): *Shell*: minute, depressed, similar in form to *Hawaiia minuscula*; whitish corneous, somewhat translucent, fragile, the umbilicus wide, its width contained 2.5 times in the greatest diameter of the shell. Surface marked with very fine but rather sharp growth striae, and crowded, microscopic spirals throughout, the spirals conspicuous to the apex. *Whorls*: 3.5, quite convex, the last everywhere well rounded. *Aperture:* round-lunate, the penultimate whorl excising about ¼ the circumference of the peristome; lip thin and acute, a little dilated at the columellar margin.

SIZE: SL nearly 0.8 mm, greatest dia. 1.7 mm, umb. width 0.5 mm. Another specimen was about 2 mm.

TYPE LOCATION: Dripping Spring, Organ Mountains, New Mexico. Lectotype, ANSP 77564; paralectotypes, 12170.

JUNIOR SYNONYMS: *Zonitoides neomexicanus* (Cockerell and Pilsbry) Pilsbry, 1900a; *Zonitoides minuscula neomexicana* Pilsbry and Ferriss, 1906; *Punctum pygmaeum albeolum* Dall, 1926; *Psuedovitrea minuscula neomexicana* (Pilsbry and Ferriss) Baker 1929a; *Hawaiia minuscula neomexicana* (Pilsbry and Ferriss) Baker 1930b.

NOTES: Smaller than other discoid species in Utah except *Punctum minutissimum*, which is even smaller, and *H. minuscula*, which has a smaller umbilicus. Little is known about the biology of this species. Whether *neomexicana* should remain a subspecies (as recognized by Pilsbry and Ferriss [1906], H. B. Baker [1930b], and Pilsbry [1946]) or be considered a distinct species as originally proposed by Pilsbry (1899a) is unresolved based on current data.

DISTRIBUTION: Mexico; United States, New Mexico, Texas. Known from two locations in eastern Washington County (Gregg 1940) and one location in southwestern Garfield County (Gregg 1942). To date, there are no museum specimens from Utah for this species.

Pristiloma subrupicola Dall, 1877 Southern Tightcoil

DESCRIPTION (Dall 1877, p. 163): "*H. subrupicola*, while exhibiting radiating lines of growth, some which are more conspicuous than others, does not show any such well-marked grooves or indentations as are figured by Morse (Land Shells of Maine) in *indentata*, and which form its most striking specific character. The former has five-and-a-half whorls, with the greatest diameter in the largest specimen of 0.14 in. (3.5 mm), while *indentata* has but little more than four, with a diameter of 0.20 in. (5.1 mm). The former is perfectly pellucid (translucent),

Pristilomatidae

FIG. T20. *Pristiloma subrupicola*, ANSP 178008 topotype. Right: ANSP 158711. Left: from Lake Point, Utah, near Clinton's Cave. Credit: ANSP.

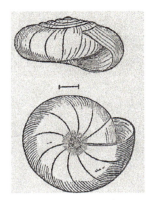

FIG. T21. *Pristiloma subrupicola*, original drawing. Credit: Dall 1877.

while the latter has a peculiar whitish spermaceti-like luster. *H. subrupicola* has the last whorl smaller proportionally than *indentata*, and in fact the increment of the whorls in the former is much more regular and even. The umbilicus in both is precisely similar (fissure-like to narrowly umbilicate)."

SIZE: 2.7–5.5 mm dia. Pilsbry (1946) suggested that the number of whorls is likely 3.6 to 4.5 and that 5.5 whorls was likely a mistake.

ANIMAL (Chamberlin and Jones 1929): "The animal of *subrupicola* varies from whitish to slaty; the granules of the upper surface of the foot are remarkably coarse and well-marked. The tentacles are, as contracted in alcohol, hardly perceptible; the eye-peduncles, are from the same cause, not extended, but appear to be as usual in the genus, and to possess normal ocular bulbs." Sole is narrowly rounded, almost pointed, posteriorly. Jaw is thin, narrow, and transparent; radular formula: 11–5–1–5–11, with 68 transverse rows; 5th tooth transitional, but all marginals are unicuspid.

TYPE LOCATION: Clinton's Cave, Lake Point, Tooele County, Utah.

JUNIOR SYNONYMS: *Hyalina subrupicola* Dall, 1877; *Vitrea subrupicola* Dall, 1895; *Ogaridiscus subripicola* (Dall) Chamberlin and Jones 1929, Burke 2013; *Pristiloma subrupicola* (Dall) Baker 1930c.

NOTES: Much smaller umbilicus than for *H. neomexicana* or *Punctum minutissimum*, but similar to that of *Glyphyalinia indentata*. *P. subrupicola* lacks the incised radial grooves of *G. indentata* and *G. umbilicata* (Chamberlin and Jones 1929); more regular increments in whorl size, and a more transparent shell.

DISTRIBUTION (Pilsbry 1946; Burke 2013; Ibase): CA, OR (Umatilla County, Josephine County), Idaho (Shoshone Co.); In Utah, only known from Clinton's Cave, at Lake Point near Saltair on the Great Salt Lake.

SPF: LIMACOIDEA Batsch, 1789

Agriolimacidae Wagner, 1935

Wagner (1935) formed the subfamily Agriolimacinae, which features small slugs. His description (Google translation from Hungarian): medium or small animals. Their skin is relatively thin and smooth. They are monochrome or bright, in the latter case they are usually mesh-like. They have a well-developed, sometimes large, mantle that always completely covers the limestone slab beneath it. Their short tentacles never reach the mantle. Their mucus is clear or white. The medial tooth of the radula is tricuspid. The intestine has four bends. Very often they have ancillary organs on their penis, the appendix, and stimulus body. The penis and the right retractor muscle are parallel to each other. Hausdorf (1998) also notes that family characters include the mantle covering more than a third of the body, pneumostome surrounded by a well-delimited round plate, and the central field of the sole has V-shaped grooves. Bank et al. (2001) recognized the family as Agriolimacidae. There are 113 recognized species within 5 genera: *Deroceras, Furcopenis, Krynickillus, Megalopelte,* and *Lytopelte. Deroceras* Rafinesque, 1820, is the largest by far, with 104 species, 2 of which are found in Utah.

Deroceras laeve Müller, 1774 Meadow Fieldslug

DESCRIPTION (Müller 1774; Burke 2013): Nearly uniformly colored, sometimes with gray flecks; Color is various shades of amber, reddish-brown, dark brown to blackish. The mantle may be a little paler. The pneumostome is situated posteriorly in the mantle and has a slightly lighter border around it. Mantle with fine concentric lines, oval, fleshy. Back has elongated furrows and tubercles. Mucus is thin and clear. Posterior end is keeled very shortly.

FIG. T22. *Deroceras laeve*, California. Credit: Cedric Lee, iNaturalist.org.

SIZE (Burke 2013): 15–25 mm; shell is about 4 mm long, rounded anteriorly, somewhat pointed posteriorly.

ANIMAL: Hindgut with no caecal diverticulum. Hermaphrodite gland hidden in visceral mass. Penis terminates in a recurved or spirally curved gland extending beyond the insertion of the vas deferens. Anterior penis with a glandular external layer and the cavity contains a conic stimulator; above this stimulator, the cavity contains two fleshy ridges; penial retractor muscle weak or wanting.

TYPE LOCATION: Denmark, in moss.

JUNIOR SYNONYMS (Cockerell 1893a; H. B. Baker 1930b): Synonyms of the genus: *Agriolimax* Mörch, 1865; *Krynickia* Kaleniczenko, 1839; *Krynickillus* Kaleniczenko, 1851; *Malino* Gray, 1855; *Hydrolimax* Malm, 1868; *Chorolimax* Westerlund, 1894. Synonymous species: *Krynickia americana* Tate, 1870; *Limax laevis* Müller, 1774; *L. brunneus* Draparnaud, 1801; *L. gracilis* Rafinesque, 1820; *L. campestris* Binney, 1842; *L. parvulus* Normand, 1852; *L. semitectus* Mörch, 1857; *L. weinlandi* Heynemann, 1862; *L. arenarius* Gassies, 1867; *L. guatemalensis* Crosse and Fischer, 1870; *L. (Eulimax) campestris* var. *occidentalis* Cooper, 1872; *L. stenurus* and *L. berendti* Strebel, 1873; *L. montanus* Ingersoll, 1875 (Ingersoll 1876); *L. castaneus* Ingersoll, 1875; *L. ingersolli* Binney, 1875; *Agriolimax montanus* forms *typicus*, *intermedius*, and *tristis* (Ingersoll) Cockerell, 1888c; *Agriolimax berendti* var. *pictus* Cockerell, 1897a; *Limax hyperboreus* (Westerlund) Dall, 1905; *Limax laevis* var. *americana* von Ihering, 1885; *Limax hemphilli* Binney, 1890; *Agriolimax campestris* var. *zonatipes* Cockerell, 1892b; *Agriolimax laevis campestris* form *nigrescens* Cockerell, 1893a; *Agriolimax campestris* var. *plumbeus* Sterki, 1907; *A. guatemalensis montaguensis* Cockerell, 1914; Last change by H. B. Baker (1930b) to *Deroceras laeve* (Müller, 1774).

NOTES (Wagner 1935; Pilsbry 1948; Burke 2013): The animal is smaller in size than *D. reticulatum*; its body is lighter colored, normally poor in pigmentation, sometimes almost white, free from all dark spots; generally with thin, fairly smooth skin. Mucus is watery, not turning milky when handled as for *D. reticulatum*.

DISTRIBUTION (Burke 2013; ANSP; Ibase): Holarctic; Jamaica, Bermuda, Haiti; Central America; Peru; Chile, Colombia; Indonesia; Madagascar, Namibia, Kenya. Widespread in the United States from Arkansas to Maine, south to Florida, Texas, and California. In Utah, museum records from Summit Canyon (ANSP 69004); Cache, Salt Lake, Grand, Washington, Iron, Sevier, Summit, and San Juan counties. Jones (1935): 3 miles east of Echo City; Park City; between Peoa and Rockport. Wheeler (2018) noted it in Zion National Park.

Deroceras reticulatum Müller, 1774 Gray Fieldslug

DESCRIPTION (Pilsbry 1948; Burke 2013): Similar color between mantle and skin of the back. Color whitish to buff to light to dark gray; may be mottled with gray or black flecks. Tentacles dark. Mantle slightly longer than $1/3$ the slug length, with fine concentric wrinkles. Rest of body with low, long tubercules. Pneumostome on right side, about 80% back from mantle front edge, encircled with lighter border. Tail end has a short keel, tip tapering quickly. Tripartite sole. Mucus is clear but becomes white when animal is disturbed. Shell is thin, slightly convex, showing faint lines of growth.

SIZE (Pilsbry 1948): 35–50 mm long.

ANIMAL (Pilsbry 1948): Short rectal caecum (~2.5 mm) on hindgut. Large ovo-testis, reaching more than half the distance from caecum insertion to apex of the visceral mass. Seminal receptacle small, oval. Penis with a large conic stimulator and several irregular pads and ridges; interior minutely grooved or striate. Vas deferens opening and retractor muscle insertion are near the posterior end, in front of recurved terminal penial gland, which is variously digitate or has crimped borders.

FIG. T23. *Deroceras reticulatum*. Cache Valley, UT. Credit: E. Wagner.

TYPE LOCATION: Gardens of Rosenburg and Fridrickshal.

JUNIOR SYNONYMS (Cockerell 1893a): *Limax reticulatus* Müller, 1774; *Agriolimax reticulatus* (Müller) Luther 1915; *Limax agrestis* Leidy, 1851; *Agriolimax obliquus* Brard, 1815; *A. tunicatus* Gould, 1841; *A. niciensis* (Bourguignat) Nevill 1880; *A. agrestis griseus* Cockerell, 1889; *Agriolimax agrestis* (L.) Chamberlin and Jones, 1929.

NOTES (Pilsbry 1948): Larger and more strongly marked than *D. laeve*. The milky mucus when disturbed also differs from the clear mucus of *D. laeve*. Smaller than *L. maximus*. Commonly found in and around moist wood, stones, vegetation, riparian areas, and moist urban gardens and flower beds. Often a pest in gardens and agricultural fields. They will also consume mushrooms, dead slugs, earthworms, and other animal matter. They reproduce from spring to late fall, or year-round depending on the climate. Individuals have been known to produce nearly 700 eggs/year. There are a number of slugs that are not known from Utah but may possibly appear with greenhouse plants or via other vectors. The reader is referred to Burke (2013) for more details on slugs (and snails) from the Northwest.

DISTRIBUTION (Ibase; Chamberlin and Berry 1929): Native to western Europe and the British Isles. Argentina, Australia; Chile; New Zealand; Nicaragua; Widely distributed in the United States and Canada. In Utah, records from Cache, Davis,

Weber, San Juan, Grand, Wayne, and Salt Lake counties. Probably distributed statewide in suitable habitat.

Limacidae Batsch, 1789

Limacidae features slugs characterized by an oval mantle on the anterior part of the back and a shell that is reduced to a flat plate (covered in most species). Foot narrow, lacking a caudal pit, the sole tripartite, locomotion rhythmic, with direct waves over the middle field. Breathing pore is on the right edge of the mantle, behind a short slit to the edge. Marginal teeth of radula simply thorn-shaped or bifid. Duct of spermatheca short, usually opening directly into the atrium. Tentacular and buccal retractors united posteriorly into a single band (Pilsbry 1948).

Currently, Limacidae has 96 species within 12 genera and two subfamilies (Limacinae, Eumilacinae) that are recognized as valid taxa (Mbase). The genus *Limax* Linnaeus, 1758, Latin for slug, has the most species (52). The genus features large spotted or striped slugs, mostly native to Europe. Two species have been introduced into Utah.

Limacus flavus Linnaeus, 1758 Yellow Garden Slug

DESCRIPTION (Linnaeus 1758; Forsythe 2004; Welter-Schultes 2012): Yellowish-brown to gray-greenish-olive, with gray mottling and elliptical light spots. Sole milky-yellow; tentacles pale blue-violet. Mantle mottled gray, 20% of body length, with fine fingerprint-like ridges, pneumostome posterior of midline. Back rounded, ~10–15 mm of keel at tail end. Body mucus yellowish; foot mucus clear.

SIZE: 75–100 mm long.

ANIMAL: Third intestinal loop short; caecum long. Penis about 1/6th of body length. Spermatheca duct unites with oviduct, and both open together into the atrium as a flattened broadening (see Barker 1999; Quick 1960).

FIG.T24. *Limacus flavus*. Washington Co., UT. Credit: Inaturalist.org, above, © Klarenz. Right: © Kevin Wheeler.

TYPE LOCATION: Unknown.

JUNIOR SYNONYMS: *Limax flavus* L.; *Limacella unguiculus* Brard, 1815; *Limacus breckworthianus* Lehmann, 1864 (type spp. for genus); *Limax baeticus* Mabille, 1868; *Limax bicolor* Selenka, 1865; *Limax canariensis* d'Orbigny, 1839; *Limax companyoi* Bourguignat, 1863; *Limax deshayesi* Bourguignat, 1861; *Limax ehrenbergii* Bourguignat, 1853; *Limax eubalius* Bourguignat, 1864; *Limax megalodontes* Quoy and Gaimard, 1824; *Limax olivaceus* Gould, 1852; *Limax umbrosus* Philippi, 1844; *Limax variegatus* Draparnaud, 1801.

NOTES: Larger than the *Deroceras* slugs. Differs from *L. maximus* in color (body more yellowish and tentacles bluish, not reddish brown) and lacks the lateral bands.

DISTRIBUTION (Ibase; Forsythe 2004; Welter-Schultes 2012): Europe, North Africa, and Middle East. Introduced into Argentina, Chile, China, Colombia, Hong Kong, Kenya, Mexico, Netherlands, New Zealand, South Africa, and British Columbia. United States: Pacific Coast, Gulf Coast states, IL, KS, MO, OK, PA, SC, TN. Utah records: Zion National Park (Wheeler 2018).

Limax maximus Linnaeus, 1758 Giant Garden Slug

DESCRIPTION (Pilsbry 1948): Yellowish-gray, usually spotted with black; on the shield the spots are scattered or coalesce into irregular blotches or marbling. Behind the shield, the spots are usually arranged in three bands of black spots lengthwise on each side, or one or two bands may be continuous. Neck, sole, and foot fringe are pale. Mucus colorless, not very sticky. Internal shell is oblong, thin, nearly flat, covered with a thin, yellowish epidermis, projecting at the edges, lower face white.

SIZE: When extended, reaching 100 mm or more. Shell length 10–12 mm.

ANIMAL (Pilsbry 1948; Forsythe 2004): Third intestinal loop long; rectum without a caecal diverticulum. Penis with a terminal retractor muscle and lacking an appendix; broad lamellar fold within the cavity of the penis, the penis wall thin and smooth on one side of the fold, thick and transversely wrinkled on the other. The longitudinal fold is abruptly reduced to a low ridge in the contracted anterior neck of the penis. Lower part of the prostate gland is free from the oviduct. For anatomical illustrations of the animal, see Barker (1999) and Quick (1960).

TYPE LOCATION: Sweden

JUNIOR SYNONYMS (Mbase): synonyms of the genus include *Eulimax* Moquin-Tandon, 1855; *Chromolimax, Gestroa, Opilolimax,* and *Stabilea* Pini, 1876; *Heynemannia* Malm, 1868; *Limacella* Brard, 1815; *Macroheynemannia* Simroth, 1891; *Prolimax* Simroth, 1906. Other synonyms: *Limacella parma* Brard, 1815; *Krynickillus mamelianus* Bourguignat, 1869; *Limax maculatus* Leach, 1852; *Limax sylvaticus* Morelet, 1845.

FIG. T25. *Limax maximus*. Centerville, Utah. Credit: iNaturalist.org.

NOTES (Pilsbry 1948): This slug is easily differentiated from the *Deroceras* slugs based on its much larger size and spotting. It forages at night. Typically found in moist urban habitats like gardens, cellars, springhouses, and leaf litter. It lays about 60 eggs at a time, each of about 4.5 mm diameter. Eggs hatched early in the season reach full size by autumn but do not sexually mature until the following year. They are estimated to live about 2.5–3 years. *L. maximus* Linnaeus, 1758, is the type species for *Limax*.

DISTRIBUTION (Pilsbry 1948): Europe, Asia Minor, Algeria; introduced into North and South America, South Africa, Australia, and Hawaii. Utah records (iNaturalist.org) from Cache, Weber, Utah, Salt Lake, and Davis counties.

Vitrinidae Draparnaud, 1801

Vitrinidae features snails with shells that are very thin, of few rapidly enlarging whorls, imperforate or very narrowly perforate, and the aperture is very large with a simple, thin lip. The foot is narrow, tripartite, with pedal grooves but no caudal pit. Mantle with ample body and shell lobes. Kidney is short. Marginal teeth with two or more points (Pilsbry 1946).

There are two fossil genera within the family (*Planellavitrina* Magry, 2018; *Provitrina* Wenz, 1919), and 18 Recent genera within two subfamilies, Plutoniinae and Vitrininae (Mbase). Within the genus *Vitrina* Draparnaud, 1801, there are 8 recognized species, one of which is represented in Utah.

Vitrina pellucida Müller 1774, Western Glass Snail

DESCRIPTION (Pilsbry 1946): *Shell*: vitreous, somewhat convex, greenish buff, polished. *Whorls*: 3½, rapidly enlarging, about equally raised on both sides, lower lip of last whorl descending. *Aperture:* moderate, rounded but wider than tall; columella somewhat straightened at base; peristome thin, brownish.

SIZE (Pilsbry 1946): 2 mm tall × 5 mm dia.; exceptionally to 10 mm dia., but usually 6.0–7.4 mm.

ANIMAL: bluish-gray, head black; mantle edge bluish-gray, densely black speckled; the hind part of the foot pale gray. Foot is long and narrow; sole tripartite. Lobe of mantle is very small.

FIG.T26. *Vitrina pellucida*, Mono Co., CA. Credit: Cedric Lee, iNaturalist.org.

TYPE LOCATION: near hot springs of Godhavn and Sukkertoppen, Greenland.

JUNIOR SYNONYMS: *Helix pellucida* Müller, 1774; *Hyalina pellucida* and *Vitrina angelicae* Beck, 1837; *Vitrina alaskana* Dall, 1905; *Vitrina pfeifferi* Newcomb, 1861; *Vitrina rhodopensis* (Wagner) Wohlberedt 1911.

NOTES: Distinguished from similar looking discoid shells by the distinctive shell, with few rapidly enlarging whorls, a large subtransversely rounded aperture, and a shell that is very thin, exceptionally fragile, and transparent. *Microphysula ingersoli* has a similar transparent shell, but has more whorls (4.5–5.75) and is less convex (more discoidal), with a nearly flat spire. *V. pellucida* is a common species, usually found in leaf litter.

DISTRIBUTION (Henderson & Daniels 1916; Jones 1935; 1940a, b; Gregg 1940; Woolstenhulme 1942a; Pilsbry 1946; Oliver and Bosworth 2000; Wheeler 2018; Ibase; ANSP): Europe, Russia, Pakistan, Greenland, Sweden, United Kingdom, and Canada. United States: AK, AZ, CA, CO, HA, ID, ME, MT, NM, OR, SD, WA, WY. Widespread in Utah. Oquirrh Mountains; Tooele; Brian Head Peak area; Zion National Park; Salt Lake City; near Morgan; Dry, Red Butte, Bell's and City Creek

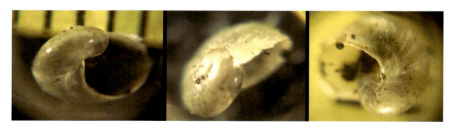

FIG. T27. *Vitrina pellucida*, Middle Fork Ogden Canyon. Credit: E. Wagner.

canyons (Salt Lake City), Panguitch, Hominy Creek (southern slope Uinta Mountains), near the head of Provo Canyon, and Jordan Narrows. Museum records (UMNH; FMNH) exist for Salt Lake County, Tooele County, LaSal Mountains, Wasatch Mountains Near Strawberry Reservoir, Timpanogos Cave, and Mammoth Creek. In recent surveys, the author found it near the Middle Fork Odgen River, Cache County, and in an aspen grove on the north slope of the Uinta Mountains.

SPF: PUNCTOIDEA Morse, 1864
Discidae Thiele, 1931 (1866)

Discidae contains three Recent genera (*Anguispira, Canaridiscus, Discus*) and three fossil genera (Yanes et al. 2011; Cameron et al. 2013; Mbase). *Atlantica* was a genus that Yanes et al. (2011) erected for some Canary Islands snails, but Cameron et al. (2013) later moved the genus to Gastrodontidae based on anatomical studies (it also has a few "teeth" on the inner palatal wall of the body whorl) and elevated *Canaridiscus* to generic rank. Snails in *Discus* and *Anguispira* are primarily found in woodlands. *Anguispira* is endemic to North America but is not known to exist in Utah. Junior synonyms for Discidae include Patulidae and Gonyodiscidae (Bouchet and Rocroi 2005).

Discus Fitzinger, 1833, is characterized by disk-shaped shells, wider than tall, that are openly umbilicate, usually finely ribbed, the aperture toothless (in Utah species) and the lip thin and simple. The foot is long and narrow, with pedal grooves. The jaw is arcuate and vertically striate. The central teeth of the radula are tricuspid, nearly as wide as the laterals. The lateral and marginal teeth have an ectocone but no entocone. The penis lacks an epiphallus and papillae. *Discus* has a holarctic and eastern Atlantic Ocean distribution, with 18 species known, including two found in Utah (Pilsbry 1948).

Genera that are junior synonyms of *Discus* include *Goniodiscus* (misspelling of *Gonyodiscus*) and *Gonyodiscus* Fitzinger, 1833; *Euromphala* Beck, 1837; *Helix* (*Patula*) and *Patula* Held, 1837; *Patularia* Clessin, 1876; and *Pyramidula* (*Gonyodiscus*) Fitzinger, 1833 (Adams and Adams 1855; Pilsbry 1948). In Pilsbry (1948), *Discus* was listed under the family Endodontidae. It was later elevated to family status (Solem 1978), and recognized in the superfamily Punctoidea in the classification scheme of Bouchet and Rocroi (2005).

Discus shimekii Pilsbry, 1890 Striate Disk

DESCRIPTION: Pilsbry (1948): *Whorls* are much more robust than *D. whitneyi*. It has a low conic spire, rounded periphery and rather narrowly umbilicate base, the umbilicus contains about 3.7–4 times in the diameter. The first whorl projects

FIG. T28. *Discus shimekii*. Paralectotype, Iowa City, IA, ANSP 451604. Credit: ANSP.

somewhat, the first 1.5 whorls smooth; following whorls regularly and rather strongly rib-striate. The ribs are about as wide as their intervals, regularly developed on the penult and next earlier whorls, but becoming somewhat lower and irregular on the last whorl, where they disappear in the peripheral region, the base being marked only with weak wrinkles of growth. The *aperture* is subcircular, about 1/5th the circumference.

SIZE (Pilsbry 1948): Iowa City specimen was 4 mm tall × 6 mm dia.; Edmonton shell, 3.7 × 6.5 mm; both 4½ whorls.

ANIMAL: No data (original description was of a fossil).

TYPE LOCATION: Near Iowa City, Iowa (Type ANSP 12297); Type for *Zonites randolphi* from Lake Lindeman at the head of the Yukon River (Type ANSP 73659).

JUNIOR SYNONYMS: *Zonites shimekii* Pilsbry, 1890; *Pyramidula shimekii* (Pilsbry) Shimek 1901; *Gonyodiscus shimekii* (Pilsbry) Baker 1927; *Patula ruderata cronkhitei* form *viridula* Cockerell, 1890; *Pyramidula cockerelli* and *Zonitoides randolphi* Pilsbry, 1898b; *Gonyodiscus shimekii cockerelli* Pilsbry and Ferris, 1909; *Pyramidula cockerelli cronkhitei* Hanna and Johnston, 1913; *Discus shimeki cockerelli* Henderson, 1936.

NOTES (Pilsbry 1948): Shell differs from *D. whitneyi* by its smoother base, which is only lightly striate, not rib-striate; rib-striae weaker on the last whorl. The whorls of *shimekii* are more robust, and the umbilicus diameter is smaller (about a quarter of the shell diameter versus a third for *D. whitneyi*). Apex is smooth and projecting somewhat, though the spire of the Rocky Mountain race *cockerelli* is more depressed than eastern populations. The aperture is more circular than many other small glossy discoid shells. Named for the boyhood friend of Henry Pilsbry.

DISTRIBUTION (Chamberlin and Jones 1929; Chamberlin and Berry 1929; Woolstenhulme 1942a; Pilsbry 1948; Oliver and Bosworth 2000; UMNH records; Ibase): western Canada, AK, AZ, CA, CO, OR, IA, IL, MO, MT, SD, IA, NM, NE, WY. In Utah, reported from Mount Tukuhnikivatz southeast of Moab; San Juan and Daggett counties; Logan, Beaver, Mill Creek, City Creek, and Red canyons; Hominy Creek (southern slope Uintah Mountains); LaSal and Blue Mountains; Green River Gorge near Green's Lake; Fruita; Fish Lake; and Panguitch Creek.

Discus whitneyi Newcomb, 1865 Forest Disk

DESCRIPTION (Newcomb 1867; Pilsbry 1948): *Shell:* depressed, rather thin, light ochraceous-buff to light brown, with low conoid spire and open, perspective umbilicus, contained about 3 times in the diameter and plainly showing all the whorls. *Whorls:* 3.7–4.5, cylindrical, the last equably rounded peripherally with strongly convex base. First 1½ whorls are smooth, the rest with sculpture of regular retractive riblets, separated by wider intervals, and continuing over the base, suture wide and deep. On the upper surface, there is some rather indistinct, irregular granulation between the riblets. *Aperture:* rounded, a little larger than the umbilicus; peristome thin, simple, dilated toward the columellar insertion.

SIZE: Type specimen 3.1 mm tall × 5 mm dia.; 3¾ whorls. Other specimens ranged in shell height from 2.7 to 3.6 mm and diam. from 5.5 to 6.7 mm, with whorls of 3⅔ to 4½.

ANIMAL: The back and tentacles are blackish; the sides toward the edges of the foot and tail are translucent pale gray. The sole is pale gray, lighter posteriorly, narrow, its width when the animal is moving, about $\frac{1}{6}$ the length; length about 1¼ times the diameter of the shell. The surface is copiously lubricated, no muscular waves are seen on the sole in movement.

TYPE LOCATION: Klamath Valley, Oregon.

FIG. T29. *Discus whitneyi*, apical and umbilical views. Credit: Lois & Mark Ports, iNaturalist.org.

JUNIOR SYNONYMS: *Helix cronkhitei* Newcomb, 1865 (Newcomb 1867); *Gonyodiscus cronkhitei* (Newcomb) Berry 1922; *Pyramidula cronkhitei* (Newcomb) Dall 1905; *Gonyodiscus cronkhitei anthonyi* Henderson, 1924; *Discus cronkhitei cronkhitei* and *Discus cronkhitei anthonyi* Henderson, 1936; *Helix striatella* Anthony, 1840; *Patula striatella* (Anthony) Morse 1864; *Patula striatella* form *albina* Cockerell, 1890; *Pyramidula striatella* var. *alba* Walker, 1894; *Pyramidula striatella* var. *albina* Walker, 1906; *Pyramidula cronkhitei anthonyi* Pilsbry, 1906. Last revision by Roth (1987) to *Discus whitneyi*.

FIG. T30. *Discus whitneyi*. Dougherty Basin Lake, UT. Credit: E. Wagner.

NOTES: Distinctive ribbing, channeled suture, larger umbilicus, and smaller size distinguishes this species from *D. shimekii*. Larger aperture than for *Zonitoides* species. May be found in rotten wood and rotting leaves and grass in riparian areas. Some Maine varieties are white (form *albina*). Weaker ribs on the base of the shell are found in some western populations (e.g., California, Colorado, New Mexico; Pilsbry 1948).

DISTRIBUTION (Henderson and Daniels 1916, 1917; Vanatta 1921; Jones 1935; Brooks 1936; Gregg 1940, 1941; Woolstenhulme 1942a, b; Pilsbry 1948; Oliver and Bosworth 2000; Meretsky et al. 2002; Ibase): Widespread in Canada, northern United States from Maine to California, south to Kentucky, New Mexico, and Arizona. Widespread in Utah: Wasatch Mountains, Zion National Park, Cedar Breaks National Monument, Kanab Creek, between Marysvale and Richfield, Beaver Canyon, Fruita, Logan ("near divide"), Bear Lake, Utah Lake, Provo Canyon; Glenwood, Moroni, Cedar Valley (Oquirrhs) and Clover, Utah; Ballard Springs near Providence; Mill Creek, City Creek, Emigration, and Red Butte canyons near Salt Lake City; Tooele; Chalk Creek, Weber Canyon, East Canyon, Bell Canyon, Clear Creek Canyon (Deep Creek Mountains), 3 miles east of Morgan; Daggett, Uinta, Cache, Washington, and San Juan counties and other locations.

Helicodiscidae Baker, 1927

Pilsbry (1948, p. 622): "*Helicodiscus* is strongly individualized by the peculiar shell, the blind animal, the tricuspid lateral and narrow, short-cusped central teeth of the radula, the plaited jaw and by the genitalia, differing from Punctinae and the larger Endodontidae by the singular undivided subcylindric ovotestis, and with the hermaphrodite duct not convoluted." See H. B. Baker (1927) for more on the anatomy. The shell is small, disk- or coin-shaped, with a nearly flat spire and broadly open umbilicus; pale, unicolored, typically spirally striated or lirate, the embryonic 1¾ whorls often smoother; whorls narrowly coiled, of small caliber. At all stages of growth, the last whorl usually has 1–3 pairs of small conical teeth at irregular intervals within the outer and basal walls of its cavity (spiral threads and teeth wanting in subgenus *Hebetodiscus*). Aperture lunate, lip unexpanded, sharp. Sole shows no division and no waves in progression, pedal furrows distinct. Eyestalks rather stout, not swollen at the ends and without pigmented eyes; tentacles short. Mantle edge orange tinted, but animal is otherwise translucent whitish throughout. Jaw arcuate, closely plaited, the flat plaits fully united, in places appearing merely as striae. Radula having about 77 rows of 12–1–12 to 15–1–15 teeth. Central tooth is decidedly narrower than the laterals, with a very short mesocone and minute side cusps. Lateral teeth with large, square basal plates, tricuspid, the mesocone as long as the basal-plate, entocone and ectocone subequal, strong, with short cutting points. Marginal teeth low and wide, with the ento- and ectocones split into 2 or 3 cusps.

Helicodiscus eigenmanni Pilsbry, 1900 Mexican Coil

DESCRIPTION (Pilsbry 1900b): *Shell:* as above, with threads strong on first whorl. *Whorls:* $4^{2}/_{3}$–5, opaque, latter part of last whorl falling below the preceding whorls; the umbilicus moderately deep, cup-shaped, contained about $2^{1}/_{3}$ times in the diameter. *Aperture* lunate, the peristome thin.

SIZE: Height 1.5–1.9 mm, diameter 4–5 mm.

TYPE LOCATION: Beaver Cave near San Marcos, Texas (ANSP #78730).

JUNIOR SYNONYMS: *Helicodiscus eigenmanni arizonensis* Pilsbry and Ferriss, 1906.

NOTES: Large number of slowly increasing whorls, with small teeth within the last whorl, distinguishes this shell from similar discoid shells. Striae in the direction of whorls on a nearly flat shell is also a key feature.

FIG. T31. *Helicodiscus eigenmanni.* ANSP 87077 lectotype for synonym *H. eigenmanni arizonensis.* Credit: ANSP.

DISTRIBUTION (Chamberlin and Berry 1929; Pilsbry 1948; Ibase; ANSP): Mexico; AR, AZ, CO, KY, NM, OK, SD, TX. In Utah, recorded from San Juan County.

Oreohelicidae Pilsbry, 1939

Oreohelix features large herbivorous land snails with an opaque shell that is wider than tall, with a depressed conical shape (though varying from discoidal to pyramidal) and large umbilicus. Whorls: 4–6, tubular or carinate; typically with two dark brown bands, but with many bands to none; embryonic whorls carinate (~2.0–2.5 whorls), with radial striae or riblets and usually some spiral sculpture. Juvenile shells are carinate, lenticular, and usually dark brown. *Aperture:* rounded or angular, toothless, columellar margin dilated, lip otherwise not expanded or reflected (Pilsbry 1939).

Oreohelicidae is composed of about 84 species in two genera, *Radiocentrum* and *Oreohelix*; only *Oreohelix* is represented in Utah (Nekola 2014). Anatomy and reproduction mode define the two genera. In the genus *Oreohelix*, snails are viviparous, the embryonic shells have >2 whorls, the epiphallus is shorter than the penis sac (preputium), and the penial retractor muscle attaches to both the penis sac and epiphallus. In *Radiocentrum*, snails are oviparous, the embryonic shell has 1.5 whorls, the epiphallus is about as long as the penis, and the retractor muscle is attached only to epiphallus. In both genera, the penis is truncate posteriorly and lacks a verge or papillae; the vagina is relatively long, and the spermatheca is globose, on the end of a long duct, relatively large, and usually pigmented. The type species (*Helix strigosa* Gould, 1846) was later transferred to *Patula* (Binney 1878). Pilsbry (1904; 1939) later assigned the snails to *Oreohelix* and the subfamily Oreohelicinae, which was later elevated to family (Wurtz 1955; Solem 1978). *Oreohelix* Pilsbry, 1904, has about 79 currently recognized species and subspecies, though recent genetic analyses have suggested the synonymy of many of these (Weaver et al. 2008; Linscott et al. 2020). To date, 31–32 chromosomes (haploid) have been documented in Oreohelicidae species studied (Babrakzai et al. 1975).

It takes about 5 years for the snail to attain a size of about 20 mm (Beetle 1997). Size is also dependent on environmental conditions; for example, Beetle (1987) noted that both the height and diameter of shells were greater in moist areas than exposed locations. Beetle (1997) kept *Oreohelix* snails alive for as long as 8 years. Often found at the base of limestone cliffs in the crevices where there are shade and moisture or under tall shrubs in riparian vegetation (Pilsbry 1939; Oliver and Bosworth 2000). Meadows (2002) demonstrated a significant preference for leaf litter. Habitats where *Oreohelix* were found near Brian Head, Utah, included limestone substrates, basaltic rock with limestone, and basalt; snails were found under the rocks in close association with dense clumps of currants

(*Ribes* spp.), ground juniper, conifers, and some forbs and grasses (Oliver and Bosworth 2002).

Colonies of *Oreohelix* have been noted to be highly variable in the height of the spire, convexity of whorls, banding patterns, width of the umbilicus, and the descending of the last whorl (Henderson and Daniels 1916; Pilsbry 1939; Beetle 1987). Sinistral, albino, and dark variants are also known to occur. As Beetle noted (1987, p. 72), "extremes within a colony could be designated as different species or subspecies, yet a series of shells can be selected leading from one to the other." Pilsbry (1905, p. 270), in reference to the large number of named subspecies and forms, remarked that "the minor modifications can be so overnamed that the wider distinctions become altogether lost, as in the Utah series." It is clear that variants in shell morphology are

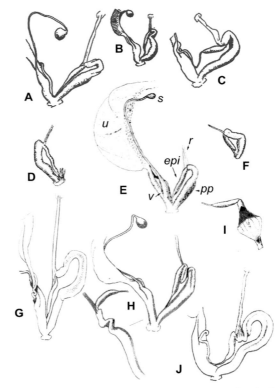

FIG. T32. Comparison of penis morphology among *Oreohelix* groups found in Utah. *O. subrudis* group A–C: A. *O. subrudis* large form from Yellowstone Nat. Park; B. *O. subrudis*, Gleneyre, CO; C. *O. subrudis* Black Range, NM. *O. yavapai* group D–F: D. *O. yavapai*, Yavapai Co., AZ; E. *O. yavapai* var. *extremitatis*, Shell, WY; F: *O. yavapai neomexicana*, Beulah, NM. *O. strigosa* group G–J: G. *O. strigosa* (*depressa* form from Ogden Canyon, UT). H. *O. strigosa* (*rugosa* form, Clarkston, UT), J. *O. strigosa* (*depressa* form from Oquirrh Mts., UT. I. cutaway view of interior preputium showing longitudinal muscular folds/ribbing and upper papillate portion. Note proportionately longer epiphallus in *O. yavapai* compared to other forms. Abbreviations for parts detailed in E: epi = epiphallus, pp = preputium (penis is epi1pp), r = retractor muscle, v = vagina, u = uterus, s = seminal receptacle. Credit: Pilsbry 1905, 1916c.

not all different species. Genetic analyses have revealed that shell ornamentation (i.e., keels, spiral ribbing, and radial ribbing) has arisen many times in separate groups indicating ornamentation is not a good taxonomic character by itself (Linscott et al. 2020). Pilsbry (1939) identified three main groups of *Oreohelix* based on penial morphology: *O. strigosa-haydeni-idahoensis*, *O. yavapai*, and *O. subrudis*. The *strigosa* group is characterized by a long cylindrical preputium in which the internal longitudinally ribbed portion (pillars or folds of muscle) is less than half the entire length. In the *yavapai* group, the preputium is swollen, and the ribbed portion is more than half the total length. Also, the proportion of epiphallus length is generally greater than in the other two groups. In the *subrudis* group, the preputium is not swollen or is only slightly so, but it also has more than half of the preputium ribbed. For radular dentition in the penial groups, the central and the first lateral teeth of the *O. subrudis* and *strigosa* groups are unicuspid. The *O. yavapai* group contains species with either unicuspid and bicuspid lateral and central teeth. Some *Oreohelix* species with bicuspid laterals include *O. idahoensis, hemphilli, hendersoni, barbata, carinifera, vortex*, and *waltoni* (Pilsbry 1916c, 1939; Solem 1975).

Recent genetic research (Weaver 2008; Linscott et al. 2020) has supported clades for these three penial groups, and others, suggesting there are about 15–16 North American species in Oreohelicidae. Following these genetic data and the penial morphology grouping given by Pilsbry (1939), nominal *Oreohelix* species in this guide are organized within these groupings. Whether or not the nominal species within a grouping are synonymous will require more research (e.g., hybridization tests, genetics, anatomy, distribution, life history, and study of ontogenic changes in diagnostic characters).

The species of the family are distributed primarily in the Great Basin and Rocky Mountains of the United States but are found from Canada to Mexico; outlying species have been found westward on Catalina Island, California, and eastward to the Black Hills, South Dakota, and eastern Iowa.

Oreohelix strigosa group

Preputium cylindrical, internal longitudinally ribbed portion is less than half the entire length; central and lateral radular teeth without side cusps.

Oreohelix haydeni Gabb, 1869 Lyrate Mountainsnail

DESCRIPTION (Gabb 1869; Berry 1932; Pilsbry 1939; Fairbanks 1975): *Shell:* orbicular, depressed shell is solid and white (dull ashy gray in live specimens), with a low conical spire (though varied from high spired to flat in museum specimens from the type locale); *Whorls:* 5–5.5 (6 in largest specimens), rounded, with 8–13 prominent ribs and concave interspaces, the suture well marked, the last whorl descending very slightly above to the aperture, the first whorl very finely striate, the next with 2–3 spiral threads; later whorls have coarse irregular striae of growth and strong raised spiral cords on both the upper surface and base, one at the periphery a bit more prominent; between some of them weak spiral lines occur; nuclear whorls 2¼. *Umbilicus:* funnel-shaped, perspective, about a fourth of the base to 5X in diameter. *Aperture:* circular to slightly wider than high, oblique,

FIG. T33. *Oreohelix haydeni.* Holotype from Weber Canyon, ANSP 23048. Credit: ANSP.

margins simple or very slightly thickened, peristome blunt, crenulated by the spirals, the margin joined by a thick parietal callus.

SIZE: 11.6 × 17.7 to 16.5 × 22.3 mm. Berry (1932): dia. 17.7–22.3 mm, SL 10.5–16.5 mm, SL/dia. ratio 0.505–0.740

ANIMAL: Pilsbry (1939) examined the genitalia of seven of the races of *O. haydeni* described, and all were found to be the same as that of *O. strigosa*, that is, the ribbed anterior portion of the penis is less than half of the total length (usually ¼–⅓). The radula of a specimen of *O. haydeni oquirrhensis* from Devil's Slide, Utah, had 30–1–30 teeth; the central and lateral teeth had well-developed, but short, ectoconal cutting edges. Those of *O.h. betheli* were similar. *O. h. corrugata* had longer cutting edges, a small mesocone on the centrals, and 9 laterals. In Montana, Fairbanks (1975) found the number of radular teeth per row varied from 44 to 62 among four populations.

For the form initially described as *O. haydeni corrugata* Henderson and Daniels, 1916, the last whorl is only scarcely carinated at the periphery on elevated specimens; about 13 strong, sharp ridges, interspaces much broader and occupied by 3–6 spiral riblets or threads; numerous crowded, irregular, transverse riblets and growth lines roughen the shell; color pinkish-white to white, the first 2–3 whorls dark horn color; umbilicus deep and narrower than typical *haydeni*; Type and cotypes dimensions, respectively: 14 mm tall × 18 mm dia., 13 mm tall × 18.5 mm, 14 mm × 19.7 mm. *O. haydeni hybrida* Hemphill, 1890b, has 4.5–5 whorls that are flattened above, rounded below, the last descending in front and striped with two chestnut bands; umbilicus large. Dimensions: 11.2 mm tall × 18.7 mm dia., 9.7 × 14.4 mm (4.5 whorls).

TYPE LOCATION: Weber Canyon, Utah; holotype is ANSP #28048. *O. h. corrugata* type was found in Cache Valley, Utah (Richmond Knoll, per Clarke and Hovingh 1994), and is held in the University of Colorado Museum, cotype in ANSP. *O. h. hybrida* type was found near Logan, Utah.

JUNIOR SYNONYMS: *Helix haydeni* Gabb, 1869; Genus change to *Oreohelix* by Pilsbry (1904). Various subspecies have been described for *O. haydeni* including *oquirrhensis* (Oquirrh Mountains, Utah); *perplexa, hesperia* Pilsbry, 1939 (Idaho); *corrugata* Henderon and Daniels, 1916; *Patula strigosa* var. *hybrida* Hemphill, 1890b; *alta, betheli* Pilsbry and Cockerell, 1913 (Glenwood Springs, Colorado); *bruneri* Ancey, 1881 (Montana), *gabbiana* Henderson, 1912, and *mixta* Pilsbry, 1916c.

NOTES: Strong corrugations in direction of the spiral of the whorls separates this species from other Utah *Oreohelix*. Fairbanks (1975) conducted some of the first genetic work on *Oreohelix* comparing four Montana populations of *O. haydeni* using starch gel electrophoresis and morphometrics; height/diameter ratios varied significantly among populations and esterase patterns differed. Gabb (1869) noted *Helix cooperi* Binney, 1858b (now known as *Oreohelix strigosa cooperi* Pilsbry, 1939) in the same population on the Weber River. As Pilsbry (1939, p. 463) noted, "there seems to be ground for the hypothesis that the weakly sculptured forms, such as *gabbiana, utahensis, hybrida,* and *mixta,* which still exist in the Colorado, Utah, and Montana areas, are similar to the primitive form of the species, which attain a wide distribution; then in several parts of its range strongly lirate forms arose independently—typical *haydeni, oquirrhensis, corrugata, betheli* and *hesperia.*" Clarke and Hovingh (1994) noted that, of 198 shells from Quarry Canyon, 127 (64%) had strong spiral sculpturing, 28 (14%) had weak or sporadic spiral sculpturing, and 43 (22%) had no visible spiral sculpturing; the authors also note that *O. strigosa* was found on the east-facing slope of the same canyon, whereas *O. haydeni* was found only on the xeric west-facing slope above the riparian zone under sagebrush or, more commonly, under Gambel oak. *O. haydeni corrugata* in Cache Valley were associated with antelope bitterbrush, mule ear, and with giant sagebrush. Berry (1932) noted that *O. haydeni* was found under the dead leaves of serviceberry *Amelanchier alnifolia,* near the base of the shrub. Recent genetic analyses by M. Linscott et al. (2020) have indicated that the lirate forms like *O. haydeni* should not be recognized as separate species based solely on that character.

DISTRIBUTION (Vanatta 1921; Berry 1932; Jones 1935; Pilsbry 1939; Clarke and Hovingh 1994; UMNH; Ibase): CA, CO, MT; John Day Creek, Twilegar Gulch (near Lucile), and St. Charles Canyon, Idaho; In Utah, *O. haydeni* has been reported from Quarry and Dry Creek canyons (tributaries of Weber Canyon, west of cement plant); Garden City near Bear Lake; Deweyville; Weber Canyon; Wasatch Mountains (Wheeler Expedition); Thistle Junction (American Fork Canyon); Filmore Canyon; Zion National Park; Box Elder, Cache, and Salt Lake Counties; Skull Valley; and the Oquirrh and Stansbury Mountains.

Oreohelix parawanensis Gregg, 1940 Brian Head Mountainsnail

DESCRIPTION (Gregg 1940): *Shell:* rather small, depressed, sublenticular, with a moderately carinate periphery and a perspective umbilicus; radial striations, with faint spiral striations over the base of the body whorl and a suggestion of spiral sculpture on the 2nd whorl. Two chestnut-colored bands, one above the keel and one close below; the rest of the shell varies from cinnamon-brown at the apex to a light buff on the later portion of the body whorl. *Whorls:* 4 $^1/_3$, convex below the suture, prominent in the middle, and then flattened above the keel; In the final third of the last whorl, there is a pronounced fading out of the keel so that the peristome is nearly circular. The last third of the body whorl descends slightly, bringing the suture line below the keel of the preceding whorl. *Aperture:* nearly round, peristome simple and connected by a faint callus over the parietal wall. *Umbilicus:* ~3.5X in the diameter of the shell, all whorls visible.

FIG. T34. *Oreohelix parawanensis*. Topotypes collected November 2018. Credit: E. Wagner.

SIZE: Type specimen: SL 5.4 mm, dia. 10.5 mm, umbilicus 3.0 mm wide. Oliver and Bosworth (2002; mean [range]): SL 4.15 (2.34–6.48) mm, dia. 6.81(3.72–9.62) mm, umbilicus 1.50 (0.78–2.25) mm wide, diam./umb. 4.66 (3.93–5.78), dia./SL 1.65 (1.44–1.90), whorls 4.14 (3.0–5.0); embryos from four intact dead shells (parent shells 5.68–9.32 mm dia.; 3 with 1 embryo each, 1 with 2 embryos) were 1.8–2.4 mm dia., with 2.0–2.25 whorls.

TYPE LOCATION: Southwest slope of Brian Head Peak (ca. 11,000 ft elevation), Brian Head, Iron County, Utah. Holotype ANSP 176907. Oliver and Bosworth (2002) noted that holotype 176907 is missing from the collection, though paratype ANSP 340315 is present and the Los Angeles County Museum also has 19 paratypes. Another, more representative holotype was assigned by Oliver and Bosworth (2002), ANSP 401984.

JUNIOR SYNONYMS: None

NOTES: *O. parawanensis* cannot be differentiated from other Utah oreohelicids with a rounded periphery, given the similarities in shell morphology and the lack of any published anatomical data. Identification is based primarily on location. Recent genetic analysis by Linscott et al. (2020) suggests that this species is synonymous with *O. strigosa*. Herein it is listed separately until more complete studies (e.g., anatomical, genetic, and hybridization research) on the population are done.

DISTRIBUTION: Only records are from the Brian Head Peak area near Parawan, Iron County, Utah.

Oreohelix peripherica Ancey, 1881 Deseret Mountainsnail

DESCRIPTION (Pilsbry 1939): *Shell:* light buff to nearly white with dull pinkish spire and sometimes a faintly traced subperipheral line. Sculpture varies from quite coarse to fine. Varies widely in size, color, degree of elevation, development of ribs and in being plain or banded. *Whorls* 4.5–5.5. The *binneyi* Hemphill variant has strong, rough wrinkles (~50 on first whorl) rather than ribs and an occasional lower columellar tubercle. The *multicostata* Hemphill variant has coarse ribs (~70 on first whorl), 2 revolving chestnut bands, and occasional tubercles as well. The

FIG. T35. *Oreohelix peripherica weberiana*. Holotype, ANSP 113572. Credit: ANSP.

gouldi Hemphill variant has rough wrinkles on the last whorl (~62), 2 revolving color bands. The *albofasciata* Hemphill variant has a broad white band at the periphery and white around the umbilicus; some individuals have the two chestnut bands or the tooth on the peristome. The *castanea* Hemphill variant has wrinkles less developed than in the other previous variants and is a uniform chestnut color, except around the umbilicus. Pilsbry (1939) recognized three subspecies found in Utah, *O. p. weberiana* Pilsbry, 1935, *O. p. newcombi* (Hemphill) Binney, 1878, and *O. p. wasatchensis*. *O. p. weberiana* was described as coarsely ribbed, with a depressed conic shape and a moderate umbilicus (~6.5X in dia.). *O. p. newcombi* also was described as coarsely ribbed, with a small umbilicus (5.5–9X in dia.). *O. p. wasatchensis* similarly was coarsely ribbed, but pyramidal in aperture view, the last whorl had a strong peripheral keel and is narrowly umbilicate; 18–23.3 mm dia., Height/Dia. 0.73–0.85.

SIZE: Type dimension: 9 mm high, 14 mm diameter. Diameter up to 20 mm with 5.5 whorls.

ANIMAL (Pilsbry 1939): Genitalia are similar to *O. strigosa depressa* and *O. haydeni*, that is, ribbed portion of the penis is < ½ of the total penis length. Central and inner lateral teeth of the radula have no side cusps. There were about 12 lateral teeth on a small specimen from below Cache Junction, Cache County. A snail from near Newton, Utah, had a radula formula of 17–13–1–13–17. The transition from laterals to marginal teeth is gradual, so the exact numbers of laterals is subjective.

TYPE LOCATION: Utah; *O. p. weberiana* type was from west side of Weber River, 4 miles west of Coalville (ANSP #113572); *O. p. newcombi* (Hemphill) Binney, 1878 type was from the "mountains north of Ogden, among bushes on steep sides of a gulch facing north, in continual shade." *O. p. wasatchensis* type was found in the Wasatch Mountains near Ogden, Utah, among quartzite boulders about a mile south of the Ogden Canyon mouth, on a river terrace in a thicket of scrub oak and mountain maple.

JUNIOR SYNONYMS: *Patula cooperi* (strongly ribbed variety, Hayden Survey, Bear River, Utah) (Binney) Ingersoll, 1876; *Helix idahoensis* var. *peripherica* Ancey, 1881; Hemphill's varieties of *Patula strigosa*—var. *binneyi*, *multicostata*, *gouldi*, *albofasciata*, *newcombi*, and *castaneus*; *O. peripherica castanea* Henderson, 1929a.

NOTES: Strong axial ribbing distinguishes this species from other *Oreohelix* in Utah. Recent genetic work by Linscott et al. (2020) suggests that the strong ribbing is a character that has arisen several times in different taxa and may be a poor diagnostic character. *O. peripherica wasatchensis* was petitioned for listing as endangered in 1994, but so far it has not been listed formally for protection under the U.S. Endangered Species Act. Weaver et al. (2008) genetically compared

O. peripherica from the type location with *Oreohelix* snails at other Wasatch Mountain locations, as well as other Utah, Nevada, and Colorado sites.

DISTRIBUTION (Ibase; ANSP): ID, MT, and OR. In Utah, reported from along the Bear River in Box Elder and Cache counties, the Wasatch Mountains (upper Weber, North Ogden Canyon, Morgan); Millard, Sanpete, Tooele, and Weber counties.

Oreohelix strigosa Gould, 1848a Rocky Mountain Snail

DESCRIPTION (Gould 1848a; Pilsbry 1933; Pilsbry 1939; Jones 1944): *Shell* circular, depressed, rough, widely umbilicate, ashy-gray, mottled with dusky or rusty brown, linear revolving bands of light brown. *Whorls:* 5, convex, the last angled (carinate) near the aperture. Embryonic shell has 2.5 whorls; there is usually a sharp line of demarcation between the embryonic shell and subsequent whorls. The new growth lacks the spiral striae, and radial striae form coarse riblets. For synonym *O. howardi*, the umbilicus was described as about a sixth of the shell diameter, and it was widely open at 2.5 whorls ($1/3$ the diameter at this size). *Aperture:* deflexed, circular, with a simple continuous lip. For synonym *O. howardi*: aperture of variable shape, axis at 15–30 degrees from shell axis.

The *albida* variant (Hemphill 1890b) described from near Logan, Utah, is white, tinged with horn color; surface covered with fine oblique striae and fine microscopic revolving lines: whorls 6, convex, the last falling in front; spire depressed; aperture oblique, nearly round. Hemphill's (1890b) *carnea* variant, found near Salt Lake City is dark horn color, sometimes faintly banded, but most of the specimens are plain and without bands; surface somewhat uneven and covered with irregular oblique striae; whorls 5.5, convex, the last faintly subcarinated in the depressed specimens, falling in front, spire subconical. *O. strigosa* var. *depressa* Cockerell, 1890, is generally lighter colored, the striation is finer and weaker compared to typical *strigosa*, and the color bands on the base below the subperipheral band are very rare. The *depressa* form in the Great Basin is about 4–5 mm less in diameter (mean 15–18 mm among Great Basin ranges) than the *strigosa* of Utah's Wasatch Range (Ports 2004). The *tooelensis* form is chalky white, giving the appearance of dead weathered shells, and the color bands are narrow. The *rugosa* variant, found near Brigham City, has an elevated spire, ranging from 54 to 64% of diameter. The *magnicornu* variant (Pilsbry 1916d) is carinate in front, the carina weakening to an angle on the last $2/3$ of the last whorl, very weak near the outer lip; deeply descending in front; umbilicus 5.1 times in shell diameter.

Oreohelix howardi was described by Jones (1944) from Mill Creek Canyon, Salt Lake County, Utah; it was differentiated from typical *O. strigosa* var. *depressa* by the narrowness of the two sharply margined bands. No animal data exists to date to differentiate this species from others in Utah. The wide variation among individuals in banding forms, shell shape, and size (Pilsbry 1939; Beetle 1987), as well

Oreohelicidae

FIG. T36. *Oreohelix strigosa.* ANSP 23058: var. *hybrida*, holotype from near Logan Canyon, UT; ANSP 23051: *O. strigosa utahensis* holotype, Oquirrh Mts.; ANSP 23052: *O. strigosa oquirrhensis* holotype, Oquirrh Mts. Credit: ANSP.

FIG. T37. *Oreohelix howardi* topotypes collected 2019 from Mill Creek Canyon, Salt Lake Co., UT.

as recent genetic data (Linscott et al. 2020), indicate that this nominal species cannot be differentiated from *O. strigosa*, which has taxonomic priority. Even Jones (1944) notes that bands are not found on about 1 in 16 shells. Clarke and Hovingh (1994) also considered *O. howardi* a synonym and ecophenotype of *O. strigosa depressa*. Herein, *O. howardi* is considered a synonym of *O. strigosa* until new animal data indicates otherwise.

SIZE: Type: 23 mm dia. × 10 mm tall. Variants: SL 12.7–19 mm, dia. 15–25.4 mm. For synonym *Oreohelix howardi*, holotype: 25 mm dia. × 15 mm high (H:D 0.60), with 5.25 whorls and an umbilicus of 4 mm. Paratype H:D ratio ranged from 0.58 to 0.68 (12–28 mm dia.), whorls 4 –5.5.

ANIMAL: Penis (Fig. T32a) is relatively long (⅔–¾ of SW), its anterior third or slightly more is ribbed inside, the ribs and intervals usually minutely porous or spongy. Vas deferens enters the epiphallus at one side of the apex of the latter, not centrally, and it usually lies coiled around the vagina. Among eight Great Basin populations, the radula formula was 30–1–30, penis length/shell diameter ratio averaged 42–66%, and the ribbed portion (section of preputium nearest the external orifice with longitudinal muscular pillars) averaged 33–38% of the preputium length (Ports 2004).

Type location (Gould 1848a): "Interior of Oregon." Allyn Smith (1937) deduced the location to be near the confluence of the Entiat and Columbia rivers, where he also found specimens (Pilsbry 1939). *O. strigosa* is the type species for the genus *Oreohelix*. Etymology: *strigosus* = lean. For synonym *O. howardi*, Mill Creek Canyon, Utah, holotype at UMNH was transferred to UMMZ.

JUNIOR SYNONYMS (Pilsbry 1939): *Helix strigosa* Gould, 1848a; *Patula strigosa* (Gould) Binney, 1878; Hemphill's (1890) varieties: *subcarinata*, *bicolor*, *lactea*, *fragilis*, *parma*, and *picta*; *Pyramidula strigosa iowensis* Pilsbry, 1898a (fossil); *Oreohelix strigosa stantoni* Dall, 1905; *Oreohelix strigosa canadica* Berry, 1922; *O. variabilis* Henderson, 1929a; *O. strigosa delicata* Pilsbry, 1933; *O. s.* form *capax* Pilsbry and Henderson, 1937; *O. strigosa metcalfei* Cockerell, 1904; *O. howardi* Jones, 1944; *Pyramidula strigosa huachucana* Pilsbry, 1902. In that 1902 publication, Pilsbry alluded to needing a new genus for *strigosa*, but he did not name it *Oreohelix* until his 1904 publication.

NOTES: This species was the first *Oreohelix* named, so many varieties and shells attributed to this species may be separate species. Pilsbry (1939) observed 13–18 embryonic shells in specimens from Oregon, Idaho, and Washington. Recent genetic analyses (Linscott et al. 2020) suggest that many of the *Oreohelix* found in Utah along the Wasatch Range and I-15 corridor are a single species. Ports (2004), however, noted lower radula counts associated with smaller shells and lower penis length/shell diameter ratios, which he identified as *O. hemphilli*. It should be pointed out, however, that variations in radula, that is, the width of cusps, the number of teeth in a row, and the number of rows, have been noted to vary with size and environment (H. B. Baker 1922; Weatherburn 1964; Bertsch 1976; Andrade and Solferini 2006; Weaver et al. 2008). Habitats where these are found include riparian areas with aspen and cottonwood trees as well as pinyon pine and juniper habitats (Ports 1996). Jones (1940c) found that the shell was 98.3% calcium carbonate (aragonite).

DISTRIBUTION (ANSP; Ibase; UMNH; Vanatta 1921; Brooks 1936; Pilsbry 1939; Woolstenhulme 1942a, b; Ports 2004): British Columbia; AZ, CA, CO, IA, ID, MT, NV, NM, OR, SD, TX, WA, WY. Utah records: Garden City/Bear Lake; Cache County; between Onya and Inkom; South Fork Raft River; Bennington Canyon; Wasatch Front Canyons including Upper Lambs, Box Elder, Mill Creek, and Weber Canyon; Tucker, southeast and northeast of Tooele and Stansbury Range, Tooele County; Kamas and Woodland; Vernal; Polar Mesa, Grand County; American Fork and Sixth Water canyons; LaSal and Blue Mountains; Navajo Mountain; Cache, Millard, Morgan, Kane, San Juan, and Uinta counties; Eureka; House and Deep Creek Ranges, Juab County; Red Pine Canyon (near Kamas); near Green's Lake (Green River Gorge); Cedar Canyon, Iron County; Zion Canyon, and Wheeler Peak. Jones (1940) reported *O. strigosa depressa* from several Bonneville Basin sites (Bingham Canyon, Cedar Valley, Clover, Grantsville, Mecur, and the mouth of Butterfield Canyon). Gregg (1940, 1941) noted *O. s. depressa* at Cedar Breaks National Monument and on the southeast slopes of Brian Head Peak.

Oreohelix subrudis group

Preputium cylindrical or slightly swollen, internal longitudinally ribbed portion more than half the entire length; central and lateral radular teeth without side cusps.

Oreohelix subrudis 'Pfeiffer 1854' Reeve, 1854 Subalpine Mountainsnail

DESCRIPTION (Reeve 1854; Pilsbry 1939): *Shell:* umbilicate, depressed, somewhat solid; obliquely, rather roughly striate and under the lens decussate (interwoven) with close spiral striae; opaque, whitish, encircled with a wide violaceous-brown band at the suture and some other obsolete ones. Spire depressed conoid, the apex a little obtuse, corneous. *Whorls:* 5, somewhat convex, slowly increasing, the last tubular, not descending. *Umbilicus* nearly $1/3$ of the shell diameter. *Aperture:* a little oblique, lunate rotund; the peristome simple, straight, its margins converging and the columellar narrowly spreading.

SIZE (Pilsbry 1939): Type: dia. 16.75 mm × 11 mm high; umb. 3 mm wide. diameters up to 17.5–25 mm and L/W ratios of 0.65–0.76. The var. *apache*, from Apache County, Arizona (Fig. T38), reaches 22–26 mm diameter (Height:Dia. 0.62, umbilicus 4.5 mm).

FIG. T38. *Oreohelix subrudis*. synonym syntype ANSP 117287 (original combination: *Oreohelix cooperi* f. *obscura*, WY; bottom row: ANSP 109184, holotype, original comb. *O. cooperi apache*, Black River, AZ. Credit: ANSP.

ANIMAL: Lower part of the penis (preputium) contains 2 or 3 longitudinal fleshy ridges, the upper ends of which project a little into the cavity of the thin-walled portion. The internally plicate part of the long penis is half or more than half of the total length of the penis (shorter in *O. strigosa*), the anterior half of which is not swollen or is only slightly so (swollen in *O. yavapai*). Radula for *O. subrudis rugosa* specimen from Clarkston, Utah (Pilsbry 1916c): 17–11–1–11–17; lateral teeth without side cusps; gradual transition to marginal teeth.

TYPE LOCATION: Not provided by Reeve (1854) or Pfeiffer (1854). Type is in the British Museum.

JUNIOR SYNONYMS: *Helix subrudis* (Pfeiffer) Reeve, 1854; *Oreohelix subrudis* Henderson, 1936; *Helix cooperi* Binney, 1858; *Patula strigosa* var. *cooperi* Cockerell, 1890; *Patula strigosa* form *sinistrorsa* Cockerell, 1893b; *P. strigosa* form *globosula* Cockerell, 1890; *P. strigosa* form *globulosa* Pilsbry, 1894 (correction for *globosula*); *Patula cooperi* (Binney) Cockerell, 1889; *Pyramidula strigosa* var. *cooperi* Elrod, 1901; *Oreohelix cooperi* (Binney) Henderson, 1912; *O. cooperi obscura* Henderson, 1924; *O. cooperi* form *apache* Pilsbry & Ferris, 1919; *O. cooperi* form *maxima* Pilsbry, 1916c; Last change to *Oreohelix subrudis* (Reeve) by Pilsbry (1933).

NOTES (Pilsbry 1939; Karlin 1961; Beetle 1987; van Paridon et al. 2017): Shell lacks the keel (in larger shells) found in *O. eurekensis* and *O. yavapai*; rounded as for *O. strigosa*. Shell is taller than *O. strigosa depressa* and has a more rounded last whorl and smaller umbilicus. Highly variable in size, shape, umbilical width, and color, even in the same colony. Penis of *subrudis* differs from *O. strigosa*, *haydeni*, and *O. peripherica* in that the internally costate part of the penis is longer than the papillose part. The shell is usually more distinctly striate spirally than for *O. strigosa*. *O. subrudis* is an intermediate host for the liver fluke *Dicrocoelium dendriticum*. Found under logs and leaves in heavy timber, in sparse cottonwood stands, deep humus of deciduous trees, in aspen, mixed conifer woods, under sagebrush and other shrubs, along stream banks, and under talus and at cliff bases. Varieties described include *Patula cooperi* var. *typica* from Cañon City and Manitou, Colorado, var. *trifasciata*, a 3-banded shell from Mesa County, Colorado; *Patula strigosa* form *globosula* is from Summit County, Colorado; var. *elevata* (higher spire) and *minor* (small size) Hemphill from Utah.

DISTRIBUTION (Brooks 1936; Pilsbry 1939; Roscoe 1954; ANSP; Ibase): British Columbia, Alberta; OK, SD, OR, TX, Rocky Mountain and Great Basin regions, south to higher elevations of AZ and NM. Other Utah records: Clarkston (*O. subrudis rugosa*), Garden City, Blue Mountains of Monticello, Zion National Park; Eureka, Spanish Fork Canyon, Fillmore Canyon, Ogden Canyon; Brighton; Cache, Carbon, Davis, Rich, Summit, Salt Lake, Grand, San Juan, Tooele, Uinta, Utah, and Weber counties, South Fork Raft River (Box Elder County) and Deep Creek, LaSal, and Oquirrh Mountains. Ports (2004) suggested that *O. subrudis* and *O. eurekensis* reported in the Deep Creek Range are actually *O. strigosa* and *O. hemphilli* based on shell morphology and genitalia.

Oreohelix yavapai group

Preputium noticeably bulged, internal longitudinally ribbed portion more than half the entire length; central and lateral radular teeth either unicuspid or bicuspid.

Oreohelix eurekensis Henderson and Daniels, 1916 Eureka Mountainsnail

DESCRIPTION (Henderson and Daniels 1916, p. 321): "*Shell* small, sublenticular; spire slightly elevated; whorls 4.5–4.75, strongly carinated at the periphery, the carina having a tendency to disappear toward the aperture in adults; *whorls* rounded above, sloping roundly in to the suture so as to form an excavated suture, and on the other hand sloping flatly to the periphery; transverse sculpture well marked, irregular; spiral sculpture consists, in the type, of 6 minute, beaded lines below the periphery, with very indistinct lines in the interspaces and in the edge of the umbilicus; similar sculpture above, but not so well defined nor so plainly of two grades; on the cotypes the lines are not so well defined and not so plainly of two grades below; umbilicus wide, exhibiting all the volutions; apical whorls brown, very dark brown in the type, changing to dirty white on the last whorl; two very obscure dark spiral bands, one above, the other barely below the periphery." *Aperture*: subcircular, peristome thin, its insertions connected by a thin parietal film; whorls: 4.3–4.5 (Pilsbry 1939). The subspecies *O. eurekensis*

FIG. T39. *Oreohelix eurekensis.* UMNH 1.012095. Eureka, UT. Credit: E. Wagner, courtesy UMNH.

uinta Brooks, 1939, differed from the form described above primarily by having a wider umbilicus (~3.75X in diameter) and slightly fewer whorls (4.25).

SIZE: type: 5.5 mm high, greater dia. 9.7 mm, lesser 8.8 mm. Cotype: 6.5 mm high × 9.3 mm dia. Umbilicus: 4.4 to 5 times in diameter.

ANIMAL (Pilsbry 1939): The topotype dissections indicated that the snail is allied with *O. yavapai*, having the internally ribbed part of the penis more than half the total length, the latter less than the diameter of the shell. There are distinct side cutting edges on the central tooth and 2 or 3 lateral teeth of the radula, after which there are distinct side cusps. There are about 7 lateral teeth, though the transition to marginals is very gradual.

TYPE LOCATION: Eureka, Utah, on north side of Godiva Mountain. Holotype held in University of Colorado Museum; cotype at ANSP (#113287). *O. e. uinta* was found at Hominy Creek near Whiterocks, Uinta County, Utah; holotype is in the Carnegie Museum, and paratypes are in ANSP.

JUNIOR SYNONYMS: *Oreohelix hemphilli eurekensis* Henderson and Daniels, 1916. Pilsbry considered *eurekensis* a subspecies of *O. hemphilli*, differing only in having fewer whorls, possibly due to the smaller size of the specimen (Henderson and Daniels 1916). It was elevated to *O. eurekensis* by Henderson (1924), which Pilsbry similarly recognized as a valid species (Pilsbry 1939).

NOTES: Typically, smaller than other keeled *Oreohelix* in Utah. Endemic to Utah. Recent genetic analyses by Linscott et al. (2020) suggest that *eurekensis* is synonymous with *O. strigosa*. Surveys by Clarke and Hovingh (1994) suggested that a population at Mammoth Peak-Godiva Mountain, Juab County, contained about 50,000 to 500,000 individuals; Only a single shell was found on neighboring Lime Peak.

DISTRIBUTION: Nevada and Utah. Utah records from Juab, Duschesne, San Pete, Grand, Tooele, and Uinta counties. Clarke and Hovingh (1994): Northern part of

East Tintic Mountains, Juab and Utah counties. Subspecies *uinta* reported from Daggett and Uinta counties.

Oreohelix hemphilli Newcomb, 1870 White Pine Mountainsnail

FIG. T40. *Oreohelix hemphilli*, holotype, ANSP 23060. Credit: ANSP.

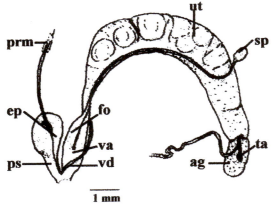

FIG. T41. *Oreohelix hemphilli* genitalia. Credit: Ports (2004), drawing by Lois K. Ports. prm = penial retractor muscle, ep = epiphallus, ps = penis, vd = vas deferens, va = vagina, fo = free oviduct, ut = uterus, sp = spermatheca, ag = albumin gland, ta = talon.

DESCRIPTION (Newcomb 1870; Pilsbry 1939; Ports 2004): *Shell:* thin, depressed, with a low-conic, pale-brown spire and whitish base with gray radial streaks, carinate periphery, and perspective umbilicus contained 5X in diameter. *Whorls:* 2.5 embryonic whorls that are finely striate radially, becoming coarser after the second whorl and with some subgranose spirals; the second whorl is concave above the suture; whorls generally strongly convex below the suture, prominent in the middle and concave above the keel, which is irregularly crenulate; The last whorl is clouded and streaked with white and two brown bands, is coarsely and irregularly striate, with a few weak widely spaced spirals, descends slowly to the aperture, and has a strong keel in front that weakens in the last half turn. Basal and apical surfaces have distinct whorled lirae. *Aperture:* roundly oval, peristome thin, margins joined by a thin parietal callus.

SIZE (Ports 2004): mean shell diameter was 8.0–12.5 mm among three Great Basin populations; Height/Dia. averaged 0.60– to 0.64; umbilicus width averaged 2.4–3.1.

ANIMAL (Binney 1875; Pilsbry 1939; Ports 2004): GENITALIA: Penis length averaged 33 to 38% of shell diameter among three Great Basin populations. The ribbed portion of the preputium varied from 36 to 60% of the total preputium length.

RADULA with 22–1–22 to 24–1–24 teeth, the central and laterals with ectoconal cutting edges; a distinct ectocone appearing about the 7th tooth. Marginals with two simple cusps. Jaw without ribs, wrinkles, or striae, but with a median projection of cutting edge.

TYPE LOCATION: Nevada, "White Pine Mining District, 8,000 feet." Holotype and juvenile paratypes are in ANSP (23060).

JUNIOR SYNONYMS: *Helix hemphilli* Newcomb, 1870; *Patula hemphilli* (Newcomb) Binney, 1878; *Patula strigosa* var. *hemphilli* Binney, 1886–1888.

NOTES: Keeled periphery, perspective umbilicus, and concavity of upper whorls are distinctive characters for differentiation from other *Oreohelix*. Radular teeth differ from *O. yavapai*, which lack the ectocones on the central and lateral teeth. Habitats where these are found include riparian areas with aspen and cottonwood trees as well as pinyon pine and juniper habitats (Ports 1996).

DISTRIBUTION (ANSP collection; Ports 2004; Ibase): CA, MT, NV, NM; Lost River Mountains and Portneuf River, Idaho. In Utah: Salt Lake, Cache, Garfield, Millard (Kings Canyon), and Juab counties; Deep Creek Range, House Range, and Stansbury Mountains.

Oreohelix yavapai Pilsbry, 1905 Yavapai Mountainsnail

DESCRIPTION (Pilsbry 1905, 1939): *Shell:* depressed, subconical, thin, whitish with a dull brown spire and a faint brown band above and below the periphery; A peripheral keel extends to the aperture but is pinched up less than in the subspecies *O. y. neomexicana*. *Whorls:* ca. 5.3; embryonic whorls $2\,^1/_3$, the sharp oblique lines cut by a few spiral lines; first whorl nearly smooth, convex, the next more flattened, finely, densely striate obliquely, and very strongly striate and ribbed spirally. Last whorl barely descends in front and has more spirals. The larger spirals, especially on the base, emphasized as series of granules (bearing short cuticular processes on fresh shells). *Umbilicus:* 3.75X in diameter of the shell. *Aperture:* oblique, rounded, with a thin lip.

SIZE (Pilsbry 1905): SL 8.7, 9.5 mm, dia. 15.2, 16.6 mm; *O. yavapai neomexicana*: typically 7.5 to 8.8 mm tall × 14.6 (4.75 whorls) to 15.8 (5.25 whorls) mm dia. Shells from the northern side of the Sandia Mountains measure about 7.4 × 12.5 mm, 4.5 whorls, umbilicus 5.5X in the diameter; variety *fortis* diameter: 19.7–25.8 mm.

Oreohelicidae

FIG. T42. *Oreohelix yavapai*. Top row: ANSP 79145 lectotype, AZ; middle row: ANSP141875, synonym *O. yavapai fortis*, holotype, Grand Canyon; bottom row: ANSP 84297, *O. yavapai neomexicana*, lectotype, Cañon Diablo, NM. Credit: ANSP.

ANIMAL: Penis short (e.g., 5 mm), the basal half swollen, not much longer than the distal portion, the latter not kinked. Radula: 26–1–26, with unicuspid central and inner lateral teeth; outer laterals with a strong outer cutting point, becoming a well-developed ectocone on the marginals.

O. yavapai neomexicana Pilsbry 1905 (San Miguel County, New Mexico): Differs from *O. yavapai* s.s. by being more depressed, with a stronger keel, the surface above and below it concave, and the whorls are conspicuously swollen below the suture. Wrinkle striation is typically rude and irregular but variable. Embryonic whorls 2–2$^{1}/_{3}$, impressed above the suture, densely, finely striate, and with faint spirals on the second whorl. Umbilicus about 4X in the diameter. The radula has 19–1–19 teeth, similar in shape to those in *O. yavapai* (Pilsbry 1939); marginals bicuspid.

Several other subspecies have been described (Pilsbry 1939). *O. y. compactula* Cockerell 1905 (Pecos Canyon, New Mexico) is smaller and has a higher spire and narrower umbilicus (5.5X in shell diameter) than typical *O. y. neomexicanus*. *O. y. cummingsi* "Ferriss" Pilsbry 1933 (Navajo Mountain, Utah/Arizona) is shaped like typical *neomexicana*, but the shell is always smaller, with the last whorl more swollen below the suture, and is uniform brown; 6 × 12 mm, umbilicus 3 mm, 4.5 whorls. This form was reported to be abundant in the Abajo Mountains, San Juan County (Ferriss 1920; Pilsbry 1939). *O. y. clutei* (Ferriss) Pilsbry, 1933 (Navajo Mountain at New Trail Spring, Arizona; Holotype: ANSP 159216) is pale brownish, suffused with opaque white, with a heavy parietal callus; 5.3 whorls, the last strongly angular in front, the angle disappearing in the last third, where the whorl descends slowly, well below the periphery of the preceding whorl. A variant of this form descends but little. *O. y. fortis* Cockerell (Grand Canyon) is sharply angular in front of the aperture but soon becomes rounded; the umbilicus is broadly open, 3.5–4.4X in diameter, large (19.7–25.8 mm). *O. y. profundorum* has 4.5–5 whorls, a very oblique aperture that tends to point down to the earth, and has a slightly thickened peristome. *O. y. extremitatis* has a depressed conic shape, 4.75 whorls, a body whorl, with the last third to half acutely carinate and not descending much, and widely spaced granose crystals on the base in front of the aperture. Umbilicus: 4.25–2.5X in diameter. See Pilsbry (1939) for more details on the subspecific forms of *O. yavapai*.

TYPE LOCATION: Purtyman's Ranch, on Oak Creek, Yavapai County, Arizona. Holotype and paratypes: ANSP 79415. Also found on summit of Mount Mingus near Jerome, Arizona. *O. y. neomexicana* type location is Canyon Diablo, San Miguel County, near Rowe, New Mexico. Holotype, ANSP 84297.

JUNIOR SYNONYMS: None

NOTES (Beetle 1987; Pilsbry 1905): Identification of this species is generally based on geography and penial morphology since shell characters are too similar to other *Oreohelix* species. *O. yavapai extremitatis* found generally in drier habitats than other oreohelicids; found at the base of cliffs, in talus or on steep slopes. Tend to be smaller at higher elevations. Older shells tend to descend more in the last whorl. In one individual, 10 embryos were found in the uterus.

DISTRIBUTION (Ibase; ANSP): AZ, CA, ID, MT, NE, NM, NV, SD, WY. In Utah, museum records from Navajo and Blue Mountains; San Juan, Millard, and Summit counties.

Punctidae Morse, 1864

This family is characterized by minute snails commonly referred to as spots. The snails have umbilicated shells and a micro- and macro-radial postapical structure. Whorl count and shape are highly variable. Foot of animal is undivided, with prominent pedal and suprapedal grooves that unite above the tail without forming a caudal pit. Radula: central tooth tricuspid, latero-marginals bicuspid with three tiny accessory cusps, major cusps becoming reduced on outer teeth but not tending to split into more cusps. Jaw of separated square plates, partly fused in larger species (Solem 1982). Morse (1864) named the subfamily, Punctinae, which was later elevated to family by Solem (1976, 1982), who split the large family Endodontidae into the families Punctidae, Charopidae, and Endodontidae. Morse defined Punctidae based on the radula and buccal plate characteristics.

Currently, there are 31 genera in the family, including *Punctum* Morse, 1864 in the subfamily Punctinae (Mbase, accessed January 2020). There are 33 species within the genus *Punctum*, one of which is known from Utah. Synonyms of the family include Laomidae (Laominae) Suter, 1913; Paralaomidae Iredale, 1941, and Patulastidae Steenberg, 1925.

Punctum minutissimum Lea, 1841 Small Spot

DESCRIPTION (Lea 1841; Morse 1864; Pilsbry 1948): *Shell*: minute, subdiscoidal with a broad, convex spire, umbilicate, delicate striae with or without spaced riblets, and very minute spiral striae. Periostracum brownish-horn, raised in coarse ridges running parallel with the incremental striae. The ridges become more prominent as they approach the umbilical region and coalesce at or near the suture. Faint revolving lines are more prominent near the umbilicus and appear to be arranged in pairs. *Whorls:* 3.75–4.25, convex, the first 1.5 smooth or lightly striate spirally; last whorl cylindric, suture descending to about the periphery of previous whorl. Umbilicus about 3.7 times in the shell diameter. *Aperture:* lunate-rounded, with a simple, thin lip.

SIZE: Diameter 1.1–1.51 mm × 0.69–0.94 mm.

FIG. T43. *Punctum minutissimum.* Credit: above: ANSP. Below: redrawn from Pilsbry 1948.

ANIMAL (Pilsbry 1948): Jaw arcuate or crescentic, with 13–19 rhombic plates, loosely connected by a thin transparent membrane, and are overlapping. Buccal plate divided into 16 distinct pieces. Central teeth somewhat narrower than laterals, tricuspid, the mesocone shorter than the basal plate, side cusps small. Basal plates of lateral teeth much longer than the cusps. Foot with distinct pedal grooves, obtuse posteriorly. Kidney U-shaped and lung with a branched pulmonary vein.

TYPE LOCATION: Vicinity of Cincinnati, Ohio.

JUNIOR SYNONYMS: *Helix minutissima* Lea, 1841; *Punctum minutissimum* (Lea) Morse, 1864; *Punctum pygmaeum* (Draparnaud) Binney, 1878; *Microphysa pygmaea* (Draparnaud) Binney, 1885. *Punctum minutissimum* is the type species for the genus *Punctum*.

NOTES: The small size for a shell with 3.75–4.25 whorls differentiates this shell from other disk shells. Found in dense hardwood growth in rotten bark of beech trees and in the large fungi such as *Polyporus* and *Boletus* (Morse 1864). Chamberlin and Jones (1929) found *Punctum* shells in leaves, rotten wood, and aspen groves. Chamberlin and Jones (1929) noted that *Punctum pygmaeum* Draparnaud, 1801 was found in Utah, which at the time was considered synonymous with *P. minutissimum*. *P. pygmaeum* is from Europe, and H. B. Baker (1930b) and Pilsbry (1948) note that they are not synonymous; *P. minutissimum* differs in whorls that increase more gradually, is smaller and higher, and the last whorl descends to a greater degree than *P. pygmaeum*. Chamberlin and Jones (1929) noted that Utah specimens are a rich red-gold color.

DISTRIBUTION (Morse 1864; Chamberlin and Jones 1929; Jones 1935; Pilsbry 1948): Mexico (Puebla), Newfoundland, Ontario, Maritime Provinces; ME, MA, NY, NJ, PA, DE, MD, VA, WV, NC, KY, TN, AL, FL, MI, OH, IL, IA, ID, MI, SD, CO, ID, OR, NM. Utah records (*P. pygmaeum/minutissimum*): south of Moroni; Kamas; North Fork Provo River; Big Cottonwood, Lamb's, and Logan canyons.

SPF: **PUPILLOIDEA Turton, 1831**

Cochlicopidae Pilsbry, 1900c (1879)

DESCRIPTION (Pilsbry 1948, p. 1045): "The shell is small, elongate, imperforate, smooth and glossy, subtranslucent, with the ovate aperture longer than wide; lip not expanded, thickened within; parietal wall steeply sloping. Columella slightly sinuate or truncate at base. Penis with well-developed epiphallus to which the retractor muscle, which is not forked, attaches, and an appendix. The prostate gland is of the long and band-like type. Spermathecal duct of medium length (with a diverticulum in *Cionella*). The arcuate jaw is delicately and closely plaited. Radula with few (about 20–1–20 to 24–1–24) teeth. Centrals decidedly narrower than the laterals, tricuspid or with the ectocones subobsolete. Laterals bicuspid with quadrate basal plates; marginals with 4–6 cusps. Differs from the Pupillidae mainly by the characters of the shell and by having a long prostate gland." Found in the Palearctic Region worldwide, but there is only one species in North America, *Cochlicopa lubrica*.

Genus *Cochlicopa* Férussac, 1821, description (Pilsbry 1948): The shell is oblong-conic or oblong-cylindric, imperforate, smooth and glossy, composed of 5–7 slightly convex whorls. Aperture small, ovate, nearly vertical, toothless. Outer and basal lips arcuate, obtuse, thickened within by a callous rim which is continuous to the upper insertion; columella short, concave, or straightened, very slightly sinuate at the base; parietal callus very thin throughout. There are 13 recognized fossil species in the genus and 7 Recent species (Mbase).

Cochlicopa lubrica Müller, 1774 Glossy Pillar

DESCRIPTION: Pilsbry (1948, p. 1048): "The shell is imperforate, oblong, the spire gradually tapering to an obtuse apex; thin, smooth, yellowish corneous, subtransparent and very glossy. Whorls 5.5–6, moderately convex. Aperture subvertical, ovate, toothless; outer lip evenly arcuate, obtuse, bordered with yellow or reddish outside, having a narrow, smooth, and continuous callus rib within. Columella somewhat straightened, calloused, often very indistinctly notched or sinuous at its junction with the basal lip. Parietal callus thin, translucent."

SIZE: Length 5–5.8 mm, diameter 2.2–2.5 mm.

TYPE LOCATION: Not given.

JUNIOR SYNONYMS (Pilsbry 1948): *Helix lubricus* Müller, 1774; *Bulimus lubricus* (Müller) Gould 1841; *Bulimus lubricoides* Stimpson, 1851; *Cionella lubrica* (Müller) Pilsbry 1948; *Cionella subcylindrica* L. Binney and Bland, 1869; *Ferussacia subcylindrica* L. Binney, 1878; *Zua buddii* Dupuy, 1849; *Zua lubricoidea* (Stimpson) Morse 1864. Roth (2003) presented a convincing case for naming the family Cionellidae Clessin, 1879, which has precedence in time, but in both Bouchet and Rocroi (2005) and Bouchet et al. (2017), Cochlicopidae is given priority.

FIG. T44. *Cochlicopa lubrica.* ANSP 45876. Credit: ANSP.

NOTES: The narrow columnar shape and shiny luster distinguish this shell from other shells in Utah. The New Zealand mud snail has a similar shape and number of whorls, but it has a more acute (pointed) apex and the aperture is rounder. Genetic analyses have indicated that *Cochlicopa* is closely related to the genera *Leptachatina* and *Vallonia* (Wade et al. 2006). Often found in rotten wood and damp leaf litter in riparian areas.

DISTRIBUTION (ANSP): China, Tibet, Japan, Denmark, Greenland, Ireland, Europe, Russia, Romania, Sweden, and the United Kingdom. In North America, *C. lubrica* is widely distributed from Alaska to Labrador and Newfoundland, south to Washington, DC,

FIG. T45. *Cochlicopa lubrica.* Logan Canyon, UT. Credit: E. Wagner.

southern Missouri, and the Sierra Madre of Mexico, and west to California. Utah records: Blue Mountains, Hidden Lake (Glendale), 3 miles east of Morgan, Monroe Canyon, Marysvale, Weber Canyon, and Zion National Park (Jones 1935; Woolstenhulme 1942a; ANSP records; Wheeler 2018). The author found it at China Row Spring in Logan Canyon in bank detritus and dead wood (Fig T45), Green Canyon (Cache County), Box Elder Canyon near Mantua, Swan Creek (Bear Lake, Rich County), Daniels Canyon (Whiskey Spring), and in Beaver Creek above Kamas, Utah.

Pupillidae Turton, 1831

Pupoides species have small (2.75–4 mm tall), elongate, cylindrical shells with rounded ends that are reminiscent of insect pupae; they are rimate or umbilicate, with or without lamellae (informally called teeth) in an aperture that is truncate oval or rounded (Pilsbry 1948). When teeth are present in juvenile shells, they are not continuous with or correspond to adult dentition. Nekola et al. (2015) noted that shell apertural features used for classifying species are highly plastic. For example, populations expressing poorly developed lamellae or callus tended to be at sites with low calcium availability. However, shell surface sculpture and architecture characteristics were more closely allied to the genetic data. Suture depth, apex architecture, and shell width were also good characters. The pupillids lack an oviducal cul-de-sac and have a short prostate; penis and retractor are bifid, although the epiphallar arm is weakly demarcated (H. B. Baker 1935).

The type genus is *Pupilla* (Leach) Fleming, 1828 (Bouchet and Rocroi 2005). The genus is characterized by a narrowly reflected (flared) peristome that lacks a basal fold or teeth in immature forms; deeply placed parietal, columellar, and palatal teeth when present; short but distinct inferior tentacles; and a foot about half as long as the shell (Pilsbry 1948). *Pupoides* differ from *Pupilla* by having a tapering spire, longer and more loosely coiled whorls, a longer aperture with no crest behind the lip, and the oblique angle of the parietal margin of the aperture.

Pupillidae is distributed worldwide (Pilsbry 1948). The family once contained over 40 genera and nearly 700 species (Pilsbry 1948), including the species now allocated to the closely related families Valloniidae, Gastrocoptidae, and Vertiginidae. These groups were subfamilies based on anatomical differences described by H. B. Baker (1935), later elevated to family. Currently, Pupillidae has 41 fossil and 68 Recent species recognized within seven genera within two subfamilies, Pupillinae and Pupoidinae, and one fossil genus *Albertanella* (Mbase). *Pupilla* has 36 recognized species and *Pupoides* has 19. See Fig. T47 for a comparison of Utah *Pupilla* species.

Pupilla blandi Morse, 1865 (1867) Rocky Mountain Column

FIG. T46. *Pupilla blandi*. ANSP 104005, Orig. comb. *P. muscorum xerobia* lectotype. Credit: ANSP.

DESCRIPTION (Morse 1867; Pilsbry 1948; Nekola et al. 2015): *Shell*: cylindrical, shiny, delicately striated, opaque, light brown, apex domed, umbilicus rimate. *Whorls*: 6, the nucleus with microscopic granulations, sutures shallow, subconvex, the last ascending at the aperture, rapidly expanding, with an external whitish callus, between which and the peristome there is a deep constriction. *Aperture*: small, nearly circular to slightly wider than tall, teeth variable (0–3: parietal, columellar, and palatal far within at the base of the aperture). Peristome unreflected to subreflected; callus variably thickened; crest, when present, weak to strong.

SIZE: SL 2.30–3.25 mm, SW 1.2–1.6 mm. Type, 3.25 × 1.5 mm.

TYPE LOCATION: "Drift on the Missouri River near Fort Berthold."

JUNIOR SYNONYMS (Pilsbry 1948; Nekola et al. 2015): *Pupilla blandii* Morse, 1867; *Pupa sublubrica* Ancey, 1881; *Pupa blandi* (Morse) Binney, 1885; *Pupa blandi* forma *obtusa* Cockerell, 1892a; *Pupilla blandi* mut. *alba* Cockerell, 1888b; *Pupa blandi* var. *edentata* Squyer, 1894; *Pupilla muscorum xerobia* Pilsbry, 1914; *Pupilla muscorum*, in part. Based on DNA evidence, Nekola et al. (2015) has transferred *Pupilla blandi pithodes* Pilsbry and Ferriss, 1917 to *Pupilla hebes pithodes* (Pilsbry and Ferriss) *comb. nov.*

NOTES (Henderson and Daniels 1917; Nekola et al. 2015): *P. blandi* microsculpture consists of weak radial threads and a shiny luster, differing from *P. hebes,* which has sharp radial threads and a silky luster. Fewer whorls and dextral compared to *P. syngenes*. Genetic analyses indicate that *blandi* is closely related to *P. hebes* (Nekola et al. 2015). Nekola et al. (2015) considered *P. blandi* to be limited to the Plains (northeast New Mexico to northwest Minnesota and south-central Canada) and noted that *P. hebes* is the form in the Great Basin and Colorado Plateau. Some *blandi* records may need to be transferred to *P. hebes,* especially west of the continental divide. Also, *P. muscorum xerobia*, described from Duran, New Mexico, was found to be genetically synonymous with *P. blandi*.

FIG. T47. Comparison of apertural variation in some North American *Pupilla* species. Names represent those supported by DNA sequence analysis (sample no. in parentheses, cf. Nekola et al. 2015). *Pupilla blandi* (1st row): A. Ute Creek Canyon, CO (AP37); B. Irvine, Alberta (AP34); C. Moose Jaw, Saskatchewan (AP35); D. Bannon Ranch, NM (ET7 was lost, so a similar shell from the same population was used). *Pupilla hebes pithodes* (2nd row): E. Tusas Ridge, NM (AP38); F. Bullion Canyon, UT (AP 27); G. Bullion Canyon, UT (AP28); H. Bear Wallow, AZ (P6). *Pupilla hebes* (3rd row): I. Loope East, CA (P14), J. Bullion Canyon, UT (P17); K. Ruby Mountains, NV (P16); L. Kaibab Plateau, AZ (P1); M. East Tintic Range, UT (P2). *Pupilla sonorana*: N. Sacramento Mts., NM (P12). *Pupilla* n.sp. (central-eastern N. American taiga & tundra): O. Lake Bemidji, Minnesota, USA(AP33). *Pupilla syngenes*: P. Mogollon, NM (AP30); Q. Kaibab Plateau, AZ (P11). Credit: © Jeff Nekola.

DISTRIBUTION (Henderson and Daniels 1917; Jones 1940a; Gregg 1940, 1941; Woolstenhulme 1942a, b; Oliver and Bosworth 2000, 2002; Nekola et al. 2015; UMNH): Rocky Mountains and Plains (northeast New Mexico to northwest Minnesota to southern Saskatchewan and Alberta). Utah records: Cannonville, Brian Head Peak area, Cedar Breaks Nat. Monument, Zion Canyon, Wilson Arch, Twin Creeks (Fish Lake), Orderville, Hidden Lake (Glendale), north of Eureka, Oquirrh Mountains, near Tooele, Fairfield, Tooele County, Weber and Red Butte canyons, Raft River Mountains, Logan Canyon, Promontory Point, Chalk Creek, Lofgren, Hominy Creek (southern slope Uinta Mountains) and upriver of Moab. Some *Pupilla muscorum* records should also be noted here.

Pupilla hebes Ancey, 1881 Crestless Column

DESCRIPTION (Pilsbry 1948; Nekola et al. 2015): *Shell*: cylindric-ovoid, silky, rather thin, rimate, obtuse at the apex, upper $1/3$–$1/4$ tapered, corneous-tawny, with sharp, very minute striae. *Whorls:* 6–7, strongly convex, regularly increasing, joined by a normal to deep suture, regularly increasing, the last swollen towards the aperture, then deeply contracted. *Aperture:* truncate round to taller than wide; teeth 0–3 (weak parietal, columellar, and/or palatal lamellae). Peristome thin, reflected or unreflected; weak to strong crest; callus absent to strong, white to brown.

FIG. T48. *Pupilla hebes.* ANSP 115361 orig. comb. *P. blandi pithodes* holotype. ANSP 103283, orig. comb. *P. hebes kaibabensis* lectotype. Credit: ANSP.

FIG. T49. *Pupilla hebes*, albino variant, ANSP 45843. Credit: ANSP.

Pupilla hebes kaibabensis Pilsbry & Ferriss, 1911 (Fig. T48, ANSP 103283), found north of the Grand Canyon, was synonymized with *Pupilla hebes* by Nekola et al. (2015). Pilsbry (1948) considered it to be a "hunger form," diminished in size due to harsh environmental conditions.

Sinestral and albino (Fig. T49) variants have been reported in Arizona (Pilsbry and Ferriss 1910). DNA analysis by Nekola et al. (2015) indicated that snails identified as *Pupilla blandi pithodes* (Fig. T48), are genetically more related to *P. hebes* than *blandi*, and so they were renamed *P. hebes pithodes*. This subpopulation has a weaker or absent crest, and the shell is wider; it ranges from eastern Arizona and central Utah to Colorado, New Mexico, and Texas.

SIZE: SL 2.6–3.5 mm, SW 1.4–1.7. Type: SL 3.25 mm, SW 1.5 mm; L/W 2.17

TYPE LOCATION: White Pine, Nevada.

JUNIOR SYNONYMS: *Pupa hebes* Ancey, 1881; *Pupa arizonensis* (Gabb) Binney, 1885; *Pupilla hebes kaibabensis* Pilsbry and Ferriss, 1911; *Pupilla muscorum idahoensis* Henderson and Daniels, 1917; *Pupilla hebes* form *nefas* Pilsbry and Ferriss, 1910; *Pupilla blandi charlestonensis* Pilsbry, 1921; *Pupilla blandi* in part; *Pupilla muscorum*, in part. *Pupilla hebes* (Ancey) Pilsbry and Ferriss 1911.

NOTES (Pilsbry 1948; Nekola et al. 2015; Ports 2019): *P. hebes* microsculpture consists of sharp radial threads and the periostracum is silky, whereas *P. blandi* has weak radial threads and is shiny. The shell tapers for the upper $1/3–1/4$ of shell height, whereas the apex of *P. blandi* is more domed. Found in cottonwoods, conifers, aspen groves, shrubs, and rock slides. Recent genetic analyses have indicated that shells from the Rocky Mountains and High Plains of the United States with characteristics ascribed to *P. muscorum* (smooth cylindrical shell, 0–2 parietal teeth, shallow suture, strong crest, thick white callus) are *P. hebes* or *P. blandi*. Similarly, some putative *P. blandi*, were genetically determined to be *P. hebes* (Logan Canyon) or *P. hebes pithodes* (Wilson Arch). So, some Utah records for *muscorum* or *blandi* should be transferred to *P. hebes*. *P. muscorum* still exists as a species, but its range is now narrowed to Europe and parts of the eastern United States where it was introduced.

DISTRIBUTION (Pilsbry 1948; ANSP; Ibase): Chihuahua, Mexico; AZ, NM, NV, CO, ID, MT, NV, SD, WY, WA. Utah records (Gregg 1940, 1941; Oliver and Bosworth 2002; Nekola et al. 2015; ANSP; UMNH; FMNH): Brian Head Peak area east of Parowan; Cedar Breaks National Monument; Beaver Canyon, Rainbow Bridge, Abajo Mountains (pass about 3.5 miles west of Innes Sawmill), Navajo, Blue, and Henry Mountains; East Tintic Range; Bullion Canyon; Kane, Box Elder, Tooele, San Juan, and Rich counties.

Pupilla syngenes Pilsbry, 1890 Top-heavy Column

DESCRIPTION (Pilsbry 1948): *Shell*: sinestral, cylindrical, but somewhat wider toward the large, obtuse apex, blunt at each end; cinnamon brown, or a little darker. Surface dull when fresh, delicately obliquely striate. *Whorls:* 8, the last one compressed and flattened around the lower-outer portion, its last third ascending on the previous whorl, and elevated into a high rounded ridge or crest a short distance behind the outer lip. *Aperture:* slightly oblique, truncate-oval in form; the outer lip narrowly expanded, basal and columellar margins broader; about the middle of the parietal wall, or nearer the upper end, there is a small parietal lamella about ¼ of whorl long. Far within there may be a blunt columellar tooth (lamella); most specimens have a tubercular lower palatal fold far within the outer lip. *P. s. dextroversa* differs from *P. syngenes* only in the dextral aperture (sinestral in *syngenes;* see ANSP 79460, Fig. T50).

SIZE: 3.5 mm tall, 1.3 mm wide; L/W 2.69

TYPE LOCATION: Arizona. San Rafael and Grant, Valencia County, New Mexico (holotype 79460 ANSP).

JUNIOR SYNONYMS: *Pupa syngenes* Pilsbry, 1890; *Pupilla syngenes* Pilsbry and Ferriss, 1911. Subspecies include *P. s. avus* and *P. s. dextroversa* (Pilsbry 1921) and mutation *nivea* (2nd row in Fig. T50, ANSP 45852; Henderson 1924).

FIG. T50. *Pupilla syngenes.* Above: *P. syngenes avus*, Grand Canyon, ANSP holotype 94220. Middle: *P. syngenes nivea*, Black Mesa, AZ, lectotype ANSP 45852. Below: *P. syngenes dextroversa*, San Rafael, NM, lectotype ANSP 79460.

NOTES: Sinestral, club-shaped form and large number of whorls will distinguish this species from similar pupilliform species.

DISTRIBUTION (Pilsbry 1948; ANSP; Ibase): AZ, NM, MT. Utah records (FMNH; UMNH; Jones 1935; Pilsbry 1948; Wheeler 2018): Bryce Canyon; Zion National Park, Oakley, east of Kamas, and Moab; Garfield, Sevier (Fish Lake), Washington, Tooele, and Wayne counties. Woolstenhulme (1942b) recorded it from Kamas as *P. syngenes dextroversa*.

Pupoides albilabris Say, 1821 White-lip Dagger

DESCRIPTION (Say 1821; Pilsbry 1948): *Shell*: turreted, slowly tapering to the obtuse apex, pale horn color or dusky to cinnamon or slightly darker, somewhat glossy, obsoletely wrinkled across, sutures deeply impressed, umbilicus distinct and minutely perforate to rimate. *Whorls:* 6, strongly convex, the last half whorl somewhat compressed laterally, tapering to the narrowly rounded base. *Aperture:* suboval, truncated transversely above by the penultimate whorl; nearly ⅓ the length of the shell, with a nearly transverse labium that is the color of the shell exterior, labrum equally widely reflected, thickened within, its face flattened, white; the outer lip is more strongly arched near the upper insertion.

FIG. T51. *Pupoides albilabris*. Left, center: Credit: ©Rick Fridell. Right: original figure from Gabb (1866) of *P. arizonensis*, a junior synonym.

SIZE (Say 1821; Pilsbry 1948): SL 5.1 mm, SW 2.2 mm. Size varies with location, 4.2–5 mm long in Philadelphia, 4 mm (~5 whorls) in Arizona, and 5 × 2 mm (6.5 whorls) in Alabama.

Pupa arizonensis Gabb, 1866, a synonym of *albilabris*, was described as having sides more parallel, diverging convexly from the apex. It also had an apex more convex, was imperforate and fusiform, and had 5.5 whorls. The lip was thickened, strongly reflected, white, opaque, acute internally, not constricted behind the reflection; the peristome was not continuous on the body whorl; a slight emargination exists on the inner edge of the peristome, near the posterior end of the outer lip.

TYPE LOCATION: Upper Missouri. *P. arizonensis* was from Fort Grant, at the junction of the Arivapa and San Pedro rivers, Arizona.

JUNIOR SYNONYMS (Pilsbry 1948): *Cyclostoma marginata* Say, 1821. *Pupoides marginatus* (Say) Pilsbry and Vanatta 1900; *Pupa fallax* (Say) Gould 1843; *Pupa arizonensis* Gabb, 1866. Because Say's species differed from the *Cyclostoma marginatum* of G. Fischer (1807) and *Pupa marginata* of Draparnaud (1801), Adams (1841) renamed it *Pupa albilabris*. Say (1825) described *Pupa fallax,* which he noted "closely resembles *P. marginata.*" Say received *P. fallax* from a correspondent in Massachusetts, but it was actually a stray example of *Ena obscura* Müller, 1774, of Europe. The same specimen apparently served for type of *Pupa placida* Say, 1829 (Pilsbry 1948).

NOTES (Pilsbry 1948): The tapering, lustrous spire and white, thickened lip differentiate this species from the pupa-shaped forms of *Gastrocopta*, *Vertigo*, and *Pupilla*. *P. albilabris* differs from *P. hordaceus* by having a smoother shell, lacking the fine ribbing of *hordaceus*. This species likes limestone soils but may be found elsewhere. It lives under stones, at the roots of grass, in well-drained, often sunny areas. It may be found on tree trunks after rains. Sinestral variants have been found.

DISTRIBUTION (Pilsbry 1948; ANSP; Ibase): West Indies, Mexico, Peru, and Australia. North America from Ontario and Maine to the Gulf of Mexico, west to the Dakotas, Colorado, Texas, western Arizona, northern Mexico (islands in the Gulf of California), and California. Utah records: Zion National Park (FMNH; Wheeler 2018) and Salt Lake City.

Pupoides hordaceus Gabb, 1866 Ribbed Dagger

DESCRIPTION (Gabb 1866; Pilsbry 1948): *Shell*: very small, cylindrical; apex obtuse. *Whorls*: 6, convex; suture well impressed, smooth, thin, horn color. *Aperture*: small, rounded below, unarmed, lip narrowly reflected and white; base umbilicate, the umbilicus bounded by an angle.

SIZE: Shell length 2.8 mm × 1.0 mm wide.

The synonym *P. eupleura* Chamberlin and Berry, 1931, was subcylindrical, light horn color, rimate, with a blunt apex, moderately impressed sutures, and 5.5 whorls. First whorl is smooth, 2nd gently striate, the remaining three with elevated, sharp, and distant ribs. Body whorl is over half as long as the entire shell. *Aperture:* truncate-ovate, columella is straight and slightly dilated, peristome white, thickened, and broadly reflected. Length 3.7 mm × 1.9 mm wide; last whorl 2.2 mm, aperture 1.5 mm.

FIG. T52. *Pupoides hordaceus*. Left: ANSP 70463, lectotype for *Pupa gabbi mexicanorum*, a junior synonym. Credit: ANSP. Right: Original figure, Credit: Gabb 1866.

TYPE LOCATION: Fort Grant, at the junction of the Arivapa and San Pedro Rivers, Arizona. For *P. eupleura*, Henry Mountains, Utah, west of King's Ranch (holotype, UMNH No. 1777, paratypes No. 1836).

JUNIOR SYNONYMS: *Pupa hordacea* Gabb, 1866; *Pupoides hordaceus* (Gabb) Pilsbry and Vanatta 1900; *Pupa arizonensis* (Gabb) Binney 1869 (not *P. arizonensis* Gabb); *Pupa gabbi* Dall, 1897; *Bifidaria hebes* (Ancey) Pilsbry 1898 (not *Pupa hebes* Ancey); *Pupa gabbi v. mexicanorum* Cockerell, 1897c; *Pupoides eupleura* Chamberlin and Berry, 1931.

NOTES (Pilsbry 1948): Distinguished from *albilabris* by the slender, spaced riblets; fewer whorls than *P. syngenes*.

DISTRIBUTION (ANSP; Ibase): AZ, CO, KS, MT, NM, TX, & WY. In Utah, records (FMNH) from Garfield County (Henry Mountains). The form *P. eupleura*, described by Chamberlin and Berry (1931), was found in the Henry Mountains (Wayne and Garfield counties) and Cannonville, Utah.

Valloniidae Morse, 1864

Small (< 3.5 mm diameter) discoid or subglobose shells, often, but not always, ribbed or with flared apertures. Found under wood, stones, at the roots of plants, mossy cliffs, and in wet meadows. Also found in streams where fine drift settles, likely washed in by heavy rain. Morse (1864) assigned snails to the subfamily Valloniinae based on the dentition of the radula: 80 or 90 rows of plates averaging 26 plates in a row; laterals and unicini distinct (broad, short, and minutely serrated); central plate is square with 3 cusps; laterals 4–5, square, and bidentate.

In Valloniidae there are 43 fossil and 62 Recent species currently recognized in the following Recent genera: *Acanthinula* Beck, 1847 (synonyms: *Aulaca* Westerlund, 1902; *Euacanthinula* Westerlund, 1889); *Pupisoma* Stoliczka, 1873 (synonyms: *Imputegla* Iredale, 1937; *Parazoogenetes* Habe, 1956; *Ptychopatula* Pilsbry, 1889), *Salpingoma* Haas, 1937; *Spermodea* Westerlund, 1902. *Vallonia* Risso, 1826 (synonyms: *Amplexis* Brown, 1827; *Circinaria* Beck, 1837; *Glaphyra* Albers, 1850; *Pulchelliana* Caziot, 1910; *Zurama* Turton, 1831), *Pupisoma* Stoliczka, 1873, *Planogyra* Morse, 1864, *Salpingoma* Hass, 1937; *Spermodea* Westerlund, 1902; *Plagyrona* Gittenberger, 1977; *Gittenbergia* Guisti, Castagnoli, & Manganelli, 1985, and *Zoogenetes* Morse, 1864 (Mbase). *Vallonia* is the second largest genus, with 16 fossil and 22 Recent species. Within Utah are representatives from two genera, *Vallonia* and *Zoogenetes*.

In *Vallonia*, the shell is discoid, umbilicate, with an expanded peristome and 3–4.5 rounded whorls. The animal is oviparous. The absence of a secondary ureter is characteristic of the genus, a dart sac is present, and the penis has a flagellum (Sterki 1893). The foot and head are translucent; sole with many minute white dots; and locomotion is in wave-like undulations. Eye peduncles slender; inferior tentacles short but distinct (Sterki 1893). Jaw is arcuate, about 4–6X wider than tall, rounded or slightly angular at the ends. See Sterki (1893) for figures of radula.

In *Zoogenetes*, the shell is ovately conic (taller than wide), fragile, narrowly umbilicate, with few, rapidly increasing convex whorls, the first two rather smooth, the rest with delicate, widely spaced, oblique riblets; the aperture is ovate and oblique, with a simple margin, dilated near the columellar insertion (Pilsbry 1948). The animal is ovoviviparous, foot margin crenulated, head with crenulated labial processes, and short, inferior tentacles. The ureter is heavily pigmented anteriorly, the end appearing as a black spot through the mantle. The penis has a long appendix, an epiphallus which is thick posteriorly, and a forked retractor muscle, but it lacks the two accessory diverticula of *Acanthinula* (Pilsbry 1948). To date, there is only one species in the genus, *Z. harpa*.

Vallonia cyclophorella (Ancey) Sterki, 1893 Silky Vallonia

DESCRIPTION (Sterki 1893; Pilsbry 1948): *Shell*: thin, pale grayish-horn colored or whitish translucent, ribbed. Ribs fine, crowded (~60 on last whorl), with fine membranes, rather regular, though often irregular, with fine striae between them. Most specimens are dull, but the surface of some populations (e.g., Walla Walla, Washington) are shiny, the shell almost colorless, thin, transparent, and relatively large. *Whorls*: about 4, the last depressed above, suture moderately deep; last whorl somewhat widening toward the aperture, in its last ⅓ distinctly

FIG. T53. *Vallonia cyclophorella.* Left, ANSP 115197, orig. comb. *Vallonia cyclophorella septuagentaria* lectotype. Credit: ANSP; right, UMNH #1.003737. Credit: E. Wagner, courtesy UMNH.

ascending, then rapidly descending, somewhat more at the suture, so that the margins are near each other; nucleus with slightly irregular, nearly obsolete revolving lines. Umbilicus large (~ 1 mm), varying among specimens; some shells are tightly coiled so the umbilicus is about 3X in diameter, others more loosely coiled have the umbilicus about 2.6X in the diameter. *Aperture*: oblique, transversely elongate, but nearly round, upper margin markedly less curved than the lower margin, peristome slightly everted, except near the suture.

SIZE: Dia. 2.6–2.7 mm × 1.0–1.2 mm tall; umb. large (~1 mm dia.).

ANIMAL (Sterki 1893): Jaw with stout, irregular rib-striae, though smooth near side margins. Radula: 63 transverse rows of 23–25 teeth. There are 5 laterals, the fifth with a small plate, simple to bicuspid. The first marginal (6th tooth) has a large mesodont and 2–3 smaller cusps. The subsequent marginals are comparatively small, about six, the mesodont barely exceeding the other cusps only in the 2–3 first teeth; the last ones very short and with very small cusps.

TYPE LOCATION: West Cliff, Colorado, and Walla Walla, Washington

JUNIOR SYNONYMS: *Helix pulchella costata* form *cyclophorella* (Ancey) Cockerell 1890; *Vallonia cyclophorella septuagentaria* Pilsbry and Ferriss, 1918.

NOTES: The peristome is slightly everted in *cyclophorella* but is not as thickened as for *gracilicosta;* rougher sculpture than for *V. pulchella*, but not as strongly ribbed as *perspectiva*.

DISTRIBUTION (Henderson and Daniels 1917; Berry 1931; Jones 1935; Gregg 1940; ANSP collection; Ibase): western North America from Alberta south to Arizona and west from Minnesota and Colorado to California. Idaho: St. Charles Canyon; by Franklin. Utah records: Rainbow Bridge, Blue Mountains, Brian Head Peak area, Bryce Canyon, Lamb's and American Fork canyons, Eureka, near

Clinton's Cave (Tooele County); counties of Cache, Rich, Garfield, Morgan, Salt Lake, Sevier, Summit, Iron, Millard, Kane, Wayne, Weber, and San Juan.

Vallonia gracilicosta Reinhardt, 1883a Multirib Vallonia

DESCRIPTION (Sterki 1893): *Shell*: flat, with very low conic spire; silky; fine ribs, rather crowded, but regularly spaced (~40–55 on last whorl); widely umbilicated (~3x in shell dia.); whitish-gray. *Whorls:* 3.5–4, convex, with deep sutures; last whorl well rounded or slightly flattened above and below the periphery giving an angular appearance around the umbilicus, strongly expanding toward the aperture, slightly ascending in last ¼ before descending. Nucleus with indistinct microscopic revolving lines. *Aperture:* moderately oblique, subcircular to transversely oval (upper margin curved but little, lower margin more so, being almost obtusely angular), appearing slightly triangular; broad lip is strongly everted and white.

ANIMAL: Radula 0.27 mm wide with 33(35) teeth, formula 4 + 2:10(11). Jaw is 0.31 mm wide.

SIZE (Sterki 1893; Frest and Johannes 1993): Usually 2.5–3.0 mm diameter × 1 mm tall.

FIG. T54. *Vallonia gracilicosta.* ANSP 112012, holotype, Big Hatchet Mts., NM, orig. comb. *Vallonia sonorana* ANSP 11723 lectotype, orig. comb. *Vallonia costata montana*, Rocky Mts. Credit: ANSP.

TYPE LOCATION: Unknown. For synonym *V. albula*: St. Joseph, Quebec, Canada

JUNIOR SYNONYMS (Gerber 1996): *Vallonia albula* Sterki, 1893; *Vallonia sonorana* Pilsbry, 1915

NOTES: Everted lip separates *V. gracilicosta* from *cyclophorella;* fine ribbing separates it from *pulchella*, which is smoother in sculpture and from *perspectiva*, which has more pronounced ribbing and a wider umbilicus.

DISTRIBUTION (ANSP; Ibase): Ontario, Quebec, Manitoba; United States: AZ, CA, CO, IA, IL, IN, MI, MN, MO, NE, OK, KS, MT, NV, NM, ND, SD, TX, WA, WI, WY. Widespread in Utah. Museum records from Zion National Park; Logan and Box Elder canyons; between Manning and Mercur; North Creek Gulch (west of Monticello); Panguitch Creek; Cedar Canyon; Marysvale; counties of Cache, Garfield, Grand, Iron, Juab, Kane, Piute, Salt Lake, San Juan, Sanpete, Sevier, Summit, Tooele, Washington, Wayne, and Weber. Specimens from Logan Canyon, Utah, found by Hemphill and labelled *Helix pulchella* var. *costata* in the ANSP collection were thought by Sterki (1893) to be *V. gracilicosta*. Other Utah records (Berry 1931; Jones 1935, 1940; Brooks 1936; Gregg 1940; Woolstenhulme 1942a, b; Wheeler 2018): near Brian Head Peak, Fremont Canyon, Zion Canyon; 2.8 miles west of Vernal; Mill Creek; Chalk Creek; Weber River; City Creek, Salt Lake City; Grantsville; Fairfield; Clear Creek (Raft River Mountains); Red Butte, Lamb's, Bell's, Ogden, and Provo canyons.

Vallonia perspectiva Sterki, 1893 Thin-lip Vallonia

DESCRIPTION (Sterk 1893): *Shell*: small, spire flat or slightly elevated, with a very wide perspective umbilicus, widening for the last half whorl. *Whorls:* 3⅓, gradually increasing, a little flattened above and below the periphery, with a deep suture; last whorl rounded, comparatively narrow, little expanded toward the aperture, rather rapidly descending in toto. Nucleus without revolving lines. Ribs are moderately strong, somewhat regularly spaced, ~35 on last whorl, with fine striae between them. *Aperture:* is very inclined and oblique, almost tangentially, transversely ovoid or oblong to pear shaped; lip continuous, shortly, but not abruptly, everted except near the suture. Pale horn to colorless, thin, translucent.

SIZE: Typically, 2.0 (1.7–2.1) mm dia., 0.7 mm tall.

ANIMAL (Sterki 1893): Radula with 77 transverse rows of 25 teeth: Radula with 3 laterals, 2 intermediate tricuspid teeth (large mesodont, ectodont two-pointed), 6th tooth (from center) with 2 distal cusps, marginal teeth wide, short, with 4–6 cusps; last few are very small with indistinct cusps.

TYPE LOCATION: Knoxville, Tennessee, and Jackson County, Alabama

Valloniidae

FIG. T55. *Vallonia perspectiva*. ANSP 109594, Eagle Cr., AZ. Credit: ANSP.

JUNIOR SYNONYMS: None

NOTES: Distinguished from other *Vallonia* by its slightly smaller size, wider umbilicus, comparatively narrow last whorl, which is less expanding and descends in toto to the aperture, which is smaller and not circular (wider than tall); ribs also are further apart than for *cyclophorella* (Sterki 1893). Noted on wooded talus slopes (Frest and Johannes 1993).

DISTRIBUTION: North America. Utah records from Zion National Park (ANSP; Wheeler 2018).

Vallonia pulchella Müller, 1774 Lovely Vallonia

DESCRIPTION (Sterki 1893): *Shell*: discoid, shiny, spire is convex or depressed conic; pale horn or straw-colored, transparent or milky opaque; finely and densely striate (stronger at the suture and umbilicus). Striae irregular, varying with wear, but under the microscope, ribs near suture or umbilicus are 30–35 μm apart. *Whorls*: 3⅓–3½ (only largest have 4), smooth at the nucleus, rapidly increasing in size, with a deep suture; last whorl is well rounded, little expanded toward the aperture, not descending in front or slightly so at the suture. Widely umbilicated, widening near aperture. *Aperture:* moderately oblique and inclined, ⅚ circular; strong, white lip abruptly everted (flared), with umbilical margin a little straighter and slightly protracted.

SIZE: 2.4 (2.0–2.7) mm diameter × 1.2 mm tall.

ANIMAL (Sterki 1893; Welter-Shultes 2012): Animal milky white, tentacles short, foot rounded posteriorly. Jaw (0.13–0.23 mm wide × 0.065–0.070 mm high) is strongly curved with obtuse ends and no median projection on the cutting edge. Radula with 65–70 transverse rows of 27 teeth (Morse 1864 counted 23, Binney 1876 counted 21). Three lateral teeth, 2–3 bicuspid to tricuspid intermediate teeth, marginals with 5–6 cusps, moderately long, but shorter on the last marginals, reduced to finely serrate or with only a trace of a cusp.

TYPE LOCATION: not given.

FIG. T56. *Vallonia pulchella*. Left, live animal from Italy. Credit: Danio Miserocchi, iNaturalist.org; Center: ANSP 218605, Nordhausen, Germany. Credit: ANSP. Right: Logan Canyon, UT. Credit: E. Wagner.

JUNIOR SYNONYMS: *Helix pulchella* Müller, 1774; *H. paludosa* Costa, 1778; *H. crystallina* Dillwyn, 1817; *H. pulchella* var. *laevigata* Moquin-Tandon, 1855; *H. minuta* Say, 1817; *Vallonia minuta* (Say) Morse, 1864.

NOTES (Sterki 1893): The smooth shell with the last whorl not descending (or just slightly so) separates this from the ribbed forms of *Vallonia* (*cyclophorella, perspectiva*) in Utah. Immature forms may lack the flared lip of the aperture. Differentiated from *Hawaiia miniscula*, which it resembles, by the fewer, more rapidly expanding whorls, weaker striation and umbilicus which is narrower from the beginning. In early snail literature, specimens were assigned to *pulchella*, since there were few to no other species described at the time.

About 20 eggs (0.7–0.8 mm dia.) are laid singly (not in clutches) in soil or small crevices. Juveniles hatch after 15–20 days (field observation) or 12 days at 21–22 C. Full size is reached after about 2 months (21–22 C). About a week later egg laying begins; under optimal conditions, one egg/day is released for several months (July to September in France). The snails die after the egg-laying period. There may be 2 generations per year (Welter-Shultes 2012).

DISTRIBUTION: Found in Europe, North Africa, western and northern Asia, Australia, and North America (though scarce in the southeast). Utah records: Emigration Canyon (UMNH 014487); Magna (Jones 1940); Olivet Cemetery in Salt Lake City, Fillmore, and Weber River (Woolstenhulme 1942a, b). Wheeler (2018) found it in Zion National Park under oak and box elder overstory.

Zoogenetes harpa Say, 1824 Boreal Top

DESCRIPTION (Say, 1824, quoted; Pilsbry 1948; Welter-Shultes 2012): "Shell conic, reddish-brown; whorls four, convex, with numerous elevated, subequidistant, equal, lamelliform, acute lines across, the interstitial spaces flat and wrinkled; aperture suborbicular, truncated by the penultimate whorl, and very little oblique; labrum simple; umbilicus small, nearly concealed by the base of the

Valloniidae

FIG. T57. *Zoogenetes harpa* from Uintah Co., UT. Center image and inset show freshly born juveniles, discovered a few days after the parent snails were put into a container. Credit: Jordon Detlor.

labrum." *Shell*: ovate conic with an obtuse spire, fragile, somewhat transparent, olive-green, glossy. *Whorls*: nearly 4, first 2 nearly smooth, the rest with delicate, widely spaced cuticular ribs in the direction of growth lines, about 30 on the last whorl, crowding toward its end. *Aperture:* oblique, ovate, lip thin and simple, dilated at the axial termination.

SIZE (Say 1824; Pilsbry 1948): type: SL "rather more than one tenth of an inch" [2.5 mm]; SL 3.25 mm, SW 2.5 mm.

ANIMAL (Pilsbry 1948): Body and head slate-colored, but body, disk, and mantle with white dots. Foot whitish, as long as the shell. Superior tentacles darker, short, thick, bulbous, eyes large, distinct. Jaw semicircular; radula with 18–1–18 teeth, central tooth narrower than laterals, with a long narrow mesocone flanked by two small ectocones; lateral teeth (5) with a long narrow mesocone and one short ectocone on a nearly square basal plate; ectocone of 6th tooth bifid, transitioning to shorter serrate marginals (see Fig. 558 in Pilsbry 1948).

TYPE LOCATION: Northwest Territory [area west and northwest of Lake Superior].

JUNIOR SYNONYMS: *Helix harpa* Say, 1824; *Acanthinula harpa* (Say) Binney 1878; *Pupa costulata* Mighels, 1844; *Helix amurensis* Gerstfeldt, 1859. Change to *Zoogenetes harpa* by Morse (1864).

NOTES (Pilsbry 1948): The small ovate shell shape with a blunt spire is similar to *Amnicola* and *Pyrgulopsis* species, but the ribbing and upland habitat easily separate *Z. harpa* from members of those two genera. Found in wooded sites on calcareous soil, in leaf litter and moss, and lowlands near swamp and lake margins (Hubricht 1985; Frest and Johannes 1993). Welter-Shultes (2012) notes that it is found in coniferous forests, often on noncalcareous areas with the plant *Vaccinium*; in Switzerland on acidic soils (3.5–5.5). Life cycle of about a year: young are born in summer or early autumn, mature in the summer of the following year, produce young, and die. Uncommon. The first record of this species in Utah was April 2021, found live by Utah Division of Wildlife biologist Jordon Detlor.

DISTRIBUTION (Pilsbry 1948, Welter-Schultes 2012; ANSP; USNM; INHS): Japan, Scandinavia, Alps, northern Russia; in North America from Labrador and New England west to Alaska, British Columbia, and south to South Dakota, Colorado, Wyoming, and Utah. Only two Utah locations known to date: Dry Fork Canyon and Big Brush Creek, Uintah County.

Vertiginidae Fitzinger, 1833

Vertiginidae features columnar pupa-shaped shells, with or without teeth, found in terrestrial habitats. This family was originally assigned as a subfamily Vertigininae (Pilsbry 1948). Genera are based on characteristics of the animal and penial morphology. Species in the genera *Vertigo* and *Columella* have subobsolete or no tentacles and tricuspid lateral teeth on the radula. Species in *Gastrocopta* have tentacles present, bicuspid lateral teeth on the radula, a simple retractor, and the penis lacks an appendix. Species in Pupillidae, which bear similar shells to Vertiginidae, also have tentacles present but differ from the *Gasterocopta* by having a branched penis bearing an appendix and having a forked retractor. Species within genera are mainly differentiated by shell characteristics due to a high rate of aphallism and limited anatomical variation (Nekola and Coles 2010). However, recent genetic research by Nekola et al. (2015, 2018) has indicated that apertural features are highly plastic and may not be reliable characters for species identification. The authors suggested that shell surface sculpture and architecture are more reliable characters for identification.

Columella columella Martens, 1830 Mellow Column

DESCRIPTION: *Shell*: cylindrical, dextral, with clear, fine radial striae, greenish-brown color; glossy, delicate, semitransparent in live animals, but opaque, matte to matte-glossy and light brown in empty shells. *Whorls:* up to 7.5, penultimate and antepenultimate of similar size, the last often broader. *Aperture:* about as broad as high, peristome discontinuous, slightly turned in at the columella, forming a narrow umbilicus; no teeth.

SIZE: Up to 3.5 mm tall × 1.4 mm diameter.

TYPE LOCATION: Unknown.

JUNIOR SYNONYMS: *Pupa columella* Martens, 1830; *Pupilla alticola* Ingersoll, 1875 (Ingersoll 1876); *Pupa alticola* (Ingersoll) Binney 1878; *Sphyradium alticola*

FIG. T58. *Columella columella.* ANSP 43910. Chalk Cr., Utah (coll. by R. Chamberlin, 1917). Credit: ANSP.

(Ingersoll) Hanna 1912; *Columella alticola* (Ingersoll) Pilsbry 1926b.

NOTES (Welter-Schultze 2012): Similar to *Pupoides hordaceus,* but spire is not as tapered. Taller than *P. hebes*, which also lacks teeth. In marshy grasslands and wet subarctic woodlands, gray willow thickets, alpine meadows, on calcareous substrate. *Columella* differs from *Vertigo* by the subequal cusps of the bicuspid lateral teeth, the wide plates of the jaw, and the thin, sharp unexpanded lip of the toothless aperture. Larger than the Eurasian *C. edentula*, with a flatter apex.

DISTRIBUTION (Welter-Schultze 2012; ANSP; Ibase; Pilsbry 1948): Holarctic. Europe, Scandinavia, Russia, Kazakhstan, Nicaragua, Canada. United States: AK, CO, IA, ID, IL, KS (Pleistocene deposits), PA, MI, MO, MS, SD, WY. In Utah, museum specimens exist for Lamb's Canyon (FMNH 224531; Berry 1931) and Daggett County (CM 90940). Reported to be in Garfield County (Mammoth Creek headwaters).

Gastrocopta ashmuni Sterki, 1898 Sluice Snaggletooth

DESCRIPTION (Sterki 1898a; Pilsbry 1948): *Shell*: nearly cylindric, tapering but slightly; surface shiny, horn-colored with whitish lamellae and folds; slightly and irregularly striate and microscopically rugulose, as is also the nucleus. *Whorls:* 5, strongly convex with a rather deep suture, regularly increasing, the last becomes straightened and slightly sinuous in basal view, with a weak to strong crest or swelling some distance behind the aperture, with some shells in the same lot lacking the crest. Umbilicus: perforated-rimate. *Aperture:* strongly lateral, rounded subtriangular, equaling $1/3$ the altitude of the shell, highest near its columellar side, with a sinus above on the palatal side; margin continuous, usually free from the whorl in front, strongly everted, broadest so below, without a lip thickening; parietal lamella very large, strongly curved, nearer the periphery at its inner end; angular lamella large, at its inner end united with the side of the parietal, at the outer with the palatal margin, thus closing the sinus above; columellar lamella large, spiral, ascending to the body whorl between the parietal and columella; basal lamella and inferior palatal fold deep in the throat, the former radial, the latter above it, oblique; superior palatal short, tooth-like, rather remote from the margin.

The Terrestrial Snails

FIG. T59. *Gastrocopta ashmuni*, ANSP 162445, 78690. Credit: ANSP.

SIZE: SL 2.0 mm × 1.1 mm wide. A smaller form was also found in Nogales, Arizona, that was 1.5–1.9 mm tall, with a thinner shell and paler color, the everted part of the lip less broad, the number of whorls 4.0–4.5 (Sterki 1898a).

ANIMAL (Sterki 1898a): Foot and head almost colorless, mantle slate-colored.

TYPE LOCATION: Santa Rita Mountains, Arizona, and Cook's Peak, New Mexico.

JUNIOR SYNONYMS: *Bifidaria ashmuni* & *Bifidaria ashmuni* form *minor* Sterki, 1898b; *Gastrocopta ashmuni* (Sterki) Pilsbry 1916–1918; *Gastrocopta ashmuni imperfecta* Pilsbry and Ferriss, 1923.

NOTES: Fused and well-developed anguloparietal lamella and a strong, transverse basal lamella separates *ashmuni* from other *Gastrocopta* in Utah.

DISTRIBUTION (ANSP records; Ibase): AZ, NM, TX. Argentina, Mexico. In Utah, only reported from Zion National Park (Chamberlin and Berry 1930; Wheeler 2018).

Gastrocopta cristata Pilsbry and Vanatta, 1900 Crested Snaggletooth

DESCRIPTION (Pilsbry and Vanatta 1900): *Shell:* subcylindrical, bullet-shaped spire. *Aperture:* Angle and parietal lamellae more completely united than in *G. procera s.s.*, hardly bifid; strong columellar tooth, subcolumellar fold, and short palatal tooth present, crest behind the outer lip very strong.

SIZE: SL 2.8 mm × 1.2 mm dia.

TYPE LOCATION: Camp Verde, Yavapai County, Arizona; lectotype ANSP 78694

JUNIOR SYNONYMS: *Bifidaria procera* var. *cristata* Pilsbry and Vanatta, 1900.

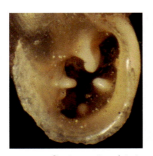

FIG. T60. *Gastrocopta cristata* aperture. Lectotype ANSP 78694. Credit: ANSP.

FIG. T61. *Gastrocopta cristata*. Lectotype, ANSP 78694, orig. comb. *Bifidaria procera* var. *cristata*. Credit: ANSP.

NOTES: Fused angular and parietal lamella but not as wide as for *G. ashmuni*; fewer palatal teeth than *pellucida,* teeth not ± even in length as in *quadridens,* and it has a stronger crest than *pilsbryana*.

DISTRIBUTION (Ibase; Bequaert and Miller 1973): Mexico; AL, AR, AZ, FL, MD, IA, KS, MO, NE, NM, OH, OK, PA, TN, TX, VA. Pleistocene fossils known from KS to TX west to AZ-NM. No museum records for Utah. Utah records: Zion National Park (Wheeler 2018).

Gastrocopta pellucida Pfeiffer, 1841 Slim Snaggletooth

DESCRIPTION (Pfeiffer 1841; Adams 1849; Pilsbry 1918): *Shell*: small, cylindric, subperforate, pellucid, glossy, pale yellowish or brownish horn, most have minute, oblique striae, the apex rather obtuse, tapering only near the summit. *Whorls:* 5–5.5, convex, with deep sutures; the diameter of the last two whorls is nearly the same, with those above tapering to an obtuse apex. The last whorl is strongly flattened over the lower palatal plica and has no trace of a crest or ridge behind the lip. Umbilicus very small. *Aperture:* oblong to semi-oval, the right side longer and shouldered above, and the transverse side a little oblique; toothed, with 2 large teeth on the columella, 3 or 4 very minute palatal teeth, not reaching the edge; the anguloparietal lamella is not very conspicuously bifid in front view (see Fig. T63 for bottom view). The columellar lamella is stout and horizontal and has a small callus below its inner end, often not seen in front view; basal fold short but distinct. Sometimes there are anomalies in the palatal teeth, for example, doubled or irregular ones interposed. Peristome simple, very slightly thickened, moderately reflected, ends remote.

SIZE: 1.5–2 mm tall (type 1.66 × 0.83 mm). For synonym *P. jamaicensis*, length 1.77 mm × 0.64 mm dia.

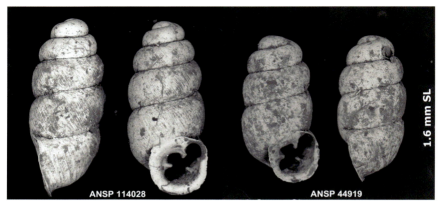

FIG. T62. *Gastrocopta pellucida.* ANSP 114028 (*G. pellucida* form *biminensis*, Bimini Islands), ANSP 44919 (*G. pellucida delicata*). Credit: ANSP.

Pilsbry (1918) described some variants of *G. pellucida*. In *G. pellucida* form *biminiensis* (left shell, Fig. T62), from the Bimini Islands, the shell is dark brown, has a crest (or trace of it) behind the lip, and the anguloparietal lamella is not bifid and is nearly straight. In *G. pellucida delicata* (right shell, Fig. T62), the shell is smaller, more delicate, without a crest; the angular lamella is very weak or low, and the basal fold is lacking or tiny when present. In *G. pellucida hordeacella* found in the United States, there is often a slight crest behind the outer lip and a somewhat longer lower palatal fold or tooth. The shell is pale brown and larger in size on average, ranging from 1.8 to 2.5 mm tall (0.76–1 mm wide), whorls 4–5.5. The anguloparietal lamella often lacks a projection on the columellar side. In the form *G. pellucida parvidens* Sterki, described from Arizona, the apex is more acute than in typical *hordeacella,* and the outline is more obovoid, the peristome is abruptly but narrowly everted, the lamella and folds are small, especially so the upper palatal, often being a mere trace; the basal is absent or very small; and the columellar tooth has no buttress below.

FIG. T63. *G. pellucida*, bottom view. Credit: Pilsbry 1918.

TYPE LOCATION: Cuba

JUNIOR SYNONYMS (ANSP; Pilsbry 1918, 1948): *Pupa pellucida* Pfeiffer, 1841; *Pupa jamaicensis* Adams, 1849–1852; *P. ovum-formicae* Weinland, 1880; *Pupa hordeacella* Pilsbry, 1890; *Bifidaria hordeacella* var. *parvidens* Sterki, 1899; *Bifidaria pellucida hordeacella* Vanatta, 1912; *Gastrocopta pellucida hordeacella* (Vanatta) Pilsbry 1916–1918; *Gastrocopta pellucida parvidens* (Sterki) Pilsbry 1917.

NOTES: Palatal teeth of *pellucida* are smaller and recessed further in the aperture than for *pilsbryana*. Teeth are not similar in length as in *quadridens*.

Distinguishing characteristics include yellowish-corneous tint; an indistinctly bifid anguloparietal lamella with a small projection on the columellar side, seen in basal view; the absence of any crest behind the lip, which is slightly thickened, but has no distinct white or brown callus; and the rather short lower palatal fold. Found in leaf litter under juniper, palo verde, and mesquite shrubs, and among grass tufts on dry bedrock outcrops and riparian sand deposits (Nekola et al. 2015).

DISTRIBUTION (Pilsbry 1918; ANSP; Ibase): West Indies, Solomon Islands, Colombia, Mexico, and Honduras. In the United States from Florida north to New Jersey. Also found in AL, AR, AZ, CO, KS, LA, MD, MI, MO, NC, NE, NV, NM, OK, SD, and TX. Wheeler (2018) found *pellucida* in Zion National Park. To date there are no museum records for Utah.

Gastrocopta pilsbryana Sterki, 1890 Montane Snaggletooth

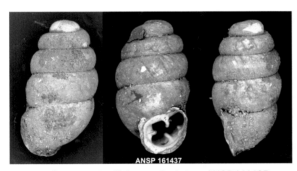

FIG. T64. *Gastrocopta pilsbryana*, lectotype ANSP 161437. orig. comb. *G. pilsbryana amissidens*, Coconino Co., AZ. Credit: ANSP.

DESCRIPTION (Sterki 1890): *Shell*: minute, narrowly perforate, cylindrical-oblong to cylindrical, somewhat attenuated toward the rather blunt apex; colorless (glassy when fresh), with a very delicate bluish tint; smooth and polished, with few, irregular, microscopic striae which are more marked near the aperture. *Whorls*: 4.5–5.5, moderately rounded with a rather deep suture, especially in the upper half, regularly and slowly increasing, the embryonal being relatively large, the last somewhat ascending toward the aperture. *Aperture*: moderate size, lateral, subovate, margins approached; peristome somewhat expanded, without a thickened lip or a callous in the palatal wall; outside is a barely perceptible trace of a crest near the margin, and behind that a slight impression most marked upon the inferior palatal fold. Lamellae 4 or 5, one parietal, rather high, of moderate length, simple; one columellar, horizontal, of moderate size, simple; basal very small or wanting; palatals the typical inferior deeper seated, of moderate size, superior small or very small. The columellar lamella projects horizontally and is a short tubercle.

SIZE: 1.5–1.7 mm tall × 0.8–0.9 mm wide. Pilsbry (1918) notes variation from 1.65 to 1.9 mm. A variant form from New Mexico has a smaller diameter and no trace of a basal lamella. The synonym *stoneri* measured 2.1 mm tall × 1 mm wide.

TYPE LOCATION: Albuquerque, New Mexico; Colorado River, Arizona.

JUNIOR SYNONYMS: *Pupa pilsbryana* Sterki, 1890; *Bifidaria pilsbryana* (Sterki) Pilsbry and Cockerell 1900; *Pupa montanella* Cockerell, 1889 *nomen nudem*, = *P. pentadon,* Cockerell, 1891b; *Gastrocopta pentodon* (Say) Henderson 1924; *Pupilla stoneri* Chamberlin and Jones, 1929; *Gastrocopta pilsbryana amissidens.*

NOTES (Sterki 1890; Pilsbry 1918; Nekola et al. 2015): Distinguished from *G. pellucida* by the shorter, simple, parietal lamella (lacks angular lamella); the palatal lamella are longer and not as recessed in the aperture as for *pellucida*. Teeth size varies, whereas in *quadridens* they are about equal. One of the most common species in mountains and high plateaus of New Mexico and Arizona. In leaf litter across a wide variety of forest sites from low to high elevation (above 4,000 ft in New Mexico and Arizona).

DISTRIBUTION (ANSP; Ibase): Mexico; IL, AZ, NM, TX. Utah (Wheeler 2018; CM; DMNH; FMNH; UF): Cedar Canyon (Iron County), Monroe Canyon, San Juan County (Indian Creek), Palisade State Park, Zion National Park, and Daggett County (Deep Creek). Chamberlin and Berry (1930) found *pilsbryana* in the Henry Mountains (Pine Springs).

Gastrocopta quadridens Pilsbry, 1916 Cross Snaggletooth

DESCRIPTION (Pilsbry 1918): *Shell*: narrowly perforate-rimate, conical-turriculate, with the apex somewhat obtuse; colorless, glassy; surface very slightly striated, shining. *Whorls:* 6, gradually increasing, with the sutures rather deep between the upper, less so between the lower, whorls; the last whorl moderately ascending at the aperture, rather rounded at the base, slightly expanded near the aperture, with an impression over the inferior palatal fold. *Aperture:* rather oval, truncated above, margins well everted, the palatal somewhat more curved than the columellar, the two connected by a thin callous; lamellae and folds four, subequal; angulo-parietal appearing almost simple, inclined toward the columella; columellar horizontal, rather short and strong, palatals rather short and stout, in normal position, the inferior somewhat larger and more remote from the margin.

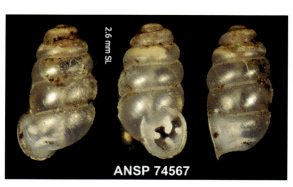

FIG. T65. *Gastrocopta quadridens*, syntype, ANSP 74567. Credit: ANSP.

SIZE: 2.4–2.8 mm tall × 1.3 mm diameter, aperture height 1.0 mm.

TYPE LOCATION: Capitan Mountains, Lincoln County, New Mexico.

JUNIOR SYNONYMS: *Bifidaria quadridentata* Sterki, 1899 (not *Pupa quadridentata* Klein, 1853); Last change to *Gastrocopta (Starotrema) quadridens* by Pilsbry 1916–1918.

NOTES: The simple anguloparietal lamella separates this from *G. ashmuni*; the four teeth about equal in length distinguishes this from the other Utah *Gastrocopta* which have teeth that are more numerous and/or are different in relative length. *G. quadridens* also has 0.5–1.0 more whorl than *G. pilsbryana* or *pellucida*.

DISTRIBUTION: AZ, NM. In Utah, ANSP record from Fish Lake (Chamberlin and Berry 1930).

Vertigo arizonensis Pilsbry and Vanatta, 1900 Arizona Vertigo

DESCRIPTION (Pilsbry and Vanatta 1900; Nekola et al. 2018): *Shell*: cylindrical-ovate, dull luster, rimate; densely, sharply, and minutely striate; light brown. *Whorls*: 4.75, convex, the last tapering below, the latter half whorl narrow as though pinched at the base, flattened over the position of the palatal folds, then rising in a low crest, obsolete except near the base. *Aperture*: two very long palatal folds, blade-like parietal tooth, and a strong angular "tooth," but no basal fold; peg-like columellar lamella obliquely entering. Peristome well expanded, irregularly truncate-oval, and brown.

SIZE: 1.7–1.9 mm tall × 0.8–0.9 mm.

TYPE LOCATION: Top of Mount Mingus, near Jerome, Arizona, about 8,500 ft elevation. Paralectotypes: ANSP 451824.

JUNIOR SYNONYMS: *Vertigo coloradensis* var. *arizonensis* Pilsbry & Vanatta, 1900.

FIG. T66. *Vertigo (Vertigo) arizonensis*. Credit: Pilsbry & Vanatta 1900.

NOTES (Nekola et al. 2018): Longer palatal tooth than other vertigos found in Utah. *V.* cf. *utahensis* is more ovate in outline and has a smaller aperture and shorter palatal lamellae. Found in mixed conifer and deciduous forests, especially in humus on talus slopes.

DISTRIBUTION (Nekola et al. 2018): Guadalupe Mountains along the New Mexico/Texas border west to central Arizona, north into central Utah and southern Colorado. Utah records: Bullion Canyon.

Vertigo arthuri Martens, 1882 Arthur's Vertigo

DESCRIPTION (Nekola et al. 2018)**:** *Shell*: cylindrical-ovate, sutures shallow to moderate, striae strong, sharp, numerous, regular; dull luster, red to yellow-brown. *Aperture:* 4–6 teeth (angular tooth none to strong, blade-like parietal, peg-like columellar, basal fold none to strong, 2 palatal teeth, the lower more deeply inserted in aperture than the upper); sinulus none to weak; crest and callus variable.

SIZE: SL 1.6–1.8 mm, SW 0.7–0.9 mm.

TYPE LOCATION: Little Missouri, North Dakota.

JUNIOR SYNONYMS (Nekola et al. 2018): *Vertigo bollesiana* var. *arthuri* Martens, 1882; *V. briarensis* Leonard, 1972 (fossil); *V. coloradensis* var. *basidens* Pilsbry and Vanatta, 1900; *V. gouldii hubrichti* Pilsbry, 1934 (Pilsbry 1927–1935); *V. hubrichti variabilis* Frest, 1991; *V. iowaensis* Frest, 1991; *V. occulta* Leonard, 1972 (fossil); *V. gouldii paradoxa* Nylander, 1900.

NOTES (Nekola et al. 2018)**:** The palatal lamella is more deeply recessed than the upper palatal, which differentiates *arthuri* from other *Vertigo* in the same subgenus. *V. berryi* and *ovata* are more egg-shaped in outline, and the striae are weaker and irregular. Apertural callus, crest, and presence/absence of basal and/or angular lamella have historically split *V. arthuri* into other taxa. However, these characters are highly variable, and these taxa are synonymized with *V. arthuri* (see Junior synonyms). Presence of a small basal tubercle defined the *basidens* variant of *V. coloradensis* (Pilsbry and Vanatta 1900). Habitat is typically upland forest, taiga, and rock outcrops. Common in herb-rich aspen groves and Douglas fir.

DISTRIBUTION: North America from Newfoundland to interior Alaska, south to upstate New York, northeastern Iowa, northwestern Minnesota, South Dakota, and the Jemez Mountains, New

FIG. T67. *Comparison of Vertigo arthuri, V. arthuri* form *basidens* and *Vertigo arizonensis*. Credit: © Jeff Nekola.

Mexico. In Utah, Jeff Nekola (pers. comm.) has found *V. arthuri* f. *basidens* in the Abajo Mountains in San Juan County and Provo Canyon.

Vertigo berryi Pilsbry, 1919 (Pilsbry and Cooke 1918–1920) Cienega Vertigo

DESCRIPTION (Pilsry 1948; Nekola et al. 2018): *Shell*: Conical-ovate, spire tapered, shiny to silky, red-brown, with moderate sutures; striae weak, many, irregular, blunt. *Whorls:* 5.5, body whorl <50% of shell height. *Aperture:* 6–7 teeth (modest angular tooth, long parietal and columellar lamellae, strong basal tooth (sometimes two), 2 palatal teeth); crest modest to strong; callus modest to strong, white; sinulus modest.

SIZE: SL 1.9–2.5, SW 1.2–1.5; ApL 0.9 mm.

TYPE LOCATION: Mill Creek Canyon at 4,600 ft elevation, San Bernardino Mountains, California

JUNIOR SYNONYMS: none

NOTES (Nekola et al. 2018): Presence of both an angular and basal tooth distinguishes *V. berryi* from *V. arizonensis, ventricosa, utahensis, V. modesta castanea*, and *V. coloradensis*. Differs from *V. ovata* in the body whorl height (<50% of SL v. >50% in *ovata*). Columellar tooth is longer than for *V. modesta concinnula* and *arthuri*.

FIG.T68. *Vertigo berryi*. Credit: © Jeff Nekola.

Habitat is wet, decaying leaf litter in low elevation wetlands in the desert southwest of the United States. Pleistocene fossils exist from southeastern Arizona into the Mojave Desert. Named for the American marine zoologist S. Stillman Berry.

DISTRIBUTION (Nekola et al. 2018): southern Utah west into southern California. GenBank samples from Mystic River seep, northwest Kane County, Utah (KY216970, KY216612, KY217378, KY216243).

Vertigo coloradensis Cockerell, 1891b Colorado Vertigo

DESCRIPTION (Nekola et al. 2018): *Shell*: cylindrical-ovate; sutures moderate to deep; striae many, sharp, regular; dull luster; brown. *Aperture:* 4 teeth (long parietal, but no angular lamella, collumellar tooth peg-like, 2 subparallel palatal teeth); weak to modest palatal depression; little to no indenting of outer lip; crest modest to strong; no callus.

SIZE: SL 1.6–1.9 mm, SW 0.9–1.1 mm.

TYPE LOCATION: Near Swift Creek, Custer County, Colorado.

JUNIOR SYNONYMS: *Pupa coloradensis* Cockerell, 1891b.

NOTES: Four teeth in the aperture, sharp and regular striae, dull luster, and a modest to strong crest distinguish this species from most other Utah *Vertigo*. *V. arthuri* differs in that the lower palatal tooth is inserted further in the aperture. *V. coloradensis* is smaller and not as shiny as the *modesta* subspecies. *V. coloradensis* lacks a weak angular tooth found in *V.* cf. *utahensis*. Found in upland taiga and high-elevation forests, especially in aspen.

FIG.T69. *Vertigo coloradensis*. Duncan Lake, British Columbia. Credit: © Jeff Nekola.

DISTRIBUTION: Alaska south along the Rocky Mountains to southeastern Arizona. Jeff Nekola (pers. comm.) found specimens in Summit County, Utah.

Vertigo modesta castanea Pilsbry and Vanatta, 1900 and *V. modesta concinnula* Cockerell 1897b Cross Vertigo

DESCRIPTION (Nekola et al. 2018): *Shell*: cylindric-ovate, with moderately deep sutures and irregular sharp striae, which are more numerous on *concinnula*. *V. m. castanea* is red- to yellow-brown, silky to shiny, whereas *concinnula* is cinnamon-colored, dull to silky. *Whorls*: 4.5–5.5, the last with a crest that is modest and blunt in *castanea*, modest to strong in *concinnula*. *Aperture:* both subspecies have a long parietal tooth and peg-like columellar lamella, but other teeth vary. In *castanea*, the angular tooth is weak to absent, the basal fold absent, and palatals are 0–2 and short, whereas in *concinnula*, the angular tooth is strong, a modest basal fold may be present, and the two palatals are long. Callus none to weak in both. *Umbilicus*: rimate, short.

SIZE: Subspecies *castanea*: 2.0–2.8 × 1.3–1.6 mm; subspecies *concinnula*: SL 2.1–2.6 mm, SW 1.2–1.4 mm

TYPE LOCATION (Pilsbry 1948):
V. m. concinnula: Brush Creek, Custer County, Colorado at 10,000 ft elevation (lectotype ANSP 59095). *V. m. castanea*: Fish Camp, Fresno County, California.

JUNIOR SYNONYMS (Pilsbry 1948; Nekola et al. 2018): *Pupa modesta* Say, 1824; *Pupa decora* Gould, 1848c; *Vertigo modesta ultima* Pilsbry, 1919 (Pilsbry and Cooke

Vertiginidae

FIG. T70. *Vertigo modesta concinnula* (left: Tin Cup, CO; center: Lemmon, AZ) and *V. modesta castanea* (Bear Cr. Summit, NV). Credit: © Jeff Nekola.

1918–1920); *V. modesta* (Say) Pilsbry and Vanatta 1900; *Isthmia corpulenta* Morse, 1867; *Pupa corpulenta* Binney 1878; *Vertigo modesta corpulenta* (Morse) Pilsbry and Vanatta 1900; *Pupa corpulenta* (Morse) var. *parietalis* Ancey, 1887b; *Vertigo modesta* mut. *parietalis* (Ancey) Pilsbry; *V. modesta ultima* Pilsbry, 1919 (Pilsbry and Cooke 1918–1920); *V. allyniana* Berry, 1919; *V. californica* (Rowell) Ingersoll, 1875 (no description); *Vertigo ingersolli* (Ancey) Cockerell, 1889 (name only); *Pupa ingersolli* (Ancey) Cockerell, 1891b (first description); *V. decora* var. *concinnula* Dall 1897; *Vertigo concinnula* Cockerell, 1897b. Nekola et al. (2018) have provisionally classified *Vertigo modesta hoppi* (syn. *Pupa hoppii* Möller, 1842; *Vertigo hoppii* [Möller] Pilsbry) as *V. (Boreovertigo)* cf. *hoppii*, genetically distinct from *V. modesta*. Nekola et al. (2018) synonymized *V. modesta insculpta* under *V. modesta concinnula*; *V. m. sculptilis* and *V. modesta microphasma* Berry, 1919 were synonymized under *V. modesta castanea*.

FIG. T71. *Vertigo modesta* subspecies types. ANSP 11655 & 10957: *V. modesta castanea*; orig. comb. 10957 *V. m. sculptilis*; ANSP 162884 & 59095: *Vertigo modesta concinnula* (orig. comb. *V. m. insculpta* (162884) and *V. concinnula* (59095). Credit: ANSP.

NOTES (Pilsbry 1948; Nekola et al. 2018): The shells of *V. modesta* subspecies are larger and shinier than *V. arizonensis* and *utahensis*. *V. berryi, ovata,* and *ventricosa* have a longer columellar tooth. The striae of *V. arthuri* and *coloradensis* are more regular, and the luster is generally duller. Albino and sinestral variants may occur. *V. modesta concinnula* habitat is usually upland high-elevation forest. *V. modesta castanea* is found in high-elevation wetlands, seeps, fens, and forest riparian areas. *V. m. concinnula* is differentiated from *V. m. castanea* and *V. modesta s.s.* by its many sharp and strong striae, dull shell luster and large apertural crest.

DISTRIBUTION (Chamberlin & Berry 1930; Berry 1931; Woolstenhulme 1942a, b; Nekola et al. 2018; ANSP; UMNH): Circumpolar in boreal habitats, alpine at lower latitudes. Kasakhstan, Greenland, Alberta, Newfoundland, South Baffin Island; AK, AZ, CA, CO, ID, IA, MO, MT, NM, OR, SD, WA, WY. The two subspecies are found in the Rocky Mountains, but *V. modesta s.s.* is found in Canada and the northeastern United States west to interior Alaska, but it does range as far south as Utah. The range for *V. m. concinnula* is the southern Rocky Mountains of the United States (AZ, NM, CO, UT). The range for *V. m. castanea* is the western United States from California (San Bernardino and Sierra Nevada ranges) east to northern Utah and southeastern British Columbia. Utah records for *V. modesta*: Mirror Lake, Clear Creek Canyon (Raft River Mts.); Box Elder, Ogden, Weber, Seven Mile, Lamb's and Bell's canyons, upper Provo River, Chalk Creek; Blue Mountains; Fish Lake; Hidden Lake (Glendale); Bullion Canyon; Salt Lake, Duchesne, and San Juan counties.

Vertigo ovata Say, 1822 Ovate Vertigo

DESCRIPTION (Say 1822; Pilsbry 1948; Nekola et al. 2018): *Shell*: broadly ovate, dextral, yellow- to red-brown, shiny; striae scattered, weak, and blunt. *Whorls*: 5, suture moderately impressed; body whorl >50% of shell height and indented near and upon labrum; columellar wall not visible. *Aperture*: semi-oval; angular tooth strong to absent, parietal and columellar lamellae long, infraparietal tooth often present, one strong basal (often a second fold too), and two long palatals (often a weak third). Lip reflected but not flattened; umbilicus distinct. Crest none to modest; sinulus none to modest; callus variable (none to strong, white).

SIZE: SL 1.6–2.4 mm, SW 1.0–1.4 mm; L/W ratio 1.9.

ANIMAL: Two tentacles, long and thick, cylindrical-obconic, retractile, with a rounded occuliferous extremity; foot white; head and neck, as far as the mantle, is black.

FIG. T72. *Vertigo ovata*, Orient, Maine. Credit: © Jeff Nekola.

TYPE LOCATION: Philadelphia, Pennsylvania

JUNIOR SYNONYMS: *Pupa ovata* f. *antiquorum* Cockerell, 1891c; *Zonites upsoni* Calkins, 1880; *Vertigo ovata mariposa* Pilsbry, 1919 (Pilsbry and Cooke 1918–1920); *V. eogea* Pilsbry, 1919 (Pilsbry and Cooke 1918–1920); *Pupa (Vertigo) hydrophila* Reinhardt, 1877. The *V. ovata diaboli* form found in Texas (Pilsbry and Cooke 1918–1920) has longer "'teeth," but the crest behind the lip is lower than in typical *ovata*. Binney (1843) suggested that *V. modesta* was a junior synonym of *V. ovata;* However, Pilsbry (1948) and Nekola et al. (2018) have maintained its specific status.

NOTES (Ports 1996; Nekola et al. 2018): *V. ovata* is more ovate than *V. arizonensis*, *coloradensis*, *V. modesta concinnula,* and *V. arthuri*. Its body whorl is >50% of SL, whereas for *V. berryi*, it is <50%. *V. ventricosa* lacks an angular tooth and the infrapalatal often found in *ovata*. Shinier luster and weaker striae than for *V.* cf. *utahensis*; stronger teeth than for *V. modesta castanea*. Prefers wet meadows and leaf litter habitats in wetlands of cattails, sedges, or *Phragmites*. Some coastal populations are limited to acidic wooded or *Sphagnum*-dominated wetlands.

DISTRIBUTION (ANSP; Ibase; Nekola et al. 2018): Argentina, Brazil, Caribbean, Canada, Ireland, Japan, Taiwan, eastern Asia, Mexico; AK, AL, AZ, CA, CO, CT, FL, GA, ID, IL, IN, IA, KS, KY, LA, ME, MD, MA, MI, MO, MS, MT, NC, NJ, NM, NY, OH, OK, PA, RI, SC, SD, TN, TX, VA, WA. Utah records from Fruita (Chamberlin and Berry 1930), Kane County (Hidden Lake, FMNH 178118; Kanab Creek, Meretsky et al. 2002; Mystic seep), and Richfield.

Vertigo cf. *utahensis* Sterki, 1900 Utah Vertigo

DESCRIPTION (Pilsbry and Vanatta 1900; Nekola et al. 2018): *Shell*: minute, cylindric-oval, perforate, thin, pale corneous-brown, semitransparent, glossy, and distinctly striate. *Whorls:* nearly 5, convex, the last expanded in a low crest very close to the lip, not noticeably constricted in front of the crest. *Aperture:* truncate oval, convex margin, peristome thin, hardly expanded; 4–5 teeth: parietal lamella short and high, weak angular tooth usually present; columellar a little smaller, lower palatal a short conic fold continued inward; upper palatal smaller, tubercular; all teeth white and the palatals showing through the outside wall.

SIZE: SL 1.8 mm × 1.0 mm dia.

TYPE LOCATION: Box Elder Canyon, Utah, at 4,500 ft elevation.

JUNIOR SYNONYMS: *Vertigo columbiana utahensis* (Sterki) Pilsbry and Vanatta 1900.

NOTES (Nekola et al. 2018): V. Sterki named *Vertigo columbiana* var. *utahensis* in *Nautilus* (VI:5), but did not provide a description. Pilsbry and Vanatta (1900) later gave a brief description based on a single shell without an angular lamella. However, all the shells of Nekola et al. (2018) possess an angular lamella but lack a basal lamella found in *V. ventricosa, V. modesta concinnula,* and *V. berryi*. *V. coloradensis* lacks an angular tooth. *V.* cf. *utahensis* differs from *V. arizonensis* and *V. arthuri* in having an ovate shell, a small wider-than-tall aperture, a strong crest, and shorter palatal teeth inserted to the same depth in the aperture. The sharper regular striae and dull luster distinguish *utahensis* from the shinier *V. modesta castanea*. Genetic analyses indicate that *Vertigo columbiana* is still a distinct species in the subgenus *Boreovertigo*. GenBank numbers for Bullion Canyon, Utah: KY217326, KY216918, KY217716, KY216577; Upper Provo River: KY217327, KY216919, KY217717, KY216578.

FIG. T73. *Vertigo* cf. *utahensis*. left: Bullion Canyon, Piute Co., UT. Credit: © Jeff Nekola.

Habitat is humus accumulations between boulders at the base of talus slopes in aspen forest.

DISTRIBUTION (Nekola et al. 2018): Endemic to central and northern Utah. Records from Box Elder Canyon, Bullion Canyon, and upper Provo River (Cobblerest Campground).

Vertigo ventricosa Morse, 1865 (1867) Five-tooth Vertigo

DESCRIPTION (Morse 1867; Nekola et al. 2018): *Shell*: umbilicate, ovate conic, smooth, polished; apex obtuse; suture deep. *Whorls:* 4, convex. *Aperture:* semicircular, with 4–5 teeth, one prominent on the parietal margin, two smaller on the columellar margin, and two prominent palatal teeth within, contracting the aperture at the base; peristome widely reflected, the right margin flexuose ("dented in"), thickened within and colored.

SIZE: 1.78 mm long × 1.14 mm wide.

ANIMAL (Morse 1867): Upper body, head, and tentacles jet black. Disk long, narrow, and rounded at extremity; anterior portion of disk dark slate, becoming lighter towards tail end. Tentacles short, very bulbous, base of tentacles approximating. Cephalic lobes conspicuous. Jaw wide, narrow, not produced in the center, but slightly curving at ends; cutting edge regularly waved. *Radula*: 98 rows of 27 teeth (13–1–13); central tooth tricuspid with large mesocone; the 6 laterals are tricuspid, 3–4 transitional teeth are serrate, remaining marginals mostly lacking

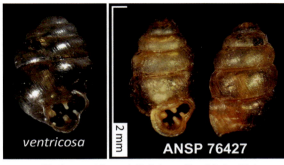

FIG. T74. *Vertigo ventricosa*. left: Salmon Brook Lake, Maine. Credit: © Jeff Nekola. right: Lectotype, ANSP 76427, orig. comb. *Vertigo elatior*/*V. gouldi* var. *lagganensis*. Credit: ANSP.

cusps or are minutely notched.

TYPE LOCATION: Maine; Concord, New Hampshire; Mohawk and Greenwich, New York.

JUNIOR SYNONYMS (Nekola et al. 2018): *Isthmia ventricosa* Morse, 1867 (read November 1865); *Vertigo ventricosa* var. *elatior* Sterki, 1894; *Vertigo gouldi lagganensis* Pilsbry, 1899a; *Vertigo gouldii loessensi* Baker, 1928; *Vertigo idahoensis* Pilsbry, 1934 (Pilsbry 1927–1935). Changed to *Vertigo elatior* (Sterki) by Pilsbry (1931) and back to *Vertigo ventricosa* (Morse) by Nekola et al. (2018) based on genetic data.

NOTES (Nekola et al. 2018): *V. ventricosa* lacks the angular tooth found in *arizonensis*, *berryi*, *utahensis*, and *V. modesta concinnula*. Proportionally taller than *V. ovata*, but with one whorl less, a less angular columellar margin, and lacking the long infrapalatal tooth of *ovata*. The columellar tooth is longer and the presence of the second columellar tooth separates *ventricosa* from *V. modesta castanea*, *V. arthuri*, and *V. coloradensis*. Found on dead leaves and twigs in wet places ranging from open to wooded, especially on grass or sedge leaves or leaf litter.

DISTRIBUTION (ANSP; Ibase; Brooks 1936; Nekola et al. 2018): Widespread in Canada. United States: AZ, CA, CO, IL, IA, IN, MA, ME, MI, MN, MO, MT, NC, ND, NM, NY, OH, PA, SD, TN, VA, WY, WV. No museum records for Utah. Found in northern Kane and Uintah counties.

SPF: SUCCINEOIDEA Beck, 1837

Succineidae Beck, 1837

Succineids are air-breathing land snails with a worldwide distribution. About 48 species are found in the United States (Nekola 2014). Their shells are characteristically thin, translucent, of few whorls (≤ 4), large apertures, and short spires, imperforate, and are amber-colored, hence the common name for the group—Ambersnails (Miles 1958; Perez et al. 2008). There are four genera within the family, differentiated by penial morphology. Representatives from three genera are found in Utah: Genus *Oxyloma*—penis with a sheath and preceded by an epiphallus with an appendix; Genus *Succinea*—penis without appendix, also within a sheath; and Genus *Catinella* (formerly *Quickella*)—penis without a sheath or distinctly differentiated epiphallus, penial appendix moderately to strongly developed (Branson 1963). This appendix is an inconspicuous lateral protuberance at the apex, or a large sac midway on the penis (Pilsbry 1948). Succineidae have a unique jaw that features a large, squarish accessory plate (Miles 1958; Fig. T75). See Branson (1963) for more on the taxonomic history of *Catinella*. *Succinea* and *Oxyloma* shells have large body whorls and short spires, whereas *Catinella* features a longer spire approaching that of the length of the aperture. *Succinea* shells are more oval, whereas *Oxyloma* shells are more elongate and narrow (Perez et al. 2008). The earliest known Succineidae are from the Paleocene of Europe and from Tertiary fossils in Africa, Europe, and North America (Barker 2001).

From Pilsbry (1948, p. 771): "The very thin shell is usually external, ovate, imperforate, of few (up to 4) whorls, the spire usually short, sometimes wanting; the aperture is large, ovate, with thin simple peristome. The sole is tripartite. Pedal grooves define a narrow foot-margin. The lung is short. The alimentary canal is of the usual four folds, and there is a short pyloric caecum between the two liver ducts. The tentacular and buccal muscles are free to their insertion on the columella, the buccal dividing far back. The right ocular retractor lies between male and female branches of genitalia. The genital atrium is usually shallow, behind and below the right eye-stalk. The seminal vesicles or talon are usually paired but often very unequal. The compact prostate gland is shorter than the sacculated oviduct. The jaw has a median projection on the cutting edge. The radula has ectocones on all teeth, usually split on the marginals; endocones are united with mesocones on the lateral teeth, but distinct on the marginals."

The taxonomy of the species in this family needs more research effort, combining data derived from new, modern genetic studies with biogeographical and morphological (animal and shell) data (Nekola 2014). Martinez-Cruz (2018) and Rundell et al. (2004) have initiated this work for some species. Miller et al. (2000) and Martinez-Cruz (2018) noted that *Oxyloma* and *Succinea* are intermixed in phylogenetic trees. Also, *Oxyloma effusa* was demonstrated to be a junior synonym of *O. salleana,* which also grouped with a Wyoming *Succinea* sample. Rundell et al. (2004) studied Hawaiian succineids relative to other succineids from the Pacific islands and Japan and similarly found that *Catinella* and *Succinea* species were intermixed. These data suggest that characters used to classify a species to one of the three genera are flawed. The lack of a penial appendix in *Succinea* may not be a valid character for defining the genus; Franzen (1963) studied anatomical variation in *Oxyloma retusa* and found that within a population some snails lacked an appendix and others varied in length. Miles (1958) has made similar observations. Chromosome counts appear to differ markedly among the species examined to date, with diploid values observed ranging from 10 for *Catinella rotundata* to 44 for *Succinea putris* (Burch et al. 1966). These differences could help with defining species and genera, but more work is needed to get chromosome numbers for species that have not been studied. The preliminary data by Burch et al. (1966) suggests that *Catinella* may have characteristically fewer chromosomes (e.g., 10–12) than *Oxyloma* and *Succinea* (34–44).

Catinella avara Say, 1824 Suboval Ambersnail

DESCRIPTION (Say 1824; Morse 1864; Burke 2013): *Shell:* suboval, pale reddish-yellow, subdiaphanous, fragile, covered with an earthy crust. *Whorls:* 3, minutely wrinkled; body whorl very large; spire small. *Aperture:* large, subovate, about ⅔ of the whole length of the shell. The posterior margin of the aperture attaches to the penultimate whorl at a near perpendicular or slightly anterior angle.

SIZE: Length 3/20th of an inch (3.8 mm); Specimen from Logan Canyon (ANSP #144611; Fig. T76) was 6.5 mm but may reach 7–11 mm × 4–6.8 mm wide. Width is about 60% of the length.

ANIMAL (Morse 1864): Buccal plate broad, narrow, strongly arcuate, having one central projection on its cutting edge, and a slight depression on its inferior edge. Lingual membrane with 39 plates in a row, with central plates broad, square, and having one long and two short denticles; laterals seven, longer than broad, angular, bidentate, inner side of larger tooth shouldered, marginals denticulated.

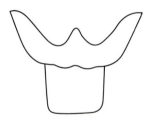

FIG. T75. Jaw of *Catinella avara*. Credit: Morse 1864.

TYPE LOCATION: Northwest Territory.

JUNIOR SYNONYMS: *Succinea avara* Say, 1824; *Succinea vermeta* Say, 1829; *Mediaappendix vermeta* (Say, 1829) Burke 2013. Adams (1841) considered *avara* to be a juvenile of *S. vermeta* and noted that it was found in the same populations as *S. obliqua* Say, 1824.

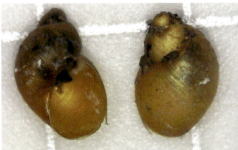

FIG. T76. *Catinella avara*. Left: Zion N. Park. Credit: K. Wheeler, iNaturalist.org; right: ANSP 144611, Logan Canyon, UT (collected by Henderson and Daniels, 1916). Credit: ANSP.

NOTES: Smaller shell and shorter aperture than for *Succinea* and *Oxyloma* species. *C. avara* is a little longer spired than *C. stretchiana*. Fewer whorls than for *S. grosvenorii*. Branson (1959) found this species in abundance associated with the spherical colonies of the alga *Nostoc*; densities of about 31/ft^2 were noted. Later in the year, they were crawling on *Nelumbo lutea* (pond lily) and cattail *Typha latifolia* in the pond. Branson noted that this species was kept with *Succinea grosvenorii* in an aquarium with *Elodea* for over a year.

DISTRIBUTION: Widely found in Canada and the United States. (Branson 1959; Beetle 1989; Burke 2013). Utah: Cedar Breaks National Monument (Gregg 1941); Zion Canyon; Marysvale; Fish Lake; Cache, Kane, Summit and Uinta counties, Red Butte, Odgen, and Weber canyons (Henderson and Daniels 1916, 1917; Jones 1935; Brooks 1936; Woolstenhulme 1942a, b; Wheeler 2018; UMNH; DMNH).

Catinella stretchiana Bland, 1867 Sierra Ambersnail

DESCRIPTION (Bland 1867): "Shell globose conic, thin, pellucid, shining, striatulate, greenish horn color; spire short, rather obtuse; suture deep; whorls 3, convex, the last roundly inflated; columella arcuate, lightly thickened, receding; aperture oblique, roundly oval; peristome simple, with the margins joined by a thin callus."

SIZE: SL typically 6.0–6.25 mm (max. 8.5 mm), SW 5 mm; ApL 5 mm, ApW 4 mm; last whorl 5.5 mm long.

TYPE LOCATION: Little Valley, Washoe County, Nevada, on eastern slope of the Sierra Nevada, 6,500 ft elevation. Holotype was found under dry cow dung at the edge of a swamp by R. H. Stretch.

JUNIOR SYNONYMS: *Succinea stretchiana* Bland, 1867; Pilsbry 1948.

NOTES: Shorter than typical *C. avara* and whorls not quite as convex, though Pilsbry (1948) notes that shell lots from other locations have longer shells, suggesting it may be synonymous with *C. avara*. No animal data available.

DISTRIBUTION (ANSP; Ibase): CA, ID, NV, OR, WY. Utah records: near Brigham City and Cache Valley.

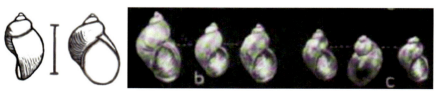

FIG. T77. *Catinella stretchiana*. Left: original figure from Bland 1867. b. Red Meadow, CA, c. Palisade Creek, CA. Credit: Pilsbry 1948.

Oxyloma haydeni Binney, 1858 Niobrara Ambersnail

DESCRIPTION (Binney 1858a; Pilsbry 1948; Franzen 1964): *Shell*: elongate-oval, thin, translucent, amber-colored; spire short, acute. *Whorls:* 3–3 ⅝, convex, the last marked with wrinkles of growth and irregular, heavy spiral furrows; suture moderate; columella covered lightly with callus and allowing all the interior whorls to be seen from below to the apex. Revolving lines sometimes continuous over entire body whorl, but they generally are interrupted or confined to the interstices of the incremental striae or wrinkles. *Aperture:* oblique, oval, 5/7th the shell length, lower portion of its margin considerably expanded.

SIZE: Holotype SL 21 mm, SW 9 mm. Paratypes 21.3–21.5 × 10.2–11.2 mm. Means and ranges from Franzen (1964) for shells >11 mm long: SL 16.4 mm (11.1–22.7); SW 8.07 mm (5.7–11.2); W/L ratio 49.5% (43–58); ApL 12.1 mm (7.9–16.6), ApW 6.9 mm (4.6–9.0); ApL/SL 73.7% (69–80); ApW/SW ratio 85.0% (73–93); ApW/ApL 57.0% (47–65). For smaller shells 9.5–10.5 mm long, W/L ratios averaged higher (56%) and aperture proportions were less (62%, 59–64% of shell length); ApW/ApL was greater (73%, 71–74). Putative *haydeni* shells from Kansas (University of Kansas Museum of Natural History) were 15–17 mm long (Miles 1958).

ANIMAL (Franzen 1964): Body wall is light cream, with patches of black flecks, and it is finely and irregularly tuberculate. Pigment patches converge between rear tentacles, fanning from there to form 3 double-rowed bands that extend across the posterior dorsal surface of the body, terminating within 0.5–1.0 mm of the attachment of the mantle to the body wall; in some individuals the bands are barely discernible. Pigmentation may be concentrated on upper and anterior parts, or it may extend over the entire surface, continuing onto the ventral foot. Lateral body wall does not tend to form a band as in *Oxyloma retusa*. Mantle is generally darkly speckled. Usually, a darkly pigmented band on the mantle outlines the posterior margin of the kidney, which appears as an orange band

FIG. T78. *Oxyloma haydeni.* Credit: (left) Tryon 1866, (center and right) Cache Valley, UT, Credit: E. Wagner.

through the mantle. Shallow vertical grooves incise the pedal groove and the very shallow suprapedal groove, producing a series of shallow scallops along the ventral margin, especially when the animal is in a partially contracted state. Albumen gland is about ¾ length of the prostate gland. Lobes of twinned seminal vesicles subequal to unequal in length.

FIG. T79. *Oxyloma haydeni kanabensis*, Topotype (1953) ANSP 345170. Credit: ANSP.

Pilsbry (1948, for the *kanabensis* form): Mantle over the lung not pigmented. Hermaphrodite duct is very large and swollen. Prostate gland is long. Penis short, swollen above, where it is abruptly bent, with a small tapering appendix and an epiphallus that makes about one spiral turn.

GENITALIA: The genital aperture is a slit (or crescent in contracted state), 0.8–1.2 mm long, surrounded by an oval tumid lip, which usually has scattered flecks of pigment. The penis is elongate, encased in a slightly speckled sheath, with an appendix (bulbous at base, finger-like at terminus, 0.6–1.2 mm long) forming a blunt hook or broad arc. The vas deferens enters the sheath at its posterior extremity. Penis sheath and vagina about equal in length. Oviduct and duct from seminal vesicle enter the vagina terminally. See Pilsbry (1948), Clarke (1991), Stevens et al. (2000), and Culver et al. (2013) for figures of the genitalia and other parts of the anatomy.

RADULA (Franzen 1964): Rows range from 66 to 96; teeth per row and number of lateral and marginal teeth vary. Ratio of laterals to marginals is about 1:3–1:4. The tooth formula varies among individuals and among rows within an individual; for example, row 12 had 9 marginals and 8 laterals and rows 49 and 50 each had 43 marginals and 8–9 laterals; other individuals had 41–44 marginals and 8–10 laterals (row 63), 30–38 marginals and 11–12 laterals (row 74), or 22–32 marginals and 8–10 lateral teeth (row 69). As in other succineids, the tricuspid central tooth has a mesocone, flanked by two ectocones. Bicuspid laterals have a mesocone and an ectocone. Marginals are tricuspid, with the ectocone subdivided into 3 cusps. In the outermost marginals, the lateral cusp of the ectocone tends to be longer and more tapering than that of *Succinea* or *Catinella*. The jaw does not differ from that of *O. retusa*; it has a median fold that projects anteriorly, but it lacks the small lateral folds found in *Succinea ovalis*.

TYPE LOCATION: Nebraska, between Loup Fork and L'eau qui Court rivers. *S. haydeni* var. *minor* from "Red River of the North." For *O. haydeni kanabensis*: "'The Greens' 10 km above Kanab, Utah on Kanab Wash, on a wet ledge among moss and cypripediums" (Pilsbry 1948). Holotype is ANSP #103166 (Topotype #345170, collected in 1953, with broken lip, is shown in Fig. T79).

JUNIOR SYNONYMS: *Succinea haydeni* Binney, 1858a; probably *Oxyloma retusum* Lea, 1834 (= *O. retusa*) in part, for old western records. Pilsbry (1948, p. 796) noted that *Oxyloma sillimani*, described by Bland (1867) from a single shell from Elko County, Nevada, is likely synonymous with *O. haydeni* given that "specimens from the western edge of Elko Co., Nevada, are partly very much like Bland's figure, but in most of them the last whorl is decidedly more convex." Genetic data by Stevens et al. (2000), tying Nevada *Oxyloma* specimens to other *haydeni*, also supports synonymy. The snail, which until recently was known as *O. haydeni kanabensis*, was first discovered in 1909 by Ferriss (1910) in the Kanab Creek drainage and was first thought to be *Succinea hawkinsi* Baird, 1863. These shells are in the Illinois Natural History Survey collection (#74710; see also CM 107348). Pilsbry (1948) later transferred it to the genus *Oxyloma* as *O. haydeni kanabensis*. Harris and Hubricht (1982) elevated *kanabensis* to species status; However, the U.S. Geological Survey (Culver et al. 2013) recognized the snail as a subspecies of *haydeni*, and it was listed as an endangered subspecies in 1992 (USFWS 1992b). According to Culver et al. (2013), the genus name *Oxyloma* is a neuter noun, so they named the form *Oxyloma haydeni kanabense*. However, according to rules of the International Commission on Zoological Nomenclature, although recommending gender matching when creating names, the original spelling and gender remain even if a species is assigned to a genus of a different gender (ICZN Code, Article 32, www.iczn.org). Based on the work of Culver et al. (2013) and the genetic work discussed below, the Kanab ambersnail is not considered a valid subspecies and is a synonym of *O. haydeni*.

NOTES: Succineid identification and taxonomy have been traditionally difficult, and more work is needed on a broad scale. As in other families, species, subspecies, and varieties have been described based on minor differences in shell morphology, without an understanding of population variation. For example, Binney (1865) described a variety he called *S. haydeni* var. *minor*, which was 15 mm long but otherwise had the characteristics already given for *S. haydeni*. There has been a recent focus on a former subspecies described by Pilsbry (1948) as *Oxyloma haydeni kanabensis*, the Kanab ambersnail. Pilsbry (1948) noted that the body whorl was more slender and drawn out than in *O. haydeni* (14–19 mm long × 7–9 mm wide), and the lower lip of the aperture is not as deeply curved. However, Stevens et al. (2000) noted that the overlap in shell morphology among *Oxyloma* species is too great to use for species diagnosis. Culver et al. (2013), came to a similar conclusion with a more in-depth study. A series of genetic analyses (Miller et al. 2000; Stevens et al. 2000; Meretsky et al. 2002; Culver et al. 2013) found that the Kanab ambersnail is not genetically distinct from other ambersnails in the region (Nevada, Colorado River, Grand Canyon, Sevier River drainage, Escalante River, upper Virgin River drainage, and Kanab Creek, Utah), indicating that subspecific designation and endangered subspecies status is unwarranted. The U.S. Fish and Wildlife Service (2020) has formally requested that the subspecies be removed from the list of threatened and endangered wildlife species. *O. haydeni* cannot be separated from *O. retusa* by shell, radula, or jaw characteristics. However, Franzen (1964) notes that the lateral body wall pigmentation in *haydeni* does not assume the form of a broad band as in *retusa*, and overall pigmentation is lighter in *haydeni*. Also, the penial appendix is longer in *haydeni* than in *retusa* (though variable in the latter; Franzen 1963).

These snails are found in forest, parkland, and wetter portions of the tall grass prairie zones (Harris and Hubricht 1982). In the southwest, they are found in wet meadow and marsh habitat or in vegetated seeps at the base of sandstone cliffs. Clarke (1991) also noted them at the mouth of vole burrows and at the edge of thick cattail (*Typha*) stands. Snails reproduce in early to midsummer among individuals ≥9 mm. Fecal analysis suggests that they feed on watercress (*Nasturtium officinale*) and decaying plant matter, and possibly also on fungi and bacteria associated with the decaying matter. In the Grand Canyon, these snails also occur on monkey-flower (*Mimulus cardinalis*), water sedge (*Carex aquatilis*), and bent-grass (*Agrostis stolonifera*). The snails are estimated to live 12–15 months. Robins have been observed to feed on the snails. Named in honor of Dr. F. V. Hayden, a pioneering American geologist.

DISTRIBUTION (Henderson and Daniels 1917; Chamberlin and Jones 1929; Woolstenhulme 1942a; Baily and Baily 1952; Harris and Hubricht 1982; Spamer and Bogan 1993; Stevens et al. 2000; ANSP): OR, WA, ID, MT, WY, NE, ND, AZ. Common in the Plains region of southern Canada and northern United States; Weston, Idaho, along Bear River. Dawson (1875) reported it (var. *minor*) from Pembina Mountain (North Dakota) near the 49th parallel. Hendricks (2012) noted that populations in Montana were found on both sides of the continental divide. Utah records: Kanab Creek and the upper Virgin River, west of Wood's Cross, 1 mile north of Vernal, Garden City, shores of Utah Lake, near Springville, near Salt Lake City, Weber Canyon, Box Elder County, and Cache Valley.

Oxyloma nuttalliana Lea, 1841 (Lea 1846a) Oblique Ambersnail

DESCRIPTION (Lea 1846a): *Shell*: long-ovate, oblique, transparent, striate, pale yellow; spire rather elevated; sutures impressed. *Whorls:* 3, somewhat convex. *Aperture:* long-ovate, ~3/4 of total shell length.

SIZE: SL 13 mm, SW 6.3 mm.

Subspecies *O. nuttalliana chasmodes* Pilsbry, 1948 (Fig. T80), was described as elliptical-ovate, thin, fragile, pale-buff, with a very large and broad aperture, occupying 85–90% of the length and short spire of 2.5 whorls. The last whorl is rather convex in the upper part on the left margin (ventral view) but later becomes more flattened there.

FIG. T80. *Oxyloma nuttalliana*. ANSP 5609 holotype. Credit: ANSP.

ANIMAL (Pilsbry 1948): Lung is dark gray. The mantle edge, foot, and head are peppered with black, more or less in spots or stripes. The hermaphrodite duct is less bulky than that in most species, not very convoluted, and dark gray. Prostate gland is rather large. Seminal vesicle has a solid black lateral projection. Penis: cylindrical, with a thin sheath, coiled in the upper part (1 revolution) in the middle of which is a moderately long, recurved appendix. This appendix is longer and the epiphallus stouter and less convoluted than related eastern species. The vagina is long and, in some individuals, angular at the insertion of the spermathecal duct. The large globular spermatheca is on a tapering duct, which is a little dilated at its base.

TYPE LOCATION: Oregon; *O. nuttalliana chasmodes* Pilsbry, 1948 holotype was from Stocton, California.

JUNIOR SYNONYMS: *Succinea nuttalliana* Lea, 1846a.

NOTES: Smaller and less elongated than *O. retusa* and *haydeni*, and inferior part or base not as retuse (rounded tip with a shallow notch). The appendix on the penis is longer and the epiphallus stouter and less convoluted than those in eastern succineids. Lea (1867) thought *nuttalliana* might be synonymous with *S. rusticana* Gould, but Pilsbry (1948) recognized it as a separate species. Henderson (1924) suggested that Utah records for *nuttalliana* should be referred to as *haydeni*.

DISTRIBUTION: ANSP: Alberta, British Columbia, AZ, CA, CO, ID, IL, MT, NV, ND, OR, WA. Utah records: Bear Lake (Pilsbry 1948; Baily and Baily 1952); Utah Lake (Henderson 1924); Warm Springs near Salt Lake (Ingersoll 1876).

Oxyloma retusa Lea, 1834 Blunt Ambersnail

DESCRIPTION (Lea 1834, quoted, p. 117; Franzen 1963; Miles 1958): "*Shell*: ovately oblong, very thin, pellucid, yellowish, spire short; whorls three; aperture below dilate and drawn back." *Whorls:* 2.5 to 3.5, the surface marked with irregularly spaced and oblique striae; nuclear whorl finely stippled and white; body whorl large. *Aperture:* ovate, with a deeply arcuate base and sharply pointed apex. Peristome sharp, callus very thin, outer lip ± straight. Sometimes the columella emerges below the apex of the aperture and continues along the margin of the last whorl in the form of a spiral plait.

FIG. T81. *Oxyloma retusa*. Credit: left, Rutland Co., VT, Pam Darrow, iNaturalist.org; Center: ©Erica Mitchell, iNaturalist.org. Right: original figure from Lea 1834.

SIZE (Lea 1834; Franzen 1963): Holotype was 7.6 mm × 18 mm. SL 8.3–19.8 mm, ApL/SL 66–84%; W/L 46.7–60%; ApW/ApL 49–70%. *S. retusa magister*: to 18 mm × 9.5–10 mm, ApL 13–14 mm (Pilsbry 1899a). *S. retusa higginsi*: 15.5–16.3 × 7.7–8.7 mm, ApL 11.6–12 mm (Pilsbry 1948).

ANIMAL (Franzen 1963, p. 88): "The body wall is light cream colored, finely and irregularly tuberculate, and peppered with flecks of black pigment. Over the dorsal surface of the head, up to the posterior tentacles, the flecks occur in irregular patches. At the level of the posterior tentacles, the flecks are arranged in three not sharply defined bands. The median dorsal band divides as it extends toward the mantle collar and sometimes does not extend that far. The median band is flanked on either side by an equally wide band which extends to the mantle collar. The lateral body wall is pigmented by a broad band, which becomes lighter ventrally and terminates above the ventral margin leaving a white band along the ventral border of the body wall corresponding in length to that of the foot. The mantle is generally darkly and uniformly speckled. Sometimes light blotches along the anterior margin produce a mottled or broadly striped effect. Through the mantle the kidney is seen as an orange band following the contour of the body. Frequently a darkly pigmented band on the mantle outlines the posterior margin of the kidney. The degree of pigmentation on the body wall and on the mantle is variable from very light to very heavy. A few very darkly pigmented (essentially black) individuals were found. Towards the ventral margin, shallow vertical grooves incise the very shallow suprapedal groove and the pedal groove producing a series of shallow

Succineidae

FIG. T82. *Oxyloma retusa*, ANSP 58289, lectotype for *O. retusa magister*, Rock Island, IL. Credit: ANSP.

scallops along the ventral margin, especially when the animal is in a partially contracted state." Örstan (2010) measured the penial appendix of four specimens: 0.55 ± 0.17 (SD) mm. The pigmentation of Örstan's specimens did not form any distinct patterns on the mantle but did form longitudinal bands in front of the head between the tentacles and formed splotches along the side of the foot.

RADULA/JAW (Franzen 1963): Basal plate is typical of *Oxyloma*, longer and more tapering than that of *Succinea* or *Catinella* teeth. Radula with 70–112 rows of teeth. Number of teeth per row varied from 77 to 103. Marginal teeth ranged from 31 to 42 with 4–5 cusps, laterals from 7 to 11, bicuspid, with smaller ectocone, though outermost laterals have an endocone as well. Ratio of laterals to marginals is about 1:3 or 1:4. Central tooth is tricuspid, with larger mesocone and smaller ectocones. Jaw is amber-colored, with a median fold that projects anteriorly; it lacks the small lateral folds characteristic of *Succinea ovalis* (Franzen 1959). See Franzen (1963) for images of representative teeth and the jaw.

GENITALIA (Franzen 1963): Genital slit ranges in length from 0.6 to 0.9 mm and is surrounded by an oval white lip, tumid to a varying degree. Penis and vagina are in the right anterior part of the animal and are about equal in length. As in other *Oxyloma*, the penis and epiphallus are enclosed within a penis sheath. In *O. retusa*, the sheath has a slight and variable amount of black flecking over its distal two-thirds. The epiphallus enters the penis sheath at its distal end, subterminally (as in other *Oxyloma*), and is coiled and recurved around the penis in no regular fashion before entering the penis. The sheath is too short to fit both the penis and epiphallus without the penis being bent or recurved. Sometimes as much as the distal third of the penis is recurved anteriorly. The penis may be twisted a half to full turn. There is a slender, finger-like, penial appendix, usually projecting ventrally from a point near the epiphallus junction. Variations in the appendix: straight, bent, or hook-shaped; inflated; length varying from none (lacking an appendix) or reduced to "pronounced" (but shorter than in *O. haydeni*). Seminal vesicle is bilobed, the lobes varying in size (equal, subequal, or one or the other longer); the distal portion is pigmented, varying in intensity among individuals (some nearly black). The fertilization sac varies in size from an inflated sac to one scarcely differentiated from the seminal vesicle and duct between the follicular albumin and prostate glands. Prostate is smaller than albumin gland and unpigmented.

TYPE LOCATION: Ohio, near Cincinnati. Synonym species *Succinea higginsi* (Bland) Tryon, 1866a, was from Put-In-Bay, Lake Erie. *S. retusa magister* Pilsbry, 1899 type (Fig. T82) was from Rock Island, IL. *S. calumatensis* Calkins, 1878, type was from the banks of the Calumet River, Cook County, IL.

JUNIOR SYNONYMS (Pilsbry 1948): *Succinea retusa* Lea, 1834; *Succinea higginsi* (Bland nov. spec.) Tryon, 1866a; *Succinea retusa magister* Pilsbry, 1899; *Succinea calumetensis* Calkins, 1878.

NOTES: Pilsbry (1948) noted that *O. retusa* differs from *O. gouldi* by its larger size and broader, more retracted and less deeply curved basal margin of the aperture, though some races of *retusa* have a deeply arched basal arc. Pilsbry also notes that the genitalia are most like *O. haydeni kanabensis*, but that species has twinned seminal vesicles, a shorter penis and greatly swollen convolutions of the hermaphrodite duct. Franzen (1963) observed that this species has a shorter penial appendix than *O. haydeni*. It was described from a single shell. Binney (see Lea 1864a) suggested that *retusa* was a junior synonym of *S. ovalis*, with which Lea (1864a), and later Pilsbry (1948), disagreed.

The snail is found near water, typically in wetland vegetation in marshes and riparian areas (Hubricht 1985; Örstan 2010). In a Maryland study (Örstan 2010), snails reproduced from late March to the end of June, when they reached their maximum size and died off. The smallest mating snail observed was 6.2 mm long. Mating lasted 63–97 min. The progeny grew and reproduced near the end of August. Both the spring and fall progeny hibernate until the next spring to renew the cycle. There are 38 chromosomes in diploid *O. retusa* (Burch et al. 1966).

DISTRIBUTION (ANSP; Ibase): British Columbia, Nova Scotia, Ontario, Prince Edward Island, Quebec, Lake Superior, St. Lawrence River; AK, AZ, AR, CA, CO, IL, IN, IA, ME, MD, MI, MN, MO, MT, ND, NJ, NY, OH, OR, PA, SD, VT, WA, WI, WY. Utah records: Wild's Ranch, Ouray, Utah (CM 115220); Logan Canyon (DMNH 171177); Rich County (DMNH 157729); Weber Canyon (CM 107376); Deception Lake near Kanab (ANSP), Kanab Canyon, and other Kane County Sites (Meretsky et al. 2002).

Succinea grosvenorii Lea, 1864a Santa Rita Ambersnail

DESCRIPTION (Lea 1864a; Pilsbry 1948, quoted, p. 821): *Shell:* oblique-ovate, striate, semitransparent, straw-colored, thin; spire exserted, sutures very impressed. *Whorls:* 4, convex. *Aperture:* nearly round, broadly ovate, about 6/10 the total shell length; outer lip expanded; columella bent in and twisted. "This is a rather short, inflated shell with strongly convex whorls, very deep suture and usually

FIG. T83. *Succinea grosvenorii*, ANSP 183154 (*S. grosvenorii mooresiana*, syntype, Platte R., NE), ANSP 65369 (*S. grosvenorii greeri*, lectotype, Vicksburg, MS) ANSP. Credit: ANSP.

somewhat coarse sculpture in places, rarely showing some irregular and interrupted spiral impressions in the peripheral region. It varies from thin and pale yellow to rather opaque, and is never transparent."

SIZE: Holotype SL 13 mm × 8.1 mm wide. Specimens measured by Pilsbry (1948) that had 3.5 whorls were 11.4–15.5 mm long × 6.9–9.0 mm wide (L/W 1.56 to 1.72); a smaller specimen with 3 whorls (8.8 mm × 6.0 mm wide) had L/W 1.47; apertures were 61–68% of total shell length (smallest shell, 69%).

FIG. T84. *Succinea grosvenorii*, ANSP 12429 (*Succinea lineata* from Payson, UT, Wheeler Expedition). Credit: ANSP.

ANIMAL (Pilsbry 1948): Mantle is light gray, with more distinct short gray streaks behind the edge; the thick mantle edge and entire head and foot are cream-white. The genital orifice is in a longitudinal pit or slit. The prostate gland is moderately sized, positioned far forward. Vas deferens is large and short. Penis is stout, swollen near the apex, where its cavity contains a small fleshy nodule on the outer wall. Passage into the epiphallus is marked by a circle of small projections into the cavity. The epiphallus has thinner walls and some low longitudinal internal ridges. The globose spermatheca is on a very slender long duct, which enters low, leaving a quite short vagina.

TYPE LOCATION: Santa Rita Valley, Kansas; Alexandria, Louisiana.

JUNIOR SYNONYMS (Pilsbry 1948): *Succinea grosvernorii* Lea, 1864a; *Succinea lineata* Binney, 1857; *Succinea mooresiana* Lea, 1864a; *Succinea greerii* Tryon, 1866a; *Succinea lineata* forma *elongata* Cockerell, 1892a.

NOTES: More whorls and more opaque than other succineid species found in Utah. Shimek (1936) noted that the habitat of *S. grosvenori* in Iowa was on the loess river banks or bluffs. The animal would press the aperture against the face of the bluff where they could find shade and form a barrier against desiccation, moving when moister conditions prevailed.

DISTRIBUTION (ANSP; UMNH; Henderson and Daniels 1917; Pilsbry 1948; Beetle 1989): Widely distributed in the United States and Canada. Preston and Weston, Idaho. Utah records: Salt Lake, Grand (UMNH #1.0121272, 1.012123), and Tooele (Lakepoint) counties; Payson, Cache Valley, and the Oquirrh Mountains. Ingersoll (1876) noted a Smithsonian record of *S. lineata* from the Yellowstone River of Utah.

Succinea missoula Harris and Hubricht, 1982 Ninepipes Ambersnail

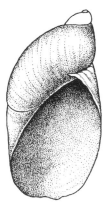

FIG. T85. *Succinea missoula*. Credit: Harris and Hubricht (1982).

DESCRIPTION (Harris and Hubricht 1982): *Shell*: oblong-ovate, pale amber, pellucid, very thin and fragile. *Whorls:* 3; spire about ⅓ the length of the shell, conical with rounded whorls and deep sutures, nuclear whorl elevated; sculpture of numerous, irregular, coarse, growth wrinkles. *Aperture:* oblique, ovate, lip thin.

SIZE: Holotype SL 14.5 mm, SW 7.5 mm, L/W ratio 1.93; ApL 10.5 mm (72% of SL), ApW 6.0 mm.

ANIMAL: Grayish-brown, mantle with dark gray spots and streaks; penis stout, straight, truncated, without an appendix, or with a mere vestige, within a thin sheath, epiphallus about as long as the penis; vagina about as long as the penis, free oviduct a little longer than the vagina; spermathecal duct very slender throughout its length; seminal vesicle (talon) not bifurcate, dark, brownish-gray; hermaphrodite duct slender throughout, black and greatly convoluted.

TYPE LOCATION: Ninepipes National Wildlife Refuge, Lake County, Montana. Holotype 200994 and paratypes 200995 in Field Museum of Natural History, Chicago.

JUNIOR SYNONYMS: *Oxyloma missoula* Harris and Hubricht 1982. Harris and Hubricht (1982) assigned this species to *Oxyloma*, differentiating it from other *Oxyloma* species by the lack of penial appendix. However, this characteristic currently defines the genus *Succinea* (Pilsbry 1948), differentiating it from other Succineidae species. This species may be synonymous with *S. rusticana*, but additional research comparing topotypes of *rusticana* with *S. missoula* topotypes is needed to clarify the relationship.

NOTES (Harris and Hubricht 1982): Differs from *Oxyloma* species in the lack of an appendix on the penis, and the seminal vesicle (= talon) is not bilobed. Shell is more translucent than that for *S. grosvenorii* and with fewer whorls. *S. missoula* cannot be separated from *S. rusticana*, since animal data on that species is lacking and shell measurements overlap.

DISTRIBUTION (Harris and Hubricht 1982): Montana (5 sites) and Utah (Farmington and Uinta Mountains [4 km north of Heber]). Historical distribution in the former Lake Bonneville and Glacial Lake Missoula basins.

Succinea oregonensis Lea, 1841 Oregon Ambersnail

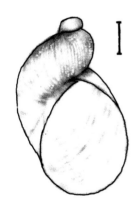

FIG. T86. *Succinea oregonensis*. Credit: Pilsbry 1948.

DESCRIPTION (Lea 1841, p. 32; Pilsbry 1948, p. 842): "*Shell* oblique, thin, rugosely striate, reddish, subdiaphanous; spire exserted: sutures much impressed; *whorls* 3, inflated; aperture large, wide-ovate." Strongly convex whorls; the first is smooth, the second is sharply striate. *Aperture:* rounded, about $^2/_3$ the length of the shell. The upper part of outer lip joins the body whorl to form an approximate right angle with columellar lip. Spire more elevated than for *avara*.

SIZE: 3.8 diameter × 7.6 mm tall; ApW of holotype is 62% of ApL.

TYPE LOCATION: Oregon (holotype, USNM 117935).

JUNIOR SYNONYMS: None

NOTES: Fewer whorls than *S. grosvenorii* and generally shorter, relative to its width, than for *Oxyloma* species. Lea (1841) described this species from a single shell. Burke (2013) refers specimens identified as *S. oregonensis* Lea "of many collections not of Lea" to *Catinella rehderi* Pilsbry, 1948. Pilsbry (1948) considered the *S. oregonensis* figured in Binney's Terrestrial Mollusks to be different from the holotype shell. No animal descriptions have been published yet.

DISTRIBUTION (ANSP; Ibase): AL, AR, AZ, CA, CO, FL, IL, ID, KS, LA, TX, MO, MN, MT, NE, ND, NM, SD, WA. Henderson and Daniels (1917) found it near Franklin, Idaho, among boulders and into Cache Valley of Utah. Utah records: Arches National Park (CM 107852); Moab (UMNH 1626, 1637), Blanding (UMNH 1599), between Blanding and Verdure (UMNH 1647, 1649), Brigham City (CM 107833; University of Florida 111518); near Garfield, Salt Lake County (CM 108299); Payson (Wheeler Expedition); Cache Valley; and Lake Point, Tooele County.

Succinea rusticana Gould, 1846 Rustic Ambersnail

FIG. T87. *Succinea rusticana*, ANSP 12485, Blue Lake, WA. Credit: ANSP.

DESCRIPTION (Gould 1846; Pilsbry 1948): *Shell*: elongate, ovate-conical, spire acute, shell rather large, thin, and fragile; pale greenish horn-color, surface rude and without luster, coarsely and irregularly marked by the lines of growth. *Whorls:* three or more, moderately convex, sutures well impressed; last whorl large and long, narrowing toward the base; body portion of the face of the shell moderately large. *Aperture:* ovate, 3/4th the length of the shell; fold of the columella distinct.

SIZE: 12.7 mm tall × 6.3 mm diameter.

ANIMAL: No data.

TYPE LOCATION: Oregon (U.S. Exploring Expedition)

JUNIOR SYNONYMS: Lea (1864a) suggested that *S. rusticana* and *nuttalliana* are synonymous, but Pilsbry (1948) recognized the two as separate species.

NOTES: The last whorl is more oval and the suture less deeply impressed than in *S. oregonensis* or *S. grosvenorii* (Pilsbry 1948). Cannot be differentiated from *S. missoula, O. retusa, O. nuttalliana,* and *O. haydeni* based on overlapping shell characters and lack of animal data for *S. rusticana*.

DISTRIBUTION: British Columbia; CA, OR, WA, (Pilsbry 1948); St. Charles Canyon near Bear Lake. In Utah, there are records from Weber Canyon (Henderson and Daniels 1917) and Salt Lake City (Woolstenhulme 1942a; UMNH #1.003749).

SPF: **TROCHOMORPHOIDEA Mörch, 1864**

Euconulidae Baker, 1928

Euconulidae features glossy, beehive-shaped (conic or biconvex) shells with a narrow umbilicus and slowly increasing whorls. Penis bearing a digitiform appendix, a terminal retractor, and short epiphallus, without a lime sac or flagellum. Spermatheca small and short (Pilsbry 1946). Junior synonym, Naninidae Geyer, 1909. H. B. Baker (1928) defined the family based on dentition of the marginal teeth of the radula. The radula has tricuspid central and lateral teeth, the marginals with 2 (*Euconulus* Reinhardt, 1883b) or 3 cusps (*Guppya* Mörch, 1867). Also, in *Euconulus*, the shell has axial striation (observed microscopically) and there is no 'horn' on the tail, whereas *Guppya* lacks the axial striation, but has the horn on the tail over the junction of the pedal furrows (Pilsbry, 1946).

Euconulidae were formerly positioned with the superfamily Gastrodontoidea (Hausdorf 1998), but new genetic data (Wade et al. 2006; Hyman et al. 2007; Teasdale 2017) led Bouchet et al. (2017) to transfer it to the superfamily Trochomorphoidea (infraorder Limacoidei). Euconulid snails in the subfamily Euconulinae Baker, 1928, are oviparous and in Microcystinae Thiele, 1931, are ovoviviparous (Hausdorf 1998). Worldwide, there are currently 51 accepted genera within the family, including *Euconulus*, which has 15 species, 2 of which are fossils. *Helix fulva* Müller, 1774, is the type species, currently known as *Euconulus fulvus*. Recent genetic analyses by Horsáková et al. (2020) revised some *Euconulus* species (originally described as *Helix fulva*; *Helix egena* Say, 1825; *H. fulva* var. *alderi* Gray, 1840, *Conulus praticola* Reinhardt, 1883a, a junior synonym of *alderi*, fide Welter-Schultes 2012; *C. polygyratus* Pilsbry, 1899b; *Euconulus trochiformis* [Montagu] Dall 1905). These taxa now are redefined as five separate taxa: *E. fulvus* (Europe), *E. polygyratus* (northeastern North America), *Euconulus alderi* (Atlantic Europe to western North America), *E. fresti* (new North American species), and *E. fulvus egenus* (Central Asia to Atlantic North America). The latter two are represented in Utah. *E. alderi* has not been found in Utah yet but may be present, and so is also described.

Euconulus alderi Gray, 1840 Brown Hive

DESCRIPTION (Gray 1840; Horsáková et al. 2020): *Shell*: dark cinnamon-brown, very glossy, roundly pyramidal, wider than tall. *Whorls*: 4.4 (4.0–5.3); protoconch microsculpture with rounded, widely spaced radial ribs but strongly reduced in teleoconch microsculpture. Typically with strong parallel microfurrows (sillons) observable, with magnification, on the base of the shell (see the figure in keys). *Aperture:* crescent shaped, transverse, narrow, with a simple edge; outer lip smoothly arched, the columellar lip joining the shell at the center axis.

SIZE (mean, range, n = 27, Horsáková et al. 2020): SL 2.10 (1.74–2.78) mm, SW 2.75 (2.44–3.53) mm, L/W 0.76 (0.71–0.84), height body whorl 1.59 (1.40–1.92 mm), ApL 1.08 (0.96–1.30) mm (68–92% of body whorl height), ApW 1.37 (1.13–1.78 mm, ApW/SW 0.5 (0.45–0.53), SW/No. whorls 0.62 (0.57–0.69).

ANIMAL: Dark, with mantle uniformly and darkly colored.

TYPE LOCATION: Great Britain

JUNIOR SYNONYMS: *Helix fulva* var. *alderi* Gray 1840;

FIG. T88. *Euconulus alderi*. ANSP. Credit: left: © Michal Horsák, right: live animal from Slovakia, © Radovan Coufal (Horsakova et al. 2020).

NOTES (Horsáková et al. 2020): Shell color is dark cinnamon-brown, and protoconch microsculpture of *alderi* features fine, widely spaced radial ribs, whereas *E. fresti* and *E. fulvus egenus* have lighter colored, less glossy shells, lack the protoconch ribbing, and the animal is not as dark. The coil expansion rate is greater than for *E. fresti*; *alderi* also lacks the keel in the body whorl. Genetic analyses have indicated that *E. alderi* is a monophyletic clade using either nuclear DNA or mitochondrial DNA. *E. alderi* is restricted to base-rich wetland and riparian habitats, ranging from open fens to wet swampy forests.

DISTRIBUTION: Atlantic Europe east across Eurasian and Alaskan taiga and tundra to the west shore of Hudson's Bay in the North American Arctic, south along the Western Cordillera to the southern Sierra Nevada in California. Distribution in Utah still unknown.

Euconulus fresti Horsáková, Nekola, and Horsák, 2020 Keeled Hive

DESCRIPTION (Horsáková et al. 2020): *Shell*: dark cinnamon-brown, glossy, squat conical shape, sutures moderate, strong but sparse furrows paralleling whorls, no umbilicus. *Whorls:* 4.8–5.0 in fully adult specimens, relatively tightly coiled, with whorl width increasing at a constant rate of 1.5–1.8X per rotation; periphery keeled even in fully adult specimens; protoconch microsculpture reduced or absent, limited to very weak spiral lines; teleoconch microsculpture features distinct spiral lines and weaker thread-like ribs. *Aperture:* crescent shaped with a simple edge.

SIZE: Holotype SL 1.9 × 2.6 mm dia. Range SL 1.9–2.1 mm, SW 2.5–2.7 mm, L/W ratio 0.7–0.8 (holotype 0.75); SW/number of whorls ratio 0.52–0.61 (holotype 0.54).

FIG. T89. *Euconulus fresti.* Left three images: holotype (ANSP 478687); far right, paratype from calcareous seep, Kane Co., Utah. Credit: ©Michal Horsák (Horsakova et al. 2020).

ANIMAL: Mantle is mottled; animal is black. See also H. B. Baker (1928).

TYPE LOCATION: Martelle Fen, Jones County, Iowa, in sedge mat in a pasture (holotype ANSP 478687; paratypes ANSP 478688). Paratypes from calcareous seep near East Fork Virgin River, Kane County, Utah (ANSP 478690); Wesley School, Washington County, Maine (ANSP 478689), sedge mat at Kelly Creek Fen, Incomappleaux River Valley, British Columbia (ANSP 478691); and marly sedge mat at Tiplady Fen, Livingston County, Michigan.

JUNIOR SYNONYMS: *Euconulus alderi* (in part), *E. praticola* Reinhardt, *E.* aff. *alderi* Horsáková, Nekola, and Horsak 2019.

NOTES: Keeled margin, tighter coils, mottled mantle, and protoconch with little to no microsculpture differentiates it from *E. alderi. E. polygyratus* is lighter colored and more tightly coiled (SW/number of whorls ratio <0.5, whereas other U.S. *Euconulus* are >0.5). Darker red-brown shell, and animal body is black compared to tawny-yellow shell and pale gray body of *E. fulvus*. Microsculpture also differs: spiral lines stronger than ribs, whereas for *E. fulvus* the spiral furrows are weaker and ribs are stronger. Common in open sedge mats of fens, rich conifer/ash swamps, sedge meadows, and shrubs. Named in honor of Terrence J. Frest, a North American malacologist. Genetic analyses by Horsáková et al. (2019, 2020), using both nuclear and mitochondrial DNA, indicate that this species is in a very highly supported monophyletic clade. The closest genetic relative is *E. polygyratus*, which has a similar protoconch microsculpture. GenBank numbers: MK266537,

MK266543-6; MK299610, MK299616-9; MK299700, MK299707-10; MK299793; MK299800-3; MN706207; MN706200-3.

DISTRIBUTION: Ontario, Manitoba, British Columbia, Yukon, but absent in the Arctic; Northern United States to Iowa, Ohio, down the Rocky Mountains. to northern New Mexico. In Utah, the paratype is from Kane County. Some previous records for *E. fulvus* likely need to be transferred to this species.

Euconulus fulvus egenus Say, 1825 Conical Leaf Snail

DESCRIPTION: (Say 1825; Pilsbry 1946; Horsáková et al. 2020): *Shell*: convex, polished, with close microscopic striae along lines of growth, and faint spirals; thin, conic, cinnamon or dilute tawny, the summit paler. Spire conic with slightly convex outlines and obtuse apex, the periphery rounded or weakly angular, base convex. Umbilicus rimate (indented) or minutely perforate. *Whorls:* 4.13–5.0, not distinctly wrinkled, rounded. *Aperture:* lunate; narrow, transverse, wider than high; labium simple, the inferior end terminating at the center of the shell's base; peristome thin, dilated near the columellar insertion.

SIZE: Type: SL 2.4 mm, dia. 3.1 mm; 5 ½ whorls; L/W 0.77. Mean (range, n = 35; Horsáková et al. 2020): whorls 4.56 (4.13–5.00), SL 2.24 (1.89–2.69) mm, SW 3.00 (2.60–3.44) mm, L/W 0.74 (0.68–0.84), ApL 1.16 (0.92–1.33) mm, ApW 1.48 (1.26–1.72) mm, ApW/SW 0.49 (0.47–0.52), SW/no. whorls 0.66 (0.57–0.72), ApL/body whorl height 0.88 (0.77–0.96).

FIG. T90. *Euconulus fulvus egenus*. ANSP 461186 synonym *E. fulvus alaskensis*, topotype, Dyea Valley, Alaska, Credit: ANSP; bottom row Credit: ©Michal Horsák; live animal from western Siberia, Russia (Horsáková et al. 2020).

ANIMAL: Grayish with still darker tentacles, which are long; mantle with large black blotches; liver orange, overlain by dark pigment at sutural edge. Sole is very long and slender, tripartite, with median zone about $^2/_3$ as wide as lateral one; snake-like locomotion. Tail is weakly keeled above, truncate, projection quite low and rounded. Mantle collar narrow with prominent right and left neck lappets and double free edge. Lung about 5.5× as long as its base (3X the length of the kidney). For additional anatomical data see H. B. Baker (1928).

TYPE LOCATION: Bank of the Delaware River, about 10 miles from Philadelphia.

JUNIOR SYNONYMS (H. B. Baker 1928; Pilsbry 1946; Horsáková et al. 2020): *Helix fulva* Müller, 1774, *Helix egena* Say, 1825; *Helix parramattensis* Cox, 1864; *Helix fabricii* Beck, 1837; *Zonites callopisticus* Bourguignat, 1880; *Conulus fulvus* Schepman, 1882; *Zonites (Conulus) fulvus* Binney, 1885, *Euconulus trochiformis* (Montagu) Dall, 1905; *Helix mortoni* Jeffreys, 1833; *Conulus chersina* (Say) Morse, 1864, *Conulus fulvus* var. *alaskensis* Pilsbry, 1899b; *Euconulus fulvus* (Müller) Pilsbry 1908a; *Hyalinia fulva* (Müller) Taylor 1914.

NOTES: The small size and beehive shape of this glossy, nearly imperforate shell easily distinguish it from other Utah species except *E. fresti*. Differs from *E. fresti* based on lighter- colored shells, differences in animal body color (gray v. black in *E. fresti*), and microsculptural ribs that are stronger than spiral lines. Fine radial striae, appearing as a fine thread wrapped side-by-side around the whorls, helps differentiate *E. fulvus* juveniles from similar-looking juveniles of other species (Burke 2013). Whorls of *E. fulvus egenus* tend to be more loosely coiled than those for *E. fulvus fulvus* and the rate of expansion is more discontinuous, though specimens from cool, humid sites may have tighter coiling and reduced microsculpture. Found across a wide gradient of acidity and soil moisture conditions ranging from forests to grasslands among damp leaves, rotten wood, and under stones in well-shaded areas (Karlin 1961). May also appear in stream drift debris.

Among the populations from around the world genetically analyzed by Horsáková et al. (2019, 2020), two were from northwestern Kane County, Utah; one, taken from an aspen fringe and south-facing talus, was named *E. fulvus egenus* (GenBank numbers MK266559, MK299632, MK299817, MK299724). The second was in a North American clade separate from, but allied to, *E. alderi*; it was named *Euconulus fresti*.

DISTRIBUTION (Horsáková et al. 2020; UMNH; Jones 1935, 1940a; Brooks 1936; Gregg 1941; Woolstenhulme 1942a; Oliver and Bosworth 2000; Meretsky et al. 2002; Wheeler 2018): from east of the Ural Mountains of Central Asia to the Atlantic Coast in northeastern North America north into the arctic tundra and south into Mexico along the Rocky Mountains. Utah records (for *E. fulvus* or *E. fulvus alaskensis*; some may need to be transferred to *E. fresti* or *E. alderi*): Tooele County, Oquirrh Mountains (South Willow Canyon near Granstville; Butterfield Canyon),

Grantsville, Bell's Canyon, Red Butte Canyon, Cedar Breaks National Monument, Zion Canyon, Kanab Creek, Fish Lake, 2.8 miles west of Vernal, Cedar Canyon, Hidden Lake (Glendale), Clear Creek Canyon (Raft River Mountains), Weber Canyon, Chalk Creek, near the head of Provo Canyon, Hominy Creek (southern slope Uintah Mountains), Verdure, Utah, and the LaSal Mountains. The author found *E. fulvus* near Manning Meadow Reservoir in the Monroe Mountains (dead) and near Tall Four Lake (live) in the Boulder Mountains, Utah.

Utah Bivalvia Key

1	Hinge lateral teeth finely serrated (inset, Fig. B1); stout ovoid shell with raised concentric ridges and prominent beak; adult shell >24 mm long (Cyrenidae)...8
1'	Shell less than 24 mm long, ovoid, lateral hinge teeth, if present, not finely serrated (Sphaeriidae)...5
1"	Shell longer/taller than 24 mm, oblong or triangular, lateral hinge teeth, if present, not finely serrated...2
2(1")	Triangular shells, with byssal threads used for substrate attachment, and usually with alternating dark and light bands ("zebra stripes"), 25–40 mm...*Dreissena rostriformis bugensis* (quagga mussel, Fig. B2).
2'	Oblong shells without byssal threads, color generally uniform and not banded...3
3(2')	Shell heavy, oblong, nacre usually purple, cardinal teeth well developed, lateral teeth incompletely developed...Genus *Margaritifera* (1 species, *M. falcata*)
3'	Shell thinner, oblong, lacking cardinal teeth...4 (3 choices)
4 (3')	Shell with a broad triangular projection on hinge side as in Fig. B3, upper right shell (Note: projection not as prominent on larger individuals, Fig. B3, lower right)...*Anodonta nuttalliana*
4'	Shell oblong oval (about twice as long as wide), lacking the triangular projection and

FIG. B1. *Corbicula* shell showing cardinal teeth (c) and serrated lateral teeth (inset). Credit: E. Wagner.

FIG. B2. *Dreissena rostriformis bugensis*. Credit: iNaturalist.org, Jeff Skrentny.

FIG. B3. Left (3 panels): *Utterbackia imbecilis*. Far Right: *Anodonta nuttalliana*. Credit E. Wagner.

	beak is not raised... *Utterbackia imbecillis* (Fig. B3, left)
4"	Large oval (not oblong) shell with a raised beak (Fig. B4)... *Pyganodon grandis*

FIG. B4. *Pyganodon grandis*. Credit: Chance Broderius, Utah Div. Wildlife Resources.

5(1')   Anterior part of shell valve longer than posterior end, hinge ligament on the shorter side, adult shells usually <4 mm tall (Fig. B5)... Genus *Pisidium* (to identify *Pisidium* species the reader is referred to Mackie 2007). See also Table B1 and notes for each species.

5'   Anterior part of shell valve shorter than posterior end, hinge ligament on the longer side; adult shells to about 4–9 mm tall... 6

6(5')   Nipple-like umbo; Nepeonic valves (distinct little caps on the umbo) inflated, separated from adult growth by a distinct sulcus (furrow); shell often thin and fragile, hinge plate narrow (~ equal to thickened end of cardinal tooth C3), hinge teeth usually weak (*Musculium*)... 7

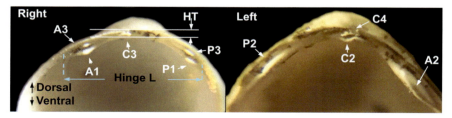

FIG. B5. Right and left sphaerid valves showing how hinge thickness (HT) is estimated; position and notation of cardinal teeth (C2, C3, C4), posterior (P1, P2, P3) and anterior (A1, A2, A3) lateral teeth. Note difference in shell length between anterior side (left of midline at C3) and posterior side (right of C3) in upper shell (*Pisidium*). Credit: E. Wagner.

6' Nepeonic valves not separated from the rest of the shell by a sulcus, shell thick, adults large (shell to 15 mm long), hinge plate about twice the width of cardinal tooth C3; hinge teeth usually stout (Fig. B6)...*Sphaerium* (for identification of N. American *Sphaerium* species, see Mackie 2007).

7(6) Shells to 8 mm tall, beaks pointed toward each other; posterior ventral margin angulate; dorsal margin often openly curved...*Musculium lacustre*

7' Shells to 9.5 mm tall with a square-like outline, beaks pointed vertically, beak broader than for *M. lacustre*, ventral margin roundly angulate, dorsal margin ± straight (Fig. B7)...*Musculium partumeium*

FIG. B6. *Sphaerium striatinum*, Cache Co., UT. Credit: E. Wagner.

8(1) Shell outline is ovate-triangular with a rounded base, height of adult shell typically <25 mm; shell width:height:length ratio 1:1.28 (± 0.32):1.30 (± 0.38)...*Corbicula fluminea*

8' Shell outline is tall triangular with a rounded base; height of adult shells

FIG. B7. *Musculium lacustre*, Summit Co., UT (left, middle), *Musculium partumeium*, Rich Co., UT (right). Credit: E. Wagner.

>30 mm; shell width:height:length ratio 1:1.45 (± 0.28):1.61 (± 0.31)... *Corbicula fluminalis*.

Table B.1 Comparison of characters of *Pisidium* species found in Utah. H = height, L = length, C = cardinal tooth, Dor = Dorsal, Ant = anterior, Pos = posterior, jct = junction or angle, max = maximum, usu. = usually, dist. = distal, prox. = proximal, ± = more or less/approximately, ND = no data.

Species: Character	casertanum	compressum	insigne	lilljeborgii	Pisidium milium	rotundatum	subtruncatum	variable	ventricosum
Outline	ovate	trigonal	inequilateral subquadrate oval	asymmetric, pentagonally rounded	ovate	rounded oval	oblique, asymmetric oval	short, triangular to longer and oval	oval; nearly spherical in side view
L, typical (mm)	4.5–5.0	4.2–4.7	2.29	4.0	3.0	3.0	3.2	5.5	2.8
Length, max. (mm)	6.0	5.0	ND	5.0	3.5	3.5	5.0	6.0	3.0
H/L	0.86 ± 0.06	0.90 ± 0.04, rarely to 1.0	0.78	0.93 ± 0.05	0.62–0.88	0.90 ± 0.08	0.88 ± 0.06	0.84 ± 0.04	0.95 ± 0.05
W/L	0.62 ± 0.08	0.60 ± 0.05	ND	0.65 ± 0.06	0.62–0.95	0.78 ± 0.08	0.54–0.74	0.60 ± 0.05	0.90 ± 0.05
L (mm) newborn	1.00–1.75	ND	ND	1.0–1.3	1.0	0.80	0.60–1.00	0.90–1.30	0.75–0.90
Beak	broad, low, subcentral to posterior	elevated, narrow, prominent	broad, low, posterior	prominent, posterior, broad and tumid	prominent, posterior, swollen	slightly post., well elevated above hinge line, rounded	very posterior, high, narrow, rounded to pointed	beaks large, prominent, margins abrupt	small, prominent, post. of center
Beak projection direction	backward	vertically	barely projecting	ND	ND	medially	backward	medially	medially
Scutum-Scutellum	usually present	absent	ND	present	ND	poorly marked	ND	poorly marked	poorly marked
Dor.-Ant. jct.	rounded	rounded	rounded to slightly angled	rounded angle	rounded to slightly angled	rounded	slight angle	angular in triangular forms	slightly rounded angle
Dor.-Pos. jct.	rounded	rounded, low arc	rounded	rounded angle	rounded angle	rounded	slight angle	angular in triangular forms	slightly rounded angle
Ven.-Ant. jct.	rounded	angular	rounded to slightly angled	acute rounded angle	acute rounded angle	rounded	rounded	rounded point	rounded

Species: Character	casertanum	compressum	insigne	lilljeborgii	Pisidium milium	rotundatum	subtruncatum	variable	ventricosum
Ven.-Pos. jct.	rounded *casertanum*	rounded *compressum*	rounded *insigne*	rounded *lilljeborgii*	rounded *Pisidium milium*	rounded *rotundatum*	rounded *subtruncatum*	rounded *variable*	rounded *ventricosum*
C3	bifid, curved, thick	bifid, curved	short, slightly curved, "toothbrush"-like	long, curved	long, of even thickness, straight to curved	curved club shape	short, variable shape, rarely bifid	thin, slightly bent midway, post. end bifid	short, club-shaped, occasionally bifid
C2	chevron shaped, low, short	tall, peg-like or incisor-like	varies, short to tall, curved or sigmoid	short, incisor-like, ant. end merges with A2	parallel with C4, but shorter	parallel with C4, incisor-like	slightly shorter than C4, similar H and shape	curved, short, low, canine-like	peg- or canine-like, short, low
C4	low, lamelliform	long, tall, lamelliform	diagonal to hinge plate	narrow, straight	slightly curved to sigmoid	subequal to C2 in L, H	lamelliform, parallel with C2 and hinge	long, lamelliform or incisor-like, diagonal	subequal to C2 in L, H; lamelliform or incisor-like
Lateral cusp position (relative to center line)	A1, A3, P1, P2, P3 dist.; A2 central to prox.	P1, A2, P2 central or dist., A1 dist.	all distal	A2 central to prox.; all others distal	A2 and P2 central to slightly distal	A2 prox, P2 central (±)	A2, P2 central to dist.	A2, P1, P2 central or distal side of center; A1 dist.; A3, P3 subcentral	A1, P1, central or distal; A2 P2, P3 distal
Ant. and Post. cusps	A3 and P3 short, pointed; others low	A3 and P3 low, blunt	tall, blunt	A2 and P2 tall, pointed	A1, A2, P1, P2 arise from hinge	tall, pointed	A2, P2 tall, blunt; A1, A3, P1, P3 short, blunt	all low, blunt	A3 absorbed into hinge; P3 low, half the L of P2
Sulci of right valve lateral teeth	short and wide	deep, reduced to slit at both ends	narrow "V," its inner margin tuberculate; opened dist., a slit prox.	V-shaped, open dist., slit prox.	opened on both ends; post. sulcus often V shaped	closed dist. in ant. laterals, closed prox. in post.	open at both ends; prox. side a slit, distal end wide	deep, long, narrow; proximal end closed, distal end a long, narrow slit	closed prox., sometimes distally

Mussels and Clams

CLASS: Bivalvia
ORDER: Unionida Gray, 1854
SPF: UNIONOIDEA Rafinesque, 1820

Margaritiferidae Henderson, 1929b (1910)

Margaritiferidae, known as the pearl mussels, has two subfamilies with 16 different species within them, 5 of which are found in the United States (Smith 2000b; Williams et al. 2017; Lopes-Lima et al. 2018). The type species for the family is *Margaritifera margaritifera* L. Margaritiferidae are found in North America, Europe, North Africa, the Middle East, and southern and eastern Asia. The species are confined to streams and rivers, living in waters that range from weakly acidic to alkaline (Smith 2000b). All species are normally short-term spring, summer, or fall brooders, diecious (male and female in separate individuals), though hermaphroditic individuals or populations of *Margaritifera falcata* and *M. auricularia* exist (Smith 2000b). Like other Unionids, these species produce glochidia, a parasitic stage of their life history that attaches to fish, where they mature and metamorphose into the adult form. Glochidia attachment is induced by mechanical stimulation, which automatically closes the valves upon the gill or fin (Arey 1932). Margaritiferidae branched off from the Unionidae at least 230 million years ago (Curole and Kocher 2002). The genus *Cumberlandia* Ortmann, 1912, is a junior synonym of *Margaritifera* (Bolotov et al. 2016; Araujo et al. 2017; Williams et al. 2017). Unfortunately, the abundance of mussel species is declining in many locations for a variety of reasons, including overharvesting, water withdrawals, reduced abundance or unavailability of host fish, pollution, competition with introduced exotic species, and habitat degradation (Bogan 2008; Hastie and Toy 2008; Varandas et al. 2013).

DESCRIPTION OF MARGARITIFERIDAE (Smith 2000b, p. 34): "Shell elongate, compressed, rhomboid and often arcuate, particularly in older individuals. Hinge teeth always present in the juvenile stage, often reduced in the adult. Small mantle attachment scars present on inner surface of shell extending diagonally from beak cavity ventrally and posteriorly and limited by the pallial border. Shell conchiolin consists of one differentiated layer; if homogeneous, unlike thin homogeneous layers of Unionidae. Periostracum almost always without rays or pigment patterns during any life stage, as a rule light brown or greenish brown in young animals, ranging to black in oldest individuals. Gill demibranchs equipped with separate solid vascularized interlamellar junctions, becoming variously coalesced or fused to form incomplete septa, arranged in oblique linear rows. All four demibranchs marsupial; however, junctions or septa not modified for marsupial function. Gills not fused with mantle posteriorly; however, diaphragm complete, formed by coupling of gills and diaphragmatic septa on mantle lobes to functionally separate inhalant and exhalant currents. Anal (exhalant) aperture long and crenulate along mantle margin, extending dorsally to a point slightly anterior to anus; no fusion of mantle lobes, thus to supra-anal opening formed separate from anal. Branchial (inhalant) apertural margin of mantle containing bifid or branched papillae, which continue a short distance anteriorly along the ventral border."

Margaritifera falcata Gould, 1850a Western Pearlshell

FIG. B8. *Margaritifera falcata*. Upper shells from Elk River, Idaho; lower image of shell from Beaver Creek, UT, showing hinge teeth (red arrows). Credit: E. Wagner.

DESCRIPTION (Gould 1850a): Shell transverse, somewhat equilateral, falcate, anterior rounded, posterior margin angled, sharp, and subparallel; shell partially hollow, umbone obtuse, eroded; epidermis brownish; cardinal tooth in right valve elevated, triangular (Fig. B8); left valve tooth (Fig. B8, left valve) is long, compressed-triangular in shape; purple markings on a silver lining.

SIZE: length, height, width: $4 \times 1.5 \times 1$ in. ($101 \times 38 \times 25$ mm). In an Oregon study, Allard et al. (2013) noted lengths typically falling within 55–80 mm but ranging from 43 to 93 mm; the height to length ratio (about 0.47) was linear as size increased.

TYPE LOCATION: "Walla Walla, Oregon" (Washington); Sacramento River, California.

JUNIOR SYNONYMS: *Alasmodon falcata* Gould, 1850a; *Margaritana margaritifera* Linnaeus, 1758 (*Margaritifera* is still a valid species in the eastern United States and Europe, but Utah records for *M. margaritifera* should be referred to *M. falcata*).

NOTES: Host fish include rainbow trout, brown trout, cutthroat trout, Chinook salmon, and steelhead. It is more arcuate and darker in color than the *M. margaritifera* L., and the anterior tooth in the right valve is comparatively obsolete, longitudinally oblique, and lamellar in the young (Gould 1850a). Differentiated from other large bivalves in Utah by the prominent hinge teeth and elongate shape. Differentiated from *M. margaritifera* in eastern United States and Europe by the nacre color and symmetry of the left cardinal teeth. Electophoretic studies have also separated these species (Davis and Fuller 1981).

For reproduction, the males release sperm into the water. Females filter sperm from the water, and fertilization occurs in the marsupium, where glochidia develop. *M. falcata* releases conglutinates, which are aggregates of glochidia in a mucus matrix that resemble insect larvae or worms (Barnhart et al. 2008; Allard et al. 2012). The conglutinates rupture when attacked by a fish, and glochidia attach to the gills or fins. Glochidia encyst and develop into tiny mussels that are eventually released into the sediment. In the closely related *Margaritifera margaritifera*, this development period requires about 1,700–3,400 Celsius degree-days (Hastie and Young 2003; Taeubert et al. 2013). In a study on *Margaritifera margaritifera*, only 1% of glochidia survived to find a host; after release, only 5% of the juveniles released from the gills survived (Young and Williams 1984). Juvenile growth is asymptotic (Hastie et al. 2008). In *M. falcata*, glochidia were released at temperatures of 8.1–13.8°C from late April to mid-June in an Oregon study (Allard et al. 2013). The glochidia of *M. margaritifera* are subround, about 55 mm long, and lack hooks, but they have irregular small teeth at the ventral margin of the valves (Ortmann 1912; O'Brien et al. 2013). During droughts, mussels are vulnerable to direct mortality by desiccation or to greater exposure to predators like raccoons when water levels and flows are very low. Dysthe et al. (2018) have shown that analysis of environmental DNA samples can detect the presence of *M. falcata*. This tool could be used for quicker determination of the species distribution.

DISTRIBUTION (Taylor 1988b; Hovingh 2004): Northwestern United States, California, Alaska, British Columbia; upper Bear and Snake rivers in Wyoming. In Utah, the historical distribution was the Bear River drainage that was once connected to the Columbia River drainage. When the Bear River was diverted by volcanic activity into the Great Basin, the spread of fish and mussels into the basin occurred. It is also possible that some populations were established by human movement of fish infected with glochidia. Call (1884) reported it from streams around Salt Lake City and as fossils in the Sevier Desert. He also noted historical distribution from Arizona to British Columbia east to the Atlantic coastal states of Canada, and the U.S. Woolstenhulme (1942b) reported it from Kamas, Utah. Chamberlin and Jones (1929) note a record by Henderson in East Canyon, Weber County, Utah. Surveys by the Utah Division of Wildlife Resources also found a few live mussels in Beaver Creek above Kamas in 2018 and in Goose Creek, Box Elder County, in 2021.

Unionidae Rafinesque, 1820

Unionidae features freshwater mussels with a life cycle that requires a host fish. That is, fertilized eggs transform into embryos that ripen into glochidia, the first larval phase. Glochidia are released by the female and attach to the gills, fin, or skin of a host fish, which forms a cyst around the organism. After several weeks to months, the next larval phase emerges, falls off, and becomes a juvenile free-living mussel, which matures and completes the life cycle. Most unionids are dioecious (separate sexes), but some are hermaphroditic, capable of self-fertilization. The requirement for a fish host has led some species (e.g., in genus *Lampsilis*) to evolve fleshy structures that mimic a small fish, complete with false eyes and markings. These attract the host fish, which triggers the release of the parasitic glochidia.

Unionidae has a worldwide distribution. Modern genetic analyses have helped organize the family into 6 subfamilies (Ambleminae Rafinesque, 1820; Anodontinae Rafinesque, 1820; Gonideinae Ortmann, 1916; Parreysiinae Henderson, 1935; Rectidentinae Modell, 1942; and Unioninae Rafinesque, 1820) and 18 tribes (Lopes-Lima et al. 2017). In the United States there are about 54 genera and 293 species (Williams et al. 2017). Junior synonyms of Unionidae are Anodontidae and Alasmidontidae (Bouchet et al. 2010). Some early literature refers to unionids as naiads. In Utah, representatives of three genera are present, of which *Pyganodon* Crosse and Fischer, 1893 (Fischer and Crosse 1900) and *Utterbackia* Baker, 1927, are presumed to have been introduced into the state, probably via historic fish stocking.

The genus *Anodonta* Lamarck, 1799, is widespread. The type species is the Eurasian *Anodonta cygnea* Linnaeus, 1758. In the United States there are four recognized species, all of which are found in the western part of the country.

Anodonta nuttalliana Lea, 1838 Winged Floater

FIG. B9. *Anodonta nuttalliana* Lea, 1838. Left: holotype shell of Lea's. Credit: Dept. Invertebrate Zoology, USNM; Right: shells from Koosharem Reservoir, Utah. Credit: E. Wagner.

DESCRIPTION (Lea 1838): Shell winged, elliptical, flattened on the side and enlarged on the umbonial slope, submarginate at base, smooth, inequilateral; substance of the shell thin, the valves being connate over the ligament; beaks compressed and undulating at the tip; umbonial slope furnished with several impressed lines; epidermis smooth and polished, having a dark, broad band at the line of growth near the margin; cicatrices scarcely visible; cavity of the shell very small; cavity of the beaks very small; nacre white.

SIZE (Wagner, unpublished data; Koosharem and Otter Creek reservoirs; $n = 16$, mean, range): shell height (wing to ventral margin) 40.4, 30–51 mm, shell length 65.5, 44–85 mm; height/length ratio 62.2, 57.0 (largest shell)–67.9% (2nd from smallest shell).

TYPE LOCATION: Willamette River, Oregon, near its junction with the Columbia River. Holotype (Fig. B9) at Smithsonian Institute.

JUNIOR SYNONYMS (Lea 1852; Call 1884; Simpson 1900; Chong et al. 2008; Mock et al. 2010):

FIG. B10. Original figure of *Anodonta nuttalliana* and *A. wahlamatensis*. Credit: Lea 1838.

Margarita (*Anodonta*) *nuttalliana* Lea, 1838; *Margaron* (*Anodonta*) *nuttalliana* Lea, 1852; *Anodonta triangularis* Trask, 1855; *Unio cuneatus* Swainson, 1823; *Anodon nuttalliana* Catlow and Reeve, 1845; *Unio triangularis* Barnes, 1823; *Anodon triangularis* (Barnes) Sowerby, 1870; *Anodonta californiensis* (in part), *A. wahlamatensis* Lea, 1838. Synonyms of *A. wahlamatensis* include *Margarita wahlametensis* Lea, 1838; *Anodonta rotundata* Trask, 1855; *Anondon rostratus* Sowerby, 1867 (Sowerby 1867–1870); and *Anodonta laosensis* Fischer, 1891.

NOTES: Chamberlin and Jones (1929) summarized data for four nominal species of *Anodonta* reported to be found in Utah: *A. californiensis, A. nuttalliana, A. oregonensis*, and *A. wahlametensis*. Mock et al. (2004) initially noted very little genetic divergence among *A. californiensis, A. oregonensis,* and *A. wahlametensis* morphotypes, but the work of Chong et al. (2008) and Mock et al. (2010) suggests that these morphotypes are not congruent with genetic divergence. *A. wahlamatensis* Lea, 1838 was described as being more inflated than *A. nuttalliana* and different in outline, but the figure provided by Lea (1838) shows a very similar winged shape (Fig. B10). *A. wahlametensis* was considered a junior synonym of *A. nuttalliana* by Call (1884) and more recently by Turgeon et al. (1998). This synonymy was also supported by recent genetic and morphological analyses (Chong et al. 2008).

Work by Chong et al. (2008) and Mock et al. (2010) indicated that *A. oregonensis* is genetically quite distinct from *A. nuttalliana* (despite both coming from the same type location). Further, these authors discovered that (i) *A. californiensis* and *nuttalliana* formed one genetic lineage and were likely synonymous, (ii) *A. oregonensis* and *A. kennerlyi* formed a separate lineage and were also likely synonymous, and (iii) these two lineages reflected an ancient subdivision and may be separate genera. Although these changes were not yet recognized in Williams et al. (2017), for the purpose of this publication the *A. californiensis/nuttalliana* lineage is considered as *A. nuttalliana*, and the *A. oregonensis/kennerlyi* lineage as *A. oregonensis*, recognizing that these names are currently under formal revision (K. Mock, pers. comm.). In Utah, all known extant populations of *Anodonta* are *A. nuttalliana* (Mock et al. 2010), and comprise a Bonneville Basin subgroup that is genetically distinct from other western U.S. hydrologic basins. The habitat for this species varies from shallow ditches to oligotrophic lakes where perennial water and muddy or sandy substrate exist.

The spade-shaped glochidia of *A. californiensis* have hooks on each shell lip, an attachment thread, the larval organism, and an adductor muscle; They averaged 246 ± 17 μm in Spring Rivers (2007) and 276 μm long × 269 μm wide in O'Brien et al. (2013). The cysts in the fins or gill tissue of mosquitofish *Gambusia affinis* lasted 26–27 days at 20°C (D'Eliscu 1972); the cysts open and release juvenile mussels. *A. nuttalliana* is a generalist with respect to glochidial hosts, based on data for *A. californiensis* (D'Eliscu 1972, Lang 1998, Spring Rivers 2007; O'Brien et al. 2013; Maine et al. 2016). These hosts include mosquitofish, three-spine stickleback, cyprinids (speckled dace, long-nosed dace, native hardhead, pit roach, Sacramento pikeminnow, but not common carp), Sacramento sucker, tule perch, margined sculpin, pit sculpin, torrent sculpin, and non-native centrarchids (sunfish/bass). Studies have shown that *Margaritifera,* especially juveniles, are negatively impacted by fine sediment, preferring larger sand substrates (>250 μm particles; Hyvärinen et al. 2021). New environmental DNA detection methods have been developed to facilitate species distribution assessment (Rodgers et al. 2020).

DISTRIBUTION: Specimens identified as *A. nuttalliana* in the Smithsonian Institute collection have been reported from British Columbia, AZ, CA, OR, WA, ID, NV, WY, UT, Portland, ME. Historical distribution records for Utah indicate that it was found in the Sevier River (Yarrow 1875), Sevier Lake (fossil), Utah Lake, near Salt Lake City, Junction (old trout pond south of town, probably there as a result of stocking fish infected with glochidia), Farr West, Bear River and Bear Lake, Calleo, and Farmington Canyon (Chamberlin and Jones 1929; USNM collection records; Bean Museum, Provo, Utah). Mock et al. (2004) found live *A. nuttalliana* at six Bonneville Basin sites: Bear River, Redden Spring, Pruess Lake (=Garrison Reservoir), Piute Reservoir, Otter Creek Reservoir, and Burriston Ponds. Torrey Rogers (pers. comm., 2021) found live mussels in the Raft River. The author has also found shells (Fig. B9) and living mussels at Salt Creek Wildlife Management Area, Tremonton, and Koosharem Reservoir, Utah.

Pyganodon grandis Say, 1829 Giant Floater

DESCRIPTION (Say 1829; Binney 1858c, p. 139): "Shell very large, subovate; disk unequally wrinkled and undulated transversely, dark yellowish brown; umbo elevated; beak slightly elevated, with generally, two or three small sinuous, acute undulations; hinge margin slightly arquated, sometimes nearly rectilinear, somewhat angulated at its anterior termination, thence the edge descends by a nearly rectilinear, or slightly concave line to the anterior margin, which is considerably narrowed; sinus of the hinge margin concave; posterior margin widely rounded; within white margined, particularly before, with dusky."

FIG. B11. *Pyganodon grandis* from 21st Street Pond (a.k.a. Goode Ski Lake), Ogden, UT. Credit: Chance Broderius, Utah Division of Wildlife Resources.

OTHER DESCRIPTIVE DATA (Utterback 1915–1916; Clarke 1981; Mulcrone 2006): Shell highly variable in form, but typically ovate, inflated, lacking hinge teeth and lateral teeth, and is thin and fragile. The anterior end is broadly rounded, and the posterior end is bluntly pointed. The dorsal hinge line is slightly curved, and the ventral margin is straight or slightly curved. Surface smooth and shiny, except where roughened with low, concentric wrinkles and growth rests. Umbonal cavities are large and deep, especially in female shells. Periostracum varies from yellowish-brown to greenish, greenish-brown, or blackish, tending to be browner in older specimens. Shell often with indistinct green rays and concentric lighter and darker bands. Nacre white or bluish white, rarely pinkish. Elevated umbone located about 30% of the distance from anterior to posterior. Beak sculpture ordinarily heavy, double-looped, and with the loop apices elevated and forming 2 radial rows of tubercles.

ANIMAL (Utterback 1916, p. 112): "Branchial opening with rather long yellowish papillae; anal directed upward, smooth; supra-anal separated from anal by long mantle connection, small, almost closed in some instances; inner gills wider and longer, inner laminae entirely free from visceral moss [sic]; palpi very large, united antero-dorsad about one-half of their length; anterior portion of pericardial region thick and watery; color of gills usually dark brown, mantle edge at siphonal openings blackish, palpi cream to purplish, remaining parts mostly tan or soiled white. Marsupium occupying outer gills only, when gravid pad-like, distended at ventral edge, secondary water canals present, undivided ovi-sacs in center, laminae very delicate, rupturing at slight touch; sterile marsupia thickened at edges to allow for distention; glochidium largest on record (0.400 × 0.395 mm), spadiform, spined, russet color, straight hinge line; no conglutinates, glochidia held in loose mosses [sic] by brownish mucus and tangles of crinkled larval threads."

SIZE (Binney 1858c): nearly 5 in. long (127 mm); breadth over 7.5 in. (190 mm); convexity 3.25 in. (82.5 mm). Shell wall about 8 mm thick near anterior pallial line (Clarke 1981). May reach up to 25.4 cm long (10 in.; Mulcrone 2006). A few juvenile shells had a height/width ratio of 0.60–0.69; this ratio decreased in older shells (Utterback 1916).

TYPE LOCATION: "Fox River of the Wabash" (IL, near New Harmony, IN).

JUNIOR SYNONYMS (Utterback 1916): *Anodonta grandis* Say, 1829; *A. opaca* Lea, 1852; *A. dakotana* Utterback, 1915.

NOTES (Utterback 1916; Tucker 1928; Clarke 1981; Mulcrone 2006): This species is characterized by the inflated ovate form of the shell and double-looped and nodulous beak sculpture. Compared to other large Utah mussels, it is not as elongate as *U. imbecilis,* which also has a flattened umbo; *P. grandis* lacks both the hinge teeth of *M. falcata* and the triangular "wing" of *A. nuttalliana.*

Occurs in permanent ponds, lakes, and rivers in mud as well as sand and gravel. River-dwelling forms tend to be thicker, more compressed, and more elongated. Females observed by Utterback (1916) were gravid with glochidia from December until March, but they lacked glochidia from April to September. Breeding season in Michigan's Huron River runs from early August to the following April or May (Lefevre and Curtis 1912; Watters 1995). Sexes are separate (dioecious), though hermaphroditic specimens have been noted. Fertilized eggs incubate in marsupia up to 11 months. The larval glochidia are released after hatching within the female. The glochidia are triangular-ovate, with spines, measuring 310–398 μm × 280–390 μm high. Several different fish species are known as hosts for the next phase of the life cycle (Lefevre and Curtis 1910; Tucker 1928; Arey 1932; Penn 1939; Trdan and Hoeh 1982; Howells 1997). Hosts include representatives from Catostomidae (suckers), Centrarchidae (sunfishes), Cyprinidae (minnows, carps), Lepisosteidae (gars), Poecillidae (topminnows), Percidae (perches, darters), and Gasterosteidae (sticklebacks). Duration of glochidial infection was 17–20 days in a study using centrachids (Tucker 1928). Trdan and Hoeh (1982) observed an average of 6 days for the parasitic period in fish held at 21 C.

DISTRIBUTION (Clarke 1981): Canada (Ontario to Alberta), Great Lakes–St. Lawrence River system, Ohio–Mississippi River drainage, and Gulf of Mexico drainages in Louisiana and Texas. Introduced into Utah, likely via stocked fish. Only known from one location in Utah, discovered in 2017: 21st Street Pond (a.k.a. Goode Ski Lake), Ogden.

Utterbackia imbecilis Say, 1829 Paper Pondshell

DESCRIPTION (Say 1829, p. 140): "Transversely oblong subovate, very thin and fragile; disks convex, green, with darker green obsolete rays, and three obvious rays on and above the umbonial slope; hinge margin rectilinear, terminating before in an angle; beaks a little undulated and not elevated above the general curvature; from the anterior tip of the hinge margin the slope is rectilinear to the anterior margin; within bluish white, iridescent before; hinge perfectly rectilinear; posterior margin rounded. Length over one inch. Breadth, over two inches. Convexity, three-fifths of an inch."

FIG. B12. *Utterbackia imbecilis*. Cutler Reservoir, Utah. Credit: E. Wagner.

SIZE (Clarke 1981): up to about 90 mm long, 50 mm high, 40 mm wide. Shell wall 1 mm thick at midanterior.

TYPE LOCATION: Wabash River, Indiana

JUNIOR SYNONYMS: *Anodonta imbecilis* Say, 1829; *Margaron (Anondonta) imbecillis* Lea, 1852; *Anodon imbecillis* (Say) Sowerby 1870; *Anodon horda* Gould, 1855, *Anodonta hordeum* Paetel, 1890. F. C. Baker (1927) created a new genus *Utterbackia*, with *A. imbecilis* as the type species. Hoeh's (1990) genetic data supported the separate taxon.

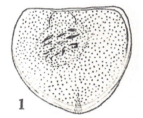

FIG. B13. Glochidium of *Utterbackia imbecilis*. Credit: Baker 1928.

NOTES: Differentiated from western pearlshells by the lack of cardinal teeth and from *A. nuttalliana* by the lack of the triangular projection of the shell and a beak that is not raised above the general curvature of the valve; not as ovate as *P. grandis*. Lives in muddy to sandy habitats in slow-moving rivers, canals, and lakes but rarely on gravel bottoms.

Glochidia are roughly triangular, with hooks, and measure about 0.23 mm in height and length (Fig. B13; F. C. Baker 1928). Glochidia of *U. imbecilis* are able to infect a wide variety of fish hosts from multiple families as well as amphibians (Tucker 1928; Trdan and Hoeh 1982; Howells 1997; Watters and O'Dee 1998). Fish families with susceptible host species include Centrarchidae, Cichlidae, Cyprinidae, Characidae, Gasteropelecidae, Callichthyidae, Fundulidae, Belontidae, Atherinidae, Cobitididae, Loracariidae, Percidae, Siluridae, Pimelodidae, Pangasiidae, Gyrinochellidae, and Gymnotidae. Bluegill have been shown to have reduced infection rates after multiple exposures to the glochidia (Rogers and Dimock 2003). Exposure to glochidia of other species of unionid mussels also increases host resistance and helps reduce infection rates (Dodd et al. 2005). Attachment of glochidia to bluegills is enhanced by the stress hormone cortisol, which is produced by the host when glochidia densities are high (≥2,000 glochidia/L) or the fish is otherwise stressed (Dubansky et al. 2011).

An estimated 7,700 (± 2,700) juveniles are produced per female. Gravid mussels may be found nearly year-round (Coker et al. 1919; Van der Schalie 1938). This species is hermaphroditic and able to complete glochidial metamorphosis within the marsupium rather than a fish host when the fish host is not available (Howard 1914; Allen 1924; Heard 1975; Dickinson and Sietman 2008). Glochidial metamorphosis in the host lasts about 8 days (Trdan and Hoeh 1982).

DISTRIBUTION: Native to Mississippi River drainage, eastern Gulf of Mexico southwest to Matamoras, Mexico, and Atlantic slope (North Carolina to Georgia) drainages (Simpson 1900). Introduced into Utah. Known to inhabit Cutler Reservoir, Cache County, Utah and downstream the Bear River to Willard Bay. Distribution within a water body may be affected by aquatic macrophyte abundance, for example, reduced at high densities of the invasive Eurasian watermilfoil *Myriophyllum spicatum* (Burlakova and Karatayev 2007).

ORDER: Venerida Gray, 1854
SPF: CYRENOIDEA Gray, 1840

Cyrenidae Gray, 1840

Shells of Cyrenidae are ovate or triangular, heavy, with prominent concentric striae and 2–3 cardinal teeth. Lateral teeth are serrated in both valves. Periostracum yellow, greenish, or brown. Found in brackish and freshwater (Mackie 2007).

The family Cyrenidae includes *Corbicula, Batissa, Cyanocyclas, Geloina, Polymesoda,* and *Villorita* as genera. Two genera are represented in the United States: *Corbicula* Muhlfeld, 1811, and *Polymesoda* Rafinesque, 1820. Bivalves in Cyrenidae were formerly in Corbiculidae Gray, 1847, but Cyrenidae has precedence (Bouchet et al. 2010). Other family synonyms include Serrilaminulinae Lindholm, 1933, Geloinidae Prashad, 1932, and Polymesodinae Habe, 1977. The type genus for the family is *Corbicula* Muhlfeld, 1811, and the type species is *Tellina fluminalis* Müller, 1774 (now considered *Corbicula fluminalis*). *Cyrena* Lamarck, 1818, is a synonym of *Corbicula* (Mbase). Although hundreds of species have been described and assigned to the genus, about 62 species in *Corbicula* are considered valid (Mbase). Two of these species, both introduced, are represented in Utah.

Corbicula fluminea Müller, 1774 Asian clam

DESCRIPTION (Mackie 2007): Adult shell subovate, trigonal, or trigonal ovate, greatly inflated, broadly rounded anteriorly, subtruncated posteriorly. Ventral margin usually well rounded, swinging high and joining anterior margin high with a rounded angle. Dorsal margin short and angulate. Ligament wing-like, posterior to umbone. Umbones prominent, roundly acuminate, often eroded. Surface sculpture of usually regular-spaced strong concentric ridges, the ridges tending to be more irregular on the older parts of the shell. Periostracum usually glossy, yellow, brownish, or black, sometimes greenish. Interior of shell with a white, light blue, or lilac-colored porcellaneous layer. Hinge plate heavy with anterior cardinal teeth greatly impressed distally and proximally by the muscle scars that impinge upon them. Three cardinal teeth unequal in length, the central usually bifid, the anterior the smallest. Lateral teeth nearly equal in length, narrow, finely serrated (Fig. B15).

SIZE: North American specimens have a ratio of shell width:height:length 1:1.28(± 0.32):1.30(± 0.38). See notes for veliger data.

TYPE LOCATION: China ("In arena fluviali *Chinae*" Müller 1774). Lectotype in Natural History Museum of Denmark, Københavns University (BIV-000035).

JUNIOR SYNONYMS (Morton 1986; Lee et al. 2005; Mackie 2007): *Tellina fluminea* and *Tellina fluviatilus* Müller, 1774; *Venus fluminea* and *V. fluviatilus* Chemnitz, 1783 (Chemnitz 1780–1795); *Cyclas chinensis* Lamarck, 1806; *Cyrena orientalis*, *C. fuscata*, and *C. fluminea* Lamarck, 1818; *Cyrena woodiana* Lea, 1837; *Corbicula cor* (Lamarck) Deshayes, 1853; *Corbicula fuscata* Benson, 1842; *C. grandis* Adams, 1854; *C. primeana* Morelet, 1862; *C. pexata*, *C. chemnitziana*, *C. mulleriana*, *C. leana* and *C. pfeifferiana* Prime, 1867; *C. ovata* and *C. inflata* Clessin, 1877–1879; *C. yunnanensis* and *C. andersoniana* Nevill, 1877; *C. sandai* Reinhardt, 1878; *C. adunca*, *C. aquilina*, *C. astronomica*, *C. aurea*, *C. bezauriana*, *C. bicolor*, *C. bilineata*, *C. cheniana*, *C. columbeliana*, *C. concinna*, *C. conica* and vars., *C. cordieriana*, *C. delavagana*, *C. diminuta*, *C. eleciana*, *C. ferriginea*, *C. fluitans*, *C. foukiensis*, *C. gentiliana*, *C. gravis* and var., *C. grilloana*, *C. gryphaea*, *C. ignobolis*, *C. iodina*, *C. ingloriosa*, *C. indigotina* and var., *C. iridina*, *C. lapicida*, *C. montana*, *C. obtruncata*, *C. orcellanea*, *C. polychromatica*, *C. portentosa* and var., *C. praeterita*, *C. rathousiana*, *C. schelastica*, *C. sphaerica*, *C. squalida*, *C. subquadrata* *C. uncinulata*, *C. variegata*, and *C. vicina* Heude, 1883; *C. manilensis* Philippi, 1884; *C. crebricostis* Westerlund, 1885; *C. fulgida* Bullen, 1901; *C. elatior* and *C. producta* von Martens, 1905; *C. suifuensis* and subsp. *finitima* Lindholm, 1925, 1928. Form "C" (see Notes) was formerly considered *C. largillerti* Philippi, 1844. Last change to *Corbicula fluminea* (Müller) by Prashad (1929).

NOTES: Easily differentiated from Utah's native bivalves of similar shape by the large size (>2 cm), stout shell, prominent striae, and serrated lateral teeth. Differs

Cyrenidae

FIG. B14. *Corbicula fluminea*, Utah Lake, UT. Credit: E. Wagner.

from *Corbicula fluminalis* Müller, 1774, which is also found in the United States, in its smaller maximum size (<25 mm long), more ovate (less triangular) shape, and an exhalant siphon that is surrounded by a ring of papillae (*fluminalis* has only one or two papillae).

Fertilization and embryo development occur in the brood pouch of the female. The preshell stage develops in the female, whereas in dreissenids, fertilization and larval development occur outside the female (Nichols and Black 1994). The larval trochophore stage lacks a shell, is ovoid, lacks a velum, and is about 190 μm long (Fig. B16 C; Kraemer and Galloway 1986). In about 24–48 h, the trochophore is transformed into the veliger stage. The veligers or shelled larvae are grouped into four types: straight-hinged, umbonal, pediveliger, and plantigrade. The first stage of the shelled larva is the D-shaped straight-hinge form; a foot is also present at this stage. The velum is present for a short time, then shed. This pediveliger stage lasts about 3–5 days. Late pediveligers and early to late juveniles are about 230 μm, the stages usually released by the parent (Kraemer and Galloway 1986). The straight-hinged juvenile grows into an umbonal juvenile at about 500 μm, the latter looking like a tiny version of the adult.

In a Texas population, *C. fluminea* spawned twice a year (late March to July, late August to November). *C. fluminea* is estimated to produce an average of 68,678 juveniles per parent (Aldridge and McMahon 1978). Population density ranged from 305 to 16,198 clams/m^2 (McMahon and Williams 1986). Smaller clams (5 mm long) grew faster than larger clams (30 mm long; 0.8 mm/month), adding length at a rate of 5.4 mm/month. Increasing temperatures had a logarithmic effect on growth rate. Optimum temperatures for growth are in the mid-20 °C range (Mattice and Wright 1986). Life span is estimated to be 2.5–7 years (Sinclair and Isom 1963; Mouthon and Parghentanian 2004). White and White

(1977) noted that this species preferred sand to mud or silt and was found at shallow depths; this propensity facilitated population control by reservoir drawdown (98% had died within 12 days).

Morton (1973, 1977) posited that U.S. specimens > 50 mm must be *C. fluminalis*, based on growth studies of oriental populations of both species. Morton (1982) later noted that both species reach different lengths in various extremes of their range.

Variation in shell form and color, as well as cryptic hybrids and variations in ploidy (diploid, triploid, and tetraploids) have been documented (Morton 1977; Pfenninger et al. 2002; Lee et al. 2005; Tiemann et al. 2017). Populations of clones, featuring sperm with two flagella, and sexual populations, with monoflagellate sperm, also add to the diversity of forms of *Corbicula* (Lee et al. 2005). There are four distinct freshwater morphotypes (Lee et al. 2005; Tiemann et al. 2017):

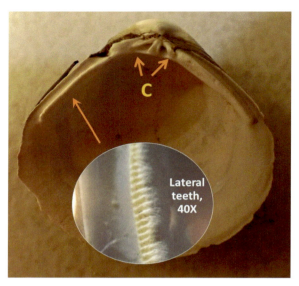

FIG. B15. *Corbicula* shell showing cardinal teeth (C) and serrated lateral teeth (insert). Credit: E. Wagner.

1. Form A, a light yellowish morph, with a more trigonal shell shape, taller and more inflated umbo, nacre of white with occasional suffusions of pink or light purple especially around the teeth, and more widely spaced external ribbing (6–10/cm),

2. Form B, a purple (nacre/lateral teeth) morph, with less space between the ribs, which are not as elevated; shell is more oval and its exterior is dark olive to brown,

3. Form C, a genotype currently found in South America, which has a thinner, less inflated shell, with a less prominent umbo, darker coloration, and finer external shell sculpture than Form A.

4. Form D, pyramidal in shape, with weakly elevated ribbing, a creamy-white nacre, purple lateral teeth, and rust-colored rays radiating out from the umbo.

For genetic-based identification on *Corbicula* species and haplotypes, see Siripattrawan et al. 2000, Lee et al. 2005, Gomes et al. 2016, Tiemann et al. 2017, and references therein.

DISTRIBUTION: Native to temperate and tropical Asia, west to the eastern Mediterranean and Africa, and south to southern Asia islands and Australia (Morton 1986). It is considered an invasive species in both North and South America, as well as Europe. It has been widely distributed in the United States.

In Utah it has been found in Washington County (Quail Creek and Gunlock reservoirs and the Santa Clara/Virgin River confluence), Escalante River, Lake Powell, Jordan River/Utah Lake, Yuba Reservoir (specimen 52431, Ohio State University, collected 1978), Goshen Warm Springs, Cutler Reservoir, Salt Creek Wildlife Management Area, Bear Lake, and small streams near Brigham City (Hovingh 2018; author's collection).

Corbicula fluminalis Müller, 1774 Asian clam

DESCRIPTION (Müller 1774): Shell thick, hard, swollen, opaque; wider anterior of the cardinals than posterior; exterior green with imbricated striae one after the other; Striae apertures parallel. Interior cyan, six medial cardinal teeth, with 3 in each valve, each ligament near the margin and each lateral elongate, evenly serrated.

Skuza et al. (2009): Shells oval-triangular, strongly convex, asymmetrical; umbo above the hinge, slightly rotated and directed to the front of the shell. Periostracum glossy, olive-green, ribbed. The number of ribs per 10 mm of the shell surface: 12–16. Interiorly, intensely violet in the ventral, posterior, and anterior parts, whereas middle part and under the umbo is white-violet with orange spots. Pallial line and adductor scars distinct.

SIZE (Mackie 2007): Width:height:length ratio of 1:1.45 (± 0.28):1.61 (± 0.31). *C. fluminalis* has a theoretical maximum length of 54 mm in southern China (Morton 1973, 1982). Research by Mouthon and Parghentanian (2004) in French canals noted a maximum length of 24 mm. The type shell measured 29.9 mm long, 29.7 mm high, 11.1 mm wide (1 valve), H/L 0.99, 2W/H 0.75 (Skuza et al. 2009). A shell from the Zoological Institute in St. Petersburg was 22.4 × 22.2 × 8.3mm (L × H × W(1 valve)), H/L 0.99, 2W/H 0.75. Average values (± SD) for 20 shells from Poland were length, 19.0 ± 3.6 mm; height 19.1 ± 3.9, width (1 valve) 15.9 ± 3.4; H/L 0.99 ± 0.03; W/H 0.83 ± 0.02 (Skuza et al. 2009).

TYPE LOCATION: "In fluvio Asiae Euphrat" (western Asia's Euphrates River). Lectotype in Natural History Museum of Denmark, Københavns University (BIV-000034).

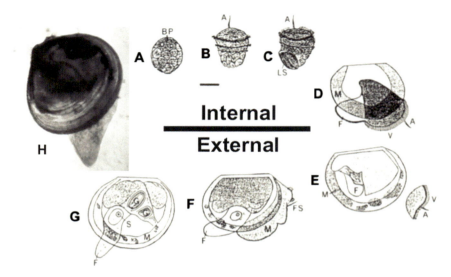

FIG. B16. Developmental stages of *Corbicula fluminea*. A, gastrula stage (post fertilization, cleavage, and blastula stages); B, trochophore; C, veliger; D, pediveliger; E, early straight hinged juvenile with recently cast off velum; F, early straight-hinged juvenile; G, late straight-hinged juvenile, and H, umbonal juvenile. Stages A to D, usually develop internally in the parent, D-H develop after release into the environment. Credit: images adapted from Kraemer and Galloway (1986). A = apical cilia, BP = blastopore, F = foot, FS = fecal strand, G = gill, LS = shell, M = mantle, S = statolith, V = velum.

JUNIOR SYNONYMS

(Morton 1986; Mackie 2007; Korniushin 2004): *Tellina fluviatilis* Müller, 1774; *Cyclas laevigata* Schumacher, 1817; *Corbicula difficilis* and *C. purpurea* Prime, 1867; *C. delessertiana* Prime, 1870; *Cyrena consobrina* Cailliaud, 1823 (Cailliaud 1823–1827). Morton (1986) considered *C. japonica* Prime, 1867 to be synonymous with *C. fluminalis*, but Korniushin (2004) later noted that a nonincubating species from Chinese estuaries previously considered to be *fluminalis* had different anatomical and reproductive characters and was reconsidered as *C. japonica* Prime, 1867.

FIG. B17. *Corbicula fluminalis*, Salt Creek Wildlife Management Area, UT. Credit: E. Wagner.

NOTES (Morton 1986; Rajagopal et al. 2000): See notes for *C. fluminea* for differentiation from that species. Although morphologically similar to *C. fluminea*, ecologically there are major differences between the two species. *C. fluminalis* occurs in estuaries and tolerates higher salinities than *C. fluminea*. Sexes are separate, with a trend toward protogyny (more females); although *C. fluminea* is also dioecious, there is a tendency toward greater percentages of hermaphrodites for that species. Fertilization is external and eggs are not incubated, whereas in *C. fluminea*, egg are incubated. However, demibranchs in *C. fluminalis* have incubatory glands, suggesting it may be possible.

Breeding occurs over winter, when temperatures are low. The gonads enlarge between February and April, continuing to mature into early summer. Ripe testes and ovaries are found from early summer to October–November. A single growth ring is produced annually in the shell. Lifespan is estimated to be up to 4 (Mouthon and Parghentanian 2004) –10 years (Morton 1986). There are 18 chromosomes (haploid), and polypoidy occurs. Preferred habitats are sandy and muddy river bottoms (Skuza et al. 2009).

DISTRIBUTION (Morton 1986; Kinzelbach 1991; Skuza et al. 2009): Native to western Asia. Found in Pleistocene deposits in Europe. Introduced elsewhere, including the United States, France, Portugal, Netherlands, Argentina, North Africa, and Israel. In Utah, found in the Salt Creek Wildlife Management Area west of Tremonton. A record from iNaturalist.org also notes they are in the Jordan River.

SPF: **DREISSENOIDEA Gray, 1840**

Dreissenidae Gray, 1840

Dreissenidae is a family of freshwater mussels, with seven living species currently recognized as members (Rosenberg and Ludyanskiy 1994). Two species, *Dreissena polymorpha* (zebra mussel) and *Dreissena rostiformis bugensis* (quagga mussel), have invaded North America and have adapted to living in various regions of the United States and Canada. Dreissenids reproduce sexually. Instead of glochidia or use of host fish, they have free-swimming veliger larvae that mature to adults. Veliger larvae develop several hours after fertilization and are free-swimming for about 1–5 weeks (Claxton and Boulding 1998). They use byssal threads to attach to surfaces. They are triangular-shaped shells, about 25–40 mm, with a distinct inside curve and a ridge. Some have stripes on their outer shells.

Dreissena rostriformis bugensis Andrusov, 1897 Quagga Mussel

DESCRIPTION (Pathy and Mackie 1993): Quagga mussels have dark concentric rings on the shell, asymmetrical valves, a rounded triangular shape, with a

FIG. B18. *Dreissena rostiformis bugensis*. Credit: iNaturalist.org, left: Jeff Skrentny; center: wini56; upper right: Bridget Gruber; lower right: Joel M.C.

distinct inside curve and ridge. Often there is a white stripe running from the umbone to posterior end. Color variants include black, brown, or white, with various striping patterns as well as all white or all black. The ventral margin (cross section) is convex, with a rounded ventrolateral shoulder. The dorsal margin is rounded, often with a wing-like extension. The umbone is pointed. The posterior end is rounded ventro-posteriorly. The interior has a broad and well-developed myophore plate, which lacks an apophysis (a small triangular tooth-like projection within the valve, extending from myophore plate). The hinge teeth are vestigial. Anterior muscle scars are located on the myophore plate. The pallial line is entire and rounded. A pallial sinus is absent. The shell is composed of aragonite and lacks microtubules (microscopic pores in shell). The mussels attach using byssal threads.

A deepwater ecotype, "profundal," has been described (Dermott and Munawar 1993); it is characterized by its white color, elliptical shell with a distinctive basal knob, and a dorsal swelling between the umbo and the pedal gap. In ventral view, the margin is straight or slightly convex, not sinusoidal as in typical quagga mussels. Shells tend to be narrower than typical quagga, and the byssal-umbo distance (1.8–4.1 mm) is shorter. Shell profile in side view is affected by depth (dorsoventrally compressed at depth).

SIZE: Height 25–40 mm.

TYPE LOCATION (Andrusov 1897): "Liman von Bug bei Nikolaew" (Port Bug near present-day Mykolaiv, Ukraine on Pivdennyi Buh River). Original images of *D. rostriformis bugensis* in Andrusov (1897) are shown in Fig. B19.

JUNIOR SYNONYMS (Rosenberg and Ludyanskiy 1994): synonyms of *D. rostriformis* include *Dreissena pontocaspica, D. distincta, D. compressa, D. grimmi*, as well as fossil species *D. tschaudae* and *D. rostriformis* vars. *gibba* and *vulgaris*. Rosenberg

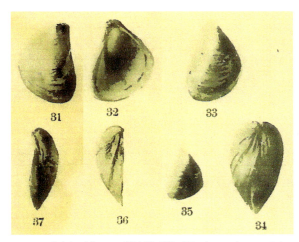

FIG. B19. Original figures (XV:31-37) of *Dreissena bugensis* by Andrusov (1897).

and Ludyanskiy (1994) proposed *Dreissena bugensis* as the name for the form found in the Great Lakes based on comparisons with type specimens of Andrusov (1897). Based on genetic testing, Therriault et al. (2004) observed little genetic divergence from *D. rostriformis* (0.3–0.4%), suggesting that *D. bugensis* and *rostriformis* are the same species. The two differ ecologically, however, with *bugensis* found in freshwater (<3 ppt) and *rostriformis* found in a more saline habitat (<13 ppt). Therriault et al. (2004) therefore considered the quagga mussel to be a subspecies of *D. rostriformis* Deshayes, 1838, as previously proposed by Mordukhai-Boltovoskoi (1960).

NOTES: Differentiated from other Utah bivalves by the byssal threads, long-triangular shape, and "zebra striping" on the shell. Very similar to zebra mussel, *Dreissena polymorpha* Pallas 1771, but when placed on a surface, zebra mussels are stable on their flattened underside while quagga mussels, lacking a flat underside, will fall over. Overall, quaggas are rounder in shape and have a small byssal groove on the ventral side near the hinge, and they lack the acute shoulder or ridge located ventrolaterally in *D. polymorpha* (Pathy and Mackie 1993). However, Beggel et al. (2015) noted discrepancies between genetic analyses and identifications based on shell characteristics. Veligers of the two species must be genetically analyzed (polymerase chain reaction assay) to separate them (Claxton and Boulding 1998; Hoy et al. 2010). Smith (1999) noted differences between the two species in the extent of sensory papillae above the exhalant siphon and the point of union of the middle mantle fold. In *D. bugensis*, the sensory papillae form a triangular pattern around the exhalant siphon that is broader and shorter than that found in *D. polymorpha*. The quagga mussel also has slightly larger sperm (9–12 um) than the zebra mussel (7–9 um; Nichols and Black 1994).

Quagga mussels can live in the soft silt of the profundal zone as well as at shallower depths, often spaced apart by the length of their siphon (Dermott and Kerec 1997). Quagga mussels compete with other benthic invertebrates for food and space (Karatayev et al. 2015). Quagga mussels live in freshwater but can tolerate salinities up to 1–5 ppt (Mills et al. 1996). They have been observed to spawn at 9°C. They tolerate temperatures up to about 27–30°C, where mortality starts to occur, with some variation in survival based on acclimation and duration (Spidle 1994; Mills et al. 1996); Temperatures estimated to kill 100% in probit analyses were 39.2–45.2°C (Spidle 1994), but observations in the Ukraine populations by Antonov and Shkorbatov (1990; as cited by Mills et al. 1996), suggest 32–35°C as more realistic thermal limits. Quagga mussels are dioecious (separate sexes) and fertilization is external (Ram et al. 2012).

DISTRIBUTION: Native to the Dnieper and Pivdennyi Buh river drainages that flow into the Black Sea of western Asia (Mills et al. 1996). Introduced into western Europe in early 2004 (Heiler et al. 2013). The quagga mussel is an introduced invasive species now found in the Laurentian Great Lakes of North America, New York, and the Mississippi River system (Mills et al. 1993, 1996). It was found in Lake Mead in the Colorado River system in 2007 (Hickey 2010), and it was discovered upstream in Lake Powell in 2013. It was introduced to the United States via the ballast water of ships, and its spread continues via attachment to watercraft and other means.

SPF: **SPHAERIOIDEA Deshayes, 1855 (1820)**

Sphaeriidae Deshayes, 1855 (1820)

The species within this family are variously known as the seed clams, fingernail clams, pill clams, or pea clams. These bivalves are ovoviviparous, brooding and nourishing their embryos within the shell (Mackie 1979; Korniushin and Glaubrecht 2002). Based on genetic analyses, Lee and O'Foighil (2003) recognized five genera within the subfamily Sphaeriinae: *Afropisidium, Odhneripisidium, Pisidium, Cyclocalyx,* and *Sphaerium*, the latter including *Musculium* as a subgenus (Herrington 1962; Lee and O'Foighil 2003). Within North America, Mackie (2007) recognized four genera within the family: *Eupera, Pisidium, Sphaerium,* and *Musculium*. In this guide, *Musculium* is recognized as a separate genus based on a larger number of embryos in the genus than for other genera in the family (Herrington 1962), and on the more delicate shell characteristics (Herrington 1962; Mackie 2007). Other genetic testing has supported separation of the two as distinct taxa in one study (Hornbach et al. 1980) but not others (Lee 2004).

Fossil specimens in Sphaeriidae date back to the Cretaceous (Keen and Dance 1969). As Clessin (1877–1879) and Sterki (1916) have noted, the taxonomy of the species within Sphaeriidae has been difficult due to the variation among individual bivalves, the poor descriptions provided in the literature, the difficulty in finding original descriptions, the lack of comparison of North American forms with European species, limited morphological characters, and collections in which species were identified using a very limited list of known options. The taxonomy and synonomy followed in this summary are largely derived from the work of

Gerald Mackie and his collaborators (2007), who studied this family in great depth.

The genus *Eupera* features only one species in North America, *E. cubensis,* which is not found in Utah. In *Eupera* all the embryos are produced at one time (synchronous), and no brood sac is used for incubation, whereas in *Pisidium*, also a synchronous spawner, there is a brood sac. *Eupera* also lacks the cardinal tooth C4 found in the other genera (Korniushin and Glaubrecht 2002).

Genus *Musculium* Link, 1807 Fingernail Clams

Shell thin and fragile; suborbicular, triangular, or rhomboidal; smooth, shining, striate moderately fine to very fine; beaks usually calyculate ("capped") and directed medially and anteriorly; cardinal teeth minute, sometimes obsolete. Periostracum silky or slightly glossy, cream-colored or dark. Ligament very narrow and short, not visible externally. Hinge plate relatively long and narrow. Laterals very thin, long, and distinct, the anterior lateral dipping inwardly at proximal ends and the posterior ones straight, forming a gentle inclined plane. Cardinal teeth are small, located closer to anterior laterals (Mackie 2007).

Musculium differs from *Sphaerium* by having a narrow hinge plate between the umbones ($\leq$thickened end of the cardinal tooth C3; Mackie et al. 2007), whereas in *Sphaerium* the hinge plate is usually more than twice as wide as the thickened end of C3. Also, in *Musculium*, siphons are united for the greater part of their length, whereas in *Sphaerium*, the siphons are separate for most of their length (Chamberlin and Jones 1929; Korniushin 1998).

The type species for the genus is *Tellina lacustris* Müller, 1774 (currently *Musculium lacustre*). Generally, shells do not exceed 8 mm in length, but shells as long as 13.5 mm may be encountered.

Musculium is an asynchronous spawner; that is, there are paired brood sacs in which the various ages of embryos are found (Van Cleave et al. 1947). Accounts of spawning timing have varied in the literature. In a laboratory study, Thomas (1959) documented self-fertilization in *Musculium partumeium*, noting the production of 3 to 6 generations in a 15-month period, varying with individual genetic lines. Thomas (1959) also observed progeny produced in a shallow pond from mid-March to early April, followed by a second period of production from early June to July, when the pond dried up. Mitropolskji (1965; as cited by Mackie 2007) noted a summer-born cohort that died after releasing progeny in the fall and a fall cohort that overwintered and died after releasing young in midsummer. Mackie (1979) studied spawning in two ponds in Ontario, Canada. *Musculium* in one pond had peak spawning in late July–early August, with half of the progeny growing to adult size by October and producing a subsequent generation the next spring. Of the other half from the summer spawn, most died during the winter. However, the survivors, plus the fall cohort began growth in the spring of the next year, producing offspring in that summer, then dying. So, it appears that the life span varies from about 6 months for summer cohorts to 12–14 months. The number of larvae per parent was typically 4–12, rarely up to 35 (Mackie 1979).

Musculium lacustre Müller, 1774 Lake Fingernail clam

DESCRIPTION (Müller 1774; Herrington 1962): Shell thin, little to considerably inflated, anterior end not as high as posterior end; beaks somewhat toward anterior end, swollen and full, varying in height, usually capped, but not always; cap size varies; striae moderately fine to fine, uneven (not as smooth as in *Musculium partumeium*); periostracum a slightly dulled gloss; dorsal margin long, slightly to considerably curved; ventral margin varying from considerably curved to a little flattened; anterior end rounded or with a rounded slope (joining ventral margin in more of an angle), joining dorsal margin with a small angle; posterior end almost straight, joining the dorsal margin with a sharp or slightly rounded angle and the ventral margin with a slightly rounded angle. The ends are seldom parallel but slope up toward the dorsal margin. Sometimes the posterior end has a much longer slope than the anterior, in which case the lower part extends farther out. Hinge very long, slightly to considerably curved, usually with a bend behind the cardinal teeth; hinge plate long and narrow, sometimes almost absent. Lateral teeth slim but distinct. There is a slight dip at the proximal end of the anterior laterals, and A1 and A2 appear to swing under the hinge plate at their proximal ends. The posterior laterals form a gentle inclined plane; all cusps are distal, only anterior ones have any prominence. Cardinals are weak and variable in shape, located closer to anterior laterals; C3 is short, parallel to the hinge plate, more or less roundly curved, posterior end enlarged and usually bifurcate; C2 short and slim, C4 also short and slim, straight, roughly parallel with C2, directed at or outside cusp of P2.

TYPE LOCATION: Europe

SIZE (Mackie 2007): Usually < 8 mm long but some specimens up to 10 mm occur. H/L ratio 0.83–0.90; W/L ratio 0.60–0.69.

JUNIOR SYNONYMS (Herrington 1962; Burch 1975; Mackie 2007): *Tellina lacustris* Müller, 1774; *Calyculina lacustris* (Müller, 1774) Clessin 1879; *Cyclas jayensis* Prime, 1851a;

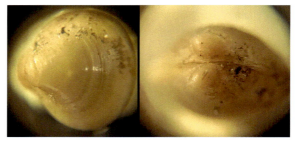

FIG. B20. *Musculium lacustre*. Henrys Fork, Uinta Mts, UT. Credit: E. Wagner.

Cyclas ryckholti Normand, 1844; *Sphaerium ryckholti* (Normand) Adams and Adams 1858; *Cyclas steinii* Schmidt, 1850; *Cyclas rosacea* Prime, 1852; *Cyclas jayensi* Prime, 1852; *Sphaerium lenticula* Prime, 1865; *Sphaerium raymondi* Cooper, 1892; *Musculium winkleyi* Sterki, 1909b; *M. pusillum* Sterki, 1910; *M. declive* Sterki, 1912a; *M. rosaceum* var. *fuliginosum* Sterki, 1916. Last revision: *Musculium lacustre* (Müller) Herrington 1962.

NOTES: Nipple-like umbo with beaks pointed toward each other rather than vertically as in *M. partumeium;* also, not as squarish-shaped in outline. Some *M. lacustre* shells have a similar shape to *Musculium partumeium*; however, the anterior end of *M. lacustre* is less rounded and joins the ventral margin lower down. The ventral margin is less curved, the striae coarser and less even, and the shell has less gloss. Found in lakes, ponds, bogs, rivers, and creeks, usually in silt.

In a Canadian study (Mackie 1979), newborns appeared in late June and grew to full size (6.5–7.5 mm) in 50–60 days. Litter size of fetal larvae ranged from about 5–12 per parent, but prodissoconch and extramarsupial larvae litters were usually 4 or less. Growth was asymptotic, peaking at 4–6 mm in length.

DISTRIBUTION: Circumpolar. Widely distributed in the United States from Maine to Florida west to Washington and California, though not recorded from the Southwest. Utah records: (Chamberlin and Jones 1929; Herrington and Roscoe 1953) Newton Reservoir, Cache County and Fish Lake, Sevier County (UMNH 847 and 814). A specimen from V. Sterki exchanged with Chamberlin and Jones (authors of the 1929 Utah guide to mollusks) is also at the museum (No. 1563). Specimens of *M. lacustre* from Aspen Grove, Utah, are in the Monte Bean Museum, Provo, Utah. The author has found it living in a sedge-dominated seep at the edge of Mill Hollow Reservoir and in a marsh along the Henry's Fork River of the Uinta Mountains.

Musculium partumeium Say, 1822 Swamp Fingernail Clam

DESCRIPTION (Say 1822, p. 380): "Shell thin and fragile, transversely suborbicular, with small, irregular, inequidistant, concentric wrinkles, and larger adventitious undulations; base rounded; anterior and posterior edges regularly, equally, and very obtusely curved; beak nearly central; hinge teeth prominent and distinct; lateral teeth prominent, white; within impressed by exterior undulations, and bluish-white on the margin and submargin. Length nine-twentieths; breadth eleven-twentieths of an inch."

ADDITIONAL DESCRIPTIONS (Herrington 1962; Mackie 2007): Shell somewhat short in outline, striae fine and evenly spaced; periostracum glossy and smooth, yellow to light-greenish horn or dark; beak usually directed dorsally; dorsal margin almost straight and about as long as ventral margin; ventral margin well curved; anterior end usually well rounded, but sometimes slightly truncate, joining the dorsal margin with an angle and the ventral margin without an angle; posterior end truncate, slightly rounded, at right angles to the dorsal margin, but union with ventral margin is rounded. Hinge plate long and narrow, with a slight bend behind the cardinal teeth; lateral teeth: left valve and inner ones of right valve are slim but distinct; proximal ends of anterior laterals dip slightly; none appear to swing under hinge plate at proximal end; the very low posterior cusps are at distal end of laterals, forming a gentle inclined plane; anterior cusps rise more distinctly from the dip, and are distal, but sometimes on the distal side of center; cardinals much closer to anterior cusps, weak; Cardinal teeth highly variable; C3 short, slightly curved, enlarged a little at posterior end, parallel to hinge plate which is so narrow that the tooth partly overhangs the valve cavity; C2 is short, sometimes little more than a peg, usually with a curve at the posterior end; C4 very slim, about as long as or a bit longer than C2, directed toward the cusp of P2 or a little inside.

FIG. B21. *Musculium partumium*. Little Creek Reservoir, Rich Co., UT. Credit: E. Wagner.

Size (Van Cleave et al. 1947; Herrington 1962; Mackie 2007): Shell usually <9 mm long, rarely up to 13.5 mm (Texas, UMMZ 199649). H/L ratio in adult shells 0.85 ± 0.03, W/L ratio 0.60 ± 0.06. Newborns are 1.75 ± 0.35 mm long and more laterally compressed (W/L ratio 0.53 ± 0.03).

ANIMAL (Van Cleave et al. 1947): Brood chambers are borne on the inner gills, with a larger and smaller pouch in each inner gill. Size at maturity is about 4 mm long. There are 8–18 young produced per parent. Mackie (2007) noted that 2–5 per parent is typical, but extremes of 30–36 young per parent have been observed. Marsupial young in a given parent are commonly of two different sizes. Soon after the fully formed young are set free, a new cohort of embryos starts to develop.

TYPE LOCATION: pond near Germantown, Pennsylvania.

JUNIOR SYNONYMS (Mackie 2007): *Cyclas calyculata* Draparnaud, 1805; *Cyclas partumeia* Say, 1822; *Cyclas elevata* Haldeman, 1841a; *Cyclas orbicularia* (Barratt) Linsley, 1845; *Cyclas truncata* (Linsley) Gould, 1848d; *Cyclas pellucida* (Stimpson, 1851) Prime, 1853; *Cyclas caerulea* Prime, 1852; *Cyclas mirabilis* Prime, 1852; *Cyclas eburnea* (Anthony) Prime, 1853; *Sphaerium contractum* Prime, 1865; *Calyculina hodgsonii* Sterki, 1902; *Calyculina ferrissi* Sterki, 1902; *Musculium truncatum* Sterki, 1916; *Musculium orbiculare* Sterki, 1913; *Musculium partumeium* var. *globosum* Sterki, 1916; *M. truncatum* var. *albidum* Sterki, 1916.

NOTES: Differentiated from *M. lacustre* by the nearly straight dorsal margin, giving the outer dorsal margins a shouldered appearance. Also, the beaks are generally pointed vertically, rather than toward each other as in *M. lacustre*. The number of young produced per parent varied from 2 to 30 (mean of 10) in a study by Thomas (1959). Mean size of young produced varied from 1.38 × 1.06 mm to 1.63 × 1.28 mm among individuals, but extremes of 0.93 × 0.72 mm to 1.85 × 1.49 mm were noted. Final size ranged from 4.31 × 6.15 mm to 7.37 × 6.20 mm (mean adult size, 4.54 × 3.92 mm). Ripe eggs and sperm appear when the shell is at least 2.1 mm long. Gilmore (1917) described some of the anatomy but did not differentiate between the two species he described, *Sphaerium simile* and *M. partumeium*. Specimens from the southern United States are larger and thicker (Herrington 1962). Life span is about 13 months and can survive in ephemeral ponds (Way et al. 1980). Densities ranging from 35 to $6,094/m^2$ have been noted in permanent ponds (Way et al. 1980).

DISTRIBUTION (ANSP, Ibase): Argentina; Canada; Mexico; Trinidad and Tobago; widespread in the United States (Maine to Washington, south to California, Texas, and Florida). One old museum record for Murray, Utah (FMNH 179015). Recently found by the author in Little Creek Reservoir, Rich County, Utah.

Genus *Pisidium* Pfeiffer, 1821 Pill Clams

DESCRIPTION (Clessin 1879; Woodward 1913; Mackie 2007): Shell: thin, small, ovoid to orbicular, equal shelled, unequal sided, the anterior part lengthened, vortex approaches the trailing edge and the posterior shortened very much; concentrically striate; ligament short, of shell substance, overbuilt. Cardinal teeth 2/2 or 2/1. Posterior teeth: 1 in left and 2 in right shell; teeth in right shell higher and stronger; anterior teeth more like cardinal teeth than the rear ones.

ANIMAL: Small, siphons very short, only slightly over the edge of the mantle, grown together to the mouth; Foot narrow, tongue-shaped; external gills very short, covering almost half of the interior; inner and outer gills large and well developed, with ascending and descending lamellae, and the dorsal loop or lobe of nephridia is cleft. The maximum life span of *Pisidium* may range from 4 months to 4 years (Holopainen and Hanski 1986).

Pisidium casertanum Poli, 1791–1827 Ubiquitous Peaclam

DESCRIPTION (Clessin 1879; Mackie 2007): Adult shell long in outline, typically ovate but sometimes rounded or triangular. Dorsal margin long, usually gently curved, but may be greatly curved. Scutum and scutellum usually present. Ventral margin very long and gently curved. Anterior and posterior ends well rounded, joining dorsal and ventral margins without angles. The upper margin of the shell falls in a rather oblique line toward the front edge; rear of shell truncated, slightly bent; slightly sharpened at the front edge. Sometimes posterior margin is vertical

FIG. B22. *Pisidium casertanum*, UMMZ specimens. 190529: Telephone Lake, WY, 187069 Rice Lake, Ontario. 196134: Ham's Fork River, WY. 219490: Cache Co. spring, UT. 190478: Pond NE of Star Lake, Uinta Mts, UT. 161735: near Kanab, UT. Credit: UMMZ.

and truncated, and anterior margin is a steep, straight slope. Walls thin, moderately inflated. Beaks broad, depressed, projecting backward, subcentral to slightly posterior. Striae fine, faint, or irregular. Periostracum moderately dull to slightly glossy, of bright horn color. Ligament long and thick, the lower edge somewhat sinuous.

Inside the shell, mother-of-pearl weak, whitish; muscle scars weakly marked. Hinge well developed, moderately long and broad; cardinals are near the outer edge and near anterior cusps. Edge sharp, with a limited light band; weakly pointed swirls approach the posterior edge. Left shell has two very short cardinal teeth, the outer one (C2) being slightly bent or chevron-shaped, low, thin, cutting, ± parallel with, and centered on hinge plate. The inner tooth (C4) is worm-shaped or lamelliform, low, thin, slightly curved, its anterior end near the apex of C2 and its posterior end directed toward inside of posterior laterals. The gap between the two teeth is long and wide. Posterior teeth simple, high, and pointed at broad base. Right shell has one very short cardinal tooth (C3), curved to strongly bent, thickened and usually bifid posteriorly. Posterior teeth double, quite stout, the outer strong, short, and of equal height to inner teeth; rear posterior tooth high and pointed, the anterior flatter, less pointed; gutter short, and wide.

Laterals, except A3 and P3, are short, with tall, pointed cusps. Cusps of A1, P1, P2 distal or on distal side of center, of A3 and P3 very low, short, and distal, and of A2 central to proximal.

SIZE: Clessin's (1879) measurements of synonym *P. abditum* were 4.5 × 3.9 × 3 mm (L, W, D) (Mackie 1979): length 5 mm, width 3.8 mm, thickness 1.8 mm. Mackie (2007): Maximum length about 6.00 mm, H/L 0.86 ± 0.06; W/L 0.62 ± 0.08. Newborns are 1.00–1.75 mm long, W/L 0.42 ±0.03. Haldeman's (1841a) measurements of *Pisidium abditum:* length 4 mm, height 3 mm, diameter 2 mm. Clessin (1879) noted that *P. casertanum* and *P. fossarinum* were very similar to *P. abditum* and likely of the same species, differing only in the posterior leg of the right cardinal tooth, which is missing.

TYPE LOCATION: Italy

JUNIOR SYNONYMS (Prime 1862; Clessin 1879; Herrington 1954; Mackie et al. 2007): *Cardium casertanum* Poli, 1791; *P. cinereum* Alder, 1838; *Cyclas minor* Adams, 1841; *Cyclas steenbuchi* Möller, 1842; *Pisidium abditum* Haldeman, 1841a + varieties; *P. roseum* Scholtz, 1843; *Pisidium minus* Stimpson, 1851; *P. kurtzi, P. obscurum,* and *P. zonatum* Prime, 1851a; *P. arcuatum, P. notatum,* and *P. regulare* Prime, 1852; *P. noveboracense* Prime, 1858 + var. *P. n. elevatum, fraturnum, lineatum, proclive, quadrulum,* and *expansum* Sterki, 1906a; *P. resartum* (Ingalls, 1855) Prime, 1862; *P. plenum* (Lewis, 1855) Prime, 1862; *P. occidentale* Newcomb, 1861; *P. arcticum* Westerlund, 1883; *P. politum* Sterki, 1895; *P. randolphi* Roper, 1896; *P. trapezoideum* Sterki, 1896 + var. *P. t. protensum, P. streatori* Sterki, 1901; *P. roperi* Sterki, 1898; *P. strengi* Sterki, 1902; *P. complanatum, P. cuneiforme,* and *P. rowelli* Sterki, 1903a; *P. ashmuni* and *P. danielsi,* Sterki, 1903b; *P. atlanticum* Sterki, 1905; *P. a. huachucanum* Pilsbry and Ferriss, 1906; *P. fragillimum, P. friersoni, P. levissimum, P. proximum, P. neglectum* var. *corpulentum,* and *P. subrotundum* Sterki, 1906a, b; *P. succineum* and *P. superius* Sterki, 1907; *P. albidum* and *P. dispar* Sterki, 1911; *P. alleni* Sterki, 1912b; *P. columbianum, P. nevadense* + var. *P. n. medicum,* and *P. furcatum* Sterki, 1913; *P. abditum lacteum, P. ovum, P. fabale, P. subrotundum* var. *pumilum* + var. *olofi* and *P. hannai* Sterki, 1916; *P. griseolum, P. paradoxum,* and *P. orcasense* Sterki, 1922; *P. lucidum* and *P. mirum* Sterki, 1923; *P. tenellum* Gould, 1850b; *P. rubellum* Prime, 1852; Herrington (1954) listed several synonymous species ascribed to V. Sterki including *P. anceps, P. barryi, P. capax* (nomen nudum), *P. concinnulum, P. devium, P. egregium, P. eyerdami, P. fidalgoense, P. isabellaneum, P. mamillanum, P. pumilum, P. rugosulum,* and *P. striggill'm*. Adams and Adams (1858) transferred a few of these synonymous species from *Pisidium* to the genus *Musculium,* including *M. abditum, M. minus, M. rubellum, M. obscurum, M. kurtzii, and M. zonatum.* Using genetic analysis, Schultheiss (2007) and Lee and O'Foighil (2003) have found that specimens determined to be *P. casertanum* based on morphology may be polyphyletic (multiple species). So, more uncertainty can be expected in the taxonomy of this group.

NOTES: Highly variable in form; those individuals in rivers tend to have a medium to large oval form with a robust hinge and well-curved C2 and C3, while those of streams are smaller, but similar in shape; shells in ponds and marshes tend to be more circular in outline, large, with straighter and more narrow hinges (Mackie 2007). Baršienè et al. (1996) reported chromosome counts of 150 in somatic nuclei for *P. casertanum* from Parra Spring, and about 180 for specimens from Balsillas Spring, Spain. Based on diploids having about 30 chromosomes (Baršienè et al. 1996), that suggests *P. casertanum* individuals are polyploid (10n–12n).

This species is more ovate than *P. compressum, P. lilljeborgii,* and *P. variable,* and generally are larger as adults than *P. insigne, Pisidium milium, P. subtruncatum,* and *P. ventricosum*. The presence of scutum and scutellum also separates it from all but *P. lilljeborgii* . The chevron shape of C2 also helps to distinguish this species from other *Pisidium* species.

P. casertanum had asynchronous development of embryos, with embryos at different stages of development found in a single brood sac (Bespalaya et al. 2015). Some of the embryos are released and others retained for development within the shell. Older and larger embryos may profit at the expense of the younger embryos. The species was a significant component of the benthic community in high-altitude lakes, often dominant. Mackie (1979) observed a wide range of size classes in a Canadian pond. Newborns (1.25–1.75 mm) appear in July and parents die soon afterward (having about a 12-month lifespan). In another population, there were two generations per year. Embryos first appear in shells of 1.5–2.0 mm and grow with the parent. Four juvenile stages are recognized: embryo (fertilization to gastrulation); fetal larvae (end of gastrulation to start of shell formation); prodissoconch larvae (start of shell formation to escape from brood sac); and extramarsupial larvae (shelled larvae broken free of brood sac but still in marsupium). A given parent will only have one larval stage present. Litter size per parent varies from 4 to 16 fetal larvae, but later stages found in parents ranged from 4 to 12 per parent (Mackie 1979). Gravid parents were found throughout most of the year.

DISTRIBUTION: *P. casertanum* is a cosmopolitan species, found worldwide in habitats ranging from ephemeral pools to large lakes. *Pisidium abditum* was reported to be found in the Raft River drainage (Cooper 1868–1872a, b) and in City Creek near Salt Lake City (Call 1884). Baily and Baily (1951) reported the species (as *P. occidentale*) at Saratoga, Provo, and Ideal Beach (Bear Lake). Woolstenhulme (1942a, b) reported it (as *P. abditum*) from Echo and Red Butte canyons, Hayden's Pass (Uinta Mountains), Strawberry River, Twin Creeks at Fish Lake, and Maxwell Spring in Beaver Creek Canyon near Kamas. Also known in Snake Valley (Hovingh 1993).

Pisidium compressum Prime, 1851a Ridged-beak Peaclam

DESCRIPTION (Prime 1851a, 1852, p. 356): "Shell rather small, oblique, triangular, tumid, ovate in adult, compressed in young, heavily striated (very finely) in adult, less so in young; color varying from yellow, gray, and brown, with a zone of yellow on the margins, occasionally spotted on the beaks; beaks small, very prominent, very distant; hinge margin angular; cardinal teeth situated centrally, double, small; lateral teeth elongated."

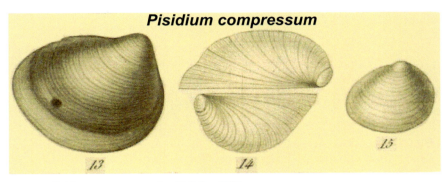

FIG. B23. *Pisidium compressum*. Credit: Prime 1852.

From Mackie (2007, p. 289): "Adult shell of medium size, trigonal, varying from short and high to moderately long. Walls heavy and moderately inflated. Beaks elevated, rather narrow and prominent, apex usually with a ridge on each side. Striae of medium coarseness to moderately fine, regularly spaced or irregular. Periostracum dull to silky, color yellowish, darker in older specimens. Ligament rather short and thick. Dorsal margin short and round. Scutum and scutellum absent. Ventral margin long (3X dorsal) and curved, joining posterior end without an angle. Anterior end begins near beaks without an angle, has a rather steep, straight slope and joins ventral margin low with an angle. Posterior end roundly truncate, vertical or slightly cut under. Hinge very long and heavy, moderately to steeply curved. Cardinals central, occupying most of the thickness of hinge plate. C3 curved, greatly enlarged posteriorly and usually bifid. C2 in lower half of hinge plate, rather tall and peg-like (i.e., rather tall and flattened on top) or incisor-like. C4 in dorsal half of hinge plate slightly curved, lamelliform, moderately long and tall, directed inside posterior laterals. Laterals heavy and rather short, cusps blunt on top. Cusps of P1, A2 and P2, central or on distal side of center, of A1 distal or on distal side of center. A3 and P3 with very low and blunt cusps. Sulci of laterals in right valve rather deep and closed proximally and distally as broad slits."

SIZE (Mackie 2007): up to 5 mm. H/L ratio usually 0.90 ± 0.04, rarely to 1.0. W/L ratio 0.60 ± 0.05, including newborn. Cotype 4.2 mm H, 4.7 mm L.; *P. altile* cotype 3.7 H, 4.2 mm L.

ANIMAL (Prime 1852, p. 356): "Foot very long, narrow, issuing from the inferior opening of the mantle; syphon short." The gross anatomy has not been described.

TYPE LOCATION: Fresh Pond, near Cambridge, Massachusetts, Cotype MCZ 19789. *P. altile* cotype MCZ 23607.

JUNIOR SYNONYMS (Mackie 2007): *Pisidium altile* (Anthony) Prime, 1852; *Pisidium peraltum* Sterki, 1900; varieties of *Pisidium compressum* by Sterki, 1905: var. *arrosum, contortum, contrarium, laevigatum, limnicalum, opacum, rostracum, smithii* and by Sterki, 1916: var. *curvatum, illinoisense, pellucidum*; *Pisidium fradulentum* Sterki, 1912b; *Pisidium compressum mutatum* Sterki, 1922.

FIG. B24. *Pisidium compressum*, UMMZ collection. 199552: Trout Lake, Ontario. 198432: Indian River, Ontario. 109020: Columbia River, Oregon. 219504: Weber River, UT. Credit: UMMZ.

NOTES (Prime 1851a, 1852; Heard 1965; Way and Wissing 1982; Mackie 2007): Compared to *P. variable*, it is less inflated, smaller, and more oblique, and it differs in color. Beak more prominent than in *P. casertanum* or *P. insigne*, but the beak is not as broad as in *P. milium* or *P. rotundatum*. H/L ratio greater than for *P. subtruncatum*. In outline, the junction of dorsal margin and anterior margin is usually rounded, whereas in *P. lilljeborgii* the transition is more angular. *P. compressum* is found in both flowing and flat-water habitats. Described from a population found in sympatry with *P. variable*. Life span is about 1–2 years. Peak gametogenesis was June–October in a Michigan stream, and mature gametes were most abundant from December to March. Average brood size of 6–20 larvae per adult, rarely up to 42. Minimum size at birth is about 0.90 mm.

DISTRIBUTION (Nylander 1900; Mackie 2007; Ibase): British Columbia, Alberta, Saskatchewan, Ontario, Prince Edward Island; Mexico. Widely distributed in the United States, especially the northern states, though found as far south as Florida and Texas. Utah records (Call 1884; Jones 1935; Woolstenhulme 1942b; Baily and Baily 1951–1952; Hovingh 1993): Utah Lake, Weber River drainage, Kamas, Bear Lake, and Snake Valley. ANSP, FMNH, MCZ, and UMMZ records for Utah: Richfield, Beaver Creek above Kamas, Rich County, above Glenwood, trout pond south of Junction in Piute County; Box Elder, Cache, Grand, Iron, Kane, Morgan, Rich, Salt Lake, Summit, Sevier, Weber, and Washington counties.

Pisidium insigne Gabb, 1868 Tiny Pillclam

FIG. B25. *Pisidium insigne*. UMMZ 202292. Credit: UMMZ.

DESCRIPTION (Gabb 1868, quoted, p. 69; Mackie 2007): "Shell minute, transverse, oval, subquadrate, very inequilateral, compressed. Anterior side produced, obliquely truncated above; posterior side regularly rounded; beaks very small, hardly projecting beyond the outline of the shell; hinge delicate, the lateral teeth long and slender; surface ornamented by a few minute striae; color light yellowish brown."

Shell elongate-oval, compressed, with thin walls. Beaks low, broad, posterior and not very prominent. Striae very fine to fine, irregular. Periostracum slightly glossy, usually covered with foreign material, yellowish to brown. Ligament long and very thick with ligament part extending $2/3$ or more of hinge plate thickness. Dorsal margin moderately long, openly curved, usually with a long shallow dip between cardinals and anterior laterals. Anterior end long and roundly pointed, joining dorsal and ventral margins with slightly rounded angle or no angle. Posterior end rounded, joining dorsal and ventral margins without angles. Ventral margin long and evenly curved. Hinge short, evenly rounded. Hinge plate thin, slightly arched, cardinals small and close to anterior cusps. C3 short, slightly curved to almost straight on its dorsal margin, thickened ventrally at the posterior end, giving C3 a "toothbrush" appearance. C2 varies: tall, short, curved, or sigmoid, ± parallel with hinge plate. C4 similar in height and length to C2, but straighter and diagonal to hinge plate. Laterals long and slim, cusp blunt but tall. All cusps distal to, or on the distal side of, center. Sulci of laterals in right valve opened distally and closed in long slits proximally producing long, narrow V-shaped cavity. Inner margins of sulci are tuberculated.

SIZE (Gabb 1868): 1.78 mm H × 2.29 mm L; H/L 0.78

TYPE LOCATION: "Spring at Fort Tejon" (presumably the fort at Lebec, California); Syntype at ANSP (281351).

JUNIOR SYNONYMS: none

NOTES: The small size, subquadrate outline, and very low beak distinguishes this species from most other Utah *Pisidium* species except *P. ventricosum*, which has a higher H/L ratio (0.90–1.00). Nothing is known about the life history and anatomy of this species.

DISTRIBUTION (ANSP; Ibase; www.idigbio.org): Ontario, British Columbia, Northwest Territories; AZ, CA (type location), ID, ME, MI, MT, NV, NM, NY, OH, OR, PA, TX, WA, WI, WY. In Utah, UMNH record: spring at Camp Timpanogos, American Fork Canyon (#1.012118). FMNH records: Kane County (179066), American Fork Canyon (178996), and Logan Canyon (108899).

Pisidium lilljeborgii Esmark and Hoyer, 1886 Lilljeborg Peaclam

DESCRIPTION (Esmark and Hoyer 1886): Shell very asymmetric, very inflated, irregularly striped, of yellow horn color; anterior part very short, trimmed, rounded; posterior part rounded. Umbone inflated and protruding. Upper margin arched, very narrow, limited by weakly marked corners of the shell and scutellum. Anterior margin short, steeply sloping. Ventral margin is very curved, without any notable border as it transitions to lateral margins. Posterior margin short, steeply sloped, a little arched. Ligament short, strong. Teeth not very prominent. Nacre slightly whitish; muscle scars hardly deepened.

Mackie (2007) adds: adult shell short in outline, obliquely rounded, pentagonal or rounded oval. Walls thin, usually moderately inflated, asymmetrical. Beaks very prominent, posterior, broad and tumid. Striae: coarse, strong. Periostracum: silky to glossy, yellowish horn color. Dorsal margin very short, somewhat posterior, straight to slightly curved, with distinct scutellum and scutum, and usually joining the ends with angles. Anterior margin long, with a slightly curved slope. Posterior margin roundly truncate to round. Ventral margin long, unevenly curved, arching higher posteriorly as it smoothly joins the posterior margin without an angle. It joins the anterior end low with an acute rounded angle. Hinge short, ligament long and narrow. Hinge plate moderately heavy to thin, slightly arched to curved. Cardinals close to anterior cusps, rather large and prominent. C3 rather long, curved, or bent where posterior end begins to expand; ± parallel with dorsal margin. C2 short, but raised, incisor-like, its posterior end appearing to rise from the hinge plate, and its anterior end from the proximal end of A2. C4 narrow, ± straight, about 1.5X as long as C2. Laterals in left valve long, with tall, pointed cusps. A2 cusp is situated central to proximal; P2, distal or on distal side of center. Laterals in right valve long; all cusps distal or on distal side of center and the sulci are both V-shaped, being divergent and opened distally and closed in a long narrow slit proximally.

Sphaeriidae

FIG. B26. *Pisidium lilljeborgii* from UMMZ collection. Upper left and upper center: MI (45668); upper R., Saskatchewan (195662); bottom row: Summit Co. near Elk Lake, UT (195775). Credit: UMMZ.

SIZE (Mackie 2007): The length is typically 4 mm, rarely exceeding 5 mm. H/L 0.93 ± 0.05, W/L 0.65 ± 0.06; newborns are 1.0–1.3 mm long with similar H/L and W/L ratios as adults.

TYPE LOCATION: Norway

JUNIOR SYNONYMS (Mackie 2007): *Pisidium alpicola* (Clessin) Suter, 1889 (*nomen nudum*); *P. loveni* Clessin, 1890 (*nomen nudum*); *P. scutellatum* Sterki, 1896; *P. marci* Sterki, 1909a; *P. scutellatum* form *cristatum* Sterki, 1928.

NOTES (Mackie 2007; Welter-Schultes 2012): The rounded angles of the dorsal margin of *P. lilljeborgii* give a rounded pentangular outline that differs from other Utah *Pisidium* species, though some individuals may be more rounded. Like *P. milium, P. rotundatum,* and *P. variable*, it has a very tumid, broad beak, but in *milium* and *variable* the cusp of lateral tooth A2 is central to distal (v. proximal in *lilljeborgii*) of a median line. *P. rotundatum* differs in the sulcus of the right valve lateral teeth, that is, closed distally in anterior teeth (open in *lilljeborgii*). The presence of a scutum and scutellum also differentiates it from most other *Pisidium* species with a prominent beak.

Usually found in cold lakes up to 10 m deep (rarely to 40 m), rarely in flowing water. Adults begin to develop gonads at a length of 2.0–2.7 mm. Usually there are 4–5 larvae/parent, but up to 13 have been observed.

DISTRIBUTION (Mackie 2007; www.idigbio.org; Ibase): England, northern Eurasia. Widespread in Canada. AK, CO, IN, IL, MA, MN, MI, MT, NM, NY, OH, TN, WA,

WI. Utah records: Summit County (UMMZ 0195775; small lake north of Elk Lake), Sevier County (NCSM 51237, Koosharem Reservoir), and Uintah County (NCSM 51234, Barker Spring).

Pisidium milium Held, 1836 Quadrangular Pillclam

DESCRIPTION (Mackie 2007): Shell ovate in outline, with very fine to coarse striae, often with "rest period" marks. Beaks posterior, greatly swollen and very prominent. Periostracum glossy, whitish, horn-colored or dark horn. Dorsal margin evenly and considerably curved, short, joining anterior margin with a well-rounded or no angle, and joining the posterior end with a rounded angle. Anterior margin long, with a steep, evenly curved slope, joining ventral margin low with a rounded point. Posterior margin roundly truncate, almost vertical above the median horizontal line, but below this line it swings under and joins the ventral margin without an angle. Ventral margin long and slightly curved.

Hinge short, hinge plate usually narrow, openly curved. Cardinal teeth subcentral (slightly anterior) and prominent. C3 long, ± of even thickness throughout, slightly expanded posteriorly; straight to slightly curved. C2 and C4 parallel to each other. C4 overlaps most of C2 (looks like the equals sign, ==), both slightly curved or sigmoid, of similar height, C2 slightly shorter. Laterals of moderate length, narrow, cusps in right valve tall and pointed, those in left valve pointed, but shorter. Cusps of A2 and P2 central, on distal side of center, or somewhat distal. Cusps of A1 and P1 central or on distal side of center. A1 and A2, and to some extent P1 and P2, appear to arise from below the hinge plate. Sulci of laterals usually opened proximally and distally, but the sulcus of the posterior laterals may often be V-shaped. For a description of the anatomy, see Odhner (1929).

SIZE (Mackie 2007): up to 3.5 mm long; average about 3.0 mm. H/L 0.62–0.88; W/L 0.62–0.95. Newborn are about 1.0 mm long, with equally variable H/L and W/L ratios.

TYPE LOCATION: unknown

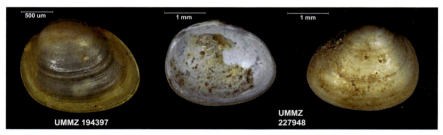

FIG. B27. *Pisidium milium*. Left: from Parawan Reservoir, UT; Center, Right, Elko Co., NV. Credit: UMMZ.

JUNIOR SYNONYMS: none

NOTES (Odhner 1929; Mackie 2007): Prominent swollen beak separates this species from most Utah *Pisidium* species except *P. lilljeborgii*, *P. rotundatum*, and *P. variable*. The lower H/L ratio separates it from *lilljeborgii*; the right valve lateral teeth sulci of *P. milium* are open on both ends, whereas they are closed proximally in posterior laterals of *P. variable* and *P. rotundatum*. In the Takern River of Sweden, young are produced from June to September by specimens 2.4–2.8 mm long. Capable of self-fertilization. Young were 0.9 mm long at birth. Brood size is up to 11 young per parent.

DISTRIBUTION (Nylander 1900; Mackie 2007; Ibase): Great Britain, Holland, Germany, France, Switzerland, and Russia. Widespread in Canada. AK, CA, CO, GA, ID, IL, MA, ME, MI, MT, NV, OH, PA, WA, WI. For Utah, museum specimens exist from Fish Lake, Sevier County (UMNH; FMNH 108897, 1799018); Silver Lake (FMNH 179016; UMMZ 28380); Big Cottonwood Canyon (FMNH 179017); and Koosharem Reservoir (North Carolina Museum of Natural Sciences 51250).

Pisidium rotundatum Prime, 1851a Fat Peaclam

DESCRIPTION (Prime 1851a, p. 164): "Shell small, somewhat globose, tumid, anterior and inferior margins rounded, posterior somewhat abrupt; beaks very large, tumid, rounded, approximate, removed slightly from the center, and inclining towards the posterior, surface smooth, striae very minute; color yellow, somewhat darker on the beaks" Mackie (2007): Adult shell is globose, inflated, rounded-oval in outline, with very thin walls. Striae are distinct and ± uniformly spaced. Beaks slightly posterior, well elevated above the hinge line, rounded. Periostracum is glossy, yellowish, brownish, or whitish horn. Dorsal margin very short, rounded. Scutum and scutellum poorly marked. Anterior and posterior ends well rounded, joining dorsal margin without angles (occasionally, a rounded angle is found above the anterior lateral cusps). Ventral margin is long and well curved. Hinge very short and light. Ligament very thick and short, the pit extending to near the inner edge of the hinge plate. Hinge plate is slightly arched and very narrow at the cardinals. Cardinals prominent, very close to anterior cusps. C3 slightly curved on dorsal side, club-shaped. C2 and C4 subequal in length and height, straight or slightly curved, incisor-like, more or less parallel with each other and with hinge plate. Laterals short, cusps tall with rather pointed tops.

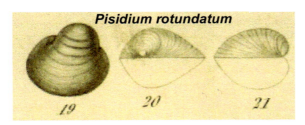

FIG. B28. *Pisidium rotundatum*. Credit: Prime 1852.

FIG. B29. *Pisidium rotundatum* specimens, UMMZ collection. 194501: Napanee River floodplain, Ontario. 228636: Jackson Lake, WY. 194511: Haystack Lake, Summit Co., UT. 194470: swamp in Ontario. Credit: UMMZ.

Cusp of A2 proximal; cusp of P2 central or on proximal or distal side of center. Sulcus closed distally in anterior laterals and proximally in posterior laterals of right valve. Cusps of A1 and A3 proximal or on proximal side of center; cusps of P1 and P3 distal or on distal side of center.

SIZE (Mackie 2007): <3.5 mm, with average about 3.0 mm long; H/L 0.90 ± 0.08; W/L 0.78 ± 0.08. Newborns are about 0.80 mm long, with similar H/L and W/L ratios. Prime (1852) noted a length of 0.095 in. (2.41 mm), a latitude of 0.075 in. (1.90 mm), and a diameter of 0.08 in. (2.03 mm).

TYPE LOCATION: Lake Superior.

JUNIOR SYNONYMS (Mackie 2007): *Musculium rotundatum* Adams and Adams, 1858.

NOTES (Prime 1851a): This species resembles *P. ventricosum* but is less inflated and more equilateral, with the margins more rounded, and the beaks are larger and more tumid. Differs from *P. milium, P. lilljeborgii,* and *P. variable* in lateral teeth sulci characteristics.

DISTRIBUTION (ANSP; Mackie 2007; Ibase; www.idigbio.org): Mexico, Northwest Territories of Canada, Alberta, British Columbia, Ontario, Manitoba, New Brunswick, Nunavut, Quebec, Saskatchewan, Yukon, Lake Superior, Lake Michigan. CA, CO, CT, FL, ID, IL, IN, KS, MA, MI, ME, MN, MT, NY, NJ, OH, OR, VT, WI, WA,

WY. In Utah, one record from Haystack Lake, Summit County (UMMZ 194511; Fig. B29).

Pisidium subtruncatum Malm, 1855 Short-ended Peaclam

DESCRIPTION (Mackie 2007): Adult shell obliquely oval or asymmetric in outline, inflated, and with thin walls. Striae moderately fine, evenly spaced. Beaks very posterior, tilted back, high, narrow, rounded to pointed. Periostracum light yellow or horn, glossy. Ligament long and white. Dorsal margin short, rounded, posterior, joining lateral margins with slight angles at or near lateral cusps. Anterior margin has a long, almost straight slope beginning above anterior cusps and joining the ventral margin in a low, rounded point. Posterior margin rounded or roundly truncate, smoothly joining ventral margin without an angle. Ventral margin long, curved.

FIG. B30. *Pisidium subtruncatum*, UMMZ collection. 192447: Lake Nipissing, Ontario. 192757: Gull and Sylvan Lakes, Alberta. Credit: UMMZ.

Hinge plate slightly arched, of ± uniform width between lateral teeth; hinge short, light. Cardinals nearer to anterior cusps. C3 short, of variable shape but usually only slightly expanded and rarely bifid posteriorly; parallel to hinge plate. C2 usually slightly shorter than C4 and more posterior, but of similar height and shape (lamelliform) and parallel with each other and hinge plate. Laterals in left valve short, composed mainly of cusps. Cusps of A2 and P2 tall and blunt, situated central to distal of median line. In right valve, A1 and P1 are long, narrow, with short, blunt, subcentral cusps. A3 and P3 are very short and ridge-like, the ridges being half the length of the inner laterals and ± parallel with them. Sulci open at both ends, but proximal opening is narrow and slit-like; the distal opening is wide.

SIZE (Mackie 2007): up to 5.0 mm long; mean maximum is 3.2 mm. H/L 0.88 ± 0.06; W/L 0.54–0.74. Newborns are 0.60–1.00 mm long; most about 0.80 mm long.

TYPE LOCATION: unknown

JUNIOR SYNONYMS (Clessin 1877–1879; Mackie 2007): *Cyclas obtusalis* Nilsson, 1822; *Pisidium dupuyanum* Normand, 1854 (Gassies 1855); *P. henslowianum* v. *dupuyanum* Baudon, 1857; *Pisidium alpicola* (Clessin) Suter, 1889 (*nomen nudum*); *P. marci* Sterki, 1909b; *P. overi* Sterki, 1913; *P. apiculatum* Sterki, 1922.

NOTES (Mackie 2007): The high, narrow beak of *P. subtruncatum* differentiates it from most other *Pisidium* species in Utah except *P. compressum*, which has a more triangular outline, and *P. variable*, which tends to have more angular junctions between the dorsal margin and the sides. Also, sulci of laterals are a narrow slit distally (wider in *subtruncatum*). For anatomy, see Odhner (1929). *P. subtruncatum* matures at about 2.00 mm in length, and gravid adults may be found from June to September. Brood size is typically 4–5 but may range from 1 to 11. Two litters have been noted (Ladle and Baron 1969). The life span is about a year.

DISTRIBUTION (ANSP; Mackie 2007; Ibase): Algeria, Austria, Canada, Denmark, France, Egypt, Germany, Hungary, Iceland, Ireland, Italy, Norway, Macedonia, Netherlands, Poland, Portugal, Romania, Russia, Norway, Sweden, Switzerland, United Kingdom, Ukraine. AL, AK, CA, CO, ID, MI, MN, MT, NY, ND, OH, OR, PA, WI, WY. In Utah, USNM record from Mount Leidy (187491).

Pisidium variable Prime, 1851a Triangular Peaclam

DESCRIPTION (Prime 1851a, p. 163): "Shell small, stout and heavy, very oblique, rather inflated than otherwise, posteriorly subtruncated; beaks large, prominent, but not approximate, margins rather abrupt; color dark olive green, generally with a zone of yellow on the margins; striations rather heavy for so small a shell." Mackie (2007): Adult shell varies from short, high and triangular in outline to longer and oval. Walls usually heavy and moderately inflated. Striae fine to

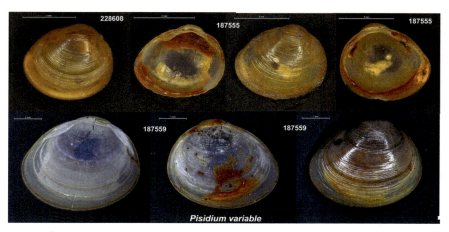

FIG. B31. *Pisidium variable*, UMMZ collection. 228608: Arizona Lake, WY. 187555: Ontario. 187559: near Wall Lake, UT. Credit: UMMZ.

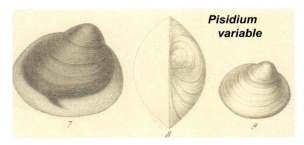

FIG. B32. *Pisidium variable.* Credit: Prime 1852.

coarse. Periostracum glossy, yellowish or brownish. Beaks prominent, broad, and situated somewhat posteriorly. Ligament strong and thick. Dorsal margin short and round, joining sides with distinct angles in triangular forms or with more rounded angles in oval forms. Scutum and scutellum poorly marked. Anterior end rather long, with a long, steep, straight or slightly curved slope, joining ventral margin with a rounded point. Posterior margin well rounded or roundly truncated, arching well out from dorsal margin and joining ventral margin without an angle. Ventral margin long and evenly and amply curved. Hinge short, well rounded. Hinge plate very heavy in triangular forms, lighter in oval forms. Cardinals slightly anterior of center, mostly in dorsal half of the hinge plate. C3 thin, slightly bent midway, ventral-posterior part thickened and usually bifid and parallel to hinge plate. C2 curved, short, low, canine-like, parallel to hinge plate. C4 long, thin, low, lamelliform or incisor-like, diagonal and directed toward outside posterior cusp. Laterals short, incorporated into hinge plate, with low, very blunt cusps. A2 and P2 central or on distal side of center. Cusps of A1 distal of center; P1 central or on distal side of center. Sulci of right valve laterals deep, long, narrow; proximal end closed, distal end a long, narrow slit. A3 and P3 cusps low, blunt, subcentral. Prime's original figures are shown in Fig. B32.

SIZE (Mackie 2007): <6 mm long, averaging about 5.5 mm in maximum shell length H/L 0.84 ± 0.04; W/L 0.60 ± 0.05; newborn are 0.90–1.30 mm long (mean 1.20 mm) with W/L of 0.50 ± 0.03.

TYPE LOCATION: Fresh Pond near Cambridge, Massachusetts.

JUNIOR SYNONYMS (Prime 1869–1870; Mackie 2007): *Pisidium cicer* Prime, 1853; *Pisum variable* Adams and Adams, 1858; *P. grande* (Whittemore, 1855) Prime, 1869; *P. compressum cicer* Prime, 1865; *P. palustre* (Lewis) (Prime 1869); *P. mirable* (Whittemore) Clessin, 1879; *P. variable* var. *brevius* Sterki, 1906a, *P. variable* var. *hybridum* Sterki, 1906a; *P. variable* var. *magnum* Sterki, 1916; *P. variable cicer* Sterki, 1916; *P. decisum* Sterki, 1922; *P. probum* Sterki, 1923.

NOTES (Mackie 1979): Not as compressed as *P. compressum*, and with larger beaks; larger adult shell than *P. rotundatum* or *P. ventricosum*. Two generations were produced annually in a Canadian study. The life span appears to be about 1 year. Birth of newborns occurs throughout the summer. Litter size of fetal larvae ranged from 2 to 10, and extramarsupial larvae averaged up to 6 per parent.

Embryos first appear when adults are 2.0–2.5 mm, fetal larvae when adults are 2.5–3.0 mm, prodissoconch larvae appear at 3.0–3.5 mm, and extramarsupial larvae when adults are 3.5–4.0 mm. Growth is asymptotic, with shell length peaking at 4–5 mm.

DISTRIBUTION (Nylander 1900; Mackie 2007; Ibase): Widespread in Canada. In the United States from Washington to Maine, south to Florida and Mexico, west to California. Also found in the Colorado River at Lee's Ferry, Arizona (Spamer and Bogan 1993). Jones (1935, 1940a, b) reported this species from the Weber R. drainage and Fairfield, Utah. Other records from the University of Utah collection (Woolstenhulme 1942b) were from "1 mile N of Vernal," Oakley, and Kamas, Utah; Maxwell Spring, Beaver Creek Canyon; Seven-Mile Creek at Johnson Valley Reservoir, and Smith-Morehouse Canyon (upper Weber River drainage).

Pisidium ventricosum Prime, 1851b Globular Peaclam

DESCRIPTION (Prime 1851b): Shell small, globose, inflated, short and subtruncate, whitish, glossy, thin, striae concentric, umbo prominent, the ends approaching each other. Mackie (2007): Adult shell oval in outline,

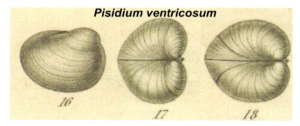

FIG. B33. *Pisidium ventricosum*. Credit: Prime 1851b.

ventricose (almost spherical in some specimens), somewhat oblique, with thin walls. Striae fine to very fine, somewhat irregular. Beaks small but prominent and situated posterior of center. Periostracum is yellowish and glossy. Dorsal margin short, well rounded, joining ends with slightly rounded angles. Anterior margin with a long, steep, slightly curved slope, joining the ventral margin low without an angle. Posterior end well rounded. Ventral margin long, well curved. Scutum and scutellum not well marked. Ligament short, thick; hinge very short, rounded. Hinge plate heavy, amply arched. Cardinals very close to anterior cusps, mainly in dorsal half of hinge plate. C3 short, posterior end club-shaped, occasionally bifid, somewhat diagonal on hinge plate, the anterior end being close to the dorsal margin. C2 somewhat peg-like or canine-like, short and low, ± parallel to the hinge plate. C4 often slightly longer but usually subequal in height and length to C2, more lamelliform or incisor-like, diagonal to hinge plate, and pointing to posterior cusp. Laterals short and stout, cusps of A2 and P2 distal or on distal side of center. Cusp of A1 and P1 central or on distal side of center. Cusps of A3 usually absorbed into hinge plate. P3 cusp very low, distal and about half the length of P1. Sulci in right valve closed proximally, occasionally also distally (in *P. rotundatum*, the sulcus is always closed only distally in anterior laterals).

Sphaeriidae

FIG. B34. *Pisidium ventricosum*, UMMZ collection. 247781: Whitehorse, Yukon; 112894: Lovely Brook, Maine; 228353: Lake Desolation, Jordan River drainage, UT; 194719: Gull and Sylvan Lakes, Alberta; 194538: Copeland Lake, Ontario; 112891: Waltham, MA. Credit: UMMZ.

SIZE (Mackie 2007): up to 3 mm long. H/L 0.95 ± 0.05; W/L 0.90 ± 0.05. Shells of newborn are 0.75–0.90 mm long. Holotype: 2.79 m long, 2.41 mm height, 2.16 mm diameter.

TYPE LOCATION: Fresh Pond, Cambridge, Massachusetts

JUNIOR SYNONYMS: *Pisidium obtusale* Pfeiffer, 1821; *P. ovum* Sterki, 1916; *P. vesiculare* var. *striatellum* Sterki, 1916. *P. rotundatum* Prime, 1851a was considered a junior synonym of this species by Herrington (1962), but Mackie (2007) noted that the lateral teeth differences separate the two species.

NOTES: More spherical (W/L 0.90 ± 0.05) than other *Pisidium* species in Utah. Also, anterior cusps of lateral teeth are central or on the distal side of center in *P. ventricosum,* whereas the cusps are proximal, or on the proximal side of center in *P. rotundatum.*

DISTRIBUTION (ANSP; Nylander 1900; Mackie 2007; Ibase; www.idigbio.org): Canada's Northwest Territories, Yukon, Saskatchewan, Quebec, Ontario, and Newfoundland. AK, CA, CO, CT, ID, IN, KY, MA, ME, MI, MN, ND, NJ, NH, NY, OH, PA, SD, WA, WI, WY. In Utah, UMMZ record (194706) from Summit County and from the Jordan River drainage (228353). There is also a USNM record (905148) from the Santa Clara River, Washington County.

Genus *Sphaerium* Scopoli, 1777 Fingernail Clams

Sphaerium has 8 species recognized in North America, including the introduced type species *Sphaerium corneum* L. (Mackie 2007). Shell is thin, oval, oblong, or nearly circular and more or less inflated. Beaks subcentral or directed slightly forward. Posterior part of the shell slightly longer than the anterior. Shell surface smooth or concentrically striate. Cardinal teeth small, one in the right and two in the left valve. Lateral teeth thin and lamelliform, two anterior and two posterior lateral teeth in the right valve, one anterior and one posterior lateral tooth in the left valve. Adult shell usually longer than 7 mm. Nepionic valves not distinctly separated from subsequent growth of the shell. Siphons united at their base but separate for most of their length (Mackie et al. 2007). In *Sphaerium* there are 1 to 4 brood sacs. Spawning is sequential, with various ages of embryos at different stages of development found in the sacs (Cooley and O'Foighil 2000). Extramarsupial larvae are usually >4 mm.

Sphaerium nitidum Westerlund, 1876 Arctic Fingernail Clam

DESCRIPTION (Westerlund 1876, Mackie 2007): Shell globose, ventricose (swollen), with thin walls; beak tumid, upper portion large, central, low, and rounded. Striae moderately fine, uniformly spaced and maintaining their size up and over the beaks. Scutum and scutellum absent. Periostracum very glossy to a dull gloss, creamy in juveniles, brown in adults. Dorsal margin short, slightly rounded. Ventral margin very long, gently rounded, joining the anterior end much higher than the posterior end. Posterior margin inclined toward dorsal margin, creating a rounded angle with the ventral margin and a distinct bend at the dorsal margin. Anterior margin round, joining ventral margin near midline without an angle and the dorsal margin with a sharp angle.

Hinge very short, relatively narrow, widening slightly at the cusps below the dorsal-anterior and dorsal-posterior margins. Ligament short, relatively thick. Cardinals small and thin; interior cardinal tooth of left valve slightly curved, only the inner half slightly obscured. C3 is parallel with the narrow hinge plate, at or below the median line; posterior end of C3 often bifid, and only slightly thicker, but much shorter than the anterior end close to the anterior lateral teeth. C2 straight, incisor shaped, parallel with hinge plate. Anterior half of C4 overlapping, and parallel with C2, the posterior part inclined toward inner margin of hinge plate and directed slightly inside cusp of P2. Cusps of all laterals distal or on distal side of center, low and slightly pointed with steep sides, except P2, which is often low and blunt with slightly inclined sides.

Call (1886, p. 8; for synonym *Sphaerium uintaense*): "Shell thin, small, globose, ventricose, slightly inequilateral, posterior and anterior margins well rounded, very slightly produced posteriorly; umbones large, subcalyculate, full, rounded, dark, retaining embryonic shell, approximate; basal margin rounded, thus giving a circular outline to shell; epidermis shining, dark straw or olive colored, substriate, light yellowish on basal margin; cardinal teeth microscopic, slightly in advance of the middle region of the umbones, not widely separating; lateral teeth small, short, somewhat upcurved. Viewed in profile from in front, the point of junction of lower portion of valves with the embryonic shell appears as a well-marked obtuse angle."

FIG. B35. *Sphaerium nitidum* (original figure of synonym *S. uintaense* Call, 1886. Credit: Call 1886).

SIZE (Mackie 2007): Usually <8.0 mm long. H/L 0.83 ± 0.02; W/L 0.58 ± 0.04. Newborn shells are usually 2.0–2.6 mm long and are thinner (W/L 0.33 ± 0.03) than adults, though H/L ratios are similar among age groups. *S. uintaense*: 4.76 mm long, diameter 4.02 mm.

TYPE LOCATION: "Siberia prope Jenissei ad Dudino (lat. 69° 15') et Lusin (lat. 68° 40')." *S. uintaense:* "A lake in the Uinta Mountains, Utah, at an elevation of 10,500 ft."

JUNIOR SYNONYMS: *Sphaerium uintaense* Call, 1886; *S. walkeri* Sterki, 1901; *S. tenue walkeri* Sterki, 1916; *Musculium uintaense* "Call" Sterki 1916.

NOTES: Distinguished from *S. striatinum* by the more inflated, roundly oval form of the shell. Odhner (1929) has described some of the anatomy. Herrington (1950) found no evidence of a breeding season in Great Slave Lake, Canada. Clarke (1973) and Heard (1977) found gravid clams in summer, but spring and fall data are lacking. Specimens have been found with up to 13 larvae (Heard 1977).

DISTRIBUTION: UMNH record from stream leading into Fish Lake, Sevier County, Utah. UMNH record from Francis, Utah, as *Musculium uintaense*.

Sphaerium occidentale Prime, 1853 Fingernail Clam

DESCRIPTION (Prime 1853, p. 276, for *Cyclas ovalis*): "Shell: small, pellucid, fragile, transparent, equilateral, somewhat elongated, not much inflated; outline of the valves oval; beaks small, rounded, not prominent; lines of growth light and regular; color in some specimens of a light yellow, in others of a greenish yellow; hinge margin very gently rounded; teeth small, cardinal teeth double."

Mackie (2007): Adult shell nearly oval in outline, moderately inflated, with thin walls. Striae fine, becoming faint near the beaks; usually at least one annulus (growth rest mark). Beaks large, rounded, slightly elevated above dorsal margin. Periostracum dull or with a dull gloss, yellowish-brown or cream. Ligament long and thick.

FIG. B36. *Sphaerium occidentale.* Brooks Lake Creek Falls, WY 192390; Spokane Falls, WA 104259; Weber Canyon, UT 104286; Lincoln, MT 192372; Napanee River, Ontario, Canada 191422, Franklin, ID 104260. Credit: UMMZ.

Dorsal margin moderately long, gently curved (almost straight in newborn) joining ends with only very slight angles. Anterior end more broadly curved than posterior end. Most specimens have a ridge on the inside of the shell about midway between the end and extending from near the beaks to the ventral edge of the shell.

Hinge very long (>90% shell length). Hinge plate long, narrow to heavy. Cardinal teeth large and distinct, closer to anterior laterals than to posterior laterals. C3 mostly toward the outside of, and parallel with, the hinge plate, curved or bent, the posterior part enlarged and often bifid. C2 usually relatively straight, sometimes canine-shaped in heavier specimens, ± parallel with the hinge plate. C4 incisor-shaped, low, often inconspicuous, its anterior third overlapping the posterior part of C2, and angling gently across the hinge plate. Laterals fairly slim and long, except A3 and P3, which have very short, low, blunt, distal cusps (i.e., A3 and P3 are mostly cusps, with no sides). Cusps of A2 central or proximal. Cusps of P1 and P2 central, proximal, or distal. Cusp of A1 central or on proximal side of center. All cusps, except A3 and P3, relatively tall and pointed or slightly blunt on top.

SIZE (Herrington 1962; Mackie 2007): rarely exceeds 8 mm in shell length, average about 6.5 mm, typical range 2.3–7.0 mm; height 1.8–6.0; diameter 1.0–4.1. H/L ratio 0.83 ± 0.02; W/L 0.54 ± 0.03. Newborn are 1.9–2.2 mm long and laterally compressed (W/L 0.41 ± 0.03). Prime (1853) type: 6.60 mm long, 5.69 mm wide, 4.32 mm diameter.

TYPE LOCATION: Oswego and Greenwich, New York; Columbus, Ohio.

JUNIOR SYNONYMS (Prime 1895; Mackie 2007): *Cyclas ovalis* Prime 1853 (preoccupied); *Sphaerium tenue* Prime; *Sphaerium occidentalis* Prime, 1860; *S. occidentale amphibium* Sterki, 1907. Last change to *Sphaerium occidentale* by Prime, 1865.

NOTES: More circular in outline than *S. striatinum*. Life span of up to 3 years (Herrington 1948; McKee and Mackie 1981). Only clams >3.0 mm contain embryos; extramarsupial larvae (1.50–2.20 mm long) are found in individuals >5.5 mm shell length. The number of shelled larvae per parent ranges from 11.5 ± 1.4 in November to 6.2 ± 1.5 in April. Newborn appear generally twice a year (spring and fall), although ontogenetic stages are present in the population throughout the year. The estimated mitotic chromosome number was 189–213 (most were 204–209; Petkevičiūtė et al. 2007).

DISTRIBUTION: Alberta, British Columbia, Manitoba, Ontario, New Brunswick, Quebec; AL, AR, DE, FL, GA, ID, IL, IN, KS, LA, MA, MI, MN, MS, MT, NJ, NY, NC, OH, OK, OR, PA, SC, TN, VT, VA, WA, WI, WY. Utah record from Weber Canyon (University of Florida, 88310; UMMZ, 104286).

Sphaerium striatinum Lamarck, 1818 Striate Fingernail Clam

DESCRIPTION (Mackie 2007): Adult shell somewhat elongate, inequipartite, compressed or inflated. Young shells are rectangular in outline. Beaks vary from low and slightly raised above dorsal margin to high and swollen. Shell wall moderately thin to fairly thick. Striae irregular; some specimens heavily striated over entire shell; some have heavy striae in beak region only, others have weak striae in the region of beaks, but striae become increasingly heavier toward the growing edge of shell. Still others may have weak striae over the whole shell. Scutum and scutellum usually well marked. Periostracum dull, color corneous, dark in older specimens or with dark patches on different parts of the shell. Ligament long and thick. Hinge relatively long, greatly or unevenly curved with a slight to moderate dip between the cardinals and anterior lateral teeth. Dorsal margin arched slightly to greatly. Ventral margin broadly rounded, joining anterior margin high, with a less rounded angle than posterior margin. Posterior edge usually a slope, joining margins with or without an angle.

Inner anterior lateral teeth project considerably into shell interior. Hinge plate fairly long, narrow to moderately heavy. Laterals short, somewhat curved, proximal ends of A1 and P1 often dipping under the hinge plate. A1 and A3 very short, cusps low and blunt, central to distal of center; sulcus often closed proximally and usually conspicuously tuberculated. P1 and P3 longer, cusps low, blunt and distal, or on distal side of center. A2 and P2 tall, cusps of P2 more blunt than A2, but P2 usually more truncated. Cardinals rather small, closer to anterior laterals, and occupy most of the thickness of the hinge plate. C3 curved or bent, ± parallel with hinge plate; posterior part usually thickened and bifid, and close to the inner margin of hinge plate; the anterior part of C3 is usually thin and slightly below outer margin of the hinge plate. Sometimes C3 is of uniform thickness throughout, in which case it is diagonal to hinge plate. C2 slightly inclined on hinge plate, usually stump-like with end thickened near inner margin of hinge plate; if thickened toward outer margin, C2 often low and inconspicuous. C4 rather straight in dorsal half of hinge plate and inclined toward inner edge of anterior laterals. C4 begins outside the center of C2.

FIG. B37. *Sphaerium striatinum.* Older shells on the left and center have lost the dark periostracum (pigmented epidermal layer) seen on fresh shells (right). Credit: E. Wagner.

SIZE (Mackie 2007): Shell length rarely > 8 mm; usually about 6.5 mm maximum length. H/L ratio 0.83 ± 0.02; W/L ratio 0.54 ± 0.03. Newborn are usually 1.9–2.2 mm long at birth and are laterally compressed (W/L 0.41 ± 0.03).

TYPE LOCATION: unknown

JUNIOR SYNONYMS (Prime 1895; Herrington and Taylor 1958; Johnson 1959; Burch 1975; Mackie 2007): *Cyclas striatina* Lamarck, 1818; *Cyclas sulcata* Lamarck, 1818 (*nomen nudum*); *C. triangularis* Say, 1829; *C. edentula* Say, 1829; *C. staminea*

Conrad, 1834b; *C. dentata* Haldeman, 1841b; *C. flava, C. emarginata, C acuminata, C. solidula, C. modesta, C. aurea, C. albula, C. distorta, C. inornata, C. simplex,* and *C. tenuistriata* Prime, 1852; *C. bulbosa* (Anthony) and *C. furcata* (Rafinesque) (Prime 1853); *C. fuscatum* (Rafinesque) (Prime 1860); *Sphaerium vermontanum* Prime, 1861; *S. tumidum* and *S. spokani* Baird, 1863; *S. mormonicum* Sowerby, 1878; *S. lilycashense* Baker, 1898; *S. jalapensis* Pilsbry, 1903; *S. hendersoni* Sterki, 1906c; *S. stamineum forbesi* Baker, 1906; *S. pilsbryanum* Sterki, 1909c; *S. acuminatum* and *S. ohioense* Sterki, 1913; *S. torsum, S. stamineum* var. *wisconsinense,* and *S. striatinum* var. *corpulentum* Sterki, 1916; *S. declive* Sterki, 1922; *S. notatum, S. notatum neoshense,* and *S. notatum gibbosum* Sterki, 1927; *S. bakeri* (Sterki) Baker, 1928; *S. solidum* var. *winnebagoensis* Baker, 1928; *S. flavum* var. *foxense* Baker, 1928. Brooks and Herrington (1944) synonymized many of Sterki's species with *S. striatinum* including *S. striatinum attenuatum* (*nomen nudum*), *S. striatinum badium, S. browni, S. cerinum, S. canadense, S. concinnum, S. cumberlandicum, S. striatinum decorum, S. acuminatum diaphanum, S. elegans, S. eminens, S. notatum glabrum, S. acuminatum lacuum, S. stamineum laeve, S. laevigatum, S. striatinum novangliae* (*nomen nudum*), *S. nylanderi, S. obtusum*; *S. ornatum, S. redense, S. regulare*; *S. striatinum rugosum, S. striatinum solidulum, S. striatinum tenerrum,* and *S. wrighti.*

NOTES (Herrington and Taylor 1958): Found in a variety of habitats from Great Lakes to small lakes, rivers, and creeks in mud, sand, gravel, or the cracks of rocks; However, it is usually not found in ponds, bogs, or swamps. Canadian specimens are smaller and the heavier ones among them have a shorter outline than fossils. Lee (1999) estimated that there were about 152 chromosomes in *S. striatinum,* with a probable base haploid number of 19.

DISTRIBUTION (Herrington and Taylor 1958): Historically found widely in North America from Panama to the Northwest Territories of Canada. In Utah, it has been found living in Tony Grove Lake and Hyrum Reservoir, Cache County, and below Cutler Reservoir in Box Elder County. Call (1884) noted this species as *Sphaerium dentatum,* found abundantly in Utah Lake and as a semi-fossil from the Sevier Desert (Sevier Lake) and near the mouth of the Jordan River in the Great Salt Lake. Baily and Baily (1951–1952) reported *S. pilsbryanum* from Bear and Utah lakes. The Smithsonian has a specimen from the mouth of the Jordan River.

Henderson and Daniels (1916) found dead shells in Cache Valley.

Bibliography

Adams, A. 1854. "Description of Twenty-Seven New Species of Shells from the Collection of Hugh Cuming, Esq." *Proceedings of the Zoological Society of London* 22:311–317.
Adams, C. B. 1840. "Description of Thirteen New Species of New England Shells." *Boston Journal of Natural History* 3:318–331.
———. 1841. "Catalogue of the Mollusca of Middlebury, Vermont, and Vicinity, with Observations." *American Journal of Science and Arts* 40:266–277.
———. 1842. Chapter VI. "Invertebral Animals of Vermont." In *History of Vermont, Natural, Civil, and Statistical: In Three Parts, with an Appendix. Vol. 1*, edited by Z. Thompson, 151–173. Burlington, VT: Self-published.
———. 1849. "Description of Supposed New Species and Varieties of Helicidae from Jamaica." *Contributions to Conchology* 1:17–38.
Adams, H., and A. Adams. 1858 (1854–1858). *The Genera of Recent Mollusca: Arranged According to Their Organization*. (In three volumes). London. Dates: pp. 1–92 (1854); 93–284 (1855); 285–412 (1856); 413–540 (1857); 541–660 (1858).
Adanson, M. 1757. *Histoire Naturelle du Sénégal. Coquillages*. Paris: Jean-Baptiste Pauche.
Albers, J. C. 1850. *Die Heliceen, nach Natürlicher Verwandtschaft*. Berlin: T. C. F. Enslin.
Albrecht, C., K. Kuhn, and B. Streit. 2007. "A Molecular Phylogeny of Planorboidea (Gastropoda, Pulmonata): Insights from Enhanced Taxon Sampling." *Zoologica Scripta* 36:27–39.
Alda, P., M. Lounnas, A. A. Vazquez, R. Ayaqui, M. Calvopiña, M. Celi-Erazo, R. T. Dillon Jr., et al. 2021. "Systematics and Geographical Distribution of *Galba* Species, a Group of Cryptic and Worldwide Freshwater Snails." *Molecular Phylogenetics and Evolution* 157:107035.
Alder, J. 1838. "Supplement to a Catalogue of the Land and Fresh-Water Testaceous Mollusca, Found in the Vicinity of Newcastle." *Transactions of the Natural History Society of Northumberland, Durham and Newcastle upon Tyne* 2:337–342.
Aldridge, D. W., and R. F. McMahon. 1978. "Growth, Fecundity, and Bioenergetics in a Natural Population of the Asiatic Freshwater Clam *Corbicula manilensis* Philippi, from North Central Texas." *Journal of Molluscan Studies* 44:49–70.
Allard, D., M. Koski, and T. A. Whitesel. 2012. *Western Pearlshell Mussel Reproduction in Merrill Creek, Oregon: Timing; 2010 Annual Report*. Vancouver, WA: U.S. Fish and Wildlife Service, Columbia River Fisheries Program.
———. 2013. *Western Pearlshell Mussel Reproduction in Merrill Creek, Oregon: Timing; 2011 Annual Report*. Vancouver, WA: U.S. Fish and Wildlife Service, Columbia River Fisheries Program. https://www.fws.gov/columbiariver/publications/Merrill_Creek_2011_Final.pdf
Allen, E. 1924. "The Existence of a Short Reproductive Cycle in *Anodonta imbecilis*." *Biological Bulletin* 46:88–94.
Alonso, A., and P. Castro-Diez. 2012. "The Exotic Aquatic Mud Snail *Potamopyrgus antipodarum* (Hydrobiidae: Mollusca): State of the Art of a Worldwide Invasion." *Aquatic Science* 74:375–383.
Ancey, C. F. 1881. "De Quelques Mollusques Nouveaux ou Peu Connus." *Le Naturaliste* 3(#51):403–404.
———. 1886. "Diagnoses of a Few Subgenera in Helicidae." *The Conchologists Exchange* 1(5):20.
———. 1887a. Correspondence (no title, re: *Pristiloma, Averellia, Pilsbrya*). *The Conchologists Exchange* 1:54–55.

———. 1887b. "Description of North American Shells." *The Conchologists Exchange* 2:63–64, 79–80.

Andrade, S. C. S., and V. N. Soferini. 2006. "Transfer Experiment Suggests Environmental Effects on the Radula of *Littoraria flava* (Gastropoda: Littorininidae)." *Journal of Molluscan Studies* 72:111–116.

Andrusov, N. I. 1897. "Fossil und Lebende Dreissenidae Eurasiens: Atlas von XX Phototypischen Tafeln in 4°." *Travaux de la Société des Naturalistes de St. Pétersbourg. Section de Géologie et de Minéralogie* 25:285–286.

AnimalBase 2019. http://www.animalbase.uni-goettingen.de/zooweb/servlet/AnimalBase/list/genera?family=93

Annandale, N. 1920. "Materials for a Generic Revision of the Freshwater Gastropod Molluscs of the Indian Empire." *Records of the Indian Museum* 19:107–115.

Anthony, J. G. 1840. "Description of Three New Species of Shells." *Boston Journal of Natural History* 3:278–279.

Antonov, P. I., and G. L. Shkorbatov. 1990. "Ecological–Physiological Characteristics of *Dreissena* of the Lower Reaches of the Dnieper River." In *Vid i Yego Areale: Biologiya, Ekologia i Prodktivnost Vodnykh Bespozvonochnykh* [Species in its distribution range: Biology, ecology and production of aquatic invertebrates], 126–130. Minsk: Navuka I Technika Publ. [in Russian].

Araujo, R., S. Schneider, K. J. Roe, D. Erpenbeck, and A. Machrodom. 2017. "The Origin and Phylogeny of Margaritiferidae (Bivalvia: Unionoida): A Synthesis of Molecular and Fossil Data." *Zoologica Scripta* 46:289–307.

Arey, L. B. 1932. "The Formation and Structure of the Glochidial Cyst." *Biological Bulletin* (Woods Hole) 62:212–221.

Askenova, O. V., I. N. Bolotov, M. Y. Gofarov, A. V. Kondakov, M. V. Vinarski, Y. V. Bespalaya, Y. S. Kolosova, et al. 2018. "Species Richness, Molecular Taxonomy and Biogeography of the Radicine Pond Snails (Gastropoda: Lymnaeidae) in the Old World." *Scientific Reports* 8, Article 11199. https://www.nature.com/articles/s41598-018-29451-1

Babrakzai, N., W. B. Miller, and O. G. Ward. 1975. "Cytotaxonomy of Some Arizona Oreohelicidae (Gastropoda: Pulmonata)." *Bulletin of the American Malacological Union* 40:4–11.

Baily, J. 1957. "Opinion 432, Rejection as an Unpublished Proof of the Paper by Binney (W. G.) dated "9th December 1863" and entitled *"Synopsis of the Species of Air-Breathing Mollusks of North America"* (Confirmation of Ruling Given in Opinion 87) and Validation under the Plenary Powers of the Generic Name "*Carinifex*" Binney, 1865 (Class Gastropoda)." *Opinions and Declarations Rendered by the International Commission of Zoological Nomenclature* 14:374–392.

Baily, J. L., and R. I. Baily. 1951. "Further Observations on the Mollusca of the Relict Lakes in the Great Basin." *Nautilus* 65(2):46–53.

———. 1952. "Further Observations on the Mollusca of the Relict Lakes in the Great Basin (Part 2)." *Nautilus* 65(3):85–93.

Baird, W. 1863. "Descriptions of Some New Species of Shells, Collected at Vancouver Island and in British Columbia by J. K. Lord, Esq., Naturalist to the British North-American Boundary Commission, in the Years 1858–1862." *Proceedings of the Zoological Society of London*: 66–70.

Baker, F. C. 1897. "Notes on Radulae." *Journal of the Cincinnati Society of Natural History* 19:81–92.

———. 1898. "A New *Sphaerium*." *Nautilus* 12:65–66.

———. 1902. *The Mollusca of the Chicago Area*. Bulletin No. 111 of the Natural History Survey, Chicago Academy of Sciences.

———. 1905a. "A New Species of *Lymnaea* from Ohio, with Notes on *Lymnaea parva* Lea." *Nautilus* 19:51–53.

———. 1905b. "Critical Notes on the Smaller Lymnaeas." *Nautilus* 18:125–127.

———. 1906. "A Catalogue of the Mollusca of Illinois." *Bulletin of the State Laboratory of Natural History* 7:53–136.

———. 1907. "Description of a New Species of Lymneae." *Nautilus* 20:125–127.

———. 1908. "Note on *Lymnaea desidiosa* Say." *Nautilus* 22:20–23, Plate 3.

———. 1909. "A New Species of *Lymnaea*." *Nautilus* 22:140–141.

———. 1911. *The Lymnaeidae of North and Middle America, Recent and Fossil*. Special Publication No. 3. Chicago: Chicago Academy of Sciences.

———. 1912. "A New *Lymnaea* from Montana." *Nautilus* 26:115–116.

———. 1919. "Freshwater Mollusca from Colorado and Alberta." *Bulletin of the American Museum of Natural History* 41:527–539.

———. 1920. "Notes: *Physa smithiana*, New Name for *Physa smithii*." *Nautilus* 33:142.

———. 1924. "A new *Physa* from California (*P. marci*)." *Nautilus* 38:15.

———. 1926. "Nomenclatural Notes on American Freshwater Mollusca." *Transactions of the Wisconsin Academy of Sciences, Arts, and Letters* 22:193–205.

———. 1927. "On the Division of the Sphaeriidae into Two Subfamilies and the Description of a New Genus of Unionidae, with Descriptions of New Varieties." *American Midland Naturalist* 10:220–223.

———. 1928. *The Freshwater Mollusca of Wisconsin, Part 1—Gastropoda and Part 2—Pelecypoda*. Wisconsin Geological and Natural History Survey Bulletin 70.

———. 1930. "Description of a New Variety of *Valvata lewisi* Currier (*V. lewisi ontariensis*)." *Nautilus* 44:119–220.

———. 1934. "New Lymnaeidae from the United States and Canada: 1. California, Oregon and Other Western States." *Nautilus* 48:17–20.

———. 1935. "The Generic Position of *Planorbis umbilicatellus* with the Description of a New Group of Planorbidae." *Nautilus* 49:46–48.

———. 1945. "*The Molluscan Family Planorbidae*. Urbana: University of Illinois Press.

Baker, F. C., and J. Henderson. 1929. *Fossaria perplexa*. *Nautilus* 42:103–104.

Baker, H. B. 1922. "Notes on the Radula of the Helicinidae." *Proceedings of the Academy of Natural Sciences Philadelphia* 74:29–67.

———. 1927. "Minute Mexican Land Snails." *Proceedings of the Academy of Natural Sciences Philadelphia* 79:223–246.

———. 1928. "Minute American Zonitidae." *Proceedings of the Academy of Natural Sciences of Philadelphia* 80:1–44, +8 plates.

———. 1929a. "*Pseudovitrea minuscula neomexicana*." *Proceedings of the Academy of Natural Sciences Philadelphia* 81:262

———. 1929b. "New Southern Appalachian Land Snails." *Nautilus* 42:86–98.

———. 1930a. "The North American Retinellae." *Proceedings of the Academy of Natural Sciences of Philadelphia* 82:193–219, Plates 9–14.

———. 1930b. "Mexican Mollusks Collected for Dr. Bryant Walker in 1926." *Occasional Papers of the Museum of Zoology University of Michigan* 220:1–45, Plates 7–11.

———. 1930c. "New and Problematic West American Land-Snails." *Nautilus* 43:95–101, 121–128.

———. 1931. "Nearctic Vitrene Land Snails." *Proceedings of the Academy of Natural Sciences Philadelphia* 83:85–117.

———. 1935. "Review of the Anatomy of Pupillidae and Related Groups." *Manual of Conchology* 28:191–220, Plates 1–31.

———. 1941. "Zonitid Snails from Pacific Islands Parts 3 and 4." *Bernice P. Bishop Museum Bulletin* 166:205–370.

Bandel, K., and T. Kowalke. 1999. "Gastropod Fauna of the Cameroonian Coasts." *Helgoland Marine Research* 53:129–140.

Bank, R. A. 2017. "MolluscaBase: Classification of the Recent Terrestrial Gastropoda of the World, last updated 16 July 2017." https://molluscabase.org/aphia.php?p=sourcedetails&id=278821

Bank, R. A., P. Bouchet, G. Falkner, E. Gittenberger, B. Hausdorf, T. von Proschwitz, and T. E. J. Ripken. 2001. "Supraspecific Classification of European Non–Marine Mollusca." *Heldia* 4(1–2):77–128.

Bargues, M. D., and S. Mas-Coma. 1997. "Phylogenetic Analysis of Lymnaeid Snails Based on 18S rDNA sequences." *Molecular Biology and Evolution* 14(5):569–577.

Bargues, M. D., M. Vigo, P. Horák, J. Dvorak, R. A. Patzner, J. P. Pointier, M. Jackiewicz, et al. 2001. "European Lymnaeidae (Mollusca: Gastropoda), Intermediate Hosts of Trematodiases, Based on Nuclear Ribosomal DNA ITS-2 Sequences." *Infection, Genetics and Evolution* 1:85–107.

Bargues, M. D., P. Horák, R. A. Patzner, J. P. Pointier, M. Jackiewicz, C. Meier-Brook, and S. Mas-Coma. 2003. "Insights into the Relationships of Palearctic and Nearctic Lymnaeids (Mollusca: Gastropoda) by rDNA ITS-2 Sequencing and Phylogeny of Stagnicoline Intermediate Host Species of *Fasciola hepatica*." *Parasite* 10:243–255.

Bargues, M. D., P. Artigas, M. Jackiewicz, J. P. Pointier, and S. Mas-Coma. 2005. "Ribosomal DNA ITS—1 Sequence Analysis of European Stagnicoline Lymnaeidae (Gastropoda). In *Beiträge zur Süsswaser-Malakologie, Festschrift für Claus Meier-Brook und Hans D. Boeters*, edited by P. Glöer and G. Falkner. *Heldia (Munchner Malakologische Mitteilungen)* 6: 57–68.

Bargues, M. D., R. L. Mera y Sierra, P. Artigas, and S. Mas-Coma. 2012. "DNA Multigene Sequencing of Topotypic Specimens of the Fascioliasis Vector *Lymnaea diaphana* and Phylogenetic Analysis of the Genus *Pectinidens* (Gastropoda)." *Memorias del Instituto Oswaldo Cruz* (Rio de Janeiro) 107(1):111–124.

Barker, G. M. 1999. *Naturalized Terrestrial Stylommatophora (Mollusca: Gastropoda)*. Fauna of New Zealand 38. Lincoln, New Zealand: Manaaki Whenua Press.

———. 2001. "Gastropods on Land: Phylogeny, Diversity, and Adaptive Morphology." Chap. 1 In *The Biology of Terrestrial Mollusks*, edited by G. M. Barker, 1–146. Wallingford, UK: CABI Publishing.

Barnes, D. H. 1823. "On the Genera *Unio* and *Alasmodonta*. *American Journal of Science and Arts* 6:127, 258–280.

Barnhart, M. C., W. R. Haag, and W. N. Roston. 2008. "Adaptations to Host Infection and Larval Parasitism in Unionioda." *Journal of the North American Benthological Society* 27:370–394.

Baršienè, J., G. Tapia, and D. Barsyte. 1996. "Chromosomes of Mollusks Inhabiting Some Mountain Springs of Eastern Spain." *Journal of Molluscan Studies* 62:539–543.

Batsch, A. J. G. C. 1789. *Versuch einer Anleitung, zur Kenntniß und Geschichte der Thiere und Mineralien, für Akademische Vorlesungen Entworfen, und mit den Nöthigsten Abbildungen Versehen. Vol. 2, Besondre Geschichte der Insekten, Gewürme und Mineralien*. Jena: Akademische Buchhandlung.

Baudon, A. 1857. "Essai Monographique Sur les Pisidies Francaises." *Memoires des le Societe de l'Academie Oise, Beauvais* 3:315–367.

Beck, H. H. 1837 (pp.1–100)–1838(pp. 101–124). *Index Molluscorum Praesentis aei Musei Principis Augustissimi Christiani Frederici*. Hafniae.

———. 1847. "Verzeichniss einer Sammlung von Landconchylien aus den Dänischen Staaten in Europa." *Amtlicher Bericht uber die Fünfundzwanzigste Versammlung der Gessellschaft Deutscher Naturforscher und Ärzte in Kiel im September 1846* 24:122–124.

Beetle, D. 1961. "Mollusca of the Big Horn Mountains." *Nautilus* 74:95–102.

———. 1987. "The Genus *Oreohelix* (Pulmonata: Oreohelicidae) in Two Western Canyons of the Big Horn Mountains, Wyoming." *The Festivus* 19(7):66–72.

———. 1989. "Checklist of Recent Mollusca of Wyoming, U.S.A." *Great Basin Naturalist* 49 (4):637–645.

———. 1997. "Recolonization of Burned Aspen Groves by Land Snails." *Yellowstone Science* 5(3):6–8.

Beggel, S., A. F. Cerwenka, J. Brandner, and J. Geist. 2015. "Shell Morphological Versus Genetic Identification of Quagga Mussel (*Dreissena bugensis*) and Zebra Mussel (*Dreissena polymorpha*)." *Aquatic Invasions* 10(1):93–99.

Behrens, L., and D. L. Strayer. 2007. *Impacts of an Invasive Snail on Benthic Macroinvertebrate Communities*. Undergraduate Ecology Research Report, Hamline University, St. Paul, MN. https://www.caryinstitute.org/sites/default/files/public/reprints/Behrens_2007_REU.pdf

Beiler, R. 1992. "Gastropod Phylogeny and Systematics." *Annual Review of Ecology, Evolution, and Systematics* 23:311–338.

Benoit, L. 1875. *Illustrazione Sistematica Critica Iconografica de'Testacei Estramarini della Sicilia Ulteriore e delle Isole Circostanti 8*. Nobile, Napoli.

Benson, W. H. 1842. Mollusca. In *General features of Chusan, with Remarks on Flora and Fauna of that Island*, T. Cantor, 486–490, *Annals and Magazine of Natural History: Zoology, Botany, and Geology* 9.

Bequaert, J. C., and W. B. Miller. 1973. *Mollusks of the Arid Southwest, with an Arizona Checklist*. Tucson: University of Arizona Press.

Berry, E. G. 1931. "Mollusca of Lamb's Canyon, Utah." *Nautilus* 44:113–114.

———. 1932. "The Rediscovery of *Oreohelix haydeni* (Gabb)." *Nautilus* 46:56–57, Plate 3.

———. 1943. *The Amnicolidae of Michigan: Distribution, Ecology, and Taxonomy*. University of Michigan, Miscellaneous Publications of the Museum of Zoology No. 57.

Berry, S. S. 1919. "Three New Alpine Vertigos from California." *Nautilus* 33:48–52.

———. 1922. *Land Snails from the Canadian Rockies*. Victoria Memorial Museum Biological Series No. 8, Bulletin No. 36.

Bersine, K., V. E. F. Brenneis, R. C. Draheim, A. M. Wargo-Rub, J. E. Zamon, R. K. Litton, S. A. Hinton, et al. 2008. "Distribution of the Invasive New Zealand Mudsnail (*Potamopyrgus antipodarum*) in the Columbia River Estuary and its First Recorded Occurrence in the Diet of Juvenile Chinook Salmon (*Oncorhynchus tshawytscha*)." *Biological Invasions* https://doi.org/10.1007/s10530-007-9213-y.

Bertsch, H. 1976. "Intraspecific and Ontogenetic Radular Variation in Opistobranch Systematics (Mollusca: Gastropoda)." *Systematic Zoology* 25:117–122.

Bespalaya, Y., I. Bolotov, O. Aksenova, A. Kondakov, I. Paltser, and M. Gofarov. 2015. "Reproduction of *Pisidium casertanum* (Poli 1791) in Arctic Lake." *Royal Society of Open Science* 2(1): PMC4448796. https://dx.doi.org/10.1098%2Frsos.140212

Binney, A. 1840–1841. "A Monograph of the Helices Inhabiting the United States." *Boston Journal of Natural History* 3(3):353–394, continued in 3(4):405–438, Plates 7–26.

———. 1842. "Descriptions of Some of the Species of Naked, Air-Breathing Mollusca, Inhabiting the United States." *Boston Journal of Natural History* 4(2):163–175.

———. 1843. "Minutes of the March 15, 1843 Meeting (*Pupa gouldii*)." *Proceedings of the Boston Society of Natural History* 1:104–106.

Binney, W. G. 1857. "Descriptions of American Land Shells." *Proceedings of the Academy of Natural Sciences of Philadelphia* 9:18–19, 183–192.

———. 1858a. "Notes on American Land Shells, No. 3." *Proceedings of the Academy of Natural Sciences of Philadelphia* 10:114–116.

———. 1858b. "Notes on American Land Shells, No. 4." *Proceedings of the Academy of Natural Sciences of Philadelphia* 10:197–211.

———. 1858c. *The Complete Writings of Thomas Say on the Conchology of the United States*. New York: Balliere.

———. 1859. *The Terrestrial Air-Breathing Mollusks of the United States, and the Adjacent Territories of North America, Vol. 4*. Philadelphia: Little, Brown.

———. 1865a. *Land and Freshwater Shells of North America. Part II. Pulmonata, Limnophila, and Thalassophila*. Smithsonian Miscellaneous Collections 7 (publ. 1867)(Article 2).

———. 1865b. *Land and Freshwater Shells of North America. Part III. Ampullaridae, Valvatidae, Viviparidae, Freshwater Rissoidae, Cyclophoridae, Truncatellidae, Freshwater Neritidae, Helicinidae*. Smithsonian Miscellaneous Collections 7 (publ. 1867)(Article 3).

———. 1875. "On the Jaw and Lingual Membrane of North American Terrestrial Pulmonata." *Proceedings of the Academy of Natural Sciences of Philadelphia* 27:140–243, Plates 1–21.

———. 1876. "On the Lingual Dentition and Genitalia of *Partula* and Other Pulmonata." *Proceedings of the Academy of Natural Sciences of Philadelphia* 27:244–254, Plates 19–21.

———. 1878. *The Terrestrial Air-breathing Mollusks of the United States and Adjacent Territories of North America. Vol. 5*. Cambridge: Welch, Bigelow & Co. (also issued as *Bulletin of the Museum of Comparative Zoology,* Vol. 4.).

———. 1885. "A Manual of the American Land Shells." *Bulletin of the United States National Museum* 28:1–528.

———. 1886–1888. "A Second Supplement to the 5th Volume of the Terrestrial Air-Breathing Mollusks of the United States and Adjacent Territories." *Bulletin of the Museum of Comparative Zoology* 13:23–48, Plates 1–3.

———. 1890. "A Third Supplement to the Fifth Volume of the Terrestrial Air—Breathing Mollusks of the United States and Adjacent Territories. *Bulletin of the Museum of Comparative Zoology* 19:183–226, Plates 1–11.

———. 1892. "The Terrestrial Air-Breathing Mollusks of the United States and Adjacent Territories of North America." 4th Supplement. *Bulletin of the Museum of Comparative Zoology* 22:163–204, Plates 1–4.

Binney, W. G., and T. Bland. 1869. "Land and Freshwater Shells of North America. Part 1. Pulmonata Geophila." *Smithsonian Miscellaneous Collections* 8 (Article 3[194]):1–316.

Blainville, H. M. D. de. 1824. *Mollusques. Dictionnaire des Sciences Naturelles, Tome 32*. Strasbourg: Levrault.

Bland, T. 1862. " Remarks on Certain Species of North American Helicidae. *Annals of the Lyceum of Natural History New York* 7:26–39, 115–142.

———. 1866. "Descriptions of New Species of North American Land Shells." *American Journal of Conchology* 2(4):371–374.

———. 1867. "Notes on Certain Terrestrial Mollusca with Descriptions of New Species (Read September 25, 1865)." *Annals of the Lyceum of Natural History New York* 8:155–170.

———. 1875a. "Notes on the Sub-Generic Character of *Helix jamaicensis* Chemn., and on Certain Terrestrial Mollusks from Haiti; with Description of a New Species of *Helix* from Colorado." *Annals of the Lyceum of Natural History of New York* 11:146–154.

———. 1875b. "Notes on Certain Terrestrial Mollusks, with Descriptions of New Species." *Annals of the Lyceum of Natural History of New York* 11:72–87.

Boettger, C. R. 1913. "Beiträge zur Kenntnis der Molluskenfauna Schlesiens." *Nachrichtsblatt der Deutschen Malakozoologischen Gesellschaft* 45–46:153–170.

Bogan, A. E. 2008. "Global Diversity of Freshwater Mussels (Mollusca, Bivalvia) in Freshwater." *Hydrobiogia* 595:139–147.

Bolotov, I. N., I. V. Vikhrev, Y. V. Bespalaya, M Y. Gofarov, A. V. Kondakov, E. S. Konopleva, N. N. Bolotov, et al. 2016. "Multi-Locus Fossil-Calibrated Phylogeny, Biogeography, and a Subgeneric Revision of the Magaritiferidae (Mollusca: Bivalvia: Unionida)." *Molecular Phylogenetics and Evolution* 103:104–121.

Born, I. A. 1778. *Index Rerum Naturalium Musei Caesarei Vindobonensis. Pars I. ma. Testacea*. Verzeichniss der Naturlichen Seltenheiten des K. K. Naturalien Cabinets zu Wien. Erster Theil. Schalthier (1–140) 1–458. Vindobonae: Kraus.

Bouchet, P., and J. P. Rocroi. 2005. "Classification and Nomenclator of Gastropod Families." *Malacologia* 47(1–2):1–397.

Bouchet, P., J. P. Rocroi, R. Bieler, J. G. Carter, and E. V. Coan. 2010. "Nomenclator of Bivalve Families with a Classification of Bivalve Families." *Malacologia* 52(2):1–184.

Bouchet, P., J. P. Rocroi, B. Hausdorf, A. Kaim, Y. Kano, A. Nützel, P. Parkhaev, et al. 2017. "Revised Classification, Nomenclator and Typification of Gastropod and Monoplacophoran Families." *Malacologia* 61(1–2):1–526.

Bourguignat, J. R. 1853. *Catalogue Raisonné des Mollusques Terrestres et Fluviatiles Recueillis Par M.F. de Saulcy*. Paris: Gide et J. Baudry.

———. 1861. "Des Limaces Algériennes." *Revue et Magasin de Zoologie Pure et Appliquée, Series 2*, Tome 13:299–306.

———. 1862. *Les Spiciléges Malacologiques*. Paris: Chez Balliére et Fils.

———. 1863. Mollusques Nouveaux, Litigieux ou Peu Connus. *Revue et Magasin de Zoologie Pure et Appliquée, Series 2*, Tome 15:179–187.

———. 1864. *Malcologie de l'Algérie ou Histoire Naturelle des Animaux Mollusques Terrestres et Fluviatiles Recueillis jusq'à ce Jour Dand nos Possesions du Nord de l'Afrique. Tome 2*. Paris: Challamel Ainé, Bastide.

———. 1869. "Catalogue des Mollusques Terrestres et Fluviatiles des Environs de Paris a l'Époque Quaternaire." In *La Seine–1. Le Bassin Parisien aus Áges Antéhistoriques*, 3–32, with 7 plates, F. E. Belgrand. Paris: Imprimerie Imperiale.

———. 1877. "Descriptions de Deux Nouveaux Genres Algériens, Suivies d'Une Classification des Families et des Genres de Mollusques Terrestres et Fluviatiles du Systéme Européen." *Bulletin de la Societé des Sciences Physiques et Naturelles de Toulouse* 3 (1875–1876) (1):49–101.

———. 1880. "Aperçu Monographique des Zonites Crystalliniens et Fulviens d'Europe et Descriptions d'Espécies Espagnoles." In G. Servain, *Études sur les Mollusques Recuillis in Espagne et en Portugal*, Saint-Germain: Bardin.

———. 1884. "Histoire des Melaniens du Systéme Européen." *Annales de Malacologie* 2(1):1–168.

———. 1889. *Mollusques de l'Afrique Équatoriale de Moguedouchou a Bagamoyo et de Bagamoyo au Tanganika*. Paris: D. Dumoulin et Cie.

Bowler, P. A. 1991. "The Rapid Spread of the Freshwater Hydrobiid Snail *Potamopyrgus antipodarum* (Gray) in the Middle Snake River, Southern Idaho." *Proceedings of the Desert Fishes Council* 21:173–182.

Bowler, P. A., and T. J. Frest. 1992. "The Non-Native Snail Fauna of the Middle Snake River, Southern Idaho." *Proceedings of the Desert Fishes Council* 23:28–44.

Branson, B. A. 1959. "An Ecological Observation on *Succinea avara*." *Nautilus* 72:145–146.

———. 1963. "The Recent Gastropoda of Oklahoma, V. Terrestrial Species, Valloniidae, Achantinidae, and Succineidae." *Proceeding of the Oklahoma Academy of Science* (for 1962): 73–87.

Brard, P. 1815. *Histoire des Coquilles Terrestres et Fluviatiles qui Vivent Aux Environs de Paris*. Paris-Geneva: J.J. Pashoud.

Broderip, W. J. 1839. "Malacology." *The Penny Cyclopaedia of the Society for the Diffusion of Useful Knowledge (London)* 14:314–325.

Brooks, S. T. 1936. "Some Molluscs from Utah." *Nautilus* 50:13–14.

———. 1939. "*Oreohelix eurekensis uinta*." *Nautilus* 52:105–106.

Brooks, S. T., and H. B. Herrington. 1944. "The Sphaeriidae, a Preliminary Survey." *Nautilus* 57:93–97.

Brown, T. 1827. *Illustrations of the Conchology of Great Britain and Ireland*. Edinburgh: Lizars & Lizars and S. Highley.

Bruguiere, J. G. 1792. *Encyclopedique Méthodique, Histoire Naturelle des Vers, Tome 1:* Paris: Panckoucke.

Brusina, S. 1894. "Note Préliminaire sure le Groupe des Aphanotylus, Nouveau Genre de Gastropoda de l'Horizon á Lyrcaea, et sur Quelques Autres Espéces Nouvelles de Hongrie." *Glasnik Hrvatskoga Naravoslovnoga Društva* 6:241–248.

Bibliography

Bullen, R. A. 1901. " On Two Apparently New Species of *Corbicula*." *Proceedings of the Malacological Society of London* 4:254–255.

Burch, J. B. 1960a. " Chromosome Studies of Aquatic Pulmonate Snails." *Nucleus* 3(2):177–204, 4 plates.

———. 1960b. "Chromosomes of *Gyraulus circumstriatus*, a Freshwater Snail." *Nature* 4723 (May 7):497–498.

———. 1975. *Freshwater Sphaeriacean Clams (Mollusca: Pelecypoda) of North America*. Hamburg, MI: Malacological Publications.

———. 1982. "North American Freshwater Snails: Identification Keys, Generic Synonymy, Supplemental Notes, Glossary, References, Index." Society for Experimental and Descriptive Malacology. *Walkerana* 1(4):217–365.

———. 1989. "North American Freshwater Snails: Introduction, Systematics, Nomenclature, Identification, Morphology, Habitats, Distribution." *Walkerana* 2(6):1–80.

Burch, J. B., and P. A. Ayers. 1973. "Breeding Experiments with *Stagnicola elodes* and *S. emarginata*." *Malacological Review* 6:51–52.

Burch, J. B., and Y. Jung. 1988. "Land Snails of the University of Michigan Biological Station Area." *Walkerana* 2(9):1–175.

———. 1993. "Polyploid Chromosome Numbers in the *Torquis* Group of the Freshwater Snail Genus *Gyraulus* (Mollusca: Pulmonata: Planorbidae)." *Cytologia* 58:145–149.

———. 1972. "The Systematic Position of "*Lymnaea*" *bulimoides*." *Malacological Review* 5:16–17.

Burch, J. B., C. M. Patterson, and R. Natarajan. 1966. "Chromosomes of Four Species of North American Succineidae." *Venus* 24(4): 342–353. https://www.jstage.jst.go.jp/article/venusjjm/24/4/24_KJ00004340281/_pdf

Burch, J. B., and J. L. Tottenham. 1980. "North American Freshwater Snails. Species List, Ranges and Illustrations." *Walkerana* 1(3):81–215.

Burke, T. E. 2013. *Land Snails and Slugs of the Pacific Northwest*. Corvallis: Oregon State University Press.

Burlakova, L. E., and A. Y. Karatayev. 2007. "The Effect of Invasive Macrophytes and Water Level Fluctuations on Unionids in Texas Impoundments." *Hydrobiologia* 586:291–302.

Cailliaud, F. 1823–1827. *Voyage a Méroé, au Fleuve Blanc: au-delà de Fazoql dans le Midi du Royaume de Sennâr, a Syouah et dans Cinq Autres Oasis, Fait dans les Années 1818, 1820, 1821 et 1822*. (4 vol. text, 2 vol. plates). Paris.

Calkins, W. W. 1878. "A New Species of Succinea." *The Valley Naturalist* 1(11):57.

———. 1880. "Description and Figure of a New Species of *Zonites* from Illinois." *The Valley Naturalist* 2(1):53.

Call, R. E. 1884. "On the Quaternary and Recent Mollusca of the Great Basin, with Descriptions of New Forms." *Bulletin of the U.S. Geological Survey* 11.

———. 1886. "On Certain Recent, Quaternary, and New Freshwater Mollusca." *Proceedings of the Davenport Academy of Natural Sciences* 5(1884–1889):1–8.

Call, R. E., and H. A. Pilsbry. 1886. "On *Pyrgulopsis*: A New Genus of Rissoid Mollusk, with Descriptions of Two New Forms." *Proceedings of the Davenport Academy of Natural Sciences* 5 (1884–1889):9–14.

Cameron, R. A. D., G. A. Holyoak, D. T. Holyoak, Y. Yanes, M. R. Alonso, and M. Ibáñez. 2013. "Shell Characters and Genital Anatomy of *Atlantica calathoides* and Transfer of the Genus *Atlantica* from Discidae to Gastrodontidae (Gastropoda: Pulmonata)." *Journal of Conchology* 41(3):287–294.

Campbell, D. C., S. A. Clark, and C. Lydeard. 2017. "Phylogenetic Analysis of the Lancinae (Gastropoda, Lymnaeidae) with a Description of the U.S. Federally Endangered Banbury Springs Lanx." *ZooKeys* 663:107–132.

Carpenter, P. P. 1856–1857. "Monograph of the Shells Collected by T. Nuttall, esq., on the Californian Coast, in the Years 1834–5." *Proceedings of the Zoological Society of London* 24:209–281.

———. 1864. "Supplementary Report on the Present State of Our Knowledge with Regard to the Mollusca of the West Coast of North America." *Report of the British Association for the Advancement of Science* 33:517–686.

Caruana, A. A. 1867. *Enumeratio Ordinata Molluscorum Gaulo–Melitensium of the Late Mr. Giuseppe Mamo*. Malta: British Press.

Catlow, A., and L. Reeve 1845. *The Conchologist's Nomenclator: A Catalogue of All the Recent Species of Shells Included under the Subkingdom "Mollusca," With Their Authorities*. London: Reeve Brothers.

Caziot, E. 1910. *Étude sur Les Mollusques Terrestres et Fluviatiles de la Principauté de Monaco et du Département des Alpes-Maritimes*. Monaco: Imprimerie de Monaco.

Chamberlin, R. V. 1933. "Observations on *Stagnicola kingi* (Meek), Living and Extinct." *Nautilus* 46:97–100.

Chamberlin, R. V., and E. G. Berry. 1929. "Notes on the Mollusca of Southeastern Utah." *Nautilus* 42:123–125.

———. 1930. "Mollusca from the Henry Mountains and Some Neighboring Points in Utah." *Bulletin of the University of Utah* 21(2) [Biological Series 1, Vol. 3]:1–7.

———. 1931. "A New Mollusk of the Genus *Pupoides* from Southern Utah." *Proceedings of the Biological Society of Washington* 44:7–8.

———. 1933. "Mollusks of the Pliocene Deposits at Collinston, Utah." *Nautilus* 47:25–29.

Chamberlin, R. V., and D. T. Jones. 1929. "A Descriptive Catalog of the Mollusca of Utah." *Bulletin of the University of Utah* 19(4):i–ix, 1–203.

Charpentier, J. 1837. *Catalogue des Mollusques Terrestres et Fluviatiles de la Suisse*. Neuchatel: Societe Helvetique des Sciences Naturelles.

Chemnitz J. H. (1780–1795). *Neues Systematischen Conchylien Cabinet*. Nürnberg: G. N. Raspe. Vol. 4 [1780], Vol. 5 [1781], Vol. 6 [1782], Vol. 7 [1784], Vol. 8 [1785], Vol. 9(1) [1786], Vol. 9(2) [1786]; vol. 10 [1788], Vol. 11 [1795].

Chen, H. T. 1942. "The Metacercaria and Adult of *Centrocestus formosanus* (Nishigori, 1924), with Notes on the Natural Infection of Rats and Cats with *C. armatus* (Tanabe, 1922)." *Journal of Parasitology* 28:285–298.

Cheng, Y. W., and L. L. LeClair. 2011. "A Quantitative Evaluation of the Effect of Freezing Temperatures on the Survival of New Zealand Mudsnails (*Potomopyrgus antipodarum* Gray, 1843), in Olympia Washington's Capitol Lake." *Aquatic Invasions* 6(1):47–54.

Children, J. G. 1823. "Lamarck's Genera of Shells." *Quarterly Journal of Science, Literature and the Arts* 15:243.

Chong, J. P., J. C. Brim Box, J. K. Howard, D. Wolf, T. L. Meyers, and K. E. Mock. 2008. "Three Deeply Divided Lineages of the Freshwater Mussel Genus *Anodonta* in Western North America." *Conservation Genetics* 9:1303–1309.

Clarke, A. H. 1973. "The Freshwater Molluscs of the Canadian Interior Basin." *Malacologia* 13(1–2):1–509.

———. 1981. *The Freshwater Molluscs of Canada*. National Museum of Natural Sciences, National Museum of Canada, Ottawa, Canada.

———. 1991. *Status Survey of Selected Land and Freshwater Gastropods in Utah*. Final Report to the U.S. Fish and Wildlife Service by EcoSearch Inc., Portland, TX.

Clarke, A. H., and P. Hovingh. 1994. Studies on the Status of Endangerment of Terrestrial Mollusks in Utah. Malacology Data Net (EcoSearch Inc., Portland, TX) 3(5/6):101–138.

Claxton, W. T., and E. G. Boulding. 1998. "A New Molecular Technique for Identifying Field Collections of Zebra Mussel (*Dreissena polymorpha*) and Quagga Mussel (*Dreissena bugensis*) Veliger Larvae Applied to Eastern Lake Erie, Lake Ontario, and Lake Simcoe." *Canadian Journal of Zoology* 76:194–198.

Clench, W. J. 1924. "A New Species of *Physa* from Texas (*P. bottimeri*)." *Nautilus* 38:12–13.

———. 1925. "Notes on the Genus *Physa* with Descriptions of Three New Subspecies." *Occasional Papers of the Museum of Zoology (Univ. Michigan)*161:1–10, Plate 1.

———. 1926. "Three New Species of *Physa*." *Occasional Papers of the Museum of Zoology (University of Michigan)* 168:1–6, Plate 1.

———. 1930. "Notes on Physidae with Descriptions of New Species." *Occasional Papers of the Boston Society of Natural History* 5:301–315.

———. 1935. "*Physa ampullacea* 'Gould' Binney (*Physa gouldi* n.sp.)." *Nautilus* 49:30–32.

———. 1962. "A Catalogue of the Viviparidae of North America with Notes on the Distribution of *Viviparus georgianus* Lea." *Occasional Papers on Mollusks (Museum of Comparative Zoology, Harvard)* 2(27):261–288.

Clench, W. J., and S. L. H. Fuller. 1965. "The Genus *Viviparus* (Viviparidae) in North America." *Occasional Papers on Mollusks (Museum of Comparative Zoology, Harvard)* 2(32):385–412.

Clessin, S. 1876. *Deutsche Excursions-Mollusken-Fauna. Auflage 1*. Nürnberg: Bauer & Raspe.

———. 1877–1879. "Die Familie der Cycladeen." *Systematisches Conchylien—Cabinet von Martini und Chemnitz* 9(3):1–283. Nürnberg: Bauer & Raspe.

———. 1886. "Die Familie der Limnaeiden Enthaltend die Genera *Planorbis*, *Limnaeus*, *Physa*, und *Amphipeplea*." *Systematisches Conchylein-Cabinet von Martini und Chemnitz* 1(17):1–430 (+55 plates). Nürnberg: Bauer & Raspe.

———. 1887–1890. *Die Mollusken-Fauna Mitteleuropa's. II. Tiel. Die Molluskenfauna Oesterreich-Ungarns und der Schweiz*. Nürnberg: Bauer & Raspe. Part 1: pp. 1–160 (1887); Part 2:161–320 (1887); Part 3: 321–480 (1888), Part 4: 418–624 (1889); Part 5:625–858 (1890).

Cockerell, T. D. A. 1888a. *Physa elliptica*. *Hartwicke's Science Gossip: An Illustrated Medium of Interchange and Gossip* 24:163.

———. 1888b. "Shells from Niagra, Mollusca in Colorado." *Hartwicke's Science Gossip: An Illustrated Medium of Interchange and Gossip* 24:257.

———. 1888c. "On *Agriolimax montanus* in Colorado." *Journal of Conchology* 5(12):358–360.

———. 1889. "Preliminary Remarks on the Molluscan Fauna of Colorado." *Journal of Conchology* 6:60–65.

———. 1890. "A List of the Mollusca of Colorado." *Nautilus* 3:99–103.

———. 1891a. "On the Geographical Distribution of Slugs." *Proceedings of the Zoological Society of London, for 1891*(2):214–226.

———. 1891b. "Notes (*Pupa coloradoensis*, *P. ingersolli*)." *The British Naturalist* 1 (5):99–100.

———. 1891c. "New Forms of American Mollusca." *Zoe* 2(1):18.

———. 1892a. "New Varieties of American Mollusca." *Journal of Conchology* 7:39.

———. 1892b. "New Varieties of California Slugs." *The Conchologist* 2(3):72.

———. 1893a. "A Checklist of the Slugs." *The Conchologist* 2(7–8):168–76, 185–232.

———. 1893b. "Notes on the Variation of Some North American Mollusca." *British Naturalist* 3:80–83.

———. 1897a. "A Few Notes on Slugs." *Journal of Conchology* 6(1):3–5.

———. 1897b. "*Vertigo coloradoensis* and Its Allies." *Nautilus* 10:134–135.

———. 1897c. "A New Form of *Pupa*. (*P. gabbii* var. *mexicanorum*)." *Nautilus* 10:143.

———. 1899. "Notes on the *indentata* group of *Vitrea*." *Nautilus* 12:120.

———. 1902. "*Physa virgata* mut. *alba* nov." *Journal of Malacology* 9(4):138.

———. 1904. "A new *Oreohelix*." *Nautilus* 18:113–114.

———. 1905. "A Fossil Form of *Oreohelix yavapai* Pilsbry." *Nautilus* 19:46–47.

———. 1914. "Some Slugs (*Agriolimax*) from Guatemala." *Nautilus* 28:55–58.

Coen, G. S. 1945. "Catologo dei Gasteropodi Polmonati della Colezione Coen." *Pontificale Academiae Scientiarum Scripta Varia* 3:1–99.

Coker, R. E., A. F. Shira, H. W. Clark, and A. D. Howard. 1919. "Natural History and Propagation of Freshwater Mussels." *Bulletin of the Bureau of Fisheries*, Document 893.

Colbeau, J. 1865. "Excursions et Decouvertes Malacologiques." *Mémoires de al Societe Malacologique de Belgique* 1:23–120, 2 plates.

Collado, G. A. 2014. "Out of New Zealand: Molecular Identification of the Highly Invasive Freshwater Mollusk *Potamopyrgus antipodarum* (Gray, 1843) in South America." *Zoological Studies* 53:70. http://www.zoologicalstudies.com/content/53/1/70.

Conrad, T. A. 1834a. "Description of Some New Species of Freshwater Shells from Alabama, Tennessee, etc." *American Journal of Science and Arts* 25(1):338–343.

———. 1834b. *New Freshwater Shells of the United States, with Lithographic Illustrations, and a Monograph of the Genus Anculotus of Say; Also a Synopsis of the American Naiades*. Philadelphia, PA: Dobson Publ.

———. 1855. "Description of a New Species of *Melania* (*M. exigua*)." *Proceedings of the Academy of Natural Sciences* 7:269.

Cooke, A. H. 1895. "Molluscs." In *Cambridge Natural History Vol. III*. Edited by S. F. Harmer and A. E. Shipley, 1–462. London: Macmillan.

Cooke, C. M., Jr. 1921. "Notes on Hawaiian Zonitidae and Succineidae." *Occasional Papers of the Bernice Pauahi Bishop Museum of Polynesian Ethnology and Natural History* (Honolulu, HI: Bishop Museum Press) 7(12):262–277, Plates 24, 25.

Cooley, L. R., and D. O'Foighil. 2000. "Phylogenetic Analysis of the Sphaeriidae (Mollusca: Bivalvia) Based on Partial Mitochondrial 16S rDNA Gene Sequences." *Invertebrate Biology* 199(3):299–308.

Cooper, J. G. 1868–1872a. "On Shells of the West Slope of North America." *Proceedings of the California Academy of Sciences (Series 1)* 4:150–154.

———. 1868–1872b. "The West Coast Freshwater Univalves, No. 1." *Proceedings of the California Academy of Sciences (Series 1)* 4:92–100.

———. 1872. "On New California Pulmonata, etc." *Proceedings of the Academy of Natural Sciences of Philadelphia* 24:143–154.

———. 1892. "Additional Notes and Descriptions of New Species." *Proceedings of the California Academy of Sciences (Series 2)* 3:70–90.

Correa, A. C., J. C. Escobar, P. Durand, F. Renaud, P. David, P. Jarne, J. P. Pointier, et al. 2010. "Bridging Gaps in the Molecular Phylogeny of the Lymnaeidae (Gastropoda; Pulmonata), Vectors of Fascioliasis." *BMC Evolutionary Biology* 10:381. http://www.biomedcentral.com/1471-2148/10/381

Correa, A. C., J. S. Escobar, O. Noya, L. E. Velásques, C. González-Ramírez, S. Hurtrez-Boussès, and J. P. Pointier. 2011. Morphological and Molecular Characterization of Neotropic Lymnaeidae (Gastropoda: Lymnaeoidea), Vectors of Fasciolosis. *Infection, Genetics, and Evolution* 11:1978–1988.

Costa, A. 1882. "Notizie ed Osservarzioni Sulla Geo-Fauna Sarda: Memoria Prima; Risultamento de ricerche fatte in Sardegna nel Settember 1881." *Atti Della Real Accademia Delle Scienze Fisiche e Matematiche* 9 (Article 11):1–42.

Costa, E. M. da. 1778. *Historia Naturalis Testaceorum Britanniae or The British Conchology*. London: self-published.

Cowie, R. H. 2011. Case 3518. *Cornu* Born, 1778 (Mollusca, Gastropoda, Pulmonata, Helicidae): Request for a Ruling on the Availability of the Generic Name. *Bulletin of Zoological Nomenclature* 68(2):97–104.

Cox, J. C. 1864. "Descriptions of Twenty-Six New Species of Australian Land-Shells." *Annals and Magazine of Natural History, Including Zoology, Botany, and Geology (3rd Series)* 14:180–197.

Cox, T. J., and J. C. Rutherford. 2000. "Thermal Tolerances of Two Stream Invertebrates Exposed to Diurnally Varying Temperature." *New Zealand Journal of Marine and Freshwater Research* 34(2):203–208.

Crabb, E. D. 1927a. "Genetic Experiments with Pond Snails *Lymnaea* and *Physa*." *American Naturalist* 61:54–67.

———. 1927b. "Anatomy and Function of the Reproductive System in the Snail *Lymnaea stagnalis*." *Biological Bulletin* 53(2):55–66.

Crandall, O. A. 1901. "The American Physae." *Nautilus* 15:54–58.

Bibliography

Criscione, F., and W. F. Ponder. 2013. "A Phylogenetic Analysis of Rissooidean and Cingulopsoidea Families (Gastropoda: Caenogastropoda)." *Molecular Phylogenetics and Evolution* 66(3):1075–1082.

Crosse, H., and P. Fischer. 1870. "Diagnoses Molluscorum Novorum, Reipublicae Mexicanae et Guatemalae Incolarum." *Journal de Conchyliologie* 18:297.

———. 1881. "Diagnoses Molluscorum Novorum, Reipublicae Mexicanae Incolarum." *Journal de Conchyliogie* 29 (ser. 3, t. 21):334–335.

Culver, M., H. W. Herrmann, M. Miller, B. Roth, and J. Sorenson. 2013. *Anatomical and Genetic Variation of Western Oxyloma (Pulmonata: Succineidae) Concerning the Endangered Kanab Ambersnail (Oxyloma haydeni kanabense) in Arizona and Utah*. Scientific Investigation Report 2013–5164. U.S. Department of the Interior, U.S. Geological Survey, Reston, VA.

Curole, J. P., and T. D. Kocher. 2002. "Ancient Sex-Specific Extension of the Cytochrome C Oxidase II Gene in Bivalves and the Fidelity of Doubly-Uniparental Inheritance." *Molecular Biology and Evolution* 19:1323–1328.

Currier, A. O. 1867. "Description of New Species of Freshwater Shells from Michigan." *American Journal of Conchology* 3:112–113.

Cuvier, G. 1816 (work generally dated 1817, but see Roux 1976). *Le Régne Animal Distribué d'Aprés son Organisation, Tome 2 Contenant les Reptiles, les Poissons, les Mollusques, les Annélides*. Paris: Deterville.

Dall, W. H. 1877. "*Hyalina subrupicola* n.s." In *On a New Cave Fauna in Utah*, edited by A. S. Packard Jr., 163–64. Bulletin of the U.S. Geological and Geographical Survey of the Territories (Hayden Expedition) Vol. 3.

———. 1884. "Contribution to the History of the Commander Islands No. 3. Report on the Mollusca of the Commander Islands Bering Sea collected by Leonard Stejneger in 1882 and 1883." *Proceedings of the United States National Museum* 7:340–349.

———. 1885. "Notes on Some Floridean Land and Freshwater Shells with a Revision of the Auriculacea of the Eastern United States." *Proceedings of the U.S. National Museum* 8:254–289.

———. 1895. "Description of a New *Vitrea* from Puget Sound." *Nautilus* 9:27–28.

———. 1897. "Report on the Mollusks Collected by the International Boundary Commission of the United States and Mexico, 1892–1894." *Proceedings of the U.S. National Museum* 19(1111):333–379, 3 plates.

———. 1895–1898. "Contributions to the Tertiary Fauna of Florida, with Special Reference to the Silex Beds of Tampa and the Pliocene Beds of the Calaoosahatchie River." *Transactions of the Wagner Free Institute of Philadelphia* 3 (Part 3, pp. 484–570; 1895) (Part 4, pp. 571–947, 1898).

———. 1905. "Land and Freshwater Mollusks." *Harriman Alaska Expedition* Vol. 13:1–171, Plates 1–2.

———. 1919. "The Mollusca of the Arctic Coast of America Collected by the Canadian Arctic Expedition West from Bathurst Inlet with an Appended Report on a Collection of Pleistocene Fossil Mollusca." *Report of the Canadian Arctic Expedition 1913–18, Vol. 8 (Mollusks, Echinoderms, Coelenterates, Etc.)*:3–37.

———. 1926. "Expedition to the Revillagigedo Islands, Mexico, in 1925." *Proceedings of the California Academy of Science (Series 4)* 15:467–490, Plate 36.

Darling, C. R. 1987. *Annual Narrative Report for Calendar Year 1986: Review and Approvals*. Fish Springs National Wildlife Refuge, Dugway, UT.

Davis, G. M., and S. L. H. Fuller. 1981. "Genetic Relationship among Recent Unionacea (Bivalvia) of North America." *Malacologia* 20:217–53.

Dawson, G. M. 1875. "Land and Freshwater Mollusca, Collected During the Summers of 1873–74, in the Vicinity of the Forty-Ninth Parallel—Lake of the Woods to the Rocky Mountains." In *Report on the Geology and Resources of the Region in the Vicinity of the Forty-ninth Parallel,* from *Lake of the Woods to the Rocky Mountains with Lists of Plants and Animals Collected, and Notes on the Fossils,* edited by G. M. Dawson, 347–350. Montreal: Dawson Brothers.

Dayrat, B., M. Conrad, S. Balayan, T. R. White, C. Albrecht, R. Golding, S. R. Gomes, et al. 2011. "Phylogenetic Relationships and Evolution of Pulmonate Gastropods (Mollusca): New Insights from Increased Taxon Sampling." *Molecular Phylogenetics and Evolution* 59:425–437.

De Camp, W. H. 1881. *List of the Shell-Bearing Mollusca of Michigan*. Kent Science Institute Miscellaneous Publ. No. 5.

De Kay, J. E. 1843. *Zoology of New York or the New-York Fauna. Part 5. Mollusca*. Albany, NY: Carroll & Cook.

D'Eliscu, P. D. 1972. "Observation of the Glochidium, Metamorphosis, and Juvenile of *Anodonta californiensis* Lea, 1857." *Veliger* 15(1):57–59.

Delpey, G. 1941. "Gastérpodes Marins. Paléontologie, Stratigraphie." *Mémoires de la Societé Géologique de France, New Series* 19(3–4), Mémoire 43:1–144, 28 plates.

Dermott, R., and D. Kerec. 1997. "Changes to the Deepwater Benthos of Eastern Lake Erie Since the Invasion of *Dreissena*: 1979–1993." *Canadian Journal of Fisheries and Aquatic Sciences* 54:922–930.

Dermott, R., and M. Munawar. 1993. "Invasion of Lake Erie Offshore Sediments by *Dreissena*, and Its Ecological Implications." *Canadian Journal of Fisheries and Aquatic Sciences* 50:2298–2304.

Deshayes, M. 1838. "Description des Coquilles Fossiles Recueillies en Crimée." *Mémoires de la Société Géologique de France* 3:37–69.

———. 1853. *Catalogue of the Conchifera or Bivalve Shells in the Collection of the British Museum. Part 1. Veneridae, Cyprinidae and Glaucomonidae*. London: British Museum, Taylor and Francis.

———. 1854–1855. "Description of New Species of Shells from the Collection of H. Cuming, Esq." *Proceedings of the Zoological Society of London* 22:13–16 (1854), 17–23 (1855).

Dickinson, B. D., and B. E. Sietman. 2008. *Recent Observations of Metamorphosis Without Parasitism in* Utterbackia imbecilis. Minnesota Department. Natural Resources, St. Paul. https://www.researchgate.net/profile/Bernard_Sietman/publication/325603798_Recent_Observation_of_Metamorphosis_Without_Parasitism_in_Utterbackia_imbecillis/links/5b17f103a6fdcca67b5d97d4

Dillon, R.T., Jr., C. E. Earnhardt, and T. P. Smith. 2004. "Reproductive Isolation Between *Physa acuta* and *Physa gyrina* in Joint Culture." *American Malacological Bulletin* 19(1/2):63–68.

Dillon, R. T., Jr., J. D. Robinson, T. P. Smith, and A. R. Wethington. 2005. "No Reproductive Isolation Between Freshwater Pulmonate Snails *Physa virgata* and *P. acuta*." *The Southwestern Naturalist* 50(4):415–422.

Dillon, R. T., Jr., A. R. Wethington, and C. Lydeard. 2011. "The Evolution of Reproductive Isolation in a Simultaneous Hermaphrodite, the Freshwater Snail *Physa*." *BMC Evolutionary Biology* 11:144.

Dillon, R. T., Jr., A. R. Wethington, J. M. Rhett, and T. P. Smith. 2002. "Populations of the European Freshwater Pulmonate *Physa acuta* are Not Reproductively Isolated from American *Physa heterostropha* or *Physa integra*." *Invertebrate Biology* 121(3):226–234.

Dillwyn, L. W. 1817. *A Descriptive Catalogue of Recent Shells, Arranged According to the Linnean Method, with Particular Attention to the Synonymy*. London: J. McCreery

Dodd, B. J., M. C. Barnhart, C. L. Rogers-Lowery, T. B. Fobian, and R. V. Dimock Jr. 2005. "Cross-Resistance of Largemouth Bass to Glochidia of Unionid Mussels." *Journal of Parasitology* 91(5):1064–1072.

d'Orbigny, A. 1839. "Mollusques, Echinodermes, Foraminiféres et Polypiers Recueillis aus Iles Canaries." In *Histoire Naturelle des Iles Canaries, Tome 2, Part 2 (Zoologie),* edited by P. B. Webb and S. Berthelot, 1–155, with 14 plates.

Draparnaud, J. P. R. 1801. *Tableau des Mollusques Terrestres et Fluviatiles de la France*. Paris: Bossange, Masson, et Besson.

———. 1805. *Historie Naturelle des Mollusques Terrestres et Fluviatiles de la France*. Paris: Plassan, Renaud.

Dubansky, B., B. Whitaker, and F. Galvez. 2011. "Influence of Cortisol on the Attachment and Metamorphosis of Larval *Utterbackia imbecilis* on Bluegill Sunfish (*Lepomis macrochirus*)." *Biological Bulletin* 220:97–106.

Duncan, A., and R. Z. Klekowski 1967. "The Influence of Salinity on the Survival, Respiratory Rate, and Heart Beat of Young *Potomopyrgus jenkinsi* (Smith) Prosobranchiata." *Comparative Biochemistry and Physiology* 22:495–505.

Dundee, D. S. 1974. "Catalog of Introduced Molluscs of Eastern North America (North of Mexico)." *Sterkiana* 55:1–37.

———. 1986. "Notes on the Habits and Anatomy of the Introduced Land Snails, *Rumina* and *Lamellaxis* (Subulinidae)." *Nautilus* 100:32–37.

Dupuy, D. 1849. "Catalogus Extramarinorum Galliae Testaceorum Ordine Alphabeticus Dispositus Brevioribus Specierum Nondum Descriptarum Diagnosibus." Troisième Fascicule of *Histoire Naturelle de Mollusques Terrestres et d'Eau Douce qui Vivent en France*. D. Dupuy. [12 pages lacking page numbers]. Paris: Victor Masson.

———. 1847–1852. *Histoire Naturelle des Mollusques Terrestres et d'Eau Douce qui Vivent en France*. Paris: Victor Masson. (pp. 1–106, 1847; pp.107–226, 1848, pp. 227–330, 1849, pp. 331–458, 1850; pp. 459–594, 1851, pp. 595–738, 1851–1852) 31 plates.

D'Urban, W. S. M. 1859. *Catalogue of Animals and Plants Collected and Observed in the Valley of the River Rouge and the Neighboring Township, in the Counties of Argentevil and Ottawa*. Progress Report of the Geological Survey of Canada, pp. 241–243.

Dybdahl, M. F., and S. L. Kane. 2005. "Adaptation vs. Phenotypic Plasticity in the Success of a Clonal Invader." *Ecology* 86(6):1592–1601.

Dybowski, W. 1903a. "Bemerkungen über die Gegenwärtige Systematik der Süsswasser-Schnecken." *Nachrichtsblatt der Deutchen Malakozoologischen Gesellschaft* 35(9–10):130–144.

———. 1903b. "*Limnaea* (Linnus) *lagorii*." *Bulletin de l'Académie Impériale des Sciences de Saint Petersbourg* 18:113.

———. 1913. "Mollusken aus der Ufer-region des Baikalsees." *Annuaire du Musee Zoologique de l'Académie Impériale des Sciences de Saint Petersbourg* 17:12–13, 167–218, Plates 3–7.

Dysthe, J. C., T. Rodgers, T. W. Franklin, K. J. Carim, M. K. Young, K. S. McKelvey, K. E. Mock, et al. 2018. "Repurposing Environmental DNA Samples—Detecting the Western Pearlshell (*Margaritifera falcata*) as a Proof of Concept." *Ecology and Evolution* 8:2659–2670.

Eckblad, J. W., and M. H. Shealy. 1972. "Predation of Largemouth Bass Embryos by the Pond Snail *Viviparus georgianus*." *Transactions of the American Fisheries Society* 101:734–738.

Ecosearch. 1993. *Status Survey of Fifteen Species and Subspecies of Aquatic and Terrestrial Mollusks from Utah, Colorado, and Montana*. Draft Report for the U.S. Fish and Wildlife Service, Contract 14–16–0006–91–046. Ecosearch Inc., Portland, TX.

Elrod, M. J. 1901. "Collecting Shells in Montana." *Nautilus* 15:86–89.

Esmark, F. B., and Z. A. Hoyer 1886. "Die land- und Süsswassermollusken des Arctischen Norwegens." *Malakozoologische Blatter* 8:84–123.

Etheridge, R. 1889. "The General Zoology of Lord Howe Island, Containing Also an Account of the Collections Made by the Australian Museum Collecting Party Aug–Sept. 1887." *Australian Museum Scientific Publications Memoirs* 2(1):1–42.

Fagot, P. 1883. "Diagnoses d'Espèces Nouvelles pour la Faune Française." *Bulletin de la Societe d'Histoire Naturelle de Toulouse* 17:207–224.

Fairbanks, H. L. 1975. *A Taxonomic Study of* Oreohelix haydeni *in Western Montana*. Master's Thesis, University of Montana.

Ferriss, J. H. 1910. "A Collecting Excursion North of the Grand Canyon of the Colorado." *Nautilus* 23(9):109–112.

———. 1920. "The Navajo Nation." *Nautilus* 34(1):1–14.

Férussac, J. B. L. d' Audebard de. 1807. *Essai d'Une Méthode Conchyliogique Appliquée aux Mollusques Fluviatiles et Terrestres d'Apres la Consideration de l'Animal et de son Test: Nouvelle Edition Augmentée d'une Synonymie des Espéces les Plus Remarquables, d'une Table de Concordance Systématique des Celles qui Ont eté Décrites par Geoffrey, Poiret et Draparnaud, ave Müller et Linné, et Terminé par un Catalogue d' Espéces Observees en Divers Lieux de la France, par J. Daudebard fils.* Paris: Delance.

———. 1821–1822. *Tableaux Systématiques des Animaux Mollusques, Classes en Familles Naturelles, dans Lesquels on a Etabli la Concordance de Tous les Systémes; Suivis d'un Prodrome Général pour Tous les Mollusques Terrestres ou Fluviatiles, Vivantes ou Fossiles.* Paris: Arthus Bertrand Publ.

———. 1827. "Suite du Catalogue des Especes de Mollusques Terrestries et Fluviatiles, Recueilleies par M. Rang, Dans un Voyage a Grandes-Indes." *Bulletin des Sciences Naturelles et de Geologie* (Zoologie Article 284) 10:408–413.

Fischer, P. H. 1877. "Monographische Versuche: *Paraphanta, Retinella, Mesomphix, Macrocyclis, Patera, Columna, Streptostyla, Rhynchocheila* und *Trochatella*." *Notitiae Malacologicae oder Beiträge zur näheren Kenntniss der Mollusken (von R. J. Shuttleworth)* 2(1):5–16, 30 plates.

———. 1891. *Catalogue et Distribution Geographique des Mollusques Terrestres, Fluviatiles & Marins d'une Partie de l'Indo-chine (Siam, Laos, Cambodge, Cochinchine, Annam, Tonkin).* Autun: Dejussieu Pére et Fils.

Fischer, P., and H. Crosse. 1900 (1870–1902). *Etude sur les Mollusques Terrestres et Fluviatiles du Mexique et du Guatamala. Recherches Zoologiques pour Servir a l'Histoire de la Faune de l'América Central et du Mexique. Septiéme Partie.* Paris: Imprimerie Nationale. Published in 17 parts: Vol. 1:1–152 (1870); pp.153–304 (1872); 305–464 (1873), 465–546 (1875), 547–624 (1877), 625–702 (1878). Vol. 2: 1–80 (1880), 81–128 (1886), 129–176 (1888), 177–256 (1890), 257–312 (1891), 313–392 (1892), 393–656 (1894), 657–731 (1902).

Fischer, W. G. von 1807. *Museum Demidoff, ou, Catalogue Systematique et Raisonne des Curiosites de la Nature et de l'Art: Donnees a l'Universite Imperiale de Moscou par son Excellence Monsieur Paul de Demidoff.* Vol. 3. Moscow: Univ. Imperiale de Moscou, 6 plates.

Fitzinger, L. I. 1833. "Systematisches Verzeichniss der im Erzherzogthume Oesterreich Vorkommenden Weichthiere, als Prodrom einer Fauna Desselben." *Beiträge zur Landeskunde Oesterreich's Unter der Enns.* Bd. 3:88–122.

Fleming, J. 1820. "Mollusca." In *Edinburgh Encyclopedia,* edited by D. Brewster, 14(2):598–635.

———. 1828. *A History of British Animals.* Edinburgh: Bell & Bradfute.

Forsyth, R. G. 2004. *Land Snails of British Columbia.* Royal BC Museum Handbook. Victoria: Royal British Columbia Museum.

Franke, H., F. Reidel, M. Glaubrecht, F. Kohler, and T. von Rintelen. 2007. "Evolution and Biogeography of Southeast Asian Viviparids (Gastropoda: Caenogastropoda)." In *World Congress of Malacology,* edited by K. Jordaens, N. Van Houtte, J. Van Goethem, and T. Backeljau. Antwerp, Belgium.

Franzen, D. S. 1959. "Anatomy of *Succinea ovalis* Say." *Proceedings of the Malacological Society of London* 33(November 5):193–199.

———. 1963. "Variations in the Anatomy of the Succineid Gastropod *Oxyloma retusa*." *Nautilus* 76(3):82–95.

———. 1964. "Anatomy of the Succineid Gastropod *Oxyloma haydeni*." *Nautilus* 77(3):73–81.

Frest, T. 1991. *Summary Status Reports on Eight Species of Candidate Land Snails from the Driftless Area (Paleozoic Plateau), Upper Midwest. Final Report, Contract #30181–01366.* U.S. Fish and Wildlife Service Region 3. Fort Snelling, MN.

Frest, T., and E. J. Johannes. 1993. *Land Snails of the Black Hills National Forest, South Dakota and Wyoming.* Report, Deixis Consultants, Seattle, WA.

———.1998. *Freshwater Mollusks of the Upper Klamath Lake Drainage, Oregon. 1998 Yearly Report to Oregon Natural Heritage Program.* Deixis Consultants, Seattle, WA. (not seen).

———. 2000. "An Annotated Checklist of Idaho Land and Freshwater Mollusks." *Journal of the Idaho Academy of Science* 26(2):1–51.

Gabb, W. M. 1866. "Description of Three New Species of Land Shells from Arizona." *American Journal of Conchology* 2:330–331.

———. 1868. "Description of New Species of *Pisidium* from California." *American Journal of Conchology* 4(2):69, Plate 2.

———. 1869. "Description of a New *Helix* from Utah." *American Journal of Conchology* 5:24, Plate 8.

Gangloff, M. M., K. K. Lenertz, and J. W. Feminella. 2008. "Parasitic Mite and Trematode Abundance are Associated with Reduced Reproductive Output and Physiological Condition of Freshwater Mussels." *Hydrobiologia* 610:25–31.

Gassies, J. B. 1855. "Description des Pisidies (*Pisidium*), Observées à l'état Vivant, Dans la Région Aquitanique du Sud–Oeste de la France." *Actes de la Société Linnéenne de Bordeaux* 20 (no. 1–5):330–353, 2 plates.

———. 1867. "Malacologie Terrestre et d'Eau Douce de la Région Intra-Littorale de l'Aquitaine." *Actes de la Societé Linnéenne de Bordeaux* 26(2):109–136, Plate 1.

Gebler, F. 1829. "Lettre de Mr. le Cons. de College, Dr. de Gebler, Barnaoul. le 26 Juillet 1829." *Bulletin de la Societe Imperiale des Naturalistes de Moscou* 1:184–186.

Gerard, C., A. Blanc, and K. Costil. 2003. "*Potamopyrgus antipodarum* (Mollusca: Hydrobiidae) in Continental Aquatic Gastropod Communities: Impact of Salinity and Trematode Parasitism." *Hydrobiologia* 493:167–172.

Gerber, J. 1996. "Revision der Gattung *Vallonia* Risso 1826 (Mollusca: Gastropoda: Valloniidae)." *Schriften zur Malakozoologie aus der Haus der Natur-Cismar,* Heft 8:1–227.

Germain, L. 1903. *Etude sur les Mollusques Terrestres et Fluviatiles Vivants des Environs d'Angers et du Departement de Maine-et-Loire*. Extract from Bulletin de la Societe des Sciences Naturelles de L'Ouest de la France. Nantes, France: R. Guisthau and A. Dugas. 2 plates.

———. 1911. "Mollusques Terrestres et Fluviatiles de l'Asie Antérieure (2nd note)." *Bulletin du Muséum National d'Histoire Naturelle* 17:63–67.

———. 1921. *Faune Malacologique Terrestre et Fluviatile des Iles Mascareignes*. Angers: Gaultier et Thébert.

Gerstfeldt, G. 1859. "Über Land und Süsswasser-Mollusken Sibiriens und des Amur-Gebietes." *Memoires Présentés a l'Académie Impériale des Sciences de Saint Pétersbourg par Divers Savants et dans ses Assemblées* 9:505–548, 1 plate.

Geyer, D. 1909. *Unsere Land- und Susswasser-Mollusken*. Stuttgart, Germany: Lutz Verlag. 18 plates.

Gill, T. 1871. "Arrangement of the Families of Mollusks." *Smithsonian Miscellaneous Collections* 10, Article 2(227):1–49.

Gilmore, R. J. 1917. "Notes on Reproduction and Growth in Certain Viviparous Mussels of the Family Sphaeriidae." *Nautilus* 31:16–31.

Gittenberger, E. 1977. "Beigrage zur Kenntnis der Pupillacea VII. Uber Zwei Wenig Bekannte Valloniidae." *Zoologische Mededelingen* 50:295–301.

Glöer, P. 2019. *The Freshwater Gastropods of the West-Palaearctis. Volume 1. Fresh- and Brackish Waters Except Spring and Subterranean Snails*. Self-published.

Gomes, C., R. Sousa, T. Mendes, R. Borges, P. Vilares, V. Vasconcelos, L. Guilhermino, et al. 2016. "Low Genetic Diversity and High Invasion Success of *Corbicula fluminea* (Bivalvia, Corbiculidae) (Muller, 1774) in Portugal." *PLoS ONE* 11(7):e0158108.

Goodrich, C. 1943. *The Walker–Beecher Paper of 1876 on the Mollusca of the Ann Arbor Area*. Occasional Papers of the Museum of Zoology No. 475.

Gould, A. A. 1833. *Lamarck's Genera of Shells, with a Catalogue of Species*. Translated by A. A. Gould. Boston: Allen & Ticknor.

———. 1841. *Report on the Invertebrata of Massachusetts, Comprising the Mollusca, Crustacea, Annelida, and Radiata*. Cambridge, MA: Cambridge University Press.

———. 1843. "Monograph of the Species of *Pupa* Found in the United States." *Boston Journal of Natural History* 4(3):350–360.

———. 1846. *Expedition Shells: Described for the Work of the United States Exploring Expedition Commanded by Charles Wilkes, U.S.N. During the Years 1838–1842*. Boston: Freeman & Bolles.

———. 1848a. [Untitled, describing shells of the Exploring Expedition.] *Proceedings of the Boston Society of Natural History* 2:165–167.

———. 1848b (read March 1847). "Descriptions of New Species of Limniadae from the Collection of the Exploring Expedition." *Proceedings of the Boston Society of Natural History* 2:210–212.

———. 1848c. [Untitled, describing shells collected by Dr. C.T. Jackson on the shores of Lake Superior]. *Proceedings of the Boston Society of Natural History* 2:263.

———. 1848d. "Descriptions of Shells Found in Connecticut, Collected and Named by the Late Rev. J. H. Linsley." *American Journal of Science and Arts* Series 2, 6(17):233–236.

———. 1850a. "Shells from the United States Exploring Expedition." *Proceedings of the Boston Society of Natural History* 3:292–296.

———. 1850b. "Catalogue of Shells, with Descriptions of New Species." In *Lake Superior: Its Physical Character, Vegetation, and Animals, Compared with Those of Other and Similar Regions*, L. Agassiz, 243–245. Boston: Damrell & Moore.

———. 1852. *Mollusca & Shells. U.S. Exploring Expedition during the years 1838, 1839, 1840, 1841, 1842 under the command of Charles Wilkes, U.S.N. Vol. XII*. Boston: Gould & Lincoln.

———. 1854–1856. "New Species of Land and Fresh-Water Shells from Western (N.) America." *Proceedings of the Boston Society of Natural History* 5 (1854–1856):127–130, 228–229.

Gray, J. E. 1840. *A Manual of the Land and Freshwater Shells of the British Islands (revision of W. Turton's Manual)*. London: Longman, Orme, Brown, Green & Longmans.

———. 1843. IV. "Catalogue of the Species of Mollusca and Their Shells, Which Have Hitherto Been Recorded as Found at New Zealand, With the Description of Some Lately Discovered Species." In *Travels in New Zealand, Vol. 2*, E. Dieffenbach, 228–296. London: John Murray Publ.

———. 1847. "List of Genera of Recent Mollusca, Their Synonyma and Types." *Proceedings of the Zoological Society of London* 15:129–219.

———. 1854. "A Revision of the Arrangement of the Families of Bivalve Shells (Conchifera)." *Annals and Magazine of Natural History, Ser. 2*, 13(77):408–418.

———. 1855. *Catalogue of the Pulmonata or Air-breathing Mollusca of the British Museum, Part 1*. London: Taylor & Francis.

Gregg, W. O. 1940. "A New *Oreohelix* from Southern Utah." *Nautilus* 54:95–96.

———. 1941. "Mollusca of Cedar Breaks National Monument, Utah." *Nautilus* 54:116–117.

———. 1942. "Additional Utah Records." *Nautilus* 55:143–144.

Gregg, W. O., and D. W. Taylor. 1965. "*Fontelicella* (Prosobranchia: Hydrobiidae), a New Genus of West American Freshwater Snails." *Malacologia* 3:103–110.

Griffith, E., and E. Pidgeon. 1833–1834. *The Mollusca and Radiata*. London: Whittaker.

Gude, 1911. "Note on Some Preoccupied Molluscan Generic Names and Proposed New Genera of the Family Zonitidae." *Proceedings of the Malacological Society of London* 9:269–273.

Guisti, F., L. Castagnoli, and G. Manganelli. 1985. "La Fauna Malacologica delle Faggete Italiane: Brevi Cenni di Ecologia, Elenco delle Specie e Chiavi per il Riconoscimento dei Generi e delle Entitá Più Comuni." *Bollettino Malacologico* 21(5/6):69–144.

Guisti, F., G. Manganelli, and P. Schembri. 1996. "The Non-Marine Molluscs of the Maltese Islands." *Monografie de Museo Regionale de Scienze Naturali, Torino* 15:1–607.

Gustafson, K. D., B. J. Kensinger, M. G. Bolek, and B. Luttbeg. 2014. "Distinct Snail (*Physa*) Morphotypes from Different Habitats Converge in Shell Shape and Size under Common Garden Conditions." *Evolutionary Ecology Research* 16:77–89.

Haak, D. M., B. J. Stephen, R. A. Kill, N. A. Smeenk, C. R. Allen, and K. L. Pope. 2014. "Toxicity of Copper Sulfate and Rotenone to Chinese Mystery Snail (*Bellamya chinensis*)." *Management of Biological Invasions* 5(4):371–375.

Haas, F. 1937. "Neue und Kritische Pupilliden." *Archiv fur Molluskenkunde* 69(1/2):2–18, 3 plates.

Habe, T. 1956. "Anatomical Studies on the Japanese Land Snails." *Venus (Japanese Journal of Malacology)* 19(2):109–117.

———. 1977. *Systematics of Mollusca in Japan: Bivalvia and Scaphopoda*. Tokyo: Hokuryukan Book Co.

Haldeman, S. S. 1840. *A Monograph of the Limnaides and Other Freshwater Univalve Shells of North America. No. 1*. Philadelphia: Self published, J. Dobson.

———. 1841a. "Descriptions of Four Species of *Cyclas*, Three of Which Belong to the Subgenus *Pisidium;* and Two Species of *Cypris*." *Proceedings of the Academy of Natural Sciences of Philadelphia* 1:53.

———. 1841b. "Description of a New Species of Freshwater Shell (*Cyclas dentata*)." *Proceedings of the Academy of Natural Sciences of Philadelphia* 1:103.

———. 1842. *A Monograph of the Freshwater Univalve Mollusca of the United States, Including Notices of Species in Other Parts of North America*. Philadelphia: Dorsey.

———. 1844. *A Monograph of the Freshwater Univalve Mollusca of the United States. Genera* Planorbis *and* Ancylus. *No. 7*. New York: self-published, Carey & Hart, J. Dobson & J. Pennington.

———. 1867. "Description of a New Species of *Limnea*." *American Journal of Conchology* 3:194, Plate 6.

Hall, Jr., R. O., M. F. Dybdahl, and M. C. VanderLoop. 2006. "Extremely High Secondary Production of Introduced Snails in Rivers." *Ecological Applications* 16: 1121–1131.

Hall, R., J. L. Tank, and M. F. Dybdahl. 2003. "Exotic Snails Dominate Nitrogen and Carbon Cycling in a Highly Productive Stream." *Frontiers in Ecology and the Environment* 1(8):407–411.

Hamilton, W. L. 1994. "Changing Diversity of Mollusks in Zion Canyon. Is This Fauna Recovering from a Prehistoric Flood?" *Park Science* 14:22–24.

Hanna, G. D. 1912. "The American Species of *Sphyradium* with Inquiry as to Their Generic Relationships." *Proceedings of the U.S. National Museum* 41:371–376.

———. 1924. "Freshwater Mollusks of Eagle Lake, California." *Proceedings of the California Academy of Sciences, 4th Series* 13(7):131–136.

———. 1966. "Introduced Mollusks of Western North America." *Occasional Papers of the California Academy of Sciences* 48:1–108.

Hanna, G. D., and J. Henderson. 1934. "A Review of the Genus *Carinifex* Binney." *Reports of the American Malacological Union* 1934(3):6.

Hanna, G. D., and E. C. Johnston. 1913. "A Pleistocene Molluscan Fauna from Phillips County, Kansas." *Kansas University Science Bulletin* 7(3):111–121.

Hannibal, H. 1910. "Valvatidae of the Western North America." *Nautilus* 23:104–107.

———. 1912. "A Synopsis of the Recent and Tertiary Land and Fresh Water Mollusca of the California Province, Based on an Ontogenetic Classification." *Proceedings of the Malacological Society of London* 10:112–211.

Harju, T. 2007. *Modeling Regional Distribution and Local Food Web Dynamics of the New Zealand Mud Snail (*Potamopyrgus antipodarum*).* Master's Thesis. Utah State University, Logan.

Harris, S. A., and L. Hubricht. 1982. "Distribution of the Species of the Genus *Oxyloma* (Mollusca, Succineidae) in Southern Canada and the Adjacent Portions of the United States." *Canadian Journal of Zoology* 60:1607–1611.

Hartmann, J. D. W. 1840. *Erd- und Süsswasser Gasteropoden*. London: St. Gallen, Von Scheitlin & Zollikofer.

Hartog, C. D., and L. de Wolf. 1962. "The Life Cycle of the Water Snail *Aplexa hypnorum*." *Basteria (Tijdschrift van de Nederlandse Malacologische Vereniging)* 26(5–6):61–88. http://natuurtijdschriften.nl/download?type=document;docid=596440

Hastie, L. C., and K. A. Toy. 2008. "Changes in Density, Age Structure and Age-Specific Mortality in Two Western Pearlshell (*Margaritifera falcata*) Populations in Washington (1995–2006)." *Aquatic Conservation: Marine and Freshwater Ecosystems* 18:671–678.

Hastie, L. C., and M. R. Young. 2003. "Timing of Spawning and Glochidial Release in Scottish Freshwater Pearl Mussel (*Margaritifera margaritifera*) Populations." *Freshwater Biology* 48(12):2107–2117.

Hastie, L. C., M. R. Young, and P. J. Boon. 2008. "Growth Characteristics of Freshwater Pearl Mussels, *Margaritifera* (L.)." *Freshwater Biology* 43(2):243–256.

Hausdorf, B. 1998. "Phylogeny of the Limacoidea Sensu Lato (Gastropoda: Stylommatophora)." *Journal of Molluscan Studies* 64(1):35–66.

Hayden, W. 1872. *Preliminary Report (for 1870) of the United States Geological Survey of Wyoming and Portions of Contiguous Territories.* U.S. Geological Survey, Washington, DC.

Hazay, J. 1881. *Die Mollusken-Fauna von Budapest mit Besonderer Rücksichtnahme auf die Embryonalen und Biologischen Verháltnisse Ihrer Vorkommnisse.* Cassel: Fischer.

Hazprunar, G. 2014. "A Nomeclator of Extant and Fossil Taxa of the Valvatidae (Gastropoda, Ectobranchia)." *ZooKeys* 377:1–172.

Heard, W. H. 1965. "Comparative Life Histories of North American Pill Clams (Sphaeriidae: *Pisidium*)." *Malacologia* 2(3):381–411.

———. 1975. "Sexuality and Other Aspects of Reproduction in *Anodonta* (Pelecypoda: Unionidae)." *Malacologia* 15(1):81–103.

———. 1977. "Reproduction of Fingernail Clams (Sphaeriidae: *Sphaerium* and *Musculium*)." *Malacologia* 16:421–455.

Heiler, K. C. M. A. bij de Vaate, K. Ekschmitt, P. V. von Oheimb, C. Albrecht, and T. Wilke. 2013. "Reconstruction of the Early Invasion History of the Quagga Mussel (*Dreissena rostriformis bugensis*) in Western Europe." *Aquatic Invasions* 8(1):53–57.

Held, F. 1836. "Aufzáhlung der in Bayern Lebenden Molluken." *Isis (Encyclopädsche Zeitschrift Vorzuglich für Naturegeschichte, Vergliechende, Anatomie und Physiologie von Oken, Leipzig)* 29:271–282.

———. 1837. "Notizen über die Weichthiere Bayerns." *Isis (Encyclopädsche Zeitschrift Vorzuglich für Naturegeschichte, Vergliechende, Anatomie und Physiologie von Oken, Leipzig)* 30:303–309, 901–919.

Hemphill, H. 1890a. "New Forms of Western Limniades." *Nautilus* 4(3):25–27.

———. 1890b. "New Varieties of *Patula strigosa*." *Nautilus* 4:15–18.

Henderson, J. 1912. "*Oreohelix* Colonies in Colorado." *Nautilus* 25:133–139.

———. 1919. "Nomenclature and Systematic Position of Some North American Fossils and Recent Mollusks, II." *Nautilus* 33:118–122.

———. 1924. "Mollusca of Colorado, Utah, Montana, Idaho and Wyoming." *University of Colorado Studies* 13(2):65–223.

———. 1929a. "Some Notes on *Oreohelix*." *Proceedings of the California Academy of Sciences* 18(8):221–227, Plate 24.

———. 1929b. "Non-Marine Mollusca of Oregon and Washington." *University of Colorado Studies* 17(2):47–190.

———. 1932a. "*Carinifex jacksonensis* New Species from Wyoming." *Nautilus* 45(4): 133–34, Plate 11.

———. 1935. "Fossil Non-marine Mollusca of North America." *Geological Society of America Special Paper No. 3.*

———. 1936. "Mollusca of Colorado, Utah, Montana, Idaho, and Wyoming–Supplement." *University of Colorado Studies* 23:81–145.

Henderson, J., and L. E. Daniels. 1916. "Hunting Mollusca in Utah and Idaho." *Proceedings of the Academy of Natural Sciences of Philadelphia* 68:314–339, Plate 15.

———. 1917. "Hunting Mollusca in Utah and Idaho in 1916." *Proceedings of the Academy of Natural Sciences of Philadelphia* 69:48–81.

Hendricks, P. 2012. *A Guide to the Land Snails and Slugs of Montana*. A Report to the U.S. Forest Service, Region 1. Montana Natural Heritage Program, Helena, MT.

Herrington, H. B. 1948. "Further Proof that *Sphaerium occidentale* Does Not Attain Full Growth in One Year." *Canadian Field Naturalist* 62:74–75.

———. 1950. "Sphaeriidae of Athabaska and Great Slave Lakes, Northwestern Canada." *Canadian Field Naturalist* 64:25–32.

———. 1954. "*Pisidium* Species and Synonyms, North America, North of Mexico." *Nautilus* 67:97–104, 131–138.

———. 1962. *A Revision of the Sphaeriidae of North America (Mollusca: Pelecypoda)*. Museum of Zoology, University of Michigan, Miscellaneous Publications No. 118.

Herrington, H. B., and E. J. Roscoe. 1953. "Some Sphaeriidae of Utah." *Nautilus* 66:97–98.

Herrington, H. B., and D. W. Taylor. 1958. *Pliocene and Pleistocene Sphaeriidae (Pelycypoda) from the Central United States*. Occasional Papers of the Museum of Zoology, University of Michigan No. 596.

Herrmannsen, A. N. 1846. *Indicis Generum Malacozoorum Primordia*, Vol. 1. Cassellis: Fischeri. https://www.biodiversitylibrary.org/item/40627#page/9/mode/1up

Hershler, R. 1985. "Systematic Revision of the Hydrobiidae (Gastropoda, Rissoacea) of the Cuatro Cienegas Basin Coahuila, Mexico." *Malacologia* 26:31–123.

———. 1994. *A Review of the North American Freshwater Snail Genus* Pyrgulopsis *(Hydrobiidae)*. Smithsonian Contribution to Zoology No. 554.

———. 1998. "A Systematic Review of the Hydrobiid Snails (Gastropoda: Rissooidea) of the Great Basin, Western United States." Part I. Genus *Pyrgulopsis*. *Veliger* 41:1–132.

———. 1999. "A Systematic Review of the Hydrobiid Snails (Gastropoda: Rissooidea) of the Great Basin, Western United States. Part II. Genera *Colligyrus, Eremopyrgus, Fluminicola, Pristinicola,* and *Tryonia*." *Veliger* 42(4):306–337.

Hershler, R., and T. J. Frest. 1996. *A Review of the North American Freshwater Snail Genus* Fluminicola *(Hydrobiidae)*. Smithsonian Contributions to Zoology No. 583.

Hershler, R. H., and J. J. Landye. 1988. *Arizona Hydrobiidae (Prosobranchia: Rissoacea)*. Smithsonian Contributions to Zoology No. 459:1–63.

Hershler, R. H., and H.-P. Liu. 2017. *Annotated Checklist of Freshwater Truncatelloidean Gastropods of the Western United States, with an Illustrated Key to the Genera*. Technical Note 449. U.S. Department of the Interior, Bureau of Land Management, National Operations Center, Denver, CO.

Hershler, R., H.-P. Liu, C. Forsythe, P. Hovingh, and K. Wheeler. 2017. "Partial Revision of the *Pyrgulopsis kolobensis* Complex (Caenogastropoda: Hydrobiidae), with Resurrection of *P. pinetorum* and Description of Three New Species from the Virgin River Drainage, Utah." *Journal of Molluscan Studies* 83:161–171.

Hershler, R., and W. F. Ponder. 1998. *A Review of Morphological Characters of Hydrobiid Snails*. Smithsonian Contributions to Zoology 600.

Hershler, R., and F. G. Thompson. 1987. "North American Hydrobiidae (Gastropoda: Rissoacea): Redescription and Systematic Relationships of *Tryonia* Stimpson, 1865 and *Pyrgulopsis* Call and Pilsbry, 1886." *Nautilus* 101:25–32.

———. 1988. "Notes on Morphology of *Amnicola limosa* (Say, 1817) (Gastropoda: Hydrobiidae) with Comments on Status of the Subfamily Amnicolinae." *Malacological Review* 21:81–92.

Hesse, P. 1927 (1879). "Systematische Anordnung der Extramarinen Gastropoden der Deutchen Fauna." In *Unsere land- und Süsswasser-Mollusken, Einfuhrung in die Molluskenfauna Deutchlands* (3rd Ed.), pp. 45–48. D. Geyer, Stuttgart: K. G. Lutz.

Heude, R. P. 1883. *Cochyliogie Fluviatile de la Province de Nanking et de la Chine Centrale*, Part 7. Paris: F. Savy [some figures are reproduced in *J. de Conchyliogie* 31].

Heynemann, F. D. 1862. "Einige Mittheilungen über Schneckenzungen mit Besonderer Beachtung der Gattung *Limax*." *Malakologische Blatter* 9–10:200–218.

Hibbard, C. W., and D. W. Taylor. 1960. "Two Late Pleistocene Faunas from Southwestern Kansas." *Contributions of the Museum of Paleontology, Univ. Michigan* 16(1): 1–223, 16 plates.

Hickey, V. 2010. "The Quagga Mussel Crisis at Lake Mead National Recreation Area, Nevada (U.S.A.)." *Conservation Biology* 24(4):931–937.

Hietala-Henschell, K., T. Stone, and R. Huff. 2019. *Interagency Special Status/Sensitive Species Program ISSSSP) Species Fact Sheet:* Helisoma newberryi. USDA Forest Service Region 6 and USDI Bureau of Land Management Oregon State Office. https://www.fs.fed.us/r6/sfpnw/issssp/species-index/fauna-invertebrates.html

Hinds, R. B. 1842. "Description of New Shells." *Annals and Magazine of Natural History* 10:80–84.

———. 1844. Mollusca. In *Zoology of the Voyage of the H.M.S. Sulphur*. pp. 49–72, Plates 1–21. London: Smith, Elder & Co.

Hoeh, W. R. 1990. "Phylogenetic Relationships among Eastern North American *Anodonta* (Bivalvia: Unionidae)." *Malacological Review* 23:63–82.

Holopainen, I. J., and I. Hanski. 1986. "Life History Variation in *Pisidium* (Bivalvia: Pisidiidae)." *Ecography* 9(2):85–98.

Holzmagel, W. E., D. J. Colgan, and C. Lydeard. 2010. "Pulmonate Phylogeny Based on 28S rRNA Gene Sequences: A Framework for Discussing Habitat Transitions and Character Transformation." *Molecular Phylogenetics and Evolution* 57:1017–1025.

Hornbach, D. J., M. J. McLeod, and S. I. Guttman. 1980. "On the Validity of the Genus *Musculium* (Bivalvia: Sphaeriidae): Electrophoretic Evidence." *Canadian Journal of Zoology* 58:1703–1707.

Horsáková, V., J. C. Nekola, and M. Horsák. 2019. "When Is a 'Cryptic' Species Not a Cryptic Species: A Consideration from the Holarctic Micro–Landsnail Genus *Euconulus* (Gastropoda: Stylommatophora)." *Molecular Phylogenetics and Evolution* 132:307–320.

———. 2020. "Integrative Taxonomic Consideration of the Holoarctic *Euconulus fulvus* Group of Land Snails (Gastropoda, Stylommatophora)." *Systematics and Biodiversity* 18(2):142–160.

Houbrick, R. S. 1988. "Cerithoidean Phylogeny." *Malacological Review, Suppl.* 4:88–128.

Hovingh, P. 1993. "Zoogeography and Paleozoology of Leeches, Molluscs, and Amphibians in Western Bonneville Basin, Utah, USA." *Journal of Paleolimnology* 9:41–54.

———. 2004. "Intermountain Freshwater Mollusks, USA (*Margaritifera, Anodonta, Gonidea, Valvata, Ferrissia*): Geography, Conservation, and Fish Management Implications." *Monographs of the Western North American Naturalist* 2:109–135.

———. 2010. "Distribution of a Unique Limpet (Gastropoda: Ancylidae) in the Colorado River Drainage Basin, Western North America." *Western North American Naturalist* 70(4):508–515.

———. 2018. *Extant (1984–2000) Freshwater Mollusk Distributions from the Great Basin and Adjacent Regions in the Natural History Museum of Utah Collection and the Supplemental Field Data Sheets Surveys in Western North America for Leeches, Mollusks, and Amphibians*. Self-published.

Howard, A. D. 1914. "A Second Case of Metamorphosis Without Parasitism in the Unionidae." *Science* 63:353–355.

Howells, R. 1997. "New Fish Hosts for Nine Freshwater Mussels (Bivalvia: Unionidae) in Texas." *Texas Journal of Science* 49:255–258.

Hoy, M. S., K. Kelly, and R. J. Rodriguez. 2010. "Development of a Molecular Diagnostic System to Discriminate *Dreissena polymorpha* (Zebra Mussel) and *Dreissena bugensis* (Quagga Mussel)." *Molecular Ecology Resources* 10(1):190–192.

Hubendick, B. 1951. "Recent Lymnaeidae. Their Variation, Morphology, Taxonomy, Nomenclature, and Distribution." *Kungliga Svenska Vetenkapsakadamiens Handlingar. Fjärde Serien* 3:1–223.

———. 1978. "Systematics and Comparative Morphology of the Basommatophora." In *Pulmonates, Volume 2A, Systematics, Evolution and Ecology*, edited by V. Fretter and J. Peake, 1–47. New York: Academic Press.

Hubricht, L. 1985. "The Distributions of the Native Land Mollusks of the Eastern United States." *Fieldiana: Zoology* 24:1–191.

Huchner, M. K., and F. J. Etges. 1977. "The Life Cycle and Development of *Aspidogaster conchicola* in the Snails, *Viviparus malleatus* and *Goniobasis livescens*." *Journal of Parasitology* 63:669–674.

Hurt, C. 2004. "Genetic Divergence, Population Structure and Historical Demography of Rare Springsnails (*Pyrgulopsis*) in the Lower Colorado River Basin." *Molecular Ecology* 13:255–276.

Hutton, F. W. 1880. *Manual of the New Zealand Mollusca*. Wellington, New Zealand: James Hughes Publ.

———. 1882. "On the New Zealand Hydrobiinae." *Transactions and Proceedings of the New Zealand Institute* 14:143–146, Plate 1.

Hyman, I. T., S. Y. W. Ho, and L. S. Jermiin. 2007. "Molecular Phylogeny of Australian Helicarionidae, Euconulidae and Related Groups (Gastropoda: Pulmonata: Stylommatophora) Based on Mitochondrial DNA." *Molecular Phylogenetics and Evolution* 45:792–812.

Hyvärinen, H., M. Saarinen-Valta, E. Mäenpää, and J. Taskinen. 2021. "Effect of Substrate Particle Size on Burrowing of the Juvenile Freshwater Pearl Mussel *Margaritifera*." *Hydrobiologia* 848:1137–1146.

Ibase (www.invertebase.org/portal/collections/harvestparams.php). *Database of Six U.S. Museum Mollusk Specimen Collections*.

ICZN (International Commission on Zoological Nomenclature). 1998. "Opinion 1896. *Galba* Schrank 1803 (Mollusca, Gastropoda). *Buccinum truncatulum* Müller, 1774 Designated as the Type Species." *Bulletin of Zoological Nomenclature* 55:123.

Ihering, H. Von. 1885. "Zur Kenntniss der Amerikanischen Limax-Arten." *Jahrbucher der Deutchen Malakozoologischen Gesellschaft* 12(3):201–218, Plate 5.

———. 1909. "Les Mélanidés Américains." *Journal de Conchyliogie* 57(4):289–316.

Inaba, A. 1969. "Cytotaxonomic Studies on Lymnaeid Snails." *Malacologia* 7:143–168.

Ingersoll, E. 1876. "Report on the Natural History of the United States Geological and Geographical Survey of the Territories, 1874." In *8th Annual Report of the United States Geological and Geographical Survey of the Territories (Hayden Survey for 1874)*. F. V. Hayden, 385–410. Washington, DC.

———. 1877. "On a Collection of Mollusks from Utah and Colorado." *Davenport Academy of Natural Sciences* 2:130–134.

Iredale, T. 1937. "A Basic List of the Land Mollusca of Australia." *Australian Zoologist* 8:287–333.

———. 1940–1941. "Guide to the Land Shells of New South Wales." *Australian Naturalist*, Part 1. 10:227–236; Part II. 10:262–269, Part III. 11:1–8, Part IV. 11:33–40.

Issel, A. 1866. "Dei Molluschi Raccolti Nella Provincia di Pisa." *Memorie della Società Italiana di Scienze Naturali* 2(1):1–6

Jackiewicz, M. 1959. "Badania nad Zmiennością I Stanowiskiem Systematycznym *Galba palustris* O.F. Muller." *Prace Komisji Matematyczno–Przyrodniczej Poznań-skiego Towarzystwa Przyjaciół Nauk* 19(3):89–187. [in Polish]

———. 1993. "Phylogeny and Relationships Within the European Species of the Family Lymnaeidae." *Folia Malacologica* 5:61–95.

Jay, J. 1852. *A Catalogue of Shells Arranged According to the Lamarckian System, Etc. Contained in the Collection of John C. Jay. 4th Ed., with Supplement*. New York: Craighead.

Jeffreys, J. G. 1828–1833 (read 1828). "A Synopsis of the Testaceous Pneumonobranchous Mollusca of Great Britain." *Transactions of the Linnean Society of London* 16:323–392.

———. 1872. "The Mollusca of Europe Compared with Those of Eastern North America." *Annals and Magazine of Natural History* 10(4th ser.):237–247.

Johnson, P. D., A. E. Bogan, K. M. Brown, N. M. Burkhead, J. R. Cordeiro, J. T. Garner, P. D. Hartfield, D. A., et al. 2013. "Conservation Status of Freshwater Gastropods of Canada and the United States." *Fisheries* 38(6):247–282.

Johnson, R. I. 1959. "The Types of Corbiculidae and Sphaeridae (Mollusca: Pelecypoda in the Museum of Comparative Zoology, and a Bio-Bibliographic Sketch of Temple Prime, an Early Specialist of the Group." *Bulletin of the Museum of Comparative Zoology, Harvard* 120:429–480.

———. 2003. "Molluscan Taxa and Bibliographies of William James Clench and Ruth Dixon Turner." *Bulletin of the Museum of Comparative Zoology* 158(1):1–46.

Jokinen, E. H. 1982. "*Cipangopaludina chinensis* (Gastropoda: Viviparidae) in North America, Review and Update." *Nautilus* 96:89–95.

Jones, D. T. 1935. "Mollusks from Weber Canyon, Utah." *Utah Academy of Sciences, Arts, and Letters* 12:227–228.

———. 1940a. "Mollusks of the Oquirrh and Stansbury Mountains in Utah." *Nautilus* 54:27–29.

———. 1940b. "Recent Collections of Utah Mollusca, with Extralimital Records from Certain Utah Cabinets." *Proceedings of the Utah Academy of Sciences, Arts, and Letters* 17:33–45.

———. 1940c. "A Study of the Great Basin Land Snail *Oreohelix strigosa depressa* (Cockerell)." *Bulletin of the University of Utah* 31(4):1–43.

———. 1944. "*Oreohelix howardi*, New Species." *Proceedings of the Utah Academy of Sciences, Arts, and Letters* 21:61–65.

Kaleniczenko, J. 1839. "Necrologie. Notice sur le Professor J.A. de Krynicki." *Bulletin de la Société Impériale de Naturalistes de Moscou* 12(1):25–33.

———. 1851. "Description d'un Nouveau Genre de Limaces de al Russie Méridionale." *Bulletin de la Société Impériale de Naturalistes de Moscou* 24(1):215–228.

Karatayev, A. Y., L. E. Burlakova, and D. K. Padilla. 2015. "Zebra Versus Quagga Mussels: A Review of Their Spread, Population Dynamics, and Ecosystem Impacts." *Hydrobiologia* 746:97–112.

Karlin, E. J. 1961. "Ecological Relationships Between Vegetation and the Distribution of Land Snails in Montana, Colorado and New Mexico." *American Midland Naturalist* 65(1):60–66.

Karvonen, A., S. Paukku, E. T. Valtonen, and P. J. Hudson. 2003. "Transmission, Infectivity, and Survival of *Diplostomum spathecum* Cercariae." *Parasitology* 127:217–224.

Keen, M., and P. Dance. 1969. "Family Pisidiidae." In *Treatise on Invertebrate Paleontology. Part N, Vol. 2: Mollusca 6, Bivalvia*, edited by R. C. Moore, N669–N670. Lawrence, KS: Geological Society of America and University of Kansas Press.

Keep, J. 1887. *West Coast Shells*. San Francisco, CA: Bancroft Brothers.

———. 1904. *West American Shells*. San Francisco, CA: Whitaker & Ray.

Kennard, A. S., and B. B. Woodward. 1926. *Synonymy of the British Non-Marine Mollusca*. London: R. Clay & Sons for British Museum.

Kerans, B. L., M. F. Dybdahl, M. M. Gangloff, and J. E. Jannot. 2005. "*Potamopyrgus antipodarum*: Distribution, Density, and Effects on Native Macroinvertebrate Assemblages in the Greater Yellowstone Ecosystem." *Freshwater Science* 24(1):123–138.

Kinzelbach, R. 1991. "Die Korbchenmuscheln *Corbicula fluminalis*, *Corbicula fluminea* und *Corbicula fluviatilis* in Europa (Bivalvia: Corbiculidae)." *Mainzer Naturwissenchaftliches Archiv* 29:215–228.

Klein, A. 1853. "Conchylien der Süsswasserkalkformation Wurtembergs." *Jahreshefte des Vereins fur Vaterlandische Naturkunde in Württemberg* 9:203–223.

Kobelt, W. 1879. *Iconographie der Land- & Süsswasser-Mollusken mt Vorzüglicher Berücksichtigung der Europäischen Noch Nicht Abgebildeten Arten von E.A. Rossmässler*. Wiesbaden: Kreidel. Dates: Heft 1 to 3, pp. 1–48, July 1878; Heft 4 to 6, pp. 49–158, Aug. 1879.

———. 1881. *Illustrirtes Conchylienbuch, Vol. 2*. Nürnberg: Bauer & Raspe

Korniushin, A. V. 1998. "Notes on the Anatomy of Some Species of *Sphaerium* S. (Mollusca, Bivalvia) from the Tropical Regions with Revision of their Taxonomic Status." *Vestnik Zoologii* 32(3):3–12.

———. 2004. "A Revision of Some Asian and African Freshwater Clams Assigned to *Corbicula fluminalis* (Müller, 1774) (Mollusca: Bivalvia: Corbiculidae), With a Review of Anatomical Characters and Reproductive Features Based on Museum Collections." *Hydrobiologia* 529:251–270.

Korniushin, A. V., and M. Glaubrecht. 2002. "Phylogenetic Analysis Based on the Morphology of Viviparous Freshwater Clams of the Family Sphaeriidae (Mollusca, Bivalvia, Veneroida)." *Zoologica Scripta* 31(5):415–459.

Kraemer, L. R., and M. L. Galloway. 1986. "Larval Development of *Corbicula fluminea* (Muller) (Bivalvia: Corbiculacea): An Appraisal of its Heterochrony." *American Malacological Bulletin* 4(1):61–79.

Krist, A. C., and C. C. Charles. 2012. "The Invasive New Zealand Mudsnail, *Potamopyrgus antipodarum*, Is an Effective Grazer of Algae and Altered the Assemblage of Diatoms More Than Native Grazers." *Hydrobiologia* 694(1):143–151.

Kruglov, N. D. 2005. *Mollusks of family Lymnaeidae (Gastropoda, Pulmonata) in Europe and Northern Asia*. Smolensk: SGPU Publishing. [in Russian]

Kruglov, N. D., and Y. I. Starobogatov. 1985. "Ob'yom Podroda *Galba* I skhodnykh s Nim Pofrodov Roda *Lymnaea* [the Volume of the Subgenus *Galba* and of the Other Similar Subgenera of the Genus *Lymnaea* (Gastropoda, Pumonata)]." *Zoologicheskiy Zhurnal* 64(1):24–35. [in Russian]

———. 1989a. "Mollyuski Podroda *Polyrhytis* Roda *Lymnaea* Fauny SSSR (Pulmonata, Lymnaeidae). [Mollusks of the Subgenus *Polyrhytis* of the Genus *Lymnaea* of the Fauna of the USSR (Pulmonata, Lymnaeidae)]." *Zoologicheskiy Zhurnal* 68(3):14–20. [in Russian]

———. 1989b. "Morphology and Taxonomy of the Molluscs from the Subgenus *Radix* of the Genus *Lymnaea* (Gastropoda, Pulmonata, Lymnaeidae) from Siberia and Far East of the USSR." *Zoologicheskiy Zhurnal* 68(5):17–30. [in Russian]

———. 1993. Guide to Recent Molluscs of Northern Eurasia. 3. Annotated and Illustrated Catalogue of Species of the Family Lymnaeidae (Gastropoda, Pulmonata, Lymnaeiformes) of Palaearctic and Adjacent River Drainage Areas. *Ruthenica* 3: (1) 65–92 [Part 1], (2) 161–180 [Part 2].

Küster, H. C. 1862. "Die Gattungen *Limnaeus, Amphipeplea, Chilina, Isidora*, und *Physopsis*." *Systematiches Conchylien-Cabinet von Martini und Chemnitz*, Bd. 1 Abt. 17b. Nürnberg: Bauer & Raspe.

Küster, H. C., W. Dunker, and S. Clessin. 1886 (1841–1886). "Die Familie der Limnaeiden Enthaltend die Genera *Planorbis, Limnaeus, Physa*, und *Amphipeplea*." *Systematisches Conchylien-Cabinet* 1(17). Dates: pp. 1–8 (1824), Taf. 1 (1843); 9–20, Taf. 2–4, 16 (1844); 21–28, 35–62, Taf. 5–10 (1850); 29–39, Taf. 11–39 (1884); 223–310, Taf. 40–50 (1885); 311–430, Taf. 51–55 (1886).

Ladd, H. L. A., and D. L. Rowgowski. 2012. "Egg Predation and Parasite Prevalence in the Invasive Freshwater Snail, *Melanoides tuberculata* (Muller, 1774) in a West Texas Spring System." *Aquatic Invasions* 7(2):287–290.

Ladle, M., and F. Baron. 1969. "Studies on Three Species of *Pisidium* (Mollusca: Bivalvia) from a Chalk Stream." *Journal of Animal Ecology* 38:407–413.

Lamarck, J. B. 1799. "Prodrome d'Une Nouvelle Classification des Coquilles, Comprenant une Rédaction Appropriée des Caractères Génériques, et l'Établissement d'un Grand Nombre de Genres Nouveaux." *Mémoires de la Société d'Histoire Naturelle de Paris* 1(an VII):63–91. Paris.

———. 1806. "Sur les Fossiles des Environs de Paris." *Annales du Muséum d'Histoire Naturelle* 7:419–430.

———. 1818. *Histoire Naturelle des Animaux Sans Vertébres*, Vol. 5. Paris: Deterville.

———. 1822. *Histoire Naturelle des Animaux Sans Vertébres*, Vol. 6. Part 2. Paris.

Lang, B. Z. 1998. Anodonta californiensis *from Curlew Lake, Washington*. WDFW Contract No. 53081050. [not seen, *fide* Maine et al. 2016]

Lea, I. 1834. "Observations on the Naiades, and Descriptions of New Species of That, and Other Families." *Transactions of the American Philosophical Society (Philadelphia)* (new ser., Article 5) 4:63–121.

———. 1837. "Observations on the Naiades, and Descriptions of New Species of That, and Other Families (Part 2)." *Transactions of the American Philosophical Society* (Philadelphia, new ser., Article 2) 5:23–119.

———. 1838–1839. "Description of New Freshwater and Land Shells." *Transactions of the American Philosophical Society* (new ser., Article I) 6:1–154.

———. 1841 (1844). "Continuation of 'On Fresh Water and Land Shells' Read at the Last Meeting." *Proceedings of the American Philosophical Society* (Philadelphia) 2(17):30–35, 81–83, 224–225, 234, 237, 241–243.

———. 1846a. "Continuation of 'On Fresh Water and Land Shells.'" *Transactions of the American Philosophical Society* (Philadelphia, new ser., Article 1) 9:1–31.

———. 1846b. "Description of New 'Fresh Water and Land Shells." *Transactions of the American Philosophical Society* (new ser., Article 10) 9:275–282.

———. 1852. *Synopsis of the Family Naiades, 3rd ed*. Philadelphia: Blanchard & Lea.

———. 1856. "Description of New Freshwater Shells from California." *Proceedings of the Academy of Natural Sciences of Philadelphia* 8:80–81.

———. 1858. "Descriptions of a New *Helix* and Two New Planorbes." *Proceedings of the Academy of Natural Sciences of Philadelphia* 10:41.

———. 1864a. "Description of Six New Species of *Succinea* of the United States." *Proceedings of the Academy of Natural Sciences of Philadelphia* 16:109–111.

———. 1864b. "Description of and Remarks on *Planorbis newberryi*." *Proceedings of the Academy of Natural Sciences of Philadelphia* 16:5.

———. 1864c. "Description of Five New Species of *Lymnaea* of North America." *Proceedings of the Academy of Natural Sciences of Philadelphia* 16:8.

———. 1864d. "Descriptions of Twenty-Four New Species of *Physa* of the United States and Canada." *Proceedings of the Academy of Natural Sciences of Philadelphia* 16:114–116.

———. 1866–1869. "New Unionidae, Melanidae, etc. Chiefly of the United States." *Journal of the Academy of Natural Sciences of Philadelphia* (ser. 2) Vol. 6. Published in four parts: Part I, July 1866, pp. 5–66; Part II, September 1867, 113–188; Part III January 1869, 249–302; Part IV, August 1869, 303–344.

Leach, W. E. 1852. *Molluscorum Britanniae Synopsis: A Synopsis of the Mollusca of Great Britain*. London: VanVoorst.

Lee, T. 1999. "Polyploidy and Meiosis in the Freshwater Clam *Sphaerium striatinum* (Lamarck) and Chromosome Numbers in the Sphaeriidae (Bivalvia: Veneroida)." *Cytologia* 64:247–252.

———. 2004. "Morphology and Phylogenetic Relationships of Genera of North American Sphaeriidae (Bivalvia, Veneroida)." *American Malacological Bulletin* 19(1/2):1–13.

Lee, T., and D. O'Foighil. 2003. "Phylogenetic Structure of the Sphaeriinae, a Global Clade of Freshwater Bivalve Mollusks, Inferred from Nuclear (ITS-1) and Mitochondrial (16S) Ribosomal Gene Sequences." *Zoological Journal of the Linnean Society* 137:245–260.

Lee, T., S. Siripattrawan, C. F. Ituarte, and D. O'Foighil. 2005. "Invasion of the Clonal Clams: *Corbicula* Lineages in the New World." *American Malacological Bulletin* 20:113–122.

Lefevre, G., and W. Curtis. 1910. "Reproduction and Parasitism in the Unionidae." *Journal of Experimental Biology* 9:79–115.

———. 1912. "Experiments in the Artificial Propagation of Freshwater Mussels." *Bulletin of the Bureau of Fisheries* 28:617–626.
Lehmann, D. 1864. "Neue Nacktschnecke aus Australien." *Malakozoologische Blätter* 11/12:145–149.
Lehmann, R. 1862. "Ueber eine neue Heliceen-Gattung". *Malakozoologische Blatter* 9(3):111–112.
Lehnert, E. 1884. "Alaskan Plants and Shells." *Science Record* 2(8):171–172.
Leidy, J. 1851. "Special Anatomy of the Terrestrial Gastropoda of the United States." In *The Terrestrial Air-Breathing Mollusks of the United States, and the Adjacent Territories of North America. Vol. 1*, A. A. Gould, 198–260. Boston: Little, Brown.
Leonard, A. B. 1943. "The Mollusca of Meade and Clark Counties, Kansas." *Transactions of the Kansas Academy of Science* 46:226–240.
———. 1948. "Five New Yarmouthian Planorbid Snails." *Nautilus* 62:41–47, Plate 2.
———. 1972. "A new *Valvata* from the Pleistocene of Southern Illinois." *Nautilus* 86(1):1–2.
Lesson, R. P. 1840. "Travaux Inédits. Molluscorum Species Novae." *Revue Zoologique* 1840:355–358.
Levri, E. P., A. A. Kelly, and E. Love. 2007. "The Invasive New Zealand Mud Snail (*Potamopyrgus antipodarum*) in Lake Erie." *Journal of Great Lakes Research* 33:1–6.
Lewis, J. 1855. "Remarks on the *Cyclas* and *Lymnea*." P*roceedings of the Boston Society of Natural History* 5:122–124.
———. 1860. "Catalogue of the Mollusks in the Vicinity of Mohawk, New York." *Proceedings of the Academy of Natural Sciences of Philadelphia* 12:17–19.
Lindahl, A. M. 1976. *Ecological Reconnaisance, Grapevine Spring, Zion National Park, Utah, Summer 1976*. Unpublished report to Zion National Park.
Lindholm, W. A. 1911. "Bemerkungen über Einige Hyalinien Russlands Nebst Beschreibung Einer neuen Art." *Nachrichtsblatt der Deutchen Malakozoologischen Gesellschaft* 43:94–99.
———.1925. "Ueber der Vorkommen der Gattung *Corbicula* im Ussuri-Gebiete." *Doklady Rossiyskoi Academii Nauk,* 29–32.
———.1928. "Zur Kenntnis der *Corbicula*-formen (Lamellibranchiata) Sudost-Siberiens." *Ezhegodnik Zoologicheskogo Muzeya Akademii Nauk SSSR*. 28(4):550–554.
———. 1933. "Eine Verschollene Muschel aus Zentralasien." *Archiv für Molluskenkunde* (*Internat. J. Malacology*) 65:264–268.
Link, H. F. 1807. "Beschreibung der Naturalein-Sammlung der Universitat zu Rostock." *Adlers Erben, Rostock* 3:152.
Linnaeus, C. 1758. *Systema Naturae per Regna Tria Naturae, Secundum Classes, Ordines, Genera, Species, cum Characteribus, Differentiis, Synonymis, Locis. 10th edition. Vermes. Testacea*. Salvius: Holmiae.
Linscott, T. M., K. Weaver, V. Morales, and C. E. Parent. 2020. "Assessing Species Number and Genetic Diversity of Mountainsnails (Oreohelicidae)." *Conservation Genetics* 21:971–985.
Linsley, J. H. 1845. Catalogue of the Shells of Connecticut. *American Journal of Science and Arts* 48:271–286.
Lister, M. 1823. *Historia Sive Synopsis Methodica Conchyliorum, Editio Tertia*. Oxford: Typographeo Clarendoniano.
Liu, H. P., and R. Hershler. 2007. "A Test of the Vicariance Hypothesis of Western North American Freshwater Biogeography." *Journal of Biogeography* 34:534–548.
Liu, H. P., R. Hershler, and P. Hovingh. 2018. "Molecular Evidence Enables Further Resolution of the Western North American *Pyrgulopsis kolobensis* Complex (Caenogastropoda: Hydrobiidae)." *Journal of Molluscan Studies* 84:103–107.
Liu, H. P., P. Hovingh, and R. Hershler. 2015. "Genetic Evidence for Recent Spread of Springsnails (Hydrobiidae: *Pyrgulopsis*) Across the Wasatch Divide" *Western North American Naturalist* 75(3):325–331.

Liu, H. P., J. Walsh, and R. Hershler. 2013. "Taxonomic Clarification and Phylogeography of *Fluminicola coloradoensis* Morrison, a Widely Ranging Western North American Pebblesnail." *Monographs of the Western North American Naturalist* 6:87–110.

Locard, A. 1880. *Etudes Sur les Variations Malacologiques d'Aprés la Faune Vivante et Fossile de la Partie Centrale du Bassin du Rhone*. Tome Premier. Lyon: H. Georg/Bailliére et Fils.

Locard, A. 1883. "Recherches Paleontologiques sur les Depots Tertiaires a Milne–Edwardsia et Vivipara du Pliocene in Inférieur du Département de L'Ain." *Annales de l'Academie de Macon* Ser. 6:2–166, 4 plates.

———. 1893. *Les Coquilles de Eaux Douces et Saumatres de France*. Paris: Balliére et Fils.

Lopes-Lima, M., I. N. Bolotov, V. T. Do, D. C. Aldridge, M. M. Fonseca, H. M. Gan, M. Y. Gofarov, et al. 2018. "Expansion and Systematics Redefinition of the Most Threatened Freshwater Mussel Family, the Margaritiferidae." *Molecular Phylogenetics and Evolution* 127:98–118.

Lopes-Lima, M., E. Froufe, V. T. Do, M. Ghamizi, K. E. Mock, Ü. Kebapçi, O. Klishko, et al. 2017. "Phylogeny of the Most Species-rich Freshwater Bivalve Family (Bivalvia: Unionida: Unionidae): Defining Modern Subfamilies and Tribes." *Molecular Phylogenetics and Evolution* 106:174–191.

Lorencová, E., L. Beran, M. Nováková, V. Horsáková, B. Rowson, J.C. Hlaváč, J.C. Nekola, and M. Horsák. 2021. "Invasion at the population level: a story of the freshwater snails *Gyraulus parvus* and *G. laevis*." *Hydrobiologia* 848:4661–4671.

Lu, H. F., L. N. Du, Z. Q. Li, X-Y. Chen, and J. X. Yang. 2014. "Morphological Analysis of the Chinese *Cipangopaludina* Species (Gastropoda: Caenogastropoda: Viviparidae)." *Zoological Research* 35(6):510–527.

Luther, A. 1915. "Zuchtversuche an Ackerschnecken (*Agriolimax reticulatus* Mull. und *Agriolimax agrestis* L.)." *Acta Societatis pro Fauna et Flora Fennica* 40(2):1–42.

Mabille, M. J. 1868. "Travaux Inedits, des Limaciens Européens." *Revue et Magasin de Zoologie pure et Appliquée, Series 2*, 20:129–146.

Mackie, G. L. 1979. "Growth Dynamics in Natural Populations of Sphaeriidae Clams (*Sphaerium, Musculium, Pisidium*)." *Canadian Journal of Zoology* 57:441–456.

———. 2007. "Biology of Freshwater Corbiculid and Sphaeriid Clams of North America." *Ohio Biological Survey Bulletin New Ser*. Vol. 15, No. 3.

Magry, C. J. P. J. 2018. "*Planellavitrina occulta* Gen. & Spec. Nov. a Second Fossil Vitrinid from the Canary Island of La Gomera (Gastropoda: Pulmonata)." *Basteria* 82(1–3):15–18.

Maine, A., C. Arango, and C. O'Brien. 2016. "Host Fish Associations of the California Floater (*Anodonta californiensis*) in the Yakima River Basin, Washington." *Northwest Science* 90(3):290–300.

———. 1855. "Om Svenska Landt-och Söttvattens Molluskerm Med Särskilt Afseende på de Arter och Former, som Förkomma I Granneskapet af Christianstad (C) och Götheborg (G)." *Götheborgs Kungliga Vetenskaps och Vitterhets Sämhalles Handlingar:Ny Tidsföljd* 3:73–152.

———. 1868. "Zoologiska Observationer. V. Haftet. Skandinaviska Land-Sniglar, *Limacina*, Afbildade Efter Lefvande Exemplar och Beskrivna [Scandinavian land slugs figured from living specimens and described]." *Götheborgs Kungliga Vetenskaps och Vitterhets Sämhalles Handlingar:Ny Tidsföljd* 8:25–93, Plates 1–5.

Martens, E. Von. 1869. "Mollusken." In *Reisen in Ost-Afrika in 1859–1865*: *Wissenschaftliche Ergebnisse, Dritter Band, Erste Abtheilung: Säugetheire, Vögel, Amphibien, Crustacean, Mollusken und Echinodermen*. C. C. Von der Decken, 54–66, 3 plates. Leipzig, Heidelberg: C. F. Winter'sche Verlagshandlung.

———. 1873. "*Hydrobia antipodum*. Critical List of New Zealand Mollusks." *Malakozoologische Blätter* 19:14.

———. 1874. "Sliznyaki (=Mollusca)." In A. P. Fedchenko (ed.), *Puteshestvie v' Turekestan (Expedition to Turkestan)*. Tom' II (Vol. 2), Zoogeograficheskaya Izledovaniya (Zoogeographical Investigations). Chast 1 (Part 1), *Vypusk'* (Issue 1). Izvestiya Imperatorskago Obbshchestva Lyubitelei Estestvoznaniya, Antropologii I Etnografii pri

Imperatorskom Moskovskom Universitete (Proceedings of the Imperial Society for the Amateurs of Natural History, Anthropology, and Ethnography of the Imperial University of Moscow), Tom' XI (Vol. 11), *Vypusk'* 1 (Issue 1), viii + 66 pages, 3 plates. [in Russian]

———. 1882. [no title; on collections in northwest United States, *V. bollesiana* var. *arthuri*]. *Sitzungberichte der Gesellschaft Naturforschender Freunde zu Berlin* 9:138–143.

———. 1890–1901. *Land and Freshwater Mollusca*. Biologia Centrali-Americana. London: Taylor & Francis.

———. 1905. "Koreanische Süsswasser-Mollusken." *Zoologische Jahrbücher* 8:23–70, 3 plates.

Martens, G. Von. 1830. "Natur und Vaterlandskunde: Über Würtembergs Fauna." *Correspondenszblätter des Württemgergischen Landwirtschaftlichen Vereins* 17:123–185.

———. 1865. "Ueber die Mexikanischen Binnen-Conchylien aus den Sammlungen von Deppe und Uhde im Berliner Museum." *Malakozoologische Blätter* 11–12: 1–78.

Martinez-Cruz, M. A. 2018. *Species Delimitation among Southeastern U.S.* Oxyloma *(Gastropoda: Succineidae)*. Master's Thesis, University of Texas, Rio Grande Valley.

Maton, W. G., and T. Rackett. 1807. "A Descriptive Catalogue of the British Testacea." *Transactions of the Linnean Society of London* 8:17–250, 6 plates.

Mattice, J. S., and L. L. Wright. 1986. "Aspects of Growth of *Corbicula fluminea*." *American Malacological Bulletin, Special Edition* No. 2:167–178.

McCraw, B. M. 1957. "Studies on the Anatomy of *Lymnaea humilis* Say." *Canadian Journal of Zoology* 35:751–768.

———. 1961. "Life History and Growth of the Snail, *Lymnaea humilis* Say." *Transactions of the American Microscopical Society* 80(1):16–27.

McKee, P. M., and G. L. Mackie. 1981. "Life History Adaptations of the Fingernail Clam, *Sphaerium occidentale* and *Musculium securis* to Ephemeral Habitats." *Canadian Journal of Zoology* 59:2219–2229.

McMahon, R. F. 1975. "Effect of Artificially Elevated Water Temperature on the Growth, Reproduction, and Life Cycle of a Natural Population of *Physa virgata* Gould." *Ecology* 56(5):1167–1175.

McMahon, R. F., and C. J. Williams. 1986. "A Reassessment of Growth Rate, Life Span, Life Cycles and Population Dynamics in a Natural Population and Field Caged Individuals of *Corbicula fluminea* (Müller) (Bivalvia: Corbiculacea)." *American Malacological Bulletin, Special Edition* No. 2:151–166.

Meadows, D. W. 2002. "The Effect of Roads and Trails on Movement of the Ogden Mountain Snail (*Oreohelix peripherica wasatchensis*)." *Western North American Naturalist* 62(3):377–380.

Meek, F. B. 1876. *A Report on the Invertebrate Cretaceous and Tertiary Fossils of the Upper Missouri Country*. U.S. Geological Survey of the Territories 9. (see p. 532 for *L. Polyrhytis kingii*).

———. 1877. "Part 1. Paleontology." In *U.S. Geological Exploration of the Fortieth Parallel: Professional Papers of the Engineer Department, U.S. Army, No. 18*, edited by A. A. Humphreys and C. King, 1–197, 24 plates. Washington, DC.

Meier-Brook, C. 1983. "Taxonomic Studies on *Gyraulus* (Gastropoda: Planorbidae)." *Malacologia* 24(1–2):1–113.

Meier-Brook, C., and M. D. Bargues. 2002. "*Catascopia*, a New Genus for Three Nearctic and One Palearctic Stagnicoline Species (Gastropoda: Limnaeidae)." *Folia Malacologica* 10:83–84.

Mendes da Costa, E. 1778. *Historia Naturalis Testaceorum Britanniae, or the British Conchology* (in both French and English). London: Millan, White, Emsley & Robson.

Menke, C. T. 1828. *Synopsis Methodica Molluscorum Generum Omnium et Speciearum Earum, Quae in Museo Mekeano Adservantur; Cum Synonymia Critica et Novarum Specierum Diagnosibus*. Pyrmonti: Gelpke.

———. 1830. *Synopsis Methodica Molluscorum Generum Omnium et Specierum Earum, Quae in Museo Menkeano Adservantur; Cum Synonymia Critica et Novarum Specierum Diagnosibus. Editio Altera, Auctior et Emendatior*. Pyrmonti: Uslar.

Meretsky, V. J., E. G. North, and L. E. Stevens. 2002. "Kanab Ambersnail and Other Terrestrial Snails in South Central Utah." *Western North American Naturalist* 62(3):307–315.

Mighels, J. W. 1844. [untitled, descriptions of 11 new species]. *Proceedings of the Boston Society of Natural History* 1:187–190.

———. 1848 (read 1845). "Description of Shells from the Sandwich Islands, and Other Localities." *Proceedings of the Boston Society of Natural History* 2:18–28.

Mighels, J. W., and C. B. Adams. 1842. "Descriptions of Twenty-four Species of the Shells of New England." *Boston Journal of Natural History* 4:37–54.

Miles, C. D. 1958. "The Family Succineidae (Gastropoda: Pulmonata) in Kansas." *University of Kansas Science Bulletin* 38, Part 2, No. 24:1499–1543.

Miles, M. 1861. "Chapter VIII. Report of the State Zoologist." In *First Biennial Report of the Progress of the Geological Survey of Michigan: Embracing Observations of the Geology, Zoology, and Botany of the Lower Peninsula*, A. Winchell, 213–241. Lansing, MI: Hosmer & Kerr.

Miller, M. P., L. E. Stevens, J. D. Busch, J. A. Sorensen, and P. Keim. 2000. "Amplified Fragment Length Polymorphism and Mitochondrial Sequence Data Detect Genetic Differentiation and Relationships in Endangered Southwestern U.S.A. Ambersnails (*Oxyloma* spp.)." *Canadian Journal of Zoology* 78:1845–1854.

Miller, M. P., D. E. Weigel, K. E. Mock, and B. Roth. 2006a. "Evidence for an Outcrossing Reproductive Strategy in the Hermaphroditic Heterobranch Gastropod *Valvata utahensis* (Valvatidae), with Notes on the Genetic Differentiation of *V. utahensis* and *V. humeralis*." *Journal of Molluscan Studies* 72(4):397–403.

Mills, E. L., R. M. Dermott, E. F. Roseman, D. Dustin, E. Millina, D. B. Conn, and A. Spidle. 1993. "Colonization, Ecology, and Population Structure of the Quagga Mussel (Bivalvia: Dreissenidae) in the Lower Great Lakes." *Canadian Journal of Fisheries and Aquatic Sciences* 50:2305–2314.

Mills, E. L., G. Rosenberg, A. P. Spidle, M. Ludyanskiy, Y. Pligin, and B. May. 1996. "A Review of the Biology and Ecology of the Quagga Mussel (*Dreissena bugensis*), a Second Species of Freshwater Dreissenid Introduced to North America." *American Zoology* 36:271–286.

Mirolli, M. 1958. "I. Gasteropodi Costieri del Lago Maggiore e di Alcuni Laghi Vicini." *Memorias Instituto Italiano de Idrobiologia* 10:209–316, 41 plates.

Mitchell, A. J., and T. M. Brandt. 2003. "Temperature Tolerance of Red-Rim Melania *Melanoides tuberculatus*, an Exotic Aquatic Snail Established in the United States." *Transactions of the American Fisheries Society* 34:126–131.

Mitropolskji, V. I. 1965. "Observations on the Life Cycle, Growth Rate and Tolerance of Drying in *Musculium lacustre* (Muller) (Lamellibranchiata)." *Trudy Instituta Biologii, Vnutrennikh Vod Akademiya Nauk SSSR* 8:118–124.

Mock, K. E., J. C. Brim Box, J. P. Chong, J. K. Howard, D. A. Nez, D. Wolf, and R. S. Gardner. 2010. "Genetic Structuring in the Freshwater Mussel *Anodonta* Corresponds with Major Hydrologic Basins in the Western United States." *Molecular Ecology* 19:569–591.

Mock, K. E., J. C. Brim Box, M. P. Miller, M. E. Downing, and W. R. Hoeh. 2004. "Genetic Diversity and Divergence among Freshwater Mussel (*Anodonta*) Populations in the Bonneville Basin of Utah." *Molecular Ecology* 13:1085–1098.

Modell, H. 1942. "Das naturliche System der Najaden." *Archiv für Molluskenkunde* 74:161–191.

Möller, H. P. C. 1842. "Index Molluscorum Groenlandiae." *Naturhistorisk Tidsskrift* 4:76–97.

Montfort, P. D. 1810. *Conchyliologie Systématique, et Classification Méthodique des Coquilles*, Vol. 2. Paris: Schoell.

Moore, A. C., J. B. Burch, and T. F. Duda, Jr. 2014. "Recognition of a Highly Restricted Freshwater Snail Lineage (Physidae: *Physella*) in Southeastern Oregon: Convergent

Evolution, Historical Context, and Conservation Considerations." *Conservation Genetics.* DOI 10.1007/s10592-014-0645-5.

Moquin-Tandon. A. 1855. *Histoire Naturelle des Mollusques Terrestres et Fluviatiles de France, Tome 2.* Paris: Baillére.

Mörch, O. A. L. 1857. "Description de Nouveaux Mollusques de L'Amerique Centrale." *Journal de Conchyliologie* 6:282–283.

———. 1865. "Quelques Mots sur un Arrangement des Mollusques Pulmonés Terrestres (Géophiles, Fér.) Basé sur le Systém Naturel (Suite)." *Journal de Conchologie* (Ser. 3, t.5)13:376–396.

———. 1867. "Abrégé de l'Histoire de la Classification Moderne des Mollusques Basée Principalement sur l'Armature Linguale." *Journal de Conchyliologie* 15:232–258.

Mordukhai-Boltovoskoi, F. D. 1960. *Caspian Fauna in the Basin of the Azov and Black Seas.* Academy of Sciences of USSR, Institute of the Water-Reservoirs Biology, Moscow. [in Russian]

Morelet, A. 1845. *Description des Mollusques Terrestres et Fluviatiles du Portugal.* Paris: Bailliére.

———. 1849 (Part 1)—1851 (Part 2). *Testacea Novissima, Insulae Cubanae et Americae Central.* Paris: Bailliére.

———. 1862. "Diagnoses Testarum Indo-Sinarum." *Revue et Magazin de Zoologie Pure et Appliquée* (Ser. 2) 14:477–481.

Morgan, E., and V. K. Last. 1982. "Observations on the Feeding and Digestive Rhythm of the Freshwater Prosobranch *Melanoides tuberculata* Müller." *Zoologischer Anzeiger* 209:381–393.

Morrison, J. P. E. 1940. "A New Species of *Fluminicola* with Notes on 'Colorado Desert' Shells, and on the Genus *Clappia*." *Nautilus* 53(4):124–127.

———. 1954. "The Relationships of Old and New World Melanians." *Proceedings of the U.S. National Museum* 103:357–394.

Morse, E. S. 1864. "Observations on the Terrestrial Pulmonifera of Maine, Including a Catalogue of All the Species of Terrestrial and Fluviatile Mollusca Known to Inhabit the State." *Journal of the Portland Society of Natural History* 1(1):1–75.

———. 1867 (read November 20, 1865). "Descriptions of New Species of Pupadae." *Annals of the Lyceum of Natural History of New York* 8:207–212.

Morton, B. 1973. "Analysis of a Sample of *Corbicula manilensis* Philippi from the Pearl River, China." *Malacogical Review* 6:35–37.

———. 1977. "The Population Dynamics of *Corbicula fluminea* (Bivalvia: Corbiculacea) in Plover Cove Reservoir, Hong Kong." *Journal of Zoology, London* 181:21–42.

———. 1982. "Some Aspects of the Population Structure and Sexual Strategy of *Corbicula* cf. *fluminalis* (Bivalvia: Corbiculacea) from the Pearl River, People's Republic of China." *Journal of Molluscan Studies* 48:1–23.

———. 1986. "*Corbicula* in Asia—an Updated Synthesis." *American Malacological Bulletin*, Special Edition No. 2:113–124.

Mousson, A. 1872. "Revision de la Faune Malacologique des Iles Canaries: Neue Denkschriften der Allgemeinen Schweizerischen Gesellschaft für die Gesammten Natursissenschaften." *Nouveau Memoires de la Societe Helvetique des Sciences Naturelles* (Neuchatel) 25:1–176.

Mouthon, J., and T. Parghentanian. 2004. "Comparison of the Life Cycle and Population Dynamics of Two *Corbicula* Species, *C. fluminea* and *C. fluminalis* (Bivalvia: Corbiculidae) in Two French Canals." *Archiv für Hydrobiogie* 161:267–287.

Muhlfeld, J. C. M. 1811. "Entwurf Eines euen Systems der Schaltiergehäuse." *Magazin für die neuesten Entdeckungen in der Gesammten Naturkunde von der Gesellschaft Naturforschaft Freunde zu Berlin* 5(1):38–72.

———. 1818. "Beschreibung Einiger Neuen Conchylien." *Gesellschaft Naturforschender Freunde zu Berlin, Magazin fur die Neusten Entdeckungen in der Gesammten Naturkunde* 8:2–11, Plates 1, 2.

Mulcrone, R. 2006. *Pyganodon grandis* (On-line), Animal Diversity Web. https://animaldiversity.org/accounts/Pyganodon_grandis (Accessed January 2020)

Müller, O. F. 1773. *Vermium Terrestrium et Fluviatilium, Seu Animalium Infusorium, Helminthicorum, et Testaceorum, non Marinorum, Succincta Historia. Voluminis Imi Pars Ima.* Copenhagen and Leipzig: Heineck & Faber.

———. 1774. *Vermium Terrestrium et Fluviatilium, Seu Animalium Infusorium, Helminthicorum, et Testaceorum, non Marinorum, Succincta Historia. Volumen Alterum 2.* Copenhagen and Leipzig: Heineck & Faber.

Munier-Chalmas, E. P. A. 1879. (no title, *Heterovalvata* n. gen.). *Revue de Geologie pour les Années 1876 et 1877* 15:33–34.

Nekola, J. C. 2014. "Overview of the North American Terrestrial Gastropod Fauna." *American Malacological Bulletin* 32(2):225–235.

Nekola, J. C., S. Chiba, B. F. Coles, C. A. Drost, T. von Proschwitz, and M. Horsák. 2018. "A Phylogenetic Overview of the Genus *Vertigo* O.F. Muller, 1773 (Gastropoda: Pulmonata: Pupillidae: Vertigininae)." *Malacologia* 62(1):21–161.

Nekola, J. C., and B. F. Coles. 2010. "Pupillid Land Snails of Eastern North America." *American Malacological Bulletin* 28:29–57.

Nekola, J. C., B. F. Coles, and M. Horsák. 2015. "Species Assignments in *Pupilla* (Gastropoda: Pulmonata: Pupillidae): Integration of DNA-Sequence Data and Conchology." *Journal of Molluscan Studies* 81:196–216.

Nevill, G. 1877. "List of the Mollusca Brought Back by Dr. J. Anderson from Yunnan and Upper Burma, with Descriptions of New Species." *Journal of the Asiatic Society of Bengal* 46 (Part 2):14–41.

Nevill, G. 1880. "On the Land Shells, Extinct and Living, of the Neighborhood of Menton (Alpes Maritimes); with Descriptions of a New Genus and Several New Species." *Proceedings of the Zoological Society of London* (1880):94–142.

Newcomb, W. 1861. "Description of New Shells." *Proceedings of the California Academy of Sciences (Ser. 1)* 2:91–94.

———. 1864. "Description of Nine New Species of *Helix* Inhabiting California." *Proceedings of the California Academy of Sciences (Ser. 1)* 3:115–119.

———. 1867 (1863–1867). "Description of New Species of Land Shells." *Proceedings of the California Academy of Natural Sciences* (Ser. 1) Vol. 3:179–182.

———. 1870. "Description of a New American *Helix* (*H. hemphillii*)." *American Journal of Conchology* 5:165.

Nichols, S. J., and M. G. Black 1994. "Identification of Larvae: The Zebra Mussel (*Dreissena polymorpha*), Quagga Mussel (*Dreissena rosteriformis bugensis*) and Asian Clam (*Corbicula fluminea*)." *Canadian Journal of Zoology* 72:406–417.

Nicholson, 1818. *Conchology, British Encyclopedia. 3rd Edition.* Philadelphia: Mitchell, Ames, & White.

Nilsson, S. 1822. *Historia Molluscorum Sveciae, Terrestrium et Fluviatilum Breviter Delineata.* Lundae. [Note: Woodward (1924, Proc. Malacol. Soc. 16:23) suggests that the true publication date was 1823.)

Normand, N. A. J. 1844. *Notice sur Plusieurs Nouvelles Especes de Cyclades Decouvertes dans les Environs de Valencienes.* Valenciennes: Self-published.

———. 1852. *Description de Six Limaces Nouvelles Observées aux Environs de Valenciennes.* Valenciennes: Self-published.

Norton, C. G., and J. M. Bronson. 2006. "The Relationship of Body Size and Growth to Egg Production in the Hermaphroditic Freshwater Snail, *Helisoma trivolvis*." *Journal of Molluscan Studies* 72(2):143–147.

Nylander, O. 1900. "A List of Shells from Northeastern Maine." *Nautilus* 13:102–106.

O'Brien, C., D. Nez, D. Wolf, and J. Brim Box. 2013. "Reproductive Biology of *Anodonta californiensis*, *Gonidea angulata*, and *Margaritifera falcata* (Bivalvia: Unionida) in the Middle Fork John Day River, Oregon." *Northwest Science* 87(1):59–72.

Odhner, N. H. 1929. "Die Molluskenfauna des Takern: Sjon Takern Fauna och Flora." *Utgiven av K. Svenska Vetenskapsakademien* 8:39–93.

Oliver, G. V., and W. R. Bosworth III. 2000. "Oreohelices of Utah, I. Rediscovery of the Uinta Mountainsnail, *Oreohelix eurekensis uinta* Brooks, 1939 (Stylommatophora: Oreohelicidae)." *Western North American Naturalist* 60(4):451–455.

———. 2002. "Oreohelices of Utah, II. Extant Status of the Brian Head Mountainsnail, *Oreohelix parawanensis* Gregg, 1941 (Stylommatophora: Oreohelicidae)." *Western North American Naturalist* 62(4):451–457.

Olivier, G. A. 1804. *Voyage Dans l'Empire Othoman, l'Égypte et la Perse: Fair par Ordre du Gouvernement, Pendant les Six Premiéres Années de la République. Tome 2.* Paris: Aggase.

Oplinger, R. W., and E. J. Wagner. 2016. *New Zealand Mudsnails: Effects on Native Hydrobiid Species, Reproduction after Digestion by Fish, and Update on Range Within Utah.* Utah Division of Wildlife Resources Publication 16–13.

Örstan, A. 2010. "Reproductive Biology and Annual Population Cycle of *Oxyloma retusum* (Pulmonata: Succineidae)." *American Malacological Bulletin* 28: 113–120.

Ortmann, A. E. 1912. "*Cumberlandia*, a New Genus of Naiades." *Nautilus* 26(2): 13–14.

———. 1916. "The Anatomical Structure of *Gonidea angulata* (Lea)." *Nautilus* 30(5):50–53.

Pace, G. L. 1973. "The Freshwater Snails of Taiwan (Formosa)." *Malacological Review, Supplement* 1:1–118.

Paetel, F. 1875. *Die Bisher Veröffentlichten Familien- und Gattungsnamen der Mollusken.* Berlin: Gebrüder Paetel.

———. 1889. *Catalog der Conchylien-Sammlung, Zweite Abtheilung (2nd Ed.): die Land- und Süsswasser-Gasteropoden.* Berlin: Gebrüder Paetel.

———. 1890. *Catalog der Conchlien-Sammlung. Dritte Abthelung (3rd Ed.), die Acephalen und die Brachiopoden.* Berlin: Gebrüder Paetel.

Pallary, P. 1909. *Catalogue de la Fauna Malacologique d'Égypte. Mémoires Présentes a l'Institut Égyptien. Tome VI, Fasc. 1.* Le Caire: Diemer.

———. 1920. "Récoltes Malacologiques du Capitaine Paul Martel dans la Partie Septentrionale du Maroc." *Journal de Conchyliologie* 65 (Ser. 4):131–160.

Pallas, P. S. 1771. *Reise Durch Verschiedene Provinzen des Russischen Reichs. Vol. 1.* St. Petersburg: Kayserlichen Academie der Wissenschaften.

Paridon, B. J. van, J. S. Gilleard, D. D. Colwell, and C. P. Goater. 2017. "Life Cycle, Host Utilization, and Ecological Fitting for Invasive Lancet Liver Fluke, *Dicrocoelium dendriticum*, Emerging in Southern Alberta, Canada." *Journal of Parasitology* 103(3):207–212.

Parodiz, J. J. 1969. "The Tertiary Non-Marine Mollusca of South America." *Annals of the Carnegie Museum* 40:1–242, 16 plates.

Pathy, D. A., and G. L. Mackie. 1993. "Comparative Shell Morphology of *Dreissena polymorpha*, *Mytilopsis leucophaeata*, and the 'Quagga' Mussel (Bivalvia: Dreissenidae) in North America." *Canadian Journal of Zoology* 71:1012–1023.

Paul, A. J., and H. F. Clifford. 1991. "*Acroloxus coloradensis* (Henderson), a Rare North American Freshwater Limpet." *Nautilus* 105(4):173–174.

Paulucci, M. 1882. "Note Malacologische Sulla Fauna Terrestre e Fluviatile dell'Isola di Sardegna." *Bulletino della Società Malacologica Italiana* 8 (7/16):139–381, 9 plates.

Pease, W. H. 1870. "Remarks on the Species of *Melania* and *Limnaea* Inhabiting the Hawaiian Islands, with Description of New Species." *American Journal of Conchology* 6:4–7.

Penn, G. 1939. "A Study of the Life Cycle of the Freshwater Mussel, *Anodonta grandis*, in New Orleans." *Nautilus* 52:99–101.

Perez, K. E., J. R. Cordeiro, and Coppolino. 2008. *A Guide for Terrestrial Gastropod Identification.* American Malacological Society, Carbondale, IL.

Petkevičiūte, R., G. Stanevičiūte, V. Stunženas, T. Lee, and D. O Foighil. 2007. "Pronounced Karyological Divergence of the North American Congeners *Sphaerium rhomboideum* and *S. occidentale* (Bivalvia: Veneroida; Sphaeriidae)." *Journal of Molluscan Studies* 73:315–321.

Pfeiffer, L. 1821–1828. *Naturgeschichte Deutscher Land- und Süsswasser-Mollusken.* Weimar: Commission des Grofsherzogl. Abt. 1: pp. 1–134, (1821), Abt. 2: 1–40, (1825), Abt. 3: 1–84, (1828).

———. 1840. "Uebersicht der im Januar, Februar und Marz 1839 auf Cuba Gesammelten Mollusken." *Archiv für Naturgeschichte* 6:250–261.

———. 1841–1846. *Symbolae ad Historiam Heliceorum.* Parts 1–5 (pp. 1–88, 1841); *I. Aphorismi de Distributione Familiae, II. Helicea Collectionis Pfeifferianae, III. Diagnoses 71 Specierum, IV. Synonymia Generis Helicis, V. Synonymia Generis Bulimi*). *Sectio Altera* (pp. 1–147; 1842). *Sectio Tertia* (pp. 1–100; 1846). Cassel: Fischer.

———. 1854–1860. *Novitates Conchologicae, Series Prima, Mollusca Extramarina.* Cassel: Fischer.

Pfenninger, M., F. Reinhardt, and B. Streit. 2002. "Evidence for Cryptic Hybridization Between Different Evolutionary Lineages of the Invasive Clam Genus *Corbicula* (Veneroida, Bivalvia)." *Journal of Evolutionary Biology* 15:818–829.

Philippi. R. A. 1844. *Enumeratio Molluscorum Siciliae, cum Viventium Tum in Tellure Tertiaria Fossilium, Vol. 2.* Halis: E. Anton.

———. 1886 (1841). "*Physa mexicana* Philippi, die Mexikanische Blasenschnecke." In *Die Familie der Limnaeiden, enthaltend die genera* Planorbis, Limneus, Physa, *und* Amphipeplea, edited by H. C. Kuster, W. Dunker, and S. Clessin, 5–6. Systematisches Conchylien-Cabinet von Martini und Chemnitz Bd. 1, Abt. 17.

Pieńkowska, J. R., and A. Lesicki. 2018. "A Note on the Status of *Galba occulta* Jackiewicz, 1959 (Gastropoda: Hydrophila: Lymnaeidae)." *Folia Malacologica* 26(4):231–247.

Pilsbry, H. A. 1889. "Nomenclature and Check-list of North American Land Shells." *Proceedings of the Academy of Natural Sciences of Philadelphia* 41:191–210.

———. 1890. "New and Little-Known American Mollusks, No. 3." *Proceeding of the Academy of Natural Sciences of Philadelphia* 42:296–302, Plate 1.

———. 1891. "Land and Fresh-Water Mollusks Collected in Yucatan and Mexico." *Proceedings of the Academy of Natural Sciences of Philadelphia* 43:310–334.

———. 1893–1895. *Manual of Conchology, Structural and Systematic, with Illustrations of the Species. Vol. 9 (Ser. 2, Pulmonata) (Helicidae, Vol. 7, 1894). Vol.16: Philinidae, Gasteropteridae, Aglajidae, Aplysiidae, Oxynoeidae, Runcinidae, Umbraculidae, Pleurobranchidae (1895–1896).* Philadelphia: Academy of Natural Sciences. [Note: G. W. Tryon is credited as author on title page, as he started the series, but Pilsbry wrote this section.]

———. 1896. "*Limnaea bulimoides* Lea Resisting Drought." *Nautilus* 10:96.

———. 1897–1898. "A Classified Catalogue of American Land Shells, with Localities." *Nautilus* 11:45–48, 59–60, 71–72, 83–84, 93–96, 105–108, 117–120. 127–132, 138–144.

———. 1898a. "Descriptions of New American Land Shells." *Nautilus* 11:133–134.

———. 1898b. "Description of New Species and Varieties of American Zonitidae and Endodontidae." *Nautilus* 12:85–88.

———. 1899a. "New American Land Shells." *Nautilus* 12:102–104.

———. 1899b. "Remarks on the American Species of *Conulus*." *Nautilus* 12:113–117.

———. 1899c. "Descriptions of New Species of Mexican Land and Fresh-Water Mollusks." *Proceedings of the Academy of Natural Sciences of Philadelphia* 51:391–405.

———. 1899d. "Catalogue of the Amnicolidae of the Western United States." *Nautilus* 12:121–127.

———. 1900a. "New Species and Subspecies of American Land Snails." *Nautilus* 13:114–115.

———. 1900b. "Notice of New American Snails." *Nautilus* 14:40–41.

———. 1900c. "On the Zoological Position of *Partula* and *Achatinella*." *Proceedings of the Academy of Natural Sciences of Philadelphia* 52:561–567.

———. 1902. "Southwestern Land Snails." *Proceedings of the Academy of Natural Sciences of Philadelphia* 54:510–511.

———. 1903. "Mexican Land and Freshwater Mollusks." *Proceedings of the Academy of Natural Sciences of Philadelphia* 55:761–789.

———. 1904. *Oreohelix* Is the New Genus for Rocky Mountain Helices of the *H. strigosa* Group (footnote). *Nautilus* 17:131.

———. 1905. "Mollusca of the Southwestern States I. Urocoptidae, Helicidae of Arizona and New Mexico." *Proceedings of the Academy of Natural Sciences of Philadelphia* 57:211–90, Plates 11–27.

———. 1906. "Mollusca of the Southwestern States. II." *Proceedings of the Academy of Natural Sciences of Philadelphia* 58:123–175, Plates 5–9.

———. 1908a. "On *Euconulus fulvus* and *E. trochiformis*." *Nautilus* 22:25–26.

———. 1908b. "*Valvata humeralis californica* N. Subsp." *Nautilus* 22:82.

———. 1914. "Shells of Duran, New Mexico (*Pupilla muscorum xerobia* n.subsp.)." *Nautilus* 28(4):37–38.

———. 1915. "Mollusca of the Southwestern States VI. The Hacheta Grande, Florida, and Peloncillo Mountains, New Mexico." *Proceedings of the Academy of Natural Sciences* 67:345–350.

———. 1916a. "New Species of *Amnicola* from New Mexico and Utah." *Nautilus* 29:111–112.

———. 1916b. "Hunting Mollusca in Utah and Idaho." *Nautilus* 30:96

———. 1916c. "Notes on the Anatomy of *Oreohelix*: With a Catalogue of the Species." *Proceedings of the Academy of Natural Sciences of Philadelphia* 68: 340–359.

———. 1916d. "On Some Ill-understood Oreohelices." *Nautilus* 29:139–142.

———. 1917. "Notes on the Anatomy of Oreohelix, II." *Proceedings of the Academy of Natural Sciences of Philadelphia* 69:42–46.

———. 1916–1918. "Pupillidae (Gastrocoptinae)." *Manual of Conchology* 24:1–380, Plates 1–48.

———. 1920–1921. "Pupillidae (Vertiginidae, Pupillinae)." *Manual of Conchology* (Ser. 2, Pulmonata) 26:1–254, Plates 19–24.

———. 1926a. "A Freshwater Snail, *Physa zionis,* Living under Unusual Conditions." *Proceedings of the Academy of Natural Sciences* 77:325–328, Plate 11.

———. 1926b. "Pupillidae (Oruculinae, Pagodulinae, Acantinulinae, Etc.)." *Manual of Conchology Ser. 2*, Vol. 27:1–369, Plates 19–32.

———. 1926c. "The Land Mollusks of the Republic of Panama and the Canal Zone." *Proceedings of the Academy of Natural Sciences of Philadelphia* 78:57–126, Plates 9–10.

———. 1927–1935. "Geographic Distribution of Pupillidae; Strobilopsidae, Valloniidae, and Pleurodiscidae." *Manual of Conchology* (Ser. 2, Pulmonata) 28: 1–190, Plates 24–25.

———. 1932a. "Notes and News: *Physa humerosa interioris* Ferriss 1920 is, in my opinion, a form of *Physa virgata* Gould." *Nautilus* 45:139.

———. 1932b. "*Carinifex newberryi subrotunda* N. Subsp." *Nautilus* 45:139.

———. 1933. "Notes on the Anatomy of *Oreohelix*. III. With Descriptions of New Species and Subspecies." *Proceedings of the Academy of Natural Sciences of Philadelphia* 85:383–410.

———. 1934. "Review of the Planorbidae of Florida, with Notes on Other Members of the Family." *Proceedings of the Academy of Natural Sciences of Philadelphia* 86:29–66.

———. 1935. "Western and Southwestern Amnicolidae and a New *Humboldtiana*." *Nautilus* 48:91–94.

———. 1939. *Land Mollusca of North America (North of Mexico). Volume 1, Part 1*. Academy of Natural Sciences of Philadelphia Monograph No. 3.

———. 1940. *Land Mollusca of North America (North of Mexico). Volume 1, Part 2*. Academy of Natural Sciences of Philadelphia Monograph No. 3.

---. 1946. *Land Mollusca of North America (North of Mexico). Volume 2, Part 1*. Academy of Natural Sciences of Philadelphia Monograph No. 3.

---. 1948. *Land Mollusca of North America (North of Mexico). Volume 2, Part 2*. Academy of Natural Sciences of Philadelphia Monograph No. 3.

Pilsbry, H. A., and T. D. A. Cockerell. 1900. "Records of Mollusca from New Mexico." *Nautilus* 14:85–86.

---. 1913. "A New Form of *Oreohelix*." *Nautilus* 26:144.

Pilsbry, H. A., and C. M. Cooke. 1918–1920. "Pupillidae (Gastrocoptinae, Vertiginidae)." *Manual of Conchology* 25:1–401, Plates 1–34.

Pilsbry, H. A., and J. H. Ferriss. 1906. "Mollusca of the Southwestern United States. II." *Proceedings of the Academy of Natural Sciences of Philadelphia* 58:123–60 (June 20), 161–75 (July 24).

---. 1909. "Mollusca of the Southwestern States III. The Huachuca Mountains, Arizona." *Proceedings of the Academy of Natural Sciences of Philadelphia* 61:495–516, Plates 23–24.

---. 1910. "Mollusca of the Southwestern United States: IV. The Chiricahua Mountains, Arizona." *Proceedings of the Academy of Natural Sciences of Philadelphia* 62:44–144.

---. 1911. "Mollusca of the Southwestern States: V. The Grand Canyon and Northern Arizona." *Proceedings of the Academy of Natural Sciences of Philadelphia* 63(1):174–199, Plates 12–14.

---. 1917. "Mollusca of the Southwestern States, VIII: The Black Range, New Mexico." *Proceedings of the Academy of Natural Sciences of Philadelphia* 69:83–106, Plates 7–10.

---. 1918. "New Land Shells from California and Nevada." *Nautilus* 31:93–95.

---. 1919. "Mollusca of the Southwestern States. IX. The Santa Catalina, Rincon, Tortillita, and Galiuro Mountains." *Proceedings of the Academy of Natural Sciences of Philadelphia* 70(3):282–333, Plates 3–7.

---. 1923. "Mollusca of the Southwestern States, XI: From the Tucson Range to Ajo, and Mountain Ranges Between the San Pedro and Santa Cruz Rivers, Arizona." *Proceedings of the Academy of Natural Sciences of Philadelphia* 75(1):47–104, Plates 1–8.

Pilsbry, H. A., and J. Henderson. 1937. "*Oreohelix strigosa capax*." *Nautilus* 50:101.

Pilsbry, H. A., and E. G. Vanatta. 1900. "A Partial Revision of the Pupae of the United States." *Proceedings of the Academy of Natural Sciences of Philadelphia* 52:582–611, Plates 12–13.

Pini, N. 1876. "Molluschi Terrestri e d'Acque Dolce Viventi nel Territorio d'Esino." *Bulletino della Societá Malacologica Italiana* 2(2):67–210. 2 plates.

Poli, I. X. 1791–1827. *Testacea Utriusque Siciliae Eorumque Historia et Anatome, Tabulis Aeneis Ilustrata. Tomus Primus*. Parmae: Ex Regio.

Polinski, W. 1929. "Limnoloska Ispitifanjia Balkanskog. I. Reliktna Fauna Gasteropoda Ochridskog Jezera (Fauna Reliquaire des Gasteropodes du Lac d'Ochrida)." *Glas Srpska Kral'eveske Akademije, Beograd, Prvi Razred* 137(65):129–178. [in Serbian]

Ponder, W. F. 1988. "*Potamopyrgus antipodarum*—A Molluscan Coloniser of Europe and Australia." *Journal of Molluscan Studies* 54(3):271–285.

Ports, M. A. 1996. "Habitat Affinities and Distributions of Land Gastropods from the Ruby Mountains and East Humboldt Range of Northeastern Nevada." *Veliger* 39(4):335–341.

---. 2004. "Biogeographic and Taxonomic Relationships among the Mountain Snails (Gastropoda: Oreohelicidae) of the Central Great Basin." *Western North American Naturalist* 64(2):145–154.

---. 2019. "Terrestrial Mollusks of Great Basin National Park, the Snake Range, Nevada, USA." *Western North American Naturalist* 79(2):247–59.

Potiez, V. L. V., and A. L. G. Michaud. 1838. *Galerie des Mollusques, ou Catalogue Méthodique, Descriptif et Raisonné des Mollusques et Coquilles du Muséum de Donai(sic= Douai), Tome premier*. Paris: Bailliére.

Prashad, B. 1929. "Revision of the Asiatic Species of the Genus *Corbicula*. III. The Species of the Genus *Corbicula* from China, South-Eastern Russia, Thibet, Formosa and the Philippine Islands." *Memoirs of the Indian Museum* 9:49–68.

———. 1932. *Les Lamellibraches de L'Expedition du Siboga. Partie Systematique II. Pelecypoda (exclusive of the Pectinidae)*. Siboga Expeditie Vol. 53:1–353, 9 plates.

Preston, H. B. 1907. "Description of New Species of Land and Freshwater Shells from Central and South America." *Annals and Magazine of Natural History, Including Zoology, Botany, and Geology* Ser. 7, Vol. 20 (No. 120):490–498.

———. 1913. "Characters of New Genera and Species of Terrestrial Mollusca from Norfolk Island." *Annals and Magazine of Natural History Including Zoology, Botany, and Geology*, Ser. 8, Vol. 12 (No. 72) (article LXV): 522–538.

Prime, T. 1851a. [no official title] New Species in *Cyclas* and *Pisidium*. *Proceedings of the Boston Society of Natural History* 4:155–165.

———. 1851b. [no official title] *Pisidium ventricosum*. *Proceedings of the Boston Society of Natural History* 4:68.

———. 1852. "A Monograph of the Species of *Pisidium* Found in the United States of North America, with Figures." *Boston Journal of Natural History* 6:348–368.

———. 1853. "Notes on the Species of *Cyclas* Found in the United States." *Proceedings of the Boston Society of Natural History* 4:271–286.

———. 1858 (read 1853). "Descriptions of Three New Species of *Pisidium*." *Annals of the Lyceum of Natural History of New York* 6:64–66.

———. 1860. "Cyclades." In *Checklist of Shells of North America*, I. Lea, P. P. Carpenter, W. Stimpson, W. G. Binney, and T. Prime, 1–2. Smithsonian Miscellaneous Collections 2(Article VI)

———. 1861. *Monograph of the Species of Sphaerium of North and South America*. Philadelphia: Merrihew & Thompson.

———. 1862. "List of the Known Species of *Pisidium*, with Their Synonymy." *Annals of the Lyceum of Natural History of New York* 7:94–103.

———. 1865. *Monograph of American Corbiculadae*. Smithsonian Miscellaneous Collections 7(145). i–xi, 1–80.

———. 1867. "Notes on the Species of the Family Corbiculadae, with Figures." *Annals of the Lyceum of Natural History of New York* 8:57–92; 213–238; 414–431.

———. 1869–1870. "Catalogue of the Recent species of the family Corbiculadae." *American Journal of Conchology* 5:127–187.

———. 1895. *Catalogue of the Species of Corbiculadae in the Collection of Temple Prime, Now Forming Part of the Collection of the Museum of Comparative Zoology at Cambridge, Massachusetts*. Self-published.

Quick, H. E. 1960. "British Slugs (Pulmonata: Testacellidae, Arionidae, Limacidae)." *Bulletin of the British Museum (Natural History), Zoology* 6:103–226.

Quoy, M., and P. Gaimard. 1824. "Chapter XI, Description des Mollusques." In *Voyage Autour du Monde par les Corvettes l'Uranie et la Physicienne, pendant les Années 1817, 1818, 1819, et 1820. Vol. 3 Zoologie*, 410–516. Paris: Pillet Ainé.

Rader, R. B., M. C. Belk, and M. J. Keleher. 2003. "The Introduction of an Invasive Snail (*Melanoides tuberculata*) to Spring Ecosystems of the Bonneville Basin, Utah." *Journal of Freshwater Ecology* 19(4):647–657.

Rafinesque, C. S. 1815. *Analyse de la Nature ou Tableau de l'Univers et des Corps Organisés*. Palerme.

———. 1819. "Podrome de 70 Nouveaux Genres d'Animaux." *Journal de Physique, de Chemie, et d' Histoire Naturelle et des Arts* 88:417–429.

———. 1820. "Monographie des Coquilles Bivalves et Fluviatiles de la Riviére Ohio, Contenant Douze Genres et Soixant-Huit Espéces." *Annales Génerales des Sciences Physiques* 5(5):287–322, Plates 80–82.

Rajagopal, S., G. Velde, van der, and A. bij de Vaate. 2000. "Reproductive Biology of the Asiatic Clams *Corbicula fluminalis* and *Corbicula fluminea* in the River Rhine." *Archiv für Hydrobiologie* 149(3):403–420.

Ram, J. L., A. S. Karim, F. Banno, and D. R. Kashian. 2012. "Invading the Invaders: Reproductive and Other Mechanisms Mediating the Displacement of Zebra Mussels by Quagga Mussels." *Invertebrate Reproduction and Development* 56(1):21–32.

Rath, E. 1988. "Organization and Systematic Position of the Valvatidae." In *Prosobranch Phylogeny, Malacological Review,* Supplement 4:194–204.

Raut, S. K., and G. M. Barker. 2002. "*Achatina fulica* Bowdich and Other Achatinidae as Pests in Tropical Agriculture." In *Mollusks as Crop Pests*, edited by G. M. Barker, 55–79. New York: CABI.

Reeve, L. A. 1854. *Monograph of the genus* Helix. Conchologia Iconica 7. London: self-published.

Reinhardt, O. 1877. "Bemerkungen uber Einige Transcaucasische Pupa-Arten." *Jahrbucher der Deutchen Malakozoologischen Gesellschaft* 4:76–87.

———.1878. "Ueber Japanische Corbicula-Arten." *Jahrbucher der Deutchen Malakozoologischen Gesellschaft* 5:185–194.

———.1883a. "Uber die von den Herren Gebruder Krause auf Ihrer Reise Gesammelten *Pupa*-, *Hyalina*- und *Vallonia*-Arten." *Sitzungs-Bericht der Gesellschaft Naturforschender Freunde zu Berlin* 1883:37–43.

———. 1883b. "Ueber Einige von Hungerford Gesammelte Japaniche Hyalinen." *Sitzungs-Bericht der Gesellschaft Naturforschender Freunde zu Berlin* 1883:82–86.

Remigio, E. A. 2002. "Molecular Phylogenetic Relationships in the Aquatic Snail Genus *Lymnaea*, the Intermediate Host of the Causative Agent of Fascioliasis: Insights from Broader Taxon Sampling." *Parasitology Research* 88(7):687–696.

Remigio, E. A., and D. Blair. 1997a. "Molecular Systematics of the Freshwater Snail Family Lymnaeidae (Pumonata: Basommatophora) Utilizing Mitochondrial Ribosomal DNA Sequences." *Journal of Molluscan Studies* 63:173–185.

———. 1997b. "Relationships among Problematic North American Stagnicoline Snails (Pumonata: Lymnaeidae) Reinvestigated Using Nuclear Ribosomal DNA Internal Transcribed Spacer Sequences." *Canadian Journal of Zoology* 75:1540–1545.

Richards, D. C. 2004. *Competition Between the Threatened Bliss Rapids Snail,* Taylorconcha serpenticola *(Hershler et al.) and the Invasive Aquatic Snail* Potamopyrgus antipodarum. PhD Dissertation, Montana State University, Bozeman.

———. 2016. *Unionoida Mussel and Non-Pulmonate Snail Survey and Status in the Jordan River, Utah.* Final Draft Report, prepared for T. Miller, Central Valley Water Reclamation Facility, Salt Lake City, UT. file:///C:/Users/fishc/Downloads/JordanRiverMolluskSurveyFinalReport2.1.pdf

Richards, D., L. Cazier, and G. Lester. 2001. "Spatial Distribution of Three Snail Species Including the Invader *Potamopyrgus antipodarum* in a Freshwater Spring." *Western North American Naturalist* 61(3):375–380.

Rigacci, G. 1866. *Catalogo dell Conchiglie Componenti la Collection Rigacci Classificata Col Sistema di Lamarck.* Rome: Self-published.

Risso, A. 1826. *Histoire Naturelle des Principales Productions de l'Europe Méridionale et Particuliérement de Celles des Environs de Nice et des Alpes Maritimes. Tome 4.* Paris: Levrault.

Rodgers, T. W., J. C. Dysthe, C. Tait, T. W. Franklin, M. K. Schwartz, and K. E. Mock. 2020. "Detection of Four Imperiled Western North American Freshwater Mussel Species from Environmental DNA with Multiple qPCR Assays." *Freshwater Science* 34(4). https://doi.org/10.1086/710570

Röding, P. F. 1798. *Museum Boltenianum Sive Catalogus Cimeliorum e Tribus Regnis Naturae quae Olim Collegerat Joa. Fried Bolten, MD. p.d. per XL: Annos Proto Physicus Hambergensis. Pars Segunda Continens Conchylia Sive Testacea Univalvia, Bivalvia, & Multivalvia.* Hamburg: Trapp.

Roessler, M. A., Beardsley G. L., and D. C. Tabb. 1977. "New Records of the Introduced Snail, *Melanoides tuberculata* (Mollusca: Thiaridae) in South Florida." *Florida Scientist* 40:87–94.

Rogers, C. L., and R. V. Dimock Jr. 2003. "Acquired Resistance of Bluegill Sunfish *Lepomis macrochirus* to Glochidia Larvae of the Freshwater Mussel *Utterbackia imbecilis* (Bivalvia: Unionidae) After Multiple Infections." *Journal of Parasitology* 89(1):51–56.

Rohrbach, F. 1937. "Oekologische und Morphologische Untersuchungen an *Viviparus* (*Bellamya*) *capillatus* Frauenfeld und *Viviparus* (*Bellamya*) *unicolor* Oliver, unter Berucksichtigung anderer Tropischer Formen und im Hinblich auf Phyletische Beziehungen." *Archiv fur Molluskenkunde* 69:177–218.

Roper, E. W. 1896. "Notes on the Washington Sphaeria and Pisidia, with Descriptions of New Species." *Nautilus* 9(9):97–99.

Roscoe, E. J. 1954. "Some Terrestrial Gastropods from the Deep Creek Mountains, Juab County, Utah." *Great Basin Naturalist* 14:19.

———. 1964. "Notes on the Bonneville Basin Quaternary Mollusca collected by Richard Ellsworth Call in the U.S. Geological Survey–U.S. National Museum Collections." *Sterkiana* 13:1–5.

Rosenberg, G., and M. L. Ludyanskiy 1994. "A Nomenclatural Review of *Dreissena* (Bivalvia: Dreissenidae), With Identification of the Quagga Mussel as *Dreissena bugensis*." *Canadian Journal of Fisheries and Aquatic Sciences* 51:1474–1484.

Roth, B. 1987. "Identities of Two Californian Land Mollusks Described by Wesley Newcomb." *Malacological Review* 20:129–132.

———. 2003. "*Cochlicopa* Férussac 1821 not *Cionella* Jeffreys 1829; Cionellidae Clessin 1879 not Cochlicopidae." *Veliger* 46:183–185.

Roux, C. 1976. "On Dating of the First Edition of Cuvier's Régne Animal." *Journal of the Society for the Bibliography of Natural History* 8(1):31.

Rowell, J. 1863. "Description of a New California Mollusk, Discovered by Rev. Joseph Rowell, at Marysville, in the Waters of Feather River." *Proceedings of the California Academy of Sciences, Ser. 1*, 3:21–22.

Rudolph, P. H., and J. B. Burch. 1989. "Electrophoretic Analysis of Enzymes in Three Species of *Stagnicola* (Pulmonata: Lymnaeidae)." *Journal of Medical and Applied Malacology* 1:57–64.

Rundell, R., B. S. Holland, and R. H. Cowie. 2004. "Molecular Phylogeny and Biogeography of the Endemic Hawaiian Succineidae (Gastropoda: Pulmonata)." *Molecular Phylogenetics and Evolution* 31:246–255.

Russell, R. H. 1971. "Mollusca of Fish Springs, Juab County, Utah: Rediscovery of *Stagnicola pilsbryi* (Hemphill, 1890)." *Great Basin Naturalist* 31:223–236.

Saadi, A. J., and C. M. Wade. 2019. "Resolving the Basal Divisions in the Stylommatophoran Land Snails and Slugs with Special Emphasis on the Position of the Scolodontidae." *Molecular Phylogenetics and Evolution* 139: 106529.

Sager, A. 1839. *Report of Dr. Abraham Sager, Zoologist of the Geological Survey of Michigan*. Detroit.

Say, T. 1816. "Conchology (*Helix arboreus*)." In *Nicholson's American Edition of British Encyclopedia, Vol. 2* [no page numbers]. Philadelphia: Mitchell, Ames, & White, Plate 4.

———. 1817. "Description of Seven Species of American Fresh Water and Land Shells, Not Noticed in the Systems." *Journal of the Academy of Natural Sciences of Philadelphia* I:13–18; 123–126.

———. 1818. "Conchology." In *Vol. 4, 2nd American Edition of Nicholson's British Encyclopedia of Arts and Sciences*. Philadelphia.

———. 1819. "Conchology." In *Vol. 4, 3rd American Edition of Nicholson's British Encyclopedia of Arts and Sciences*. (no page numbers) Philadelphia.

———. 1821. "Description of Univalve Shells of the United States." *Journal of the Academy of Natural Sciences of Philadelphia* 2:149–182.

———. 1822. "Description of Univalve Terrestrial and Fluviatile Shells of the United States." *Journal of the Academy of Natural Sciences of Philadelphia* 2: 370–81.

———. 1824. "Class Mollusca. Appendix Part 1 (Natural History) B." In *Narrative of an Expedition to the Source of St. Peter' River, Lake Winnepeek, Lake of the Woods, etc., Performed in the Year 1823 (under Command of Steven H. Long)*. W. H. Keating, 256–265. Philadelphia: Carey & Lea.

———. 1825. "Descriptions of Some New Species of Fresh Water and Land Shells of the United States." *Journal of the Academy of Natural Sciences of Philadelphia* 5: 119–131.

———. 1829. "Descriptions of Some New Terrestrial and Fluviatile Shells of North America." *New Harmony Disseminator of Useful Knowledge* 2:230 (see also Binney 1958).

———. 1840. "Descriptions of Some New Terrestrial and Fluviatile Shells of North America, 1829, 1830, 1831." *New Harmony Disseminator, Indiana*. [compilation and republication of previous works]

Schepman, M. W. 1882. "Die Zungen der Hyalinen." *Jahrbücher der Deutchen Malakologischen Gesellschaft* 9:236–243, Plates 6–8.

Schileyko, A. A. 2003. Treatise on Recent Terrestrial Pulmonate Molluscs. Part 10: Ariophantidae, Ostracolethidae, Ryssotidae, Milacidae, Dyakiidae, Staffordiidea, Gastrodontidae, Zonitidae, Duaudebardiidae, Parmacellidae. *Ruthenica,* Supplement 2, Part 10:1309–1466.

Schlesch, H. 1906. "Fauna der Insel Bornholm (Konigreich Danemark)." *Annales de la Société Royale Zoologique et Malacologique de Belgique* 41:175–185.

Schmidt, A. 1850. "Malakologische Mittheilungen." *Zeitschrift fur Malakozoologie* 7(8):113–120.

Scholtz, H. 1843. *Schlesien's Land- und Wasser-Mollusken: Systematisch Geordnet und Beschrieben*. Breslau: Schultz & Co.

Schrank, F. von Paula. 1803. *Fauna Boica: Durchgedachte Geschichte der in Baiern Einheimischen und Zahmen Thiere; Dritten und Lezten;* Bd. 2, Abt. 1:1–372, 3–19 Krüll: Landshut.

Schultheiss, R. 2007. "Systematics and Character Evolution of *Pisidium* (Bivalvia) in the Ancient Lakes Ohrid and Prespa." *Malacologist* 49. http://malacsoc.org.uk/the_Malacologist/BULL49/Schultheiss49.htm

Schumacher, C. F. 1817. *Essai d'un Nouveau Systéme des Habitations des Vers Testaces*. Copenhagen: Schultz.

Scopoli, J. A. 1777. *Introductio ad Historiam Naturalem Sistens Genera Lapidum, Plantarum et Animalium*. Prague: Wofgangum Gerle.

Selenka, E. 1865. "Zwei neue Nacktschnecken aus Australien." *Malakozoologische Blatter* 12:105–110.

Servain, G. 1880. *Etude Sur les Mollusques Recueillis en Espagne et en Portugal*. St. Germain: Bardin.

———. 1881. *Histoire Malacologique du Lac Balaton en Hongrie*. Paris: Poissy.

Shaw, J. N., and B. T. Simms 1929. "*Galba bulimoides* Lea as Intermediate Host of *Fasciola hepatica* in Oregon." *Science* 69:357.

Shimek, B. 1901. "*Pyramidula shimekii* (Pilsbry) Shimek." *Bulletin from the Laboratories of Natural History of the State University of Iowa* 5(1–2):139–145.

———. 1936. "The Habitats of Iowa Succineas." *Nautilus* 49:6–10.

Simpson, C. T. 1900. "Synopsis of the Naiades, or Pearly Fresh-Water Mussels." *Proceedings of the U.S. National Museum* 22:501–1044.

Simroth, H. 1891. "Die Nacktschnecken der Portugiesisch-Azorischen Fauna." *Kaiserlichen Leopoldinisch-Carolinischen Deutchen Akademie der Naturforscher* (Dresden) 56(2):204–423.

———. 1906. "Ueber Eine Reihe von Nacktschenecken, die Herr Dr. Cecconi auf Cypern und in Palaestina Gesammelt Hat." *Nachrichtsblatt der Deutschen Malakozoologischen Gesellschaft*. 38 (heft 1):17–24.

Sinclair, R. M., and B. G. Isom 1963. *Further Studies on the Introduced Asiatic Clam Corbicula in Tennessee*. Tennessee Pollution Control Board, Tennessee Department of Public Health, Nashville.

Siripattrawan, S., J. K. Park, and D. Ó Foighil. 2000. "Two Lineages of the Introduced Asian Freshwater Clam *Corbicula* Occur in North America." *Journal of Molluscan Studies* 66:423–429.

Skuza, L., A. M. Labecka, and J. Domagala. 2009. "Cytogenetic and Morphological Characterization of *Corbicula fluminalis* (O. F. Müller, 1774) (Bivalvia: Veneroida: Corbiculidae): Taxonomic Status Assessment of a Freshwater Clam." *Folia Biologica* (Kraków) 57(3,4):177–185.

Smith, A. G. 1937. "Type Locality of *Oreohelix strigosa* (Gould)." *Nautilus* 50:73–77.

Smith, D. G. 1999. "Differences in Siphonal Anatomy Between *Dreissena polymorpha* and *D. bugensis* (Mollusca: Dreissenidae) in Lake Ontario." *American Midland Naturalist* 141(2):402–405.

———. 2000a. "Notes on the Taxonomy of Introduced *Bellamya* (Gastropoda: Viviparidae) Species in Northeastern North America." *Nautilus* 114(2):31–37.

———. 2000b. "Chapter 3. Systematics and Distribution of the Recent Margaritiferidae." In *Ecology and Evolution of the Freshwater Mussels Unionoida*, edited by G. Bauer and K. Wächtler, 33–49. Berlin: Springer.

Smith, E. A. 1876. "Description of a New Species of *Carinifex* from California." *Proceedings of the Zoological Society of London* 1875: 536–537.

———. 1889. "Notes on British Hydrobiae, With Description of a Supposed New Species." *Journal of Conchology* 6:142–145.

———. 1893. "On the Generic Name to Be Applied to the *Nerita aurita* of Müller and Other Allied Species." *Conchologist* 2:141–142.

———. 1906. "Note on *Paludestrina jenkinsi*." *Proceedings of the Malacological Society of London* 7:203–204.

Solem, A. 1975. "Notes on Salmon River Valley Oreohelicid Land Snails with Description of *Oreohelix waltoni*." *Veliger* 18:16–30.

———.1976. *Endodontoid Land Snails from Pacific Islands (Mollusca: Pulmonata: Sigmurethra), Part 1. Family Endodontidae*. Field Museum of Natural History, Chicago.

———. 1978. "Classification of the Land Mollusca." In *Pulmonates, Vol. 2A, Systematics, Evolution, and Ecology,* edited by V. Fretter and J. Peake, 49–98. New York: Academic Press.

———. 1982. *Endodontoid Land Snails from Pacific Islands (Mollusca: Pulmonata: Sigmurethra), Part II. Families Punctidae and Charopidae, Zoogeography*. Field Museum of Natural History, Chicago.

Soler, J., D. Moreno, R. Araujo, and M.A. Ramos. 2006. "Diversidad y Distribución de los Moluscos de Aqua Dulce en la Communidad de Madrid (España)." *Graellsia* 62(Numero Extraordinario):201–252.

Sowerby, G. B. 1867–1870. "Monograph of the Genus *Anodon*." *Conchologia Iconica* 17, 37 plates. London: Reeve.

———. 1874. *Conchologia Iconica* 19. London: Reeve.

———. 1878. "Monograph of the Genus *Sphaerium*." *Conchologia Iconica* 20. London: Reeve

Spamer, E. E., and A. E. Bogan. 1993. "Mollusca of the Grand Canyon and Vicinity, Arizona: New and Revised Data on Diversity and Distributions, With Notes on Pleistocene-Holocene Mollusks of the Grand Canyon." *Proceedings of the Academy of Natural Sciences of Philadelphia* 144:21–68.

Spidle, A. 1994. *A Comparison of Exotic Bivalves, the Quagga Mussel (*Dreissena bugensis *Andrusov) and the Zebra Mussel (*D. polymorpha *Pallas), Using Genetic Variation and Tolerance to Temperature and Salinity*. M.S. Thesis, Cornell University, Ithaca, NY.

Spix, J. B., and J. A. Wagner 1827. *Testacea Fluviatilia Quae in Itinere per Brasiliam Annis MDCCCXVII–MDCCCXX*. Monachii: C. Wolf. 29 plates

Spring Rivers. 2007. *Reproductive Timing of Freshwater Mussels and Potential Impacts of Pulsed Flows on Reproductive Success*. California Energy Commission, PIER Energy-Related Environmental Research Program. CEC-500-2007-097.

Squyer, H. 1894. "List of Shells from the Vicinity of Mingusville, Montana." *Nautilus* 8:63–65.
Stagliano, D. M., G. M. Stephens, and W. R. Bosworth. 2007. *Aquatic Invertebrate Species of Concern on U.S.F.S. Northern Region Lands*. Report to the U.S. Forest Service, Northern Region by Montana Natural Heritage Program and Idaho Department of Fish and Game.
Starobogatov, Y. I. 1967. "On the Systematization of Freshwater Pulmonate Mollusks." *Trudy Zoologicheskogo Instituta Akademiya Nauk SSSR* 42:280–304 [in Russian].
———. 1970. *Fauna Molluskov I Zoogeograficheskoe Raionirovanie Kontinental'nykh Vodoemov Zemnogo Shara (Mollusk fauna and zoogeographical partitioning of continental water reservoirs of the world)*. Zoologicheskii Instituti Nauka, Akademiya Nauk, SSSR, Leningrad. [in Russian]
Starobogatov, Y. I., V. V. Bogatov, L. A. Prozorova, and E. M. Saekno. 2004. Molluscs. In *Key to the Freshwater Invertebrates of Russia and Adjacent Countries*, edited by S. J. Tsalolikhin, 6: 6–492. Saint Petersburg: Nauka Publishers. [in Russian]
Stearns, R. E. C. 1883. "Description of a New Hydrobiinoid Gastropod from the Mountain Lakes of the Sierra Nevada, with Remarks on Allied Species and the Physiographical Features of Said Region." *Proceedings of the Academy of Natural Sciences of Philadelphia* 35:171–176.
———. 1893. "Report of the Land and Fresh-Water Shells Collected in California and Nevada by the Death Valley Expedition, Including a Few Additional Species Obtained by C. Hart Merriam and Assistants in Part of the Southwestern United States." *North American Fauna* 7:269–283.
———. 1902. "The Fossil Freshwater Shells of the Colorado Desert, Their Distribution, Environment and Variation." *Proceedings of the National Museum* 24:271–299.
Steenberg, C. M. 1917. "Anatomie des *Acanthinula* et des *Vallonia*. les Organes Génitaux." *Videnskabelige Meddelelser fra Dansk Naturhistorisk Forening I København* 69:1–15.
———. 1925. "Études sur l'Anatomie et al. Systématique des Maillots (Fam. Pupillidae s. lat.)." *Videnskabelige Meddelelser fra Dansk Naturhistorisk Forening I København* 80:1–126.
Stein, J. P. E. F.1850. *Die Lebenden Schnecken und Muscheln der Umgegend Berlins*. Berlin: G. Reimer.
Sterki, V. 1890. "On Some Northern Pupidae, With Descriptions of New Species." *Nautilus* 3:123–126.
———. 1893. "Observations on *Vallonia*." *Proceedings of the Academy of Natural Sciences of Philadelphia* 45:234–279.
———. 1894. *The Land and Freshwater Mollusca in the Vicinity of New Philadelphia, a Contribution to the Natural History of Tuscarawas Co., Ohio*. 8th Annual Report of the Ohio State Academy of Science.
———. 1895. *Some Notes on Recent Mollusca of Ohio*. 3rd Annual Report of the Ohio State Academy of Science.
———. 1896. "New North American Pisidia." *Nautilus* 9(11):124–125.
———. 1898a. "*Bifidaria ashmuni*, a New Species of Pupidae." *Nautilus* 12:49–50.
———. 1898b. "New Species of *Bifidaria*." *Nautilus* 12:90–92.
———. 1899. "New Pupidae." *Nautilus* 12:127–129.
———. 1900. "New Pisidia, and Some General Notes." *Nautilus* 14:5–8.
———. 1901. "New Pisidia." *Nautilus* 14:99–101.
———. 1902. "Some Notes on the North American Calyculinae, with New Species." *Nautilus* 16:89–93.
———. 1903a. "New Pisidia." *Nautilus* 17:20–22, 79–82.
———. 1903b. "New North American Pisidia." *Nautilus* 17:42–43.
———. 1905. "New Varieties of North American Pisidia." *Nautilus* 19:80–84.
———. 1906a. "New Varieties of North American Pisidia." *Nautilus* 19:118–120.
———. 1906b. "New Species of *Pisidium*." *Nautilus* 20:17–20.
———. 1906c. "*Sphaerium hendersoni* n. sp." *Nautilus* 20:69–70.

———. 1907. "A Preliminary Catalogue of the Land and Fresh-Water Mollusca of Ohio." *Proceedings of the Ohio State Academy of Sciences* 4(8):367–402.
———. 1909a. "*Pisidium marci* n.sp." *Nautilus* 23:42–43.
———. 1909b. "Descriptions of Two New Species of *Musculium*." *Nautilus* 23:66–67.
———. 1909c. "*Sphaerium pilsbryanum*, n. sp." *Nautilus* 22:141-142.
———. 1910. "A New Species of *Musculium*." *Nautilus* 24:3
———. 1911. "New Pisidia from Alabama." *Nautilus* 25:2–3.
———. 1912a. "*Musculium declive*, n. sp." *Nautilus* 25:103–104.
———. 1912b. "Sphaeridae, Old and New." *Nautilus* 26:6–9, 95–96.
———. 1913. "Sphaeridae, Old and New, IV." *Nautilius* 26:136–140.
———. 1916. "A Preliminary Catalogue of the North American Sphaeriidae." *Annals of the Carnegie Museum* 10:429–477.
———. 1922. "Some Notes on Sphaeriidae with Descriptions of New Species." *Annals of the Carnegie Museum* 13:425–439.
———. 1923. "Colorado Pisidia." *Nautilus* 37:16–22.
———. 1927. "A New Species of *Sphaerium* (*S. notatum*)." *Nautilus* 41:55–57.
———. 1928. "Sphaeriidae, Palearctic and Nearctic, II." *Nautilus* 42:23–27.
Stevens, L. E., P. Keim, M. Miller, and S.-K. Wu. 2000. *Morphological and Genetic Relatedness among Succineid Landsnails in the United States and Canada, With Emphasis on the Endangered Kanab Ambersnail* (Oxyloma haydeni kanabensis). Draft Final Report, Bureau of Reclamation Contract 98-FC-40-1230. Grand Canyon Monitoring and Research Center, Flagstaff, AZ.
Stewart, T. W. 2006. *The Freshwater Gastropods of Iowa (1821–1998): Species Composition, Geographic Distributions, and Conservation Concerns*. Iowa State University, Natural Resource Ecology and Management, http://lib.dr.iastate.edu/nrem_pubs
Stimpson, W. 1851. *Shells of New England; a Revision of the Synonymy of the Testaceous Mollusks of New England, with Notes on Their Structure and Their Geographical and Bathymetrical Distribution, with Figures of New Species*. Boston: Phillips, Sampson & Co.
———. 1865a. *Researches upon the Hydrobiinae and Allied Forms*. Smithsonian Miscellaneous Collections 7 (Article 4, 201):1–59.
———. 1865b. "Diagnoses of Newly Discovered Genera of Gasteropods, Belonging to the Sub-Fam. Hydrobiinae, of the Family Rissoidae." *American Journal of Conchololy* 1:52–54.
Stoliczka, F. 1873. "On the Land Shells of Penang Island, with Descriptions of the Animals and Anatomical Notes; Part Second, Helicacea." *Journal of the Asiatic Society of Bengal* 42:11–110.
Strebel, H. 1873. *Beitrag zur Kenntnis der Fauna Mexikanischer Land- und Süsswasser-Conchylien*. Abhandlungen aus dem Gebiete der Naturewissenschaften hereausgegeben vom dem Naturewissenschaftlichen Verein 4(1). Hamburg.
Streng, L. H. 1896. "A New Variety of *Lymnaea*." *Nautilus* 9:123.
Suter, H. 1889. "Beitrage zur Schweizerischen Mollusken-Fauna." *Malakozoologische Blatter* 1889–1891:1–26.
———. 1904. "Revision of the New Zealand Species of the Genus *Potamopyrgus*, with a Description of New Species." *Transactions and Proceedings of the New Zealand Institute* 37:258–267.
———. 1913. *Manual of the New Zealand Mollusca, with an Atlas of Quarto Plates*. Wellington, New Zealand.
Swainson, W. 1823. "The Specific Characters of Several Undescribed Shells." *The Philosophical Magazine* (London) 62:401–403.
———.1840. *A Treatise on Malacology or The Natural Classification of Shells and Shell Fish*. London: Longman, Orme, Brown, Green, Longmans, & Taylor.
Taeubert, J. E., B. Gum, and J. Geist. 2013. "Variable Development and Excystment of Freshwater Pearl Mussel (*Margaritifera* L.) at Constant Temperature." *Limnologica* 43(4):319–322.

Tappan, B. 1839. "Description of Some New Shells." *American Journal of Science and Arts* 35:268–270.

Tate, R. 1870. "On the Land and Freshwater Mollusks of Nicaragua." *American Journal of Conchology* 5:151–162.

Taylor, D. W. 1950. "Three New *Pyrgulopsis* from the Colorado Desert, California." *Leaflets in Malacology* 1:52–54.

———. 1954. "A New Pleistocene Fauna and New Species of Fossil Snails from the High Plains." *Occasional Papers of the Museum of Zoology, University of Michigan* 557:1–16.

———. 1966. "Summary of North American Blancan Nonmarine Mollusks." *Malacologia* 4(1):1–172.

———. 1970. "American Malacological Union Symposium: Rare and Endangered Mollusks. 4. Western Freshwater Mollusks." *Malacologia* 10(1):33–34.

———. 1975. "Index and Bibliography of Late Cenozoic Freshwater Mollusca of Western North America." *University of Michigan Papers on Paleontology* 10:1–384.

———. 1981. "Freshwater Mollusks of California: A Distributional Checklist." *California Fish and Game* 67:140–163.

———. 1987. "Freshwater Mollusks from New Mexico and Vicinity." *Bureau of Mines and Mineral Resources Bulletin* 116:1–50.

———. 1988a. "New Species of *Physa* (Gastropoda: Hygrophila) from the Western United States." *Malacological Review* 21:43–79.

———. 1988b. "Aspects of Freshwater Mollusk Ecological Biogeography." *Palaeogeography, Palaeoclimatology, Palaeoecology* 62:511–576.

———. 2003. "Introduction to Physidae (Gastropoda: Hygrophila). Biogeography, Classification, and Morphology." *Revista de Biologia Tropical (International Journal of Tropical Biology and Conservation)* 51 (Suppl. 1).

Taylor, D. W., and R. C. Bright. 1987. "Drainage History of the Bonneville Basin". In *Cenozoic Geology of Western Utah*, Publ. 16, Utah Geological Association, 239–256.

Taylor, D. W., H. J. Walter, and J. B. Burch. 1963. "Freshwater Snails of the Subgenus *Hinkleyia* (Lymnaeidae: *Stagnicola*) from the Western United States." *Malacologia* 1:237–276.

Taylor, J. W. 1914. *Monograph of the Land and Freshwater Mollusca of the British Isles. Zonitidae, Endodontidae, Helicidae*. Leeds: Taylor Brothers.

Te, G. A. 1978. *A Systematic Study of the Family Physidae (Bassommatophora: Pulmonata)*. PhD Diss., University of Michigan, Ann Arbor.

———. 1980. "New Classification System for the Family Physidae (Pulmonata: Bassomatophora)." *Archiv für Molluskenkunde* 110:179–184.

Teasdale, L. C. 2017. *Phylogenomics of the Pulmonate Land Snails*. PhD diss., University of Melbourne.

Terry, C. H., and T. F. Duda. 2021. "Consequences of Captive-rearing and Exposure to Cues from Potential Predators on Shell Sizes and Shapes of North American Stagnicoline Gastropods (Family Lymnaeidae). *American Malacological Bulletin* 38(2):89–97.

Therriault, T. W., M. F. Docker, M. I. Orlova, D. D. Heath, and H. J. MacIsaac. 2004. "Molecular Resolution of the Family Dreissenidae (Mollusca: Bivalvia) With Emphasis on Ponto-Caspian Species, Including First Report of *Mytolopsis leucophaeata* in the Black Sea Basin." *Molecular Phylogenetics and Evolution* 30:479–489.

Thiele, J. 1925. "Prosobranchia." In *Handbuch der Zoologie 5(1)*, edited by W. Kükenthal and T. Krumbach, 40–94. Berlin: Walter de Gruyter & Co.

———. 1931. "Gastropoda: Opisthobranchia und Pulmonata." *Handbuch der Systematischen Weichtierkunde*; Bd. 1, Zwiter Teil, 377–778. Stuttgart: Fischer.

———. 1998. *Handbook of Systematic Malacology, Part 3 (Scaphopoda/Bivalvia/Cephalopoda) and Part 4 (Comparative Morphology/Phylogeny/Geographical Distribution)*. Smithsonian Institution translation by R. Bieler and P. M. Mikkelsen, Washington, DC.

Thiroit-Quiévreux, C. 2003. "Advances in Chromosomal Studies of Gastropod Molluscs." *Journal of Molluscan Studies* 69:187–201.
Thomas, G. J. 1959. "Self-Fertilization and Production of Young in a Sphaeriid Clam." *Nautilus* 72:131–140.
Thompson, F. G. 1977. "The Hydrobiid Snail Genus *Marstonia*." *Bulletin of the Florida State Museum, Biological Sciences* 21:113–158.
Thompson, F. G., and R. Hershler. 2002. "Two Genera of North American Freshwater Snails: *Marstonia* Baker, 1926, Resurrected to Generic Status, and *Floridobia*, New Genus (Prosobranchia: Hydrobiidae, Nymphilinae)." *Veliger* 45(3):269–271.
Tiemann, J. S., A. E. Haponski, S. A. Douglass, T. Lee, K. S. Cummings, M. A. Davis, and D. Ó Foighil. 2017. "First record of a putative novel invasive *Corbicula* lineage discovered in the Illinois River, Illinois, USA." *BioInvasions Records* 6(2):159–166.
Tillier, S. 1989. "Comparative Morphology, Phylogeny and Classification of Land Snails and Slugs (Gastropoda: Pulmonata: Stylommatophora)." *Malacologia* 30(1–2):1–303.
Trask, J. B. 1855. "Three Specimens of Naiades, With Descriptions, from the Sacramento River, and Lagoons." *Proceedings of the California Academy of Sciences* 1:28–29.
Trdan, R. J., and W. R. Hoeh. 1982. "Eurytopic Host Use by Two Congeneric Species of Freshwater Mussel (Pelecypoda: Unionidae: *Anodonta*)." *American Midland Naturalist* 108:381–388.
Tronstad, L. M., and M. D. Andersen. 2018. *Aquatic Snails of the Snake and Green River Basins of Wyoming*. Report prepared by the Wyoming Natural Diversity Database for the Wyoming Game and Fish Department.
Tryon, G. W., Jr. 1863. "Descriptions of New Species of Fresh Water Mollusca Belonging to the Families Amnicolidae, Valvatidae, and Limnaeidae Inhabiting California." *Proceedings of the Academy of Natural Sciences of Philadelphia* 15: 147–150.
———. 1865a. "Descriptions of New Species of North American Limnaeidae." *American Journal of Conchology* 1(3):223–231.
———. 1865b. "Catalogue of the Species of *Lymnaea* Inhabiting the United States." *American Journal of Conchology* 1:247–251.
———. 1866a. "Monograph of the Terrestrial Mollusca of the U.S." *American Journal of Conchology* 2(3):218–277.
———. 1866b. "Descriptions of New Fluviatile Mollusca." *American Journal of Conchology* 2:111–114.
———. 1866c. "Descriptions of New Fresh-water Shells of the United States." *American Journal of Conchology* 2:4–7.
———. 1866d. "Review of 'Researches upon the Hydrobiinae and Allied Form' by W. Stimpson." *American Journal of Conchology* 2:152–158.
———. 1867. "Notices and Reviews of New Works (*Planorbella binneyi*)." *American Journal of Conchology* 3:195–197.
———. 1870. *Monograph of the Fresh-Water Univalve Mollusca of the United States*. Conchological Society of the Academy of Natural Sciences of Philadelphia.
Tucker, M. E. 1928. "Studies on the Life Cycles of Two Species of Fresh-Water Mussels Belonging to the Genus *Anodonta*." *Biological Bulletin (Woods Hole)* 54:117–127.
Turgeon, D. D., A. E. Bogan, E. V. Coan, W. K. Emerson, W. G. Lyons, W. L. Pratt, C. F. E. Roper, et al. 1998. *Common and Scientific Names of Aquatic Invertebrates from the United States and Canada: Mollusks. 2nd Ed*. American Fisheries Society Special Publication 26.
Turton, W. 1831. *A Manual of the Land and Fresh-Water shells of the British Islands*. London: Longman, Rees, Orme, Brown, & Green.
USFWS (United States Fish and Wildlife Service). 1992a. *Endangered and Threatened Wildlife and Plants: Determination of Endangered or Threatened Status for Five Aquatic Snails in South Central Idaho*. Federal Register 57:59244–59257.

———. 1992b. "Endangered and Threatened Wildlife and Plants: Final Rule to List the Kanab Ambersnail as Endangered." Federal Register 57 (No. 75):13657–136661.

———. 2015. *New Zealand Mudsnail (*Potamopyrgus antipodarum*), Ecological Risk Screening Summary.* U.S.F.W.S. https://www.fws.gov/fisheries/ans/erss/highrisk/Potamopyrgus-antipodarum-ERSS-revision-June2015.pdf

———. 2020 (January 6). "Endangered and Threatened Wildlife and Plants: Removing the Kanab Ambersnail from the List of Endangered and Threatened Wildlife." 50 CFR, Part 17, RIN 1018–BD49. Federal Register 85(3) govinfo.gov/content/pkg/FR-2020-01-06/pdf/2010-28352.

Utterback, W. I. 1915–1916. "The Naiades of Missouri." *American Midland Naturalist* Part 1, 4(3):41–53; Part 2, 4(4):97–152, Part 3, 4(5):181–204; Part 7, 4(10):432–464. Also available as combined offprint from University of Notre Dame, IN. 28 plates.

Vanatta, E. G. 1902. "General Notes: *Planorbis parvus walkeri* N. Var." *Nautilus* 41:58.

———. 1910. "Bermuda Shells." *Proceedings of the Academy of Natural Sciences of Philadelphia* 62:664–672.

———. 1912. "Land Shells of Southern Florida." *Nautilus* 26:16–22.

———. 1921. "Shells of Zion National Park, Utah." *Nautilus* 34:140–141.

Van Cleave, H. J., A. G. Wright, and C. W. Nixon. 1947. "Preliminary Observations on Reproduction in the Molluscan Genus *Musculium*." *Nautilus* 61:6–11.

Van der Schalie, H. 1938. *The Naiad Fauna of the Huron River, in Southeastern Michigan*. Miscellaneous Publication 40, University of Michigan Museum of Zoology, Ann Arbor.

Varandas, S., M. Lopes-Lima, A. Teixeira, M. Hinzmann, J. Reis, R. Cortes, J. Machado, et al. 2013. "Ecology of Southern European Pearl Mussels (*Margaritifera margaritifera*): First Record of Two New Populations on the Rivers Terva and Beça (Portugal)." *Aquatic Conservation: Marine and Freshwater Ecosystems* 23:374–389.

Vinarski, M. V. 2012. "The Lymnaeid Genus *Catascopia* Meier-Brook et Bargues, 2002 (Mollusca: Gastropoda: Lymnaeidae), Its Synonymy and Species Composition." *Invertebrate Zoology* 9(2):91–104.

Vinarski, M. V. 2013. "One, Two, or Several? How Many Lymnaeid Genera Are There?" *Ruthenia* 23(1):41–58.

Vinarski, M. V., O. V. Aksenova, Y. V. Bespalaya, I. N. Bolotov, M. Y. Gofarov, and A. V. Kondakov. 2016. "*Ladislavella tumrokensis*: The First Molecular Evidence of a Nearctic Clade of Lymnaeid snails Inhabiting Eurasia." *Systematics and Biodiversity* 14:276–287.

Vinarski, M. V., O. V. Aksenova, and I. N. Bolotov. 2020. "Taxonomic Assessment of Genetically-Delineated Species of Radicine Snails (Mollusca, Gastropoda, Lymnaeidae)." *Zoosystematics and Evolution* 96(2):577–608.

Vinarski, M .V., I. N. Bolotov, K. Schniebs, I. O. Nekhaev, and A. K. Hundsdoerfer. 2017. "Endemic or Strangers? The Integrative Re-appraisal of Taxonomy and Phylogeny of the Greenland Lymnaeidae (Mollusca: Gastropoda)." *Comptes Rendus Biologies* 340:541–557.

Vinarski, M. V., and A. Eschner. 2016. "Examination of the Type Material of Freshwater Mollusk Species Described by J. P. R. Draparnaud." *Annalen des Naturhistorischen Museums in Wein, B*, 118:29–53.

Vinarski, M. V., and P. Glöer. 2008. "Taxonomic Notes on Euro-Siberian Freshwater Molluscs. 3. *Galba occulta* Jackiewicz, 1959 is a Junior Synonym of *Lymnaea palustris* var. *terebra* Westerlund, 1885." *Mollusca* 26:175–185.

Vinson, M., T. Harju, and E. Dinger. 2007. *Status of New Zealand Mud Snails (*Potamopyrgus antipodarum*) in the Green River Downstream from Flaming Gorge Dam: Current Distribution; Habitat Preference and Invertebrate Changes; Food Web and Fish Effects; and Predicted Distributions*. National Aquatic Monitoring Center (Utah State University) Final Report for Project Agreements USFWS-601815G405, NPS-J1242050058, BLM-JSA041003.

Wade, C. M., P. B. Mordan, and F. Naggs. 2006. "Evolutionary Relationships among the Pulmonate Land Snails and Slugs (Pulmonata, Stylommatophora)." *Biological Journal of Linnean Society* 87:593–610.

Wagner, H. 1935. "Magyororszag, Hovatorszag es Dalmacia Hazatlan Csigai: Die Nacktschnecken Ungarns, Croatiens und Dalmatiens." *Annales Historico-Naturales Musei Nationalis Hungarici, Pars Zoologica* 29:169–212.

Wagner, E., J. Detlor, R. Gibbs, and J. Hudson. 2018. *Aquatic Invasive Species Inspections, 2018 Annual Report.* Utah Division of Wildlife Resources, Salt Lake City, Utah.

Walker, B. 1892. "The Shell Bearing Mollusca of Michigan." *Nautilus* 6:31–35.

———. 1894. *A Review of Our Present Knowledge of the Molluscan Fauna of Michigan.* Thomas Smith Press, Michigan. (reprinted in 1965 in Sterkiana 17:10–25).

———. 1906. *An Illustrated Catalogue of the Mollusca of Michigan. Part 1. Terrestrial Pulmonata (Land Snails).* Report of the State Board of Geological Survey of Michigan for the Year 1905.

———. 1908. "New Michigan *Lymnaeas.*" *Nautilus* 22:9, 163, Plate 2.

———. 1918. "A Synopsis of the Classification of the Freshwater Mollusca of North America, North of Mexico, and a Catalogue of the More Recently Described Species, with Notes." *Michigan University Museum of Zoology Miscellaneous Publication* 6:1–213.

———. 1925. "New Species of North American Ancylidae and Lancidae." *Occasional Papers of the Museum of Zoology, University of Michigan* 165.

Walker, B., and H. A. Pilsbry. 1902. "The Mollusca of Mt. Mitchell Region, North Carolina." *Proceedings of the Academy of Natural Sciences of Philadelphia* 54:413–442, Plates 24, 25.

Walther, A. C., J. B. Burch, and D. O'Foighil. 2010. "Molecular Phylogenetic Revision of the Freshwater Limpet Genus *Ferrissia* (Planorbidae: Ancylinae) in North America Yields Two Species: *Ferrissia* (*Ferrissia*) *rivularis* and *Ferrissia* (*Kincaidilla*) *fragilis.*" *Malacologia* 53(1):25–45.

Waltz, J. 2008. *Chinese Mystery Snail Review.* Fish 423 Report, University of Washington. http://depts.washington.edu/oldenlab/wordpress/wp-content/uploads/2013/02/Bellamya-chinensis_Waltz.pdf

Warwick, T. 1944. "Inheritance of the Keel in *Potamopyrgus jenkinsi* (Smith)." *Nature (London)* 154:798–799.

Watson, H. 1934. "Genital Dimorphism in Zonitoides." *Journal of Conchology* 20:33–42.

Watters, G. 1995. *A Guide to the Freshwater Mussels of Ohio.* Ohio Department of Natural Resources, Columbus.

Watters, G. T., and S. H. O'Dee. 1998. "Metamorphosis of Freshwater Mussel Glochidia (Bivalvia: Unionidae) on Amphibians and Exotic Fishes." *American Midland Naturalist* 139(1):49–57.

Way, C. M., D. J. Hornbach, and A. J. Burky. 1980. "Comparative Life History Tactics of the Sphaeriid clam, *Musculium partumeium* (Say), From a Permanent and a Temporary Pond." *American Midland Naturalist* 104(2):319–327.

Way, C. M., and T. E. Wissing. 1982. "Environmental Heterogeneity and Life History Variability in the Freshwater Clams, *Pisidium variable* (Prime) and *Pisidium compressum* (Prime) (Bivalvia: Pisidiidae)." *Canadian Journal of Zoology* 50:2841–2851.

Weatherburn, M. 1964. "Radulae of Ottawa River Snails (Abstract)." *American Malacological Union Annual Reports for 1964* (30th Annual Meeting), p. 13.

Weaver, K. F., M. Perez-Losoda, R. P. Guralnick, A. Nelson, S. Blatt, and K. A. Crandall. 2008. "Assessing the Conservation Status of the Land Snail *Oreohelix peripherica wasatchensis* (Family Oreohelicidae)." *Conservation Genetics* 9: 907–916.

Weinland, C. D. F. 1880. "Zur Molluskenfauna von Haiti." *Jahrbucher der Deutchen Malakozoologischen Gesellschaft* 7:338–378, Plate 12.

Welter-Schultes, F. W. 2012. *European Non-Marine Molluscs, a Guide for Species Identification.* Göttingen, Germany: Planet Poster Editions.

Welter-Schultes, F., C. R. Altaba, and C. Audibert. 2013. "Comment on *Cornu* Born, 1778 (Mollusca, Gastropoda, Pulmonata, Helicidae): Request for a Ruling on the Availability of the Generic Name." *Bulletin of Zoological Nomenclature* 70(1):41–42.

Wenz, W. 1919. "Zur Systematik Tertiarer Land- und Susswassergastropoden. I." *Nachrichtsblatt der Deutchen Malakozoologischen Gesselschaft* 51(2):76–79.

Westerlund, C. A. 1876. "Neue Binnenmollusken aus Sibiren." *Nachrichtsblatt der Deutchen Malakozoologischen Gesselschaft* 8:97–104.

———. 1881. "Malakologiska Bidrag." *Öfversigt af Kongliga Vetenskaps Akademiens Förhandlingar* 4:35–69.

———. 1883. "Von der Vega-Expedition in Asien Gesammelte Binnenmollusken." *Nachrichtsblatt der Deutchen Malakozoolischen Gesellschaft* 15(3–4):48–59.

———. 1885. *Fauna in der Paläarktischen Region, Lebenden Binnenconchylien. Vol. 5 Fam. Succinidae, Auriculidae, Limnaeidae, Cyclostomidae & Hydrocenidae.* Lund: Håkan Ohlsson.

———. 1886. *Fauna in der Paläarctischen Region, Lebenden Binnenconchylien. Vol. 6. Fam. Ampullaridae, Paludinidae, Hydrobiidae, Melanidae, Valvatidae, and Neritidae.* Lund: Håkan Ohlsson.

———. 1894. "Specilegium Malacologicum. Neue Binnen-Conchylien aus der Paläarktischen Region." *Nachrichtsblatt der Deutchen Malakozoologischen Gesselschaft* 26(9/10):163–177, 190–205.

———. 1889. *Fauna in der Paläarctischen Region (Europa, Kaukasien...) Lebende Binnenconchylien. II. Gen. Helix*, p. 1–473. Berlin: Frielander.

———. 1897. "Beiträge zur Molluskenfauna Russlands." *Annuaire du Musée Zoologique de L'Académie Impériale de Sciences de St. Pétersbourg* (*Ezhegodnik Zoologicheskogo Muzeya Imperatorskoi Akademii Nauk*) 2:117–143.

———. 1902. "Methodus Dispositionis Conchyliorum Extramarinorum in Regione Palaearctic Viventium, Familias, Genera, Subgenera, et Stirpes Sistens." *Rad Jugoslavenske Akademije Znanosti I Umjetnosti, Matematicko–Prirodoslovni Razred* 151(32):82–139.

Wethington, A. R. 2004. *Family Physidae. Workbook*. www.researchgate.net/profile/Amy_Wethington/publication/242143007_Family_Physidae/links/0a85e53372c2a0aeec000000.pdf

Wethington, A. R., and C. Lydeard. 2007. "A Molecular Phylogeny of Physidae (Gastropoda: Basommatophora) Based on Mitochondrial DNA Sequences." *Journal of Molluscan Studies* 73:241–257.

Weyrauch, W. K. 1964. "Nomenklatorische Bemerkungen." *Archiv fur Molluskenkunde* 93(3/4):169.

Wheeler, K. 2018. *Preliminary Report of Land Snails of Zion National Park*. Field Report, Washington County Field Office, Utah Division of Wildlife Resources.

White, D. S., and S. J. White. 1977. "The Effect of Reservoir Fluctuations on Populations of *Corbicula manilensis* (Pelecypoda: Corbiculidae)." *Proceedings of the Oklahoma Academy of Science* 57:106–109. http://digital.library.okstate.edu/Oas/oas_htm_files/v57/p106_109nf.html

Whiteaves, J. F. 1863. "On the Land and Fresh-Water Molluca of Lower Canada." *Canadian Naturalist and Geologist* 8:50–65, 98–113.

Wilke, T., G. M. Davis, X. Gong, and H. X. Liu. 2000. "*Erhaia* (Gastropoda: Rissooidea): Phylogenetic Relationships and the Question of *Paragonimus* Coevolution in Asia." *American Journal of Tropical Medicine and Hygiene* 62:453–459.

Wilke, T., G. M. Davis, A. Falnowski, F. Giusti, M. Bodon, and M. Szarowska. 2001. "Molecular Systematics of Hydrobiidae (Mollusca: Gastropoda: Rissooidea): Testing Monophyly and Phylogenetic Relationships." *Proceedings of the Academy of Natural Sciences of Philadelphia* 151:1–21.

Wilke, T., M. Haase, R. Hershler, H. P. Liu, B. Misof, and W. Ponder. 2013. "Pushing Short DNA Fragments to the Limit: Phylogenetic Relationships of 'Hydrobioid' Gastropods (Caenogastropoda: Rissooidea)." *Molecular Phylogenetics and Evolution* 66:715–736.

Williams, J. D., A. E. Bogan, R. S. Butler, K. S. Cummings, J. T. Garner, J. L. Harris, N. A. Johnson, et al. 2017. "A Revised List of the Freshwater Mussels (Mollusca: Bivalvia: Unionida) of the United States and Canada." *Freshwater Mollusk Biology and Conservation* 20:33–58.

Wilson, K., K. Wheeler, and E. Betram. 2017. *Mollusks of Utah, A Simple Guide*. Utah Division of Wildlife Resources, Salt Lake City, Utah.

deWinter, A.J., S. van Leeuwen, and A. Hovestadt. 2015. "A New Species of *Glyphyalus* (Gastropoda, Pulmonata, Oxychilidae) from the Dutch Caribbean Island of St. Eustatius." *Basteria* 80(1-3):39–46.

Winterbourn, M. 1970. "The New Zealand Species of *Potamopyrgus* (Gastropoda: Hydrobiidae)." *Malacologia* 10(2):283–321.

Wohlberedt, O. 1911. "Zur Molluskenfauna von Bulgarien." *Abhandlungen der Naturforschenden Gesellschaft zu Görlitz* 27:167–234.

Woodward, B. B. 1913. *Catalogue of the British Species of Pisidium (Recent and fossil)*. London: British Museum.

Woodward, S. P. 1856. "On the Land and Fresh-Water Shells of Kashmir and Tibet, Collected by Dr. T. Thomson." *Proceedings of the Zoological Society of London*. Part 24:185–187.

Woolstenhulme, J. P. 1942a. "New Records of Mollusca." *Bulletin of the University of Utah* 32(11) [*Biological Ser.* 6(9)]: 1–14.

———. 1942b. "Uinta Mountain Mollusks." *Nautilus* 56:50–55.

Wurtz, C. B. 1955. "The American Camaenidae (Mollusca: Pulmonata)." *Proceedings of the Academy of Natural Sciences of Philadelphia* 107:99–143.

Yakhchali, M., and L. J. Deilamy. 2012. "Radular Variations in Freshwater Snails of the Family Lymnaeidae (Mollusca: Gastropoda: Basommatophora)." *American Malacological Bulletin* 30(2):323–326.

Yanes, Y., G. A. Holyoak, D. T. Holyoak, M. R. Alonso, and M. Ibáñez. 2011. "A new *Discidae* Subgenus and Two New Species (Gastropoda: Pulmonata) from the Canary Islands." *Zootaxa* 2911:43–49.

Yarrow, H. C. 1875. "Report upon the Collections of Terrestrial and Fluviatile Mollusca Made in Portions of Colorado, Utah, New Mexico, and Arizona during the Years 1872, 1873, and 1874." *Report upon Geographical and Geological Explorations and Surveys West of the 100th Meridian (Wheeler Survey)* 5:923–954.

Yen, T. C. 1947. "Pliocene Fresh-Water Mollusks from Northern Utah." *Journal of Paleontology* 21(3):268–277.

Young, M., and J. Williams. 1984. "The Reproductive Biology of the Freshwater Pearl Mussel *Margaritifera margarifera* (L.) in Scotland. 1. Field Studies." *Archives of Hydrobiology* 99(4):405–422.

Zoological Nomenclature Commission. 1998. "Opinion 1896. *Galba* Schrank, 1803 (Mollusca, Gastropoda): *Buccinum truncatulum* Muller 1774, Designated as the Type Species." *Bulletin of Zoological Nomenclature* 55(2):123.

Glossary

Abaxial: Outward, away from the shell axis.

Acuminate: Shape of a tip that tapers to a point; the sides of the point are concave and the point is extended (Fig. G1).

Adaxial: Inward, toward shell axis.

Adductor: The muscle that closes the valves of bivalved mollusks.

Adnate: Joined to or fused with another part or organ, as parts not usually united.

FIG. G1

Alate: Wing-like.

Antepenultimate: Preceding the penultimate, for example, the whorl before the second-to-last whorl.

Anterior: Situated on the body toward the head; on shells the aperture end is the anterior end. On bivalves, the anterior end of the right valve is to the left when the umbo is up and to the right on the left valve (valve with cardinal teeth C2 and C4 in Sphaeriidae).

Aperture: The opening of a snail shell, from which the snail extends its head and foot.

Apex: The top or most central whorls of a snail shell, where the earliest growth occurred.

Apical: On the top of a shell, opposite the base.

Appressed: Closely connected to, or abutting; for example, between the body whorl and aperture lip.

Auriculate: Ear-shaped (usually refers to aperture shape).

Basal: The lower or ventral surface of the shell.

Base: The underside or ventral side of a shell, opposite the apical side.

Beak: The earliest-formed part of a bivalve shell, often the highest feature on the valve.

Beehive: Shell-shaped as a traditional beehive (Fig. G2).

Biconvex: Convex on both sides.

FIG. G2

Bicuspid: With two points or cusps.

Bifid: Forked; with two branches.

Bivalve: A mollusk with two hinged shells, including freshwater and saltwater clams, mussels, and oysters.

Body whorl: The outermost and largest whorl of a shell; a complete round from the aperture.

Glossary

FIG. G3

Bulimoid: A squat shell shape that is higher than wide, but with a broad angle formed by the spire outline and shell heights that are usually less than twice the width (Fig. G3).

Byssus/byssal threads: Mass of thread-like fibers secreted by some bivalves for attachment.

Callus: A thickened area of shell material; usually referring to the columellar region.

Calyculate: Cup-like; as for the umbo of *Musculium* shells in which the cup is separated from the rest of the shell by a distinct mark.

Cardinal teeth: The hinge teeth of bivalves that have them.

Carina (carinae, plural; **carinate**, adj.**):** keel or raised ridge-like part of some shells that winds spirally.

Cicatrices: Recently formed connective tissue on a healing wound; scar tissue.

Collabral: Oriented at the same angle or arc as the aperture; that is, like the aperture.

Columella: The central axis of a spiral shell.

Conical: A shell shape that is broad at the base and tapers to a point.

Connate: Congenitally or firmly united; innate.

Convex: Inflated or curved outward, as in a spire or whorl.

Costate: Ribbed.

Crest: A wave-like ridge of the shell just behind the aperture lip. Seen in side view, especially in pupillid shells.

Ctenidium (ctenidia, plural**):** Comb-like structure, such as the respiratory apparatus of a mollusk.

Cusp: Tooth or point; often used when describing radular teeth and the number of points on a given buccal plate.

FIG. G4

Depressed heliciform: A shell shape that is wider than high but still features a slightly raised spire (Fig. G4).

Dextral: "Right-handed." Used to describe the direction of the twist of the shell for snails. If, when holding a snail with the spire up and the aperture toward you, the aperture is on your right, then the shell is dextral. Opposite of sinistral.

Diaphanous: Translucent, allowing light to pass through.

Dioecious: Having male or female reproductive organs in distinct individuals; having separate sexes.

FIG. G5

Discoidal: A very flattened, disk-like, wider-than-high shell shape (Fig. G5).

Distal: Away from; toward the tip; opposite of proximal.

Dorsal: The back or top of; in bivalves, the dorsal area is the part with the umbones and ligament.

Ectocone: Outer cusp of a radular tooth.

Endocone: The inner (medially) cusp of a radular tooth.

Epiphallus: Enlargement of the vas deferens as it enters the penis. This may include the penis sheath if present, the penis, and possibly an appendix. The epiphallus, if present, attaches to the larger preputium that is last element of the penial complex.

Epiphragm: A thin membrane of dried mucous that seals the aperture of a snail without an operculum when it is dormant.

Extramarsupial larvae: Referring to the stage of development in Sphaeriidae (Bivalvia), after the prodissoconch stage, in which shelled larvae have broken free from the brood sacs but are still contained in the marsupium prior to birth.

Fetal larvae: Referring to the stage of development from completion of gastrulation through the beginning of shell formation in viviparous bivalves (precedes the prodissoconch and extramarsupial stages).

Foot: The flat, muscular surface of the body of a snail used for crawling.

Gastropod: A one-shelled mollusk; includes both aquatic and terrestrial snails, slugs, and limpets.

Geniculate: Bent at an abrupt angle, like that of a bent knee.

Globose: A squat shell shape that is rounded overall and nearly as wide as tall (Fig. G6).

FIG. G6

Glochidium: Parasitic larva of some bivalves that attaches itself to the gills or fins of fish. Plural: glochidia.

Growth lines: Crosswise ridges on the shell surface that are formed during growth of a snail.

Head: The portion of the body of a snail that contains the tentacles and mouth; anterior.

Height: The measurement of a shell from the apex to the most basal part of the shell, parallel to the columella. In bivalve shells the height is measured as the maximum distance between the dorsal hinge and the opposing ventral margin, perpendicular to the length measurement.

Hermaphrodite: An organism having both male and female reproductive organs.

Hinge: The dorsal part of a bivalve where the left and right valves attach; it is composed of the ligament and hinge teeth (if present).

Hirsute: "Hairy"; a descriptive term for having "hairs" (wisps of periostracum) on the surface of the shell.

Holarctic: Adjective for the zoogeographic region that includes the northern areas of the earth (divided into Nearctic and Palearctic).

Holotype: Original archival specimen that was used to define and represent a species.

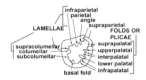

FIG. G7

Imperforate: Lacking an open or perforate umbilicus.

Inflated: Describing a bivalve shell as puffed up or expanded versus flat.

Keel (of the shell): A sharp edge of the shell periphery, particularly prominent in some families and species.

Keel (of the tail): A ridge on the tail; present in some species.

Labium/labrum: Edge, rim, or lip; referring to aperture margin.

Lamella (lamellae, plural**):** Folded structure formed by the shell appearing as a thin ridge or little tooth (Fig. G7). Pilsbry and Vanatta (1900) defined lamellae as those folds within the parietal and columellar area of the aperture, differentiated from plicae (basal and outer wall folds). Herein, lamella/lamellae is used in the broad sense.

Lateral teeth: For radulae, laterals are the teeth immediately to either side of the central/rachidian tooth of a common form, transitioning distally to intermediate and marginal teeth of different shapes or number of cusps; for bivalves, lateral teeth are the cusps/sulci or serrated teeth on the posterior and anterior parts of the shell, on either side of the central cardinal teeth.

Lectotype: Archival specimen designated as the holotype when the holotype has been lost or destroyed.

Length: In gastropod shells, the maximum height, between extreme ends of the columellar axis, perpendicular to the diameter or width of the shell. In bivalves, the length is the maximum distance between the anterior and posterior end (perpendicular to the dorsal-ventral axis).

Lentic: Adjective referring to still or standing water.

Lip/apertural lip: The rim of the aperture of the shell, may be either sharp or thickened.

Lirae: Raised spiral cords on a snail shell.

Lotic: Adjective referring to flowing or moving water.

Malacology: The study of mollusks.

Malleated: Dented surface, as if repeatedly hit with a ball-peen hammer.

Mantle: The tissue that covers the organs of a mollusk. In most snails, it is within the shell, and only the edge of the mantle is visible at the aperture. In native slugs, it is located behind the head and forms a hump.

Mesocone: Central cusp of a radular tooth.

Microsculpture: Fine textural features on the surface of a shell that are best seen with a microscope.

Mollusk: A member of the animal phylum Mollusca. Mollusks have a soft body, and most have a shell or shells but lack vertebrae. They live in aquatic or moist habitats. Mollusks include snails, slugs, clams, octopi, limpets, and similar animals.

Nacre: Composite material making up an inner shell layer. The color of the nacre can be used to describe some species.

Nearctic: Adjective referring to the zoogeographic region that includes the Arctic and northern (temperate) areas of North America and Greenland.

Nephridium: Excretory organ that functions like a kidney (plural: nephridia).

Neritiform: Shaped like shells in the Gastropod genus *Nerita*, which are subglobose with large oblique apertures and very short spires.

Nomen nudum: New species named without a description.

Obtuse: An angle exceeding 90°.

Operculum: A hardened plate that covers the aperture when the snail is withdrawn into its shell. Common in several aquatic snails; not present in most terrestrial snails.

Orthocline: Straight or upright plane, usually referring to aperture axis relative to shell axis

Osphradium: Single or paired olfactory organ found in certain aquatic mollusks, linked with the respiratory organ of a snail. It is located just ventral to the base of the ctenidium (gill). It consists of a patch of sensory epithelium on the afferent gill membranes. Its position relative to the ctenidium and its general shape are used as diagnostic characters differentiating among taxa (Hershler and Ponder 1998).

Ovate: Egg-shaped.

Oviparous: Producing eggs that hatch outside of the parent after being deposited.

Palatal: Generally, the dorsal area of the aperture from where the lip joins the penultimate whorl to the outer margin. For shells higher than wide, the palatal area refers to the outer lip down to the basal area.

Palearctic: Adjective referring to the zoogeographic region that includes Europe, the northwestern coast of Africa, and Asia north of the Himalayas.

Pallial: Of or pertaining to the mantle of a mollusk.

Pallium: Mantle of a mollusk.

Paratypes: Archival specimens collected at the same time as the holotype from the type location.

Parietal: The region of the aperture of a gastropod shell adjacent to, or pressed against, the preceding whorl.

Parietal denticle (tooth): A projection from the body whorl within the aperture, present in some terrestrial gastropod species.

Parthenogenesis: Asexual reproduction in which a female develops embryos without fertilization of eggs by a male to produce clonal offspring.

Patulous: Spreading or expanding from a center; usually referring to the shell aperture lip, spreading laterally and anteriorly (bottom of shell when facing the aperture).

Paucispiral: Of few whorls or turns; a diagnostic type of pattern on some species' operculae.

Pedal grooves: Linear furrows or indentations on the foot of some snails between the outer margin and the shell.

Pellucid: Translucent, allowing light to pass through.

Periostracum: The outer skin-like membrane of a snail shell; contains any color (pigment) or texture that the shell has.

Peristome: The border or rim of the aperture, reflected or thickened.

Plait: A spirally flattened ridge on the columella.

Plicae: Folds of the shell (ridge- or tooth-like) within the basal and outer walls of the aperture. See also Lamellae.

Pneumostome: The opening in the mantle that allows air to pass and gas exchange through the vascular tissue.

Posterior: Directional term meaning toward the tail or rear; in gastropod shells, toward the apex of shell or rear of the animal. Opposite of anterior (see Anterior for details on bivalves).

Preputium: Penis sac, located anterior to penis sheath into which the vas deferens enters. Within the preputium there are usually several muscular pillars that aid in extrusion of the penis.

Prodissoconch larvae: The larval stage of sphaerid clam development from the start of shell development until escape from the brood sac.

Prosobranch: Any of a subclass (Prosobranchia) of gastropod mollusks that have gills, osphradia, the loop of visceral nerves twisted into a figure eight, the sexes usually separate, and usually with an operculum.

Prosocline: With the plane of the aperture inclined away from the axis in its upper part and toward the axis in the lower part, as in most prosobranch gastropods.

Protoconch: The whorls (few to several) at the center of the coil completed in the egg during embryonic development.

Proximal: The nearest end, nearest the body or point of origin.

Pseudocardinal teeth: Triangular, often serrated structures located near the hinge of some bivalves.

Quadrate: Squarish; more or less shaped like a square or rectangle.

Glossary

Radial: The transverse direction of lines and sculpture, that is, outward, perpendicular to the spiral lines and the central axis, across the whorl.

Radula: Teeth-like structures in the mouths of gastropods that are used to scrape algae from surfaces or feed in other ways. Individual teeth within a radular ribbon may vary in number, shape, and size, which may be used for separating different taxa. Usually, there is a larger central radular tooth, flanked symmetrically on either side (going distally) by lateral, inner marginal, and outer marginal teeth. The central tooth may also have a characteristic dentition and "tongue" shape.

Ribs: Raised ridges on the surface of a shell that run in an axial or crosswise direction (radially).

Rimate: An adjective describing an umbilicus shaped like a narrow slit.

Sarcobelum: Fleshy ring of tissue at the upper or inner end of the preputium that is an excitatory organ.

Scalar/scalariform: Form similar to steps in a staircase, for example, shell spire with shouldered whorls or umbilicus with stepped levels.

Sculpture: Shell surface characteristics, for example, raised markings, striae, descussate, punctate (pitted), ribbing, and microstructure.

Scutellum: The projecting or pinched parts of the shell in front of the beaks in bivalves.

Scutum: The projecting or pinched parts of the shell behind the beaks.

Shoulder: The shelf created on a whorl, adjacent to the sutures of a shell before convexly tapering downward; shaped like a shoulder.

Sinistral: "Left-handed." A term used to describe the direction of the twist of the shell for snails. If, when holding a snail with the spire up and the aperture toward you, the aperture is on *your* left, then the shell is sinistral. Opposite of dextral.

Sinulus: A wave; usually referring to the indented outer margin of the aperture in some Vertiginiidae.

Slug: A snail with a shell that is absent or much reduced.

Spiral: The direction of the coil of the whorls; opposite of axial.

Spire: The pointed top of the shell of a snail, includes all the whorls except for the body (last) whorl.

Statocyst: A small organ of balance in usually aquatic invertebrates, consisting of a fluid-filled sac lined with sensory hairs containing statoliths (calcareous structure).

Striae: Indented lines or grooves on the surface of a shell; can be in either spiral or axial direction.

Glossary

FIG. G8

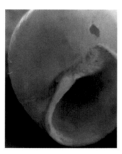

FIG. G9

Subcylindrical: A shell shape that is higher than wide (Fig. G8, b).

Subglobose: Rounded or nearly spherical; slightly wider than high (Fig. G8, a).

Sublenticular: Lens-shaped (bi-convex).

Succiniform: A shell shape that is higher than wide, with a very large aperture and last body whorl typical of snails in the family Succineidae (Fig. G8, c).

Sulcus (sulci, plural): A shallow trough-like depression or furrow; In bivalves, these features may be on the outer surface of a bivalve shell that extends concentrically from the beak or referring to the gap between lateral teeth. In gastropods, the sulcus may refer to the groove or trough between radial ribs.

Suture: The seam where the whorls of a shell join. Sutures may be deeply or shallowly impressed, depending on species.

Syntype: Cotype; one or more archival specimens used in the original species or subspecies. description, when no holotype was designated; may become lectotype if designated as such.

Talon: Part of the snail reproduction system associated with the albumen gland, darkly pigmented, often recurved like a raptor's claw.

Teleoconch: The portion of the shell that develops after the protoconch.

Tentacles: The sensory appendages of a snail containing the eyes.

Topotype: Archival specimens collected from the type location, but at a later date than when the species was originally described.

Trochoid: Roulette-like curve traced by a point on a radius or an extension of the radius of a circle that rolls along a line (from Greek trochos, wheel).

Tubercle: Small bump or raised area about as wide as long.

Turbinate: Shaped like a top.

Umbilicus: An opening in the middle of the whorls at the base (bottom) of a snail shell. In shells of Lymnaeidae, a columellar flap may create a small opening, also referred to as the umbilicus (Fig. G9). It may or may not be present. The umbilicus may be perforate (with an opening), imperforate (with no umbilicus), or rimate (with a fissure-like crack instead of a hole).

Umbo: The raised dorsal portion of a bivalve shell near the hinge. Also called the beak.

Uncinate: Hooked (adj.)

Unicini: Teeth at the margins of the radula.

Glossary

Valve: One shell of a two-shelled mollusk (bivalve).

Varix: Prominent axial ridge or protrusion formed by expansion of the shell aperture during a previous stage of growth.

Veliger: The free-swimming larvae of some bivalves (e.g., Dreissenidae, Corbiculidae).

Velum: Structure in some larval bivalves that forms as an outgrowth of a protoconch. In some species it aids in swimming. Velar cilia in *Corbicula* move food particles. In some larval gastropods, the velum is a locomotory ciliated ring, arising anterodorsally, and circumscribes the apical area. In viviparous pulmonates, the velum is reduced or absent.

Ventral: Lower portion or underside. In bivalves, the ventral portion is the region opposite the beaks and hinge.

Verge: Organ that bears the penis in some male gastropods.

Viviparous: Bearing live young that are hatched and nourished within the parent.

Whorl: One complete round of the spiral of a snail shell. Whorls are counted from the smallest central whorl outward toward the last body whorl (Fig. G10).

Width: The width of a gastropod shell is measured as the maximum distance perpendicular to the columellar axis. Also referred to as the diameter, especially in depressed and discoid shells. In bivalves, the width is the thickness of the two valves together (Fig. G11).

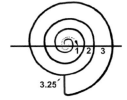

FIG. G10

FIG. G11